T0142243

Lecture Notes of the Institute for Computer Sciences, Social Informatics and Telecommunications Engineering 466

More information about this series at https://link.springer.com/bookseries/8197

Mian Ahmad Jan · Fazlullah Khan (Eds.)

Application of Big Data, Blockchain, and Internet of Things for Education Informatization

Second EAI International Conference, BigIoT-EDU 2022
Virtual Event, July 29–31, 2022
Proceedings, Part II

Springer

Editors
Mian Ahmad Jan 🆔
Department of Computer Science
Abdul Wali Khan University Mardan
Mardan, Pakistan

Fazlullah Khan 🆔
Department of Computer Science
Abdul Wali Khan University Mardan
Mardan, Pakistan

ISSN 1867-8211   ISSN 1867-822X (electronic)
Lecture Notes of the Institute for Computer Sciences, Social Informatics
and Telecommunications Engineering
ISBN 978-3-031-23946-5   ISBN 978-3-031-23947-2 (eBook)
https://doi.org/10.1007/978-3-031-23947-2

This Springer imprint is published by the registered company Springer Nature Switzerland AG
The registered company address is: Gewerbestrasse 11, 6330 Cham, Switzerland

Preface

We are delighted to introduce the proceedings of the second edition of the European Alliance for Innovation (EAI) International Conference on Application of Big Data, Blockchain, and Internet of Things for Education Informatization (BigIoT-EDU 2022). BigIoT-EDU aims to provide a platform for international cooperation and exchange, enabling big data and information education experts, scholars, and enterprise developers to share research results, discuss existing problems and challenges, and explore cutting-edge science and technology. The conference focuses on research fields such as big data and information education. The use of artificial intelligence (AI), blockchain, and network security lies at the heart of this conference as we focus on these emerging technologies to excel the progress of Big Data and information education.

BigIoT-EDU has three tracks: the Main Track, the Late Track, and a Workshop Track. BigIoT-EDU 2022 attracted over 700 submissions, and Each submission was reviewed by at least Three Program Committee members in a double blind process, resulting in the acceptance of only 205 papers across all three tracks. The workshop was titled "International Workshop on IoT-enabled Big Data Analytics using Machine Learning for Smart Societies" and co-chaired by Muhammad Babar and Mian Muhammad Aimal from Allama Iqbal Open University Islamabad, Pakistan, and the Virtual University Lahore, Pakistan, respectively. The workshop aimed to focus on advanced techniques and algorithms to excel big data analytics and machine learning for advancement of smart societies.

Coordination with the steering chair, Imrich Chlamtac, was essential for the success of the conference. We sincerely appreciate his constant support and guidance. It was also a great pleasure to work with such an excellent organizing committee team for their hard work in organizing and supporting the conference. In particular, we are grateful to the Technical Program Committee, who completed the peer-review process for the technical papers and helped to put together a high-quality technical program. We are also grateful to Conference Manager Martin Vojtek for his constant support along with the whole of the EAI team involved in the conference. We must say that they have been wonderful and it is always a pleasant experience to work with them. Also, we would like to thank all the authors who submitted their papers to the BigIoT-EDU 2022 conference.

We strongly believe that the BigIoT-EDU conference provides a good forum for all researchers, developers, and practitioners to discuss all science and technology aspects that are relevant to big data and information education. We also expect that the future

BigIoT-EDU conferences will be as successful and stimulating as this year's, as indicated by the contributions presented in this volume.

Mian Ahmad Jan
Fazlullah Khan
Mengji Chen
Walayat Hussain
Shah Nazir

Organization

Steering Committee

Imrich Chlamtac	University of Trento, Italy
Mian Ahmad Jan	Abdul Wali Khan University Mardan, Pakistan
Fazlullah Khan	RoZetta Institute, Australia

Organizing Committee

General Chairs

Mian Ahmad Jan	Abdul Wali Khan University Mardan, Pakistan
Fazlullah Khan	RoZetta Institute, Australia
Mengji Chen	Guangxi Science and Technology Normal University, China

Technical Program Committee Chairs

Fazlullah Khan	RoZetta Institute, Australia
Mian Ahmad Jan	Abdul Wali Khan University Mardan, Pakistan
Walayat Hussain	Victoria University, Australia
Shah Nazir	University of Swabi, Pakistan

Sponsorship and Exhibit Chairs

Sahil Verma	Chandigarh University, India
Lan Zimian	Harbin Institute of Technology, China
Izaz Ur Rehman	Abdul Wali Khan University Mardan, Pakistan
Sara Karim	Abdul Wali Khan University Mardan, Pakistan

Local Chairs

Huang Yufei	Hechi Normal University, China
Wan Haoran	Shanghai University, China

Workshops Chairs

Zhang Yinjun	Guangxi Science and Technology Normal University, China
Rahim Khan	Abdul Wali Khan University Mardan, Pakistan

| Abid Yahya | Botswana International University of Science and Technology, Botswana |
| Syed Roohullah Jan | Abdul Wali Khan University Mardan, Pakistan |

Publicity and Social Media Chairs

| Varun G. Menon | SCMS Group of Educational Institutions, India |
| Aamir Akbar | Abdul Wali Khan University Mardan, Pakistan |

Publications Chairs

| Mian Ahmad Jan | Abdul Wali Khan University Mardan, Pakistan |
| Fazlullah Khan | RoZetta Institute, Australia |

Web Chairs

| Mohammad Imran | Abdul Wali Khan University Mardan, Pakistan |
| Yar Muhammad | Abdul Wali Khan University Mardan, Pakistan |

Posters and PhD Track Chairs

| Mengji Chen | Guangxi Science and Technology Normal University, China |
| Ateeq ur Rehman | University of Haripur, Pakistan |

Panels Chairs

| Kong Linxiang | Hefei University of Technology, China |
| Muhammad Usman | Federation University, Australia |

Demos Chairs

| Ryan Alturki | Umm Al-Qura University, Saudi Arabia |
| Rahim Khan | Abdul Wali Khan University Mardan, Pakistan |

Tutorials Chairs

Wei Rongchang	Guangxi Science and Technology Normal University, China
Muhammad Zakarya	Abdul Wali Khan University Mardan, Pakistan
Mukhtaj Khan	University of Haripur, Pakistan

Session Chairs

Ryan Alturki	Umm Al-Qura University, Saudi Arabia
Aamir Akbar	Abdul Wali Khan University Mardan, Pakistan
Mengji Chen	Hechi University, China

Vinh Troung Hoang	Ho Chi Minh City Open University, Vietnam
Muhammad Zakarya	Abdul Wali Khan University Mardan, Pakistan
Yu Uunshi	Shanxi Normal University, China
Ateeq ur Rehman	University of Haripur, Pakistan
Su Linna	Guangxi University, China
Shah Nazir	University of Swabi, Pakistan
Mohammad Dahman Alshehri	Taif University, Saudi Arabia
Chen Zhi	Shanghai University, China
Syed Roohullah Jan	Abdul Wali Khan University Mardan, Pakistan
Qin Shitian	Guangxi Normal University, China
Sara	Abdul Wali Khan University Mardan, Pakistan
Mohammad Wedyan	Al-Balqa Applied University, Jordan
Lin Hang	Beijin Linye University, China
Arjumand Yar Khan	Abdul Wali Khan University Mardan, Pakistan
Liu Cheng	Wuxi Technology University, China
Rahim Khan	Abdul Wali Khan University Mardan, Pakistan
Muhammad Tahir	Saudi Electronics University, Saudi Arabia
Tan Zhide	Anhui University, China

Technical Program Committee

Mian Yasir Jan	CECOS University, Pakistan
Abid Yahya	Botswana International University of Science and Technology, Botswana
Noor Zaman Jhanjhi	Taylor's University, Malaysia
Mian Muhammad Aimal	Virtual University, Pakistan
Muhammad Babar	Iqra University, Pakistan
Mamoun Alazab	Charles Darwin University, Australia
Tao Liao	Anhui University of Science and Technology, China
Ryan Alturki	Umm Al-Qura University, Saudi Arabia
Dinh-Thuan Do	Asia University, Taiwan
Huan Du	Shanghai University, China
Sahil Verma	Chandigarh University, India
Abusufyan Sher	Abdul Wali Khan University Mardan, Pakistan
Mohammad S. Khan	East Tennessee State University, USA
Ali Kashif Bashir	Manchester Metropolitan University, UK
Nadir Shah	COMSATS University Islamabad, Pakistan
Aamir Akbar	Abdul Wali Khan University Mardan, Pakistan
Vinh Troung Hoang	Ho Chi Minh City Open University, Vietnam
Shunxiang Zhang	Anhui University of Science and Technology, China

Contents – Part II

Research on Educational Informatization from the Perspective of Pedagogy 1
  Hong Liang

Somatosensory Dance Interaction System Based on AdaBoost Algorithm 10
  Jiahong Li

Value Reconstruction and Path Innovation of Blockchain Technology
for the Development of Higher Education 21
  Donghong Zhang

Research on the Design of Automatic Accompaniment System of Piano
Teaching Audio Database Under the Background of the Internet 31
  Li Guo

Research on the Evaluation of College English Classroom Teaching
Quality Based on Triangular Fuzzy Number 39
  Ning Chong

Study on the Interactive Education System of Motion Evaluation Algorithm ... 45
  Ping Yao

Research on the Evaluation of Constructive English Teaching Model
Based on RBF Algorithm 56
  Liping Du

Algorithm and Implementation of College English Teaching
Comprehensive Ability Evaluation System 67
  Hui Zheng

Design of English Teaching Resource Management System Based
on Collaborative Recommendation 78
  Mingming Ding

Analysis of College English Teaching Under the Network Teaching
Platform 89
  Jianli Chen, Yanping Shan, and Changqing Yu

Design and Realization of the Innovation and Entrepreneurship Experience
System of Data Dynamic Innovation Model 100
  Xiaoli Xie and Xiaowei Hu

Application of Random Simulation Algorithm in Physical Education
Teaching Evaluation 110
   HuiYang and Chengliang Zhang

Application of Improved Association Rule Algorithm in E-commerce
English 116
   Xiaojia Lai

Application of Risk Assessment Model of Accounting Resource Sharing
Management in Education and Teaching 126
   Chang Xia Ren

Innovation Analysis of English Education in Higher Vocational Colleges
Based on Multi-objective Genetic Algorithm 135
   Chuanwei Zhang

Design of Taijiquan Multimedia Distance Teaching System Based on ASP
Technology 146
   Xueqin Wu

Innovation of Film and Television Screenwriter Education in the Era
of Mobile Internet 156
   ChunLiang Wang

Innovative Analysis of Sports Competition Training Integrating Interactive
Digital Media 165
   Jinghua Li

Design Teaching and Implementation of Data Mining Algorithm
in Business Management System 177
   Mengzhen Hao and Haiqin Shao

Input and Understanding of Chemical Symbols in Multimedia Education
Software 188
   Wei Li and Yiping Wang

Investigation and Analysis on Learning Attitude of Public Pedagogy
Under the Background of Big Data 195
   Hong Liang

Multi-color Garment Cutting and Decoupling Optimization Teaching
Method Based on Data Mining Algorithm 204
   ShanShan Li

Development of Computer Intelligent Proofreading System
from the Perspective of Medical English Translation Application 211
  Yan Zhang

On the Application and Significance of Simulation Technology in Film
Creation 223
  Chun Liang Wang

On the Design of Student Employment Module in Higher Education
Management System Based on Genetic Algorithm 232
  Gao Fei

Discussion and Practice of Online and Offline Mixed Teaching of Track
and Field Course Based on OBE Concept 243
  Xiaoyu Shi and Jianxin Zhang

Research and Application of Software Testing Method Improvement
Based on Big Data Information 254
  Peng Gao, GuoXing Chi, YuLing Liu, and WeiPeng Sun

Establishment and Application of Quality Evaluation System of College
Students' Psychological Education Based on Genetic Algorithm 262
  Xiaozhen Zhao and Bo Chen

Research on Coordination Between Power Information Security System
and Environment Based on Fusion Mechanism 275
  Hong Zhang Xiong and Xiaokun Yang

Research on Economic Management Experiment Teaching Management
System Based on Computer 286
  Xiaosu Feng, Weiwei Miao, Pengcheng Cao, and Wenguo Zhao

Research on the Design of Psychological Quality Education of Violin
Course in Colleges and Universities Under Virtual Technology 292
  Juanjuan Zhang

Study on Corrosion Wear and Protection of Coal Preparation Equipment
Based on PLC Centralized Control System 298
  Wenjuan Sun and Guozhi Liang

Summary of Research on Learning Analysis Based on Educational Big Data ... 309
  Weijuan Wang

Research on the Influencing Factors of the Endangered Inheritance of Folk
Intangible Cultural Heritage and the Educational Protection Based on Big
Data Technology 314
    Yafang He

Teaching Practice and Research of Recognition System in Art Teaching
Based on Visual Communication 325
    Guiping Li

Research on the Integration Design of Algorithm Teaching
and Mathematics Curriculum Under Information Technology 331
    Guomin Fang

The Application Design of Modern Educational Information Technology
in Kindergarten Teaching 344
    Linjiao Liu and Chao Gong

Research on the Management System of an Internet Big Data Analysis
Platform Based on Machine Learning 350
    LinHao Liu

Construction of Maker Education Resource Sharing Platform Based
on Web Technology 361
    Kan Wang

The Application of Documentary New Media Communication Platform
in Education and Teaching 368
    Te Zhai

Research on the "Online and Offline" Operation Education and Teaching
Mode of Cross-Border E-commerce Business Based on the Internet 379
    Jihong Zhang

Construction of Large-Scale Chinese-English Bilingual Corpus
and Sentence Alignment 389
    Sun Jie

The Application of Graphic Composition Design in Computer Vision Art
Teaching 400
    Chunyuan Wu

Research on the Quality Evaluation of College Students' Innovation
and Entrepreneurship Education Based on Ant Colony Algorithm 412
    XingRong Zhang

The Application of Hierarchical Teaching Mode Based on Hybrid
Criterion Fuzzy Algorithm in Higher Vocational English Education 424
  Chuanwei Zhang

Research on the System Design of Primary School Science Multimedia
Teaching 431
  Yanmei Zhao

Research on the Teaching Application of the Improved Genetic Algorithm
in E-commerce 443
  Sisi Zhang

Construction of a Mathematical Model Based on the Big Data Information
Platform 454
  Lei Huang, Yan Wang, and Li Zhang

Construction and Development of Chemistry Teaching Platform in Higher
Vocational Colleges Under the Background of Artificial Intelligence 463
  Yiping Wang and Wei Li

Construction and Application of Computer Network Experimental
Teaching Platform Based on Big Data 472
  Zhangsheng Zhong

Computer Ability Education and Training of Tourism Talents in the Era
of "Internet + Tourism Big Data" 481
  Li Xing and Yanhong Dong

Comparison Between American Restorative Justice and Chinese People's
Mediation System in the Era of Big Data Intelligence 488
  Yang Xiao, Yanhong Gan, and Leihan Yu

Evaluation Method of English Teaching Quality Based on SOFM Neural
Network 497
  Jing Sheng

Communication Path and Influence Analysis of Drama, Film
and Television Performance of Data Technology 503
  Yan Zhang

Evaluation Model of College English Teaching Effect Based on Big Data
Platform 512
  Suyun Gan

Based on C4 Design and Implementation of College Health Sports System
Based on 5 Algorithm 523
  Shaorong Lin

Evaluation Model of College Students' Psychological Education Quality
Based on Data Technology 535
  Bo Chen and Xiaozhen Zhao

Classification Method of Educational Discourse Power Imbalance Data
Set Based on Mixed Big Data Analysis 546
  Jinzhi Teng

Evaluation of Business English Practical Teaching Based on Decision Tree 558
  Xiaojia Lai

Application of VR Technology in Practical Courses of Preschool
Education Specialty 569
  Lijuan Liao

Evaluation of English Teaching Quality in Higher Vocational Colleges
Based on Artificial Intelligence Optimization Network 580
  Lingli Zhang

Application of Virtual Reality Technology in Environmental Art Design 591
  Liao Wang

Exploration and Practice of Experimental Teaching Mode of Online
and Offline Virtual Reality Combined with Hybrid Computer Network
Course 602
  Zhangsheng Zhong

Application of Web Data Mining Algorithms in Information Management
Education 612
  Li Liu

Application Progress of Particle Swarm Optimization in Modern Literature 618
  Dong Zhang and Beibei Li

Exploration of Personalized Foreign Language Teaching Model Based
on the Integration of Multimedia Means and Traditional Methods 629
  Fei Gao

Fast Conversion of Material Parameters of Asphalt Mixture by Laplace
Transform 635
  Nan Zhang, Pei Sun, and Ting-ting Ling

Higher Education Evaluation System Based on Computer Network 647
  Guangjuan Gu

Author Index 661

Research on Educational Informatization from the Perspective of Pedagogy

Hong Liang[(✉)]

Cavite State University, Shandong 276000, China
13153907567@163.com

Abstract. China's basic education informatization began in the 1980s and has a development history of more than 20 years. Since entering this century, educational informatization has shown a trend of rapid development. Both research literature and total investment are growing at a high speed. At present, behind the prosperity, there are also insurmountable problems in the theory of educational informatization, such as the deep integration of information technology into education. Education is a conscious social activity with the direct goal of affecting people's physical and mental development. Pedagogy is to study how to make people independent, self-improvement and self-reliance. Therefore, based on the research on educational informatization from the perspective of pedagogy, this paper considers educational informatization from the dimension of information technology, which is the pedagogical perspective of educational informatization research.

Keywords: Pedagogical perspective · Educational informatization

1 Introduction

At present, the development of educational informatization in China has entered a more critical period. On the whole, the construction of educational informatization in eastern China has been basically in place, and the construction of educational informatization has gradually transferred to the central and western regions. When the software and hardware conditions for educational informatization are basically met, if information technology can not be deeply integrated into education and teaching and can not have "resonance" with the life growth of teachers and students, information technology may be marginalized in education, and China's educational informatization may fall into stagnation or even retrogression. In view of the problems in the field of educational informatization practice, educational informatization theory must give its own answers. The shackles of the research perspective make it difficult for the theoretical research of educational informatization to achieve a transformational breakthrough under the framework of technology, and it is also difficult to achieve "educational informatization drives and promotes the leapfrog development of basic education" "This grand idea. Therefore, if the educational informatization theory itself wants to seek a breakthrough

© ICST Institute for Computer Sciences, Social Informatics and Telecommunications Engineering 2023
Published by Springer Nature Switzerland AG 2023. All Rights Reserved
M. A. Jan and F. Khan (Eds.): BigIoT-EDU 2022, LNICST 466, pp. 1–9, 2023.
https://doi.org/10.1007/978-3-031-23947-2_1

and change the research perspective from the perspective of technology to the perspective of pedagogy, it may be a prerequisite change.

We believe that studying educational informatization from the perspective of pedagogy may change our understanding of the essence of educational informatization, the value orientation of educational informatization research, the research object of educational informatization and other theoretical issues, and then realize the overall change of educational informatization research, that is, the transformation of educational informatization research. The core of this transformation is the deep integration of information technology into education Activities bring new possibilities to the life growth of teachers and students, the structural block diagram of educational informatization is as follows.

Technology and Intel join hands to introduce the new Intel ® vPro ® Platform and other products and technologies, combined with its intelligent desktop virtual cloud classroom solution, have brought higher quality and safe teaching experience to university teachers and students, reduced the maintenance pressure of IT department and improved the utilization efficiency of information-based teaching environment (Fig. 1).

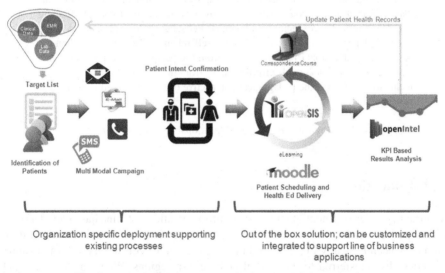

Fig. 1. Structural block diagram of educational informatization

We need educational informatization with the following functions:

Openness

In order to ensure the openness of the system, the world's mainstream hardware platform (host, network equipment, etc.) and software platform shall be used in the system construction. Based on the industry's open standards, various network protocols, hardware interfaces and data interfaces involved in the system construction shall be supported to lay the foundation for the future system expansion.

Flexibility and scalability
The system should have good openness and scalability, and can efficiently adapt to the changing needs of laboratory management in the future. Various parameters are configurable to ensure the data flexibility and scalability of the system.

Safety and reliability
Security mechanism can not only define the security of data, but also define the security of application level. The security management of the system can be integrated with other applications through portal.

Practicability
Practicability is the main standard for evaluating the management system of off campus practice, which can play a positive role in improving the efficiency and management level of off campus practice management.

Easy to operate
The operation process is simple, which is convenient for personnel at all levels to quickly master the operation process and be familiar with the key points of work.

2 Related Work

[2] evaluate the effect of Korea's education informatization policy qualitatively. [3] explore the informational teaching model under the background of educational informationization at the present stage, combining with the talents training objectives of high-level cognition and evaluation. [4] introduce the problem of formation of ICT competence of future teachers. The objective of [5] is to study the path of improving the effectiveness of Ideological and political education (IAPE) from the perspective of educational informatization. [4] analyze the data of Guangxi in the construction of rural basic education informatization in the aspects of fund investment, school running conditions, teacher training, platform construction and so on in the last five years, so as to analyzes the existing problems theoretically, and puts forward some improvement strategies on how to solve the problem. [8] discuss the teaching concept, platform selection, study situation analysis, resource preparation, curriculum implementation, summary and reflection and other aspects of the curriculum under the background of educational informatization, so as to do a good job in the organization and management of online teaching under the background of educational informatization, and lay a foundation for the innovative practice of information-based leading educational concept and education mode. Other influential work includes [1, 7, 9, 10].

3 Concept and Characteristics of Educational Informatization

3.1 Concept of Educational Informatization

The concept of educational informatization was put forward with the construction of information highway in the 1990s. The Clinton administration put forward the "national information infrastructure" plan (NII) in 1993, its core is to develop a comprehensive information service system with the Internet as the core and promote the wide application of information technology in various fields of society, especially taking the educational application of information technology as an important way to implement the educational reform facing the 21st century. This move of the United States has aroused positive reactions from all countries in the world, and many governments have formulated plans to promote their own educational informatization.

Since the 1990s, with the rapid popularization of network technology, the relationship between the development of the whole society and information technology has become closer and closer. People pay more and more attention to the impact of information technology on social development. The formulation of "social informatization" began to appear[1]. In the field of education, "educational informatization" At present, the concept of "educational informatization" has been officially used in various government documents, and attaches great importance to the work of educational informatization.

It is worth pointing out that the concept of "informatization" is basically the product of Oriental language thinking. In many Eastern countries, including China, Japan, South Korea and Russia, the concept of "informatization" is generally used, while in the literature of western countries, there are few "informatization" and "educational informatization" They often use many different names, such as e-education, network based education, online education, cybereducation, etc.

3.2 Characteristics of Educational Informatization

There are three main external characteristics of Educational Informatization: first, it refers to people's educational concept, educational theory and educational model; second, it is material, mainly teaching media; third, it is educational management system; first, it plays a decisive role. Among these three external characteristics, there is an internal characteristic of educational informatization, which is the democracy of education, This is the essence and soul of educational informatization.

In ancient times, education informatization was not emphasized. At that time, students were regarded as the appendages of students. Students became the private property of students at the spiritual and cultural level. Students attached to students, and even had a certain degree of personal attachment. Confucius honored 72 sages and 3000 disciples. Socrates was in trouble because of the degeneration of youth thought and the tendency of anarchy. Now, the school is engaged in education and teaching With the informatization, the role of teachers has changed. Teachers are no longer the main body, but become the guide of learning, the organizer of learning activities, the manager of learning resources, the coordinator of the team and the developer of courses. The role of teachers has diversified, and the skills of teachers have been improved[2]. They are both service providers and researchers. Students engage in diversified learning methods in diversified learning organizations and are no longer passive educated The school's educational system, educational concept, teaching content, teaching mode, teaching method and teaching evaluation should change and develop, and the soul of democracy should be reflected everywhere and anytime.

4   Research on Educational Informatization

4.1   Problems Caused by Excessive Emphasis on Technology in Educational Informatization

From the development of education informatization, the "technology" of Education Informatization " Attribute to a certain extent, it has changed the teaching methods, provided diversified communication media for education, changed the breadth and depth of cultural communication, and enabled people to quickly and effectively obtain information and transcend the limitations of time and space. The emergence of network education and distance education has blurred the boundaries of schools, and some network-based teaching methods such as virtual classroom, online community and discussion area have also begun It has been widely popularized, which has changed the previous school-centered education system, and education is developing towards openness and lifelong. Information technology emphasizes independent, cooperative and inquiry problem-solving, and learners' personality has been fully reflected[3]. The vivid expression of multimedia technology can promote effective memory and improve the effectiveness of knowledge acquisition When the development of technology brings positive impact to educational informatization, it also leads people into a misunderstanding that educational informatization is "technology" Application in education. People rely too much on media and technology, so that people lose their nature and are controlled by technology, so that the technology that should be dominant in educational informatization controls people's life all the time, from an independent, free and personalized individual to a technical person in technology. The educated have high emotion, cooperative spirit, interpersonal communication and other abilities In order to solve various problems caused by the technological development of educational informatization, we need to analyze the connotation of educational informatization from different perspectives, depth and breadth. We should answer the question of educational informatization through the Paradigm Research of quantitative, qualitative, comprehensive, critical and interpretation of educational informatization "What is" rather than "why".

4.2   Highlight the Core Issue of Educational Informatization is Education

The core of educational informatization lies in its life form, so the core of educational informatization is not a "tool" problem or a "technology" problem, but a "adult" in the information technology environment Problems. Educational informatization should pay attention to the development and alienation of people in the process of educational informatization. The main object of educational informatization implementation is people. It should be a dynamic, step-by-step and continuous process, and its essence and core is education. It is a conscious social activity in the digital virtual world with the direct target of affecting people's physical and mental development. People's life The problem of existence and development began to enter the vision of educational informatization research. The product of educational informatization is specific individuals, and the talents in education are the core of educational informatization. Therefore, education is a good way to solve the problems of information technology.

Educational activities focus on how to mobilize and realize people's potential to the greatest extent, and how to fully generate people's internal spirituality and possibility. Education is more important than the education of people's soul, rather than just the accumulation of rational knowledge and understanding[4]. The origin of education is life, and life is the origin of education. People regulate these information through educational activities to affect education The quality, ability and concept of educators, guide and expand the essence, purpose and function of education at a deeper and wider level, have a comprehensive and scientific understanding of the self teaching process and various elements constituting the teaching process, study education from the practical level, and use educational principles, methods and ways to solve specific educational problems.

5   Educational Informatization from the Perspective of Pedagogy

5.1   Environmental Construction of Educational Informatization

Educational informatization is inseparable from the construction of three environments: hardware environment, software environment and humanistic environment.

The hardware environment includes various education and teaching media, various education and teaching equipment and facilities, and the surrounding environment of the school. Without these hardware environments, normal education and teaching activities cannot be carried out.

The software environment includes the software recording education and teaching information in different media, the conception, content and quality of the software.

Humanistic environment includes educational thought, educational theory, educational concept, educational system, educational laws and regulations, people's modern educational consciousness and the degree of mastering modern educational technology, etc.

The construction of hardware environment is the foundation, the construction of software environment is the guarantee, and the construction of humanistic environment is the key. There are no educators who have modern educational ideas, concepts and consciousness, master modern educational theory and modern educational technology, no educational system, policies and regulations in line with educational laws and China's national conditions, no good modern educational social atmosphere, no matter how good modern educational technology conditions, Will be difficult to play a role, no matter how good modern educational technology and equipment are difficult to be equipped in place.

5.2   The Renewal of Educational Concept is the Premise of Educational Informatization

Educational informatization is first of all the modernization of educational ideas. Any system innovation and system innovation depend on the renewal of ideas. Therefore, whether the leaders of educational competent departments, principals, teachers and students should carry out a revolution in educational ideas. Changing ideas is the primary task of educational informatization. The process of educational informatization can not be simply regarded as an information machine The introduction process of information technology can not be simply equivalent to computerization or networking. The process of educational informatization is the process of the transformation of educational ideas and educational ideas, and the process of systematic analysis and understanding of the process of knowledge transfer from the perspective of information. Only on this basis can we guide the application of information technology in the field of education. Educational informatization is not fashionable and should have a sense of urgency. At the same time, school leaders should also change their ideas and should not think that educational informatization is optional, early or late. School leaders should actively guide, create necessary conditions for educational informatization and strengthen teacher training, Teachers are encouraged to make full use of existing facilities and make full use of information means for teaching and scientific research.

At present, China's educational informatization is moving towards a new stage of digital transformation. The implementation of educational digitization strategy is a process of promoting the deep integration of emerging technologies such as Internet, big data, artificial intelligence and fifth generation mobile communication with education and teaching, using emerging technologies to update educational ideas, change educational models, and comprehensively promote the transformation of educational digitization. In accordance with the general requirements of "application is king, service is supreme, concise and efficient, and safe operation", the transformation and upgrading of digital enabled education management is essentially to apply digital technology and digital thinking to the whole process of education management with emerging technology as the main means and information data as the core elements, and carry out all-round, intelligent and comprehensive research on the ways, processes, means and tools of education management, education decision-making and education services Systematic function remodeling and process reengineering; Its essence is to improve the efficiency of education management, help the education system improve and create new governance capabilities, and use the same resources to run higher quality and fairer education.

Educational information requires teachers to change from the traditional knowledge imparter to the learning organizer and coordinator, that is, to guide, plan, organize and coordinate students' learning activities, and pay attention to cultivating students' ability of self-learning and acquiring information and knowledge. In the past, cultivating students' ability of self-learning emphasized the use of two tools, That is, dictionary and library. In the future, to add a tool, we should emphasize learning through the Internet. Teachers should pay attention to the improvement of their own quality and the development of curriculum courseware by using new technology. Teachers who have used a teaching plan for many years must be eliminated by the information society.

As far as students are concerned, educational informatization cannot be equated with the concept of simple Internet. Students should turn information network and technology into a tool for conscious learning, self discovery and independent exploration under the guidance of teachers. There is a conceptual problem here. We should not only think that learning is only when we enter the classroom, knowledge is only what teachers speak, and ability is only explained by test scores. We should comprehensively and correctly understand educational informatization, as shown in Fig. 2.

The Internet not only provides new educational means and contents, but also has an important impact on the cultivation of talents, the transformation of learning methods, the generation of new cultures and values, and even the evolution of language. In the whole process, it is also the publicity and dissemination of a national culture and values. If a nation does not seize this opportunity, it will be unable to stand on its own in the forest of nations in the world in the future.

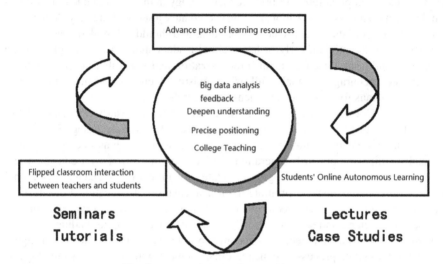

Fig. 2. Internet information teaching mode

6   Conclusion

In short, educational informatization plays a positive role in changing educational ideas and concepts, promoting teaching reform, accelerating educational development and the modernization of management means, especially in creating a social system of national learning and lifelong learning, deepening the reform of basic education, improving the quality and efficiency of higher education, and cultivating "Facing Modernization, the world and the future" The process of educational information construction and its all-round application is not only an effective way to reform the traditional educational model, but also an important measure to improve the national quality, and the only way for the Chinese nation to truly integrate into the international community.

References

1. Yu, S., Wang, M., Che, H.: An exposition of the crucial issues in china's educational informatization, Edu. Technol. Res. Develop. (2005)
2. Kim, J., Lee, W.: An analysis of educational informatization level of students, teachers, and parents: in Korea, Comput. Educ. (2013)
3. Wei, C., Yuan, L.: Reflection on college informationized teaching model under the background of educational informationization. In: 2019 IEEE International Conference on Computer Science and Educational Informatization (CSEI) (2019)

4. Gennadievna Matviyevskaya; E., Grigorievna Tavstukha, O., Vladimirovna Galustyan, O., Aleksandrovich Ignatov, P., Miroshnikova, D.: Formation of Information and Communication Competence of Future Teachers. IJET (2019)
5. Zhou, J.: The Path of Improving the Effectiveness of Ideological and Political Education from the Perspective of Educational Informatization (2020)
6. Wang, M., Wei, Y., ; Lu, X., Fang, J.: The research the informatization of rural basic education in guangxi from the perspective of educational modernization. In: 2020 International Conference on Big Data and Informatization Education (ICBDIE) (2020)
7. Shi, Y.: The relationship between educational informatization and regional economy and its coordinated development path in fragile ecological region. Int. J. Electr. Eng. Edu. (2021)
8. Dong, X., Chen, X.: Research on Online Teaching of College Teachers Under The Background of Education Informatization. In: Matec Web of Conferences (2021)
9. Wei, C., Zhong, L.: Research on the problems and countermeasures of higher education management informatization development in the computer internet era. J. Phys. Conf. Ser. (2021)
10. Tingting, W.: Policy analysis of educational informatization based on the perspective of policy tools. Adv. Educ. (2021)

Somatosensory Dance Interaction System Based on AdaBoost Algorithm

Jiahong Li[✉]

Lanzhou Resources and Environment Voc-Tech University, Lanzhou 730021, Gansu, China
lixdong@lzre.edu.cn

Abstract. As a new interdisciplinary subject, dance science is gradually absorbed by China's dance education with its scientific, healthy function and unique training value. It pays attention to scientific training methods, pays attention to the feeling process of movements, and emphasizes making up for many deficiencies in dancer training. Based on dance science training, this paper studies the somatosensory dance interaction system based on AdaBoost algorithm, and discusses its positive role in ontology. It has played a positive role in promoting the movement perception ability, the improvement of movement stability, the breakthrough of dynamic shaping and injury prevention in dance training.

Keywords: AdaBoost algorithm · Somatosensory interaction system · Dance

1 Introduction

Dance science training has been developed and applied in western countries in the 20th century. So far, it has developed many training forms, such as floor ballet, yoga, Pilates, Alexander and so on. Because dance scientific training pays more attention to noumenon feeling and pays attention to the training part ignored by dancers in a scientific way, more and more dance educators gradually change from teaching skills to paying attention to scientific training methods and enhancing the physical quality of dancers [1]. On the basis of traditional dance training, adding dance scientific training can enable dancers to quickly find effective practice methods. The practice process can strengthen dancers' perception of movements, improve the texture of dance movements, help dancers break through the plateau period in training, and enhance dancers' physical stability, It also plays an active role in preventing dance injuries.

The construction of dance theory "Mu class" teaching platform meets the needs of diversified teaching management. Generally speaking, "Mu class" teaching platform mainly includes the functions of student management, teaching plan management and teaching resource mobilization management [2]. It breaks through the limitations of traditional teaching methods and promotes the maximization of teaching resource sharing; "Mu class" teaching platform makes data statistics from the course dimension and user maintenance, which greatly enriches the data and report functions, provides more comprehensive and accurate query services for managers, teachers and learners, greatly

M. A. Jan and F. Khan (Eds.): BigIoT-EDU 2022, LNICST 466, pp. 10–20, 2023.
https://doi.org/10.1007/978-3-031-23947-2_2

reduces the daily workload of teachers, and plays a vital role in the development and promotion of dance.

To sum up, gradually cultivate the awareness of large-scale online open courses and promote the Internet of dance teaching services [3]. In order to change the traditional primary means of dance teaching and educational administration, we should modestly learn and learn from the advanced technology at home and abroad, or introduce high-tech application software at home and abroad, or our own research and development platform, and integrate the advantages and disadvantages. In order to make better use of dance teaching and improve the utilization of teaching resources, The development of "Mu class" teaching platform with dance course as the pilot is already a general trend [4]. At the same time, it is also hoped that the "Mu class" teaching system developed by taking the "Mu class" teaching of dance theory as an example will be effectively promoted in schools and other colleges in the future. Using the "Mu class" teaching platform for teaching can update the information of modern dance learning in a more timely manner, Make dance teaching reach a new level.

With the continuous development of human-computer interaction technology, people's demand for more natural interaction is becoming increasingly prominent. At the same time, the traditional interaction mode gradually shows some shortcomings. The human action has many forms of expression, including body posture or movement process such as arm, head, face and limbs [5]. The human movement belongs to the information interaction between human and environment, which can reflect the inner thoughts of human beings to the greatest extent. Therefore, using human action for human-computer interaction has become a novel and natural way of interaction. Therefore, this paper studies the somatosensory dance interaction system based on AdaBoost algorithm.

2 Related Work

2.1 Somatosensory Interaction Technology

As a kind of intelligent interaction, somatosensory interaction, also known as "motion sensing interaction technology", is a technology that directly uses body movements, sounds, expressions and other ways to interact with computer equipment or environment, and the computer interprets and recognizes the user's body movements and sounds, and makes relevant feedback. It emphasizes the use of body movements, gestures, voice and other existing ways in real life to interact with computers, so as to reduce people's dependence on unnatural control methods such as mouse and keyboard, and make users pay attention to the task itself.

In recent years, somatosensory interaction technology has played an important role in education and teaching. It plays an important role in physical education teaching and enhances learners' sense of participation and immersion. The learning environment combining somatosensory interaction technology and motion perception can fully mobilize learners' multi sensory organs, closely combine learning and motion, and enhance human-computer interaction, which is conducive to learners' health and greatly increase learners' interest [6]. It plays an important role in sports evaluation. It improves the traditional test method and realizes objective quantitative evaluation. It plays an important role in teaching practice, provides teaching tools, learning resources and learning environment for situational teaching, personalized teaching and game teaching, and changes the way of learning and evaluation. Somatosensory interactive games are becoming more and more popular among students, especially special children, which is helpful for special children's learning and rehabilitation training. Somatosensory interaction method directly uses gesture limbs instead of mouse and keyboard operation, which increases the interaction in teaching. It is used to make various learning tools to make teaching more visual, animated and lively in learning and promoting effective learning in games, and finally compensate for the shortcomings of human-computer interaction in traditional mouse and keyboard mode [7]. Somatosensory interaction has improved the enthusiasm of teaching and learning, but there are also some problems, such as difficult development, rapid technology renewal and limited teaching effect. The application of somatosensory interaction technology in education and teaching still needs to be developed and studied.

Somatosensory technology is that people can directly interact with surrounding devices or scene objects through human actions without mouse and keyboard. According to the different ways and principles of user somatosensory, the mainstream somatosensory technologies can be roughly divided into the following four categories.

(1) Inertial sensing. This technology is mainly based on inertial sensors. It mainly obtains the user's physical data such as motion acceleration, angular velocity and magnetic field through gyroscopes, gravity sensors and other equipment, and then analyzes these data to determine the user's action changes in the scene space.

(2) Optical sensing. This technology mainly collects the information in the surrounding environment and user shadow through optical sensors The image data is then processed by computer to interact with the corresponding content. As early as 2004, Sony launched EYETOY optical sensing equipment, which is mainly based on 2D plane. Firstly, it obtains the user's image data, and then through the analysis and processing of the image data, users can interact with the game through their own body movements [8]. In 2010, Microsoft released a new somatosensory suite Kinect, which can obtain human depth images and motion data through laser and infrared cameras, and is not limited by the influence of light. In 2014, the second generation Kinect somatosensory device was launched. The device supports the windows operating system and can recognize human graphics data, voice data and motion data. It is cheap and can complete natural human-computer interaction without other external auxiliary devices [9]. It is suitable for laboratory research and is favored by the majority of developers.

(3) Inertial and optical joint sensing. This technology combines the advantages of inertial sensing and optical sensing, has simple structure and more accurate data detection. The Wii launched by Nintendo in 2006 mainly detects the displacement and acceleration of the user's hand in space through two sensors, so as to identify some simple limb movements of the user. In 2010, Sony launched the joystick move, which can be used to detect the movement and rotation of users' hands in space.

(4) Other body sensing. Such as other sensing technologies based on muscle electrical signal or WiFi signal. Based on the above comparative analysis, Kinect V2 is selected as the user's somatosensory data acquisition equipment to design and develop the hydraulic turbine teaching system. Kinect is a somatosensory device developed by Microsoft, including three cameras and four microphones. The device can realize the functions of

depth image data acquisition, human motion data tracking, audio processing and gesture recognition. The specific equipment is shown in Fig. 1.

Fig. 1. Kinect

2.2 AdaBoost Algorithm

AdaBoost algorithm is one of the ten classical algorithms in data mining. The most representative algorithm in the boosting algorithm group is AdaBoost algorithm. The origin of boosting algorithm series comes from the PAC learning theory proposed by valiant. PAC theory studies what kind of problem can be learned and the specific algorithm of learnable problem. In the PAC learning model, the question whether the weak learning algorithm can be promoted to the strong learning algorithm was first proposed by valiant and Kearns. In 1994, schapire gave a positive answer to this question. In 1995, schapire and frenund proposed an improved boosting algorithm based on the online allocation algorithm. It is called AdaBoost algorithm [10]. Compared with boosting algorithm, this algorithm is more efficient and simpler.

AdaBoost algorithm is an important feature classification algorithm in machine learning. It has been widely used in facial expression recognition, image retrieval and other applications. AdaBoost algorithm has good performance. First, AdaBoost algorithm can greatly improve the accuracy of decision tree. Second, the algorithm runs fast and basically does not need to call parameters. Third, the algorithm has almost no over fitting problem [11]. These advantages of AdaBoost algorithm make it widely used in classification and regression problems. AdaBoost mainly solves two kinds of problems, multi class single label problem, multi class multi label problem, regression problem, etc.

The calculation process of adabost algorithm is: given the training set: (x1, Y1),..., (xn, yn) where Yi $\in \{-1,1\}$, which is the label of Xi, I $= 1,...,$ n. Then the initial distribution of the sample is:

$$\|\Delta x_{k+1}(t)\| \leq k_f \int_0^t \|\Delta x_{k+1}(t)\| d\tau + m_1 \int_0^t \|\Delta u_k(\tau)\| d\tau \qquad (1)$$

The flow chart of AdaBoost algorithm is shown in Fig. 2.

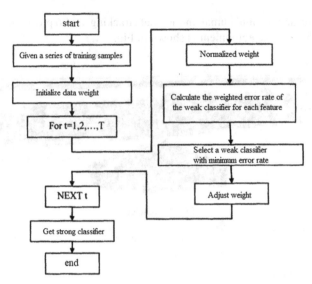

Fig. 2. AdaBoost algorithm flow chart

3   Demand Analysis of Somatosensory Dance Interaction System

3.1   System Design Principles

The system scheme design shall meet the following principles:

(1) Ease of use.
The original intention of the development of somatosensory interactive dance teaching system is to build a bridge between dance teachers and students in Colleges and universities. The simplicity and operability of the system is very important. The ease of use of the system directly affects the confidence of both parties in the use of the remote system. In particular, college students enrolled at this stage are students who pursue innovation and trend. They have high requirements for the beauty of the user system interface and the ease of use of the system. Moreover, in terms of user-oriented document online production and training material upload, they should have a large number of processing mechanisms to adapt to the big data problems in the current society [12]. Therefore, ease of use is also a key requirement for designing an efficient and reusable system.

(2) Security.
Security is mainly aimed at whether users have done just perfect in account login and password protection when using the system, because the leakage of accounts or passwords may cause great loss to the distance teaching system, because the login accounts are often ID number or ID card number, which both give the criminals the opportunity to take advantage of the system. To a certain extent, it does not have security, and also loses the requirements of the system for privacy. Criminals will even extort money by using the courseware or image and video materials uploaded by the teachers Upload the network, which will leak the privacy of teachers, so the security requirement is a more important requirement index in the process of system design.

(3) Reliability.

Reliability is also an important index for examining a system, especially for the software failure that may occur when users use the system. However, the frequency statistics of software failure is the key factor to measure a system, and it is also a more important factor for other aspects such as the severity, recoverability and predictability of system failure, However, the former is the main factor and the latter are secondary factors.

(4) Stability.

System stability refers to the phenomena of memory leakage, sudden interface crash and system crash during the user's use of the system. Imagine that if the picture is suddenly interrupted due to the instability of the system, or the interface collapses due to long-time operation, it is tantamount to causing a teaching accident, but the responsibility is not caused by the teacher, This is the problem of system development, maintenance and stability, which will damage everyone's confidence in using the distance learning system.

(5) System performance.

System performance refers to the additional attribute indicators of the distance teaching system, mainly including system response time, throughput, accuracy, effectiveness, resource utilization, average button response frequency and other indicators. The whole system (including database and service components) adopts cluster architecture, and the internal load balancing mechanism is realized through optimized algorithms to avoid single point of failure [13]. After a large number of preliminary tests, the system can ensure trouble free operation for 24 * 7 h. In case of any problem, ensure that the system can resume normal operation within two hours. Database resources should be backed up regularly (at least daily).

3.2 System Design Objectives

The design goal of dance somatosensory interactive teaching platform is to closely combine Internet technology with dance teaching, make up for the shortcomings of traditional dance teaching mode, such as lack of high-quality teachers and resources, lack of manpower, and lack of guarantee for teaching quality and process, and create a joint construction and sharing, benign and effective interaction between teachers and students, centered on the "Mu class" course of dance theory Massive quality dance teaching resources converge, with advanced, sustainable, iterative and upgrading development to meet the needs of our school dance teaching online education platform, thereby improving the level of dance teaching management and teaching, improving students' ability of active learning and innovative learning, and meeting the increasing demand of dance teaching in the society [14].

(1) Fully demonstrate the construction of school dance curriculum. On the platform, the school's dance curriculum construction resources are displayed in an all-round way, promote the co construction and sharing of high-quality curriculum resources, help the school build a high-quality dance teaching team, provide the school with effective dance curriculum production tools, and accelerate the transformation and innovation of dance teaching concepts.

(2) Establish an open and sharing platform for large-scale dance teaching. The sharing of curriculum resources among teachers in the school allows students to enjoy more high-quality teaching resources. The sharing of possible contents between teachers and students, including problem discussion, mid-term and final exams, mutual evaluation of homework, and integration with curriculum learning, is conducive to students' autonomous learning potential, and also provides a shortcut for inter school curriculum resource exchange and sharing.

4 Somatosensory Dance Interaction System Based on AdaBoost Algorithm

4.1 Overall Architecture

The system design method of the dance physical interaction system adopts a three-layer structure, which are data layer, control layer and performance layer.

1) The data layer is mainly responsible for reading the song profile and evaluation criteria profile, and the iterator is used as an intermediate abstraction layer to provide a convenient data access interface for the control layer and the performance layer. The song configuration file stores the beat type, number of beats, beat interval of action similarity evaluation and beat interval of action cue picture display for each song; the evaluation standard file stores the action similarity score and the correspondence of its level.

2) The control layer includes music beat control, movement sequence pre-processing, movement similarity evaluation and dance flow control system. The motion sequence pre-processing module uses interpolation wavelets to reduce the noise of the collected motion sequences. The movement similarity evaluation module scores user movements in real time. Based on the song configuration and the time manager of Unity3D engine, the beat control module passes the strong and weak beat messages to the movement evaluation module and the performance layer part of the module. The dance process control module is responsible for the overall process control, including the music and dance animation synchronization, pause and dance end judgment and other functions.

3) The performance layer includes the visual elements in the 3D scene and the user interface, which is used to receive the data input from users and display the data to provide users with a physical virtual interactive scene. Among them, the user points module is used to accumulate the points of each action evaluation and display; the action prompt module is used to display the prompt map of the previous, current and next action; the scene interaction module controls the three-dimensional model in the scene to synchronize with the user's action; the evaluation display module is used to display the evaluation of the user's dance action in real time, where the data comes from the action evaluation module in the logic layer; the completion display module The animation control module realizes the playback of the standard dance movements collected by the motion capture system on the 3D model in advance. The system structure is shown in Fig. 3.

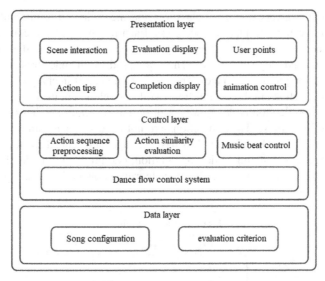

Fig. 3. System structure diagram

4.2 Module Division Design

The production of somatosensory dance interactive system based on AdaBoost algorithm consists of planning, art and program. Planning to carry out system design in the early stage and system module integration in the later stage, including the preparation and modification of planning scheme and game synthesis; The work of art is to make relevant art resources used in the game, including 2D pictures, 3D models, special effects, etc. the main needs are described by the planning, and the art is made according to the overall style of the system and the needs of the planning scheme; The work of the program is to divide the planned and designed game into different modules and realize these modules, including system design, scene construction, UI control and somatosensory control of somatosensory game.

The system data layer is responsible for storing the configuration file and parsing the configuration file. The storage configuration file module stores the song configuration data at runtime as an XML file according to the predefined rules. A special parsing configuration file module is set up to parse the XML, and the data is written into the data structure at runtime. This data configuration method can keep the data in the configuration file consistent with the actual dance beat. The accuracy of the systematic movement evaluation and the overall dance experience have been greatly improved.

4.3 Implementation of Action Recognition

The definition of human bones in openni is composed of joint points. Each joint point has two key parameters: position and direction. Openni defines a total of 24 joint points. At present, when using the plug-in nite for motion recognition, only 15 joint points are supported at most.

Openni defines a very important class to act as the basic unit of internal communication, which is called production node class. Each production node class has a clear production function. For example, the user production node class is used to process user data information and judge user status; The depth production node class is used to read depth images or output depth images. The production node is in charge of all the basic and necessary functions in the openni framework. Development using openni is inseparable from the production node. However, openni also defines another kind to realize some advanced functions. These functions are not necessary and can be called when developers need them. This kind of class has an image name called capability class.

In the process of realizing action recognition, one production node class and two capability classes are mainly used. The core algorithm flow is shown in Fig. 4.

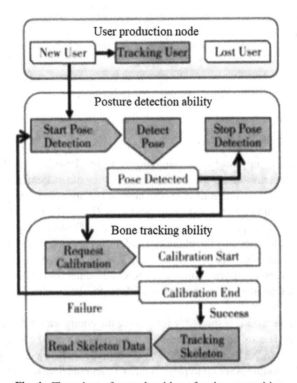

Fig. 4. Flow chart of core algorithm of action recognition

Before starting to identify user actions, you first need to call the user production node class to detect the user. The production node class is used through the callback function. Therefore, when initializing the user's production node class, newuser and lostuser callback functions are registered, corresponding to the two events of user occurrence and user departure. When the user is successfully detected, the newuser function will be called to start tracking the user and trigger the pose detection capability class. The function of pose detection capability class is to judge whether the user makes a specific calibration pose. The detected user needs to make the calibration pose before triggering the next capability class. The callback function posedetected is registered in the pose detection capability class. When a new user is detected, it will start to detect and wait for the user to make a calibration pose. When the calibration pose is detected, the function posedetected will be activated, and then send a request for bone information calibration to the bone tracking ability class, and stop the detection of the calibration pose.

After receiving the bone information calibration request, the bone tracking ability class starts bone information calibration through the callback function calibrationstart. When the user's posture and calibration posture reach a certain degree of confidence, use the callback number calibrationend to complete the calibration and start bone tracking. If the bone information calibration cannot be carried out within a certain time, the posture detection ability class will be triggered again to detect the calibrated posture in a cycle.

According to the above algorithm flow, the system compiles a set of scripts in the script editing environment of unity 3D. Its main function is to detect the user, calibrate and track the user's bone data, and transfer the data to the virtual character's bone in real time. Its core structure is as follows:

```
public class OpenNIUserTracker{
void Star().
void Update().
public void UpdateSkeleton().
void userGenerator. NewUser().
void userGenerator_ LostUser().
void poseDetectionCapability PoseDetected().
void AtemptCalibrationForAllUsers().
void skeletonCapbility. CalibrationEnd().
```

The script registers five important functions to call the five core callback functions required for action recognition, namely new user, lost user, pose detected, calibration start and calibration end in the core algorithm (Fig. 4). The start function in the script calls five core functions, which will be executed first each time the script is called to realize user initialization and action calibration. The update function determines whether the user's distance from Kinect is appropriate when rendering each frame. The updateskeleton function is called by each joint point of the virtual character bone to traverse and update the position and direction of each joint point, so as to complete the action recognition of the whole bone in this frame.

5 Conclusion

With the more and more extensive application of computers, people's demand for human-computer interaction technology is not improved in modern life. Under this background, human-computer interaction technology has become a research hotspot, and somatosensory technology is the mainstream of research. This paper studies the somatosensory dance interaction system based on AdaBoost algorithm. The system consists of motion capture system, real-time somatosensory motion evaluation system and data configuration tool. Combined with appropriate post-processing, get the standard dance movements; The Kinect somatosensory camera is used as the action acquisition device to evaluate the user's action based on AdaBoost algorithm; The data configuration tool provides developers with a workflow to make dance song configuration files quickly and accurately.

References

1. Pan, S.: Design of intelligent robot control system based on human–computer interaction. Inte. J. Syst. Assur. Eng. Manag. 1–10 (2021). https://doi.org/10.1007/s13198-021-01267-9
2. Zhu, Y.X., Jin, H.R.: Speaker localization based on audio-visual bimodal fusion (2021)
3. Xu, L., Hou, J., Gao, J.: A novel smart depression recognition method using human-computer interaction system. Wirel. Commun. Mob. Comput. **20**, 1–8 (2021)
4. Wang, C.J.: Deep Learning Strategies in Media Teaching System Based on ADABoost Algorithm (2021)
5. Volik, M., Kovaleva, M., Khachaturova, E.: The concept of implementing a customer interaction system based on CRM Bitrix24. In: SHS Web of Conferences (2021)
6. Zhang, D.: Intelligent recognition of dance training movements based on machine learning and embedded system. J. Intell. Fuzzy Syst. **1**, 1–13 (2021)
7. Zhong, L.K., Xie, C.L., Jiang, S., et al.: Prioritizing susceptible genes for thyroid cancer based on gene interaction network. Front. Cell Develop. Biol. **9**, 740267 (2021)
8. Lokare, V.T., Netak, L.D.: Concentration Level Prediction System for the Students Based on Physiological Measures Using the EEG Device (2021)
9. Wang, H., Qi, X.: V-E algorithm: A new vital vertex identifying algorithm based on vertex-edge interaction. Asia-Pacific J. Oper. Res. (2021)
10. Brenneis, D., Parker, A.S., Johanson, M.B., et al.: Assessing human interaction in virtual reality with continually learning prediction agents based on reinforcement learning algorithms: A pilot study (2021)
11. Cataldo, A., Hagura, N., Hyder, Y., et al.: Touch inhibits touch: sanshool-induced paradoxical tingling reveals perceptual interaction between somatosensory submodalities. Proc. R. Soc. B: Biol. Sci. **2021**(288), 20202914 (1943)
12. Wang, C.M., Lin, Y.H.: Construction of a somatosensory interactive system based on computer vision and augmented reality techniques using the kinect device for food and agricultural education. Int. J. Eng. Sci. Technol. **5**(2), 1–37 (2021)
13. Gb, A., Epb, C., Glb, C., et al.: Somatosensory inputs modulate the excitability of cerebellar-cortical interaction. Sci. Dir. (2021)
14. Wilson, A., Nodarse, C.L., Peraza, J., et al.: Examining somatosensory function by age, testing site, and modality. J. Pain **22**(5), 590 (2021)

Value Reconstruction and Path Innovation of Blockchain Technology for the Development of Higher Education

Donghong Zhang[✉]

Medical College, University of Business Management, Yunnan 650106, China
zdh123450701@163.com

Abstract. As an integrated application of distributed data storage, point-to-point transmission, consensus mechanism, encryption algorithm and other technologies, blockchain has become a hot spot in the research and application of the United Nations, the International Monetary Fund and other international organizations as well as in the field of education in recent years. This paper discusses the value reconstruction of blockchain technology on the development of higher education from three perspectives: college student credit investigation management mode, digital education resource service supply mode and collaborative development mode of public service platform of higher education. The theoretical mechanism and logical basis of integration can be grasped from the multiple perspectives of system theory, discipline theory, innovation theory, overall education theory and knowledge theory. The path of integration includes: the nature of education, the pluralistic integration of "Trinity"; Type generation; Multi level and multi type school integration; The way of running a school, the two-way integration of "combination of work and study, school enterprise cooperation", and the improvement and integration of system construction, supporting facilities and system.

Keywords: Blockchain · Higher education · Path innovation · Value reconstruction

1 Introduction

The rapid development of information technology has improved the degree of informatization in various fields of society and accelerated the process of a new round of technological revolution. As an emerging technology, blockchain technology has attracted extensive attention all over the world. Some developed countries such as the United States, Britain, Russia and Japan have actively studied it and accelerated the application and development of blockchain technology [1]. The white paper on China's blockchain technology and application development, prepared with the participation of the Ministry of industry and information technology, summarizes the core technology, development route and trend of blockchain, and raises the research of blockchain technology to the national level. The use of blockchain technology to promote industrial development

M. A. Jan and F. Khan (Eds.): BigIoT-EDU 2022, LNICST 466, pp. 21–30, 2023.
https://doi.org/10.1007/978-3-031-23947-2_3

plays a positive guiding role and also brings unprecedented opportunities for innovation and development in the field of education [1]. The blockchain technology framework is shown in Fig. 1 below.

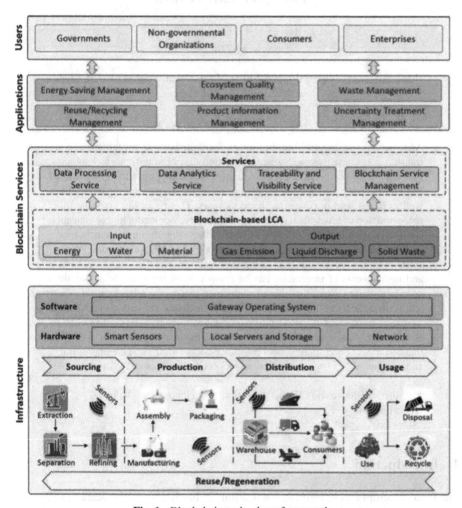

Fig. 1. Blockchain technology framework

The innovative development of education is not realized through the independent role of technologies such as big data, MOOCS, Internet of things, virtual reality and artificial intelligence. Instead, new things are formed based on these technologies and realized and transformed through the blockchain known as the second generation Internet, so as to promote the innovative development of Education. In the long run, "blockchain + education" is an irresistible development trend [2]. Therefore, studying the potential value of blockchain technology for educational innovation and development has certain theoretical value and practical significance.

Blockchain technology is another new technology that has attracted great attention from governments and enterprises around the world after cloud computing, the Internet of things and big data. Even under the serious impact of the global COVID-19, blockchain still maintains the trend of rapid development. While most industry personnel are facing the risk of unemployment, especially the education industry, the work related to blockchain is increasing, Blockchain technology has also become a popular hard core skill. The trend of blockchain development is shown in Fig. 2 below.

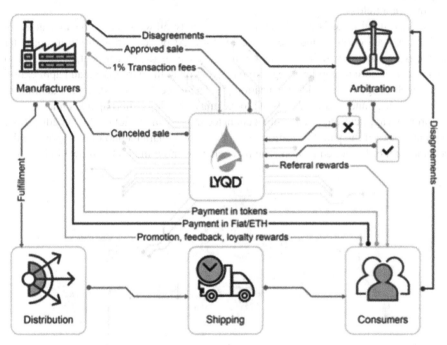

Fig. 2. The trend of rapid development of blockchain

"Education" is an important industry related to the national economy and the people's livelihood. As a populous country in the world, China is one of the largest education markets in the world [3]. In recent years, with the development of the national economy, people have become more and more aware of the importance of education. The state has also begun to pay more and more attention to education, and has issued a number of incentive policies to promote the continuous and good development of the education industry.

In june,2020, the Ministry of Education issued the guiding opinions on strengthening the regular learning of disabled children and adolescents at the stage of compulsory education, which made it clear that we should play the role of resource center and encourage the use of big data and blockchain technology to improve the accuracy of services [4].

In June, 2021, the Ministry of education and other six departments issued, pointing out that the new generation of information technologies such as 5 blockchain should be deeply applied to give full play to the role of data as a new production factor and promote the digital transformation of education.

In addition, provinces and cities in China have also successively issued policies related to "blockchain + education" to promote the specific application of blockchain technology.

It is believed that blockchain, artificial intelligence and big data will become the three technical pillars in the field of financial technology in the future, and blockchain may be the "Internet" in 10 years. Do not know what impact blockchain will have on the education field?

At present, with the further development of society, all walks of life begin to actively explore, pay attention to and use this technology. At present, in addition to applying blockchain technology to the familiar fields of finance, medical treatment, energy and so on, more and more researchers begin to pay attention to the exploration and application of this technology in the field of education [5]. Therefore, by introducing the definition, core technology and characteristics of blockchain technology, this paper summarizes the research and application status of blockchain technology in the field of higher education, and puts forward the path innovation research of blockchain technology to promote the development of higher education. The blockchain worked method is shown in Fig. 3.

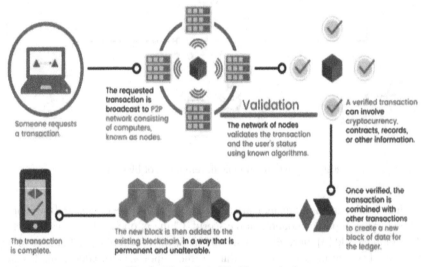

Fig. 3. Blockchain Working method

2   Overview of Relevant Technologies

2.1   Blockchain Technology

The concept of blockchain originated from bitcoin. Bitcoin is a virtual cryptocurrency that adopts point-to-point network and consensus mobility and takes blockchain as the underlying technology. Blockchain technology is a data structure that combines blockchains. It uses the network to record and store information in a distributed way, rather than using the central organization to organize and manage. The information to be processed recorded in a block consists of two parts: the block header and the block body. They are generated in a certain order. The block header and the block body have their own roles. The former is responsible for connecting to the next block through the main chain, and the latter is responsible for storing and analyzing information. The operation principle of blockchain has changed the traditional billing method that is recorded and managed uniformly by the central organization into a bill that is publicly available in all networks and jointly maintained by all nodes [6]. This new method enables each transaction information to be published in the whole network and publicly available to all accounts, so that everyone can check it together, It ensures the authenticity and reliability of transaction information. The education blockchain technology is shown in Fig. 4 below.

In recent years, with the rapid growth of China's economy, the acceleration of the process of wealth and urbanization, and the adjustment of economic and social structure, people's demand has gradually risen from the material level to the spiritual level. Cultural consumption has increasingly become the main daily expenditure of people. The demand of urban residents for cultural consumption has increased significantly, and the proportion of people's expenditure on education and training in consumer expenditure has gradually increased.

In 2019, the per capita consumption expenditure on education, culture and entertainment was 2513 yuan, an increase of 12.9%, accounting for 11.7% of the per capita consumption expenditure. In the first three quarters of 2020, due to the impact of COVID-19, the per capita consumption expenditure on education, culture and entertainment was 1276 yuan, down 27.7%, accounting for 8.6% of the per capita consumption expenditure [7].

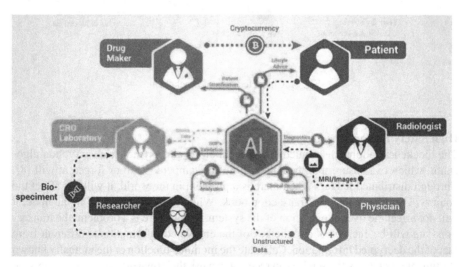

Fig. 4. Education blockchain Technology

With the population increasing year by year, the reform of education system and the influence of Chinese traditional culture, it is predicted that the scale of China's k12 education market will reach about 946.8 billion yuan in 2025 according to the development of China's k12 education industry in recent years.

2.2 Characteristics of Blockchain

The blockchain is linked in a decentralized manner, so that any node can directly realize data transmission and verification without the need for a third-party platform or other facilities. Data runs from point to point, saving a lot of cost and transaction time. The characteristics of blockchain are shown in Fig. 5 below.

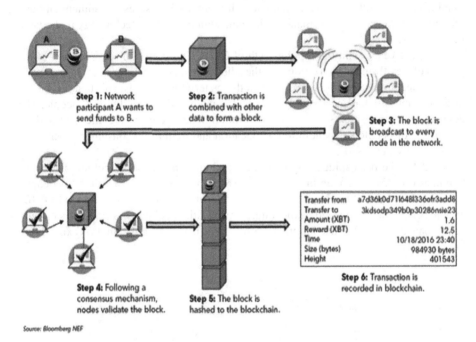

Fig. 5. Characteristics of blockchain

High Safety Factor

The blockchain adopts distributed ledger technology and asymmetric encryption algorithm, which can ensure that the data will not be tampered with or forged at will [8]. Through distributed ledger; When there is a problem in the world, it will not affect the country. Users need to add a transaction book. When there is a problem in the node, it will not affect the overall operation of the system. When there is a problem, the transaction data will be encrypted, and the key of the encrypted information is different from that of the decrypted information. Calculate the modulus function of the mutually known starting number. Only the sender and receiver can use their own different private keys for encryption and decryption, and need to be publicly verified through the key [9]. Any user can encrypt the information with the public key to ensure the authenticity and reliability of the information, and the owner of the information can decrypt the information with the private key to make the information more secure [10].

Information Transparency

Users can access, read, write and trade information according to their own permissions and authentication. Except that private information encryption is not accessible, any data on other blockchains can be accessed unrestricted, and the information of the whole system is highly transparent. Blockchain technology can also promote the transparent sharing of data between different organizations and strictly supervise the opening of data. Figure 6 below shows the information transparency process.

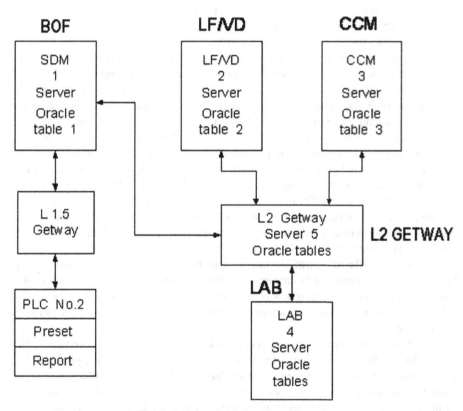

Fig. 6. Information transparency process

High Trust

The blockchain system adopts the mode of smart contract. According to the set code, only those who meet the conditions can automatically execute the program, which can avoid transaction interference and tampering and ensure the reliability of program operation [11]. In addition, the blockchain is connected by a 256 bit random number password, and the transaction is completed through the connection address, public key signature, private key verification signature, etc., which greatly reduces the trust risk of the system.

5. Users have Self Sovereignty

Users can strengthen self identification while maintaining control over the storage and management of their personal data, and the recorded content is not easy to be modified by other users.

3 Value Reconstruction and Path Innovation of Blockchain Technology for the Development of Higher Education

In the existing educational institutions, course teachers and student counselors should evaluate students, especially course teachers, need to provide a lot of learning materials to support it. The traditional educational administration management system, because the development company is aimed at most colleges and universities, so teachers use it more cumbersome and backward, which makes the office efficiency very low. In view of this situation, relevant personnel can use blockchain to solve this problem and separate teachers' teaching and educational affairs [12]. On the one hand, they can establish a separate blockchain for teachers and students, and teachers can record students' classroom performance. On the other hand, they can establish a blockchain for teachers and counselors to facilitate counselors to pay attention to students' learning status.

Due to the regional characteristics of our country, the educational resources in the north, South and East are seriously uneven, which limits the effective utilization of higher education resources. The traditional practice is that colleges and universities turn their own resources into electronic resources to realize sharing, but this cycle is long, the information is inaccurate, and the sharing effect is also very poor. Blockchain technology has changed the traditional way of resource sharing. By using point-to-point data storage, each teacher can make full use of his own block to upload teaching data materials, verify the reliability of information in the period through consensus, and realize synchronous sharing of all information. In this way, students can query relevant data in the fastest and most concise way, which saves time, improves efficiency and achieves the purpose of balancing educational resources [13].

The unique consensus and traceability of blockchain technology make every recorded information verified and added in order. This unique feature can protect copyright. When each submitted work is recorded in the blockchain as information, it will automatically generate a time point to ensure the accuracy of the information, and will be protected by the unique electronic signature technology. In this way, even if the work is continuously reproduced and cited, the information of the original work can still be found through the blockchain technology to protect the rights and interests of the original work.

Blockchain technology promotes the innovation and development of higher education, which requires strong information technology original innovation and integrated innovation ability [14]. Pay attention to technological innovation, consolidate the development foundation, pay attention to talent training, optimize the development environment, issue incentive policies, and increase support.

4 Blockchain Information Management Mode

Academic fraud, paper fraud, job resume fraud, employers and colleges lack verification means, suffer the loss caused by information asymmetry, and reduce the trust between schools and enterprises, colleges and universities [15].

In the next few years, based on the promotion of "Internet + education" application demonstration and "artificial intelligence + education" application scenarios by the education department, it is necessary to deeply explore vocational education, continuing education and other fields, and build exemplary "blockchain + education" application models in online teaching, teaching experiments, libraries and other teaching scenarios [16].

5 Conclusion

As a new technology, blockchain has attracted more and more attention, and its application field has gradually expanded to all walks of life. Many scholars at home and abroad have conducted relevant research on blockchain technology, which has laid a good theoretical foundation for people to better understand its operation mechanism and application value. For the field of education, blockchain technology is still mysterious, but its opportunities and potential value for education development are becoming increasingly prominent. We should continue to explore in depth and work together to draw the blueprint of "blockchain + education".

Although the government, educational administrative agencies, universities and traditional primary and secondary schools have recognized the great potential of blockchain in promoting education development, they have carried out practices such as infrastructure, technical architecture and application mode based on blockchain, and have produced certain results. However, based on the continuous promotion of blockchain practice and application, it faces the lack of normative and guiding policies and documents.

Therefore, it is an urgent need to formulate policies and standards related to "blockchain + education". The international standards organization IEEE is preparing the "blockchain vertical industry standard" (p2418, ISO). There are three working groups (foundation, security, privacy and identity authentication, smart contracts and their applications) and three research groups (use cases, governance and interoperability). ITU has carried out research on blockchain standards in "SG13/16/17/20".

References

1. Hua, D.: Value reconstruction and Path Innovation of blockchain technology for the development of Higher Education. Mod. Educ. Technol. **10**, 55–60 (2017)
2. Xianmin, Y., Xin, L., Huanqing, W., et al.: Application mode and practical challenges of blockchain technology in Education. Modern Distance Education Research **2**, 34–44 (2017)
3. Qing, L., Xin, Z.: Blockchain: promoting openness and public trust in education with technology. J. Dist. Educ. **1**, 36–44 (2017)
4. Jiayang, X.: Research on innovation of cross-border payment system based on blockchain technology. Financial Education Research **6**(9–14), 25 (2017)

5. Hyeok, K.M., Jin, L.W., Hee, L.D., et al.: Development of nanofiber reinforced double layered cabin air filter using novel upward mass production electrospinning set up. J. Nanosci. Nanotechnol. **18**(3), 2132–2136 (2018)
6. Saratov, A.A.: Synchronizing the operation of workshops in custom production. Autom. Remote. Control. **82**(3), 481–489 (2021)
7. Xu, J., Tran, H.M., Gautam, N., Bukkapatnam, S.T.S.: Joint production and maintenance operations in smart custom-manufacturing systems. IISE Trans. **51**(4), 406–421 (2019)
8. Kovacs, K., Ansari, F., Sihn, W.: A modified Weibull model for service life prediction and spare parts forecast in heat treatment industry. Proc. Manuf. **54**(9), 172–177 (2021)
9. Rocha, C., Miron, L.G.: The house factory: a simulation game for understanding mass customization in house building. J. Profess. Issues Eng. Educ. Pract. **144**(1), 01–08 (2018)
10. Siderska, J., Jadaan, K.S.: Cloud manufacturing: a service-oriented manufacturing paradigm. A review paper. Eng. Manag. Prod. Serv. **10**(1), 22–31 (2018)
11. Fathi, M., Ghobakhloo, M.: Enabling mass customization and manufacturing sustainability in Industry 4.0 context: a novel heuristic algorithm for in-plant material supply optimization. Sustainability **12**(16), 6669 (2020)
12. Liu, C., Yao, J.: Dynamic supply chain integration optimization in service mass customization. Comput. Ind. Eng. **120**(07), 42–52 (2018)
13. Zabatiero, J., Straker, L., Mantilla, A., Edwards, S., Danby, S.: Young children and digital technology: Australian early childhood education and care sector adults' perspectives. Australas. J. Early Childhood **43**(2), 14–22 (2018)
14. Naslund, J.A., Aschbrenner, K.A.: Digital technology for health promotion: opportunities to address excess mortality in persons living with severe mental disorders. Evid. Based Ment. Health **22**(1), 17–22 (2020)
15. Aujla, G.S., Kumar, N., Zomaya, A.Y., Ranjan, R.: Optimal decision making for big data processing at edge-cloud environment: an SDN perspective. IEEE Trans. Industr. Inf. **18**(000), 1 (2018)
16. Valerio, P., Antonio, P., Antonio, P., Sperli, G.: Benchmarking big data architectures for social networks data processing using public cloud platforms. Futur. Gener. Comput. Syst. **89**(11), 98–109 (2018)

Research on the Design of Automatic Accompaniment System of Piano Teaching Audio Database Under the Background of the Internet

Li Guo[✉]

Tongling College, Anhui 244000, China
guoli_1010@126.com

Abstract. With the rapid development of Internet technology, China has entered the era of Internet plus. In order to comply with the trend, colleges and universities have also established a relatively perfect campus network system, which provides strong technical support for teaching, scientific research and various types of activities. The interactive teaching theory of education cloud provides a solid theoretical support for the implementation of the integrated piano teaching mode of "teaching, scientific research and artistic practice", which makes piano teachers and students get all-round development.

Keywords: Internet background · Education cloud · Research on the mode of integration

1 Introduction

Nowadays, the research on the field of piano subject information has attracted the attention of experts and scholars. More and more people realize the significance of information teaching methods for the improvement of piano teaching quality. Interactive piano course based on education cloud has two forms: individual class and collective class. Six weeks as a teaching cycle can be used to summarize and analyze the weekly class situation in the form of experimental data tracking. The first, second and fifth weeks are in the form of individual courses, while the third, fourth and sixth weeks are collective courses. From the first week to the sixth week, the corresponding teaching methods are carried out respectively, which can be accepted by the students step by step. The data are obtained by combining the recognition degree and effect feedback of the students every week, and finally check the students' completion, thus reflecting the advantages of a new piano teaching mode in the information technology environment.

Education cloud can effectively integrate the data resources generated in the process of educational informatization, provide a low-cost, convenient, efficient and rich resource platform for teachers and students, and provide powerful technical support for the reform of educational information. The application of cloud platform in piano teaching makes

M. A. Jan and F. Khan (Eds.): BigIoT-EDU 2022, LNICST 466, pp. 31–38, 2023.
https://doi.org/10.1007/978-3-031-23947-2_4

the teaching cost greatly reduced, and more funds can be invested in improving teaching hardware facilities, high-quality learning resources are widely used, the shortage of piano teachers in western region has been improved, and teachers and students have also improved their comprehensive quality in network teaching. The relevant research of the information piano teaching has been more adequate, and many music colleges of comprehensive universities are also in the preliminary application. This paper takes the students of music major in the music college of comprehensive university as the audience, and analyzes the integrated mode of piano teaching, scientific research and art practice based on the education cloud[1].

2   Piano Education Cloud Information Platform

2.1   Interactive Piano Teaching Platform

For the general education system, the intelligent and multimedia teaching system has entered people's vision as early as the 1990s. Of course, many courses in music colleges have also been widely used in these technologies, which has greatly changed the teaching methods and effects of music education" But the piano teaching process is extremely complex, the course involves music aesthetics, teacher-student emotional exchange, performance technology, music theory and other aspects, so it is not enough to teach students knowledge in one direction. In the past, the information technology means such as network classroom can only assist piano teaching, and the teaching process has no substantial change. Network classroom can not play the main role in teaching, and has no good effect on the innovation of teaching mode.

Taking education cloud as the infrastructure of educational informatization construction, we should establish a unified, open and flexible piano teaching information platform. Based on the modern information technology environment and the existing discipline resources on campus network, the basic starting point is to build a learning environment for learners to learn, and take the education cloud as the basic framework of educational informatization construction, and establish a unified, open and flexible piano teaching information platform [2].

The platform divides the user system into student and teacher system, and searches for the required learning materials through the search engine system based on Lucene, an open source project; At the same time, the search information is recorded; The recommendation system can automatically recommend the relevant learning materials to the user by obtaining the relevant information of the user in the database (see Fig. 1).

The use of interactive teaching platform makes the source of data resources more extensive, not only teachers upload learning materials, but also students can share learning experience and Piano data through the platform, which can enrich and diversify the content of the resource base, and bring the source of the construction of the resource base. Interactive platform can also collect data about students' learning progress, and then feed back to teachers. It greatly facilitates teachers to design teaching plans, adjust curriculum arrangement, improve teaching methods, etc.

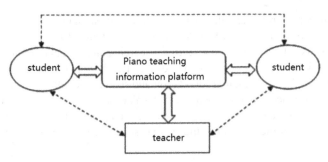

Fig. 1. Information piano platform

2.2 Intelligent Assessment

The information age makes students enjoy abundant electronic education resources, but they are often faced with serious problem, information overload. Most college students have been familiar with the use of network resources. However, there are many kinds of electronic music, books and documents, video and audio resources on the network, and various sources. For students still in the learning stage, there is a difficult situation to choose. Due to the lack of cognitive ability and knowledge reserve, the information that does not meet their actual situation may be used, Thus, the efficiency and quality of students' knowledge acquisition are greatly limited. The intelligent resource base will be classified according to the categories and difficulties of learning resources, and the students' learning level will be evaluated by the student model constructed in the education cloud, and the learning resources will be selected accurately according to the actual needs of students.

Students register personal information in cloud platform, select grade, major, piano years and other information, and then participate in basic music common sense network examination. The system first classifies the students' level, then evaluates the piano teachers' performance on the spot. The teacher records the evaluation information into the system, and then the system accurately positions the students. When students learn new works, the system provides students with relevant materials according to their level of learning. If students have strong musical literacy, the system will provide them with multiple versions of music and video for their own comparative study. The text materials will select the text with detailed music and sound analysis for them, so that students can understand the background knowledge of the work in detail. If the students' level is shallow, the system recommends a most famous and popular version of the music and video, and then provides the plain and easy to understand text for their reading, preliminary understanding of the work, and after the knowledge is improved, more detailed information will be prepared for them [3].

3 Scientific Research Management and Teaching Platform

The traditional scientific research management mode of colleges and universities is relatively conservative and single, the management thinking is not open enough, the sense of cooperation is not strong, and the various scientific research resources cannot be integrated to the maximum extent, which leads to the problems of low efficiency and low innovation results, which makes the scientific research management of many universities difficult to break through. This problem is especially obvious for colleges and universities with weak scientific research foundation and scarce scientific research personnel. Piano, as a performance oriented discipline, is weak in scientific research ability of some teachers and students. Therefore, it is of theoretical and practical significance to manage and disseminate scientific research achievements scientifically by using cloud platform.

3.1   The Mode and Platform Structure of Scientific Research Teaching

(1)   Integrate resources and personnel

Cloud platform provides a free and open communication space, which presents project flow through pictures, words and audio and video forms, including declaration, closing, investigation report, paper, supporting materials, etc., and enables the instructor to communicate with students or project team members through email, message, forum and message, and hold virtual academic seminars, It is convenient for the instructor to understand the real-time progress of the project, give specific guidance, so that the project leader can control the progress of scientific research. Through the contact of virtual platform, the project members are integrated into one, and a consensus can be reached effectively in the process of project implementation [4].

(2)   Mutual cooperation

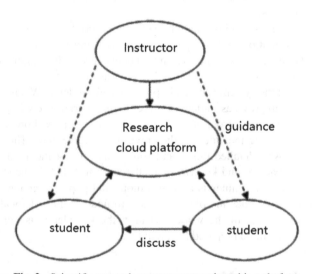

Fig. 2. Scientific research management and teaching platform

Each student uploads all the materials related to their own scientific research on the cloud platform, and the project members share with each other, so as to timely understand the progress of the members and their ideas, so as to make the cooperation closer. According to the content presented by the platform, the instructor puts forward modification suggestions and feeds them back to the project members to guide the follow-up work, as shown in Fig. 2.

3.2 Research Management Mode and Platform Architecture

(1) Management mode

The scientific research plate of cloud platform is built with colleges and universities as the unit, and then the scientific research space is set up with colleges as the second level. Each level of platform is managed by professional researchers, and the project development team is composed of teachers and students. Teachers or students establish their own research topics and design implementation plans, and first submit them to the research space of the college. The full-time researchers of the college provide suggestions for improvement, and finally screen out feasible projects and hand them over to the university level platform for review. After the conclusion, select excellent projects to show on the platform for other teachers and students to learn. Managers at all levels rely on the cloud platform for dynamic management of scientific research, which can track the project application, project funds, research results and scientific research progress in real time, so as to make corresponding decisions and achieve efficient management.

(2) Management module

It can be divided into two levels of management to improve the management efficiency, integrate the management module into the human integrated cloud platform, upload and download data easily and quickly, and make targeted public presentation after the scientific research project is completed, for other teachers and students to learn from.

4 Art Practice Cloud Platform

At present, the Piano Majors in the Conservatory of music of comprehensive universities generally don't pay enough attention to the art practice. Students often only show up in the final professional examination every semester. Piano as a performing subject, not only to impart knowledge, but also to cultivate students' performance technology, artistic aesthetics, emotional expression, the final form of achievement display is inseparable from the stage, for students' interest in learning, learning enthusiasm, self-confidence, sense of achievement is helpful. Therefore, in the whole piano learning career, students need to often participate in art practice activities to exercise their psychological quality and accumulate stage experience. Therefore, practical education is an indispensable part of art education activities in Colleges and universities.

4.1 The Problems of Piano Art Practice in Traditional Colleges and Universities

(1) Lack of art practice platform. In various comprehensive universities and independent art colleges, the number of students majoring in piano or musicology is very

large, so it is difficult to provide each student with the opportunity to show on stage, and the professional examination has become the only practical opportunity for most students. In the newly established comprehensive universities of music major, there is often no concert hall, so there is no professional platform for Piano Majors to participate in art practice. As an extremely complex musical instrument, piano is not easy to transport due to its volume and weight, which limits the stage of piano display.

(2) The form of art practice is single. The piano art practice in traditional colleges and universities is mainly presented in the form of solo concert, piano competition, art guidance and instrumental ensemble. In view of the shortcomings in the performance, we can only get the guidance of our professional teachers and students, which limits the development of the follow-up learning and improvement work. The application of network technology has become an indispensable part of the comprehensive quality. Nowadays, the traditional form can not meet the needs of cultivating comprehensive talents who serve the society.

4.2 Cloud Platform Art Practice Mode

(1) Live on the piano network. With the popularity of the Internet in the whole country, a new Internet industry is rising rapidly, that is, the webcast platform. Now the live broadcasting platform has entered the 3.0 mobile video live broadcasting era of "go, watch and play". More and more people are willing to participate in and use the live broadcasting platform, and the nationwide live broadcasting has gradually become a trend. Webcast platform has the characteristics of openness, real-time communication and interaction, authenticity that can not be tampered with, so it has its unique communication advantages.

(2) Piano network classroom. The piano network classroom mainly takes the digital piano room, multimedia classroom, Internet plus and so on as the main implementation environment, designs typical teaching activities sequence, realizes human-machine interaction through the "cloud" platform, breaks through the limitation of traditional teaching time and space, saves teaching costs, and promotes feedback after class, and ultimately promotes the improvement of teaching quality.

(3) Digital music experiment teaching system. The traditional performance mode of piano concerto is the live performance of orchestra and piano, with a large number of people, which needs a lot of human, material and financial support. And the digital Orchestra, is the piano concerto Orchestra part through the combination of multimedia technology and MIDI music technology into music software, the score of each note to restore to each instrument, output in audio format, easy for students to carry, to achieve "one person" band effect. Experiments show that the digital experimental teaching system can improve the single status of teaching equipment and teaching environment, optimize the classroom, enrich teaching forms and improve teaching efficiency.

5   Integrated Teaching Mode of Teaching, Scientific Research and Art Practice

With the emergence of the trend of interdisciplinary integration, comprehensive talents are more and more popular in the society. Comprehensive talents not only need to be outstanding in professional aspects, have rich professional experience, but also need to have a certain ability in all aspects. In the process of learning, the Contemporary Piano majors should not only improve their performance level, but also pay attention to the improvement of Humanities and Social Sciences, artistic accomplishment and other aspects, and put an end to the "behind closed doors" learning style. Most of the students will go to teaching posts in the future, so we must be familiar with the multimedia teaching mode, master a variety of teaching methods, and adjust the teaching methods according to the characteristics of students, so as to teach students in accordance with their aptitude.

5.1   The Combination of Theory and Performance Technique

Theory guiding practice is the most common guiding ideology of higher education activities. Piano teaching can not only teach performance skills in class, students need to have enough thinking process to get real improvement, summarize the knowledge taught by teachers, and even derive and expand research. Writing papers can promote students to think, digest the knowledge learned in class, and students will take the initiative to collect extra-curricular knowledge in order to enrich the content of papers, which promotes the accumulation of students' knowledge from the side. The cloud platform provides a rich resource library, which is convenient for students to search, and also presents the process of students' research and thinking.

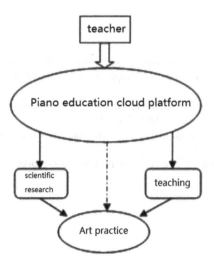

Fig. 3. Piano education cloud platform

5.2 Autonomous Learning Piano Ecosystem

Internet plus Internet plus Internet plus teaching, Internet + autonomous learning, Internet plus feedback and other teaching activities are the core of the cloud platform piano network section (see Fig. 3). Teachers only participate in the process of teaching plan making, process guidance and achievement review, and delegate more initiative to students, so as to promote students' autonomous learning by using the intelligent and interactive characteristics of cloud platform. Break through the limitation of traditional teaching practice and space, and realize the new teaching structure.

6 Conclusion

Piano education is a complex and long process. Information teaching will make up for and improve the content that cannot be completed and realized in traditional piano teaching. The role of teachers and students in the information process will change. The new teaching mode will change the previous "one-to-one" face-to-face teaching form, effectively reduce the psychological pressure of students in class, and turn students into the protagonists in the learning process, Stimulate students' interest in learning and enhance their ability of independent exploration. Cloud platform for College Piano Majors to find a convenient way to learn, establish a piano learning ecosystem supported by the network, make piano teaching keep up with the pace of the times, conform to the trend of the times.

Acknowledgements. Philosophy   and   Social   Science   Planning   Project of Anhui province:Innovative Research on the Protection and inheritance of Guichi Luotian Folk Songs (Item number: AHSKQ2016D100).

References

1. Haisheng, L., Chunqing, L.: Informatization construction of university scientific research management under Internet environment. Comput. Knowl. Technol. **10**(18), 4352 – 4353 + 4355 (2014)
2. Liu, Y.: Discussion on piano teaching reform in normal universities under the background of information age. Popular Literat. Art **9**, 256 (2013)
3. Cheng, Q.: On the art practice management of Shanghai Conservatory of music. Shanghai Conservatory of music (2012)
4. Cao, X.: Art and technology in art education in the background of Internet plus, **29** (3), 355 (2016)

Research on the Evaluation of College English Classroom Teaching Quality Based on Triangular Fuzzy Number

Ning Chong[✉]

Department of Basic Courses, Modern College of Northwest University, Xi'an 710130, Shanxi, China
chongning1028@163.com

Abstract. With the advent of globalisation in China, English courses have become a key element of the university teaching system, and in order to change the traditional 'duck and fill' approach to teaching, reform of university English teaching has become an important project in the construction of the higher education curriculum in China. The classroom model has changed considerably in the course of deepening teaching reform, such as catechism and flipped classroom, which provide an online learning platform for students to study online, thus effectively improving the quality of university English teaching. Based on this, this paper first examines the impact of catechism on the classroom model in the reform of university English teaching, and then proposes some specific reform strategies in the hope of providing valuable references.

Keywords: Computer aided system · English vocabulary query · Page tedious · Struts · Query module · JSP page

1 Introduction

The goal of teaching English at university is to cultivate students' comprehensive application of English, especially their listening and speaking skills, so that they can use English to communicate effectively both orally and in writing in their future work and social interactions, as well as to enhance their independent learning ability and improve their comprehensive cultural literacy to meet the needs of China's social development and international exchanges. This is the general requirement put forward by the Ministry of Education in February 2004 for the university English teaching curriculum, which focuses on comprehensively improving the comprehensive English application ability of university students, so that when they graduate, they can basically understand English broadcasts, communicate in simple English and have a certain degree of writing and translation ability.

To date, although China's university English teaching has made great achievements, there are still some shortcomings and problems, for example, the development of university English teaching is unbalanced, the overall level is not high, the content is repeated

M. A. Jan and F. Khan (Eds.): BigIoT-EDU 2022, LNICST 466, pp. 39–44, 2023.
https://doi.org/10.1007/978-3-031-23947-2_5

with the high school curriculum, the emphasis is on the transmission of knowledge rather than the cultivation of ability, the teaching concept is lagging behind, the teaching mode is single, the teaching methods are old, the teaching methods are backward, and the main role of students' learning has not been fully appreciated, The problems of students' comprehensive English application ability (especially listening and speaking ability) exist to varying degrees in the English teaching of all universities in China.

The reform of English teaching in universities is an important breakthrough in the cultivation of talents and teaching reform in higher education. With the development of the economy and the advent of the globalization era, the traditional teaching mode of university English has failed to meet the needs of higher education and the requirements of the times for high quality and innovative talents. In this situation, the Ministry of Education has adjusted the syllabus of university English to change the emphasis on reading, writing and translating to listening and speaking, and to improve students' comprehensive application ability, which has put forward new requirements for the teaching methods and teaching ideas of university English teachers [1]. It has become an urgent task for every college English teacher who devotes himself to education and cultivates really useful talents for the development of society to fully understand the importance of college English teaching in the cultivation of talents.

2 Analysis of the Impact of MU on the Classroom Model

2.1 The Design of Rich Classroom Activities to Develop Students' English Language Skills

In the traditional teaching mode, students have little opportunity to practice their language skills as the teacher is trying to complete the teaching task at a fast pace. In the flipped classroom model, students have already completed the MU materials and understood the basic content of the lesson, thus saving a lot of time in the classroom and allowing teachers to create tasks that give students more time to use English in the classroom. Teachers can organise flipped teaching around online learning and offline assignments in the form of English dialogues, mock performances, oral presentations, speeches and debates. The ease of the digital age also stimulates students' creativity, as teachers can encourage students to write English blogs, produce videos, publish video work and create their own learning products. This is what the new age demands of English learning.

2.2 Sharing Resources and Personalising Learning

MU can provide a large amount of data and resources for university English teaching, effectively alleviating the problem of unbalanced teaching resources in China, in the context of MU, students only need to use mobile phones, computers and other smart devices to learn English, this means of learning is not limited by time and space, students can search for teaching resources contained in MU according to their actual needs, providing students with Personalised services. For example, if students are interested in the cultural differences between Chinese and American numbers, they can use the

Internet to search for teaching resources in this part of the course. Two does not have a special meaning, but only has a certain derogatory meaning when used to describe a person. In addition, the number four is particularly taboo in China, as it is a resonance of death, so it is usually avoided in hospitalisation and in house selection for residents, but in the US the number four represents fairness and justice. This shows that students can acquire some knowledge outside the textbook through the catechism and meet their individual needs, as shown in Fig. 1.

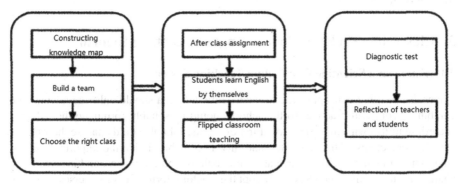

Fig. 1. Classroom model after class

2.3   Pay Attention to the Subject Status of Students

In the traditional classroom teaching mode, teachers are usually in the dominant position, and students can only passively accept teaching knowledge. This teaching mode of teaching by words and deeds will make the classroom boring, reduce students' interest in learning and affect the quality of the classroom. The application of admiring classes has promoted the reform of English teaching mode in Colleges and universities, and truly realized the flipped classroom, Make students become masters of learning. As Mu class is an educational model combining Internet and education, teachers should give targeted guidance to students' learning. For example, when teaching students the pronunciation of phonetic symbols, teachers can first use multimedia to collect the audio of phonetic symbols, stimulate students' learning enthusiasm through multimedia teaching, and then teachers should lead the reading [2]. After the reading, they can use the group cooperation learning mode to learn phonetic symbols, so that students can master the pronunciation law of each phonetic symbol. At the end of the class, teachers should recommend some excellent English pronunciation videos and movies to students for after-school learning, and implement teaching through the combination of class worship and actual teaching, reflecting the teaching mode of student-centered and teacher-assisted. In addition, students can also use the network evaluation system to evaluate the curriculum and teachers' teaching methods, so as to enable students to participate in the teaching reform and reflect students' right to speak.

2.4 Formative Evaluation of Diversification

Teachers use the traditional teaching mode for teaching. The formative evaluation of students mainly adopts the form of questionnaire survey or classroom observation. The work efficiency is low and can not supervise students' learning status at any time, but the application of class worship has effectively changed this situation. Mu class can monitor students' learning process at any time through clearance questions, online tests and comments, and teach according to students' learning status, so as to lay a good foundation for students' development.

3 Classroom Model in College English Teaching Reform

3.1 Establish a Scientific Curriculum Teaching System

Under the teaching concept of the new curriculum, China should cultivate talents who combine theory and practice, so the school should reasonably formulate the syllabus according to its own actual situation. First of all, the school should analyze the English teaching objectives of this semester, and then reasonably divide the important knowledge points of each semester, such as theme, culture and grammar, combined with the characteristics of micro courses, and adopt the teaching form of micro courses to enable students to learn at any time [3]. Through this teaching form, students can preview and review the key contents of the course, find their problems in the learning process, and take appropriate measures to solve them, so as to effectively improve students' self-study ability. For example, when students study the UK country profile, teachers can record the major events in each period according to the time clue and make it into PPT, so that students can review the contents after class.

3.2 Innovative Teaching Mode

In teaching, teachers should change the traditional teaching method of "blackboard + blackboard writing", pay attention to the main position of students, give full play to students' subjective initiative, and make students actively participate in classroom teaching. For example, when explaining drama, teachers can use multimedia to provide background pictures and sound effects, so that students can adopt the learning mode of group cooperation, select the plot related to the course content for performance, and students can refer to other excellent videos before performance, so as to cultivate students' performance ability and language application ability. In addition, teachers can also use network technology to provide students with some class content related to drama content, and master students' learning about drama through game passing tests. This student-centered teaching method can effectively stimulate students' learning enthusiasm, improve students' participation and further improve the teaching quality.

With the promotion of the new teaching concept and the new college English teaching model in Chinese colleges and universities, the roles of teachers and students in the process of teaching and learning are bound to change fundamentally. In recent years, the College English teaching model of "students as the main body and teachers as the leading" has been widely concerned by the majority of English teachers. As shown in Fig. 2, active learning methods such as discussion, practice and teaching others can achieve better learning results [4]. Therefore, it should be emphasized that any language teaching should regard the individual learner as the main body of learning, and all teaching activities should take analyzing and meeting the needs of students as the starting point. The English classroom under this teaching mode is a cooperative classroom between teachers and students. As the main body of learning, students directly participate in the decision-making process of teaching content and teaching implementation means. The purpose of teaching is to develop students' language skills and learning skills, enhance students' awareness as learners, and clarify students' learning objectives and learning needs. In this process, teachers no longer simply teach language knowledge and skills, but should be student-centered, not only teach general language knowledge and skills, but also pay attention to cultivating language application ability and autonomous learning ability. Encourage students to actively participate in the whole teaching process and adopt heuristic teaching to improve students' practical ability of foreign language application in the rich and colorful teaching process.

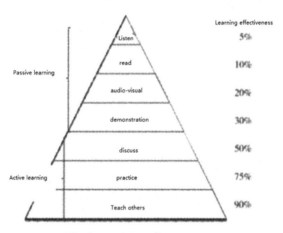

Fig. 2. Learning effect pyramid

4   Conclusion

To sum up, College English teaching reform has an important impact on the classroom model. It not only realizes resource sharing and personalized learning, but also pays attention to the dominant position of students and realizes diversified formative evaluation. Therefore, teachers should pay more attention to the reform of College English teaching. Through the investigation, it is found that the effect of College English Teaching in China is not ideal. Schools can take measures such as establishing a scientific curriculum teaching system and innovating teaching modes to improve the teaching level of College English, so as to lay a good foundation for the development of students.

Acknowledgements. This work was supported by "the 14th Five-year Plan" Education Scientific Research Project of Shaanxi Province in 2021, a Research on "Half-flipped Classroom" Model in College English Teaching for Students Majoring in Art (SGH21Y0492).

References

1. Lu, H.: Feasibility analysis of the application of flipped classroom model based on micro class in college English teaching. Foreign Lang. Telephone Teach. **4**, 33–36 (2014)
2. Sun, J., Zhu, J.: Research on college English teaching reform in the era of Mu class. J. High. Educ. **19**, 66–69 (2017)
3. Hu, J., Wu, Z.: Research on college English flipped classroom teaching model based on MOOC. Foreign Lang. Telephone Teach. **6**, 40–44 (2014)
4. Tang, M., Mu, K.: Revolution-how the Internet Changes Education. CITIC press, Beijing (2015)

Study on the Interactive Education System of Motion Evaluation Algorithm

Ping Yao$^{(\boxtimes)}$

Zhengzhou University of Science and Technology, Zhengzhou 450064, Henan, China
`ieuniversity@163.com`

Abstract. This research is about the interactive education system of motion evaluation algorithm. The main goal of this work is to create an educational tool that can be used in the classroom environment, which will allow students to learn how to program using Python as their main language. To achieve this goal, we have developed a prototype application that allows students to interact with animations created by our team. The main purpose of this study is to study the effectiveness of using computer-based interactive education system in teaching basic algebraic operations and their applications. The main hypothesis to be tested in this study is: "using the computer-based interactive education system, students can learn basic algebraic operations and their applications more effectively than the traditional way. This hypothesis will be tested through three independent variables: 1) students' motivation; 2) students' ability; 3) students' interest.

Keywords: Square dancing · Somatosensory games · Kinect · Action evaluation

1 Introduction

First of all, education is about learning. How to teach should be based on how to learn, and what content of education should be based on how to give full play to one's greater ability in the goal of improving society. Interactive education is to explore this problem.

Is it OK to learn cramming? Yes, but the effect is not good. First of all, students do not have a thorough understanding of knowledge. They do not know how knowledge comes. They only know that this is OK. Is this education? No, this is indoctrination, which is very useful for replication technology, but not for innovation. For example: what did we learn about the chapter of collections? The nature of set, the operation of set, the representation of set, etc., but the more important one is how to abstract the concept of set from the real world; For this concept, what we need is to study the nature of this concept. How to study the nature, put forward in specific things, and how to extract it? Why and how to establish a representation? How to establish operations, how to establish operations? These problems are based on the study of a problem, and these studies have some common attributes, which can help to understand new knowledge points faster. This is a change in content, and the real advantage of interactive education lies in the carrier [1]. It is used on computers, such as web pages. It can use big data to teach

M. A. Jan and F. Khan (Eds.): BigIoT-EDU 2022, LNICST 466, pp. 45–55, 2023.
https://doi.org/10.1007/978-3-031-23947-2_6

students in accordance with their aptitude, customize exercises according to students' understanding, and review in time. Learning itself is nonlinear, but it can establish a linear learning process through computers. Of course, there are many more. The linear learning process is shown in Fig. 1 below.

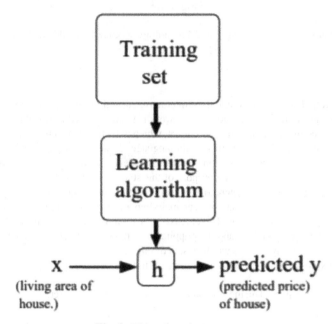

Fig. 1. Linear learning process

From the perspective of cognition, the internal basis of interactive teaching method is constructivism theory. "Constructivism theory believes that learning is realized through the active rather than passive construction of learners, and emphasizes the need to give play to the enthusiasm of learners". Constructivist theory holds that the construction and formation of knowledge by students or learners are completed from three levels: first, on the basis of existing knowledge accumulation, start to explore, digest and understand new knowledge, and form knowledge update; Secondly, through the accumulation of new knowledge (including language and cultural knowledge), the whole knowledge is updated; Finally, using the updated and accumulated new knowledge to re understand and analyze the new things and complete the construction of new knowledge. During this period, due to the different accumulation of individual knowledge, different people often have different understandings and conclusions about the same thing [2]. The comprehensive cognition of new things requires mutual communication and questioning, and finally a tacit understanding is reached, that is, the construction of new knowledge. In the teaching process, students' knowledge construction needs the interaction and cooperation among teachers, students and textbooks. The learning process is also the construction process in the interactive form.

Cognitive theory emphasizes the gradual process of contact, acceptance and absorption of knowledge by students or learners in the learning process, rather than simple transmission, storage and accumulation. Only after the knowledge is transformed and processed by itself can it be truly internalized into the learners' own knowledge, and the teaching process is to promote the transformation and Realization of this behavior process. In the process of teaching, students are the main body and implementer of learning behavior, the acquirer of knowledge, and the receiver, receiver and user of knowledge transmission. However, the total amount of acceptable and digestible knowledge formed in the process of knowledge transmission depends on the total amount of knowledge output by teachers on the one hand, and on the total amount of autonomous choice, acceptance, digestion and absorption by students or learners on the other hand. The logical starting point of learning is the selective perception of environmental information, and teaching is to promote the production of selective perception. The emphasis of cognitive psychology on the internal needs and motivation of students provides a theoretical basis for the application of interactive teaching methods and the development of teaching activities.Based on this, this paper studies the interactive education system of motion evaluation algorithm.

2 Related Work

2.1 Characteristics of Interactive Teaching Methods

The interactive teaching method emphasizes that teachers play the role of organizers of classroom activities, guides of learning activities and promoters of learning strategies in the teaching process, and highlights the principle of students' subjectivity in classroom teaching. The organization and development of teaching activities should follow the principles of cooperation and strategy. Teachers should properly set up teaching situations and take the forms of cooperation and dialogue between teachers, students and students, Promote students to actively participate in classroom teaching activities to achieve the purpose of understanding articles, mastering knowledge and improving ability. Studying the characteristics and teaching principles of the interactive teaching method can promote the effective combination and application of the interactive teaching method and the teaching practice of the intermediate and advanced reading class of Chinese as a foreign language [3].

Characteristics of Interactive Teaching Method
The basic characteristics of interactive teaching method are embodied in the teaching process that students are the main body of classroom teaching and the center of teaching activities, while teachers are the organization planners of classroom teaching activities, the controllers of classroom rhythm and the guidance promoters of students' learning strategies and methods. In the practical application of classroom teaching, it usually organizes students to integrate into classroom teaching by means of dialogue and cooperation, promotes students to think and learn actively and participate in classroom teaching activities, and teachers guide and evaluate students' classroom feedback and learning activities. In the process of interactive teaching, teachers set, implement and complete the strategies of interactive teaching, and students are both the actors and executors of

strategies in the process of strategy implementation. The interactive task-based teaching framework is shown in Fig. 2 below.

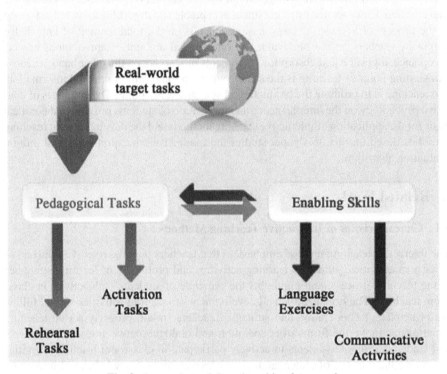

Fig. 2. Interactive task-based teaching framework

Generally speaking, the interactive teaching method is that teachers design and create teaching situations, take corresponding teaching strategies according to the actual situation of students, enable students to independently carry out learning activities within the framework of teaching design set by teachers, and carry out communication and interaction between teachers' teaching and students' learning around teaching objectives, so as to achieve the goal of cultivating students to master knowledge, learn methods and improve their abilities.

The teaching principle of interactive teaching method.

(1) Principle of subjectivity.

The principle of subjectivity determines the object and subject of teaching implementation in teaching design. The principle of subjectivity clarifies and highlights the subjective status of students in the teaching process, and emphasizes that students, as the receivers of knowledge, are the main actors of knowledge transformation and processing. When the knowledge is internalized by the students themselves, the teachers' analysis and explanation and teaching behavior become external causes, and the students' independent thinking and learning and digestion behavior become internal causes. Therefore, all kinds of methods and strategies designed and implemented in classroom teaching activities should be based on the student-centered principle.

(2) Cooperative principle.

The cooperative principle determines the activity mode of the teaching subject in the teaching design. The principle of cooperation emphasizes that in the process of carrying out teaching and achieving goals, teachers and students should fully carry out cooperation and exchange activities between each other, so as to promote students or learners to renew their original knowledge and accumulate and construct new knowledge, so as to promote students to achieve individual progress and overall development of students. In the activities, the leading role of teachers and the main role of students should be played to ensure the cooperation between teachers and students, rather than the transmission and transmission of simple information.

(3) Strategy training principles.

The principle of strategy training determines the mode of teaching activities in teaching design. The principle of strategy training refers to that during the teaching process, teachers should fully understand the cultural background, knowledge level, existing problems and needs of the teaching objects according to the teaching tasks of the intermediate and advanced reading class of Chinese as a foreign language, as well as the teaching objectives of cognition, skills and emotions, and adopt appropriate teaching methods and strategies to promote students to implement and complete classroom teaching activities according to the teaching design [4]. It emphasizes the strategic training for students in the process of interactive activities such as participating in activities, carrying out learning and cultivating their abilities. The principle of strategic training is an important theoretical basis of interactive teaching method and an important activity form of teaching design, which runs through the whole process of teaching Chinese as a foreign language.

2.2 Somatosensory Interaction Equipment

Somatosensory interaction equipment is the hardware basis of providing somatosensory technical support. It obtains the user's action information through sensors, so as to realize the interaction with programs. So far, many devices for somatosensory interaction have been developed at home and abroad, including Wii, PlayStation move, leap motion and Kinect. Wi is a home game console launched by Nintendo. Playstation move is a somatosensory controller produced by Sony. Both devices need to use motion sensing handles similar to remote controls to realize somatosensory detection. The Wii controller monitors the movement and rotation of the hand in three-dimensional space by capturing the light emitted by the handle sensing strip.

Playstation move recognizes the trajectory of the top ball through Playstation eye, and uses gyroscope to help increase its recognition range. Compared with Wii, it has the advantages of wireless connection, fewer keys, no battery change and more intelligence. But generally speaking, the interaction mode of the two is very similar, and both need additional handheld devices. For children, it is necessary to learn how to use the handle, and the hand movement is always limited. Leapmotion is a somatosensory controller launched by leap company, which tracks the precise movement of the hand through infrared ray. The user's hand in the real world corresponds to the hand model in the application, and the infrared camera obtains the relevant data of each frame of the user's hand in real time to drive the hand model; In addition, developers can define hand posture in the program to represent a command [2]. It can work in parallel with hardware devices such as mouse and keyboard, and supports two operating systems: windows and MAC. Users only need to open the running program of the controller, and then insert the device into the computer to realize easy interaction with the application with both hands and fingers [5]. The main recognition object of leap motion is gesture. Although its tracking speed and recognition accuracy are very high, its recognition range is very limited, sometimes even overly sensitive.

Kinect is a somatosensory transmission peripheral developed by Microsoft. The Xbox 360 version was launched in 2010. Two years later, the Kinect version adapted to Windows system came out, which once set off a crazy sales boom. It is mainly composed of three cameras: the leftmost one is the camera that emits infrared. When Kinect is started normally, the infrared light here can be seen by the naked eye; In the middle is the RGB color camera used to obtain color images [3]; On the far right is the camera used to sense the depth of the human body from Kinect. In addition, Kinect also combines the focusing technology. Similarly, after its normal startup, the base will automatically rotate and adjust according to the human body on the focus. At the same time, there are four microphone arrays on both sides of Kinect, which can realize speech recognition and sound source location. Figure 3 shows the appearance of Kinect.

Fig. 3. Kinect

3   Somatosensory Dance Interaction System Based on Motion Evaluation Algorithm

3.1   Motion Evaluation Algorithm

Motion estimation: the technology of estimating the motion displacement between two frames of images is called motion estimation, and motion compensation: aligning the images according to the estimated motion displacement is called motion compensation (making the residual value smaller after subtracting the current frame from the reference frame). The most important thing of the background subtraction method is the establishment of the background image. Then, the difference operation between the established background image and each frame image is used to determine whether it is a moving region, in which the pixel region with large difference is used as the moving region, and the pixel region with small difference is used as the background region. In the background subtraction method, the background image will change in real time due to the influence of external light and other external environment changes, so the key of the background subtraction method is background modeling and background update [6].

Adaptive Gaussian mixture background modeling is an important method of image background modeling. Its working principle is to obtain the color distribution of pixels based on the distribution of pixels in the time range in the video image, so as to achieve the purpose of background modeling.

$$E(t)\Delta \dot{x}_{k+1}(t) = f(t, x_d(t)) - f(t, x_{k+1}(t)) + B\Delta u_k(t) - \Gamma_{p1}C(\dot{x}_d(t) - \dot{x}_{k-1}(t)) - M_1 C(\dot{x}_d(t) - \dot{x}_k(t)) - M_2 C(\dot{x}_d(t) - \dot{x}_{k+1}(t))$$
(1)

In this work, a novel adaptive warping layer is proposed to aggregate bilinear deformation and kernel convolution in one step. This layer uses optical flow and interpolation kernel to deform the pixels of the input frame. For the video frame insertion task, because the intermediate frame ° is not originally available, the author estimated the flow of the front and rear reference frames, and then projected it to simulate the flow between the intermediate frame and the reference frame. This operation can be realized through the flow projection layer (the proposed layer).

Adaptive deformation and flow projection layer are the two main technical innovations of this algorithm. The author summarizes their advantages in the following two aspects. First [4]. The required parameters are defined as shown in Fig. 4 below.

Traditional MEMC methods rely on manual features (for example, SIFT for motion estimation, or Gaussian weight map for motion compensation), and the adaptive deformation layer proposed in this paper allows us to extract data-driven features for motion estimation and motion compensation at the same time [7]. Therefore, the model in this paper has better generalization ability to deal with the video framing and enhancement tasks of their own scenes. Secondly, the adaptive deformation layer closely combines two learning based methods, namely, flow based method and kernel based method.

3.2 Overall Architecture

The basic mode of cramming education is that teachers teach in the classroom and students listen below. Interactive education is that every student has a device such as a computer, and on a software such as a browser, he can browse the content of this class. These content is not made by the teachers in class, but by teachers with many years of teaching experience combined with the opinions of offline teachers, that is, everyone's is the same, However, there are simple mode, ordinary mode and hell mode, which are used to match students of different levels. Each student learns according to actual needs. The basic content of this page is: text, images, videos, animations, etc. These are interactive.

```
n_a = 64
n_values = 1
batch_size = 32
input_len = Y.shape[0]
epochs = 15000
print(input_len)
x_train = X;
y_train = Y;
plt.plot(x_train[1:5000, :])
plt.plot(y_train[1:5000, :])
plt.legend(['Input', 'Expected output'])
plt.title('Input')
plt.show()
```

Fig. 4. Define required parameters

Text can be clicked. For pre knowledge, you can view the knowledge that needs to be supplemented through text hyperlinks ° to prevent a vicious circle, There are some words that can give some additional supplements. The image can be more specifically displayed to give a better understanding. The video is interactive, that is, it will explain a knowledge point first, and then give several questions. If the answer is correct, the video can continue. If not, it will relearn until it is understood. If you really don't understand, you can ask the teachers present to answer. The progress of each student may be different. Those who fall behind can review and keep up at night. Teachers can check the progress of each student and provide help. In this way, the basic mode of education is not to teach and learn one by one, but that students actively explore knowledge with the help of computers, complete self-study, and cultivate self-study ability. Because there is video explanation, it is not different from in class [8]. The difference is that each student can learn according to his own progress and catch up in time.

The system structure is shown in Fig. 5.

4   Teaching Suggestions

In the research and discussion of the application of interactive teaching method to the teaching of Chinese as a foreign language, according to its theoretical principles and method characteristics, and combined with the reading teaching theory and strategy, a specific teaching design has been formed. After teaching practice, on the basis of the feedback from students and teachers and the evaluation and summary of teaching

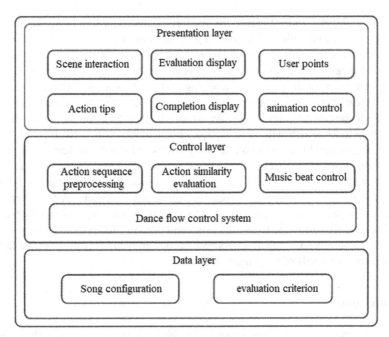

Fig. 5. System structure diagram

practice, this paper analyzes the advantages and disadvantages of teaching design, and puts forward some suggestions on how to solve the problems existing in the current reading teaching and teaching design, which can be criticized and studied by other teachers of Chinese as a foreign language.

(1) Teachers should strengthen the research and practice of interactive theory. Adhere to the interactive teaching method throughout the whole process of teaching design and teaching implementation of Chinese reading as a foreign language. The theory of interactive teaching method plays a unified theoretical guiding role in the whole process of teaching design research and teaching practice. The implementation of various strategies and activities adopted in the process should focus on the subjective principle of "taking students as the center". In the teaching process, we should fully respect the students' dominant position, guide students to actively participate in classroom interaction activities, give full play to students' autonomy, initiative and creativity in learning, and transform students from passive receivers of knowledge to active constructors of knowledge. Through constructive cooperation and interaction, we can promote the completion of teaching objectives and realize the coordinated development of students' individuality and collectivity [9]. The strategy training for students will run through the whole teaching process, so that students can gradually form learning strategies and methods that conform to their own style and characteristics, so that they can correctly understand the language and express their ideas in interactive activities.

(2) Teachers should clarify and adhere to the teaching objectives of reading class. To clarify and adhere to the teaching objectives of reading class, which are to train students to understand the reading content, accumulate language knowledge and improve

their reading ability. Understanding the reading content and mastering the language knowledge are the foundation. Accumulating the language knowledge and improving the reading ability are the main purposes. Organizing and implementing various classroom activities, strategies and training is an important means and guarantee to achieve the teaching objectives. In the process of teaching design and teaching practice, we should always be clear about the teaching objectives, so as to determine the teaching focus and achieve the expected teaching effect. Avoid the situation of practice for practice and activity for activity, which will cause the teaching activities to lose the focus.

(3) Teachers should adhere to the self-improvement focusing on learning new theories and new knowledge. Teachers of Chinese as a foreign language need to constantly update their teaching theory, language culture and other knowledge, constantly enrich and improve themselves [10]. Only when they interact with students with different cultural backgrounds, social experiences and ideas can they better understand the teaching objects, accurately formulate teaching design and organize teaching according to local conditions. Generally speaking, teachers need to constantly improve their comprehensive ability to meet the needs of teaching tasks.

5 Conclusion

Research on interactive education system of mobile evaluation algorithm This research aims to find a method to evaluate movies. Motion evaluation algorithm has been widely used in many educational applications, such as learning and teaching materials, games, etc., but the human-computer interaction is not good and needs to be improved. In addition, some problems need to be solved before applying the motion evaluation algorithm to the interactive education system. Therefore, we have studied these problems in order to improve the interaction between human and computer in the interactive educational environment. In order to choose the best movie. In this study, we used two different methods - first, we selected a set of moving images, and then used these two methods to evaluate their motion. We also compare the two methods with each other. The purpose of this study is to study the interactive education system of sports evaluation algorithm and its application. The main goal is to develop a new interactive education system to evaluate the quality of animation by using motion analysis. The system can be used in various applications, such as quality control, training and production. The results show that there is no significant difference between the two methods. Therefore, it can be concluded that either of these two technologies can be used as an alternative technology to evaluate films.

Acknowledgements. 1. Research on the Industrialization Development of Dance Culture in Henan in the New Era. Research Project of Henan Federation of Social Sciences and Henan Federation of Economic Organizations, 2018. Project Host: Ping Yao.

2. Research on the Development of Dance Education Industry in Zhengzhou. Social Science Research Project of Zhengzhou, 2018. Project Host: Ping Yao.

References

1. Wei, J., Mo, L.: Open interactive education algorithm based on cloud computing and big data. Int. J. Internet Protoc. Technol. **13**(3), 151 (2020)
2. Wang, J., Zhao, B.: Intelligent system for interactive online education based on cloud big data analytics. Journal of Intelligent and Fuzzy Systems **40**(1), 1–11 (2020)
3. A motion planning algorithm for the feed support system of FAST. **20**(5), 10 (2020)
4. Han, K., Wang, Q.: Research on 020 platform and promotion algorithm of sports venues based on deep learning technique. Int. J. Inf. Technol. Web Eng. (2018)
5. Liu, Y.: Interactive system design of entrepreneurship education based on internet of things and machine learning. J. Intell. Fuzzy Syst. **39**(4), 5761–5772 (2020)
6. Nie, A.: Design of English interactive teaching system based on association rules algorithm. Secur. Commun. Netw. (2021)
7. Qin, J., Zhang, L., Dong, Q., et al.: Torque Interactive Control System of Upper Limb Rehabilitation Robot Based on Servo Motor. Beijing Biomedical Engineering (2019)
8. Jing-Hua, Y.U., Wang, Q., Chen, H.: Motion Sensing Dance Interaction System Based on Motion Evaluation Algorithm. Computer and Modernization (2018)
9. Chai, G., Wen, Q.: An interactive English–Chinese translation system based on GLA algorithm. J. Inf. Know. Manag. **21** (2022)
10. Qian-Shuai, M.A., Wang, E.M., Center, E.T.: Design and Implementation of the Control System in Four-Axis Stacking Robot. J. Tianjin Univ. Technol, Edu. (2018)

Research on the Evaluation of Constructive English Teaching Model Based on RBF Algorithm

Liping Du[✉]

Xi'an Conservatory of Music, Xi'an, Shaanxi 710061, China
anniedu888@163.com

Abstract. The evaluation of constructive English teaching model based on RBF algorithm is a new method to evaluate the effectiveness of different types of corrective feedback to improve learners' English level. The purpose of this study is to determine whether there are differences between students who receive corrective feedback and students who do not receive corrective feedback, and its effectiveness in improving their language skills. In this paper, we will focus on its application in English Teaching (ELT). In ELT, RBF algorithm can be used to evaluate students' writing quality and measure their progress in learning new vocabulary or grammatical structures. You can also use this method to evaluate content based on specific criteria, such as lexical density (the number of unique words). The results showed that students who received corrective feedback scored higher than those who did not receive any correction at all, but they also differed from each other according to the type of correction they received. This finding shows that teachers should choose the appropriate type of feedback for students,the English learning platform plays a good and positive auxiliary role for students to learn English. As a better means of English education, it has certain research value and positive significance for the research of English teaching.

Keywords: RBF algorithm · Constructive · English teaching · Evaluate

1 Introduction

Therefore, when people talk about "constructivist teaching", they think of discussing the teaching mode. In order to emphasize "learner centered", the discussion teaching mode is more called "discussion learning method". This statement is also easier to understand: learners learn, grow and construct in discussion.Discussion learning mode is put forward from the persp. Figure 1 below shows the framework of the discussion teaching mode.

The effectiveness of teaching strategies belongs to a higher level, including many specific and different operation methods and methods. Careful readers will find that the action learning method, which is popular all over the world and extremely popular in China in recent years, is a discussion learning mode.

M. A. Jan and F. Khan (Eds.): BigIoT-EDU 2022, LNICST 466, pp. 56–66, 2023.
https://doi.org/10.1007/978-3-031-23947-2_7

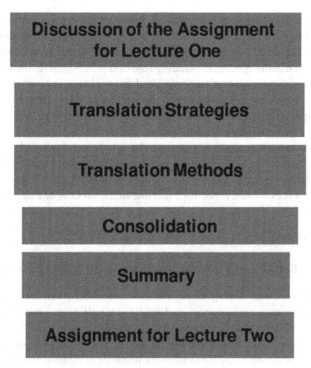

Fig. 1. Discussion teaching model framework

Through the theoretical research of RBF based neural network algorithm, the practical exploration of constructive English learning platform is carried out to immerse students in English learning situations. And in the current international, the practice of online teaching platform is very widely used.

As far as English teaching is concerned, there are two teaching modes: Teacher centered teaching mode and student-centered teaching mode. Before the 1990s, it was mainly embodied in the "teacher" centered teaching model. The advantages of the "teacher" centered teaching model are: it is conducive to teachers to play a leading role, to teachers to monitor and organize the progress of the whole teaching activities, and to the emotional communication between teachers and students, so as to help systematically impart scientific knowledge, Fully consider the key role of emotional factors in the learning process; Its deficiency is that teachers completely dominate the classroom and ignore the role of students' cognitive subject, which is not conducive to the growth of creative talents with innovative ability and innovative thinking [1]. On the contrary, the "student- centered" teaching model requires students to change from the object of knowledge indoctrination and the passive recipient of external stimulation to the subject of information collection and the active constructor of knowledge meaning, so that teachers can change from the indoctrinator and imparter of knowledge to the instructor and promoter of students' active meaning construction, Teachers are required to use the latest teaching mode and educational thought in the teaching process. This teaching mode pays attention to that students are the main body of the cognitive process and the active constructor of meaning. Its effect is to facilitate students' active discovery and exploration and to cultivate creative talents; The disadvantage is that this teaching model, because it emphasizes students' "learning", usually ignores the leading role of teachers, and ignores the important role of emotional communication and emotional factors between teachers and students in the learning process. In addition, due to the neglect of the leading role of teachers, once the free space for students' autonomous learning is too large, it is often easy to deviate from the requirements of teaching objectives.

Based on the teaching personality analysis based on neural network algorithm, this paper uses the constructive teaching mode to establish the model of English autonomous learning. Finally, by designing and realizing the platform of autonomous learning, we hope to provide a feasible reference for everyone in the process of English learning.

2 Related Work

2.1 Difference Between RBF Neural Network and BP Neural Network

Neural RBF network and neural BP network are nonlinear multi feedback networks, both of which represent general approximation. For each BP neural network, RBF neural network is replaced. Vice versa, but there are many differences between the two networks. This paper compares RBF neural network with BP neural network in the aspects of network structure, training calculation, network resource utilization and AP approximate efficiency.

1. In terms of network structure, BP neural network realizes permission link, and RBF neural network has direct link from input layer to hidden line layer and permission link from hidden line layer to output layer. The transfer function of BP hidden line unit of neural network generally adopts nonlinear function (inverse tangent function, etc.), and the transfer function of RBF hidden line unit of neural network includes centrosymmetric RBF (Gaussian function, etc.). BP neural network is a static neural network with three or more upper layers. It is difficult to determine the number of hidden layer and hidden layer nodes, and there are no generally applicable rules. After defining the network structure, the network structure will not be changed in the training stage. RBF neural network is a three-layer static feedback neural network [2]. The number of implicit layer units, that is, the structure of the network, can adapt to the specific problems studied in the training stage and improve the applicability of the network. As shown in Fig. 2 below, the RBF neural network structure is created.

2. The wild counted by training. The parameters that BP neural network must determine are link weights and thresholds. The most important training algorithm is BP algorithm, which is the same as the improved BP algorithm. However, BP algorithm is easy to be limited to the local minimum value, and the convergence speed of the learning process is slow, which confirms the number of hidden layer and hidden layer nodes. Importantly, the new BP neural network system can converge after training. The training sample cover, the selected algorithm and the network structure (input node, implicit node, output node, transfer function of output node), pre error, are closely related to the training level [3].

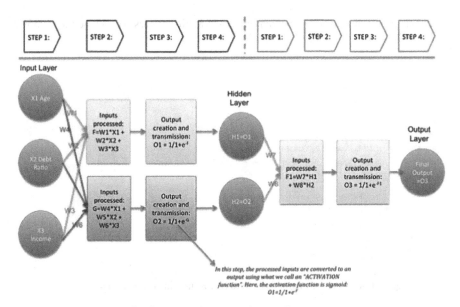

Fig. 2. Create RBF neural network structure

The algorithm of RBF neural network is introduced. IKEA, many RBF neural network training algorithms support online and offline training. Dynamically determine the expansion constants of network structure, data center and hidden layer units. It has faster learning speed and better efficiency than BP algorithm.

3. In the field of network resource utilization, the principle, structure and particularity of neural RBF network learning algorithm can be based on the cover, type and distribution of training samples to confirm the school of implicit elements. When the nearest distance classification method is used to train the network, the location of hidden layer units in the network depends only on the distribution of the training mode and the width of hidden layer units, but the same task. According to the distribution of invisible units, the reflection relationship between input and output is realized through the weight between invisible units and output units. Well, the impact between different tasks is relatively small [4].

2.2 RBF Algorithm

The correlation function of RBF network, P is the R * q-dimensional matrix composed of Q groups of input vectors; T is the s * q-dimensional matrix composed of q-group target classification vectors; Goal is the mean square error goal, which is 0 by default; Spread is the expansion speed of radial basis function, which is 1 by default; Mn is the maximum number of neurons, and the default is Q; DF is the number of neurons added between two displays, which is 25 by default; Net is the return value, an RBF network, TR is the return value, training record. Using newrb () to create RBF network is not only a trial process, but also needs to continuously increase the number of middle layer neurons and until the output error of the network meets the value of chromodin. The radial basis function is used to realize nonlinear function regression. The code is shown in Fig. 3 below.

```
from keras.initializers import Initializer
from sklearn.cluster import KMeans

from keras import backend as K
from keras.engine.topology import Layer
from keras.initializers import RandomUniform, Initializer, Constant
import numpy as np

from keras.models import Sequential
from keras.layers import Dense
from keras.losses import binary_crossentropy
from keras.optimizers import Adam
```

Fig. 3. Radial basis function is used to realize nonlinear function regression

The transformation from the input layer to the hidden layer is nonlinear. The hidden layer node is composed of a certain action function, but the transformation from the hidden layer to the output layer is linear. The weight from the input layer to the hidden layer is fixed to 1, and only the weight from the hidden layer to the output layer is adjustable. As shown in Fig. 4 below, it is a very classic neuron model of input.

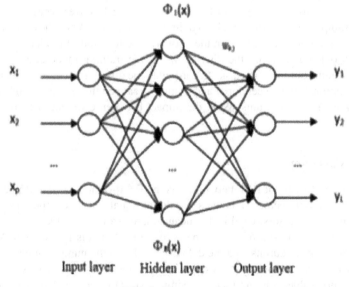

Fig. 4. Neuron model

The transformation function of the hidden layer is a non negative linear function distributed locally and attenuated radially symmetrically about the central point, which is usually a Gaussian function:

$$e(w, b)\frac{1}{2}(t - a)^2 = \frac{1}{2}(t - wp)^2 \tag{1}$$

The output of the network can be expressed as:

$$\Delta w(i, y) = -\eta \frac{\partial e}{\partial w(i, y)} \tag{2}$$

The constructive English learning mode based on RBF algorithm is to add the idea of algorithm to the design of the platform, fully reflect the algorithm in the process of writing code, and realize it in the interface function of the platform, so that it can be reasonably combined with the constructive learning mode to reflect its advantages of developing individual learning characteristics [5].

2.3 Constructive Teaching Mode

The constructive teaching mode is based on students' intelligent adaptive learning, pays attention to the perspective of teaching and learning, and comprehensively improves students' skill learning ability through the use of science and technology, computer network technology and even multimedia technology, so as to finally achieve the goal of "double main and equal emphasis" teaching structure. Compared with the teaching of other subjects, the focus and goal of English teaching lies in application, mainly because English itself is a skill, including various practical abilities such as listening, speaking, reading and writing [6]. The application pays more attention to the environment, and the constructive teaching mode is established under the premise of environmental teaching.

The teaching modes of the teaching structure of "paying equal attention to learning and teaching" mainly include individual counseling mode, teaching mode, exploratory learning mode, discussion learning mode and cooperative learning mode.

Under the thinking of China's current English education reform, according to China's current modern computer network technology and multimedia technology environment, the constructive network teaching mode has become a reality. Firstly, the core of National English teaching reform is to adopt advanced modern educational technology to promote English teaching relying on network technology.

Secondly, only with the help of network environment can we carry out the innovative mode of combining classroom teaching and students' autonomous learning through network multimedia. This model focuses on student-centered, allowing students to experience in learning and learn in experience, that is, students understand and control the learning process, choose the learning content and learning methods, and evaluate their learning results.

Thirdly, the network-based multimedia network classroom vividly reflects the boring and boring classroom knowledge in sound, film and television, image and animation, which greatly enhances the students' participation initiative.

3   Research on the Evaluation of Constructive English Teaching Model Based on RBF Algorithm

An open learning environment can provide students with a lot of extra-curricular learning space. Students can study independently after class and use multimedia and network technology to integrate the learned English knowledge with new language knowledge, so as to enhance learning efficiency. In this way, they can actively and confidently participate in classroom discussion in class, It can not only share the achievements of self-study with other students, but also experience the joy of learning success, obtain a sense of achievement and improve self-confidence.

Finally, the networked communication environment provides a platform for students and teachers to verify and evaluate English learning achievements. Therefore, the constructive teaching model not only enhances students' learning skills and shows the purpose of teachers' leading role, but also integrates teaching resources, creates an open English teaching system by using modern multimedia technology and computer network technology, and comprehensively improves students' autonomous learning ability and skill level [7].

The constructive English learning mode based on RBF algorithm is to add the idea of algorithm to the design of the platform, fully reflect the algorithm in the process of writing code, and realize it in the interface function of the platform, so that it can be reasonably combined with the constructive learning mode to reflect its advantages of developing individual learning characteristics.

It mainly solves the needs of two parts: teachers track and analyze students' information and arrange teaching plans; The collection of various learning information and learning effects of students is shown in Table 1 below.

Table 1. Problems to be solved by algorithm model

Teacher level	What kind of academic achievement is qualified or good, and what are the quantitative indicators of academic achievement
	Actual performance of each student and implementation of learning plan
	Whether the matching relationship among learning time, learning methods and learning materials is appropriate in order to maximize the effect
Student level	Solve the problem of real reaction of learning state (time, mode and data)
	Solve the problems of follow-up review and schedule of new tasks after the completion of current tasks
	Solve the planning problem of completing each task every day
	Solve the time arrangement problem of increasing learning tasks with ultra-low grades

Firstly, the platform analyzes the learning behavior and results of excellent students who have used the platform and passed the national CET-4 and CET-6 through neural network technology (there is a learning courseware database in the platform, and all courseware correspond to the hidden label: "vocabulary, field, knowledge points and grammar", then each courseware can reflect the attributes of the courseware [8]. Neural network technology is to logically analyze the attributes of the courseware used by each user of the platform and the corresponding performance results), formulate a general learning plan and method for everyone, and apply it to each student who uses the platform for the first time. When each student continues to analyze the error of the student's learning plan through the neural network algorithm in the application process, it is found that the part with insufficient learning and the lowest learning efficiency (that is, the part with errors in training or examination) will be studied as the focus in the new learning plan.

1. Construct a relational learning database, and each learning material constructs a relational transformation function:

$$W = (w1, w2, ..., w_n) \tag{3}$$

2. Initialize the collection of learning materials and convert the learning contents submitted by students into time pattern vectors:

$$y = \varphi(v) = \varphi(wx + b) \tag{4}$$

3. Platform operation, given time mode vector × As input, operate with the correlation function, and take the result as the input of the next stage of the platform to continue;

4. The platform converges to a stable state. When the platform has associated the whole cycle chain, that is, the learning materials corresponding to the weakness information are extracted, the platform stops running and returns to extract the learning materials;

5. Results screening: the results returned by the platform are screened by neural network, and the processing results are returned to students.

4 Simulation Analysis

The discussion of English teaching mode solves the problem of poor structure. The so-called problem includes three factors: "a" (actual situation), "B" (target situation), "C" (solution). The problem of poor structure refers to: either "a" (actual situation) is not clear, or "B (target situation) is not clear, or" a "and" B "are not clear, then the path and method from" a "to" B ", that is," C "is diverse. This is also the basic idea advocated by Constructivist English Teaching: because the structure of the problem is bad, there are many solutions; Because the situation of learners is different, they can choose and agree with different schemes. Because people learn by experience, and a person's experience is always limited, we need to work together to learn [9].

Therefore, constructivism mainly solves the problem of poor structure. As for those well structured problems, it is not necessary to use constructivist English teaching. Of course, in order to make learners better understand and master, direct English teaching mode can be used, which can not only enable learners to construct, but also improve efficiency [10].

However, for complex problems with poor structure, one's experience is always limited, which requires special and in-depth discussion as a theme to jointly solve problems through collective wisdom. The most common "brainstorming" and "brainstorming" in life In fact, this method is adopted.

The RBF layer is constructed through data editing, as shown in Fig. 5 below:

```
## RBF layer
class RBFLayer(Layer):
    def __init__(self, output_dim, initializer=None, betas=1.0, **kwargs):
        self.output_dim = output_dim
        self.init_betas = betas
        if not initializer:
            self.initializer = RandomUniform(0.0, 1.0)
        else:
            self.initializer = initializer
        super(RBFLayer, self).__init__(**kwargs)

    def build(self, input_shape):

        self.centers = self.add_weight(name='centers',
                                       shape=(self.output_dim, input_shape[1]),
                                       initializer=self.initializer,
                                       trainable=True)
        self.betas = self.add_weight(name='betas',
                                     shape=(self.output_dim,),
                                     initializer=Constant(
                                         value=self.init_betas),
                                     trainable=True)

        super(RBFLayer, self).build(input_shape)
```

Fig. 5. Data editing to build RBF layer

The normalization function of test data is constructed as shown in Fig. 6 below:

```
def maxminnorm(array):
    maxcols=array.max(axis=0)
    mincols=array.min(axis=0)
    data_shape = array.shape
    data_rows = data_shape[0]
    data_cols = data_shape[1]
    t=np.empty((data_rows,data_cols))
    for i in range(data_cols):
        t[:,i]=(array[:,i]-mincols[i])/(maxcols[i]-mincols[i])
    return t
```

Fig. 6. Construct test data normalization function

In terms of autonomous learning control, students can carry out offline learning and online learning. No matter which learning method, learning control technology runs through the learning process. The system's offline learning control technology for students is to use various methods such as time recording, link process control, achievement evaluation and so on. All kinds of data controlled by the offline learning system can be automatically saved on the student's computer. These data are encrypted and can also be transmitted to the online management system for storage. The core function module of the software system is the learning control module. According to the record of students' learning behavior and learning progress, transfer in the corresponding learning content and the process of neuron RBF algorithm in the transfer stage, and display it according to the corresponding template. Automatically record the learning process, test results, learning time, etc. [11, 12].

The system is easy to operate and uses realizable and easy to operate technology to design a clear navigation. The learning system framework adopts a three-level system structure, and the learning navigation menu can be viewed at any time. The interface design is simple, the elements are unified, and the general button identification is used.

5 Conclusion

Based on the logical analysis of the relationship between RBF and individual learning, this paper establishes the optimal algorithm of RBF, which is based on the logical analysis of the relationship between the content of English learning plan and the effect of individual learning. Collaborative learning is the most basic feature of constructive learning and one of the four elements of constructivism teaching. Collaborative learning includes the cooperation between teachers and learners, as well as the cooperation between learners. In the discussion teaching mode, collaborative learning emphasizes more "cross-border" collaborative learning.

As mentioned earlier, the theory teaching mode solves the problems of poor structure, which are very complex. We need to understand, understand and solve problems from different angles, and everyone solves problems based on experience. Therefore, people from different fields, backgrounds and specialties need to get together and use cross-border ideas and methods to solve these problems together. Develop and implement an autonomous. At the same time, adjust and improve the configuration of software platform support equipment according to customer feedback.

References

1. Bb, A., Nah, B., Skc, D., et al.: YUKI algorithm and POD-RBF for Elastostatic and dynamic crack identification. J. Computat. Sci. (2021)
2. Rc, A., Rr, B., Rm, C., et al.: Enhanced the moving object detection and object TRACKING for traffic surveillance using RBF-FDLNN AND CBF algorithm (2021)
3. Li, L., Fan, X., Gong, H., et al.: Intelligent equalization based on RBF LSSVM and adaptive channel decoding in faster-than-nyquist receiver. Int. J. Pattern Recog. Artif. Intell. (2021)
4. Angleitner, N., et al.: $\mathcal{H}$-inverses for RBF interpolation (2021)
5. Peng, X., Yu, H., Zhu, X., et al.: Electro-hydraulic proportional position control using auto disturbance rejection based on RBF neural network. J. Beij. Inst. Technol. **30**, 121–128 (2021)

6. Jt, A., Zheng, Y.B., Rz, B., et al.: RBF neural network modeling approach using PCA basedLM-GA optimization for coke furnace system. Appl. Soft Comput. (2021)
7. Zhou, X.L., Liu, M.W., Wang, L., et al.: Multi-objective function optimization for environmental control of a greenhouse based on a RBF and NSGA-II. **28**(1), 15 (2021)
8. Hashim, S., Yusoff, N.M.: The use of reflective practice towards achieving effective English language teaching at primary schools. Int. J. Eval. Res. Edu. **10**(1), 364 (2021)
9. Qoura, A.: New trends in English language teaching and learning new trends in ELT&L (2021)
10. Li, C.: Implementation and analysis of intelligent inquiry teaching model in primary school English teaching. (2021)
11. Zhao, W.: An empirical study of english teaching model in higher vocational colleges based on data analysis (2021)
12. Coniam, D., Lampropoulou, L., Cheilari, A.: Online proctoring of high-stakes english language examinations: a survey of past candidates' attitudes and perceptions. Eng. Lang. Teach. **14**(8), 58 (2021)

Algorithm and Implementation of College English Teaching Comprehensive Ability Evaluation System

Hui Zheng(✉)

Xi'an Haitang Vocational College, Xi'an, Shaanxi 710038, China
jqmzhzy@126.com

Abstract. The traditional methods of university quality evaluation must also be abandoned. In order to improve the teaching quality of the school, English teaching ability has been developed. However, assessing English learning opportunities is a very complex and time-consuming task. The main purpose of the comprehensive evaluation system of College English teaching ability is to evaluate students' comprehensive ability. According to the system design, English learning refers to all students' English knowledge and skills. The design of College English teaching ability evaluation system is to test college students' English teaching ability. The purpose of this test is to evaluate the effectiveness and efficiency of English teaching, which can be used as a reference for evaluating teachers' performance. The test consists of five parts: listening, speaking, reading, writing and grammar. Each part has two levels: easy level and difficult level. Students must answer questions according to the difficulty they face during the examination. The assessment process should be based on these four elements, including motivation, learning attitude and communicative competence. The comparison of the comprehensive teaching quality of different classes or classes objectively reflects the overall teaching level of the school.

Keywords: English teaching · Evaluation system · Fuzzy algorithm

1 Introduction

The application of computer and Internet technology in the field of education is becoming more and more popular, and people pay more attention to the data resources. With the arrival of the big data era, learning evaluation emphasizes the combination of quantitative and qualitative. In other words, we should pay attention not only to the results of learning, but also to the process and benefits of learning. Using massive data to carry out formative evaluation and performance measurement has become a new hotspot in the field of education, and the quantification of education has become a trend [1]. The international new media Consortium (NMC) has predicted and analyzed this phenomenon in the horizon report (Higher Education Edition) published in recent years. Learning measurement is a process of objectively quantifying the results of students' learning

M. A. Jan and F. Khan (Eds.): BigIoT-EDU 2022, LNICST 466, pp. 67–77, 2023.
https://doi.org/10.1007/978-3-031-23947-2_8

according to certain rules. In 2015, this concept was first proposed in the report and listed as a medium-term development trend. It is believed that in the next three to five years, learning measurement will be increasingly valued by people. In the reports of 2016 and 2017, it still ranks among them. Learning measurement is considered to be an important means to improve the quality of education in the era of big data, and is one of the key technologies affecting the development of education informatization. It can meet the current educational field's attention to evaluation and the needs of students' learning preparation, progress and skills acquisition through evaluation, recording and measurement [2]. In the big data environment, higher education is increasingly affected by learning measurement. Neither the current popular adaptive learning and learning analysis, nor the ever-growing MOOC and data mining can lack the important premise of learning measurement. It is an important link in learning evaluation and provides a data base for scientific and accurate learning analysis. With the optimization and upgrading of the social and economic structure, the state and employers have made new adjustments to the ability and quality standards of the labor force. Therefore, under the requirements of the new era, colleges and universities also need to reconsider how to cultivate and measure students' Comprehensive English ability.

In the previous evaluation model, it is basically evaluated by three parties: students, teachers and teaching supervisors (experts). When choosing the effect evaluation method, the traditional way of questionnaire is usually used to judge teachers' Comprehensive English teaching ability through the checked options. This one-way evaluation method can not provide. And some teachers can not accept the evaluation results in this simple form, which will not only affect teachers' teaching mentality, but also affect. and the evaluation results can not be distinguished only by good or bad [3]. Therefore, an evaluation system that can dynamically monitor the teaching process by communicating with teachers, carefully consulting relevant evaluation materials of colleges and universities, and actively participating in project discussion, so as to replace the manual operation in the traditional evaluation mode, so that the evaluation of teachers' Comprehensive English teaching ability can be scientific and reasonable. Promote the fairness of teachers' comprehensive ability evaluation of English teaching.

For most colleges and universities, English teaching comprehensive ability evaluation is an important content in teaching work, and a variety of teaching evaluation methods have been adopted to study teachers' teaching methods and teaching results. And some colleges and universities also regard it as an indispensable and important link of teaching management. No matter what kind of school, it is a routine work in teaching management once a year. Under the comprehensive ability evaluation, universities as a whole, stimulate teachers' enthusiasm for teaching work, universities, reflect on the current teaching model, and continuously optimize and reform the original teaching model through the evaluation results, It is of overall teaching ability of colleges and universities. The management of teaching evaluation system is also an important task. How to guide the school's and reform through scientific results, so as teachers' and the teaching quality of colleges and universities [4].

Therefore, to study and build a comprehensive, fair and scientific evaluation is an provide excellent talents for social enterprises. It is an important content to enrich the theoretical research work of teaching evaluation reform in China's informatization. It has extensive and far-reaching significance.

2 Related Work

2.1 English Teaching Evaluation

In Chinese, evaluation means to evaluate value. Teaching evaluation is a process of measuring the teaching process and results and giving value judgment based on the teaching objectives, according to scientific standards and using all effective technical means. It includes the evaluation of students' academic achievements and the evaluation of teachers' teaching quality. The concept of teaching evaluation includes three meanings:

First, teaching evaluation should be based on teaching objectives and certain value standards. Teaching objectives and value standards are not fixed. They are constantly changing with the development of society and the progress of science. Therefore, the basis and standard of teaching evaluation are essentially determined by social development [5].

Second, teaching evaluation should adopt various scientific and feasible methods and technologies to collect teaching information, so as to ensure the smooth development of teaching evaluation activities and obtain rich teaching information.

Third, teaching evaluation is the evaluation of the whole process of teaching activities, which involves all fields of teaching.

English teaching evaluation refers to the qualitative and quantitative measurement of the educational process and the results produced according to the educational objectives and principles of English subjects in English teaching activities, so as to make a value judgment and provide a basis for the development of children and the improvement of teaching.

English teaching evaluation plays an important role in English teaching. It is not only a measuring tool for judging and selecting students, but also can stimulate students' interest in learning and arouse their enthusiasm for learning with its own encouragement and promotion. It can also enhance students' self-confidence, sense of satisfaction and success, And lay a good foundation for their further English learning [6].

The evaluation of College English teaching can be oral or written; According to the evaluation object, it can be divided into self-evaluation, mutual evaluation, parent evaluation and teacher-student evaluation; According to the timeliness of evaluation, it can be immediate evaluation or delayed evaluation; According to the evaluation results, it can be divided into formative evaluation and summative evaluation.

There are many ways of teaching evaluation, which need to be further summarized and summarized to sort out suitable evaluation methods and form models for English teaching, so as to improve the efficiency of English teaching, establish students' self-confidence in learning English, stimulate students' interest in learning, and promote the good development of students' learning and body and mind.

2.2 Fuzzy Algorithm Evaluation

The advantage of fuzzy comprehensive makes a comprehensive and comprehensive evaluation of things affected by many factors through the operation of the method provided by fuzzy mathematics. so as to provide basis for correct decision-making. The comprehensive fuzzy evaluation method has many advantages

(1) The comprehensive fuzzy evaluation method can minimize the gap between the evaluation results and the objective results to the greatest extent, and has strong immunity. It can transform incomplete information and uncertain information into fuzzy concepts, quantify qualitative problems, and improve the accuracy and credibility of the evaluation.

$$U = \{u_1, u_2, ...u_N\} \tag{1}$$

$$V = \{v_1, v_2, ...v_M\} \tag{2}$$

$$A = \{a_1, a_2, ...a_n\} \tag{3}$$

$$R_i = \{r_{i1}, r_{i2}, ...r_{in}\} \tag{4}$$

$$R = \begin{pmatrix} r_{11} & r_{12} & \cdots & r_{1m} \\ r_{21} & r_{22} & \cdots & \\ \cdots & \cdots & \cdots & \cdots \\ r_{n1} & r_{n2} & \cdots & r_{nm} \end{pmatrix} \tag{5}$$

(2) Comprehensive fuzzy evaluation method uses digital means to deal with fuzzy teaching effect evaluation. Although fuzzy mathematics is used, the mathematical model is simple and easy to master, and the teaching effect is comprehensively evaluated.

(3) Comprehensive fuzzy evaluation method has no strict definition standard for the evaluation of each factor affecting education and teaching performance, and the rather than a point value, which overcomes the "disadvantage" of the only solution in traditional mathematics. It eliminates the traditional one size fits all teaching evaluation system, can obtain a relatively fair and just, and makes the results of teaching evaluation more scientific, reasonable and close to the actual teaching evaluation.

Therefore, evaluation method to construct an effective teaching evaluation model, solve the problems existing, optimize the work of teaching evaluation and improve the accuracy. so that the imprecise and fuzzy evaluation can quantitatively and qualitatively describe the quality of classroom teaching, overcome the subjectivity and unfairness of previous evaluation, provide an effective evaluation method for classroom teaching, and also provide a reliable basis for improving teaching quality[7]. As shown in Fig. 1.

When we evaluate something, some of the content in the natural language we use cannot be accurately quantified, such as "probably", "very good", "less", etc. When the application computer reads these data, if these quantifiers that clarify the situation of things are not quantified, the computer will not be able to "understand" these information. Similarly, there will be similar situations in the teaching quality evaluation system [8]. Therefore, such problems must be changed into words that can be read by the computer according to certain principles before the teaching quality evaluation can be completed with the help of the computer.

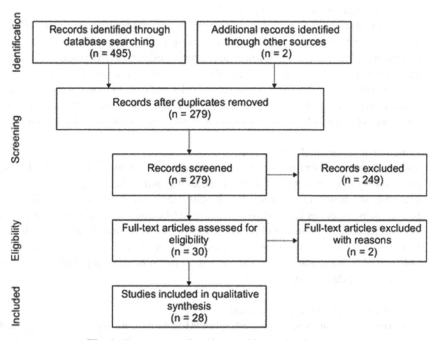

Fig. 1. Fuzzy comprehensive teaching evaluation model

This uncertainty caused by inaccurate quantification also exists in the knowledge base technology and standard fuzzy division applied in teaching quality evaluation. Moreover, in some cases, this qualitative problem also needs to be handled by the quantitative methods. Therefore, the standardization of teachers' fuzzy evaluation words can better give an accurate evaluation of teachers' teaching quality.

3   An Analysis of the Comprehensive Ability Evaluation System of College English Teaching

3.1   Principles of Construction of Teaching Ability Evaluation Index System

There are various expressions about the principles that the teaching evaluation system should follow, but all of them should be extended according to the objective laws of the teaching evaluation system, which are used to guide the items of teaching evaluation, and then formulate various principles for carrying out teaching evaluation activities according to the items. College English teaching has its own unique particularity. The construction principles of its teaching evaluation system must be based on the characteristics of directional learning and the laws of directional teaching ability evaluation, combined with the principles of College English teaching, and objectively put forward the principles to be followed in constructing the evaluation index system of College English teaching ability.

(1) Comprehensive and systematic principle

The comprehensive and systematic principle is to consider various factors affecting the evaluation of PE Teachers' directional sports teaching ability in all aspects and from multiple angles, and combine the main and secondary factors, subjective experience and objective facts differently. According to the actual situation of the teaching process, under the premise of unified standards, the indicators are determined comprehensively and systematically by levels and periods, and according to the objective requirements, so as to achieve both comprehensive and systematic[9].

(2) Principle of scientific development

The principle of scientific development means that the indicators, methods and procedures of evaluation must be reasonable. It requires that the evaluation of orienteering teaching must respect the objective laws, adhere to the scientific attitude of being rigorous and realistic, select scientific and effective evaluation forms and methods, start from the objective reality of Orienteering Teaching in Henan Province, take the development of teachers' teaching ability as the long-term goal, not limited to the evaluation of the current situation of teaching ability From the perspective of development.

(3) Principle of conciseness and pertinence

The principle of conciseness and pertinence is to select the most concise and targeted representative indicators in the process of selecting and refining indicators according to the specific sports characteristics of orienteering and the actual teaching needs of Orienteering of PE teachers in primary and secondary schools in Henan Province, so as to extract the most valuable and effective information, More objective and accurate feedback on the teaching ability of physical education teachers.

(4) Applicable feasibility principle

The applicable feasibility principle means that the system is applicable to the evaluation of PE Teachers' orienteering teaching, and each link in the implementation process can be accepted by the evaluator and the evaluator, and can be operated and implemented. It conforms to the basic teaching concept of PE teaching and orienteering teaching in primary and secondary schools in Henan Province, integrates and refines the influencing factors according to specific teaching practice, and makes the index system of teaching evaluation clear, concise and detailed, At the same time, according to the actual teaching process, teaching evaluation is carried out to achieve the ultimate goal of improving teachers' teaching ability.

3.2 College English Teaching Comprehensive Ability Evaluation System

Whether formative evaluation or summative evaluation, the use of multiple evaluation can efficiency to the greatest extent. The "evaluation suggestions" in the new English curriculum standards emphasize that the evaluation function has changed from focusing on screening and selection to incentive, feedback and adjustment; the evaluation content has changed from paying too much attention to academic work to paying attention to the potential of multifaceted development; the evaluation technology has changed from too much emphasis on quantification to more emphasis on visual analysis; the evaluation subject has changed from single to multiple, and the evaluation angle has changed from summative to process and development, Pay more attention to the individual differences of students; The evaluation methods are more open and diversified, such as observation and interview, investigation, work display, project activity report and so on, rather than relying on the results of the written examination, paying more attention to the current situation [10].

Through analysis, this civilization confirms the attribute of school English teaching quality evaluation: the attribute is divided into internal and external. You can't unilaterally. Our understanding must be multifaceted. Therefore, the characteristic of English teaching evaluation system is the combination of internal qualification factors, external factors and financial resources. Especially personal factors, environmental factors and tuition fees. The structure of English teaching evaluation system is shown in Fig. 2.

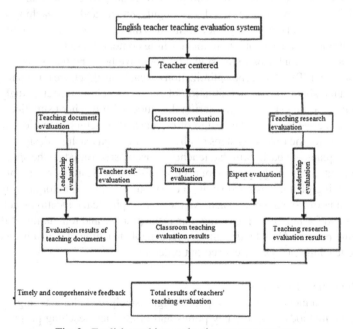

Fig. 2. English teaching evaluation system structure

4 College English Teaching Comprehensive Ability Evaluation System

4.1 Comprehensive Ability of College English Teaching

(1) Teaching structure design ability

The teaching structure design ability focuses on the analysis of students' learning status, the analysis of teaching resources and the design of teaching plans. Adhere to the development of students as the center, reflected in the improvement of expansibility, and promote the comprehensive and coordinated development of teenagers. It is necessary to understand and investigate the characteristics of the audience group, including grade age, theoretical level, cognitive and understanding ability and physical quality. In particular, students should make clear the original basis and existing problems of the topic they are talking about, so that the teaching content can meet the actual needs of students and be targeted. Considering the students' characteristics and varying degrees, classroom teaching cannot meet the needs of all students, but it should meet the needs of most students. In order to achieve efficient teaching, we should not only carefully study, analyze and understand the teaching resources and the key and difficult points of classroom teaching, but also fully consider the different characteristics of students and understand the actual situation of students. Teachers should understand the materials and data related to the topic in advance, understand difficult problems, carefully consider and analyze the teaching resources word by word, thoroughly understand the teaching materials, and be sure to find out the key issues related to the teaching process and the key and difficult points of each content in the teaching content. Design the "entry point" of the course that conforms to the students' cognitive law, and reasonably design the teaching plan. To achieve the optimization of teaching effect, we must pay attention to the analysis of the current situation of specific teaching objects. Analyzing the students' learning situation, mastering the students' pre-school situation, and providing effective basis for the design of orienteering teaching activities are the key conditions for the following steps of physical education teaching design. Designing teaching plans is a basic skill that teachers must master. Based on the specific physical education teaching situation of each school and the learning reality of students, the teaching plan is designed so as to carry out teaching in an organized, orderly and standardized manner and achieve the goal of physical education teaching. The design and formulation of teaching plan is the premise and foundation of the whole teaching process. Only by designing a reasonable teaching plan in advance can the whole teaching process be carried out orderly.

(2) Teaching plan design ability

The basic elements of teaching plan design usually include: teaching objectives, contents, methods, teaching key points and difficulties, teaching progress, etc. In the theory and method of instructional design, the purpose of the design must be clear. Before the implementation of teaching, the teacher must make clear "where to go" to optimize and achieve the expected teaching objectives. The selection of teaching content, determination and application of teaching methods must be set around the realization of teaching objectives. According to the characteristics of orienteering teaching content in primary and secondary schools, adopt high-quality and scientific teaching process, and gradually spread and teach the knowledge and skills of Orienteering to students. The design of objectives is the basis for evaluating teaching results. Analyzing and determining the teaching objectives is conducive to selecting the best teaching methods and helping learners meet the requirements. In fact, the teaching content is the "core skeleton" of the whole teaching process. From the point of view of curriculum theory, the curriculum standard of physical education and health in compulsory education puts forward the directionality of the curriculum design of "objective leadership content", in short, to reasonably select the appropriate teaching content according to the teaching objectives. The purpose of education restricts the teaching methods. The selection and application of teaching methods are aimed at achieving good teaching results. When selecting teaching methods, teachers must master the characteristics of students. They should follow the teaching idea of "there are methods in teaching, but there are no fixed methods, and the most important thing is to adapt to the situation". The purpose is to study the laws of physical education teaching, update the traditional teaching methods, comply with the development needs of modern physical education teaching in China, create appropriate physical education teaching methods, and start from the actual situation of students, adapt measures to local conditions, school conditions and students. The teaching progress reflects the overall progress of the teaching work. According to the actual situation of the students and the teaching hours arranged by the school, the teaching contents should be distinguished from the primary and secondary ones, and the teaching progress should be reasonably planned in a balanced manner, phase by phase, month by month, week by week. Give priority to basic knowledge and key knowledge, followed by general knowledge and secondary knowledge.

4.2 Comprehensive Ability Evaluation of English Teaching

With the development of society, the requirements of society for the evaluation of college teachers. The in-depth reform of college teaching is imminent. The educational management is constantly changing from the traditional mode to the information mode. The position of expert system in teaching organization is as light as weight. In the future, the teaching is particularly important. Therefore, it is a very important task to continuously supplement and improve the comprehensive ability evaluation system of English teaching, which requires a lot of money and energy.

1. Learning interest: it is extremely important to understand students' interest in course learning through observation, questions, discussion and questionnaire, so as to improve and maintain. Another important reason for the variation of students' learning interest is the content of teaching materials and teachers' teaching, so students' learning interest can also be used as the profile information to evaluate teachers.

2. Emotional and strategic development status: observe and understand students' active learning in students' topic listening, answering questions, students' dialogue performance, group discussion and other activities. understand whether students can adjust to different learning tasks.
3. Mastery of language knowledge and skills learned in the corresponding learning stage: test the teaching effect through classroom questioning, independent homework, stage quiz, etc. Judge students' mastery of key teaching points according to the results, and take corresponding remedial measures in time.
4. Comprehensive language skills application ability: through observing students' performance in classroom listening, answering questions, students' dialogue performance, group discussion and other activities, understand students' comprehensive application of language knowledge.

The structure of College English teaching comprehensive ability evaluation system is shown in Fig. 3.

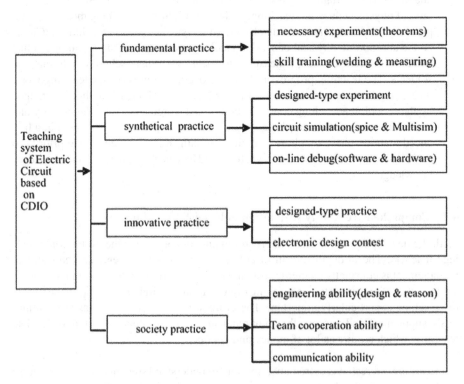

Fig. 3. The structure of English teaching comprehensive ability evaluation system

5 Conclusion

English curriculum evaluation system is a multi index (factor, attribute) evaluation model. Original design. It limits the change of the weight of evaluation indicators (factors, attributes) and the mutual constraint of evaluation indicators (factors, attributes). The comprehensive evaluation system of English learning ability is a multifaceted decision-making problem, including social environmental factors, learning environmental factors, natural environmental factors, intelligence training factors, formation factors, motivation and recruitment factors.

References

1. Chen, H.: Design and Implementation of Fuzzy Comprehensive Evaluation System for Teaching Effect of Physical Education in Colleges and Universities (2021)
2. The design and implementation of new engineering college students' intelligent evaluation system for comprehensive quality. Comput. Sci. Appl. **11**(5), 1281–1290 (2021)
3. Ma, X.: Study on college English online teaching model in mixed context based on genetic algorithm and neural network algorithm. Discret. Dyn. Nat. Soc. (2021)
4. Chen, Z.: Using big data fuzzy K-means clustering and information fusion algorithm in English teaching ability evaluation. Complexity **2021**(5), 1–9 (2021)
5. Zhao, Y.: Research on the application of university teaching management evaluation system based on Apriori algorithm. In: Journal of Physics: Conference Series, vol. 1883, no. 1, p. 012033 (6pp) (2021)
6. Feng, M.: Research on the construction of student ability evaluation system based on computer application. In: Journal of Physics: Conference Series, vol. 1915, no. 2, p. 022037 (5pp) (2021)
7. Wu, C.: Effect of online and offline blended teaching of college English based on data mining algorithm. J. Inf. Knowl. Manag. **21**(Supp02) (2022)
8. Sang, H.: English Teaching Comprehensive Ability Evaluation System Based on K-means Clustering Algorithm (2021)
9. Ji, S., Tsai, S.B.: A study on the quality evaluation of English teaching based on the fuzzy comprehensive evaluation of bat algorithm and big data analysis. Math. Probl. Eng. (2021)
10. Gao, K.: Evaluation of college English teaching quality based on particle swarm optimization algorithm. In: CONF-CDS 2021: The 2nd International Conference on Computing and Data Science (2021)

Design of English Teaching Resource Management System Based on Collaborative Recommendation

Mingming Ding[✉]

Henan University of Animal Husbandry and Economy, Zhengzhou 450000, Henan, China
1377960836@qq.com

Abstract. This study uses a system approach by relying on collaborative recommendation to provide teachers and students with the best information. The system is designed by using various tools such as LMS, e-learning platform and different types of software. It provides an integrated environment that helps provide users with a better learning experience. These systems are based on the concept of collaborative recommendation, and everyone can contribute to everyone involved in this process. This tool is used by many schools and universities around the world. The main goal is to determine how to make recommendations, how teachers use them, and what factors will affect their use. The design collaboration recommendation system requires us to first determine who will participate in making suggestions (designers), and then develop the process of design suggestions (developers). We need to understand the roles and responsibilities of the two groups so that we can ensure that the work of each group complements the efforts of the other. In addition, it is important to know what kind of information will be collected. In view of the current English teaching resources "lost" and "waste" problem. In order to realize the system, the use case of the system is analyzed firstly. Based on the use case analysis, the function and overall architecture of the system are designed respectively, and the collaborative recommendation module is designed. In order to improve the accuracy of recommendation, combined with the professional attributes and other attributes of old users, the hybrid recommendation algorithm is used to complete the recommendation of learning resources.

Keywords: Collaborative recommendation · Resource management · English Language Teaching

1 Introduction

In the process of English education, English education resources are not effectively used or the allocation of resources is unreasonable. Many students suffer from lack of good English learning channels or good learning methods to acquire English knowledge, and their English level is not improved, which makes them feel tired of learning. Moreover, most school teaching methods allow students to accept passively and lack of interaction and communication between teachers and students in teaching activities, Teachers

M. A. Jan and F. Khan (Eds.): BigIoT-EDU 2022, LNICST 466, pp. 78–88, 2023.
https://doi.org/10.1007/978-3-031-23947-2_9

rarely know what kind of teaching means students need. In the teaching process, many teachers only deal with one class, which is more difficult for students to accept [1]. This makes English learning a "death spot" for many students, which is their biggest headache, thus hindering the reform of Vocational English education?. The significance of active and rational use of English teaching resources can help teachers establish the awareness of teaching resources, establish a new concept of teaching resources, improve the knowledge level of teachers, help improve the personal quality of teachers, improve the teaching effect, and help students create an English learning environment. In this environment, students can fully perceive and experience English and the use of English, so that students can be happy physically and mentally, At the same time, it can help some students reduce their anxiety, eliminate their inferiority complex and improve their English quality effectively [2].

With the growth of modern information in Pb level, it is the focus of current computer research and thinking to strengthen the mining of these information to improve the efficiency of data utilization. In the context of massive data growth, education departments and academic institutions have accumulated a large number of teaching resources. For English education institutions, how to recommend these resources to different learners so that learners can combine their own needs and improve the application value of different teaching resources is the focus of the relevant departments of English education institutions [3]. At the same time, the problems of "resource overload" and "resource lost" are seriously troubling educational institutions. Therefore, it is urgent to introduce modern intelligent recommendation algorithm to complete the personalized recommendation of different English teaching resources in combination with English learners' interests and other actual situations, so as to improve the use efficiency of English teaching resources.

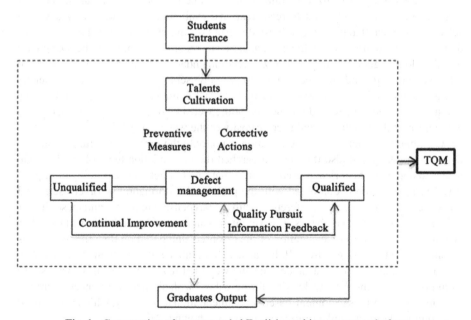

Fig. 1. Construction of recommended English teaching resource platform

In order to enable learners to quickly find resources that meet their own requirements and hobbies, Wang Linlin (2017) built an interest model and selected personalized recommendation algorithm according to English learners' interests to complete the recommendation of teaching resources. Liu Haitao (2017) combined the characteristics of users and teaching resources and adopted a hybrid recommendation method, In order to promote the efficiency of students' use of teaching resources. Based on the previous research, this paper constructs an intelligent recommended English teaching resource platform from the perspective of software design, and designs it in detail [4]. Figure 1 below shows the construction of the recommended English teaching resource platform.

2 Collaborative Recommendation Technology

2.1 Introduction of Collaborative Recommendation Technology

Foreign famous recommendation systems include GroupLens, Ringo, Amazon, etc. GroupLens is a collaborative filtering system applied to Usenet news, which is divided into client and server. It allows users to collaborate together and discover what they are interested in from a large number of Usenet news. Ringo is a music recommendation system designed by MIT. The system requires users to evaluate musicians first, then calculate the similarity of users according to the evaluation results, and then classify users. Users of the same category recommend music to each other. Amazon e-commerce website applies a typical recommendation method based on collaborative filtering. It recommends products that users may like through the user's purchase history, product evaluation and personal attributes of customers [5].

The domestic personalized recommendation is better: Douban's Douban guess. It analyzes the users' read, want to read, read and evaluation behaviors every day, and selects the content that users are interested in from the massive data to make recommendations. The more users use it, the more accurate its recommendation will be. Dangdang has also done a good job in personalized recommendation. Many other websites have introduced recommendation technology to provide users with a good user experience. The application of recommendation technology in e-commerce has increased the sales volume of products, increased the income of the website and the number of user visits, and improved the reputation and user viscosity of the website [6].

Collaborative filtering recommendation is not only the most successful recommendation technology, but also the most researched recommendation technology. Its basic idea is to obtain the historical preference information of target users explicitly or implicitly. The information is compared with the preference information of other users, and other users who have similar preferences with the target user are found, and these similar users are called nearest neighbors. The weighted evaluation value of the nearest neighbor is used as the target user's evaluation of the resource, and based on this, the resource is recommended to the target user [7]. Because collaborative recommendation technology does not use the user interest model, nor the weighted feature vector of resources, but from the user's point of view, looking for neighbors with similar preferences, there are no many shortcomings in content-based recommendation technology, which can be used to recommend objects with complex structure, as shown in Fig. 2.

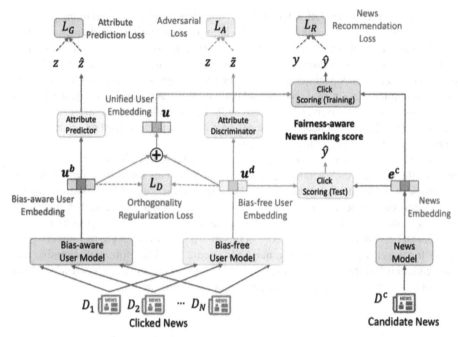

Fig. 2. Principle of collaborative filtering recommendation technology

Collaborative recommendation technology has the following advantages

① Because collaborative recommendation technology is from the user's point of view, it does not need to build complex weighted eigenvectors for resources, which reduces the system's manpower and time costs.

② Collaborative recommendation technology is based on the preferences of the nearest neighbor to recommend resources for the target user, so it can recommend some new and interesting resources that the target user does not consider. This is different from content-based recommendation, which can only recommend resources in the defined resource types in the user interest model for users.

③ Collaborative recommendation technology can make use of the feedback information of the target user and the feedback information of the nearest neighbor, so it can quickly modify the recommendation content and accelerate the speed of personalized learning [8].

2.2 Implementation Process of Collaborative Recommendation Technology

Collaborative filtering technology adopts the method based on the interest direction of neighbor users. It uses other users' preferences for resource items to obtain the similarity of users, or predicts a user's evaluation of a resource through the common likes and dislikes of similar users for some resources. The system can make personalized recommendations with high accuracy based on these data. Collaborative filtering technology is a personalized recommendation technology which has been researched more and more at present. Using it for recommendation has high personalization and obvious effect.

The basic idea of collaborative filtering is very intuitive: in daily life, people often make some choices (shopping, reading, music, etc.) according to the recommendations of friends and relatives. Collaborative filtering technology is to apply this idea to information recommendation, and recommend certain information to certain users based on the evaluation of other users. Collaborative filtering technology is the most researched and widely used recommendation system, and it is also a personalized recommendation technology with high recommendation efficiency.

Because it is difficult to collect user's historical preference information implicitly, most of the existing collaborative recommendation systems use the display method to obtain user's preference information by collecting user's score of items. All users' scores of all items constitute a user item score matrix, and each item in the matrix represents a user's score of a certain item. The recommendation process for target users is to get the nearest neighbor by using the score in this matrix, and then get the recommendation result for target users by using the neighbor's score [9]. Therefore, collaborative recommendation has three main steps: user information representation, nearest neighbor selection and recommendation result generation, as shown in Fig. 3.

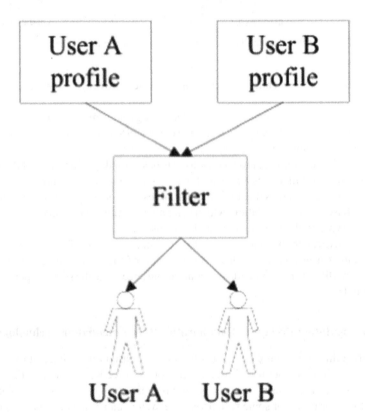

Fig. 3. Model of collaborative recommendation

According to Pearson similarity, the predicted score of user U_i and teaching resource D_m can be obtained.

$$P(i,j) = \overline{R}_i \frac{\sum_{n \in Ni} sim(i,N) \bullet (R_{n,j} - \overline{R}_N)}{\sum_{n \in Ni} sim(i,N)} \tag{1}$$

Thus, through the above prediction, we can get a recommendation set, and finally recommend it to users.

3 Analysis of English Teaching Resource Management System

3.1 Principles of Using English Teaching Resources

The use of English teaching resources is not arbitrary and needs to be regulated according to certain principles. The reason is that the connotation of English teaching resources is extremely rich and there are many kinds of English teaching resources. The use of English curriculum resources is also a huge scientific and systematic work. Therefore, we should follow the following principles in the practice of using English teaching resources:

(1) Pertinence principle

The use of English teaching resources must, on the premise of clarifying the curriculum objectives, carefully analyze all kinds of English curriculum resources related to the curriculum objectives, and understand and master their respective properties and characteristics. The use of English teaching resources should be based on the actual situation of the local and the school, give play to the regional advantages, highlight the English characteristics of the school should be based on the situation of the students, and meet the interests and development needs of the students should consider the situation of the teachers.

(2) Openness principle

The principle of openness means that in the process of using English teaching resources, we should actively absorb other people's valuable achievements, so as to absorb all human civilization achievements with an open mind. We should try our best to develop and study all the things around us that are conducive to English teaching, so as to truly achieve the goal of combining practice with teaching, instead of focusing on teaching materials as shown in many teaching activities at present, which is not conducive to improving students' enthusiasm for learning English.

(3) Adaptability principle

The principle of adaptability mainly includes three aspects. The first is to meet the needs of students. The development of teaching resources should meet the interests of students and be consistent with the scope of students' learning abilities. The next step is to adapt to the teaching level of teachers. The teaching resources that teachers can't control are of no use value, so teachers should make corresponding efforts to improve their teaching level, so as to adapt to the continuous development of the times and technology. The last is to adapt to the school's own conditions and characteristics. There are many kinds of teaching resources needed by students, and there are differences in personality. Schools can not meet the different needs of each student. Therefore, the school should base on its own actual situation, give priority to the needs of the majority of students, and seek teaching resources suitable for their development, so as to truly improve the overall level of students. The use of teaching resources should pay attention to the use of English in different disciplines, and pay attention to the relationship between English and social development, real life, scientific and technological progress [10]. At the same time, the use of English teaching resources should be able to adapt to the exploration and research activities of students. It should be conducive to students to find and put forward problems, so that students can learn by "using" or "doing", and focus on cultivating students' ability to solve practical problems in English.

(4) Developmental principle

The development of teaching resources should first promote the development of students' English level. Through the development of teaching resources, students can make better use of resources to learn, explore and practice. The second is to promote the development of teachers. The development of curriculum resources poses new challenges to teachers, so that teachers should constantly improve their own quality to meet the overall education level of the times. Because the quality and teaching level of teachers determine the identification scope, development and utilization of curriculum resources and the level of exerting benefits. Therefore, curriculum resources should also be able to promote the development of teachers, so as to form a virtuous circle between teachers and curriculum resources.

(5) Economic principle

The premise of the use of English teaching resources must be suitable for the school strength of the school. While developing English teaching resources, we must follow the principle of economy, because our goals of using educational technology are roughly three aspects: expanding the scale of education, improving the quality of teaching and improving the efficiency of teaching. While pursuing the goal, we must also achieve "more, faster, better and less". Otherwise, it will exceed the economic burden of the school. No matter how important this resource is, regardless of its cost, it is useless. Therefore, the principle of economy is one of the most basic and important principles of teaching technology. No matter what English teaching resources are used, as long as it can promote English teaching and improve students' English level. If we have neglected the principle of economy in the past, we must pay enough attention to it now.

3.2 System Design

Overall architecture: using B / S structure mode to build, the overall architecture of the system is divided into three layers: application layer, logic layer and data layer. The overall framework system is shown in Fig. 4.

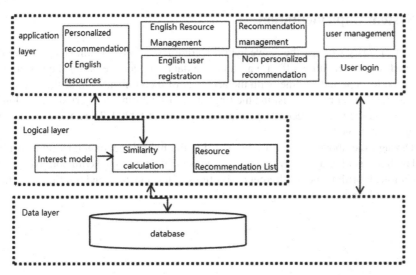

Fig. 4. Overall system architecture

In the application layer of this system, there are personalized recommendation and non personalized recommendation.

For logic layer, it mainly includes application server and personalized recommendation model. The application server mainly responds to the user's operation request. After receiving the user's request from the client, the system sends the response to the database server and sends the response result back to the client for display in front of the user's eyes.

In the process of English teaching, there are abundant extra-curricular English resources. These English resources are vivid and interesting. They can most stimulate students' interest in learning English and make them feel the charm of English. They include newspapers, magazines, literary works, film and television works and daily life English that students usually read. These English resources are an indispensable part of students' learning English, It can create a relaxed, free and happy class learning environment for students, stimulate students' thirst for knowledge, and expand the space of personality, which is conducive to the improvement of students' language ability. In the teaching process, teachers should make use of the positive influence and role of English extra-curricular resources to carry out subconscious language thinking teaching. By providing students with language materials for English construction, reasonably arranging time, effectively organizing extra-curricular teaching, finding ways to create an interactive atmosphere, meeting students' practical needs, encouraging students to actively participate in and deeply experience the language learning process inside and outside the class, and then through communication and cooperation, exploring and practicing, Build the corresponding knowledge, promote the formation and development of students' good English skills and stimulate their interest in improving their practical English application ability.

4 System Implementation

In order to verify whether the above hybrid recommendation algorithm can achieve the expected recommendation effect, based on the data set generated after the system has been used for a period of time, with the accuracy of recommendation as the evaluation standard, 2000 user records visiting the English website during this period are randomly selected, and their score records are exported, a total of 60000. Thus, the result shown in Fig. 5 is obtained.

Through the above results, we can see that the hybrid recommendation algorithm used in this paper has a slightly higher accuracy than the traditional collaborative recommendation algorithm under different proportions of test machine and training set, which shows the advantages of this algorithm.

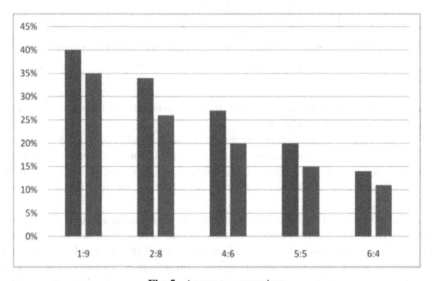

Fig. 5. Accuracy comparison

With the continuous progress of science and technology, the teaching technology has also been improved. Various advanced teaching equipment have been introduced into schools one after another, and the position and role of information technology in English teaching activities have become increasingly important. Because the teaching level of schools is inseparable from the increasingly updated knowledge with the outside world, especially for the students majoring in Business English in vocational schools, And accumulate the professional English required in future work. It can be said that information technology is the backbone of promoting English teaching reform. It provides the largest platform for global knowledge sharing and provides rich information resources for different regions. At the same time, the application of information technology in English teaching has great potential to improve the quality of English teaching environment. The rational use of information resources is of great help to help teachers enrich their teaching contents and promote students' motivation to learn English. It also plays a great role in promoting students' intellectual development and broadening their horizons. It is most appropriate to describe the great influence of information resources with the saying "scholars do not go out, but can know the world". Research shows that information technology in English teaching can more effectively stimulate students' visual and auditory systems, make students remember the knowledge they have learned more deeply, save classroom teaching time, add more rich teaching contents in a limited time, and improve teaching efficiency. Moreover, diversified information channels bring many new things, and can enhance students' curiosity and thirst for knowledge, The English knowledge required for one's major can be expressed through the real language environment, which is more effective than the teachers' simple lecture analysis in the classroom. This real language environment is not only conducive to the teachers' reserve of information resources in teaching and the accumulation of knowledge in students' learning, but also meets the needs of students' personalized learning.

The integration of information resources and teaching materials is of great help to the rational use of teaching resources other than teaching materials. Under the guidance of theory, especially under the guidance of the theory guiding teachers' teaching, it is necessary to take information resources with computers and networks as the core as an important tool to promote students' independent learning, stimulate students' sensory systems, enrich the teaching environment, Teachers can also help students to find learning materials and effectively serve students' learning. The materials needed by students for listening, speaking, reading and writing can be downloaded from the Internet, which saves a lot of costs and time and effort compared with the previous purchase.

5   Conclusion

To sum up, a teaching resource management system with collaborative recommendation function is the key to solve the problem of excessive accumulation and low efficiency of current teaching resources. This paper introduces collaborative recommendation algorithm into the teaching resource management system to recommend different types of teaching resources to suitable users. The collaborative recommendation teaching resource management system is composed of personal space management, resource management, recommendation module and system management to meet the different functional requirements of different users, In order to improve the sharing and utilization of teaching resources.

References

1. Yan, Q.: Design of teaching video resource management system in colleges and universities based on microtechnology. Secur. Commun. Netw. (2021)
2. Yuan, X.: Design of college English teaching information platform based on artificial intelligence technology. In: Journal of Physics Conference Series, vol. 1852, no. 2, 022031 (2021)
3. Huang, Y.: Design of personalised English distance teaching platform based on artificial intelligence. J. Inf. Knowl. Manag. (2022)

4. Zhu, M.: Research on English teaching model with computer aid. In: CIPAE 2021: 2021 2nd International Conference on Computers, Information Processing and Advanced Education (2021)
5. Zhou, X., Li, X., Su, N.: Design and internet of things development of network teaching resource base system for educational technology. In: Journal of Physics Conference Series, vol. 1769, no. 1, 012005 (2021)
6. Hendy, N.T.: The effectiveness of technology delivered instruction in teaching human resource management. Int. J. Manag. Educ. 19(2), 100479 (2021)
7. Nie, A.: Design of English interactive teaching system based on association rules algorithm. Secur. Commun. Netw. (2021)
8. Lin, H., Wei, Y.: Design and implementation of college English multimedia aided teaching resources. Int. J. Electr. Eng. Educ., 002072092098351 (2021)
9. Chen, C.: A method of digital English teaching resource sharing based on artificial intelligence. J. Inf. Knowl. Manag. 21(Supp02) (2022)
10. Tan, Q., Shao, X.: Construction of college English teaching resource database under the background of big data. In: Journal of Physics Conference Series, vol. 1744, no. 3, p. 032004 (2021)

Analysis of College English Teaching Under the Network Teaching Platform

Jianli Chen$^{(\boxtimes)}$, Yanping Shan, and Changqing Yu

The College of Arts and Sciences, Kunming 650000, China
2444857283@qq.com

Abstract. With the development of information technology and the increasing renewal and popularization of computer and global network technology in the twenty-first century, great changes have taken place in listening, speaking, reading, writing and translation in the process of College English learning. A single traditional teaching method can no longer meet the needs of students and society. The network has become a part of the daily life of contemporary college students. With the continuous improvement of the network teaching system, To some extent, it accelerates the transformation from traditional teaching mode to network mode. It is necessary and useful to use network resources to develop college English network teaching platform. College English teaching should make full use of multimedia and network technology, improve the single classroom teaching mode dominated by teachers, and gradually turn into a new teaching mode combining traditional teaching and network teaching. Many versions of College English online teaching platforms have been developed in China, and have been applied in many colleges and universities in China. Students can use the network to study independently. The network English teaching system provides a specific operation platform for students to learn English. This paper analyzes college English teaching based on network teaching platform.

Keywords: College English · Network teaching platform · Teaching analysis

1 Introduction

With the popularity of the network, network teaching has attracted more and more attention. A variety of network teaching software have been developed and used in teaching. The network teaching platform has become a new teaching tool and is gradually used in teaching.

Network teaching platform, also known as network teaching support platform, can be divided into broad sense and narrow sense. The generalized network teaching platform includes not only the hardware facilities and equipment supporting network teaching, but also the software system supporting network teaching. In other words, the broad network teaching platform has two parts: hardware teaching platform and software teaching platform. In a narrow sense, network teaching platform refers to a software system based on the Internet to provide comprehensive support services for network teaching

M. A. Jan and F. Khan (Eds.): BigIoT-EDU 2022, LNICST 466, pp. 89–99, 2023.
https://doi.org/10.1007/978-3-031-23947-2_10

[1]. Network teaching platform is widely used in universities and professional schools all over the world.

The traditional teaching methods and teaching platforms can not fully meet the needs of teaching and learning in today's information society. No matter in terms of methods, carriers, methods, concepts and contents, they are slowly becoming obsolete, which restricts the deepening of teaching, especially network teaching. Due to its remarkable characteristics of unlimited time and space, resource sharing, good human-computer and interpersonal interaction and real-time update, network teaching system will create a new teaching mode, so as to accelerate the reform of traditional teaching mode. Online teaching method is convenient for students' learning, helps to improve teaching efficiency and save teaching time. It is necessary to design and develop an online teaching platform. The network teaching platform is not only convenient for students to study anytime and anywhere and strengthen the communication between teachers and students, but also a resource website with complete functions and simple operation is very convenient for teachers and students [2].

English network teaching platform is also a new English education model and method with the gradual development and popularization of English education and network in China. There are two reasons for its emergence. One is the marketization of English education and training; The other is the promotion and popularization of network technology. Network teaching platform, also known as network teaching support platform, can be divided into broad sense and narrow sense [3]. The generalized network teaching platform includes not only the hardware facilities and equipment supporting network teaching, but also the software system supporting network teaching. In other words, the broad network teaching platform has two parts: hardware teaching platform and software teaching platform. In a narrow sense, network teaching platform refers to a software system based on the Internet to provide comprehensive support services for network teaching.

Through the network platform, students can easily obtain learning materials and learn courses through this system. Teachers can also conveniently manage the relevant affairs of this course through the network platform, so as to improve the efficiency. In the online teaching platform system, after registration and login, you can view the basic information of the school and leave messages through the message board [4]. Registered members only restrict the students of the school. Students can log in through student ID and password. Students can also view the homework released by the teacher through homework management, upload their homework in the form of electronic files and submit homework, In the video teaching, you can download some teaching videos and test the test questions of relevant courses in the online test.

This paper focuses on explaining the positive effect of College English online teaching software system on students' English learning [5]. The network teaching platform highlights students' independence and flexibility, and pays attention to students' individual differences, especially students' learning styles and learning strategies. "The boundless revolution in physical time and space" makes the learning in the network environment have no boundaries in the traditional sense. From the perspective of time, students can study according to their own plans rather than according to the fixed timetable. From the perspective of space, students can study in the classroom, in the dormitory, in the library or at home, So that students are no longer limited by classroom teaching time and space [6]. "The revolution in the optimization and utilization of resources" makes "people can provide the best educational resources through the network to those who cannot get them due to the obstacles of time and space through the network", so as to realize the integration and sharing of network resources, so that English language students can make full use of rich network resources for learning. Relying on the network platform, the current college English teaching system is divided into "audio-visual speaking" and "reading and writing" modules.

2   Analysis of the Current Situation of College English Teaching

The emergence of network education is gradually developed with the development of network technology. It has irreplaceable advantages when it is introduced into China and applied to English teaching. This paper will analyze the advantages of online English teaching to further elaborate the practical significance of this research. It will also introduce the three existing network teaching platforms at home and abroad in detail, so as to explain their existing problems based on user needs, and also provide a reference example for the research of this paper.

2.1   Advantages of College English Network Teaching

(1) Facilitate personalized learning
     Because of the traditional education, many people attend classes intensively and teachers teach them intensively at a moderate progress, forcing students to give up their personality. Students can only learn passively according to the teacher's progress. The result of this kind of teaching is to cultivate students into "one side of a thousand people". Let alone the ability to acquire knowledge and self-renewal. This is not only the biggest disadvantage of traditional education, but also a problem that many educators are committed to studying and solving, but it has never been able to fundamentally solve this problem [7]. The development of computer technology and network technology provides a technical platform to completely solve this problem, so that anyone can learn any course from any chapter at any time and anywhere, and students can really arrange learning according to their own situation, learn the knowledge they really need, and truly realize personalized learning.

(2) Computer network can create a good language situation for students
     The use of multimedia technology in English discipline has incomparable advantages over other disciplines. It provides more space for the development of students' personality. In English teaching, multimedia can greatly improve the breadth and depth of teaching. In traditional teaching, teachers and students have less bilateral activities, less practice, monotonous and boring scenes, learning interest will weaken or lose with the passage of time, and students' individual differences will intensify, which is not advocated by English teaching [8]. The use of multimedia teaching technology can achieve a very friendly interactive teaching environment (such as teacher-student dialogue, man-machine dialogue, student communication, situational practice, random imitation, etc.), which can greatly improve the learning efficiency and learning effect.

(3) Computer network can create an audio-visual and oral environment for students
    The virtual communication environment in the computer network promotes stu-
    dents' autonomous learning. The key to learning language lies in communication,
    and the communication activities in the classroom are often affected and restricted
    by many factors. The status of teachers and students, the difference of age and the
    level of cognition of things all lead to the difficulty of smooth communication activ-
    ities. However, due to the difference in level among students, many students dare
    not speak, fearing that they will be laughed at by their classmates for their mistakes
    [9]. However, computer network provides students with a real language communi-
    cation environment. Students can use human-computer interaction to communicate
    and learn, because students don't have face-to-face embarrassment here and don't
    have to blush because of the wrong words.
(4) English teaching based on network environment provides learners with unlimited
    learning resources
    The network environment is rich in resources and information; Fast knowledge
    updating; Lively, interesting and practical, teachers can guide students to read the
    introduction and text. Teachers present picture materials, broadcast TV and video
    clips through the network environment, and then design the following questions
    around the teaching objectives, teaching situations and teaching materials to let
    students think and explore [10]. Unlimited resources allow students with different
    English levels to choose autonomous learning and build their own learning system,
    as shown in Fig. 1.

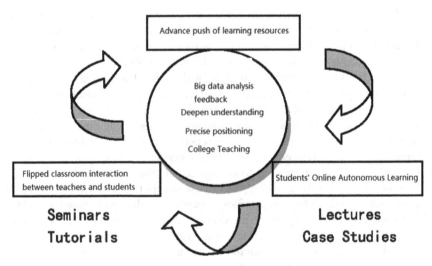

Fig. 1. Internet teaching mode

(5) Multimedia network teaching is conducive to students' autonomous learning
    Constructivism theory holds that knowledge is acquired by learners in a certain sit-
    uation with the help of others (teachers, learning partners, etc.), using necessary

learning materials and actively through meaning construction. Therefore. Students are the subject of cognition, the active constructor of knowledge meaning, not the passive receiver of external stimulation and the object of knowledge indoctrination. With multimedia network teaching, students can organize their own learning activities with the help of computers. Multimedia network teaching breaks the limitation of time and space. Students can choose learning content, learning progress and learn by human-computer interaction anytime and anywhere. In this way, teachers are no longer the only knowledge imparter and source of information. Multimedia network can realize students' autonomous learning and access to information. At the same time, in autonomous learning, learners can enjoy greater joy by constructing their own knowledge system.

(6) Network teaching platform provides a new communication platform for teachers and students

The network teaching platform has opened up a new communication platform for teachers and students in the classroom. Students can leave messages, ask questions and provide solutions to teachers and their students through the forum of the platform. Teachers can also put forward learning objectives, requirements and leave homework for learners to complete through the notice section of the platform [11]. Teachers and students can also communicate and discuss after class through e-mail and other network means. It not only facilitates the communication between students and teachers, but also promotes the increase of the frequency of communication between teachers and students.

3   Analysis of the Existing College English Online Teaching Platform

(1) Classification and characteristics of existing network teaching platforms

In this paper, the existing typical network teaching platforms are roughly divided into two categories. One is a comprehensive network teaching management platform similar to blackboard (blackboard system will be introduced in detail below). One is network courseware similar to CD courseware designed for a certain subject (for example, the new concept college English teaching system introduced below).

The characteristic of the integrated network teaching management platform is that it does not have a designed course, but provides a network platform for teachers to organize teaching courses independently. It is suitable for any discipline. Teachers use this platform to organize online classroom teaching, upload courseware, assign homework, discuss with students and other online teaching activities. Students can communicate and learn online with teachers through the platform.

The network courseware designed for a subject is another form of network teaching platform. It provides a well-designed teaching course for students to learn, practice and test. It does not support the process of teachers organizing teaching. Teachers play a role of supervision and evaluation in the whole learning process of students. The existing college English network teaching platforms for College English in China mainly belong to the latter category, which is equivalent to a kind of network courseware in terms of implementation form.

(2) Introduction and analysis of the existing college English online teaching platform
The excellent advantages of online education, such as openness, autonomy, interactivity and cooperation, make the development of online education platform a very meaningful thing. Many domestic papers have put forward many plans to establish college English online education platform, and there are many college English online education platforms in China [12]. There are four influential College English teaching systems: New Era Interactive English launched by Tsinghua University Press, college experience English launched by higher education press, new concept college English online teaching system launched by Shanghai Foreign Language Education Press, and New Vision College English launched by foreign language teaching and Research Press. These four online education platforms have also been developed and have been applied in some campuses in China, but the results are not satisfactory.

4 Improve the Ability of English Audio-Visual Teaching and Learning Through Online Teaching Platform

College English course teaching requirements: College English course aims to carry out English language quality education, cultivate students' autonomous learning ability through computer network teaching materials, and help students solve text difficulties, digest teaching priorities, and form the ability to acquire knowledge independently and self-study habits through online Q & A and multimedia face-to-face classes. In terms of English language, lay a solid foundation in pronunciation, grammar and vocabulary, cultivate skilled listening, speaking, writing and reading abilities, cultivate students' ability to actually use English language, cultivate students' logical thinking ability, independent working ability, and the ability to ask, analyze and solve problems. Multimedia network learning: the teaching of this course includes two modules: reading, writing and listening and speaking [13].

"Audio visual speaking module is to use network courseware to ask students to listen to and read relevant audio and video contents according to the teacher's teaching plan and requirements and their actual English level. They can understand key words and sentences; summarize the main idea; master details; speculate the internal meaning, etc. they can complete role play with the virtual trainer peedy built in the system and express their opinions on relevant topics The network is submitted to the teacher Teacher."

Taking the latest original English audio-visual materials as the carrier, taking students' autonomous and inquiry learning as the means, taking the cultivation of English comprehensive application ability and diversified humanistic quality as the goal, relying on Project-based language skill training to cultivate students' English comprehensive learning ability, and relying on unique task driven design to improve students' research ability and innovation ability, Develop students' learning potential by relying on the network autonomous learning mode.

Language materials on the Internet are more authentic and closer to life, which can increase the effectiveness of learning, help students' cognitive input and enhance memory. If students encounter difficulties in obtaining input information, they can search the required information on the Internet. The process of this discovery becomes passive to active, and is no longer indoctrinated. In this way, the effect of learning is positive and effective.

The role of online teaching platform for English audio-visual teaching and learning:

(1) Improve autonomy: in the College English audio-visual and oral module, students can choose different times and places to reasonably adjust their learning plans according to their own time needs and arrangements. The contact interface is similar to their familiar network, which is easy to operate, with pictures and texts. The learning mode with images can easily enable students to invest in learning. Different learning units, such as passage A: verbal task 1, verbal task 2, banked close, close, translation task 1, translation task 2, Writing task There are also passage B: reading skills, comprehension task, verbal task 1, verbal task 2, and resources for extended learning: further reading 1, further reading 2 It is not difficult to see that students can choose the learning materials they need from units of different levels and different difficulties; Design and arrange learning according to their actual needs, so that students can truly become the masters of learning and obtain a sense of achievement, so as to further stimulate their interest and autonomy in learning.

(2) Expand interactivity: the New Horizon College English online teaching platform provides a student-centered teaching model, so that teachers and students can interact. "Teaching notice and handout" can release and modify the notice and handout in time; "teaching schedule" can release and modify the teaching schedule and let students know the latest appointment schedule at the same time; the most frequently used by students is "teaching communication tool" This section can answer questions, discuss in groups, hold class forums, and send and receive emails; In addition, teachers can log in to the teacher client to control the learning process, view learning records, and provide supervision and management in real time; Students can also submit their homework through online homework. Multimedia and network technology are very beneficial to the formation and development of students' cognitive structure because they can provide an interactive learning environment with friendly interface and intuitive image [14]. It can be seen that the application of network teaching platform realizes the real teaching interaction, which is not only limited to class, but also extended to extracurricular.

(3) Enhance pertinence: in information network teaching, middle school students can learn according to the arrangement of teachers and their own actual situation, Overcome the "one size fits all" phenomenon. Students and teachers communicate online through "online Q & a", which can timely understand their progress and shortcomings; in addition, the repeatability of audio-visual and oral learning really varies from person to person, changing the traditional irreversible situation of missing a teacher's sentence; using the Internet, students can discuss in "class" The teacher can also find the common difficulties of students and the learning difficulties of individual students, so as to teach students in accordance with their aptitude, as shown in Fig. 2.

(4) Promote efficiency: students of different ages have differences in semantic memory ability, but there is little difference in situational memory ability. Vocabulary

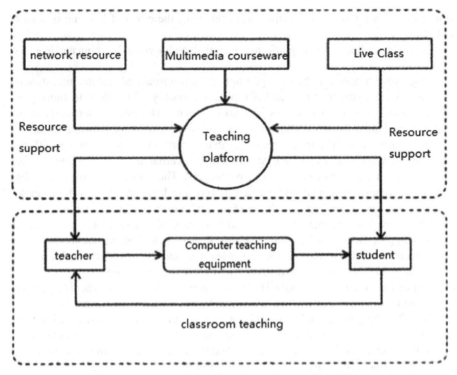

Fig. 2. Information network teaching

learning supplemented by images can better perceive vocabulary and clarify the relationship and even differences between words. In addition, learning vocabulary in context is more conducive to memory and understanding. If the text matches the animation effect, the understanding speed will be more efficient. E-learning can undoubtedly arouse students' interest, and the most important thing is to improve the quality and efficiency of learning.

(5) Deepen research: the network is more conducive to the realization of students' cooperative research-based learning. In the traditional classroom teaching process, students are limited by region and time, and cooperative learning can not give full play to its due efficiency. The real-time online and interactive functions of e-learning make cooperative research-based learning possible. For example, students cooperate with peers, experts and other students through network communication technology to publish works and communicate. Use Tencent, MSN, UC and other real-time communication software of network technology to practice oral English, BBS and e-mail, carry out cooperative learning and communication, effectively spread your questions and information to others, receive replies and comments, etc. Students can also establish personal home pages and create personalized learning platforms. Students can enhance their listening ability by listening to more English broadcasts, such as BBC, VOA and CNN; Enjoy a large number of English original films and practice listening and speaking skills. Online resources are rich and

colorful, and a large number of English websites can be directly linked, such as economist, National Geographic, etc. Online library and database are the ocean of materials for students' learning under the network environment.

5 Analysis of College English Teaching Under the Network Teaching Platform

5.1 The Reading and Writing Mode of Network Teaching Is More Humanized Than Traditional Classroom Teaching

"The reading and writing module aims to enable students to use computer network teaching materials to input language materials independently, guess the meaning of new words from the context, guess the meaning of new words from word formation, and understand the main idea and details of the article through cooperative learning and collaborative learning, so as to improve the reading speed and quality, complete relevant exercises online, and actively participate in the discussion of online community Move." Ah, teachers of traditional reading and writing courses are usually full of "cramming" teaching, because the class hours are limited and the content is limited after all. They often take into account article a rather than article B; If the vocabulary is explained in detail, there is no time to analyze the context and writing style of the article; The background knowledge of the text takes a little longer, and the practice after class may not be taken into account at all. In short, it is a common phenomenon of teaching to care for one thing and lose the other. Usually, the teaching contents are different due to the different teaching emphases of each teacher in parallel classes. The reading and writing teaching under the network teaching platform will ensure the overall consistency. Students can participate in classroom teaching activities within the scope of the outline. The knowledge points in the article are modular, clear and detailed. Students can easily carry out independent learning, but teachers should organize teaching in a planned and arranged way, and the good effect of teaching is very obvious. The background material and the context of the article flash when the student clicks the button. Of course, the role of teachers has changed significantly. They are no longer the lecturer of knowledge, but the instructor and manager. "Teaching people to fish is better than teaching people to fish". Teachers spend more time thinking about how to guide students' autonomous learning and turn their teaching attention to teaching methods, which objectively improves their professional quality and promotes the reform of College English teaching.

The reading materials of College English reading and writing module are very rich. Students can simulate the examination situation, complete reading within the specified time, exercise reading speed and skills, and improve reading quality. Some materials also have many links, which enriches students' knowledge and expands the scope of English reading.

The writing module is very independent, which makes the writing more convenient and fast. After the students complete the writing task and submit it, the system will automatically give the writing score, which greatly changes the untimely situation of traditional teaching. The teacher usually gives the evaluation after the students finish writing for a period of time.

5.2 Translation Under the Network Platform to Comprehensively Improve Students' English Ability

English learning is a process of mutual influence and gradual development of listening, speaking, reading, writing and translation. Translation, as an advanced stage of English learning, requires high ability. There are few class hours and practice opportunities involving translation in classroom teaching, which is not conducive to the cultivation of translation practice ability. Network autonomous learning of translation course has become an important means to improve translation ability. In addition, the English teaching system has its own dictionary function. Students can consult the dictionary when needed. With the help of translation software and rich network resources, it can more easily and efficiently realize the translation between Chinese and English. Some new words are difficult to obtain in high-level English dictionaries. For example, English words such as castsnap, microblogging, hikikomori and defrend have not been included in the dictionary, while words such as "selfie", "microblog", "house" and "black" have been popular for a long time; Another example is "leftover women", "Moonlight clan", "sissy", "oil tycoon", if you search ICIBA for gold miss, moonlight group, sissy boy and oil tycoon, it will pop up. With the help of the Internet, the Chinese-English translation of these words is easy and comfortable. Original films, BBC, VOA and other English materials also provide good practice materials for interpretation. Students can often browse English websites to improve their English ability in an all-round way. There are many special English language learning websites (such as pute English) that provide a large number of information input requirements for students at different levels and for different purposes. The network can easily meet the different needs of different students and improve the fluency and accuracy of students in using the target language. The network has obvious advantages in this regard.

6 Conclusion

As a modern teaching method, network has played an important role in education. Although various restrictive factors still exist: the development of network hardware construction technology is not fully mature, there are great differences in various regions, the level of teachers and students are different, but the network can bring us great convenience. If we can operate according to the actual situation of students in combination with the actual situation of regions, You'll get twice the result with half the effort. Only by making better use of the advantages of the network can we avoid its disadvantages and better promote the teaching reform. Computer technology and English are two necessary skills for talents in the twenty-first century, and the proficiency of combining these two skills determines a person's development. College English teaching aims to cultivate English talents suitable for the development of the times. Network teaching is also an irresistible trend. The online test of CET-4 and CET-6 makes use of the advantages of the network to highlight the communicative function of language, truly investigate the application and communication ability of language students, and test whether students' language ability meets the actual language needs.

References

1. Cao, S., Chen, R., Liu, H., et al.: An empirical study on multimodal discourse analysis of college English teaching in the context of new media. J. Intell. Fuzzy Syst. (2), 1–5 2021
2. Wang, L.: Analysis of college English teaching in application oriented colleges and universities based on the effect oriented concept. J. Contemp. Educ. Res. 5(2), 3 (2021)
3. Analysis of the Teaching Mode of College English Reading Teaching Based on Flipped Classroom Model. (17), 2 (2021)
4. Bao, X.: Analysis of college English teaching model based on network automation transformation. In: E3S Web of Conferences, vol. 257, 02054 (2021)
5. Gao, H.: Reform of college English teaching model under the background of artificial intelligence. In: Journal of Physics Conference Series, vol. 1744, no. 4, p. 042161 (2021)
6. Tan, Q., Shao, X.: Construction of college English teaching resource database under the background of big data. In: Journal of Physics Conference Series, vol. 1744, no. 3, p. 032004 (2021)
7. Yang, J.: The reform of college English teaching model under the OBE teaching concept. In: CIPAE 2021: 2021 2nd International Conference on Computers, Information Processing and Advanced Education (2021)
8. Liu, J.: The Influence of Modern Information Technology on College English Teaching Under the Background of Educational Information (2021)
9. Zhou, W.: The Practice of Mixed Teaching Mode in College English Teaching Under the Mobile Internet Environment (2021)
10. Liu, H., Chen, R., Cao, S., et al.: Evaluation of college English teaching quality based on grey clustering analysis. Int. J. Emerg. Technol. Learn. (iJET) 16(2), 173 (2021)
11. Li, J.: College English Teaching Mode Under the Background of Big Data (2021)
12. Zhai, Z.: A probe into the application of English euphemism in college classroom teaching under multimedia network technology. Int. J. Electr. Eng. Educ., 002072092098351 (2021)
13. Li, N.: A fuzzy evaluation model of college English teaching quality based on analytic hierarchy process. Int. J. Emerg. Technol. Learn. (iJET) 16(2), 17 (2021)
14. Zhang, M.: Analysis on cultivation of cross-cultural communication competence in college English teaching. In: 2021 2nd International Conference on Mental Health and Humanities Education (ICMHHE 2021) (2021)

Design and Realization of the Innovation and Entrepreneurship Experience System of Data Dynamic Innovation Model

Xiaoli Xie[✉] and Xiaowei Hu

Hebei Polytechnic Instiute, Hebei 050091, China
liuminggzu@163.com

Abstract. At present, we are setting off a wave of innovation and entrepreneurship, and in universities, college students' entrepreneurship is also sought after by everyone, and the work of dual innovation is promoted step by step. In order to improve the level of dual innovation of college students, help college students can better carry out entrepreneurship, save precious time of college students, and improve the management level of college students, this paper composes the entrepreneurship level of college students from three dimensions, and the preferred analysis of college students' entrepreneurship Then we summarize its characteristics and analyze the development of college students' entrepreneurship, and finally, based on the characteristics of college students' entrepreneurship, we give some guidance and develop a management system according to the national policy of importance, this system is mainly a set of system to give guidance to the current college students' dual entrepreneurship without any management experience, through the experiment, it can be seen that this system is a better solution to the current Through the experiment, it can be seen that this system can better solve the problem of insufficient management experience of college students.

Keywords: Innovation and entrepreneurship · Multidimensional dynamic innovation model · System design

1 Introduction

In recent years, with the promotion of the national development strategy and investment of education funds, the investment of colleges and universities in the news and entrepreneurship fund for students has increased annually, and the types and numbers of news and entrepreneurial projects for college students have also increased rapidly. But so far, many colleges and universities don't have the application administration of college students' news. The project application is mainly registered and accepted by experts who are inactive and difficult to manage [1].

Hao Dandan puts forward that college students' Entrepreneurship mechanism includes driving mechanism, opportunity search and financial support mechanism. He emphasizes that college students' independent entrepreneurship driving mechanism is

© ICST Institute for Computer Sciences, Social Informatics and Telecommunications Engineering 2023
Published by Springer Nature Switzerland AG 2023. All Rights Reserved
M. A. Jan and F. Khan (Eds.): BigIoT-EDU 2022, LNICST 466, pp. 100–109, 2023.
https://doi.org/10.1007/978-3-031-23947-2_11

the premise, opportunity search mechanism is the key and financial support mechanism is the guarantee. From the perspective of university entrepreneurship education, Liu Min pointed out the problems existing in college students' entrepreneurship, such as paying more attention to theory than practice, paying more attention to entrepreneurship skills training than entrepreneurship spirit and entrepreneurship awareness training, and the lack of entrepreneurship team teachers, and then put forward targeted suggestions [2]. Zhang lainan pointed out the defects of China's Entrepreneurship Policy: ① lack of systematic policy-making; ② Lack of stage segmentation; ③ Did not examine the actual national conditions; ④ Insufficient investigation on the demand side of entrepreneurship; ⑤ Lack of consideration for the new economic background of entrepreneurial economy. It is therefore urgent to develop an efficient and stable project application system. The design and implementation of the new and entrepreneurial experience of college students based on a multidimensional dynamic new mode will gradually develop simplification and simplification to diversity and intelligence. The future college student news system will be effective and stable with data-based information management [3].

News and entrepreneurship refer to entrepreneurial activities based on one or more news, such as technology news, product news, brand news, service news, commercial model news, administration news, organizational news, market news, channel news, etc. entrepreneurship is the goal of news and business. News and entrepreneurship are entrepreneurial activities based on news that differ from clean news or clean entrepreneurship. The news accepts pioneering and original, and entrepreneurship takes advantage of practical actions [4]. The fundamental difference between new entrepreneurship and traditional entrepreneurship is whether there are new factors in entrepreneurship. The news here includes not only technological news, but also administrative news, known news, processing news and marketing news.

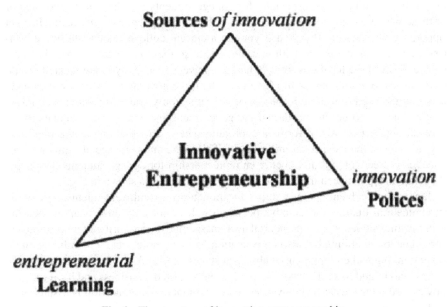

Fig. 1. The structure of innovative entrepreneurship.

In short, as long as the activities that can bring new value to resources are innovation. Innovation and entrepreneurship refers to the activities of innovation and entrepreneurship in one or several aspects. Entrepreneurship without innovation in any aspect belongs to traditional entrepreneurship. The structure of innovative entrepreneurship is shown in Fig. 1.

2 Construction and Operation Mechanism Analysis of New College Students' Entrepreneurship and Innovation Mechanism

As we all know, entrepreneur timmons created a model of entrepreneurship, this model sums up all the problems encountered in the current business, he believes that entrepreneurial activity is a high-dimensional activity, this activity is divided into three dimensions, 1. In the process of entrepreneurship, the outside world is the most important opportunity, followed by the outside world or their own mastery of resources, if these two you do not have, then entrepreneurship will be very difficult, especially at the beginning of the business, if these two you have one of the conditions, then the initial business will be relatively smooth, and also pay attention to the role of the team, when you hire a team, at the beginning of the business, must be the group as the starting point of their activities [5]. When starting a business to a certain period, the need for external funding will greatly increase. 2. In the early stage of business, you must understand the local laws and regulations, and be good at using these laws and regulations to guide your own innovative business, which can increase the atmosphere of entrepreneurship, because if the local policy is not conducive to entrepreneurship, then the good atmosphere will not make you successful in business, if the local itself has a certain entrepreneurial atmosphere, we can also call this atmosphere a good soil for entrepreneurship. This way your future financing and other business will be greatly improved. This is more favorable for you to start a business, especially for college students who have just graduated or for those who are ready to start a business, such an atmosphere can provide intellectual support for your startup [6]. And if you are a current college student starting a business, that you can cooperate with your university so that the vitality of your business is there. 3. Both the local government and the university where you are located should create a wave of entrepreneurship for all people, if the government is involved enough, then you just need to use the resources of your university, the government encourages local businesses to get involved, and the government also encourages students to get involved together, so that it forms a good atmosphere, which is one of the important ways to achieve the local economic take-off. This is the main essence of timmons. This model can effectively promote better entrepreneurship for college students in college. The relationship between innovation and entrepreneurship is shown in Fig. 2.

Innovation and entrepreneurship education aims to cultivate talents with basic entrepreneurial quality and creative personality. It is not only an education focusing on cultivating students' entrepreneurial awareness, innovation spirit and innovation and entrepreneurship ability, but also an education for the whole society to cultivate innovative thinking and entrepreneurial ability in stages and levels for those entrepreneurial groups who intend to start a business, have already started a business and have successfully started a business [7]. Innovation and entrepreneurship education is essentially a kind of practical education.

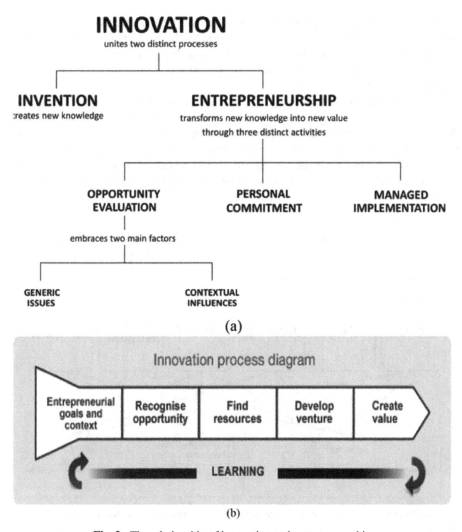

Fig. 2. The relationship of innovation and entrepreneurship

In 1991, the Tokyo International Conference on entrepreneurship and innovation education defined "entrepreneurship and innovation education" in a broad sense as: cultivating people with the most creative personality, including initiative, risk-taking spirit, entrepreneurial ability, ability to work independently, and the cultivation of technical, social and management skills.

The Ministry of education pointed out in the opinions on vigorously promoting innovation and entrepreneurship education in Colleges and universities and self entrepreneurship of college students: "To carry out innovation and entrepreneurship education in Colleges and universities and actively encourage college students to start their own businesses is a major strategic measure for the education system to deeply study and

practice the scientific concept of development and serve the construction of an innovative country; it is an important way to deepen the teaching reform of higher education
and cultivate students' innovative spirit and practical ability; it is an important measure
to implement entrepreneurship to drive employment and promote the full employment
of college graduates" [8].

The government is of great importance to implement news and entrepreneurial education in college and universities, to build a solid foundation, to build a platform and
directories, to create good news and entrepreneurial education around, to optimize the
news and business system and the service environment, to create a field of cultural environment, Who walks on news and entrepreneurship, and in full, as shown in Fig. 3, has to
do actions to build a system of university information and an entrepreneurial education
system.

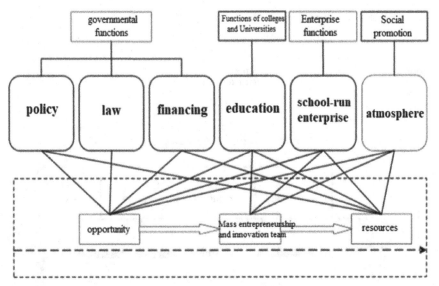

Fig. 3. Structural diagram of multidimensional dynamic innovation model (mdmi) for College
Students

3 Design of College Students' Innovation and Entrepreneurship Experience System Based on Multi-dimensional Dynamic Innovation Model

3.1 System Basic Requirements Analysis

According to the actual characteristics, this management system should mainly have
these roles, first is the project release, when the project is released, the project publisher's authority is gone, then the project applicant, the project applicant is responsible

for applying for the project, when the project application is completed, the project applicant will pass the applied project to the project reviewer, the project reviewer review the qualification of the project application and the project application, and decide whether agree to the project application. In this system, project applicants can see every step of their project application, such as viewing historical project applications, project review status, submitting applications online, including the ability to review project team members, etc. The project reviewer mainly decides to agree or disagree with the project review, other matters are not authorized to the project reviewer. The system administrator manages all the functions of the system and has the highest authority, but the project manager is not involved in all the processes and is only a technical role. The main functions of each functional module are shown in Fig. 4. Through Fig. 4, we can clearly know what role the administrator of each module plays in the system and what management is undertaken. In fact, it seems to be a very simple system, but the role of each different, the authorization received is also different, can not be because of a good relationship with the administrator, and let the administrator open the permissions without permission, so these are not tolerated, the administrator in setting up the user, the management of each module to conduct the appropriate training, so as not to cause unnecessary trouble, especially not to give the project auditor's rights to the general So generally set the project auditor as a leader or other important personnel [9]. Project applicants should not be set arbitrarily, but should also be given certain limits.

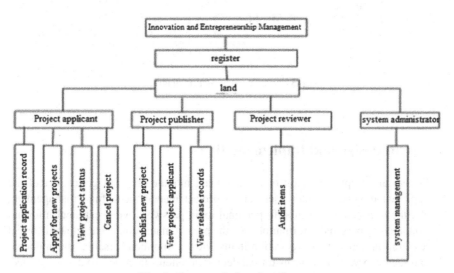

Fig. 4. System role function diagram

3.2 System Database Design

The management system, we did not use Microsoft's C++ language to write, because the use of Microsoft's programming language will cause a lot of redundant code, which is not conducive to the execution of the code, thus using the server + java programming ideas, because this method can be applied to most of the browser, and in the lower configuration of the computer is also can run smoothly, so that we can automatically according to the system access Generate mapping table, greatly improve the smoothness of the system, and improve the efficiency of the system development, as shown in Fig. 5. This also allows engineers to simplify secondary development.

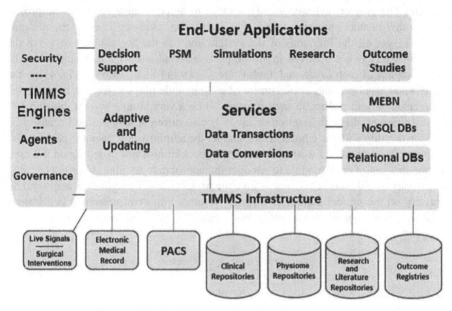

Fig. 5. System role function diagram

4   System Design and Implementation

(1) Design and implementation of the applicant module. The navigation bar of the applicant module includes user center, project management, fund management, etc. the user center can modify personal login password, view personal information, modify personal information, etc. the project management can view historical declaration items, new declaration items, view group members, etc. the applicant can see history in the view historical declaration items interface To declare project information, click the link to declare new project to enter the new declared project interface. In the declared project interface, you can see the latest project published by the project publisher [10]. The project applicant can only declare one item, and you can't declare other items after declaration. If you want to declare other items, click the link to declare new items on the interface to enter the display of declared new items In the interface, click the Cancel button to cancel a for the applied new project. In the new applied project display interface, click publish project application form to pop up the interface for filling in project application form. In the left

navigation bar, click the production viewing group member link to enter the group member display information. The project applicant can add group members, delete group members and modify group members, as shown in Fig. 6.

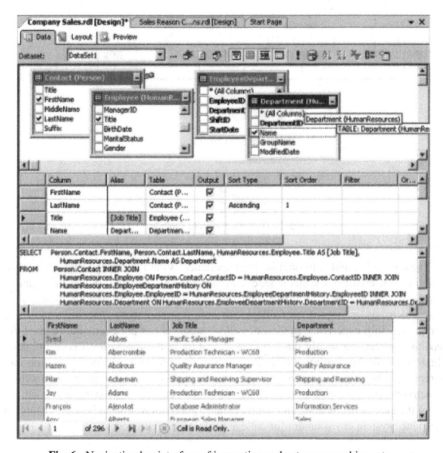

Fig. 6. Navigation bar interface of innovation and entrepreneurship system

(2) Design and implementation of the publisher module. The project publisher module has user center, project management and other navigation. The project publisher can view historical published projects, publish new projects, etc. the project publisher clicks the historical published projects link in the navigation bar to enter the interface of the project publisher's historical published projects. In this interface, the project publisher can view the details of its own historical published projects The details are the same. Click the publish new item link in the history publish item interface to pop up the publish new item interface box, as shown in Fig. 7. If the project publisher cannot publish a new item, a warning message will be issued.

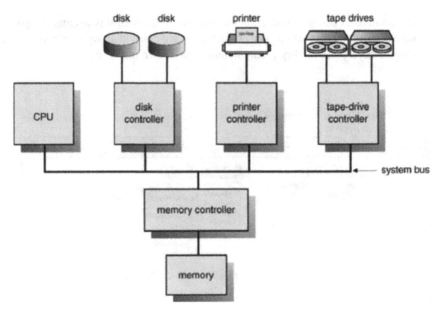

Fig. 7. System publisher module

The innovation and entrepreneurship experience system of college students has the overall characteristics of systematic, comprehensive and operable. In this mechanism, each system promotes, coordinates and restricts each other to form a dynamic process, which has an impact on College Students' entrepreneurs. The innovation and entrepreneurship experience system of college students has not been able to exert the maximum effect, especially the resource allocation at the macro level is insufficient, which needs further improvement. To optimize the college students' innovation and entrepreneurship experience system, it is not only necessary to strengthen the functions of each subsystem, but also to enhance the interaction between the systems, maximize the role of the experience system, and jointly create a good innovation and entrepreneurship experience system environment for college students' entrepreneurs.

5   Conclusion

The practical development of College Students' Entrepreneurship and innovation activities and the deepening of theoretical research provide a good way for college entrepreneurship and innovation education, provide a favorable attempt for higher education teaching reform, and achieve good social and economic benefits. This paper constructs a new multi-dimensional dynamic model, guides students to participate in the practice of higher education teaching reform research in Jiangsu Province, and successfully obtains a national university The project support of the innovation and entrepreneurship training program for college students has expanded the ideas of College Students' practical innovation and deepened the theoretical basis of College Students' Entrepreneurship and innovation activities. However, due to the limitations of the author's own theoretical foundation, the construction and expression of the model still need to be deepened and improved in order to achieve more ideal results in the practice of entrepreneurship and innovation education in the future.

References

1. Gumuskaynak, E., Toptas, F., Aslantas, R., et al.: Realization of a real-time decision support system to reduce the risk of diseases caused by posture disorders among computer users. In: Conference on Multimedia, Interaction, Design and Innovation. Springer, Cham (2022)
2. Li, L.: Design and Implementation of Innovative Entrepreneurial Experience System for College Students Based on Data Analysis Model. Springer, Cham (2021)
3. Zhong, L.: Research on the practice information system of university students' innovation and entrepreneurship based on the new computer technology support. In: Journal of Physics: Conference Series, vol. 1744, no. 3, p. 032151 (7pp) (2021)
4. Liu, F.: Design of Innovation and Entrepreneurship Teaching System for Ideological and Political Courses in Universities Based on Online and Offline Integration (2021)
5. Zhao, S.: Design of Power Integrated Energy Data Dynamic Visualization System for Integrated Construction (2021)
6. Bogacz, M., Hess, S., Calastri, C., et al.: Modelling risk perception using a dynamic hybrid choice model and brain-imaging data: an application to virtual reality cycling. Transp. Res. Part C: Emerg. Technol. **133**, 103435 (2021)
7. Toscano, M., Montalvo, W., Bastidas, C., et al.: Identification of a MIMO Twin Rotor System Using an Artificial Neural Network Trained by PSO (2023)
8. Dankesreiter, B., Serrano, M., Zhang, J., et al.: Investigating the Potential of Electrical Connection Chatter Induced by Structural Dynamics (2023)
9. Sun, T.: Design of Online Teaching System for Innovation and Entrepreneurship of Finance Major Based on Big Data (2021)
10. Nozari, H., Liaghat, A.M., Azadi, S.: Management of agricultural saline drainage using system dynamics approach. Water Environ. J. **36**(2), 299–307 (2022)

Application of Random Simulation Algorithm in Physical Education Teaching Evaluation

HuiYang and Chengliang Zhang[✉]

Qu Jing Medical College, Qujing 655000, Yunnan, China
1605857401@qq.com, 63320147@qq.com

Abstract. At present, there are many studies on the evaluation of primary physical education teaching ability, but most of them are constructed before the implementation of the new curriculum standard. This relatively old evaluation system is difficult to objectively and accurately evaluate the teaching ability of physical education teachers at this stage. Due to the inaccurate evaluation, teachers may lead to psychological imbalance and can not devote more energy to the improvement of teaching ability. Therefore, in order to improve the scientificity and objectivity of physical education teachers' teaching ability evaluation, this paper studies the application of random simulation algorithm in physical education teaching evaluation.

Keywords: Random simulation algorithm · Physical education · Teaching evaluation

1 Introduction

Physical education teachers' classroom teaching ability is the core ability in physi-cal education, because physical education teachers' comprehensive classroom teaching ability determines students' learning effect, so as to determine the core quality of the whole physical education teaching, which is also the fundamental task and main goal of physical education teaching. The evaluation of physical education teaching ability can promote physical education teachers to improve teaching methods and teaching quality, and it is also an important basis for assessing the performance of physical education teachers. However, from the current situation of the evaluation of physical education teachers' teaching ability, various educational units often ignore the evaluation of Physical Education Teachers' teaching ability; From the research results, the evaluation of physical education teaching ability by scholars is mostly limited to the overview of theory, and there is no specific operation model of evaluation [1]. The evaluation of PE Teachers' teaching ability belongs to the research category of uncertain content of fuzzy theory. Only through fuzziness, PE Teachers' teaching ability belongs to a certain area of the set level. Therefore, this paper constructs an independent advantage evaluation method that "highlights its own advantages". In the evaluation, a probability based random simulation algorithm is used to evaluate the advantages of the evaluation objects by calculating

M. A. Jan and F. Khan (Eds.): BigIoT-EDU 2022, LNICST 466, pp. 110–115, 2023.
https://doi.org/10.1007/978-3-031-23947-2_12

the degree of superiority between the evaluation objects. This method can produce evaluation conclusions in the form of probability (reliability) and have stronger explicability to practical problems. This method is proposed from the perspective of innovation The comprehensive evaluation method of "from base to top"has high independence. The evaluation link is added in the form of "component" to convert the information of the evaluation data. An example is given to verify the effectiveness of the method.

2 Stochastic Simulation Algorithm

2.1 Concept of Stochastic Process

In nature, the change process can be broadly divided into two types: one is deterministic process, and the other is uncertain process, also known as random process. Generally speaking, the so-called process is a change related to time. For example, for the motion of a free falling body in a vacuum, assuming that the initial velocity is 0 and the falling time of the object is t, the falling height $X(t) = \frac{1}{2}gt^2$ is determined by this functional relationship There is a certain causal relationship when leaving the exact position of the initial point at any time. Obviously, the falling height x is related to the time t, forming a process, which is called a deterministic process. The other kind of process has no definite change form and no inevitable change law. For example, the total daily turnover m of the mall is obviously an uncertain quantity, that is, a random variable, which is further improved The analysis shows that M is also related to time t, thus forming a process m (T), which is also called a random process. For example, the number of times x received by the paging team of the paging station every day is obviously uncertain, that is, it is a random variable. Further analysis shows that x is also related to time 1, so x (T) Similarly, air temperature, air pressure and daily customer flow of stores constitute a random process.

$$\begin{cases} E(t)\dot{x}_k(t) = f(t, x_k(t)) + B(t)u_k(t) \\ y_k(t) = C(t)x_k(t) \end{cases} \tag{1}$$

2.2 Development History of Stochastic Process

Stochastic process theory was born in the early 20th century. It is closely related to other branches of mathematics. It is an important tool to study stochastic phenomena in the fields of social science, natural science and so on. In the study of random processes, people measure the inevitable internal laws through the superficial view of contingency, and describe these laws in the form of probability. The greatest charm of this discipline is to realize necessity through contingency.

The development of stochastic process theory has a history of more than 100 years, which originated from the study of physics. Every new theory has its historical opportunity, and random process is no exception[2]. The earliest scientists paid attention to a part of the stochastic process associated with other disciplines, such as the characteristics of the independent incremental process discovered by Bachelier when analyzing the fluctuation of the stock market in 1900, the Markov chain studied by Markov, the findings of Gibbs et al. On statistical mechanics and Einstein et al. On Brownian motion. But in the real sense, the systematic and rigorous research on stochastic process theory began in the 1930s.

In the 1960s, on the basis of Markov process and potential theory, French scholars used some of their ideas and results to further expand the general theory of random process to a great extent, including section theorem, projection theory of process and so on.

In the development history of stochastic process, Chinese scholars have also done a lot of work and achieved good results. Theory comes from practice. In the development history of stochastic process, we study the actual phenomena deeply, put forward the theory to explain the phenomena, and finally verify the theory with phenomena, which is also the development process of most theories from special cases to general theories. In fact, many research directions have their practical background. When these directions are deeply studied and verified, they are used to guide practice and further expand and deepen the scope of application.

3   Construction of Evaluation Index System of Physical Education Teachers' Teaching Ability

3.1   Basic Principles of Constructing Evaluation Index System

When constructing the evaluation index system, we should strictly screen the selected indexes on the basis of following the theoretical knowledge of physical education, pedagogy, psychology and new curriculum standards. At the same time, the construction of evaluation index system must follow certain guidelines and principles.

First, the principle of integrity: that is, the constructed evaluation index system should be able to comprehensively evaluate the teaching ability of primary physical education teachers, and ensure that the selected indexes will not reappear, so as to construct hierarchical indexes at all levels, and then form a complete evaluation index system. In addition, in the process of constructing the evaluation index system, we should not only follow the commonness of the teaching ability of PE teachers in junior middle schools in the teaching process, but also highlight the characteristics of this special stage of junior middle schools.

Second, the principle of scientificity: scientificity means that the indicators should be selected on the basis of theoretical knowledge such as pedagogy and physical education. The selected indicators should not only conform to the objective truth, but also stand the test of practice [3]. They cannot be selected arbitrarily according to subjective judgment. The construction of evaluation index system is mainly to guide the teaching process scientifically and systematically, so as to improve the overall physical education teaching quality and improve teachers' teaching ability. Therefore, when constructing the evaluation index system, we should fully combine the characteristics of sports events and the actual situation of students to select the indexes at all levels.

Third, the principle of testability: testability means that the selection of indicators should be able to carry out specific operation and quantitative analysis, and make accurate judgment on the tested object through indicators. Therefore, when constructing the evaluation index system, the selection of indicators must be easy to understand and measure, reduce some vague indicators, and make each indicator reflect teachers' teaching ability in essence.

3.2 Basic Process of Constructing Evaluation Index System

The construction of evaluation index system has guiding significance for improving the teaching ability of physical education teachers and the judgment of school managers on Teachers' teaching ability. Therefore, when constructing the evaluation system, in addition to the above principles, we should also follow the strict sequence and process, so as to ensure the rationality of the evaluation system.

As shown in Fig. 1, the basic steps of constructing the evaluation index system are: (1) determine the object and goal to be evaluated; (2) Determine indicators at all levels; (3) The indexes were screened by Delphi method; (4) Calculate the weight ratio of indicators at all levels (analytic hierarchy process); (5) Complete the evaluation index system; (6) Verify the evaluation index system.

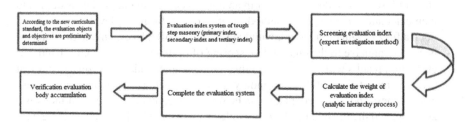

Fig. 1. Basic steps of establishing evaluation indicators

4 Application of Random Simulation Algorithm in Physical Education Teaching Evaluation

4.1 Random Simulation Algorithm is the Most Appropriate Method to Evaluate PE Teachers' Teaching Ability

The evaluation of PE Teachers' teaching ability belongs to the research category of social science, unlike the fixed data support in the evaluation standards of natural disciplines. Moreover, there is no obvious boundary for the evaluation level of physical education classroom teaching ability. In the ordinary physical education classroom evaluation, most of them make self judgment based on the evaluator's overall feeling of the main physical education classroom teaching, and sometimes there is a large gap in the evaluation level. The fuzzy matter-element clustering method solves the subjective defect in the evaluation through the qualitative and quantitative dimensions of physical education teachers' teaching ability. Therefore, the method of random simulation mathematics is feasible and the evaluation result is more reasonable.

In the calculation method, the sum of the simple difference and weight product of the two related matter elements is used as the distance between the matter element to be evaluated and the evaluation grade " In principle, the grade of the matter element to be evaluated is judged and clustered, so the calculation method is simple and easy to operate [4]. At the same time, the clustering ranking is arranged according to the distance from small to large, which makes it easy to compare the position of each physical education teacher's teaching ability in the whole and the ranks of the grade, so as to position the ability of education and teaching workers, and provide a good way to better promote the improvement of physical education teaching ability Evaluation method.

4.2 Suggestions for Model Improvement

(1) Appropriately increase the number and grade of evaluation indicators of physical education teachers' classroom teaching ability

In this study, the author only designs the evaluation indexes of one level dimension. However, in the actual social science evaluation model, in order to better reflect the scientificity and authenticity of the evaluation model, multi-level evaluation indexes can be designed to form an interrelated evaluation index system, and then calculated by using the method of progressive from low level to high level. Such a fuzzy evaluation model, with the refinement of indexes, On the one hand, it is more conducive to the quantitative scoring of evaluators. On the other hand, the evaluation results will be more objective. For example, under the primary index of action demonstration ability, secondary indicators such as action accuracy, action effectiveness and action economy can be set. The weight of each level of index is a key step, and the method of obtaining index weight can also be based on the expert weighted statistics method in this model, or Analytic hierarchy process (AHP).

(2) Try to increase the number of experts who obtain the index weight

In fuzzy evaluation, the index weight is obtained by human subjective scoring, with strong personal subjective judgment, but the weight is a key link in the implementation and operation of the evaluation model and a data-based performance that directly affects the evaluation results. In the method of obtaining the weight, first try to select well-known experts with deep academic attainments to obtain a relatively reasonable weight value. Secondly, in the number of experts It is better to select more than 30, and the more the number, the more reasonable the index weight value tends to be.

5 Conclusion

Teachers and students are the two necessary factors to constitute the physical education classroom. The role of physical education teachers has become the leader of the physical education classroom. It can even be said that the words and deeds of physical education teachers will have a profound impact on all aspects of students. This impact is reflected through the teaching ability of physical education teachers, so the teaching ability of physical education teachers is the guarantee A reasonable and sound evaluation index system can not only promote the progress of PE Teachers' teaching ability in all aspects, but also facilitate school managers to accurately judge PE Teachers' teaching ability, so as to complete the evaluation of PE Teachers' teaching ability under the new curriculum standard New requirements of physical education in junior middle schools.

References

1. Cai, W.: Matter Element Model and its Application. Science and Technology Literature Press, Beijing (1994)
2. Chen, G., Li, M.: Research on the integration of comprehensive evaluation methods based on method set. China Manag. Sci. **12**(1), 101–105 (2004)
3. Yi, P., Guo, Y.: Negotiation combination method of multiple evaluation conclusions under the characteristics of bilateral conflict. Syst. Eng. Theory Pract. **26**(11), 63–72 (2006)
4. Yi, P., Zhang, D., Guo, Y.: Stochastic simulation algorithm for comprehensive evaluation and its application. Oper. Res. Manag. **18**(5), 97–106 (2009)

Application of Improved Association Rule Algorithm in E-commerce English

Xiaojia Lai[✉]

Guinlin College, Guangxi 541004, China
xiaojia899@tom.com

Abstract. The application of the improved association rule algorithm in E-business English is to find the relationship between the two terms. It can be used to find out the similarities between the two projects, and also to find out the differences between the two projects. In this case, we use a set of rules as input data, and then apply these rules to specific projects or project groups that are similar or different from each other according to the rules. The result will be a list with some similarities and some differences. Frequent set mining is a key step of association rule mining. It determines the efficiency of association rule mining to a great extent. This paper first introduces the basic process of data mining, then introduces the association rule algorithm in E-commerce English, and focuses on how to use the improved association rule algorithm to mine the paths and page interests frequently visited by users in pattern recognition, which provides a basis for the personalized recommendation system model, This proves the application of the improved association rule algorithm in E-commerce English.

Keywords: Association rule algorithm · Electronic commerce · Data mining

1 Introduction

With the rapid development of the Internet, commercial companies are facing tremendous changes in their business models, most notably the use of trade websites. E-commerce is developing into a more and more popular business model. Whether a company can make full use of the Internet may become the key to its survival.

In the next five years, the company may become an Internet company or be destroyed. E-commerce means not only having a website to promote sales, but also having a complex relationship chain. E-commerce uses the comprehensive capabilities of the Internet and information technology to fundamentally change the key business strategies and processes [1]. The formation and development of e-commerce leads to the formation and development of E-commerce English. Under the background of economic globalization, E-business English has developed into a commonly used practical style. Obviously, it is very necessary and meaningful to study the characteristics and translation of E-business English.

Association rule mining is a branch of data mining, and it is the most typical one of many knowledge types in data mining. Rakesh Agrawal and others first proposed the

© ICST Institute for Computer Sciences, Social Informatics and Telecommunications Engineering 2023
Published by Springer Nature Switzerland AG 2023. All Rights Reserved
M. A. Jan and F. Khan (Eds.): BigIoT-EDU 2022, LNICST 466, pp. 116–125, 2023.
https://doi.org/10.1007/978-3-031-23947-2_13

problem of mining association rules between item sets in customer transaction database in 1993, and then proposed Apriori and its improved algorithm, which has become the basis of many association rule mining algorithms today. Since then, association rules have gained extensive attention and in-depth research due to their usability and easy to understand advantages [2]. Their work includes optimizing the original algorithm, such as introducing random sampling and parallel ideas, so as to improve the efficiency of algorithm mining rules and promote the application of association rules.

E-commerce refers to all business activities including business information, business management and commodity trading between traders based on computer networks and in accordance with certain rules or standards. With the continuous development of Internet technology, e-commerce has become the general trend of enterprise development.

The web data in web servers at all levels is also expanding rapidly. Although the traditional database technology and data mining technology have made great development and become more and more perfect, the web data structure has its particularity. Data mining on the web needs many technologies different from single data warehouse mining [3].

The difference between web log mining and traditional data mining lies. The object of Web log mining is the second-hand data extracted from the interaction between users and the network. These users in the web log when accessing the web, including access date, time, user IP address, URL resources requested by server IP address method.

Web log mining is to mine system log information and user registration data in order to find useful patterns and knowledge. By applying web log mining technology to the website server, we can not only improve the quality of the site, but also improve the web cache, alleviate network traffic and improve performance [4]. In e-commerce, you can also capture a large number of details of the procurement process, which makes it possible for more in-depth, so effectively service the site and increase the economic benefits of the site.

2 Association Rule Mining in E-commerce

2.1 Overview of E-commerce

The English name of e-commerce is electronic commerce, abbreviated as EC, or electronic business. The definition of e-commerce made by the Economic Commission for Europe at the Global Information Standards conference in October 1997: "business transactions between participants."

Nowadays, the benefits of e-commerce are becoming more and more obvious. Business activities through Internet have become more and more common. Some famous companies have set up e-shopping malls on the Internet, such as Amazon, Dell, Intel and CISC. In China, e-commerce has also attracted more and more people's attention [5]. Compared with traditional business activities, e-commerce has incomparable advantages, such as reducing enterprise costs, improving efficiency, improving enterprise competitiveness, users have more choices and so on. At present, major companies have launched a variety of software and hardware products to support e-commerce.

E-commerce is a new industry, and its wording is characterized by strong professionalism, but it is different from the translation of documents and contracts. Therefore, before translating the text, it is necessary to consult the literature and use professional terms as much as possible to make the translation smooth and accurate, and make all the translations have evidence to follow, simple and comprehensive. The text of E-business English (excerpts) is a practical text, which contains certain professionalism, but is not difficult to understand. In terms of terms, it is easy for customers to understand and will not cause differences and misunderstandings.

Finally, E-commerce English generally appears on major shopping websites, with the purpose of attracting customers and promoting products [6]. Therefore, when translating E-commerce English texts, we should analyze the customer base, understand the background knowledge of the website, the consumer population and the knowledge level, and conduct random surveys in the form of questionnaires to determine the areas most frequently visited by consumers in the website and the language deficiencies. Then, based on a certain social background, Start to translate the original text, make the language as beautiful as possible, and make the translation as catchy as possible under the condition that the words in the translation are accurate.

From obtaining the original text to the final completion of translation, the following steps are roughly followed:

(1) Browse the original text, and roughly understand the style of the original words and the fields involved;
(2) Learn relevant knowledge through reading references, online dictionaries and major online shopping malls;
(3) In the initial translation of the original text, emphasis should be placed on the relationship between paragraphs and on the overall handling of the article;
(4) Read the original and the translation again, and check whether there are mistakes, omissions and additions;
(5) Basically complete the translation work and submit it to the tutor for review;
(6) Revise again to determine the final translation;
(7) Self summary

E-business English translation is an open translation activity, which is not as rigid as legal texts and contract texts. Appropriate new words can be added. Therefore, the translation process of E-business English can be understood as the process of digesting the original text and reproducing the original text in a relatively creative language.

E-commerce is generally divided into six business models: B2B (between enterprises), B2C (between enterprises and consumers), C2C (between consumers), G2B (between governments and enterprises), G2C (between governments and individuals) and G2G (between governments). Among them, 132c was once the representative of e-commerce, that is, the most familiar "online store". Because B2B has absolute advantages in reducing transaction costs, shortening production cycle, reducing enterprise inventory and credit security, it can give full play to the potential benefits of e-commerce to a greater extent. It is the mainstream and direction of e-commerce development [7].

2.2   The Process of Data Mining in E-commerce

E-commerce data mining process can be subdivided into determining business objects, data collection and extraction. Among them, each step is essential. Each step is discussed below:

(1)   Definition problem

Mining data for data mining is blind and often will not succeed. When determining business objects, we should determine such questions: where to start? What data need to be mined? How much data do you need? To what extent should data mining be carried out?

In the first step of data mining, sometimes users need to provide some prior knowledge, such as concept tree and so on. These prior knowledge may be the user's business domain knowledge or the preliminary results obtained by previous data mining.

(2)   Data collection and extraction

Once the problem is defined, relevant data should be collected. For e-commerce sources of data are server data and customer registration information. E-commerce websites may have millions of online transactions every day, generating massive

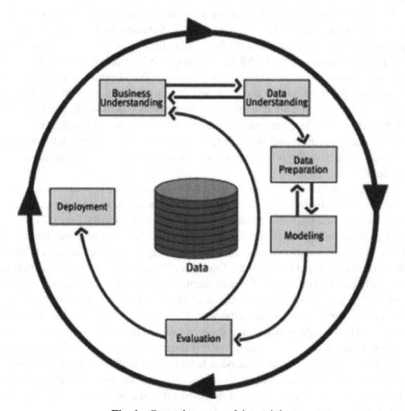

Fig. 1. General process of data mining

log files and registration forms. These massive data constitute the data source of e-commerce data mining. The extraction is to identify the data set to be analyzed, narrow the processing range quality.

(3) Data mining

The actual excavation operation is carried out at this stage. As shown in Fig. 1, select an appropriate algorithm for mining, so as to obtain effective, and knowledge from massive data. Association rules, sequential patterns commonly used in e-commerce data mining.

3   Analysis of Characteristics of E-business English

(1) The main features of E-business English are: a lot of special terms and frequent use of compound words; Derivative words are common and polysemy words are everywhere; There are many fixed sentences, many complex sentences and many rhetoric.

(2) E-business English translation usually uses some common translation skills such as "ellipsis", "addition", "Repetition", "inversion" and so on. Wherein, "Ellipsis" and "adder" are most frequently used. When E-business English is translated into Chinese, coordinate conjunctions, subordinate conjunctions, contextual connectives, etc. in the text should usually be omitted. Supplementary words are translated according to meaning (or rhetoric) And syntax needs to add some words to express the original content more faithfully and smoothly. Supplementary words are also the most commonly used alternative in translation [8]. The purpose of adding words is to make the translation more clear and the words more accessible. The supplementary words can be divided into two situations: one is to supplement the ellipsis in the original syntax; Second, according to the meaning and logical relationship of the original context and the writing habits of the target language, the words that are not literally in the original but are included in the meaning are added in the expression.

(3) The difficulties in E-business English translation are: first, how to translate professional terms accurately; The second is how to translate long sentences succinctly. In order to translate the terms accurately, we must understand the general knowledge and professional terms of the relevant industries, be good at using software and tools to find information, and spare time and energy to ensure that the corresponding terms in the target language are found. For those new terms, we must study them carefully and thoroughly understand them. Long sentence translation is always a difficult point. First of all, we should analyze the structure and components of long sentences, clarify the relationship between their form and content, read them several times, and thoroughly understand them in combination with the context; After a long sentence is correctly understood, its logical meaning relationship is accurately translated according to the expression habits of the target language. If we want to translate long sentences succinctly and incisively, we must continue to improve and improve our Chinese level. At the same time, we must revise them repeatedly, constantly improve them, and strive for perfection.

In addition, through the preparation of this paper, the author finds that it is very important to master two languages in order to translate E-business English well. If you don't know the source language well, you can't fully understand the original text, and you will make mistakes; If you are not proficient in the target language, you will make mistakes; In addition, it is essential to master the necessary professional knowledge and terminology [9]. If you do not master a certain amount of professional knowledge and terminology, you will not have the basic conditions for translating E-business English, and you will make various logical meaning errors or absurd errors in translation; When translating E-business English, we must also take translation theory as a guide and adopt appropriate translation strategies and techniques to achieve the translation purpose; In the actual translation process, it is suggested to flexibly change according to different environments and needs.

4 Improved Association Rule Algorithm

4.1 Basic Concepts of Association Rules

Association rule is an important mining pattern in data mining. It refers to the association relationship between a large number of data item sets. As shown in Fig. 2. In order to accurately express association rules, the related definitions of association rules in transaction database are given below. 1:

Definition 1: Let $I = \{I1, I2,..., in\}$ be the complete set of items. Any subset a in I is called itemset. If $|a| = k$, set a is called K itemset. Transaction database $d = \{T1,$

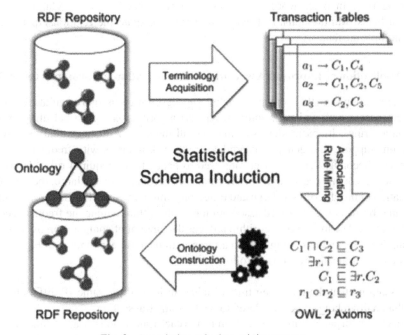

Fig. 2. Association rule data mining pattern

T2,..., TN}, where transaction t is a collection of items, which can be expressed as: T = {I1, I2,..., IP}, where p ⊆ n. For any transaction T, TID is its unique identification. Let t and a be the transaction and itemset in D respectively. If a ⊆ TK, transaction TK includes itemset a.

Definition 2 association rules: the implication of a ⇒ B, where a 88'b, B 88'i, and a ∩ B = φ₀ Where a is the premise of association rules and B is the conclusion of association rules.

Define 3 frequent itemsets: for itemset a, if support (a) ≥ min support, then a is called frequent itemset. If | a | = k, a is called a frequent k-itemset.

Define 4 strong association rules: for association rule R: a ⇒ B, if support (R) ≥ min_ Sup and confidence (R) ≥ min_ Conf, then R is a strong association rule.

According to different standards, association rules can be divided into the following types:

(1) If the element does not exist, it becomes an association rule. The logical meaning of association rule processing is divided and introduced Considering the relationship between quantitative elements or attributes, this is a quantitative correlation rule.
(2) According to the abstract data layer in rules. In level binding rules, all variables depend on elements or attributes at different levels of abstraction. Multilevel coupling rules fully consider the multilevel nature of data
(3) Based on the hierarchical structure of data coupling rules, coupling rules can be divided into one-dimensional and multi-dimensional coupling rules. If the rule only reflects one-dimensional data, it is a one-dimensional mapping rule. If a data processing rule contains multiple dimensions, it is a multidimensional mapping rule. In other words, an association rule specifies some relationships in attributes. Multidimensional association rules regulate the relationship between multiple attributes.

4.2   Application of Improved Association Rule Algorithm in E-commerce English

In pattern recognition, the corresponding mining algorithm is used to calculate the user's frequent access path and page interest. Apriori algorithm is a classical algorithm of association rules. Its basic idea is to find out all the support itemsets that exceed the minimum support, and generate candidate frequent k-itemsets with frequent (k − 1) - itemsets; Secondly, large itemsets are used to generate the required rules. However, when there are many transactions in the database and the item set is large, the scanning calculation of the algorithm is large and time-consuming. In view of these shortcomings, this paper borrows the improved association rule algorithm to mine the frequent access paths of users. The improved algorithm reduces the amount of computation by reducing the candidate set and removing redundant transactions in time, as shown in Fig. 3.

The idea of the algorithm is as follows:

(1) Assuming that the recording time of adjacent logs of the same IP differs by less than half an hour, it is considered to be the same transaction.
(2) Each item in page itemset P is a column, and each transaction in transaction database d is a row. Construct the incidence matrix M [M, n], where n is the total number of

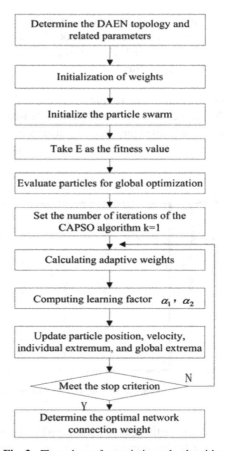

Fig. 3. Flow chart of association rule algorithm

pages in P and M is the total number of transactions in transaction database D. If the jth page is not accessed by the ith transaction, m [I, J] = 0 is defined, otherwise m [I, J] = 1.

(3) Sum each column of incidence matrix M. if the sum result exceeds the given minimum support threshold, the column is a frequent path, otherwise it is an infrequent path.

(4) Delete the column of all infrequent paths. In the deleted incidence matrix, if the element values of a row are all 0 or at most one is 1, the row will be deleted.

(5) Each column of the reduced incidence matrix is processed as follows: ① merging two columns: let the identification items of each column in the matrix be arranged in alphabetical order. If only the last identification item of a certain two columns in the matrix is different, the two identification items can be merged into a new item. The length of the new identification item is 1 more than the original one. The public part in front of the new identification item remains unchanged. The latter two items are taken from the last of the original two identification items. ② The column element of the new identification item is obtained by logical and operation

from the original two corresponding columns to form a new column. ③ Continue to find the next pair to merge until it cannot be found. The new identification item matrix formed in this way is still called incidence matrix, and the length of each identification item is the original plus 1 [10].

The following example illustrates the simplified process. The minimum support is assumed to be 0.5. ABCDE represents five visited pages. The transaction table is shown in the left table of Fig. 4. The corresponding incidence matrix is shown in the right table of Fig. 4. The correspondence between the transaction table and the incidence matrix table is shown in Fig. 4.

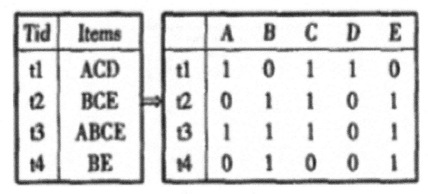

Fig. 4. Correspondence between transaction table and incidence matrix table

Based on the improved association rule algorithm, with the user's frequent access path and page interest, we can build a personalized recommendation system model. Data preparation generates log files into user files and transaction files; Specific access mining can mine users' frequent access paths and page interest. The online part optimizes the structure and page reorganization of the website by using the frequent access path and user interest generated by the offline part. In the above example, you can place some business English advertisements or carry out some promotions in the BCE page that users frequently browse.

5   Conclusion

To do a good translation, the first thing is to understand the full text, that is, on the basis of reading the full text and understanding the new words, and combining the context, go deep into every sentence, every paragraph and every word. Before translation, the author should understand the background of relevant fields, read through relevant papers, stand on the shoulders of giants, examine E-commerce English translation, and prepare for the translation of high-quality texts. After the selection of materials is determined, read the full text to have a certain understanding of the context of the whole article. Then, check the new words in the original text to further understand the context of the article.

Reading through the full text can help the translator better understand the main idea of the article, which is very important for the next translation process. Some previous working modes of E-commerce English can not meet the needs of users for the Internet. Users who often surf the Internet will find that a common problem is that in the process of browsing an e-commerce website, the current page always shows some topics they don't care about, no matter how frequently they visit the e-commerce website. The research on this problem promotes the development of e-commerce websites, that is, e-commerce websites should not only information of all users' common interests, but also pay attention to the individual information of each user's own interests. Therefore, the development trend of e-commerce websites is to provide personalized services for each user.

References

1. Das, A., Jana, S., Ganguly, P., et al.: Application of association rule: Apriori algorithm in E-Commerce. In: 2021 Innovations in Energy Management and Renewable Resources (IEMRE) (2021)
2. Zhang, C., Teng, G.: Application of an improved association rule algorithm in rural development assessment in China. In: IOP Conference Series Earth and Environmental Science, vol. 772, no. 1, p. 012089 (2021)
3. Hwa, B., Fei, W.B., Lu, Z.: Application of variational mode decomposition optimized with improved whale optimization algorithm in bearing failure diagnosis. Alex. Eng. J. $60(5)$, 4689–4699 (2021)
4. Chen, Q.: Practical Application of Improved Algorithm of Association Rules Based on Computer Technology in Teaching Evaluation (2021)
5. Yang, L., Yla, B., Yta, B., et al.: Application of improved fireworks algorithm in grinding surface roughness online monitoring (2022)
6. Song, H., Cai, M., Cen, J., et al.: Application of improved adaptive genetic algorithm in energy consumption optimization of electric refrigerated vehicles. In: Society of Photo-Optical Instrumentation Engineers (SPIE) Conference Series. SPIE (2021)
7. Zhao, W., Qu, H.: Application of improved algorithm based on sphere OBB hybrid hierarchical bounding box in Teaching. In: Journal of Physics: Conference Series, vol. 1732, no. 1, p. 012080 (6pp) (2021)
8. Sudu, L.: Design and application of vocal music teaching management system. Math. Probl. Eng. (2022)
9. Rhnisch, H.E., Eriksson, J., Lan, V.T., et al.: Improved Automated Quantification Algorithm (AQuA) and its application to NMR-based metabolomics of EDTA-containing plasma. Anal. Chem. Anal. Chem. **XXXX**(XXX) (2021)
10. Weiqing, G.E., Yanru, C.: Task-scheduling algorithm based on improved genetic algorithm in cloud computing environment. Recent Advances in Electrical & Electronic Engineering (Formerly Recent Patents on Electrical & Electronic Engineering) (2021)

Application of Risk Assessment Model of Accounting Resource Sharing Management in Education and Teaching

Chang Xia Ren[✉]

Lanzhou Resources and Environment Voc-Tech University, Lanzhou 730021, Gansu, China
lixdong@lzre.edu.cn

Abstract. The management is a method that helps to determine the risk level of each business unit and evaluate the probability of loss. It can be used as an effective tool to determine which units are most vulnerable to losses and which units are less risky. In this way, it can be used to allocate resources between different units according to the vulnerability of different units. The main idea behind this technology is that every organization has different levels of risk associated with it. Therefore, resources should be allocated accordingly so that they will not face any financial problems. The application of risk assessment model in education and teaching is to assess the risks related to the use of resources. The purpose of this model is to identify and measure the risks associated with resource use. The model also helps to determine strategies for managing risks by reducing or completely eliminating risks. It can be used as a decision-making and planning tool in financial management, human resource management and other fields. Network teaching resources are the premise and foundation of network education. It is particularly important to provide efficient storage management for accounting learning content objects and provide convenient and fast access functions for various users, so as to improve the utilization of teaching resource objects.

Keywords: Collaborative algorithm · Accounting · Resource sharing · Managing risks · Assessment

1 Introduction

With the development of famous teacher resource database, online excellent courses and online live video courses, teachers and students can obtain teaching and learning information resources more conveniently and quickly. The scope and types of teaching information resources have been expanded, including electronic textbooks, electronic courseware, electronic test questions, online courses, etc. If secondary vocational accounting teachers still only use traditional textbooks and teaching reference books to teach, it is obvious that they can't keep up with the development trend of informatization [1]. The development of informatization has brought changes to the teaching of secondary vocational accounting, and also prompted schools to build a more integrated

© ICST Institute for Computer Sciences, Social Informatics and Telecommunications Engineering 2023
Published by Springer Nature Switzerland AG 2023. All Rights Reserved
M. A. Jan and F. Khan (Eds.): BigIoT-EDU 2022, LNICST 466, pp. 126–134, 2023.
https://doi.org/10.1007/978-3-031-23947-2_14

platform for sharing teaching information resources. In the platform, courseware, teaching videos, teaching experience and so on are shared to ensure that teachers can obtain sufficient resources, And we can improve professional skills through virtual simulation system, so as to improve teachers' teaching level. As shown in Fig. 1. Therefore, this study intends to study the sharing of teaching information resources of accounting major in secondary vocational schools, so as to promote the more effective sharing of teaching information resources.

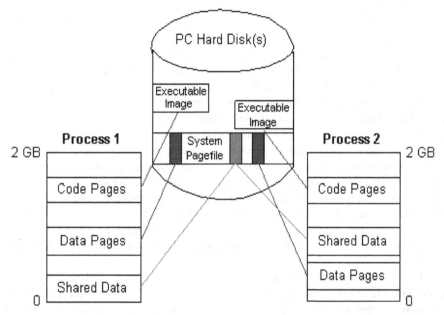

Fig. 1. Teaching resource sharing mode

On May 29, 2018, the Ministry of Education released the report on the state of Chinese language life (2018). In the past 2017, 242 new words were born, of which the word ""sharing" is the most popular. Sharing is that the relevant subjects take out their own goods for everyone to use together or take out the information they know and learn it with others. Sharing emphasizes both giving and receiving, which should be the balance of responsibility and obligation [2]. Cheng Huanwen In his book "information resource sharing", pan Yantao defined the concept of information resource sharing as "all information institutions, on the basis of voluntariness, equality and reciprocity, carry out all activities of jointly revealing, jointly building and jointly using information resources by establishing various cooperation, collaboration and coordination relations between information institutions and using various technologies, methods and ways, so as to meet the needs of users' information resources to the greatest extent". In his book "information resources and social development", Ma Feicheng proposed that "information resource sharing is trying to establish a smooth information exchange environment to ensure that anyone, at any time, at any place can obtain any information they need in any way. He also pointed out that information resource sharing is the fundamental way to solve the phenomenon of information asymmetry".

Referring to relevant literature, the sharing of teaching information resources in this study is defined as follows: teaching information resource sharing refers to all activities that teachers, students or other teaching subjects jointly reveal, jointly build and jointly use teaching information resources in the platform through relevant platforms, so as to meet the needs of all teaching subjects for teaching information resources to the greatest extent [3].

Accounting information refers to a kind of economic information generated by processing the original data of transactions and events based on the unique accounting processing methods. It is used to meet the needs of accounting management and economic pipeline. The same information demanders for purposes. Accounting information resource sharing based on Computerization means that the can be understood and used by all demanders without obstacles. For the same accounting entity, the sharing of accounting information resources includes not only sharing their own information resources with others, but also sharing and utilizing others' information resources. Referring to specific information processing systems, into three categories: original data, intermediate results and final information products [4]. According to the scope of information resource demanders, accounting information resource sharing includes the following aspects: the sharing of original data and the exchange of intermediate results among various functional modules in the information system; The exchange and utilization of economic information among various functional departments of the accounting body; The submission and distribution of financial data between entities and upper and lower levels; Disclosure of financial status and collection of economic information within the social scope.

The repeated input of some data information often results in increased workload, waste of human resources and equipment resources, and such repeated information input also increases the error rate of data to a certain extent, and reduces the accuracy and timeliness of accounting information. At the same time, from the overall external environment, although the information technology is constantly strengthened, the network environment is constantly developing, and the level of accounting computerization is also growing, people's awareness of knowledge and behavior has not been correspondingly enhanced. There is a general lack of awareness of the socialization of accounting information among the relevant strata. They do not really realize that information sharing should be paid attention to in the process of accounting computerization, and do not understand the true significance of accounting information resource sharing. Relevant managers are only limited to mastering the information of their own enterprises, and do not realize that mastering the accounting information and economic information of others can be used for their own accounting It is a good reference for the economic development of enterprises. If we fail to realize the sharing of resources, we can avoid detours and achieve win-win results [5]. This kind of blind spot in understanding makes the sharing of accounting information resources not get its due level of development. In addition, in such an open era, an era of highly developed network information, the corresponding accounting management departments do not have a good understanding of accounting information resource sharing, do not realize what role resource sharing can bring to social development, and do not realize that various enterprises can achieve win-win development results through resource sharing. This lack of understanding has led to the imperfection of the corresponding accounting policy system. It is precisely because there is no standardized accounting policy system, there is no institutional support for the sharing of accounting resource information, resulting in people's lack of awareness and the slow development of enterprises.

2   Collaborative Algorithm

2.1   Basic Idea of Coevolutionary Algorithm

The germination of the concept of synergy can be traced back to the end of the 19th century. Von ihering realized the relationship between parasites and their hosts and put forward the view that geographical isolation leads to species formation, The concept of synergy was initially formed in 1958. According to the "interaction between genes", mode considered that the continuous evolution of each gene of host resistance and each gene of parasite toxicity was a response to each other's evolution, and recently proposed a collaborative mathematical model [6].

Synergy is a common phenomenon in the bioscience community. It believes that organisms have diversity and emphasizes some inseparable links between different organisms and between organisms and the environment. When multiple biological groups reproduce and evolve, they affect and interact with each other, and gradually form a synergistic phenomenon. Synergism is mostly used to describe the relationship

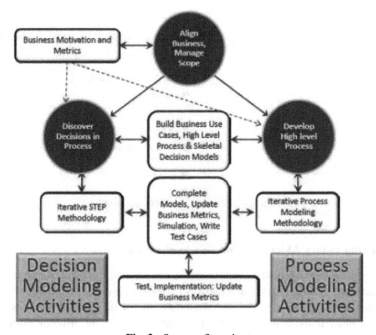

Fig. 2. Synergy flow chart

between species, emphasizing that the development and evolution of one organism evolve as a response to the behavior of another organism which is shown in Fig. 2.

Synergy is a mutually beneficial state in the evolution and development of species. Collaborative algorithm is a new intelligent evolutionary algorithm derived from the application of this collaborative mechanism to the traditional swarm intelligence optimization algorithm. The difference between CEA and classical basic swarm intelligent optimization algorithm is that in the classical intelligent algorithm, each individual represents a complete solution value, and the individual does not consider the connection links between individuals in the surrounding environment and the complex connection between biological individuals and the surrounding environment in the process of individual reproduction [7]. The cooperative algorithm fully takes into account the close relationship between biological individuals and between individuals and the surrounding natural environment, emphasizes the cooperative connection in the process of species reproduction, and breaks through the limitation of a single biological group of ordinary algorithms. The continuous set of collaboration concepts is shown in Fig. 3:

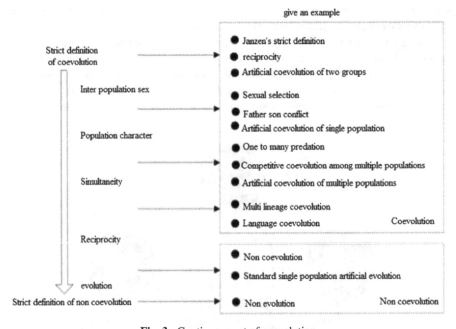

Fig. 3. Continuous set of coevolution

2.2 Coevolutionary Algorithm and Its Classification

As a coordinated development algorithm among communities, coevolutionary algorithm has multiple sub communities. The fitness of individual particles describes the viability of particles. In the classical traditional algorithm, the fitness value of particles is independent of other individuals around them. In different times or different populations, if the particles have the same velocity and position information, the fitness value is the same. However, there are many complex relationships among most species groups in ecological nature, including coevolution between individuals and coevolution between groups, and the evolution between individuals and the development and evolution of the whole community also affect each other. Therefore, coevolutionary algorithm can be classified according to different classification criteria [8]. According to the different characteristics of the relationship between species, coevolutionary algorithms can be divided into cooperative coevolutionary algorithm (COO CEA) and competitive coevolutionary algorithm (COM CEA) 6061. Based on the different ecological object models adopted by CEA algorithm, CEA algorithm can be divided into collaboration based on competitive relationship between communities, collaboration based on survival relationship between prey and hunter, and collaboration based on win-win between communities [9]. According to the different cooperation mechanisms in the population, coevolutionary algorithms can also be divided into isomorphic multi population coevolutionary algorithms and heterogeneous multi population coevolutionary algorithms.

Under the background that accountants and managers have insufficient understanding of information resource sharing, and relevant software developers lack the necessary interest drive, the government and some authoritative institutions should create an appropriate condition for accounting information sharing and provide necessary intervention and guidance for resource sharing. It is necessary to formulate some accounting related policies to enhance people's awareness of resource sharing and make them realize that in the information age, accounting information resource sharing has a positive role in promoting the development of enterprises and the progress of society. Relevant management departments can use an institutional system to strengthen the constraints on enterprises and relevant personnel, so as to promote the sharing of accounting information resources. Relevant authorities should give full play to the role of their own departments, formulate reasonable norms and institutional systems to support the sharing of accounting information resources, and set certain operating norms for the sharing of information resources, so that the sharing of accounting information resources can be effectively carried out under the constraints of laws and norms, so as to escort the development of enterprises and social economy [10].

For enterprises, the sharing of accounting information resources can effectively avoid some blind behaviors caused by insufficient experience. Under the background of market economy, enterprises can learn some relevant information of other enterprises through the sharing of information resources [11]. From the painful experience of other enterprises, they can realize that in the development of their own enterprises, they should learn from the experience of others to avoid similar mistakes. Because Daewoo Group did not make full use of accounting resource information, it made the capital structure unbalanced, the capital chain broken and finally went bankrupt in the blind capital expansion. Of course, in an environment of full resource sharing, enterprises can learn from the successful experience of other enterprises while learning from the insufficient experience of other enterprises, so that the development of the enterprise can avoid detours [12]. On the basis of resource sharing, managers can achieve better management and make better strategic decisions. Therefore, enterprise management personnel must strengthen their understanding of the sharing of accounting information resources, realize the strategic significance of establishing shared accounting information resources, and actively promote the sharing of accounting information resources.

3   Design of Risk Assessment Model for Accounting Resource Sharing Management

3.1   Selection of Evaluation Indicators

Many factors affect the management sharing It mainly includes, management factors It is difficult to analyze people, technology and management separately. As far as the security of accounting business is concerned, these three factors are opposite [13]. They are interrelated, interactive and mutually developed. Figure 4 shows the relationship between the factors affecting resource sharing in the balance sheet.

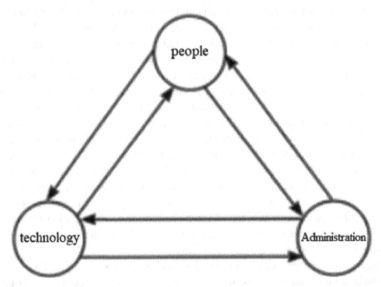

Fig. 4. Relationship diagram of influencing factors of accounting resource sharing management

3.2   Establishment of Quantitative Risk Assessment Model

Build the basic risk assessment model of accounting resource sharing management, and its expression is:

$$R = F(V, T, C) \tag{1}$$

Specifically, R is risk management based, C is the existing, V is the efficiency of resource management, and t is the risk management cycle.

The probability range of Pt threat is defined as [0.1], reflecting the possibility of dangerous events. The closer the possibility of threat, the higher the possibility of dangerous events. On the contrary, the possibility of dangerous events is very low.

PV exists objectively, but only when it is threatened will there be risks of accounting resource sharing and management. In other words, the more vulnerabilities, the greater the risk of jointly managing resources.

The effectiveness of risk control measures determines the possibility of risk events and affects the accuracy of risk assessment [14]. The more effective the risk control measures are, the lower the risk of balance sheet. The formula for calculating management measures should include:

$$\begin{cases} E(t)\dot{x}_\lambda(t) = f(t, x_\lambda(t)) + B(t)u_\lambda(t) \\ y_\lambda(t) = C(t)x_\lambda(t) \end{cases} \tag{2}$$

Specifically, NV refers to the faced by the resource sharing management system, and NR refers to the faced by the management platform.

According to events occur randomly and statistically within the framework of the resource sharing management platform. If the current λ is 10, the Poisson distribution curve is close to the normal distribution profile. As shown in Fig. 5.

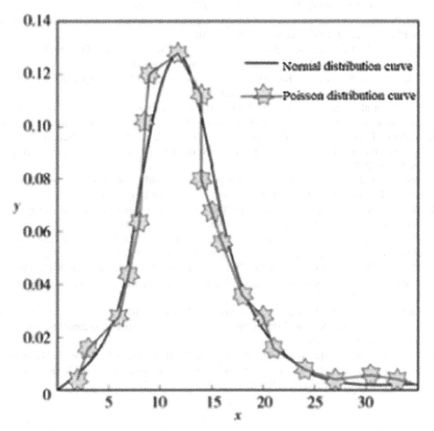

Fig. 5. λ = Poisson distribution curve and normal distribution curve of 10

4 Conclusion

The traditional risk evaluation model of management has the problems of long evaluation cycle and low evaluation accuracy. The management is effective, which can provide better security for accounting resource sharing management. Due to the difference between the environmental model and the actual conditions, there is a certain deviation in the model experimental data. In order to get more accurate experimental conclusions, the structural model needs to be further optimized.

References

1. Wang, Z., Wu, Y.: Empirical analysis of corporate bond credit risk based on contribution stochastic forest model. Econ. Math. **33**(3), 33–40 (2016)
2. Huang, Y., Lian, X.: Financial risk identification and evaluation of core enterprise supply chain. J. Beijing Univ. Posts Telecommun. (Social Science Edition) **18**(3), 44–49 (2016)
3. Li, M., Zhang, J., Wang, D., et al.: Construction of risk assessment model of problem base management based on AHP. Management **25**, 173–175 (2016)
4. Yin, X., Bao, X.: Financial risk evaluation of high-tech enterprises based on entropy weight TOPSIS method. Friends Account. **4**, 70–74 (2017)
5. Srivastava, V., Dashottar, S.: Default Probability Assessment for Project Finance Bank Loans and Basel Regulations: Searching for A New Paradigm (2019)
6. Paladino, G., Rotondi, Z.: Banking business models and risk: findings from The ECB's comprehensive assessment. Econ. Notes (2019)
7. Wu, Y., et al.: Methods to account for uncertainties in exposure assessment in studies of environmental exposures. Environ. Health: Glob. Access Sci. Source (2019) (IF: 3)
8. Abbiati, G., Broccardo, M., di Filippo, R., Stojadinović, B., Bursi, O.S.: Seismic fragility analysis of a coupled tank-piping system based on artificial ground motions and surrogate modeling (2020)
9. Tran, T., et al.: A risk assessment tool for predicting fragility fractures and mortality in the elderly. J. Bone Miner. Res.: Off. J. Am. Soc. Bone Miner. Res. (2020)
10. Ma, Y., et al.: Source quantification and risk assessment as a foundation for risk management of metals in urban road deposited solids. J. Hazard. Mater. (2020)
11. Zhou, M., Feng, X., Liu, K., Zhang, C., Xie, L., Wu, X.: An alternative risk assessment model of urban waterlogging: a case study of Ningbo City. Sustainability (2021)
12. Miao, F., Zhang, Y., Li, Y., Fang, Q., Zhou, Y.: Implementation of an integrated health risk assessment coupled with spatial interpolation and source apportionment: a case study of soil heavy metals, China (2021)
13. Qiang, Y., Wang, G., Li, R., Ding, W., Gao, Y., Hanle, L.: Risk assessment of geological hazards in mountain town scale based on FLO-2D and GIS. In: IOP Conference Series: Earth and Environmental Science (2021)
14. Wang, J., Nolte, T.M., Owen, S.F., Beaudouin, R., Hendriks, A.J., Ragas, A.M.: A generalized physiologically based kinetic model for fish for environmental risk assessment of pharmaceuticals. Environ. Sci. Technol. (2022)

Innovation Analysis of English Education in Higher Vocational Colleges Based on Multi-objective Genetic Algorithm

Chuanwei Zhang[✉]

Ganzhou Teachers College, Jiangxi 341000, China
zcwteacher@163.com

Abstract. Analysis of English education innovation in Higher Vocational Colleges Based on multi-objective genetic algorithm: This study aims to analyze the innovation process of English education in Higher Vocational Colleges Based on multi-objective genetic algorithm. The purpose is to determine the factors that affect the innovation process, and then determine how to use these factors as the basis for making innovation plans, so as to improve the quality and efficiency of English education. The main purpose is to find out the best method of English education innovation analysis in Higher Vocational Colleges Based on multi-objective genetic algorithm, and compare it with other methods. This research will be completed using genetic algorithm (GA) as a tool for innovation analysis. The purpose of this study is to determine the existing English teaching practice in Higher Vocational Colleges and its impact on students' learning outcomes. The study also aims to explore the challenges faced by these institutions and opportunities for improvement through innovative ways to improve student performance.

Keywords: Multi objective genetic algorithm · English education · Educational innovation

1 Introduction

The fundamental goal of education lies in the comprehensive development of students. The new curriculum advocates putting people first, promoting teaching through learning, teaching and learning, and pursuing the overall effect and maximum value of teaching. Conducting research on the current situation of English classroom teaching is conducive to mastering the overall situation of English classroom teaching in the school at the present stage, including teachers' teaching behavior and students' learning status; It is conducive to promoting the reform of classroom teaching [1]. Through innovative classroom teaching strategy research and practice, it advocates independent, exploratory and

M. A. Jan and F. Khan (Eds.): BigIoT-EDU 2022, LNICST 466, pp. 135–145, 2023.
https://doi.org/10.1007/978-3-031-23947-2_15

cooperative learning methods, and pays attention to the cultivation of students' innovative spirit and practical ability. It is conducive to promoting the development of students and making students become the leaders of learning; It is conducive to promoting the professional development of teachers. The research of this topic can help teachers update their educational concepts, conduct self-monitoring and self adjustment through the summary and reflection of teaching practice, optimize and improve teaching behaviors, methods and strategies, deepen the understanding of the laws of teaching activities, improve teaching ability and level, and improve the effectiveness of classroom teaching [2]. It is helpful to effectively implement the spirit of national basic education curriculum reform, deepen the experiment of curriculum reform, improve the effectiveness and quality of classroom teaching, and comprehensively promote quality education.

With the diversification of English teaching modes and methods in higher vocational colleges, the improvement of English teaching quality in higher vocational colleges has attracted more and more attention. Since the 1990s, many English teaching units in Colleges and universities in China have launched the teaching quality assurance system. Its main purpose is to improve the teaching quality through continuous monitoring of teaching quality and improving teaching measures [3].

English Teaching in higher vocational colleges is basically still in the stage of coping with the passing examination as the core, and most of the teaching is still classroom centered, book centered and teacher centered. Teachers mainly use vocabulary, grammar and translation teaching methods. Teachers generally lack the ability to comprehensively use a variety of English teaching methods. In teaching, there are many phenomena, such as paying attention to the quality of vocabulary, neglecting quantity, paying attention to intensive reading, neglecting extensive reading, paying attention to knowledge teaching, neglecting skill training, paying attention to exam oriented teaching, neglecting quality training, etc. This backward teaching method can only produce a teaching situation and effect that is full of water, ignores students' personality, lacks practical experience and consolidation, and lacks interaction between teachers and students. In addition, the teaching means are backward. Most higher vocational English teaching is still based on "teacher blackboard textbook recorder" [4]. Foreign language teaching seriously lags behind the development of modern educational technology and lacks a good hardware environment for English teaching. Figure 1 below shows English teaching problems.

The evaluation index of teaching quality is an important basis of teaching quality assurance system. The existing evaluation index mostly adopts the comprehensive evaluation method, and its index system is usually composed of multi-level indicators. For example, the first level indicators include teachers' teaching methods, teaching content, teaching quality, teaching effect, However, these traditional teaching quality evaluation methods still have some defects [5].

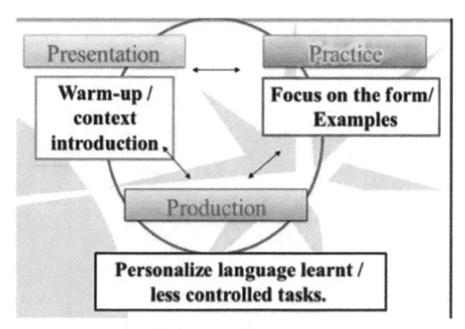

Fig. 1. English teaching problems

2   Related Work

2.1   Research Status of Multi-objective Genetic Algorithm

Since modern times, discipline differentiation has been the mainstream of discipline development; However, in recent decades, discipline integration has become a new trend. Scientific development increasingly depends on the integration, penetration and intersection of multiple disciplines, and this integration has a great impact on the development and practical application of science. J The genetic algorithm proposed by Professor Holland and others is the product of this cross discipline. Genetic algorithms (gas or GA) is an adaptive global optimization probability search algorithm formed by simulating the genetic and evolutionary processes of organisms in the natural environment, as shown in Fig. 2. As a non deterministic pseudo natural random optimization algorithm, genetic algorithm has been widely used in the past 30 years. Once proposed, it has been widely used in the field of practical engineering technology and economic management [6]. The genetic algorithm itself has also been improved and optimized in the application. However, the basic research on genetic algorithm itself is relatively few. At present, the multi-objective optimization problem is also a hot topic in the research of genetic algorithm, and the improvement of the solution to the multi-objective optimization problem is also a direction worthy of research.

Since the 1980s, multi-objective genetic algorithms (MOGA or MOGAS) have gradually become a research hotspot, and many multi-objective optimization technologies based on evolutionary methods have emerged in the past decade. In foreign countries, the research on multi-objective genetic algorithm has been more and more, especially in the application problem, multi-objective genetic algorithm has been widely used in various

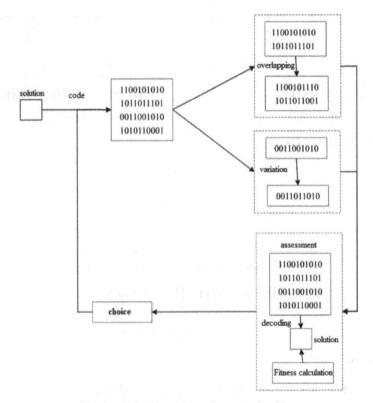

Fig. 2. Typical flow chart of genetic algorithm

fields to assist decision-making. However, the domestic research in this area is relatively weak, mainly including the comprehensive description of multi-objective genetic algorithm by Cui xunxue and Chen Huowang, and the discussion of preference based algorithm. There are not many research results. Cui Xun introduces the multi-objective evolutionary algorithm in terms of implicit building blocks and explicit building blocks, and expounds the key theory of the multi-objective evolutionary algorithm; Zheng Jinhua evaluates and compares the performance of classical algorithms and summarizes the application of algorithms. However, these overviews and descriptions are general, and the specific implementation and experiments are not described, which restricts the application and promotion of multi-objective genetic algorithm.

In recent years, in various fields of engineering application and scientific research, many experts and scholars have proposed various improved algorithms of multi-objective genetic algorithm based on domain knowledge and application, and achieved certain results in practice. Wang Xiaoqing et al. proposed a multi-objective genetic algorithm with random weight based on the retention strategy of essence by adopting adaptive niche technology, penalty technology, double round gambling and essence selection strategy. Shen Xiaoning et al. proposed a multi-objective genetic algorithm to maintain population diversity. This algorithm uses a measure based on information entropy to measure the diversity of the population in the multi-objective space. Rao Yujia et al.

Proposed a multi-objective genetic algorithm based on the best point set. The best point set genetic algorithm is a genetic algorithm that uses the theory of the best point set in number theory to redesign the crossover operation in the genetic algorithm. T. K. Liu et al. Proposed an inequality based method to solve the multi-objective optimization problem by introducing the auxiliary performance index vector. Ta Yuan Chou and others solved the scheduling of airport flight lines by using inequality based methods, and achieved certain results [7].

2.2 Multi Objective Genetic Algorithm

The research goal of multi-objective genetic algorithm is to make the algorithm converge quickly and distribute widely and uniformly in the non inferior optimal region of the problem. In the design of MOGAS, the strategy of maintaining the distribution of solutions is generally implemented in the maintenance of population. When the number of non dominated individuals exceeds a certain scale, it is necessary to use pruning operators to remove individuals. The removal of individuals is not random, but is carried out according to a certain strategy of maintaining the distribution. In NSGA-II, the clustering distance of individuals is used to maintain the population. By calculating the clustering distance of each individual in the genetic population, a partial ordered set is constructed to eliminate the individuals with small clustering distance. In this paper, based on NSGA-II, an improved non dominated sorting multi-objective genetic algorithm (NSGA-II + IMP) is proposed In its pruning operation, a new strategy is proposed, that is, selecting some individuals with a large aggregation distance from the current non dominated set to enter the new species group, forming the majority of the population; Some better individuals are selected from the lower non dominated set to enter the new species group, forming a small part of the population, thus forming the next generation population. The experimental results show that the combination of this strategy and the original algorithm improves the distribution and convergence of the original algorithm, as shown in Fig. 3.

The smallest element of chromosome is called gene, which corresponds to a characteristic of possible solution, namely design variable. After the emergence of the initial population, according to the principle of survival of the fittest and survival of the fittest, better and better approximate solutions are produced. In each generation, individuals are selected according to their fitness in the problem domain, and crossover and mutation are carried out with the help of genetic operators of natural genetics to produce a population representing a new solution set. Therefore, the performance of the solution set is improved by selection, crossover and mutation. After several generations of reproduction and evolution, the performance of the population tends to be the best [8]. The optimal individual in the last generation population can be used as the approximate optimal solution of the problem after decoding. There are some problems in the innovation of Higher Vocational English Education under the multi-objective genetic algorithm

1. Select the literary texts suitable for English Majors in higher vocational colleges. There are three principles in choosing literature textbooks

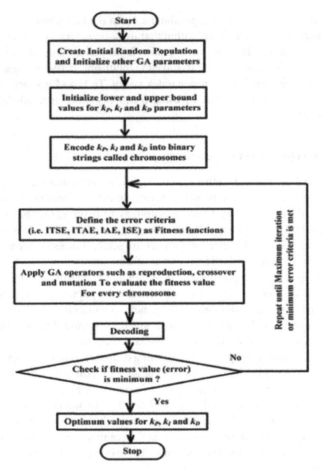

Fig. 3. Flow chart of multi-objective genetic algorithm

(1) If possible, allow yourself to choose. People can acquire knowledge from what they are interested in;

(2) It is suggested not to choose too long or too complex works, and the selected works should be suitable for students' intelligence and proficiency level;

(3) Be aware of cultural and personality differences.

2. Using a variety of teaching methods and widely using network media.
3. Improve the teaching methods of English and American literature.

An advanced multi-objective genetic algorithm is used to optimize the multi-objective function of English education innovation, so as to preliminarily test the optimization performance of the algorithm.

$$\begin{cases} f_1(x_1, x_2) = x_1^2 + (x_2 - 1)^2 \\ f_2(x_1, x_2) = x_2^2 + (x_1 - 1)^2 \end{cases} \quad 0 \leq x_1, x_2 \leq 1000 \tag{1}$$

3   Subjective Defect of Evaluation Index

Multi-objective English teaching decision-making refers to the English teaching decision-making under the condition of contradiction and competition among multiple goals. The most prominent feature of multi-objective English teaching decision-making is. The incommensurability between goals and the contradiction between goals. The so-called incommensurability of goals means that there is no unified measurement standard for each goal, so it is difficult to compare. The evaluation of action plans in multi-objective English teaching decision-making can only be carried out according to the comprehensive effect produced by multiple goals The so-called contradiction of target smell means that if a scheme is adopted to improve the value of one target, the value of another target may become worse. In the multi-objective English teaching decision-making, it often occurs that one or some of the objective functions reach the optimum, and another or some of the objective functions cannot reach the optimum. The contradiction between these objective functions determines that the multi-objective English teaching decision-making problem generally does not exist the absolute optimal solution that can make all the objective functions reach the optimum at the same time, but only the concepts of non inferior solution and satisfactory solution. Only by showing these factors can we design a scientific and reasonable English teaching model that is in line with the characteristics of English Teaching in higher vocational colleges Avoid subjective teaching quality indicators [9]. The multi-objective teaching framework is shown in Fig. 4 below.

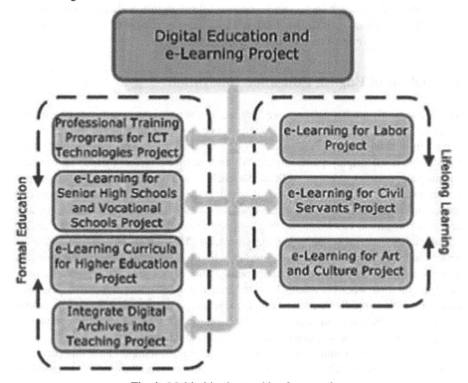

Fig. 4. Multi-objective teaching framework

Genetic algorithm is a global search algorithm, which searches in the way of quasi biological evolution, and has shown some advantages in application. The multi-objective genetic algorithm provides a solution for solving complex multivariable and high-dimensional problems, but the weighted method in its application greatly restricts its superiority. Inequality based method the parallel computing processing of multiple objectives is retained, which breaks the traditional method of changing multiple objectives into single objectives by weighting. It can maintain the independence of objectives in the process of solving and give decision makers more options. The multi-objective genetic algorithm is used to obtain Pareto minima of inequality constraints. This method does not need to calculate Pareto minima. It seeks an acceptable solution instead of necessarily Pareto minima. Unequal In the formula method, the admissible boundary E and the auxiliary performance index vector a (C, s) are introduced, the inequality constraint range is reduced by the admissible boundary, and the multi-objective problem is transformed into an inequality problem by the auxiliary performance index vector for optimization, so as to simplify the solution process and find an optimal solution.

On the one hand, in the traditional teaching quality evaluation, both peer evaluation and student evaluation cannot avoid the subjectivity and inaccuracy of the evaluation results. For example, Wei Hong and Shen Jiliang conducted an empirical study on the characteristics that affect students' evaluation results, and found that there are six characteristics that can explain 25.8% of the variation of students' evaluation results. There are some limitations in students' evaluation of teachers' teaching, which can only be used as a reference for teachers to improve teaching. On the other hand, although the evaluation results of each index can be obtained through this evaluation method, it is impossible to judge how or to what extent these indexes affect the objective teaching effect (such as the improvement of students' performance).

4   Analysis of English Education Innovation

Media, constantly modify and improve multimedia teaching courseware, teaching means refers to the teaching aids used in the teaching process, including modern teaching means and traditional teaching means, such as slides, tape recorders, small blackboard, multimedia, physical display platform, etc. Modern teaching means include multimedia teaching and network teaching. Multimedia teaching and network teaching methods are mainly used in the experiment. In the information age, the wide application of network media and multimedia provides a rich resource library for teachers and students, and provides convenient conditions for teaching and learning. The use of pictures, audio-visual, audio-visual materials in the classroom, so that students have a more intuitive understanding of a historical period, a writer, a literary work. Multimedia teaching and network teaching methods are integrated with picture, text, sound and image. It is more vivid and intuitive when presenting knowledge, and it is faster to communicate with students. It greatly simplifies the operation of teachers and improves the effect of classroom teaching. Multimedia production will be text and graphics, audio-visual integration of the screen, so that students learn to become relaxed and happy.

The theory of classroom behavior management is the most important content of classroom management, which affects the vitality of classroom and the quality of classroom teaching. Western scholars have done a lot of research on classroom behavior management, among which the more familiar ones are Kant theory, Glaser theory, coulin theory, Galton theory and Drake theory. Kanter's theory focuses on the teachers' responsibility for the students and the regular training research. He advocates that teachers have the responsibility for the classroom management, can clearly put forward expectations and requirements to the students decisively, and follow the corresponding actions. In the process, teachers can determine effective management methods according to their abilities and wishes; According to Grasser's theory, people have the need to love and be loved, and the need to expect their own value to be recognized by themselves and others [10]. This need is the driving force of students' behavior. For example, students' bad behavior is the direct result of students' failure to obtain successful recognition; Kulin's theory focuses on the preventive education routine and group management technology, emphasizing the ripple effect. He believes that when bad behaviors occur in the classroom, the same or similar behavior problems can be reduced by practicing the ripple effect. Moreover, teachers should clearly identify students with behavior problems, rather than simply punish them; Galton's theory focuses on the democratic attitude of teachers. Teachers can give up their role as authoritative figures through clear and friendly communication or by controlling bad behaviors. Through the investigation, it is found that if teachers show concern and love for students, students will show respect for teachers accordingly. However, Drake's theory focuses on students' needs and self-discipline, with the main purpose of developing students' self-discipline and educating students to be responsible for their own behavior.

(1) Cooperative teaching method.

Students are the main body of teaching activities and should participate in every link of teaching. In the teaching of English and American literature, the cooperative teaching method has its obvious advantages. For example, group tasks will be assigned to each group member, which is conducive to expanding students' participation and mobilizing their learning enthusiasm. Taking ppt production as an example, the research group takes four people as a group in teaching to form a PPT production group, which includes data collection, data analysis, PPT production and PPT demonstration. This requires four people as members of the PPT production group to perform their duties and cooperate with each other. This kind of cooperative relationship makes students learn to respect each other, communicate with each other and cooperate with others. Students' autonomy in learning is strengthened and they learn to study on their own initiative.

(2) Student centered interactive teaching method.

Students should read before class and carefully review relevant materials that need to be communicated and discussed in class. The representative writers to be studied in the English and American literature class include their literary genres, writing styles of their main works, comments and relevant literary periods, cultural backgrounds and social backgrounds. Each member of each group is responsible for one of the contents. In class, each member of the group takes turns to teach the relevant materials, information and comments they are responsible for. After the lecture, the lecturer and the students ask and answer questions to each other (the time limit for each student to explain and answer questions is 10 min). The teacher will only participate in the final discussion at this stage. Students can participate in learning freely, independently and democratically in the classroom, as shown in Fig. 5. They have the right to choose and express themselves creatively. Through their own deduction and performance, students try to understand and reproduce the classic images in their minds, and even rewrite and subvert the typical characters and scenes that have been inherent for many years.

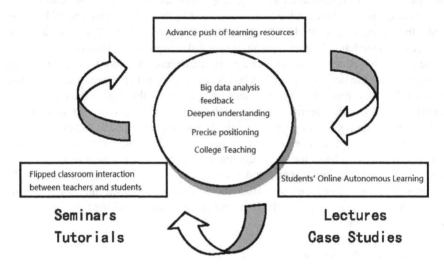

Fig. 5. Teaching mode based on multi-objective genetic algorithm

5 Conclusion

This paper proposes a multi-objective genetic algorithm based analysis of Higher Vocational English education innovation, based on multi-objective genetic algorithm data mining analysis method of Higher Vocational English teaching quality.

References

1. Wang, Q.: Research on the innovation of blended English teaching mode based on superstar platform in higher vocational colleges. In: CIPAE 2021: 2021 2nd International Conference on Computers, Information Processing and Advanced Education (2021)
2. Shi, K.: Analysis and practice of innovation and entrepreneurship activities in higher vocational colleges based on information technologies. In: 2021 2nd International Conference on Big Data and Informatization Education (ICBDIE) (2021)
3. Su, G.: Exploration of innovation and entrepreneurship education model in higher vocational colleges based on rural revitalization strategy. SHS Web of Conferences. EDP Sciences (2021)
4. Zhao, W.: An Empirical study of English teaching model in higher vocational colleges based on data analysis (2021)

5. Xie, J.: Research on the innovation of ideology education carriers in higher vocational colleges in the era of new media. Francis Academic Press **3**(6) (2021)
6. Huang, S., Cao, H., Yan, L., et al.: Teaching reform of obstetrics and gynecology nursing course in higher vocational colleges based on OBE education concept from the perspective of big data. Biomed. J. Sci. Tech. Res. **37** (2021)
7. Qiu, D.: Study on the mixed English teaching model in higher vocational colleges under the background of big data. J. Phys.: Conference Series **1852**(3), 032013 (7pp) (2021)
8. Shigeno, H., Bunno, T., Ueki, Y., et al.: The joint impact of R&D and ICT on innovation in Japanese innovative SMEs by panel data analysis based on firm-level survey data. Int. J. Innov. Technol. Manag. **19**(01) (2022)
9. Ding, Y., Sun, Y., Wang, F.: A corpus-based analysis of news on cultural industry system innovation in Shaanxi pilot free trade zone. Open Access Libr. J. **9**(5), 16 (2022)
10. Paredes-Frigolett, H., Pyka, A., Leoneti, A.B.: On the performance and strategy of innovation systems: a multicriteria group decision analysis approach. Technol. Soc., 101632 (2021)

Design of Taijiquan Multimedia Distance Teaching System Based on ASP Technology

Xueqin Wu[✉]

Martial Arts School, Wuhan Institute of Physical Education, Wuhan 430079, Hubei, China
wuxueqin202101@163.com

Abstract. With the rapid development of Internet, the continuous increase of network bandwidth and the rapid change of access technology, dynamic web page ASP technology also came into being. The web page using ASP technology has distinct personality, strong dynamic interaction and timely response to the user's client input; Be able to realize seamless integration with internal business of the enterprise; It not only improves the openness of the website, but also has good security; Web development and maintenance have good scalability, and development tools are easy to use. This paper analyzes the design of Taijiquan multimedia distance teaching system based on ASP technology, introduces the installation and use of ASP related tools and environment, and the working principle of ASP.

Keywords: ASP technology · Distance learning · System design

1   Introduction

With the human stepping into the information society and the vigorous development of the global "information highway", data communication and computer network play a more and more important role in the process of social informatization and information socialization. The Internet has become an important part of people's life, and web page production has become one of the necessary skills in the network age. The vast resources on the Internet need to be established together; Skilled web page making talents have become a popular favorite in modern society; Even ordinary netizens hope to establish a space to show themselves on the Internet by their own strength.

Modern distance education is supported by computer network and satellite digital communication technology. It has the advantages of space-time freedom, resource sharing, open system and convenient cooperation. When developing modern distance education, countries all over the world deeply realize that the sharing of learning resources and the interoperability of the system are of decisive significance to the practicability and economy of network distance education. In view of this, many countries and organizations have been committed to the research of modern distance education technology standards [1]. Vigorously developing modern distance education is of great practical significance to promote the popularization of education, establish a lifelong learning

M. A. Jan and F. Khan (Eds.): BigIoT-EDU 2022, LNICST 466, pp. 146–155, 2023.
https://doi.org/10.1007/978-3-031-23947-2_16

system and realize the great leap forward development of education. The Taijiquan multimedia distance education system based on ASP technology developed and designed in this paper is a sub function of online education, mainly to complete the teaching of Taijiquan multimedia distance education. Units carrying out distance education can use this system to conduct unified evaluation and teaching on students' learning in the form of Internet.

The remote multimedia interactive teaching system is a teaching platform that can provide text, audio and video, courseware, broadcast and electronic whiteboard interactive teaching, and runs on the Internet, intranet, campus network, LAN, and satellite network based on directpc. In the virtual reality classroom of the remote multimedia interactive teaching system, teachers and students from different places interact in real time through audio and video, as if they were in the same classroom.

The system not only supports all the functions of the current multimedia network classroom, but also highlights the communication between teachers, students and students. On the applicable network, it also extends its scope to campus network, metropolitan area network and even the Internet. The system is not limited by bandwidth, region and number of people.

The remote multimedia interactive teaching system, applied in enterprises, institutions, the military, etc., can realize remote real-time interactive teaching and training; Applied in distance universities, it can realize real-time teaching in different places and answer questions with voice and text; In the school to school environment, you can watch the on-site open classes of other schools without going out of the school; The application in campus network and multimedia network classroom can realize all the functions of the popular multimedia network classroom; It can be used in the home oriented Internet to realize hand-in-hand remote tutoring without leaving home.

The system uses network communication technology and multimedia technology to realize the cross regional nature of teaching methods at the spatial level, and provides a virtual teaching classroom for both teachers and students. Through the network, teachers' teaching screens, videos, audio, etc. are transmitted to students' computers in real time. Students can also carry out real-time two-way interactive teaching and learning activities in a timely manner through electronic hand raising questions, electronic rush answers and simple multiple-choice questions. In addition, its remote monitoring function is convenient for teachers to manage and control the dynamics of students in the network virtual classroom during distance teaching. The convenience, interactivity and practicality of the system not only enhance the communication between teachers and students, but also expand the modern teaching methods.

2   Related Work

2.1   Introduction to ASP Technology

ASP (active server pages) is a web application development technology launched by Microsoft in 1996. Microsoft claims to have designed a perfect active platform. Microsoft describes ASP as a server script environment, where dynamic, interactive and high-performance web server applications can be generated and run.

ASP is a server-side technology in ActiveX technology. It is neither a language nor a tool, but a technical framework. Its main function is to provide a powerful method or technology for generating dynamic interactive web service applications. ASP organically combines HTML, script and components to form an application that can run on the server, and sends the standard HTML page specially made according to the user's requirements to the client browser.

ASP, namely active server pages, is a server-side scripting environment developed by Microsoft, which can be used to create dynamic interactive web pages and build powerful web applications. When the server receives a request for an ASP file, it will process the server-side script code contained in the HTML (Hyper Text Markup Language) web page file used to build and send to the browser. In addition to server-side script code, ASP files can also contain text, HTML (including related client-side scripts) and COM component calls.

ASP is simple and easy to maintain. It is the choice of small page applications. When DCOM (Distributed Component Object Model) and MTS (Microsoft Transaction Server) are used, ASP can even realize medium-sized enterprise applications.

The script program in ASP runs on the server side (not on the client side), and the web page transmitted to the browser is generated on the web server. Therefore, the client browser does not process these scripts. The web server has completed the processing of these scripts and transmitted the standard HTML pages to the browser. The ASP interpreter reads and executes all script code between the <% and %> tags and generates content. Because only the execution result of the script is returned to the browser, the user cannot see the script command of the web page being browsed, but only the execution result of the script.

2.2 Design Objectives

Due to the limitations of time and space, various disadvantages of the traditional teaching mode have been exposed, which is no longer suitable for the current society. With the rapid development of network technology, many foreign universities and relevant social departments have set up distance education through the network, and realized remote education through computer network. This network teaching has incomparable advantages over the traditional teaching mode, It has the advantages of simple operation, powerful function and fast information flow. At the same time, it also adapts to the existing teaching system. Before developing this system, I read a lot of literature and related software research, understood the needs of users, and defined the functions, performance and interface of the software to be developed. In order to improve the current teaching efficiency, developers listen to various opinions, understand the whole teaching process, and use network technology to develop a suitable and efficient distance teaching system [2].

Distance teaching system realizes the networking of teaching. It creates a new teaching mode, breaks the limitations of traditional teaching mode in time and space, adopts advanced teaching means and teaching methods, makes teaching more flexible and active, greatly improves teaching efficiency and teaching effect, and improves teaching activities to a higher level. The Taijiquan multimedia distance teaching system designed in this paper well realizes the user login function. The administrator can add, delete, modify and query the information of teachers and students. Teachers can add courses, publish Taijiquan exercise videos, explain, upload courseware and answer questions online. Students can choose courses online, study online, ask questions online, etc.

What ASP has designed is a dynamic homepage, which can receive the information submitted by users and respond. The data in it can change with the actual situation, and it can meet the application needs without manually updating the web page files. For example, when you fill out a form in the browser and submit an HTTP request, you can ask the web server to execute an application set by the form, not just a simple HTML file. The application analyzes the input data of the form and transmits the corresponding execution results (usually the result set of database search) to the browser in HTML format according to different data contents. The data in the database can be changed at any time, but the applications executed on the server do not have to be changed. The web page information obtained by the client will always remain fresh and charming.

Compared with the development of web applications using visual basic, c++ or Java programming languages, ASP is a more flexible and fast method to create web applications. In addition to creating HTML interfaces for applications by adding scripts, you can also create your own com (component object model) components, and encapsulate the business logic of applications in reusable modules for calling in scripts, other components or other applications.

2.3   Design Idea of Network Distance Teaching System

As the main pillar of distance education, the design of network distance teaching system must actively apply modern educational technology, closely focus on the core subject of students, design a process of human-computer interaction, let students think, explore and discover more actively, and form a stable structure in the process of teaching activities as a model. The basic design idea of developing modern network teaching system is:

(1) Establish a teaching concept based on human development, pay attention to learners' learning needs, so as to improve learning consciousness, initiative and pertinence;
(2) Embody the idea of individualization and personalization of learning, and pay attention to individual learning process design and knowledge construction, so as to improve learners' interest and learning effect;
(3) Optimize and utilize network resources, focus on learning, accurately navigate relevant learning resources, and reasonably allocate learners' attention and time, so as to improve the effectiveness and teaching quality of distance teaching system.

ASP can obtain active X and structure support through com/dcom provided by windows. ASP uses ODBC (open database connectivity) technology to access the database. In specific applications, the database operation is generally realized through ADO (ActiveX data objects). Using ADO's connection, command and recordset objects, you can establish a connection with the database, execute sol statements, and save, traverse and display the query result set.

3 Functions of Taijiquan Multimedia Distance Teaching System

The multimedia distance teaching system of Taijiquan adopts browser / server mode, as shown in Figs. 1 and 2.

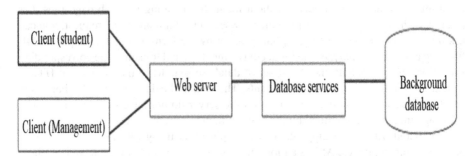

Fig. 1. Multimedia distance teaching system model of Taijiquan

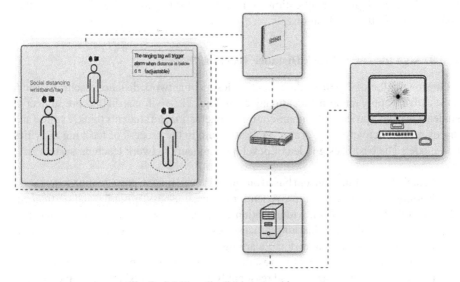

Fig. 2. Multimedia distance teaching system

(1) Assistant teaching software of network course

In order to give full play to the leading role of teachers in teaching, a flexible, convenient, beautiful and practical network assisted teaching software should be compiled according to the course content and characteristics for teachers to use in teaching; At the same time, in order to highlight the dominant position of students in learning, students should not only be able to unify the learning content on the Internet according to the teaching plan, but also be able to learn independently and choose learning according to their own time and learning situation [3]. This part mainly focuses on Web page design, so Dreamweaver is adopted, combined with fireworks, flash, Photoshop and other software, VBScript and other programming languages.

(2) Online learning resources

The system shall provide reference materials, network teaching resources and other information related to this course for students to consult. Online learning resources mainly use multimedia information such as text, picture, sound, animation and video to collect and summarize relevant learning resources in online courses, and present them in various ways such as database recording, file download, hypertext and hypermedia.

1. Use simple and easy scripting languages such as VBScript and JavaScript. Combined with HTML code, you can quickly complete the application of the website and realize the dynamic web page technology.
2. ASP file is contained in the file composed of HTML code, which is easy to modify and test, and can be interpreted and executed without compiling or linking.
3. The scripting languages used by ASP are executed on the web server. The ASP interpreter on the server will execute the ASP program on the server and send the results to the client browser in HTML format.
4. ASP provides some built-in objects that can make server-side scripting more powerful.
5. ASP can use server-side ActiveX components to perform various tasks, such as accessing database, sending email or accessing file system.
6. Because the server sends the result of ASP program execution back to the client browser in HTML format, the user will not see the original program code written by ASP, which can prevent the ASP program code from being stolen.

(3) Online Q & A, BBS discussion area and online test

Teaching and learning is a process in which teachers and students learn and promote each other. Therefore, the distance teaching system allows students to submit difficult problems or exercises to the distance teacher in time through e-mail, online BBS and other means, and the teacher will immediately make corresponding answers or modifications and feed back to the students. At the same time, students opinions or suggestions on teachers in the teaching process can be quickly fed back to teachers, so that teachers can improve teaching contents and teaching methods at any time, so as to continuously improve teaching quality and teaching effect.

The system can put forward suggested learning arrangements according to students' learning level for students' reference; In the teaching process, teachers can act as controllers and guides to ask students questions, and students communicate with teachers or learning partners through the discussion area. Through the combination of various interactive ways, teachers' teaching and students' learning are closely linked, so as to achieve the best effect of teaching and learning. Students can also carry out relevant exercises or self-test according to what they have learned at any time, and finally pass the system for automatic test paper generation. This part is the core content of the whole network distance teaching system, which is different from ordinary courseware [4]. It is not a simple repetition of the course content, but presents the interactive content between teachers and students in the course in a dynamic way. Therefore, this part of the content generally adopts dynamic web design technology ASP, and integrates it with database, ADO and other technologies, so as to realize the functions of online dynamic communication between teachers and students, random display of test questions, test paper generation and so on.

4   Main Implementation Technologies and Methods of Taijiquan Multimedia Distance Teaching System

4.1   Main Implementation Technologies

At present, the main technologies used in dynamic web page design are PHP technology, ASP technology, JSP technology and database technology. In the "online Q & a" of our Taijiquan multimedia distance teaching system, we mainly use the integrated application of ASP technology and database technology. The basic process is to store the questions raised by students and the answers of teachers in the server in the form of database. Students can raise questions and display the answers to the questions answered by teachers through the ASP program interface on the client. Teachers can input the answers through the client according to the questions raised by students, and the ASP program will automatically store the answers in the database server, Teachers can also delete unreasonable questions raised by students.

ASP is active server pages. It is a combination of HTML (Hypertext identification language), script (script) and CGI (Common Gateway Interface) developed by Microsoft. It does not provide its own special programming language, but allows users to use many existing scripting languages to write ASP applications. It runs on the web server, and then transmits the running results to the browser of the client in HTML format. Therefore, ASP is much safer than the general scripting language.

The biggest advantage of ASP is that it can contain HTML tags, directly access the database and use infinitely expanded ActiveX controls. Therefore, it is more convenient and flexible than HTML in programming. By using ASP component and object technology, users can directly use ActiveX controls, call object methods and properties, and realize powerful interactive functions in a simple way. ASP is a server-side Web page design technology, which can directly add script language to HTML web pages. It can not only easily read the contents of the database, but also easily integrate the existing client VBScript, so as to output dynamic, interactive and live web pages.

5 System Implementation Method

(1) Build database (as shown in Table 1)

Table 1. Data table of database construction

Field name	data type	title
Bh	auto number	auto number
zhang_xh	number	Chapter No
Zhang	text	Chapter title
Tmnr	text	problem
Da	remarks	answer
xzhbzh	text	Check Flag

(2) Configuring ODBC data sources
        Set up ODBC data sources in the control panel.
(3) Main design interface

① Common interface
The interface is a public interface for teachers and students, which can browse the answers to the questions answered by teachers, the questions submitted by students, enter the teacher management interface and enter the administrator interface.

a. Establish a connection with the data source;
b. Store the records of existing answers in the database into the array, and count the number of pages to be displayed (10 questions per page);
c. Display the records with answers in the database and establish a link with the answer interface;
d. Design and display corresponding page turning button and jump button;
e. Design problem submission text box and button;
f. Design teacher password submission and administrator password submission.

② The teacher answers the question interface uses the way of parameter transmission (the question to display the answer is used as the parameter) to locate the record, and store the answer entered by the teacher in the database.
③ The teacher modifies the answer interface. According to the needs, the teacher can select the questions with existing answers, re-enter the answers and store them in the database.
④ Administrator interface in this interface, you can modify administrator password, view teacher name and password, delete teacher record and new teacher registration

⑤ Enter the teacher's name and password in the new teacher registration interface, and the registration will be completed after submission. Registered teachers can answer students' questions through the public interface.

⑥ Modify the teacher password and administrator password interface. If you need to modify the password, you can enter a new password in this interface (Fig. 3).

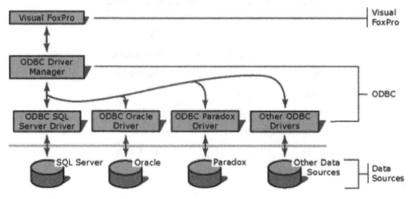

Fig. 3. ODBC SQL

An ODBC based application does not rely on any DBMS for database operations and does not directly deal with DBMS. All database operations are completed by the ODBC driver of the corresponding DBMS. In other words, whether FoxPro, access or Oracle database, ODBC API can be used for access. It can be seen that the greatest advantage of ODBC is that it can handle all databases in a unified way. Its characteristic is that ODBC technology is based on c\s structure. It makes the application and DBMS can be logically separated, and makes the application have database independence. ODBC defines an API. Each application can access different database systems and data in multiple databases by using the same source code. Compared with embedded SQL, one of the most significant advantages of ODBC is that the applications generated by ODBC are independent of the database or database engine. ODBC enables applications to have good interoperability and portability, and has the ability to access multiple DBS at the same time, thus overcoming the defects of traditional database applications.

6 Conclusion

The network Taijiquan multimedia distance teaching system developed under the Taijiquan distance education environment fully embodies the "people-oriented and teacher-student interaction" At the same time, through online Q & A and BBS discussion, it provides effective means for communication, interaction and rapid feedback between teachers and students, and represents the development trend of the new network distance teaching system. With the further development and popularization of modern educational technology and network distance education, the function of Taijiquan multimedia distance teaching system will be further improved and developed.

References

1. Shi, H., Xie, J., Peng, H.: Dynamic web page programming. Tsinghua University Press, Beijing (1), 55–76 (2009)
2. Xue, Y., Gu, J.: Design and release of Web database, pp. 55–67. Jing Hua University Press, Beijing
3. Chen, P.: Research and design of teaching platform under network mode, computer development and application, July 2006
4. Xiang, Y.: ASP + SQL Server Website System Development Project Case. Tsinghua University Press, Beijing (2007)

Innovation of Film and Television Screenwriter Education in the Era of Mobile Internet

ChunLiang Wang[✉]

School of Film and Television Media, Wuchang University of Technology, Hubei 430223, China
25356265@qq.com

Abstract. In the traditional screenwriter teaching system, the creator is difficult to control the final presentation of his works. After the completion of the script, the director modifies the script again and writes the sub lens script, which is interpreted by the actors, and completed by the cooperation of various departments such as lighting and sound on the set. In the era of mobile Internet, the content production of film and television works shows the tendency of cross media narration. A large number of short films and micro films pour into the market. Students can have faster and more access to excellent finished products, but it is difficult to obtain the original script of excellent works and understand the communication and modification between screenwriters and directors. Therefore, in order to strengthen the screenwriter students' understanding of the use of lens and the relationship between lens and script language, this paper studies the innovation of film and television screenwriter education in the era of mobile Internet.

Keywords: Film and television screenwriter · Internet · Screenwriter education

1 Introduction

From the development history of film and television drama in China, there are only a few decades, which has experienced the initial stage of development, and the development period has entered the current vigorous development period. The so-called film and television drama is a form of performance drama specially broadcast on TV or film. Film and television drama has great compatibility. It can combine the elements of film, television, drama, drama, music, dance, modeling, painting, art and other modern arts to express the charm of film and television art.

In the current Internet era, the powerful, fast and coverage of network information has brought a new and profound experience to our life and learning. The development of film and TV drama has new opportunities, especially the Internet plus era. It should combine the role of the Internet media effectively and develop the film and TV dramas in China [1]. The development of film and TV plays is also the reflection of the development of the national cultural industry. Under this background, the life style and learning habits of college students will be quite different from those of the traditional ones. This also poses a challenge to teachers' teaching, especially the teaching of film and television teachers closely related to audio-visual art, which puts forward higher requirements. In order to make students have the editing and creative ability and innovative ability to adapt to the development of the times, the reform and innovation of film and television screenwriter education and teaching is the only way. Teachers should keep up with the pace of the times and keep pace with the times.

Traditional TV Editing is carried out on the editing machine. The editing machine usually consists of a video player and a video recorder. The editor selects a suitable piece of material through the video player, records it on the tape in the video recorder, and then looks for the next shot. In addition, the advanced editing machine has a strong special effect function, which can make all kinds of superimposed drawings and images. You can adjust the picture color, or make subtitles, etc. However, because the pictures recorded on tape are sequential, you cannot insert a shot between the existing pictures or delete a shot, unless you re record all the pictures after that. So this kind of editing is called linear editing, which brings many restrictions to editors. We can see that although the traditional editing methods have their own characteristics, they all have great limitations, which greatly reduces the creativity of editors and wastes precious time in the tedious operation process.

Digital non-linear editing technology based on computer has greatly developed editing methods. This technology records the material in the computer and uses the computer to edit it. It adopts the non-linear mode of film editing, but uses simple mouse and keyboard operation instead of scissors and paste manual operation. The editing results can be played back immediately, so the efficiency is greatly improved. At the same time, it can not only provide all the special effects of various editing machines, but also provide complex special effects that the editing machine can't do through the expansion of software and hardware. Digital non-linear editing not only combines the advantages of traditional film and television editing, but also further develops it. It is a major progress in film and television editing technology. Since the 1980s, digital non-linear editing has gradually replaced the traditional method in foreign film production and become the standard method of film editing.

In China, the use of digital non-linear editing for film editing is still a matter of recent years, but it has developed very rapidly. At present, most directors have recognized its advantages. We will discuss the digital non-linear editing in detail. With the rapid development of film and television production technology, post production has shouldered a very important responsibility: the production of stunt lens. Stunt lens refers to the lens that cannot be obtained through direct shooting. Most of the early film and television stunts were completed by traditional means such as model making, stunt photography, optical synthesis and so on, mainly in the shooting stage and the development process. The use of computers provides more and better means for special effects production, and also makes many special effects that must be completed by using models and photography in the past can be completed by computer production, so more special effects have become post production work.

2 Research on the Reform Background of Film and Television Screenwriter Teaching Under the Internet Environment

Video editing: according to the requirements and script, editing and production for the purpose of highlighting a theme content, paragraph deletion, adding deleted segments, adding logo, subtitle, dubbing, montage effect, professional color matching, 3D Title customization, production gags, video format transcoding, electronic photo album, flash, etc., and editing and production according to the requirements of localization.

Material processing: provide video material with segment deletion, paragraph sequence reorganization, historical material incorporation, related material introduction and combination, etc.

Special effects processing: add transition special effects, montage effect, 3D special effects, multi picture, picture in picture effect, video picture color matching, etc. to the video material editing process.

Subtitle processing: add logo, Chinese and foreign subtitles, explanation subtitles, modified subtitles, 3D subtitles, rolling subtitles, corner subtitles, etc. for video materials.

Audio processing: add background music, special effect music, professional announcer's multilingual dubbing commentary, lip synching dubbing and music for video materials.

Packaging processing: all-round special effects packaging for video material after editing, montage effect, production of 3D title and ending, flash title and ending, image identification special effects, etc.

Output of finished products -- the produced film and television works are output to video tapes and broadcast tapes in various formats, pressed or burned to DVDs and VCDs, or output data files in various formats.

(1) The necessity of reform in the teaching of film and television screenwriter course under the Internet environment. In the Internet environment, the rise of big data, editing and creation software and even the emergence of screenwriting robots have made many students of this major question and worry about the status and professional development of film and television screenwriters. In the face of this new environment, the teaching mode in the traditional environment obviously can not adapt to the new environment. Therefore, today, when the industrialization trend of editing and creation begins to sprout, It is very necessary to explore the reform of film and television screenwriter teaching under the Internet environment.

(2) The possibility of reform in the teaching of film and television screenwriter course under the Internet environment. Under the Internet environment, the prosperity of the film market and the transmission and application of editing and creation data have brought rich IP content resources, as shown in Fig. 1. The different playback terminals brought by media technology have also brought unlimited possibilities for screenwriter editing and creation. Therefore, in the face of such an opportunity, we have the responsibility to make good use of the situation, seize the opportunity and carry out effective reform research on film and television screenwriter teaching.

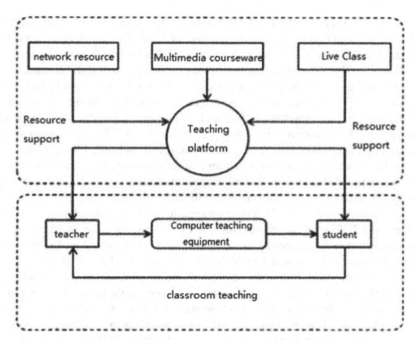

Fig. 1. Internet Film and television screenwriter Teaching

(3) The importance of teaching reform of film and television screenwriter course under the Internet environment. In the Internet environment, all kinds of script development software also bring some disadvantages, such as the similarity of script themes and insufficient type innovation. From the perspective of film and television creation, the core of film and television works is the foundation of a play. Removing the shell of fancy film and television forms often makes the audience feel that the key factor is to have a good story and the ability to tell the story well, Is what film and television screenwriters should have. It can be seen that how to cultivate students' abilities in film and television thinking, screenwriter planning and script creation in the Internet environment is particularly important for students to be invincible [2].

3   Opportunities and Challenges for the Development of Film and Television Drama in the Internet Era

3.1   The Internet Era Has Brought New Opportunities for the Development of Film and Television Dramas

The biggest advantage of new media and the Internet is fast and convenient. The Internet has brought rapid communication channels to the whole society. Whenever and wherever there is a network and terminal, you can obtain the most desired information through the Internet. The combination of TV play and Internet is the integration of resources in the Internet plus era, and brings new opportunities for the development of film and TV drama.

First, from the script of film and TV drama, in the Internet plus era, the choice of script is an important factor in winning the market. From the current development of film and television drama, the choice of script, especially in recent years, is mostly in network novels. The adaptation of online novels into scripts is the full combination of the Internet and film and television dramas. On the one hand, online novels themselves are the product of the Internet. With the help of the Internet, excellent online novels have a large number of online novel fans, who have laid the viewing foundation for the ratings of film and television dramas in the future; On the other hand, the lack of good scripts is also an important reason for the adaptation of online novels into film and television bureaus. Therefore, the combination of film and television drama with the Internet is conducive to the development of film and television drama.

Secondly, in terms of the dissemination of film and television dramas, the Internet is also a good platform for film and television dramas to let more viewers know. Especially after the SARFT reformed the broadcasting of TV dramas, the current situation of one drama and two stars has prompted that the dissemination of many film and television dramas can no longer be broadcast and publicized on every satellite TV as before. However, once the film and television drama is combined with the Internet, it can publicize and market the film and television drama at any time to ensure the favorable development of the film and television drama. As a development stage of cultural industry, film and television plays have become a part of China's important cultural industry. The opportunities brought by the Internet plus era should be fully utilized before it can bring more room for development of film and TV dramas.

3.2 Big Data in the Internet Era Has Also Brought Challenges to the Development of Film and Television Dramas

First of all, with the rise of we media, everyone has become a journalist. As long as the people have a network and terminals, they can enjoy new media and Internet resources and share resources in a fragmented way, but new media and the Internet will also have a negative impact on the development of film and television dramas. With the development of society and the rapid spread of consultation, more and more self-made dramas and film and television dramas are denounced on the Internet platform, and the audience has more and more optional rights and works [3]. Therefore, it is more and more difficult for film and television dramas to stand out. Secondly, big data has brought new challenges to the development of film and television dramas, especially the ratings and evaluation rates. Before the emergence of big data, the audience rating statistics of film and television dramas were not easy, and it was not easy to be shared by the audience for evaluation. However, the big data platform gives the audience a common platform to make their own evaluation of the film and television play, and the ratings are clear at a glance, which will become the Matthew effect affecting the development of film and television play The good will be better, and the bad will be worse. The development of film and television dramas with digital video editing is shown in Fig. 2.

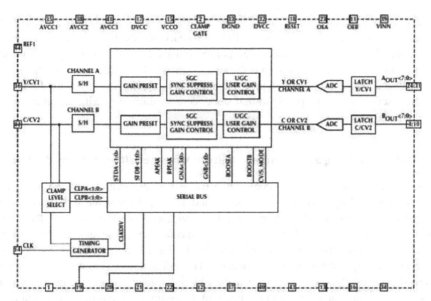

Fig. 2. The development of film and television dramas with digital video editing

4   Specific Reform Ways of Film and Television Screenwriter Course Teaching Under the Internet Environment

4.1   Build a Strong Sense of Film and Television Screenwriting

(1)   The teaching of film and television screenwriters should start with the teaching of film and television thinking. In script creation, it is no longer a traditional literary creation, but a kind of audio-visual creation. In the early writing, we should establish the awareness of photography and editing. For this, in addition to the theoretical explanation of Teachers' classroom, we can also use the comparison between film and television adapted works and original literary works for practice Join the study of photography and editing courses, so that students can establish their film and television thinking consciousness when writing, and gradually move from spontaneity to consciousness.

(2)   The teaching of film and television screenwriters should pay attention to the training of students' divergent thinking. Teachers can lead students into life, improve students' perception and imagination, or teachers can introduce hot topics, and students can make oral creation on the spot and have collective discussion, so as to truly open their thinking, so that students can gradually learn drama in the process of continuous discussion and questioning between teachers and students The basic elements of this and the novel script architecture. At the same time, the establishment of this divergent thinking should also encourage students to go out of the classroom, approach life in their spare time, observe or experience, so as to make the wings of imagination fly higher.

(3)   The teaching of film and television screenwriters should pay attention to the operability of script creation. In order to export the script creation, we should take into

account the positioning of the audience and the market, and make flexible use of the plot structure, characterization, time and space processing, so as to better meet the development needs of the contemporary film and television industry. We should not only pay close attention to it through drama skills In order to understand the audience's psychology, we should also understand the market, especially focus on the discussion of type plays, so that students can calmly deal with the changes of audience tastes.

4.2 Train the Editing and Creation Ability of One Specialty and Many Abilities

Because film and television is a comprehensive art, all the efforts of directing, photographing, recording, serving, transforming and Taoism are to achieve the script and add luster to its transformation from text to film and television. Therefore, the teaching of screenwriting course should truly reflect "one specialty and many abilities" (director, screenwriter, editing, photography and recording). That is, in the specific teaching of screenwriting major, students should understand the editing, photography and recording of a work, not just the text work, because only by truly understanding the process from text creation to film and television imaging, understanding the needs of director, camera and editing, and mastering the audience's mind, can they better complete screenwriting creation. Moreover, we should strengthen cooperation and exchange with other relevant majors, rather than being a lonely desk worker [4–6].

4.3 Set Up Rich and Colorful Classroom Teaching

In the specific teaching, the drama course should run through the four-year university from easy to difficult. In the specific teaching, we should not only understand the basic theory of script creation and master the basic elements of script, but also compare and

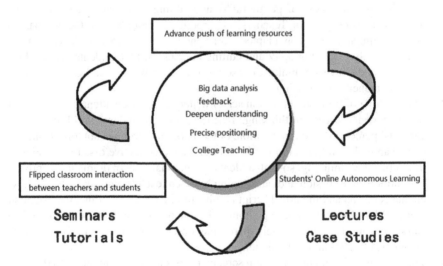

Fig. 3. Internet teaching mode

master the literary script and film and television works in the process of film pulling, and complete the creation through course practice. The Internet-based teaching mode is shown in Fig. 3.

Connect with the industry, introduce industry projects and establish cor-7-9-responding editing and creation studios [7–9]. In addition to the introduction of the project, we can also find the market trend with the help of editing and creation data development, create the most popular selling points, and win the PK by students in groups. The selected scripts will be recommended by industry experts or won prizes, with the support of professional teams and equipment, so as to complete the connection with the screenwriter industry.

5   Conclusion

In the Internet plus era, the development of screenplay education and Internet has been twice as effective. Film and television screenwriter education can integrate their own film and television drama resources with the Internet. The development of Chinese film and TV plays is an important part of the development of cultural industry, and also embodies the cultural soft power. It is an important aspect of cultural transmission in China. In the Internet plus era, whether it is the script source or the dissemination of film and TV drama, it brings new opportunities for the development of film and TV drama. Of course, the fast and fast Internet is the advantage. However, big data also brings challenges to the development of film and television screenwriter education. Teachers should take the initiative to think and actively explore. Only by identifying the direction and strategy of teaching reform can we realize the real transformation and breakthrough of teaching, so as to adapt to the new changes and developments in the current Internet Era.

Film and television media has become the most popular and influential media form. From the fantasy world created by Hollywood blockbusters, to the real life concerned by TV news, to the overwhelming TV advertising, all of them have a profound impact on our lives. In the past, the production of film and television programs was the work of professionals, which seemed to be shrouded in a mysterious veil to the public. Over the past decade, digital technology has entered the film and television production process in an all-round way. Computers have gradually replaced many original film and television equipment and played a major role in all aspects of film and television production. But until recently, film and television production has been using extremely expensive professional hardware and software. It is difficult for non professionals to see these devices, let alone skillfully use these tools to produce their own works. With the significant improvement of PC performance and the continuous reduction of price, film and television production has gradually transferred from the previous professional hardware equipment to the PC platform, and the original professional software with high status has also been gradually transplanted to the platform, and the price is becoming more and more popular. At the same time, the application of film and television production has also expanded from professional film and television production to computer games, multimedia, network, family entertainment and other broader fields. Many operators in these industries and a large number of film and television lovers can now use their computers to produce their own film and television programs.

References

1. Zhou, X.: On the teaching mode of film and television screenwriter course. West. Radio Telev. **18** (2017)
2. Zou, R.: Exploration on teaching innovation of Interactive College screenwriter course. Drama House **16** (2016)
3. Wu, R., Zhang, M.: On the characteristics and influence of network communication of film and television dramas. News World **2** (2014)
4. Li, Y.: Bottle title of the development of film and television dramas. Contemporary Television **9** (2009)
5. Liu, C., Wu, X., Mao, J., Liu, X.: Acoustic emission signal processing for rolling bearing running state assessment using compressive sensing. Mech. Syst. Signal Process. **91**, 395–406 (July 2017). View at: Publisher Site I Google Scholar
6. Paisana, F., Kaminski, N.J., Marchetti, N., DaSilva, L.A.: Signal processing for temporal spectrum sharing in a multi-radar environment. IEEE Trans. Cogn. Commun. Netw. **3**(2), 123–137 (2017). View at: Publisher Site I Google Scholar
7. Ahmad, M., Jung, L.T., Bhuiyan, A.-A.: From DNA to protein: why genetic code context of nucleotides for DNA signal processing? A review. Biomed. Signal Process. Control. **34**, 44–63 (April 2017). View at: Publisher Site I Google Scholar
8. Henry, M., Leach, F., Davy, M., et al.: The prism: efficient signal processing for the internet of things. IEEE Ind. Electron. Mag. **11**(4), 22–32 (2017). View at: Publisher Site I Google Scholar
9. Bone, D., Lee, C.-C., Chaspari, T., Gibson, J., Narayanan, S.: Signal processing and machine learning for mental health research and clinical applications [perspectives]. IEEE Ind. Electron. Mag. **34**(5), 196–195 (2017). View at: Publisher Site I Google Scholar

Innovative Analysis of Sports Competition Training Integrating Interactive Digital Media

Jinghua Li[✉]

School of Physical Education, Xianyang Normal University, Xianyang 712000, Shaanxi, China
124634903@qq.com

Abstract. In the rapid development of digital sports, digital media as a platform to provide digital communication and a medium to carry sports information. Generally speaking, the digital media refers to the digital carriers of information, including digital text, graphics, images, sounds, video images, animation and other carriers, as well as the physical media for storing, transmitting and displaying these information carriers. The function and application of digital media have contributed to the realization and extension of the digitization of sports competition and training, promoted the all-round development of "Digital Sports", provided important help for sports training, brought more sponsorship to sports events and created more commercial value. The innovation of digital sports is also of great significance to promote the development of the National Games and to improve the event quality and organizational innovation ability of the National Games.

Keywords: Digital media · Integration and interaction · Sports competition · Training innovation

1 Introduction

With the continuous close combination of digital media technology and sports, digital media technology interprets the cultural characteristics of sports, such as science and technology, fashion, extensibility and inheritance, from different perspectives. It not only shows the new characteristics of the development of sports science, but also embodies the new pursuit of cultural representation, such as multi-cultural integration of information and data, situational interpretation of sports charm, media expansion of information carrier and cultural accumulation across the digital divide. The research on the application of digital media technology in sports training is essentially an in-depth exploration of the integration of science and technology and sports. Its significance is to further show and extend the characteristics of the integration of digital technology and sports, and provide more objective, specific and rich theoretical basis and practical support for the scientific development of sports.

Interactive digital sports competition training innovation laboratory is an innovative laboratory system that applies VR / AR technology to digital sports competition training

M. A. Jan and F. Khan (Eds.): BigIoT-EDU 2022, LNICST 466, pp. 165–176, 2023.
https://doi.org/10.1007/978-3-031-23947-2_18

innovation teaching and scientific research. It provides a set of innovative construction schemes and ideas for the construction of digital sports competition training innovation and art design professional laboratories. The laboratory is mainly for the teaching and practice of undergraduate and graduate students in Colleges and universities, and for the practical application needs of the society. It not only combines students' theoretical learning with social practical application, but also provides data support and platform services for teachers and students' scientific research.

In terms of teaching, the laboratory can meet many professional teaching of digital sports competition training innovation, such as digital sports competition training innovation and production, game and three-dimensional animation design and production, virtual reality and visualization technology, human-computer interaction, nonlinear editing and video post production, computer painting, product shape concept design, etc., including image, human-computer interaction Text, audio, video and other forms. Figure 1 below shows the sports multiplayer interactive sports mode.

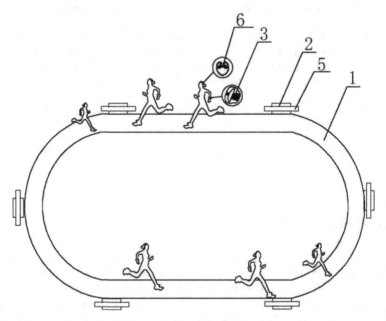

Fig. 1. Sports multiplayer interactive sports mode

In terms of scientific research, it mainly focuses on the research of innovative content processing technology of digital sports competition training, including computer graphics, image processing technology and innovative technology of multi sports competition training. Specifically, it can also be used for innovative processing and retrieval of digital sports competition training, video emotion calculation, adaptive transmission of HD and SD video content, innovative security of digital sports competition training Research on virtual experiment, innovative processing of sports competition training in multi-core environment, computer animation and film and television stunts, scientific and technological document processing, etc.

Using the teaching experimental platform of digital sports competition training innovation system, students can participate in the design and production of innovative works of actual sports competition training, so that students can understand the whole process of the production of innovative works of sports competition training, understand the integration of digital technology, art and humanistic knowledge, and understand how to combine with art and humanities personnel in the process of innovative production of sports competition training. At the same time, Further strengthen students' practical ability and practical experience.

On the basis of digital media technology, combined with the theories of communication, sports management and marketing, this paper analyzes the application of digital media by comprehensively using the research methods of literature, direct observation, field research and in-depth interview. Investigate the literature, grasp the definition, description and classification of digital media in the existing data, and understand the research situation of digital media in the field of sports [1]; Directly enter the sports events and training site, observe and collect research data; Conduct in-depth interviews with event operation managers, media or athletes to understand the innovative application mode, function and effect based on digital media, and appropriately explore and imagine the feasible application mode.

2   Related Work

2.1   New Technology of Digital Media

(1) Digital technology. Digital technology is such a technical category. It uses digital processing, computer acquisition, Internet application and communication technology to convert media information such as pictures, words, graphics and video into binary form, output and spread. Digital technology includes not only the comprehensive utilization of information system, but also various new media technologies, such as streaming media, animation, virtual technology, human-computer interaction and so on.

(2) Advantages and characteristics of digital technology. Today, with the continuous renewal and development of modern information technology, compared with the stability characteristics of traditional information technology, digital technology is unique and stands out, which fully shows that digital technology has higher foresight. This forward-looking feature reflects not only the rapidity of digital technology, but also its absolute openness. First, the characteristics of rapidity: the rapidity of digital technology is obvious. It can provide users with a simple and fast operation technology. Through the combination of software technology and hardware technology, the communication between users and computers is finally realized in time and results It has achieved two-way improvement. Second, interactive features: in the past, information content was released in one direction in the dissemination process, and users were more passive to accept. However, the emergence of digital technology has realized two-way dissemination of information. It uses the Internet platform to form interaction between users and users, users and computers. Users can fully customize and create information use opinions according to their own needs, Information resources can be shared. The third is the virtual feature: users

can form a virtual space through the simulation of digital technology. When entering this space, virtual devices can simulate the reality from various senses such as vision, hearing and touch, so that users can experience the actual feeling. The real world in the virtual world can achieve the main ideas that cannot be expressed in the actual situation. Finally, it is a comprehensive feature: digital technology can transform many information contents into binary code forms, and many information forms with different properties into information contents with unified characteristics [2]. This transformation is actually one It integrates the information content of different properties into the expression form, breaks through the information boundary, and the information content can be exchanged as long as the standards are the same. This auxiliary item can make the boundary of the segmentation result clearer, make the segmentation result more complete, and speed up the training speed of the segmentation model. The interactive training design model is shown in Fig. 2 below.

Of course, the integrated interaction module and self interaction module proposed in this paper are relatively simple, and they will be analyzed later.

$$L_{CEL} = \frac{|FP + FN|}{|FP + 2TP + FN|} = \frac{\sum(p - pg) + \sum(g - pg)}{\sum p + \sum g} \quad (1)$$

$$L = L_{BCE}(\mathcal{P}, \mathcal{G}) + \lambda L_{CEL}(\mathcal{P}, \mathcal{G}) \quad (2)$$

$$\frac{\partial L_{BCEL}}{\partial p} = -\frac{g}{p} + \frac{1 - g}{1 - p} \quad (3)$$

$$\frac{\partial L_{CEL}}{\partial p} = \frac{1 - 2g}{\sum(p + g)} - \frac{\sum(p + g - 2pg)}{[\sum(p + g)]^2} \quad (4)$$

- Reduce the difference set as much as possible to make **P** close to **G**.
- Related to all pixels in both **P** and **G**.
- Enforce a global constraint and produce more effective gradient.
- Ensure that there is enough large gradient to drive the network in the later stage of training.
- Solve the intra-class inconsistency and inter-class indistinction issues.
- Promote the predicted boundaries of salient objects to become sharper.

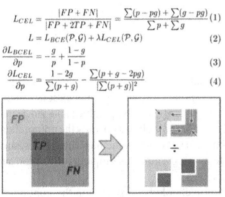

Fig. 2. Interactive training design model

The major of digital media can be explained in a sentence that everyone can understand, that is, content production, including animation, games and film and television. Therefore, in digital media related majors, we should focus on content. In the research direction, we still pay more attention to the technical realization of interaction with users, as well as the cool visual effect and sense of experience.

With such a cognition, the forms of works that digital media can design will be very rich. Such as interactive response web pages, all kinds of fun games that can solve life problems or educational significance, and even film and television animation (of course, including all kinds of carriers with sound as special artistic expression). Around these forms, we can consider and pursue the artistry, originality and professionalism of the content.

Interaction design is to trigger people's effective interaction behavior by establishing an effective way of transmitting information, so as to achieve the design purpose of effectively solving various problems encountered by people. In other words, the first problem of interaction design is how to find the problems and requirements caused by poor information transmission.

Therefore, interaction design mainly aims at solving user needs and pays attention to combing the logic and rational thinking of design; Digital media pay more attention to visual and interactive experience, and are more "free to do whatever they want" in form. The difference between the two is the driving force for their interaction and mutual inspiration.

2.2 Digital Media Technology and the Development of Sports

Digital media technology refers to the information existence and activity of binary digital operation, the technology of processing, storage, dissemination and restoration of information resources characterized by computer and network, and the multimedia network information platform that displays text, image, sound and image through the same terminal based on computer digital technology. As the latest product of the development of contemporary science and technology, digital media technology integrates material civilization and spiritual civilization, traditional culture and modern culture. While changing the form of cultural expression with the power of science and technology, it meets the material and spiritual needs of modern society with the cultural form of innovation and development. At present, with the continuous development of social needs, digital media technology is more and more closely combined with sports. Through the application in digital perception sports activities, digital sports development, multi-cultural integration of digital sports, artistic expression of digital sports, expansion of communication media of digital sports and digital development of national traditional sports, It not only shows the new characteristics of sports forms such as scientifically revealing the law of human movement and the somatosensory operation of electronic games, but also reflects the new pursuit of cultural representation such as multi-cultural integration of information data, situational interpretation of sports charm, media expansion of information carrier and cultural accumulation across the digital divide [3]. The research on digital media technology in sports training is essentially a deep exploration of the integration of science and technology and sports. Its significance is to further show and extend the cultural connotation after the integration of digital technology and sports, and provide more objective, specific and rich theoretical basis and practical support for the formed sports scientific training and the development of sports industry.

Digitalization is not only the inevitable trend of the development of sports industry and athlete training, but also the direction of reform and change of many global event leagues and teams. Swedish Ice Hockey League is one of the top event leagues in the world. Khk is a team that has won the championship of Swedish Ice Hockey League for many times. At the beginning of 2018, Tobias, the boss and chairman of khk team C. With the theme of "athlete digital training", Dr. Larsson invited blgmind innovation consulting from Shanghai, China. The two sides launched a two-year team digital change project on the latest development direction of physical training technology, the application of big data management in high-level sports teams, and the direction of artificial intelligence.

It has brought the latest enlightenment to the industry. It also brings its latest digital physical training products and research results to the ice hockey industry [4].

In order to improve students' sports awareness, use digital and information-based teaching methods to improve teaching quality, make accurate and scientific analysis on students' sports learning quality, and improve the traditional problems that students cannot be monitored and evaluated in real time, 5g intelligent bracelet is used to assist teaching and carry out healthy sports and intelligent sports classes, Let physical education insert the wings of health and science and technology, and effectively promote the all-round development of students' morality, intelligence, physique, beauty and labor.

3   Sports Competition Training Innovation Integrating Interactive Digital Media

3.1   Sports System Simulation

The characteristics of low cost and high simulation caused by virtual reality technology determine its broad application prospect in the field of sports simulation. Virtual reality technology can not only provide new and effective training means for sports dance practitioners and athletes, but also expand the application scope of system simulation, which in turn promotes the development of virtual reality technology. The so-called VR based sports simulation is to simulate the sports training process by using virtual reality technology, so that teachers and students can carry out sexual training in a virtual environment. Compared with other simulation technologies, sports simulation using virtual reality technology has obvious advantages. It can improve the level of interaction between users and sports simulation system, and significantly improve the effect of sports training. The application of virtual reality technology in sports training can not only reduce the cost and not reduce the amount of training, but also significantly improve the training level and competitive level of athletes, and greatly promote the development of sports as a national fitness sport. Virtual reality technology will play a more and more important role in the research and application of modern sports training.

In today's highly developed modern competitive sports, computer technology has been paid more and more attention by sports workers. The "scientific" training of athletes has been verified and developed in various major sports (such as the Olympic Games, the world championships, the National Games, etc.), forming a complete set of systematic and complete training system, as shown in Fig. 3. However, there are still many restrictions on the technical conditions of software and hardware of virtual reality. Various special interactive devices based on virtual reality are quite expensive [5]. The existing interactive methods are not humanized, the operation is complex, and the real-time performance and accuracy of the system are not high These restrictive factors greatly limit the popularization and application of virtual reality technology in the field of practical physical training. With the continuous progress of virtual reality software and hardware technology, more innovative and more applications can be expected in the near future.

Sports competition training is a general term of media system, which takes technology as the driving force and people as the center, and connects all media forms in the state of existence and extension. Sports competition not only means the tacit interaction between the media, but also includes the organizational construction of relations [6].

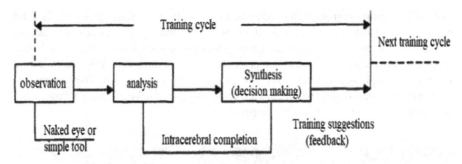

Fig. 3. Motion technology diagnosis system

The complexity of niche competition and cooperation relationship between media forms determines that sports competition communication is dynamic, nonlinear and systematic. In short, sports competition is not just the integration of multiple media in technology, but points to the ecological and systematic integration of multiple dimensions.

From the perspective of technology, the evolution of sports competition form shows a high tendency of aggregation. Sports competition means the disintegration of the previous classification standards of media technology and the breaking of the boundary of traditional media technology. Sports competition comprehensively uses a variety of technologies such as big data and artificial intelligence to collect and produce media information, and transmits the information to each receiving terminal in various forms with an ubiquitous general network platform. The audience can receive the information at any time and form communication and interaction. Therefore, technical multimedia integration is the core driving force to build sports competitions.

Sports competition communication emphasizes a variety of media symbol elements in text presentation, including the common intention mobilization and communication of text, pictures, audio, video, animation and so on. According to media psychology, compared with a single media symbol element, multi sensory stimulation based on multiple media symbol elements can often produce greater communication effect, which helps users form richer cognitive resonance.

Sports competition realizes the dynamic interactive communication of controlling multiple scenes. Through intelligent intermediaries such as mobile terminals and wearable devices, it forms a scene entrance without space-time constraints, and the scene setting is constructed by the three-dimensional presentation of different symbols. After the scene appeared, sports competition communication changed the previous mode of positioning communication of single media content, so that different media can switch and interact at will.

In the form of sports competition, omnisensory communication takes technology and environment as the communication background, breaking through the sensory bias of previous communication. Omnisensory communication enables people to realize the real "absent presence" for the first time, which is not only the original starting point of the evolution of communication form, but also the ultimate goal of the evolution of media form [7].

People in sports competition communication can be materialized into media, and the media can also be humanized. Media is the extension of human body, and people also become the extension of media. Sports competition itself is a general term. When people become media and further integrate with the media, people become invisible. They are not people in social relations, but "people" in media relations. They are media-based existence, and people and media are each other. As shown in Fig. 4 below, it is a simulation of the new era of sports competition.

Fig. 4. Simulation of sports competition in the new era

3.2 Interactive Sports Training Simulation System

The application of virtual reality technology in sports has been studied by many scholars at home and abroad in the field of competitive sports and mass fitness, and has made remarkable achievements. Amusitronix researchers have developed virtual systems such as vrbaseball, vrgolf, vrkayaking, vrtennis, vrsnow, vrskate and vrsurf. Becker et al. [8]. Established a Tai Chi trainer in the modified version of live system, which can provide better in-depth information. The system will feed back the athletes' different sports clips from the coaches and give simple comments. Virtual reality technology provides sports workers with training and teaching methods completely different from traditional methods, liberates coaches from heavy physical labor to engage in mental work, and liberates students from outdoor sports venues [9]. As long as there is a computer, they can learn from time to time and from place to place. The above characteristics of virtual reality technology determine that it has broad application prospects in sports simulation. The simulation analysis of interactive sports training simulation system is shown in Fig. 5 below.

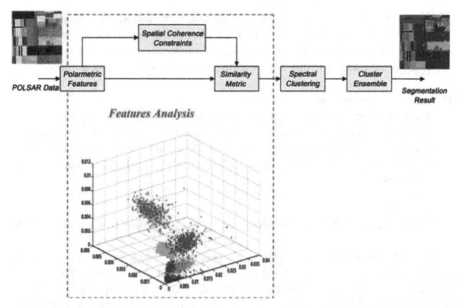

Fig. 5. Simulation analysis of interactive sports training simulation system

The sports simulation system based on the integration of interactive digital media should be able to analyze the athletes' actions and have the following functions:

(1) The corresponding virtual human model and 3D scene are constructed according to the needs of users

The system itself has a virtual human model library. Technicians or user administrators can choose different types of human models according to the requirements of users; At the same time, a virtual scene is built for users according to their actual training scene, including motion references, etc. [10].

(2) Capture motion data in real time

Generally speaking, this function is realized by two cameras and a computer. The camera obtains the video file of human motion in the process of synchronous shooting, extracts the key frame image from the video file by using the existing computer technology, and then extracts the moving human body by using the methods of artificial intelligence, mode matching and computer graphics, Finally, according to the two-dimensional information of human body at the same time, calculate the three-dimensional motion data of human body and generate computer animation.

(3) Reproduce action

This function is to reposition the human 3D motion data we obtained to the virtual human (animation), play the virtual human at a certain frame rate, and form an animation after rendering in the 3D scene [11]. The students' actions are recorded by the computer and reproduced by high-quality simulation. Students can watch their actions from multiple angles and all directions and improve. It is the core requirement of the simulation system. Coaches can also simulate some technical actions that are still under research, and can also observe students' technical actions from multiple angles in this way, so as to give students an intuitive guidance.

(4) Get motion parameters
   According to the different requirements of coaches, students and sports events, the system can feed back various parameters related to athletes and sports, such as heart rate, blood pressure and so on. In this way, it can not only objectively control the sports risk, but also conveniently and objectively quantify the students' various indicators.

4 Application of VR Technology in Sports Competition Innovation

Sports events integrate the two attributes of game and performance. Before VR, game competition was almost classified as mental competition without physical ability. After VR, maybe we can start to consider the form of combination. The sports events in VR will not be limited to the existing sports competition forms, but may develop sports events more suitable for VR equipment on the existing basis [12]. For example, table tennis turns the flat table top into a square pipe. The ball does not fly too far, which reduces the range of motion and increases some other possibilities, such as irregular pipes, special effects added for the good ball, different clothes or forms replaced for athletes, and so on.

People are lazy. If they can see, they won't move, and if they can enjoy, they won't work hard. If everyone goes to see, it promotes the performance attribute of sports. In VR, the performance attribute of sports will have more possibilities and greater play space. It is also possible to create new forms of performance.

The VR version of sports events will have greater interest space and give birth to a new model that we can't imagine now. In the VR world, all possible forms of advertising will occur and can not be avoided [13]. What everyone sees can be captured. The data is richer, the information is more transparent, and the information transmission is more direct and effective. Investors can clearly get where every penny of their investment is spent and what results are obtained.

Broadcasting sports events is still a part being explored in the VR world. The existing broadcasting media will rethink how to broadcast the Games in the holographic scene. On the one hand, in a certain trend, VR breaks the perspective choice of the existing media, and the audience will be more free to choose the content and angle they want to watch, and choose the contestants they want to watch close to watch, On the other hand, the problem for the broadcaster is that the audience may be at a loss, do not know where to look best, and have to evaluate and choose by themselves, and too many prompts will be counterproductive. This trade-off is also an issue that broadcasters need to focus on in VR content.

The implementation of force feedback is temporarily difficult to solve. In fierce sports events, the difference between athletes lies in their physical control, psychological and physical. If there are no feedback events such as touch and strength in VR, it is difficult for contestants to grasp their body [14]. For example, if a ball flies over and uses the top of the head and the top of the chest. If you don't know where the top is, you can't make a causal connection between the ejected position and your top posture. In this way, it's difficult to have accurate improvement and training direction. However, at present, this shortcoming can be compensated by new competition forms. For example, most competitions are to exercise mental skills rather than physical control, and turn some key competition objectives into mental thinking competitions. At that time, we can consider things at this time.

Similar technologies such as holoportation are immature. The advantage of the application of holoportation technology in sports events is that what you see is the image of real athletes, and athletes also play real games in real venues, so there is no problem mentioned. However, the disadvantage is that in terms of Technology: at present, the processing rate, capture range, resolution, transmission data star and time delay estimation of this technology can not meet the high requirements of sports event broadcasting [15]. If you want to add some visual effects to the sports itself, the difficulty will not be small; Competition form: This broadcasting will limit the competition form to the current sports competitions, with limited creativity. Training angle: moreover, for training and improving the angle, this technology is broadcast live, athletes will not wear sensors, and image analysis will increase the difficulty. Therefore, it is difficult to capture, analyze and improve the sports data of contestants. However, it still obtains more data than the existing competition forms. After all, you can holographic watch every movement of athletes.

5   Conclusion

The innovative design and application of digital media in sports competition training is not only reflected in the innovative application of text, picture, sound and image, but also in the high-tech improvement and application of physical media. Digital media in sports competition can assist sports training activities and provide technical support. Sports professionals who use digital media in sports training can provide practical suggestions. Therefore, sports competition and training can promote each other. This study focuses on the innovative application of digital media in large-scale events. The research results can provide reference and reference for the digital application of the National Games, so as to improve the organizational innovation ability and event quality of the National Games, and promote the application of digital media in domestic sports competition training activities.

References

1. Pace, F.D., Sanna, A., Manuri, F., et al.: Assessing the effectiveness of augmented reality handheld interfaces for robot path programming. In: EAI ICIDM 2021 - 7th EAI International Conference on Interactive Digital Media (2021)
2. Poon, S.: Designing for urban mobility: the role of digital media applications in increasing efficiency of intelligent transportation management system (2021)
3. Liu, Y., Wu, S., Xu, Q., et al.: Holographic projection technology in the field of digital media art. Wirel. Commun. Mob. Comput. **2021**(3), 1–12 (2021)

4. Nuenen, T.V., Scarles, C.: Advancements in technology and digital media in tourism. Tour. Stud. **21**(3), 146879762199041 (2021)
5. Wulaningratri, G.P., Wardhana, M.I., Hermanto, Y.: Perancangan Desain Web sebagai Media Interaktif Nusantara Wedding Expo. 2021
6. Subathra, P., Elango, M., Subramani, A.: Influence of mental training on aggression and sports competition anxiety among volleyball players. Gorteria **34**(1), 377–382 (2021)
7. Zhao, H., Liu, S.: Tracing mechanism of sports competition pressure based on backpropagation neural network. Complexity (2021)
8. Liang, D., Chen, S., Zhang, W., et al.: Investigation of a progressive relaxation training intervention on precompetition anxiety and sports performance among collegiate student athletes. Front. Psychol. **11**, 617541 (2021)
9. Li, J., Lei, H., Tsai, S.B.: Online data migration model and ID3 algorithm in sports competition action data mining application. Wirel. Commun. Mob. Comput. **2021**(7), 1–11 (2021)
10. Ramsden, R., Hewitt, D., Williams, J., et al.: Tackling student drinking within the drinking subculture of a university sports competition: a culture change approach. Health Education, 2021, ahead-of-print(ahead-of-print)
11. Sun, C., Ma, D.: SVM-based global vision system of sports competition and action recognition. J. Intell. Fuzzy Syst. **40**(2), 2265–2276 (2021)
12. Yg, A., Am, B., Pmk, C.: Recognizing the barriers to the participation of prisoners in sports competition (2021)
13. Guo, X.: Research on advertising marketing in E-sports competition in China. In: E3S Web of Conferences, 235:03040 (2021)
14. Dai, W., Shao, J., Zhang, X.: Research on the design and application of sports competition ticketing platform based on edge computing. Complexity **2021**(2), 1–12 (2021)
15. Zhang, J., Li, D.: The application of artificial intelligence technology in sports competition. J. Phys.: Conf. Ser. **1992**(4), 042006 (5pp) (2021)

Design Teaching and Implementation of Data Mining Algorithm in Business Management System

Mengzhen Hao[1]([⊠]) and Haiqin Shao[2]

[1] Saint Paul University Philippines, 3500 Tuguegarao City, Philippines
2058900819@qq.com
[2] Hebei University of Engineering, Handan 056000, Hebei, China
1626210863@qq.com

Abstract. With the development of information technology and market, database system has been widely used in all aspects. Ensuring the integrity of database has become an important topic in database technology. The emergence of data mining solves this problem. Data mining can find the hidden information in the data, which can assist enterprise managers in decision-making. Business intelligence is the specific application of data mining in enterprises. Therefore, this paper studies the design and implementation of business management system. When the database is attacked, undo and re execute the damaged things is the most commonly used mechanism. This mechanism either stops or greatly limits the database service during the repair period, resulting in unacceptable integrity loss of the database or rejecting the application service with strict requirements, or it will cause more serious damage propagation caused by new things during online data cleaning. In this case, a method to quickly repair database integrity while ensuring database availability is particularly important.

Keywords: Data mining · Business management system · Database

1 Introduction

Data is the source of knowledge. However, having a large amount of data is completely different from having a lot of useful knowledge. Over the past few years, the field of knowledge discovery from databases has developed rapidly. The broad market and research interests promote the rapid development of this field. Advances in computer technology and data collection technology enable people to collect and store information from a wider range and at a speed unimaginable a few years ago.

The quality of business management directly affects the operating efficiency of enterprises. Therefore, finding a reasonable information solution has become the strategic goal of enterprises. The implementation of business management system software has brought great convenience to enterprises. With the application of the system, a large number of original data have been accumulated, which are generally stored and managed through

M. A. Jan and F. Khan (Eds.): BigIoT-EDU 2022, LNICST 466, pp. 177–187, 2023.
https://doi.org/10.1007/978-3-031-23947-2_19

the database system. There are a lot of unknown, potential and valuable information in these massive data. If these information can be expressed, it will have great guiding significance for the daily work of business managers. However, the current database system only accesses and retrieves data records, and the information obtained is relatively "primary". For example, the business management of a quarter is nothing more than adding the business management amount of each month in that quarter. This search only gives play to the simple calculation function of the computer, and it is difficult to obtain the deep-seated mode and prediction information about the overall characteristics of the data and the development trend of the data. Therefore, it is very meaningful to mine useful information from the database, and data mining technology came into being [1].

The research of data mining (DM) has a wide application background and far-reaching theoretical significance. It is one of the hot topics of artificial intelligence and database research at present and in the future. In short, data mining is a process of mining interesting knowledge from a large amount of data stored in databases, data warehouses or other information bases.

With the development of computer technology and network technology, paperless office and enterprise management system have become the mainstream direction of modern enterprise information development, and have gradually penetrated into all walks of life, including all functional branches of modern enterprises. A perfect enterprise management system is no longer the supplement and follow-up to the routine work of the enterprise, and has become the main body of the enterprise work. Using enterprise management system to deal with the actual work has become the mainstream way of work in contemporary enterprises.

Now the functional scope of the enterprise management system is no longer limited to the original information data recording and saving functions. With the increasing complexity, relevance and timeliness of contemporary enterprise affairs, people have higher and higher requirements for enterprise management system.

The primary enterprise management system is mainly used to record and save real data. It mainly uses computer instead of manual to process low-level management transaction information. The computer has the characteristics of large storage capacity, convenient storage, strong repeatability, simple calculation and easy use, so as to realize the paperless working environment of the enterprise. Record the information data related to the basic transactions in the enterprise in the computer through the enterprise management system, so as to achieve better information preservation and exchange functions. This kind of enterprise management system is mainly used in the routine transaction processing of enterprises. It is a record of existing transaction data. It is generally used to record the incoming and outgoing equipment and materials within an enterprise and to record the enterprise transaction data.

The future enterprise management system will be fully intelligent. Automatically create a transaction model, automatically and intelligently learn, and independently judge the authenticity of data and information. Of course, to reach this stage, we need not only development and innovation in software methods and software technology, but also new development and corresponding changes in hardware and thinking mode. At present, this stage is still in the exploration and initial stage.

2 Related Work

2.1 Data Mining Technology

With the rapid development of computer hardware and software, especially the increasing popularity of database technology and application, people are facing a rapidly expanding data ocean. How to effectively use the treasure of this rich data ocean to serve mankind has become one of the focuses of the majority of information technology workers. Compared with the increasingly mature data management technology and software tools, the functions of data analysis tools that people rely on can not effectively provide decision makers with the relevant knowledge they need for decision support, thus forming a unique phenomenon "rich data, poor knowledge". In order to effectively solve this problem, data mining technology has gradually developed since the 1980s. The rapid development of data mining technology benefits from the huge data resources in the world and the huge demand for transforming these data resources into information and knowledge resources. The demand for information and knowledge comes from all walks of life, from business management, production control Market analysis, engineering design, scientific exploration, etc. Data mining can be regarded as the natural evolution of data management and analysis technology.

The huge and rapidly growing data collected and stored in many databases has far exceeded human processing, analysis and understanding ability (without the help of powerful tools), so the data stored in the database becomes a "data grave", that is, these data are rarely accessed, As a result, many important decisions are not based on these basic data, but rely on the intuition of decision makers. The reason is very simple. These decision makers do not have appropriate tools to help them extract the required information and knowledge from the data. Data mining tools can help to find the specific patterns and laws from a large amount of data, so as to provide necessary information and knowledge for business activities, scientific exploration, medical research and many other fields. The huge gap between data and information knowledge urgently needs to systematically develop data mining tools to help transform the data in the "data grave" into knowledge wealth. Figure 1 below shows the data mining process.

2.2 B/S Architecture

In the network structure design of the business management system, the B/S architecture will be selected. The B/S architecture adopts the browser and server mode. The system users can directly access the business customer management system through the Internet, and directly operate the system functions through browsers such as IE or Google. It has good convenience and also meets the technical requirements of the current software system development [2].

In the commercial customer management system, the B/S architecture mainly has three layers: user function interface layer, business logic layer and data layer. The user function interface layer is mainly oriented to users, provides the function interface of software system operation, and provides users with function access and operation. The user function interface layer is mainly arranged in the web server. The middle logic layer is mainly responsible for the system transaction logic management. The transaction logic

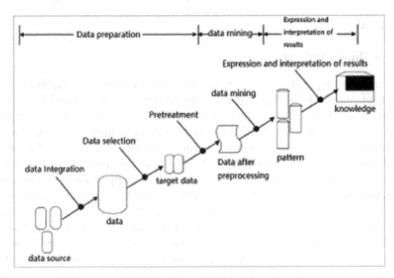

Fig. 1. Data mining process

management of the commercial customer management system is realized by the middle layer and does not need to be arranged at the front end, which is conducive to the management authority protection of the system [3]. The bottom layer is the data layer, which realizes the data management of the commercial customer management system and provides functional interfaces for data storage, modification and query. At present, with its outstanding advantages, B/S architecture has been recognized and applied by the majority of users as a typical structure form. The working principle is shown in Fig. 2:

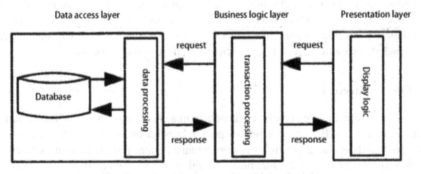

Fig. 2. B/S architecture and working principle

Using b/s model to develop applications has the following advantages.

(1) Almost unlimited client access.
(2) Development modularity.

(3) Deployment and management are extremely simplified and easy to maintain. To update an application, you only need to change a server based program, instead of updating all applications installed on the client as in c/s mode.
(4) The network load is light. The data transmitted between the browser and the server is only the condition and result of calculation, which greatly reduces the network traffic and reduces the network load.
(5) Generally, the software in b/s structure has only one-time initial investment cost; However, the software under c/s structure often requires continuous capital investment with the expansion of application scope.

Information has become an important resource of human society. The development of information technology and its industry has greatly changed the operation mode of traditional enterprises. Intranet is the development direction of enterprise management information technology. The previous management information systems will inevitably need to turn to intranet. Intranet is different from traditional management information system (MIS). It overcomes the disadvantages of traditional MIS in development and application, such as poor standard, difficult system quality assurance, poor system maintainability, long software development cycle, short software use cycle, complex training work, complex user usability, etc.; In addition, because intranet is established by using Internet technology, it has all the advantages of Internet.

The B/S architecture adopted by the commercial customer management system is conducive to the data addition, statistics and other operations of customer management. At the same time, it is also conducive to the access and security protection of system functions [4]. B/S architecture is mainly based on the principle of "low coupling and high cohesion", which can reduce system maintenance and management costs and facilitate system upgrading and expansion. B/S architecture is the most common architecture used in current system development. It is suitable for distributed data structure with large amount of data processing and is conducive to data sharing.

3 Design of Data Mining Algorithm in Business Management System

As a special social and economic system, the movement of enterprise system is to achieve the goal of enterprise. Different enterprises have different goals, and the same enterprise will also have multiple goals. However, there is always a certain gap between the goals of the enterprise and the reality of the enterprise. This gap is the "potential difference" that promotes the movement of the enterprise system, that is, the driving force of the movement of the enterprise system. How to make enterprises operate according to scientific laws is the goal of enterprise management. The gap between the operation status in line with the scientific law and the enterprise operation status is the "potential difference" of enterprise management. Under the conditions of modern information technology and network economy, enterprise digital management can make enterprises conform to the operation law of modern enterprise system. The gap between the scientific operation of modern enterprises and the current situation of enterprises has become the "potential difference" of enterprise digital management. Further decomposing these "potential differences" will form the system dynamic factor to promote enterprise digital management. These system dynamic factors answer the reasons for enterprise digital management.

The system dynamic factors of enterprise digital management mainly come from the change of enterprise management mode caused by the application of modern information technology in enterprise management and the change of enterprise business activities under the network economy environment. Digital management of enterprises is a return to the essence of information activities of enterprise management, and is the internal requirements of enterprise management. Under the conditions of modern information technology, these requirements have been met. The reasonable distribution and flow of information in enterprise organizations is one of the driving factors of digital management. At the same time, enterprises' pursuit of profits is eternal. Profit maximization depends on "export-oriented" growth based on resource investment and "inward oriented" growth based on the improvement of quality and efficiency. Information technology reduces the management cost of enterprises, and fine management brings about the improvement of quality and efficiency, and offers competitive advantages for enterprises, which is another system dynamic factor of digital management.

With the development of mobile Internet technology and software technology, more and more enterprises and adopt information management system to improve management efficiency and service level. Especially with the popularity of smart phones, people are more and more used to using mobile phones to process business [5]. Customer management system provides a good management platform for customer management. While realizing the management of basic customer data, It can make statistical analysis on the customer's behavior and transaction records, classify and summarize the customer's business, facilitate the query of customer data and the statistical analysis of customer data, and provide a good technical means for the current customer management. According to the business process analysis and system design objectives and value realization of the customer management system [6], The customer management system designed and developed in this paper mainly includes six functional modules: customer information and classification management function module, customer behavior statistics and analysis management function module, customer service and consulting management function module, financial management and financial product promotion function module, data visual display and analysis function module and decision-making auxiliary analysis function module. As shown in Fig. 3 below.

In the commercial customer management system, the decision tree algorithm in data mining is mainly used to realize the classification and judgment of customers, determine potential customers, lost customers and customer value analysis. Data mining technology is a common method in database knowledge discovery in various systems. The application of data mining technology in customer management system is mainly to search through the set mining algorithm from a large number of customer consumption data and customer business processing data, and judge the process of valuable data information hidden in the database of customer management system [7]. The application of data mining technology in customer management system is mainly realized by using the technology related to computer science, data statistics, data analysis and processing

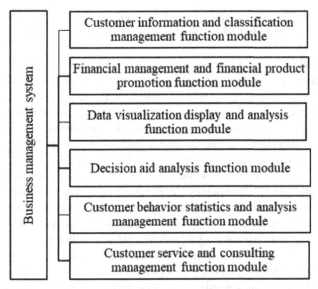

Fig. 3. Business management system design

and data retrieval. The commercial customer management system designed in this paper is mainly realized by decision tree algorithm.

In the commercial customer management system, the main decision tree algorithm is to construct the binary tree of each link data of customer management, analysis and decision-making [8]. In the structure of binary tree, the judgment conditions and results of each node constitute each node of the decision tree, in which the leaf node is the result of decision judgment.

4 Design of Data Mining Algorithm in Enterprise Management System

4.1 Digital Management Becomes an Effective Means for Enterprises to Enhance Their Core Competitiveness

With the intensification of market competition and the improvement of consumer consumption level, as well as the constant change of the internal and external environment in which the enterprise is located. The content and market environment of enterprise competitive advantage have changed. In the industrialization era, standardized products, unified market and long enough product life cycle have formed the competitive content based on scale, cost and quality; In the era of network economy, customer demand is diverse, market competition is changing rapidly, economic globalization, the content of competition has changed into mass customization, production is flexible and dynamic, and dynamic adaptive enterprise system has greater competitive advantage. The market requires enterprises to put (high-quality) products into the accurate market in the first time (quickly), and carry out a new round of design investment through (efficient) information feedback - that is, to realize the gradual transformation from "product centered" to "customer-centered".

Only enterprises with core competitiveness can survive and develop in the market. Core competence, also known as core competence. According to McKinsey & company, it refers to the combination of a series of complementary skills and knowledge within an organization, which has the ability to make one or more businesses reach the first-class level in the competitive field and have obvious advantages. Some scholars define the core competence as one or several abilities that an enterprise has to keep ahead of other competitors in the process of providing customer value. Some scholars also divide the core competitiveness into five aspects: ① knowledge and skills of the company's employees; ② Technology development and innovation capability of the company; ③ Management, production and operation capacity of the company; ④ The company's ability to create and use brands: ⑤ the company's unique culture and values.

Michael Porter put forward the value chain analysis method to determine the core competitiveness. Through the analysis of the enterprise value chain, the core competence value activities and core business processes of the enterprise are defined, and these activities and processes are optimized and reorganized through the enterprise digital management to solidify them in the enterprise management system. Under the guidance of the corresponding rules, the activities and business processes of the enterprise employees will be centered on the core competitiveness, In this way, the core competence of the enterprise can be quickly constructed and realized in the production and operation activities; At the same time, the core competence of the enterprise can be obtained partly through digital management. The knowledge and skills of the enterprise staff, the enterprise digital neural network system and digital knowledge base established through digital management can make the tacit knowledge of the enterprise explicit, and the explicit knowledge can be better shared and disseminated. The learning curve of enterprises is steeper and the learning speed of enterprises is faster. The ability of technology development and innovation based on knowledge and learning ability has been strengthened in the digital management environment. Enterprise management can transcend the limitations of time and space and rapidly deploy and implement advanced management ideas and methods; The establishment of the company's brand and corporate culture can be faster and more effective in the enterprise digital management environment; The digital management of enterprises creates a basic environment for the establishment of core competitiveness. The core competence is based on the general competence of the industry. The general competence can be established and implemented in the enterprise through digital management, creating a negative dissipative structure for the enterprise. In a state far from equilibrium, the establishment of core competence is the same as the fluctuation of internal factors (such as the establishment of core value activities and processes) to achieve a new orderly structure of the enterprise, So as to create a competitive advantage for the development of enterprises in a certain period of time.

In order to reduce the cost, improve the quality and quickly respond to the needs of customers, enterprises must use the existing computer, network technology and software technology to carry out digital management on the product R & D, production, marketing and other processes of enterprises; In order to communicate with suppliers, distributors and customers in real time and accurately, the supply chain needs digital management.

4.2   Establishment of Business Management System

The implementation of enterprise digital management is divided into the following stages: the selection and establishment of enterprise digital management mode, the overall analysis of enterprise digital management, the construction of enterprise digital nervous system, the construction of enterprise digital management, and the application and maintenance of digital management.

The establishment of an enterprise digital management system requires an in-depth and systematic analysis of the enterprise's organizational structure, business process, information content, etc., and summarizes the enterprise's digital management organizational structure, digital management business process model, information structure, etc. on this basis, the enterprise's digital neural system is established through digital means such as the drawing of information network diagram; Then, the functions of enterprise digital management are realized through enterprise digital management software, and deployed in the enterprise organization, so as to establish a digital management system in the enterprise.

The carrier of enterprise digital management is enterprise management information system (MIS). The process of enterprise digital management construction is also the process of enterprise MIS construction. The difference is that the MIS construction here is under the guidance of enterprise digital management thought, which is used to realize the enterprise MIS construction of digital management and the combination of management and technology.

After the realization of enterprise digital management through MIS construction, it will be put into specific application. The application of digital management is interactive development and dynamic change. Digital management has certain flexibility, which can be continuously improved, perfected and grown in the practice of enterprise management. This process is also the maintenance process of enterprise digital management. As shown in Fig. 4.

The realized commercial customer management system will realize the mining and analysis of customer data based on the theory of decision tree. The system will analyze and establish the customer management model based on the customer management theory, focus on the basic data management and encryption processing of customer data, and realize the basic operations such as input, modification, deletion and query of customer data [9]. At the same time, it realizes the analysis of customer behavior records, establishes customer business processing logs, and records the time, type, amount and other data of customer business processing in detail, so as to provide basic data support for customer information mining. The commercial customer management system based on decision tree will also realize customer business consultation and service processing, customer opinion collection and processing, customer data statistics and visual display and analysis. In the customer consultation and service management, the customer consultation processing process will be established to provide data management and mining analysis for customer consultation and reply, as well as satisfaction survey. At the same time, in the customer service, the business reservation and registration function will be

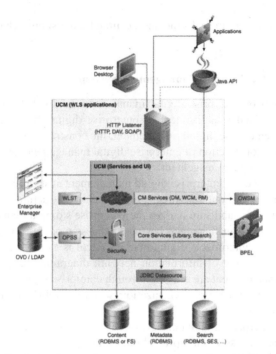

Fig. 4. Structure of enterprise management system based on Data Mining

realized to realize the customer's online reservation and business consultation [10]. The system will also realize the function of business display and promotion, and promote the latest business to registered customers. The commercial customer management system based on the decision tree will also realize the function of visual analysis and display of customer information, classify and summarize the data collected in the system, visually display, visually compare and output the customer management data, provide auxiliary support for data decision-making for the management, and help analyze and determine the business content and focus, Improve the efficiency of business and customer management, increase revenue and realize the improvement of management efficiency.

The customer information and classification management function module mainly realizes the functions of customer basic data management, contact list management and customer classification management, realizes the functions of customer data addition, modification, deletion and query, realizes the functions of contact import and export, contact list update, customer classification statistics, customer classification output and so on.

5   Conclusion

Based on the customer management theory, this paper analyzes and expounds the relevant theories and software development tools involved in the commercial customer management system based on the decision tree, the database design and data management of the customer management system, analyzes the objectives and principles of the customer management system design, tests and analyzes the realized customer management system, and constantly modifies and improves the system functions. The designed customer management system mainly realizes the basic data management and encryption processing of customer data, and realizes the basic operations such as customer data entry, modification, deletion and query. At the same time, it realizes the analysis of customer behavior records, establishes customer business processing logs, and records the time, type, amount and other data of customer business processing in detail, so as to provide basic data support for customer information mining.

References

1. Wood, D.A.: Prediction and data mining of burned areas of forest fires: optimized data matching and mining algorithm provides valuable insight. Artif. Intell. Agric. **5**(2), 24–42 (2021)
2. Cui, Z., An, F., Zhang, W.: Internet financial risk assessment based on web embedded system and data mining algorithm. Microprocess. Microsyst. **82**(3), 103898 (2021)
3. He, B., Yin, L.: Prediction modelling of cold chain logistics demand based on data mining algorithm. Math. Probl. Eng. **2021**(5), 1–9 (2021)
4. Chen, Z., et al.: Data mining algorithm and framework for identifying HVAC control strategies in large commercial buildings. Build. Simul. **14**(1), 12 (2021)
5. Zhang, F.: Construction of internal management system of business strategic planning based on Artificial Intelligence. Inf. Syst. E-Bus. Manage. (19) (2021). https://doi.org/10.1007/s10257-021-00510-x
6. Oberdorf, F., Stein, N., Flath, C.M.: Analytics-enabled escalation management: system development and business value assessment. Comput. Ind. **131**(13), 103481 (2021)
7. Harthy, A.M., et al.: The Use of Structural Equation Model (SEM) to Evaluate the Effectiveness of ISO 9001 Quality Management System (QMS) on the Performance of Oil and Gas Drilling Companies. International Journal of Business and Management, p. 15 (2021)
8. Dharaningtyas, A., Nizar, A.: An analysis on the improvement of system for proof of delivery: PT. Gunadhya Rajawali Logistik. Int. J. Res. Bus. Soc. Sci. (2147–4478). **10**(3), 53–64 (2021)
9. Laage, G., et al.: Estimating the Impact of an Improvement to a Revenue Management System: An Airline Application (2021)
10. Bassi, S.A., et al.: Environmental and Socioeconomic Impacts of Poly(ethylene terephthalate) (PET) Packaging Management Strategies in the EU (2021)

Input and Understanding of Chemical Symbols in Multimedia Education Software

Wei Li$^{(\boxtimes)}$ and Yiping Wang

Yichun Vocational Technical College, Jiangxi 336000, China
18307054939@126.com

Abstract. People's demand for knowledge and skills in work and life will increase day by day. Because multimedia education software has many advantages, such as large information content, diverse forms and strong interactive ability, it is a new teaching medium loved by home. The premise of studying chemical intelligent problem-solving is to study the input, recognition and understanding of various symbols, which is a technical difficulty in multimedia education software. This paper discusses the input of special symbols in chemistry, and designs some algorithms. These algorithms can identify all reactant molecular formulas, product molecular formulas and reaction conditions from the data structure recording a molecular formula, so as to compare and intelligently balance the answers entered by users with the standard answers.

Keywords: Multi-media · Intelligent teaching software · Pattern matching · Intelligent trim

1 Introduction

In recent years, computers have continuously penetrated into people's work, study and life. Multimedia software has developed and increasingly become a powerful helper for people. In the field of education, multimedia software has become a popular new teaching medium because of its large information content, diverse forms and strong interactive ability. Multimedia education software involves all levels of education, starting from early childhood education, covering basic education, higher education, adult education, skill training and so on. Multimedia education software can be divided into stand-alone type and network type according to the equipment used; According to the target, it can be divided into auxiliary teaching and auxiliary learning; According to the function of the software, it can be divided into teaching materials, tools and materials.

An era of knowledge explosion has come. People's demand for knowledge and skills in work and life will increase day by day. Due to the strong interactivity of multimedia education software, people can study more independently without the restriction of time and space on the one hand, and lose the guidance of teachers and experts on the other hand, You can even have real-time or non real-time conversations with the instructor. We have seen that in the information age, non degree education and even some degree education are developing towards running schools online [1].

M. A. Jan and F. Khan (Eds.): BigIoT-EDU 2022, LNICST 466, pp. 188–194, 2023.
https://doi.org/10.1007/978-3-031-23947-2_20

The premise of studying chemical intelligent problem-solving in this paper is to study the input, identification and understanding of various symbols, and then the research of intelligent problem-solving methods. The input, identification and understanding of various symbols is a technical difficulty that has not been well solved for a long time in multimedia education software. As long as this difficulty is solved, it will lay a foundation for intelligent problem solving, which will greatly enhance the interactivity and interest of multimedia education software, and be more conducive to learners to master the content.

2 Cognitive Law of Chemical Symbols

2.1 "Chemical Symbol" is the Basis for the Formation and Development of Chemical Science

Professor Yuan Hanqing, a famous chemical historian, put forward in his book important historical facts of chemistry that chemistry has experienced thousands of years of development. In fact, human society began to use chemical change long ago and made some achievements. Although people at that time did not use the term "Chemistry", they actually had the ability to deal with some chemical changes. He divided the history of chemistry into six periods: prehistoric period, alchemy period, medicinal chemistry period, phlogiston period, quantitative period and mutual penetration period of science. In each of the above periods, there were brilliant chemical achievements and accumulated a lot of chemical knowledge, but some outstanding work in the phlogiston period and quantitative period made the greatest contribution to the development of modern chemical science.

Since then, many chemists' creative research has been related to chemical symbols, the properties and representations of particles. Bezerius not only discovered new elements through experiments and published atomic weight scales, but also creatively used a set of Latin letters to represent element symbols instead of the original pictographic symbols, forming a concise and practical chemical symbol rule, which has been used until now. Many works of bezelius laid an important foundation for future generations in the fields of inorganic chemistry, analytical chemistry, organic chemistry and so on [2]. The periodic law of elements in the resumes of scientists such as Mendeleev and Meyer has become a milestone in the development of chemistry. Before and after the discovery of the periodic law, the history of chemistry can be divided into two distinct times.

2.2 "Chemical Symbols" is the Core Content of Middle School Chemistry Curriculum

The chemistry curriculum standard has made clear provisions on the study of chemical symbols. The national compulsory education chemistry curriculum standard puts forward the goal of "being able to express relevant information in words, charts and chemical language". In terms of content requirements, it specifically stipulates "remember the names and symbols of some common elements", "say the combined valence of several common elements" and "be able to express the composition of some common substances by chemical formula" "Simple calculation of material composition by using relative atomic mass and relative molecular mass", "understanding the law of mass conservation, can explain the mass relationship in common chemical reactions", "can correctly write simple chemical reaction equations and carry out simple calculation".

In the experimental textbook of the national chemistry curriculum standard for compulsory education, it is proposed that "chemical symbols should be used in learning chemistry" from Chapter 1 "opening the door of Chemistry" and Sect. 3 "how to learn and study chemistry", and began to gradually infiltrate element symbols and chemical formulas. Chapter 3 defines elements, valence, chemical formulas and related calculations, and Chapter 4 "quantitative understanding of chemical reactions" This paper discusses the writing of chemical reaction equations and their related calculations, which has been running through the study of the whole grade since then. The chemistry textbook of Shanghai compulsory education sets up a section of "world common chemical language" in Chapter 1 "the charm of Chemistry", which puts forward elements, element symbols and chemical formulas; in Chapter 2 "vast atmosphere" Systematically explain the knowledge of chemical formula, valence, quantity of substance, chemical equation, etc.

2.3 The Teaching Problem of "Chemical Symbols" Has Existed for a Long Time and Needs to Be Broken Through

"Chemical symbols" The resulting learning differentiation has puzzled the majority of chemistry teachers for many years. The research on their effective teaching has been a hot issue of concern for a long time. There are many discussants and reformers. However, due to the complex system engineering involving the content design of chemistry teaching materials, the reform of classroom teaching methods, the cultivation of students' symbolic thinking, the compilation of teaching evaluation tools and so on, it has not been summarized The teaching experience of Chinese students' cognitive law of chemical symbols, which can not increase the burden of students' memory, but also effectively slow down the differentiation of students' chemical learning. "Chemical symbols" Maintaining all the factors related to chemistry curriculum, there are many teaching problems, which is a long-standing practical subject to be broken through. Therefore, this paper studies and analyzes the input and understanding of chemical symbols based on multimedia education software.

3 System Analysis

3.1 Special Symbol Processing

Chemical symbols include not only chemical element symbols, superscripts and subscripts, but also various special symbols representing certain meanings and organic molecular formulas (such as the molecular formula of benzene ring and protein macromolecular chain), as shown in Fig. 1.

These special symbols are obviously difficult to enter with the keyboard, which is the key to the difficulty. An ingenious and easy to learn input method must be designed

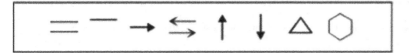

Fig. 1. Special symbol example 1

to make it convenient for users without rich computer knowledge. Solutions: first, use the keys with similar shapes on the keyboard as much as possible. Second, make some bitmap icons for the symbols that cannot be found on the keyboard. Through certain technology, click and input with the mouse to make the input process convenient and fast.

There are a large number of special characters, bitmaps and control characters in the entered chemical symbols, which increases the difficulty of computer recognition and understanding. Some algorithms must be designed. These algorithms can identify all reactant molecular formulas, product molecular formulas, reaction conditions, etc. from the data structure recording a molecular formula, so as to compare and intelligently balance the answers entered by the user with the standard answers [3].

3.2 Intelligent Trim

The intelligent balancing of chemical equations is the main part of chemical intelligent problem solving, which involves the formalization of a large number of chemical knowledge, the standardization of expression forms, the generation and calculation of complex linear equations, etc. in fact, the research of each part is an independent research topic. It can be said that the completion of intelligent balancing opens the door to chemical intelligent problem solving.

4 Treatment of Special Symbols in Inorganic Chemistry

Because inorganic chemistry and organic chemistry have their own characteristics, and the symbols of inorganic chemistry are relatively simple, we first solve the input and identification of symbols of inorganic chemistry. On the one hand, we explore a way to deal with special symbols, and on the other hand, we lay a foundation for the input and identification of symbols of organic chemistry.

4.1 Input Process Design of Inorganic Chemistry Symbols

The input of element symbols, numbers and "+" in chemical symbols is not a problem. It is mainly to design the methods for inputting other symbols (as shown in Fig. 2).

In fact, it is necessary to specify a set of rules and the input method. Through this set of rules, an inorganic chemistry equation can be entered through the keyboard. As long as users remember the regulations, they can master them in a few minutes and will not be difficult to learn. The general structure of the input and identification process is shown in Fig. 3.

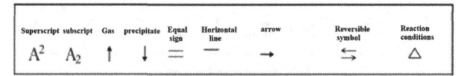

Fig. 2. Special symbol example 2

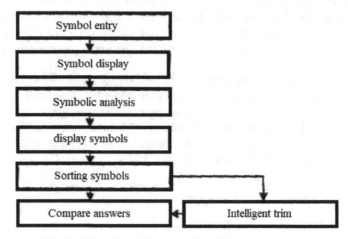

Fig. 3. Flow chart of input and identification procedures

The entered chemical symbols are stored in a string, in which there are special symbols and control symbols. Find the substrings representing molecular formulas from this string and give them a mark to prepare for the next sorting. The algorithms for analysis and recognition vary according to the above rules. According to our rules, an algorithm is given below.

First, the beginning of the string is a substring of the formula; "+", "= =", "-", "< >", "- >" not located at the superscript are all separators. Each substring is marked from front to back until the end.

4.2   Finishing Process Design of Inorganic Chemical Symbols

In a chemical equation, the order of each molecular formula entered by the user and the input order of superscript and subscript of ions are unpredictable, and it is impossible to prepare a standard answer for each possibility. Therefore, it is necessary to sort out the chemical equations entered by the user, and the sorting result will be unique. Therefore, the standard answer will also be unique. The sorting algorithm is actually a sorting algorithm. The sorting algorithm can be diverse, and the sorting basis is also diverse. Our sorting basis is dictionary order.

This process is very simple. Call the sorted string to compare with the standard answer. According to the comparison results, you can know whether the answer entered by the user is correct or not.

4.3 Intelligent Balancing of Inorganic Chemical Equations

The correct chemical equation and ion reaction formula entered by a user is a standard and unique formula after sorting, and the molecular formula or ion formula has been marked, but the coefficient before the molecular formula or ion formula has not been marked. All we have to do is calculate the correct coefficient before each molecular formula or ionic formula. This algorithm is briefly described below:

Firstly, a table containing all element symbols is established to identify various elements in the equation. The difficulty here is how to deal with ions and ion clusters. One way is to treat ion clusters as an "element", which leads to the identification of ions and ion clusters [4]. At the level of alignment, a corresponding table is established for each molecular formula or ionic formula on both sides of the equation to save the coefficients of each element symbol in the molecular formula or ionic formula, such as 2 and 3 in Fe_2O_3.

Using this method, most chemical equations can be balanced, including some simpler redox reactions. As for more complex chemical reaction equations, they need to be further refined, that is, to solve the problems of decomposition of functional groups and maintaining the dependence between elements, as shown in Fig. 4.

Example: $AB2 + C2D = = AD + BC$ trim

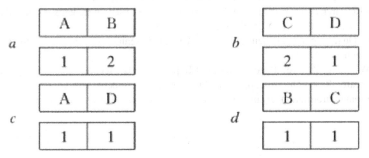

Fig. 4. Intelligent trim

The resulting linear matrix is:

$$\begin{vmatrix} 1 & 0 & -1 & 0 \\ 2 & 0 & 0 & -1 \\ 0 & 2 & 0 & -1 \\ 0 & 1 & -1 & 0 \end{vmatrix}$$

The obtained solutions are: (1 2)
That is, the coefficient of the chemical equation is: 1 1 1 2.

5 Conclusion

In recent years, the development of multimedia intelligent teaching software (ICAD) has become a booming branch in the field of computer application. It can give full play to the advantages of computer and use multimedia technology to diversify information. But in fact, multimedia application technology is quite many and complex. From the perspective of intelligence alone, there are various difficulties in improving the intelligence level in ICAI. For example, most teaching software is a difficult problem in the input and understanding of blank filling questions. This paper studies the input and understanding of chemical symbols in multimedia education software, which lays a foundation for intelligent problem solving, which will greatly enhance the interactivity and interest of multimedia education software, and is more conducive to learners to master the content.

Acknowledgements. General topic of research projects in Yichun Vocational Technical College,Construction and application of chemistry online open course for five-year primary educaiton major in vocational college from the perspective of compound talents cultivation, (No: YZ200202).

References

1. Che, Y., Shen, P., Gou, X., Song, K., Qin, H.: Application Research of Multimedia Textbook Software, Research and Application of Modern Educational Technology – Educational Information Technology for the 21st World. Higher Education Press, Beijing (1999)
2. Fu, Y.: Research on the role of chemical symbols in middle school students' chemical problem solving, master's thesis of Yangzhou University (2006)
3. Shi, W.: On the strategy of chemical symbol teaching in senior high school, chemistry teaching and learning (8) (2010)
4. Cao, W., Jiang, Z.: Web Page Design and Implementation Technology of Multimedia CAI Courseware, Research, Research and Application of Modern Educational Technology – Educational Information Technology for the 21st World. Higher Education Press, Beijing (1999)

Investigation and Analysis on Learning Attitude of Public Pedagogy Under the Background of Big Data

Hong Liang[✉]

Cavite State University, Shandong 276000, China
13153907567@163.com

Abstract. Pedagogy is a very important educational course. It plays an important role for teachers to establish correct educational concepts, master appropriate educational methods and form a certain educational ability. In the process of the implementation of pedagogy curriculum, colleges and universities have different teaching effects due to their different teaching conditions, external environment, management and other characteristics. Some normal students in Colleges and universities do not have a good understanding of pedagogy, their learning enthusiasm is not high, and even have the emotion of learning weariness. These adverse phenomena in the learning of pedagogy by normal students make us have to reflect on pedagogy teaching problems, analyze the reasons and explore countermeasures. Therefore, this paper investigates and analyzes the learning attitude of public pedagogy based on the background of big data.

Keywords: Public pedagogy · Big data · Learning attitude · Investigation and analysis

1 Introduction

In the education sector, big data has sprung up one after another. Altschool, a private school for preschool to eighth graders, attracted legendary Silicon Valley investors such as Facebook founder Zuckerberg and pay pal founder in 2015. They hope to find an answer: can "child-centered" personalized teaching absolutely not operate on a large scale and standardization like public schools? At present, they are successful. If Minerva is trying to subvert the University, alschool is exploring a new model of primary school. Altschool has created a "self-healing" education ecosystem by grasping the existing content and ideas and combining the mining and analysis of big data.

So what is the teaching status of public pedagogy as a course in the context of big data? Are there any problems? According to the personal knowledge and literature, there are the following main problems. First of all, from the perspective of curriculum content, the public pedagogy curriculum content system for vocational preparation of students majoring in normal schools is relatively complex. It integrates the basic principles, pedagogy, moral education and school management, pursues the large and comprehensive

M. A. Jan and F. Khan (Eds.): BigIoT-EDU 2022, LNICST 466, pp. 195–203, 2023.
https://doi.org/10.1007/978-3-031-23947-2_21

system, and lacks the organic integration between content structures, There are few contents that comprehensively use various theories to explore some practical problems of education (Department of Education, Nanjing Normal University 1984). Some contents in pedagogy curriculum often overlap with the teaching theories of various disciplines. What is more serious is that although Pedagogy Textbooks emerge one after another, the latest progress and theories of disciplines can rarely be quickly reflected in pedagogy curriculum. Secondly, from the perspective of the nature and tasks of the curriculum, many people in the educational circles believe that public pedagogy is not only a professional basic course, but also a strong professional practice course, but also a "professional ideological education course", which is obviously a "high expectation" for pedagogy. It can be seen that the opinions of researchers have not tended to be consistent in understanding. Thirdly, from the actual situation of teaching, most schools do not pay much attention to the teaching of public pedagogy. Students reflect that learning is useless and do not solve practical problems. Some teachers do not pay attention to the research of teaching methods and do not mobilize students' enthusiasm for learning. Therefore, this paper investigates and analyzes the learning attitude of public pedagogy based on the background of big data (Fig. 1).

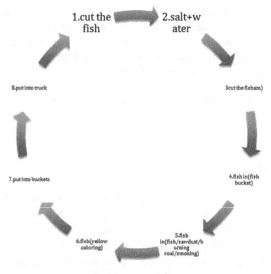

Fig. 1. The overall diagram

2 Related Work

(Suhermanto et al. 2018) usually get quality when (Suhermanto et al. 2018) discuss about industries related to the provision or delivery of services. The aim of (Galishnikova 2018) is to develop, substantiate and test the professional identity formation model of graduates in Pedagogy. Drawing on literature in public pedagogy, social movement learning and communication studies (Walker and Walter 2018) employ ethnographic content analysis to identify emergent patterns, emphases and themes in all online media coverage by the New York Times and Fox News of the Standing Rock protests from April 2016 to March 2017. To present a theoretical model that grounds teaching and learning in nursing in the focus, values, and ideals of nursing as a discipline (Chinn and Falk-Rafael 2018). Dike et al. (2020) aim to develop tacit and explicit knowledge to strengthen the values and attitudes of multicultural education in elementary schools. Unsworth and Mills (2020) show how a linguistic framework describing resources for expressing attitudinal meanings, and its extrapolation to images, informed a multimodal authoring pedagogy designed to extend year five students' repertoires for evaluative expression. Yielded add to the existing literature on the possibility of online learning as an alternative pedagogy in post COVID-19 for the education sector (Sim et al. 2021). The aim of (Alibi et al. 2021) was to identify the forms and methods of teaching physical education from the perspective of the formation of a responsible attitude of schoolchildren to their health, consolidating the skills of a healthy lifestyle in everyday life. Saboowala and Mishra (2021) address the attitude of 313 teachers towards blended learning approach and its six dimensions viz. Other influential work includes (Sharmah et al. 2018).

3   Changes in Teachers' Teaching in the Era of Big Data

The era of big data puts forward new requirements for teachers. First of all, when designing teaching, teachers must design big data experiment and practice in combination with reality. Secondly, teachers should make full use of network resources, use task-based teaching methods and diversified teaching strategies, stimulate learning and problems with innovative technologies and teaching poles, and make full use of team cooperation methods to enable students to learn cooperation, data resource sharing and collaborative learning to successfully complete the task.

3.1   Massive Teaching Resources in the Era of Big Data

At present, internet teaching information resources are quite rich, high-quality courses abound, and famous teacher courseware dazzles people. Therefore, in the era of big data, selecting online learning resources has become an indispensable learning process in the era of big data. At present, many secondary vocational schools have integrated their own school running characteristics, established teaching resources of different scales, and truly realized the learning mode without time and space restrictions by using databases, online learning networks and videos, reflecting the essence of learning, as shown in Fig. 2.

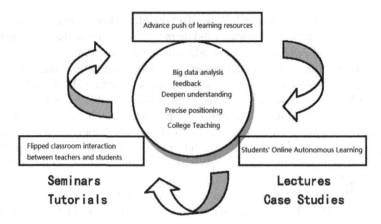

Fig. 2. Teaching mode in the context of big data

3.2 It Is So Simple for University Teachers to Predict, Understand and Evaluate Teaching Behavior According to the Times

In December 2012, the U.S. Department of Education released the report "promoting teaching and learning through educational data mining and learning analysis". The report shows that "at present, there are two applications of big data in the field of education, namely educational data mining and learning analysis". The former refers to "With the help of machine learning, data mining, mathematical statistics and other methods and technologies to analyze and process education big data, and with the help of data modeling, we can find out the relationship between learners' learning resources, content, behavior and results, so as to predict the future learning trend"; the latter refers to "Comprehensively use the theories and methods of sociology, psychology, computer science and other disciplines, process and analyze the big data of broad education, answer some questions that have a significant impact on learners' learning with the help of the existing methods and models, evaluate learners' learning behavior, and transmit artificial and adaptive feedback to learners".

Some studies mentioned that three major changes in learning were triggered by big data: feedback data that was difficult to gather or unrealistic in the past was effectively collected; personalized learning (meeting individual needs of students) could be carried out: the content, method and time of learning can be optimized with the help of probability (Guisheng, 1989). In short, after analyzing and mining education big data, we can explore the learning effect of students and learners in a series of variables such as teaching environment, method, content, time and evaluation, and play a significant role in decrypting the "teaching black box" and improving the teaching quality.

Normal colleges and universities should pay attention to the opening of open courses of pedagogy, especially the opening of courses of pedagogy and psychology, cultivate students' rational teaching attitude and working attitude through relevant courses, and enable students to carry out teaching management more rationally after entering their jobs.

1. At the same time, we should also coordinate the proportion of class hours and add pedagogical courses according to the specific situation, such as teaching theory and teaching method, which can be organized and carried out in the way of combining compulsory courses and elective courses, so as to provide more scientific and effective teaching guidance to students and promote the improvement of students' comprehensive quality.
2. Strengthen practical teaching. The educational work of preschool education major in normal colleges and universities is mostly centered on "teaching". Students often passively accept knowledge and lack learning enthusiasm and creativity.

In this regard, normal colleges and universities should actively carry out teaching reform, effectively adjust the classroom teaching content in combination with the educational development trend of preschool education, design the educational content that meets the development needs of the times and students' learning needs, and organize and carry out appropriate practical activities to realize the transformation from "teaching" to "learning", so as to improve students' learning enthusiasm, Ensure the steady progress of preschool education teaching in normal colleges and universities.

Specifically, the teaching of preschool education in normal universities has the problems of short practice time and insufficient practical activities, which affects the exercise of students' teaching skills and leads to the low overall teaching quality. For this problem, normal colleges and universities should do a good job in the organization and training of practical activities, help students combine the theoretical knowledge learned in the classroom with the actual situation, guide students to analyze and solve problems in teaching practice, and improve their teaching ability. In order to achieve this goal, normal colleges and universities should do a good job in two aspects: educational internship and educational practice, encourage students to participate in educational support activities in winter and summer vacation, or cooperate with some educational institutions to let students go to educational institutions for vacation internship, so as to increase students' practice opportunities, let them accumulate experience in the process of practice, identify deficiencies, constantly improve and improve. We can also coordinate with the surrounding primary and secondary schools to organize students to attend and give lectures regularly, broaden students' vision, improve students' teaching skills and lay a solid foundation for their future development. In a word, practice can better test theory and improve students' comprehensive quality. Therefore, in carrying out teaching reform in normal universities, we must do a good job in the organization of teaching practice activities, so that students can find their own shortcomings in practical activities and remedy them actively and effectively.

In addition to the efforts of schools and students, teachers should also play a role in the process of student training. Teachers in normal colleges and universities should constantly improve their language expression ability and teaching organization ability, so as to effectively cultivate students' moral quality and professional knowledge. In the actual teaching, teachers should reasonably grasp the teaching materials, conduct in-depth research on the teaching materials, and design more high-quality teaching contents according to the teaching materials. In addition, teachers should also note that education is not only to carry out knowledge education, but also pay attention to the cultivation of students' comprehensive quality, so as to promote students' all-round development and better be competent for teachers in the future.

4 Attribution Analysis of Public Pedagogy Learning

4.1 Course Objectives Are Not Clear Enough

Curriculum objective is the starting point and destination of curriculum implementation. It is also the basis for the selection of curriculum content and teaching methods. It not only provides the basis for the organization of curriculum and teaching, but also provides the basis for curriculum and teaching evaluation. Therefore, curriculum objective regulates the teaching of a curriculum, and the formulation of pedagogy curriculum objective plays a key role in the compilation of pedagogy teaching plan, curriculum standard and teaching materials Key role. Through investigation and analysis of literature, it is found that one of the main problems in the curriculum objectives of pedagogy is the unclear positioning of curriculum objectives, which has been a problem left over by history. After the founding of the people's Republic of China, the state has stipulated and explained the teaching hours and curriculum of undergraduate pedagogy curriculum, but has not put forward operable specific pedagogy curriculum objectives In this case, pedagogy teaching does not have a clear direction, the subjective randomness of teachers is large, and the due function of pedagogy teaching can not be brought into full play.

The theory of planned behavior is shown in Fig. 3.

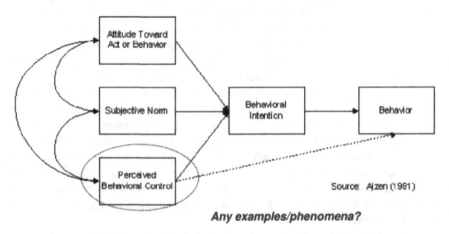

Fig. 3. Theory of planned behavior-Icek Ajzen(1991)

4.2 Unreasonable Educational Curriculum

First, in terms of the setting of educational courses. The survey found that the school's compulsory educational courses include psychology, pedagogy, subject-based teaching method and educational practice. However, the school has a certain randomness in the arrangement of which subjects should start first and which subjects should start later. Generally speaking, although the school has more categories of educational courses for pre service training of normal students However, there are some disadvantages in the setting. In addition, the theoretical subjects and educational practice subjects in the educational curriculum are separated from each other, and the learning of pedagogy does not form a benign interaction with educational practice. This separation of theoretical teaching and practical operation directly leads to the difficulty of normal college students' understanding and mechanical memory, and it is difficult to apply the learned theory to the actual situation, so that students can not perceive it What is the value of these knowledge in solving practical problems, which leads to the blind and passive situation of normal students in learning pedagogy, and even some normal students tend to oppose pedagogy and reject theory (Zhongping, 1991).

Second, in terms of the time setting of educational courses, Herbart once said: "The wrong essence of the wrong theory of freedom and the wrong psychology itself lies in the fact that all kinds of educational fallacies have replaced the real pedagogy. It is difficult for people without correct psychological views to understand the principles of pedagogy. The development process of pedagogy tells us that pedagogy itself is not an independent discipline, but is born out of philosophy and depends on psychology Before the Second World War, pedagogy research was dominated by some viewpoints of these two disciplines. From the current curriculum, the teaching time of pedagogy was arranged in the first semester of grade 3, while psychology was arranged in the second semester of grade 3. Normal students hardly studied formally and systematically before learning pedagogy Psychological knowledge has not formed a certain basic viewpoint of psychology. This "zero psychology" knowledge reserve is bound to cause obstacles to understanding the basic theoretical problems of pedagogy.

5 Some Suggestions on the Teaching Reform of Public Pedagogy

5.1 Theoretical Basis

Constructivism learning theory. Constructivism learning theory is developed on the basis of behaviorism psychology and cognitive psychology, including constructivism knowledge view, learning view, teaching view and student view. Constructivism learning view puts forward changes in learning methods, and advocates that passive learning should change to inquiry learning; individual learning should change to cooperative learning. Its core Psychology The idea is: learning is a process of construction, and learners can use existing knowledge and experience to construct new knowledge. According to the constructivist teaching view, students are not the passive recipients of knowledge, but the initiators of meaning construction. The status of teachers has also changed. Teachers become the instructors and supervisors of students' learning, fully consider students' subjective cognition, carry out teaching design and pay attention to teaching It is a challenge for both students and teachers to construct the situation of learning and pay attention to the communication between activities and subjects.

Subject education theory. In the perspective of subject education, subjects include both individual subjects and group subjects, and subjectivity focuses on people's self-development. According to the viewpoint of subject education theory, in education, we regard the educated as the subject, recognize and respect the subject status of educators, make education an activity with the educated as the subject, and stimulate the autonomy and initiative of the educated Sex and creativity (Ji, 1991). For normal students in teacher pre service education, the construction of normal students' subjectivity lies in improving normal students' subject consciousness and subject activity ability, taking teacher specialization as the yardstick and promoting people's all-round development as the foundation, building normal students' all-round development of educational science knowledge and ability, and laying the professional foundation for teaching in the future.

5.2 Transformation of Traditional Teaching Methods Based on Big Data

High quality teachers, modern teaching means and small class teaching form are important guarantees to improve teaching quality. However, from the results of investigation and analysis, the above practical conditions restricting teaching quality have not been substantially improved. If such teaching conditions are not completely changed, the quality of pedagogy will be improved Teaching quality can only be empty words. Therefore, the state and schools should further increase investment in pedagogy teaching, including improving the teaching level and academic research ability of pedagogy teachers in multiple ways, implementing small class teaching, and configuring relevant teaching aids and multimedia teaching equipment.

In addition, the teaching method directly restricts the quality of teaching. Under the current teaching situation of pedagogy, the discipline construction and textbook construction of pedagogy seem old and closed, the curriculum goal of pedagogy is not clear, and pedagogy implements a single knowledge examination method for evaluation. If teachers do not pay attention to teaching method research and do not try to reform new teaching methods, then It is not difficult for us to understand the decrease in students' satisfaction with the teaching effect. Based on the background of big data, the discipline centered and one-way teaching that regards knowledge as absolute truth obviously can not meet the needs of students, realize the transformation of teachers' role from discipline professionals to promoters and instructors of students' learning, and the student-centered teaching that encourages critical thinking is modern teaching In the specific operation, a variety of methods can be selected according to the characteristics of teaching content and available conditions.

6 Conclusion

In short, the conclusion is a big data background. It is of certain research value to take the learning attitude of college students and teachers as the research perspective, pay attention to their learning mentality, analyze their understanding, emotion and behavior of Public Pedagogy learning, and explore public pedagogy teaching problems and countermeasures. Public Pedagogy Teaching Reform is a long-term and complex systematic project, and it is not easy to get out of the teaching dilemma It is a matter of day and night, and we should think about it from more levels and a wider range.

References

Department of Education, Nanjing Normal University: Pedagogy. People's Education Press, Beijing (1984)

Chen, G.: Perplexity of pedagogy and perplexed pedagogy. J. East China Norm. Univ. (Educational Science Edition) (3), 33–40 (1989)

Hu, Z.: Some views on separating educational theory from practice. Edu. Res. (7) (1991)

Huang. J.: Review and reform of Pedagogy Teaching in public courses in normal universities. J. East China Norm. Univ. (Educational Science Edition). (2) (1991)

Suhermanto, S., Anshari, A.: Implementasi TQM Terhadap Mutu Institusi Dalam Lembaga Pendidikan (2018)

Galishnikova, E.M.: Formation of Professional Identity: Context of Training Graduates in Pedagogy (2018)

Sharma, K.K., et al.: Knowledge attitude practice and learning needs of nursing personnel related to domestic violence against women: a facility based cross sectional survey. Int. J. Commun. Med. Public Health. (IF: 3) (2018)

Walker, J., Walter, P.: Learning about social movements through news media: deconstructing New York Times and Fox News Representations of Standing Rock. Int. J. Lifelong Edu. (IF: 3) (2018)

Chinn, P.L., Falk-Rafael, A.: Embracing the focus of the discipline of nursing: critical caring pedagogy. J. Nurs. Scholar. (IF: 3) (2018)

Dike, D., Parida, L., Aristo, T.J.V., Wangid, M.N.: Strengthening tacit and explicit multicultural knowledge in elementary schools. Int. J. Educ. Vocat. Stud. (2020)

Unsworth, L., Mills, K.A.: English language teaching of attitude and emotion in digital multimodal composition. J. Sec. Lang. Writ. (IF: 3) (2020)

Sim, S.P.L., Sim, H.P.K., Quah, C.S.: Online Learning: A Post Covid-19 Alternative Pedagogy For University Students (2021)

Alibi, L., Torybayeva, J., Kishibayeva, D.D., Zhorabekova, A.: Distance learning situations and the formation of responsible attitudes to health of school children. Cypr. J. Educ. Sci. (2021)

Saboowala, R., Manghirmalani Mishra, P.: Blended Learning: The New Normal Teaching - Learning Pedagogy Post COVID-19 Pandemic (2021)

Multi-color Garment Cutting and Decoupling Optimization Teaching Method Based on Data Mining Algorithm

ShanShan Li[✉]

Shandong Vocational College of Light Industry, Zibo, Shandong 255300, China
464492354@qq.com

Abstract. In order to meet the needs of garment enterprises to reasonably formulate the plan of multi-color garment cutting and dividing bed in the production process, a decoupling optimization method of multi-color garment cutting and dividing bed based on genetic algorithm is proposed. By analyzing the characteristics of multi-color garment cutting and bed splitting problem, the actual production constraints are quantified as constraints, and a decoupling strategy based on data mining algorithm is proposed. Combined with genetic algorithm, the garment production error and the number of cutting beds put into production are optimized at the same time. In the optimization process, the nonlinear optimization problem is decomposed into a series of linear regression subproblems through the decoupling strategy, It reduces the difficulty of the problem and can be solved quickly and effectively, so as to obtain the best multi-color cutting and bed separation scheme, reduce the investment of cutting bed and cloth waste, and maximize the utilization of resources.

Keywords: Multicolor clothing · Cutting and dividing bed optimization · Data mining · Genetic algorithm (GA)

1 Introduction

With the development of modern intelligent manufacturing technology, the transformation of garment industry is facing severe technical challenges, and garment cutting sub bed is one of the core technologies. Clothing cutting and dividing bed is to design a reasonable production scheme for clothing orders by some method under the restriction of production conditions. The production scheme specifically relates to the number of cutting beds to be invested in the garment production process, the combined arrangement of different sizes (size combination scheme), and the number of cloth layers of garment samples of different colors (cloth layer scheme). The scheme of clothing cutting and bed separation is directly related to the utilization of cloth raw materials and the use of cutting equipment. For the same clothing order, the cutting and bed splitting cases obtained by using different bed splitting methods are also different. Therefore, it is of great practical significance for enterprises to improve economic benefits by optimizing the bed separation method and designing an efficient cutting and bed separation scheme, so as to reduce the manual workload and reduce the production cost.

In view of the difficulty of multi-color clothing cutting and bed optimization, this paper proposes a decoupling optimization method of multi-color clothing cutting and bed based on data mining algorithm, which solves the problem of low efficiency of the current multi-color clothing cutting and bed optimization method [1]. Firstly, binary genetic algorithm is used to optimize the number of cutting beds and size combination by linear weighting; Secondly, the decoupling method based on least square (LS) is combined to calculate the corresponding layout layer scheme, so as to avoid the direct solution of high-dimensional optimization problems by genetic algorithm falling into local optimization and improve the solution accuracy and speed. Finally, the proposed algorithm is compared with the existing methods to verify the feasibility and superiority of the algorithm.

2 Data Mining

2.1 Basic Concepts of Data Mining

Data mining refers to extracting people's interested knowledge from a large amount of data stored in databases, data warehouses or other information storage containers. These knowledge is implicit, unknown and potentially valuable useful information. It can be characterized by concepts, rules, laws, patterns, etc. Some scholars believe that knowledge discovery is the whole process of discovering useful knowledge from data, and data mining is a specific key step in this process. It uses special algorithms to extract patterns from data; Other scholars believe that data mining and knowledge discovery have the same meaning, and they can be used without distinction. In fact, they are different. KDD usually includes the following steps; Understand related fields, establish database, data preprocessing, data mining, interpret and evaluate results, and submit the discovered knowledge for use. KDD is a comprehensive process, including test record, iterative solution, user interaction, many customization requirements and decision design. Data mining is only a specific and key step in KDD.

2.2 Data Mining Process

The process of data mining generally consists of three main stages: data preparation, data analysis (mining operation) and result evaluation (expression and interpretation). As shown in Fig. 1.

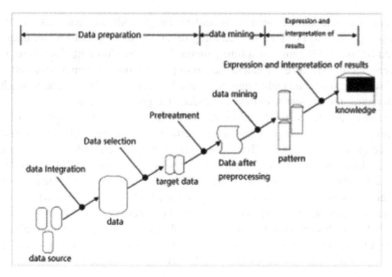

Fig. 1. Data mining process

2.3 Classification of Data Mining

The research of data mining integrates the technical achievements from different scientific fields, which makes the current data mining technology and system show a variety of forms. A clear classification of data mining technology can help potential users distinguish different systems, so as to choose the types suitable for their own needs. From different perspectives, data mining technology has several classification methods: classification according to the type of knowledge found, classification according to the type of database used and classification according to the technology used.

(1) Classification according to the type of knowledge found
Classification methods include: summary rule mining, association rule mining, feature rule mining, classification rule mining, clustering rule mining, outlier data mining, pattern analysis, trend analysis, deviation analysis, etc. A comprehensive data mining system can usually mine the above different knowledge. If the abstract level of mining knowledge is divided into: original level data mining, high-level data mining and multi-level data mining.

(2) Classification according to the type of database used
Data mining is based on relational, transactional, object-oriented, active, spatial, temporal, textual, multi media, heterogeneous databases, legacy systems, and data mining based on data warehouse.

3 Optimization Model of Multi-color Garment Cutting and Dividing Bed

3.1 Problem Description

The optimization problem of multi-color clothing cutting and dividing bed generally refers to the production of multi-color clothing orders on limited cutting equipment. By optimizing the use of the cutting bed, the combination arrangement and layout scheme of clothing samples on the cutting bed are designed as a whole, so as to obtain a cutting scheme with high production efficiency and cost saving. In actual production, garment production cost includes fabric, equipment and labor cost; Fabric cost usually accounts for 50%–60% of the total production cost, and equipment cost and labor cost also account for a large proportion. In order to minimize the production cost and reasonably use the production equipment, the multi-color cutting and bed splitting scheme often can not guarantee the flawless production of clothing orders, that is, there will be clothing production errors. Therefore, garment production error and the use of cutting machine are the general evaluation indexes of multi-color cutting and bed optimization. However, the two indexes are in conflict. Generally, reducing the number of cutting machines will often increase the production error; The pursuit of seamless production requires more cutting beds [2]. It can be seen that the essence of multi-color garment cutting optimization problem is to comprehensively optimize the number of cutting beds and garment production errors, so as to obtain the cutting scheme with the lowest cost.

The multi-color garment cutting and bed splitting optimization problem in this paper is only for garment orders with single style, single fabric, multiple colors and multiple sizes. There is a multi-color clothing order, which needs to cut y colors and N sizes. The output of clothes of the I color and j size is a. the order is shown in matrix A. Assuming that M cutting beds are required for the production of this order, the size combination scheme involved in cloth cutting can be described by the ratio matrix, and the cloth laying layer scheme can be described by the layer matrix. The combination of the matrix is the cutting and bed splitting scheme of multi-color clothing.

$$A = \begin{vmatrix} a_{11} & a_{12} & \dots & a_{1j} & \dots & a_{1n} \\ a_{21} & a_{22} & \dots & a_{2j} & \dots & a_{2n} \\ \dots & \dots & & \dots & & \dots \\ a_{i1} & a_{i2} & \dots & a_{ij} & \dots & a_{in} \\ \dots & \dots & & \dots & & \dots \\ a_{y1} & a_{y2} & \dots & a_{yj} & \dots & a_{yn} \end{vmatrix} \tag{1}$$

3.2 Mathematical Model

This paper establishes a mathematical model with the minimum garment production error and the minimum investment of cutting machine as the optimization goal, as shown below.

$$F_1 = \sum_{t=1}^{y} \sum_{j=1}^{n} \left(a_{ij} - \sum_{k=1}^{m} b_{kj} \times c_{ki} \right)^2 \tag{2}$$

According to the different color quantity of clothing orders, the cutting and bed splitting optimization problem can be divided into monochrome cutting and bed splitting optimization problem and multicolor cutting and bed splitting optimization problem. Their bed splitting schemes can be mathematically described by matrices with different dimensions and mutual coupling. Specifically, the size combination schemes of the two can be expressed by two-dimensional matrix, while the laying layer schemes are different [3]. The matrix column width of the layout layer scheme is the same as the color number of the clothing order. The layout layer scheme of the monochrome problem is a one-dimensional vector, while the layout layer scheme of the multicolor problem is a two-dimensional matrix. The difference of matrix dimension shows that the number of decision variables of the two problems is inconsistent, and the coupling degree between variables is also different. The difference between the two causes the difference in mathematical modeling and solution.

4   Decoupling Optimization Method of Multi-color Garment Cutting Bed Based on Data Mining Algorithm

Aiming at the optimization model of multi-color garment cutting and dividing bed, a decoupling optimization method of multi-color garment cutting and dividing bed based on genetic algorithm is proposed in this paper. Firstly, the size combination scheme and the number of cutting beds with relatively fixed decision space are optimized by genetic algorithm. Secondly, a decoupling strategy based on least square is designed to quickly calculate the layout layer scheme with relatively large decision space in the process of genetic optimization, which not only avoids the high-dimensional optimization problem affected by genetic algorithm from falling into local optimization and improves efficiency; Moreover, it can guide the genetic algorithm to search the optimal solution and improve the accuracy. Finally, the optimal solution searched by the algorithm is decoded to screen the optimal clipping scheme.

4.1   Decoupling Strategy Based on Least Squares

The multi-color garment cutting and bed splitting optimization problem is a high-dimensional optimization problem. Genetic algorithm is easy to fall into local optimization when dealing with high-dimensional optimization problems with many decision variables. Considering the efficiency of least square method in dealing with linear regression problems, this paper proposes a decoupling strategy based on least square, which decomposes the nonlinear optimization problem into a series of linear regression sub-problems, which reduces the difficulty of the problem. Compared with the direct global search using genetic algorithm, this strategy can quickly calculate the layer matrix with relatively large solution space, so as to improve the search accuracy and speed.

4.2   Genetic Manipulation

In this paper, the roulette selection method is used to screen the offspring. The probability of each individual being selected is directly proportional to its fitness, and the best chromosome in this generation is retained to the next generation. Although the selection operator has a certain randomness, it can ensure a certain degree of evolution, so that individuals with high fitness have a greater probability of being selected, which can make the genetic algorithm evolve in a good direction.

After retaining the new chromosome offspring, the population will change. In order to carry out the next iteration, the binary chromosome population should be crossed and mutated. Crossover operator performs crossover operation on individuals by simulating the hybridization process of natural organisms, and constantly produces new individuals. It plays a vital role in expanding the solution space and obtaining the global optimal solution. In this paper, the single point crossover operator is used, that is, the crossover points are randomly generated to exchange the gene loci of parents' chromosomes [4]. The crossover probability is recorded as PA, allowing inbreeding between similar individuals to protect excellent gene patterns to a certain extent. After the crossover operation, the mutation operator has the function of local search in the genetic algorithm, which determines the refinement ability of the algorithm. In this paper, the basic bit variation is used to mutate a gene on the chromosome according to the probability, and the variation probability is recorded as PA.

Genetic algorithm should have stop judgment mechanism. This paper sets two stop mechanisms for genetic algorithm. First, set the maximum number of iterations of the algorithm, and stop the iteration when the algorithm iterates to the maximum number of iterations. Second, the fitness value of the algorithm is unchanged, and the iteration is stopped. After the iteration, the value of the optimal chromosome in the population is output, and the chromosome carries the optimal cutting scheme.

5 Conclusion

The decoupling optimization method of multi-color garment cutting and dividing bed based on genetic algorithm designed in this paper provides a new solution for the problem of multi-color garment cutting and dividing bed in garment enterprises. The proposed method abstracts the cutting bed number and size combination scheme of multi-color garment cutting and dividing bed into the chromosome of genetic algorithm for genetic search. In the search process, the decoupling method based on least square is used to calculate the corresponding laying layer scheme, which reduces the difficulty of solution and improves the speed and accuracy of solution. Through experimental verification, the proposed method can quickly calculate the multi-color garment cutting and bed splitting scheme, effectively reduce the production error and the number of cutting beds, so as to improve the production efficiency and save the cost. For the research work of multi-color garment cutting and bed separation, the multi-objective algorithm can be used to solve the problem that the target weight needs to be set manually in the future, so as to reduce the influence of artificial super parameters on the algorithm. At the same time, how to design more complex personalized multi-color clothing cutting and bed splitting scheme more quickly and consider more detailed actual production factors for more accurate optimization is - a direction worthy of deep exploration.

References

1. Zhou, Z., Fei, S.: Research on cutting allocation optimization system based on annealing ant colony hybrid algorithm. Ind. Control Comput. **27**(11), 3941 (2014)
2. Liu, Y., Yan, S., Ji, Y., et al.: Two stage optimization method for mass customization clothing cutting and bed splitting plan. Comput. Integrat. Manufact. Syst. **18**(3), 479–485 (2012)
3. Jiang, L., Zhou, J., Dong, H.: Research on cutting and dividing bed based on adaptive acceleration factor particle swarm optimization algorithm. Comput. Measure. Control **26** (1), 181–184 + 189 (2018)
4. Zheng, P., Du, W.: Research and development of automatic dividing bed system for garment cutting. Shandong Textile Econ. **11**, 76–79 (2013)

Development of Computer Intelligent Proofreading System from the Perspective of Medical English Translation Application

Yan Zhang[(✉)]

Xi'an Medical University, Xi'an 710021, China
yiyi800510@163.com

Abstract. With the increasing improvement of China's economic status and the increase of foreign exchanges of traditional Chinese medicine, the importance of medical translation has gradually increased. The English translation proofreading system based on phrase and syntax attaches importance to the accuracy calibration of phrase and syntax, fails to solve the problem of poor contextual coherence of English translation, Based on the development and research of computer intelligent proofreading system from the perspective of medical English translation application, this paper provides a scientific teaching idea for English practical teaching, combines translation theory with TCM translation practice, and better guides students' translation practice.

Keywords: Medical English translation · Computer · Intelligent proofreading system

1 Introduction

Since the reform and opening up, China's economy has developed greatly, its international influence has increased significantly, international cooperation and exchanges have become more and more extensive, and medical academic conferences, experience exchanges and medical reports have also increased rapidly. As an important medium of medical communication on the international stage, medical English plays an increasingly prominent role, and its text translation and research become more and more important. Standardized and accurate translation not only helps to learn foreign advanced medical knowledge and medical ideas, but also promotes the dissemination and exchange of medical technology and medical knowledge at home and abroad [1]. At the same time, it is also of great significance for medical English teaching and translation research.

Medical English is a very mixed subject, which covers the grammar of almost all countries in terms of vocabulary. When a thing is first discovered by people in a country, it is named after it in the language of that country. Therefore, both grammar and pronunciation are far beyond the scope of English. The name of this subject is "medical English", um In fact, I don't know who got the name. In short, we must first have a

M. A. Jan and F. Khan (Eds.): BigIoT-EDU 2022, LNICST 466, pp. 211–222, 2023.
https://doi.org/10.1007/978-3-031-23947-2_23

concept, medical English, not English. Then, how long does it take for pure English majors to complete the translation work independently? Let me give you two examples: urgent and serious, and the difference between gout and stroke.

From the above two examples, you will find a problem. I write in Chinese, but it seems that you don't understand what it is in Chinese. Many students in my class are pure English majors. After graduation, it is difficult to learn because of the severe lack of science and engineering knowledge. The first to be eliminated in the class is British and American, which is a very strange phenomenon. Medicine is a dynamic subject, or a four-dimensional subject. Medical literature describes a dynamic process, so we must first know how to combine those things, and then we can accurately translate them.

Theoretically, it will take at least five to seven years to transfer from pure English to medical English. This is why few pure English learners turn to medical English translation. Generally speaking, medical literature is translated by medical learners themselves. Figure 1 below shows the translation of medical English body images.

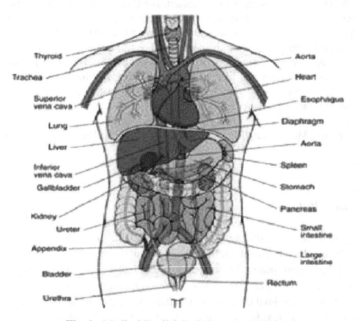

Fig. 1. Medical English body image translation

The development of Internet technology promotes the birth of a large number of English translation software. It is more convenient for people to obtain English translation results. According to its own algorithm settings, English translation software gives English translation results by searching the semantic vocabulary of the whole network. However, the reliability of these English translation results is poor and can not be used directly. A large number of manual proofreading is required in the later stage. There are two major defects in manual proofreading: the manual speed can not keep up with the proofreading demand of English translation results; With a large investment in manual proofreading, a large number of English translation computer intelligent proofreading systems came into being. Feng Zhiwei adopts the English translation proofreading system based on phrase and syntax to proofread the English translation results, paying attention to the accuracy of phrase and syntax, but ignoring the coherence proofreading of context [2]; Li Yegang is an English translation and proofreading system integrating the largest noun phrase in human bilingual. Due to the lack of records of user behavior data, it is difficult for developers to optimize the system according to the user's use. Figure 2 below shows the framework of the English translation computer intelligent proofreading system.

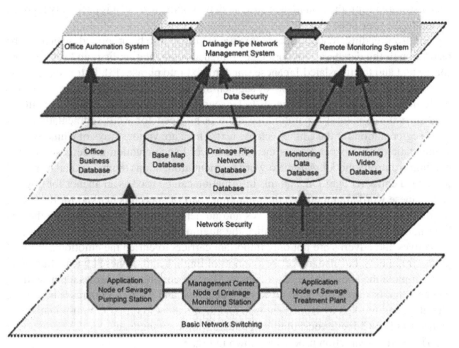

Fig. 2. English translation computer intelligent proofreading system

In view of the problems existing in the above system, based on the development and research of computer intelligent proofreading system from the perspective of medical English translation application, this paper introduces the functions and advantages of the system from two aspects of hardware and software, so as to realize the intelligent proofreading of English translation results.

2 Related Work

2.1 English Translation Computer Intelligent Proofreading Process Design

The process design of English translation computer intelligent proofreading based on phrase translation model mainly includes computer translation and intelligent proofreading. In terms of translation, after the system receives the input source text, it carries out clause preprocessing analysis The sentence segmentation results shall be kept in the state of the whole sentence or phrase, which shall be used as the retrieval unit for input retrieval. Based on the database, the phrases similar to the searched phrases are matched, returned at the same time with the corresponding translation, and sorted according to the similarity. In order to effectively improve the retrieval efficiency and accuracy and facilitate the evaluation of similarity, the system indexes the corresponding corpora of source text and translation through auxiliary translation memory. In addition, the phrase translated by the translator may have high similarity with the phrase translated by other translators, or due to the influence of context, the phrase translated by the translator appears similar reproduction in the subsequent part of the text, so it is necessary to index and store the translated phrase.

For proofreading, load the source text translation text to be proofread, which can be read through the database. Text oriented, sentence segmentation first, and segment the source text and the translated Japanese standard text into phrases [3]. In translation, text segmentation follows the principle of segmenting into the shortest language segments, while in proofreading, the text needs to be segmented into phrases. The spaces in the English text are natural separators, so there is no need for word segmentation, just word segmentation for the Chinese clause text. There are various ways of Chinese word segmentation. This paper selects the Chinese word segmentation mode based on the maximum entropy model. After text word segmentation, nouns or phrases can be parsed for named entity recognition, and this information can be used as an anchor for English and Chinese word alignment. At the same time, part of speech is marked for the text to facilitate the identification of adjectives and numerals, in which numerals are the key information of text fragments to realize the alignment of English and Chinese words; Adjectives and adverbs are not only important carriers to enrich the emotional color of phrase fragments, but also important symbols of English and Chinese lexical alignment.

Complete the above in the text segment After processing, it becomes a phrase fragment set that has been divided into word boundaries, and words and phrases have been identified and marked by named entities, and then begins to propose phrase features to realize English Chinese vocabulary alignment. Moment language.

The feature extraction process is shown in Fig. 3.

For English and Chinese phrases, feature information is extracted according to the above process and described in digital form. In English Chinese bilingual vocabulary alignment, the distance between English and Chinese phrases is calculated by increasing the weight for each dimension, and the phrase distance is evaluated based on dynamic programming method, so as to take the English Chinese alignment model with the minimum phrase distance as the final alignment result [4]. To find the aligned phrases between the source text and the target file, and find the possible inconsistent expressions, that is, editorial errors or omissions in translation, so as to realize intelligent error detection.

The bottom-up proofreading module architecture is shown in Fig. 4.

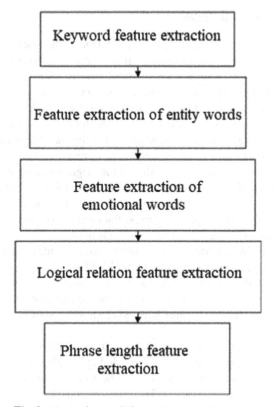

Fig. 3. Phrase feature information extraction process

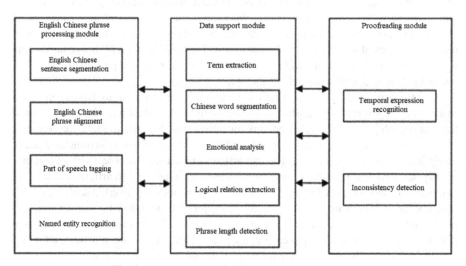

Fig. 4. Bottom up proofreading module architecture

2.2 Medical English Translation

With the improvement of science and technology and the gradual increase of international medical academic exchanges, medical English translation has become a very important subject. The demand for medical English translation is growing. To do a good job in medical English translation, we should not only master the knowledge of medical English, but also have good English level, translation skills and logical thinking ability. The following Fig. 4 shows the translation skills and logical thinking ability.

Firstly, medical English translation requires that the translation be consistent with the original content. The work of translation is to translate one language into another. The meaning of language is the same as that of the original language. Medical English translation is basically the same as translation. We must adhere to the principle of consistency and fluency. Therefore, all translations obtained from medical English translation should accurately and completely express the meaning of the original text without sentence confusion or ideology [5]. The situation is unclear.

Second, medical English translation requires correct grammar and smooth content. In order to better complete the translation of medical English, some grammatical errors should be avoided in the process of translation. Only when the grammar is completely correct can the meaning of the original text be expressed accurately and clearly. Therefore, medical English translators must have good knowledge of English grammar and be able to use it flexibly.

Third, medical English translation needs accurate translation and attaches importance to the translation of professional vocabulary. Medical English vocabulary has unique characteristics. It has strong professionalism. The meaning of many words is strictly limited by matching words and context. Therefore, medical English translation must be based on context and word collocation, combined with the article, give reasonable and accurate meaning, so that the whole translation can proceed smoothly. You can't think that every word has only one meaning. We should speculate according to the context and find the most appropriate meaning. Sometimes, in order to make the article easier to read, some parts of speech need to be converted. This puts forward higher requirements for the translator's medical English vocabulary, and we should pay attention to the understanding and application of vocabulary.

Fourth, in medical English translation, the attitude must be rigorous and pay attention to the sentence structure of translation. Medical English translation is a kind of scientific translation, which has high requirements for translation. In order to make the sentence structure rigorous, the content is logical, and the meaning of words is translated accurately [6]. Because most medical English articles emphasize the objectivity of content, mainly narrative and reasoning, many sentences in medical English articles will take on cumbersome and complex forms, such as passive sentences and inverted sentences. This requires the translator to pay attention to the sentence format, flexible conversion, and not forced translation according to the original sentence. Many medical articles involve personal information such as patient's name and doctor's name, and pay more attention to translation. We should not make mistakes to avoid misunderstanding.

The above are the four key points of how to do a good job in medical English translation, hoping to give some inspiration and help to medical translators. The following Fig. 5 shows the translation skills and logical thinking ability.

Fig. 5. Translation skills and logical thinking ability

3 Design of English Translation Computer Intelligent Proofreading System

3.1 Overall System Architecture Design

The overall architecture of the English translation computer intelligent proofreading system designed in this paper consists of work module, English translation module, English translation proofreading module, search module, user module and behavior log.

The work behavior data generated by the above five modules in the process of English translation intelligent proofreading can be recorded through the behavior log. The setting of behavior log provides a scientific basis for background engineers to view the footprint system in real time, and timely correct the problems existing in the working process of the research system, so as to improve the proofreading performance of the system.

English translation computer intelligent proofreading system is actually an English translation process. By translating English sentences and replacing the incorrect parts of the original translation results, it can realize intelligent proofreading and obtain the correct English translation results as much as possible [7]. The system searches for relevant translation information on the Internet according to the characteristics of the sentences to be proofread and stores it in the work module.

The function of the work module is the basis of intelligent proofreading of English translation. On this basis, it completes the intelligent proofreading of English translation. When the proofreading command is issued, the work module will receive the search link from the translation module. The English translation module will sort the translation results according to the similarity by analyzing the lexical features of the sentences to be proofread, and finally select the most practical translation results. Users can view the translation results at the bottom of the order in the user module for reference.

3.2 Hardware Design

(1) Search module design. The extraction and analysis of lexical features in sentences is the main function of the search module.

  When the search module receives the user input, it immediately launches vocabulary processing Work with feature search. The search module implements the basic meaning acquisition and subject content search of the words to be proofread by constructing the mapping thread [8].

(2) Behavior log. Behavior log is a record of all user behaviors in the system, which is presented in the form of data. When the user performs secondary proofreading, the behavior log records the user's footprint. If users proofread the same English translation many times, the system can intelligently increase the scope of Vocabulary Translation and search for more results that users may need, so as to improve the proofreading performance of the system and increase the accuracy of English translation computer intelligent proofreading.

3.3 Computer Intelligent Proofreading Method Based on Improved Phrase Translation Model

Therefore, the process of computer intelligent proofreading of English translation is actually the process of translating untranslated sentences, comparing and replacing the proofreading results with the initial translation results, so as to realize the intelligent proofreading of English translation [9]. The artificial neural network is introduced into the language model, and the continuous vector can replace the rough frequency with a relatively smooth probability. The model is established as shown in Fig. 6 below.

  This paper defines h as the wrong English translation result and D as the correct English translation result. The transformation from h to D is the process of English translation. The English machine translation method based on the improved phrase translation model is as follows:

$$D = argmaxM\,(D|H) = argmaxM\,(H|D) \cdot M\,(D) \qquad (1)$$

The accuracy of Vocabulary Translation in the results obtained by English machine translation methods needs to be improved, while computer intelligent English translation methods pay attention to the accuracy of vocabulary translation, that is [10], the accuracy of M(d) in Eq. (1). Therefore, on the basis of optimization formula (1) To realize computer intelligent proofreading on, the specific methods are as follows:

$$D^{\backslash} = argmaxM^{\backslash}(D|H)^{\backslash} \qquad (2)$$

In order to facilitate the expression of computer intelligent proofreading method based on improved phrase translation model H is the word to be proofread, and the word to be proofread is represented by D. It is defined that there are p characters in H, represented by H8, which correspond to the vocabulary in the phrase translation model; At the same time, Q characters exist in D, represented by di.

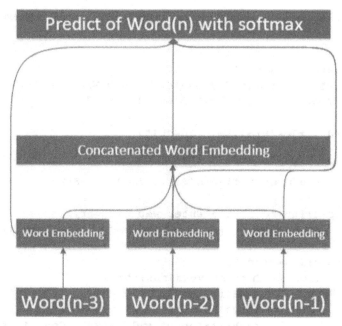

Fig. 6. Build language model

4 System Development

Medical English has experienced three main development stages: Old English, Middle English and modern English. Medical English has experienced several great changes in its long historical development, such as the Renaissance in Europe, the Norman conquest and so on. These events not only had a significant impact on politics, religion, education, justice and other fields in Britain, but also had an impact on the medical cause in Britain [11]. The direct result is that a large number of words and some structures from Latin, Greek and French have entered the medical field, become the main part of medical English, and gradually form a specific lexical structure system, specific grammatical rules and specific discourse structure. Medical English is characterized by accurate wording, objective expression, strict logic, concise writing, clear meaning, fixed meaning, and various strict application documents.

According to the classification of its subjects, medical English belongs to a member of Special English. The so-called special English refers to English related to a specific occupation, discipline or purpose. The difference from general English (also known as general English, mainly for the purpose of teaching language skills) is that special English has unique vocabulary, phrases, syntactic structure, habitual expression patterns and norms; Its purpose is to enable learners to specialize English knowledge and skills in a major or occupation based on general English.

The function of this module is to obtain the required HTML/XHTML web page code from the Internet according to the URL entered by the user, including a mobile phone login page in WML format and the web page code acquisition part of the CGI program called by it. The code of mobile phone login page in WML format is shown in Fig. 7 below:

```
<?xml version="1.0"?>
<!DOCTYPE wml PUBLIC "-//WAPFORUM//DTD WML 1.1//EN"
"http://www.WAPFORUM.org/DTD/wml_1.1.xml">
<wml>
    <card title="Html2Wml" id="01">

        <do type="accept" label="转换">

            <go href="cgi-bin/wap.py?address=$(web_site)">
        </do>
        <p align="center"> Enter web site<br/>
            <input name="web_site" value="" title="web_site"/>
        </p>
        <p align="left">
            <small> Current versions:<br/>
                    html2wml&#x2122; v1.0<br/>
                    <br/>
                    <a href="about.wml">&#xA9; Copyright BTBU
Liujie</a>
            </small>
        </p>
    </card>
</wml>
```

Fig. 7. The Pseudocode for build language model

In page conversion, because the coding of Chinese characters is different from English, page conversion should consider the recognition, conversion and display of Chinese character coding [12].

The character set of XML document is the general character set of ISO10646. At present, this character set is consistent with Unicode. WML inherits the character set of XML document. WML pages do not require full Unicode encoding. Documents that do not use UTF-8 or utf-16 encoding must declare their encoding method in XML (UTF is the abbreviation of Unicode/UCS transformation format).

Unicode is a double byte character that can represent most characters in most languages used today, including Chinese characters that we are most concerned about. UTF-8 is an unequal amplitude encoding method. In UTF-8, ASCII characters remain unchanged and are not affected at all, but other Chinese characters need to be converted by programs. Moreover, a Chinese character needs three bytes to represent. It distinguishes the length of character encoding by setting the highest bit of byte. The first bit of single byte encoding is 0; The first bit of double byte encoding is 110, and the first bit of the second byte is 10; The first bit of the three byte code is 1110, and the first bit of the second and third bytes are 10. The coding principle and characteristics of UTF-8 make it easy to make two-way free conversion between UTF-8 and Unicode. Therefore, they are consistent in coding [13].

The encoding of Unicode is different from Big5 and GB2312 commonly used by us, and the support of some WAP micro browsers for bic5 and GB2312 character sets is not ideal. Therefore, Big5 and GB2312 should be converted to unicode encoding in some cases.

5 Conclusion

Medical English, as a kind of English for science and technology, has strong knowledge and professionalism. In the process of translation, we not only need to have a clear understanding and grasp of the source language, but also need to carry out more translation practice combined with medical professional knowledge. Under the guidance of the translation theory of text typology, analyzing and studying the translation of medical English can not only have a better understanding of the vocabulary and phrase characteristics of medical English, but also better analyze and understand medical English from the sentence level, so as to better promote the dissemination and exchange of medical knowledge, serve medical English teaching and translation research. Based on the development and research of computer intelligent proofreading system from the perspective of medical English translation application, this paper uses translation model to realize the intelligent proofreading of English translation.

Acknowledgements. 2021 Shaanxi Provincial Foreign Language Special Subject "Medical College and University English Curriculum Module Construction and Ability Training of Medical Students" (Project No.: 2021ND0640).

References

1. Upadhyay, U., Chen, Y., Hepp, T., Gatidis, S., Akata, Z.: Uncertainty-guided progressive GANs for medical image translation. In: de Bruijne, M., et al. (eds.) MICCAI 2021. LNCS, vol. 12903, pp. 614–624. Springer, Cham (2021). https://doi.org/10.1007/978-3-030-87199-4_58
2. Paavilainen, P., Akram, S.U., Kannala, J.: Bridging the gap between paired and unpaired medical image translation. arXiv e-prints (2021)
3. Chen, J., Wei, J., Li, R.: TarGAN: target-aware generative adversarial networks for multi-modality medical image translation. In: de Bruijne, M., et al. (eds.) MICCAI 2021. LNCS, vol. 12906, pp. 24–33. Springer, Cham (2021). https://doi.org/10.1007/978-3-030-87231-1_3
4. Larrahondo, B.F., Valencia, J.G., Martínez-Villalba, A.M.R.: Validation of the Self Stigma of Seeking Help (SSOSH) scale in a population of Colombian medical students. Revista Colombiana de Psiquiatría (Engl. Ed.) 50, 82–91 (2021)
5. Tripathi, V.R., Kumar, J.H., Manish, P., et al.: Clinic, community, and in-between: the influence of space on real-time translation of medical expertise by frontline healthcare professionals in marginal tribal communities. J. Prof. Org. 8(3), 3 (2021)
6. Tarek, M., Rahim, C.M., Nazrul, I.M., et al.: Translation, cross-cultural adaptation and validation of the English Lequesne Algofunctional index in to Bengali. Health Qual. Life Outcomes 18, 1–9 (2021)

7. Jespersen, A.P., Lassen, A.J., Schjeldal, T.W.: Translation in the making: how older people engaged in a randomised controlled trial on lifestyle changes apply medical knowledge in their everyday lives. Palgrave Commun. **8**, 1–9 (2021)
8. Min, J.: Research on the application of computer intelligent proofreading system in college English teaching. J. Phys. Conf. Ser. **1915**(3), 032078 (2021)
9. Gao, J., Guo, Z.: Application of text proofreading system based on artificial intelligence. In: Atiquzzaman, M., Yen, N., Xu, Z. (eds.) BDCPS 2020. AISC, vol. 1303, pp. 722–727. Springer, Singapore (2021). https://doi.org/10.1007/978-981-33-4572-0_104
10. Liu, H.: Research on computer simulation big data intelligent collection and analysis system. J. Phys. Conf. Ser. **1802**(3), 032052 (2021)
11. Li, Y., Zhang, M., Chen, C.: A deep-learning intelligent system incorporating data augmentation for short-term voltage stability assessment of power systems. arXiv e-prints (2021)
12. Wu, W., Berestova, A., Lobuteva, A., et al.: An intelligent computer system for assessing student performance. Int. J. Emerg. Technol. Learn. (iJET) **16**(2), 31 (2021)
13. Sabri, Z.S., Li, Z.: Low-cost intelligent surveillance system based on fast CNN. PeerJ Comput. Sci. **7**(11), e402 (2021)

On the Application and Significance of Simulation Technology in Film Creation

Chun Liang Wang[✉]

School of Film and Television Media, Wuchang University of Technology, Hubei 430223, China
`chunliang120150284@163.com`

Abstract. Digital simulation is a process of establishing the corresponding mathematical application model by integrating the overall network of the power system and its load components, and testing and studying the mathematical model on a digital computer equipped with specific software. Simulation technology has gradually developed from mechanical stimulation to computer imaging film and television simulation technology. In the process of modern film creation, the creative techniques of on-site simulation or physical restoration using computer modeling and virtual imaging have been highly recognized by the market. Based on the emergence of simulation technology and its application in film in recent years, this paper deeply analyzes the influence of simulation technology in film creation and explores and prospects its development prospect.

Keywords: Simulation technology · Creative influence · Film creation

1 Introduction

At present, the digital simulation technology based on the digital computers has been widely used in electronic and electrical engineering, computer application engineering, engineering design, etc. the system research based on digital simulation has obtained obvious economic benefits in various application fields, accelerated the rapid development of applied research in various fields, and made great contributions to the development, testing Deployment has an obvious driving role. Since the 21st century, the rapid development of science and technology in China's information industry, including intelligent control systems, complex system research, and the promotion of national defense modernization, all have a wide demand for digital simulation technology. Therefore, the expanded virtual simulation, intelligent digital system simulation, and contemporary military system simulation have been greatly developed. The wide demand promotes the emergence of digital simulation technology science, and high-tech digital simulation technology also promotes the development of digitization, intelligence, networking, and virtualization in various fields. Although the current digital simulation technology is still in the development stage, it has become the backbone of various disciplines.

M. A. Jan and F. Khan (Eds.): BigIoT-EDU 2022, LNICST 466, pp. 223–231, 2023.
https://doi.org/10.1007/978-3-031-23947-2_24

The film has a history of more than 100 years. It was originally invented as technological innovation. Therefore, the film history in the past 100 years can also be regarded as the development history of film technology. There have been multiple creative crises in film history for more than 100 years [1]. The driving force to turn the film industry from crisis to safety, again and again, comes from the development of film technology and the resulting novel attraction. With the development of society and the improvement of people's living standards, audiences have higher and higher requirements for film quality and technology. Simulation technology is one of the important technologies to promote the development of the film. Under the unremitting pursuit of innovation by many film and television workers and the audience's expectation of novel visual effects, simulation technology has gradually developed from mechanical stimulation to computer simulation technology, which plays an increasingly important role in film creation. With its shocking audio-visual effect, Avatar has brought a refreshing feeling to the audience and once became a hot topic. It can be said that the simulation technology widely used in this film has not only promoted the continuous evolution of human appreciation and aesthetics but also promoted the formation of the industrial chain of the film and television industry.

The production of general commercial films can be roughly divided into three steps: first, the work before shooting, including proposing ideas, writing stories, dividing the scene outline, signing directors, making budgets, writing scripts, watching locations, looking for actors, and deciding on the members of the production team. Second, The work in shooting is carried out intensively under the direction of the director, and the executive producer supervises the expenditure, shooting progress, and all administrative matters. Finally, The post-shooting work includes editing, dubbing, music, subtitle design, trailer production, and pre-film publicity. In the process of shooting, the director should have a detailed division plan and draw up the shooting sequence, to achieve rapid promotion under the pressure of changing lights and being dominated by actors. For the selection of cameras and lenses, the display of lights, and the arrangement of cutting and music, the staff must closely cooperate with the director to achieve the desired effect. Therefore, a film is the creation of a group, and it is also a work of in art that the director hides his vision under various tensions. There are few restrictions on the production of privately owned films, and the production method only needs to be determined according to the film type (experimental film, feature film, or documentary film). Or make a detailed mirror division table, shoot according to the intention in advance, to save the film as much as possible; Or endless search for satisfactory shots, and then sort out a clear context from the editing stage afterward. This kind of film is most in line with personal creative desire and has the function of cultivating the mind and improving feelings, the real time digital simulation system is shown in Fig. 1.

Fig. 1. Real time digital simulation system flow chart

2 Composition and Simulation Steps of Digital Simulation Technology

1) Concept and composition of digital simulation technology

Digital simulation is the whole operation process of digital computer simulation. Through a series of digital operations and simulations, a simulation result close to the actual result is obtained. For example, digital simulation technology is widely used in some popular simulation video games. Because the simulation process completely depends on the computer, digital simulation is the abbreviation of digital computer simulation. Contemporary digital simulation has considerable influence in various fields. As early as a few years ago, the US Congress has taken digital simulation as a national resource of legislative protection to promote the development of productivity in various industries. Digital simulation technology includes three elements and three basic activities. As shown in Fig. 2.

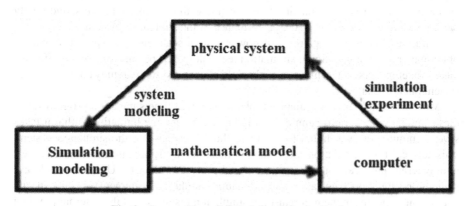

Fig. 2. Composition of digital simulation technology

The overall digital simulation technology includes two modelings and one calculation activity. The first modeling is to convert the actual physical system into a mathematical model, and the second modeling is to convert the simulated mathematical model into a simulation model. The first modeling mainly completes the identification and confirmation of the physical system, so it is called system identification technology; The second modeling involves the programming, verification, and verification of the simulation model, which is called simulation technology. The two are different and closely related to each other. The second modeling process is mainly to constantly modify the model to make it more in line with the actual process. Therefore, digital simulation is also known as the subsequent verification operation of the modeling process.

2) Digital simulation steps

The steps of digital simulation are mainly divided into seven parts. First, it is necessary to establish a mathematical model according to the description and specific requirements of the problem, conduct extensive investigation and Research on the actual physical system that needs to be studied, accurately establish a mathematical model that can describe the problem, and give the relevant performance standards for the evaluation of the simulation system; Second, prepare to establish the corresponding digital simulation model. The mathematical model needs to be improved and simplified according to the characteristics of the actual system, the specific requirements of the simulation, and the actual performance of the digital computer used for the simulation. In this step, appropriate algorithms should be selected to ensure the stability, speed, and accuracy of the calculation process and comprehensively optimize the simulation system; Third, draw the flow chart of digital simulation; Fourth, the design of the digital simulation program needs to transform the digital simulation model into a machine language program that can be recognized and executed by the computer [2]. The program needs to cover the requirements of the simulation experiment, relevant operating parameters, output requirements, and control parameters; The fifth is to test and debug the relevant programs, mainly to test the rationality and optimization of the digital simulation algorithm; Sixth, carry out digital simulation operation and debugging, and carry out relevant experiments; Finally, we need to compare the digital simulation results with the expected results, and finally make an accurate evaluation of the performance of the simulation system.

With the continuous expansion of power system scale and the rapid development of computer technology, digital simulation technology has become one of the effective means for engineers and technicians in the field of power system to study complex power system phenomena.

Most commonly used simulation tools are non real-time simulation programs. For these simulation programs running on digital computers, the limitation is that it takes several minutes or even hours to calculate the 1s response of the simulated system. This non real-time simulation speed can not meet the needs of real-time interactive test with external physical control equipment and protection devices. Usually, people use simulation simulators (such as physical dynamic simulation equipment) or some special equipment to playback the non real-time simulation results to test the external physical control equipment and protection devices.

Simulation simulators are expensive and expensive to operate. It often takes a long time to study a research project. Therefore, simulation simulators are not very popular in the world today. If the playback principle equipment is used as the test means, due to its own technical weakness, its application limitations are obvious. It takes a long time to prepare the required simulation results and cannot realize the closed-loop test. The main advantage of real-time digital simulator is that it can run in real time, and integrates the advantages of digital simulation software and analog simulator.

The emergence of real-time digital simulation system (RTDS) is the product of the development of computer technology, parallel processing technology and digital simulation technology. RTDS itself has many important characteristics: first, the adoption of parallel processing technology and specially designed hardware ensure the real-time operation of RTDS. RTDS can run at 50 μ Real-time simulation of large-scale power system on S-level step size; Secondly, the model and simulation algorithm used by RTDS to simulate various components of power system are based on the recognized standard technology of electromagnetic transient analysis software package which is widely used in modern times.

In order to enable users to concentrate on simulation research without having to worry about how to operate the simulator, RTDs provides a friendly graphical user interface running on the general computer workstation, called PSCAD. Its main functional modules include: allowing users to easily establish the simulated power system, control the simulation operation and analyze the simulation results.

With the continuous maturity of digital technology, today's animation effects and video games are becoming more realistic and realistic. Lifelike animal fur, beautiful hair fluttering in the wind, or Daji coming to you with love have already exceeded the category of "fifty cents". Not long ago, inspired by animation effects, foreign researchers successfully used an advanced computer graphics technology to simulate the motion process of a software robot.

3   The Influence of Simulation Technology on Film Creation

Simulation technology not only brings infinite charm to modern film but also brings innovation to the creative concept of film art. In particular, the development of computer technology provides a variety of possibilities for film creation. What traditional film special effects can do, it can do better and more realistic. What traditional film special effects can't do, it can also be done well. Film simulation technology not only solves some artistic creation bottlenecks but also has a far-reaching impact on the overall texture and artistic communication effect of film pictures.

Firstly, the development of simulation technology further expands the extension of film and television expression and artistic expression forms and provides a technical guarantee for the birth of various types of films. Especially with the progress of technology and the gradual reduction of cost, more film and television image effects and universal applications have become possible. In modern films, computer imaging effectively solves many difficult problems in films that are difficult to shoot or reproduce and uses modern means to show the original appearance of things more truly and clearly. In the film "emergency landing", the wing of the crashed passenger plane crossed the airport terminal. If a real aircraft is used for shooting, its shooting stability and safety factor are not high, which also makes the production cost of the whole film high and the image effect is quite poor. However, the use of simulation technology not only saves costs but also greatly improves the viewability and fidelity of the whole film. The application of simulation technology is not limited to visualization. We use the following formula to explain the visualization.

$$\ln R_u = \frac{\sum_{v=1}^{P} \phi(Z_{uv})(h(Z_{uv}) - \ln \Delta t_v)}{\sum_{v=1}^{P} \phi(Z_{uv})} \tag{1}$$

$$\phi(z) = \begin{cases} z - Z_{min}, & z \le (Z_{min} + Z_{max}) \\ z_{max} - z, & z > (Z_{min} + Z_{max}) \end{cases} \tag{2}$$

$$M_u = \frac{\sum_{v=1}^{p} Q(Z_{uv}) \cdot Z_{uv}}{\sum_{v=1}^{P} Q(Z_{uv})} \tag{3}$$

$$\begin{cases} \omega_s(m, n) = \mu_s(m, n) \\ \omega_k(m, n) = P(\omega_{k+1})\mu_k(m, n) \\ \omega(m, n) = \omega_0(m, n) \end{cases} \tag{4}$$

$$U = \sum_{v}^{a} (f(m_v) - n_v)^2 = \sum_{v}^{a} (x_0 + x_1 m_v - n_v)$$
$$\begin{cases} \frac{\partial U}{\partial x_0} = 2 \sum_{v=0}^{a} (x_0 + x_1 m_v - n_v) = 0 \\ \frac{\partial U}{\partial x_0} = 2 \sum_{v=0}^{a} (x_0 + x_1 m_v - n_v)m_v = 0 \end{cases} \tag{5}$$

Through the application of simulation technology in film and television, almost anything can be virtualized, which makes the theme of film creation infinitely possible. Especially in science fiction films, horror films, and historical films that are difficult to shoot on the real scene, the power of simulation technology can be seen at a glance. Take avatar, the landmark work of 3D film, for example. There are only a few real scenes in the whole story [3]. Most of them adopt simulation technology, and the environment and biology are virtual by using computer imaging technology. Especially in the performance of scenes that do not exist in real life, the expressiveness of computer imaging technology is very powerful. Pandora, no matter the anti-gravity mountain or the vegetation on the planet, can not be found in our real life, and it is difficult to produce it through mechanical simulation technology. At this time, the advantages of film and television simulation technology are highlighted. It can not only reach a very high simulation level, confuse the false with the real when watching on the screen, but also immerse the audience in the virtual scene, As shown in Fig. 3. The Gorilla King Kong in the new version of King Kong is also made by using simulation technology. Its shape is huge and lifelike, which makes the audience feel that the gorilla is a real creature. As a result, most of the audience will sympathize with King Kong when he died.

Secondly, the application of simulation technology has broken through the limitations of traditional film production. Film creators and producers will have more room to play. They will no longer experience multiple restrictions like traditional film teams, and the venues and various light and shadow texture effects will no longer be a headache. "The thief Shichuan five right guards gate" is a complete studio film. In the length of nearly two hours, no scene is taken out for real shooting. The crew set up scenes in the studio and combined them with film and television simulation technology to build an extremely grand Japan in the Warring States period. Of course, most films combine real scenes with post-production. First, some specific scenes required in the film are built by mechanical simulation, and then the post-production effect is produced by combining computer technology. Take the documentary Yuanmingyuan, the first large-scale use

Fig. 3. Avatar

of three-dimensional simulation film animation technology in China. Because there are only ruins on the site of Yuanmingyuan in reality, we can only shoot its basic outline, and then use computer simulation technology to reproduce the appearance of Yuanmingyuan when it was first built, which truly restores a beautiful "Garden of ten thousand gardens", At the same time, it makes a vivid narrative about the rise and fall of its history. It not only satisfies the audience visually but also shows the infinite artistic charm and great cultural value of this mysterious oriental garden in history and science.

Thirdly, the innovation of production technology also pushes back the innovation of script creation. The participation of simulation technology has a direct impact on the writers' artistic imagination and creativity so that the writers' ideas can be brought into full play to the greatest extent. In the process of film creation, technical thought has been reflected in the story outline. The planning and narrative arrangement of the script can make the creator jump out of the traditional linear thinking mode, break the concept of time and space, let the screenwriter lose his hands and feet, and give full play to his artistic imagination and form of expression. For example, the disaster blockbuster 2012 shows the doomsday world scene of the Earth destroyed by the earthquake and tsunami, the earth collapses into bottomless gullies, magma rushes into the streets, and skyscrapers overturn like dominoes; The protagonist Jackson drives his car with his family, who are forced to flee for their lives by the rapidly splitting crust, and then transfers to a small plane to leave the ground and shuttle between overturned skyscrapers. The collapsed city of Los Angeles behind him is slowly sinking into the ocean The film uses more than 500 computer-simulated special effects scenes. The lifelike disaster scenes have shocked audiences all over the world and aroused the pursuit of countless enthusiastic fans [4]. It can also be seen that the shock of disaster film largely comes from the perfect performance of simulation technology. It is undoubtedly an extremely powerful assistant for screenwriters and directors, promoting the development of film creation to unlimited possibilities.

In short, the importance of simulation technology for film creation is self-evident. Compared with the crude scenes in previous films, film and television simulation technology not only enhances its realism, enriches and expands the connotation and extension of film creation but also arouses the audience's excitement and resonance for the film.

Simulation is a technology that converts the model containing deterministic laws and complete mechanisms into software to simulate the physical world. As long as the model is correct and has complete input information and environmental data, it can basically correctly reflect the characteristics and parameters of the physical world. If the modeling of things is our understanding of the physical world or problems, then simulation is to verify and confirm the correctness and effectiveness of this understanding. The technology allows industrial enterprises to test various decisions, strategies and regulations in the virtual factory in a low-cost and zero risk way to verify the operation of different schemes. The main application areas of simulation technology in the industrial field are shown in Fig. 1, which mainly includes three categories, namely, tools, operation and industrial control.

4   Conclusion

China's film and television industries are developing by leaps and bounds. For a populous country, the demand for films can be seen from the market situation that the annual box office of films exceeds 10 billion yuan and continues to improve. Therefore, the desire for film and television talents, especially technical talents, is increasingly mentioned on the agenda of film development. We should see that the gap between the western scientific and technological level and innovation ability should not always stay in the verbal attention and appeal, but should be implemented, earnestly focus on the exploration and training of professionals, and update technical means and creative ideas. In the future market development of the film and television industry, we will continue to seek nationalized film and television simulation technology with Chinese characteristics and establish distinctive personality marks. Only in this way can we become a real film and television power.

Generally speaking, when testing relay protection products with RTDs, it shall be equipped with a voltage amplifier and current amplifier to amplify the analog output signals of voltage and current simulated by RTDS to replace the secondary side output of Pt and CT in the actual power system. Some corresponding interface circuits or supporting devices are necessary for specific simulation tests. RTDS has been used to simulate the simulation system of the second scheme of medium and long-distance line connection proposed in the technical conditions for dynamic simulation tests of line relay protection products. According to the relevant parameters of each component of the system, such a system has been established in the drawing module. In the real-time simulation, the effects of Pt and CT are compared with those of ignoring Pt and CT, and satisfactory results are obtained. The power monitoring means provided in the real-time operation module are very useful.

At present, most of our use of digital related technologies is to provide more convenient, efficient and low-cost services to the governance of various affairs in the physical world. Therefore, most of what we see are "digital applications", "digital systems" and "digital scenes", rather than "digital world". In other words, the current data has no overall structure and is scattered in all corners of the digital world. However, according to the above four rules, technology is moving the physical world and the digital world towards replication mapping interaction integration. At present, we are building a digital world that is mapped to the physical world, even larger than the physical world. For example, the game industry, including Microsoft, apple, Amazon, Facebook, and Tencent in China are all laying out metaverse, a virtual world parallel to the real world and always online. The so-called meta universe can be imagined as a virtual reality or a massively multiplayer online game (MMOG). In the virtual world, people can play games, chat, shop, take a walk, chat, watch movies, attend concerts and so on. Maybe one day, after shopping in the meta universe and returning to the physical world, express delivery has delivered everything to the door.

References

1. Wen, C.: Analysis of the impact of digital film special effects on screenwriters. Res. Visual Art Theor. (2) (2011)
2. "Nonengineering system" refers to the system formed by itself in the process of nature and human development. For details, see Chapter III of Li Qun's simulation model design and implementation, 1st edn. Electronic Industry Press (February 2010)
3. Xiangzhong, L., Yucheng, H.: Exploration on the cultivation of film special effects talents in the digital age. Modern Film Technol. (4) (2011)
4. Zhishe, C., Shuai, H.: Application of object modeling technology ithe n distributed interactive simulation system. J. Syst. Simul. 9–13 (2000)

On the Design of Student Employment Module in Higher Education Management System Based on Genetic Algorithm

Gao Fei[✉]

Wenhua College, Wuhan City 430074, Hubei, China
Wzx198909@126.com

Abstract. The design of College Students' employment management system is a process from analyzing the working environment to creating an employment management system. The main purpose of this process is to ensure that all aspects are taken into account when creating new or improving existing systems. The design phase includes analyzing and understanding how people perform their work, what problems they have, what information they need, and so on. It also includes setting goals for future development. These goals can be related to internal (employee needs) and external (customer needs). The design of College Students' employment management system based on genetic algorithm is a kind of technology that uses evolutionary principle to design computer programs. The program starts with a set of initial conditions and then uses random changes and selection to evolve its own code over time. Genetic algorithms are used to solve many problems in different fields, such as engineering, economics, biology and so on. In order to solve many problems in the manual management of employment information, the employment information management system software is developed. The software provides a good contact platform for students, parents, tour guides, departments and university employment offices, ensures the safety and consistency of graduates' employment data, improves employment efficiency, and realizes effective tracking of students' employment.

Keywords: Genetic algorithm · Employment module · Systems software

1 Introduction

With the development of China's economic construction, the "first built" management mode has been gradually implemented and popularized in all walks of life. The computer-based management technology has also made rapid development and wide application in all industries and fields. In recent years, with the continuous expansion of the scale of running schools, the number of students and the level of running schools, the management of college students has become increasingly complicated. However, the educational administration management only stays in the use of computers to replace some monotonous and mechanical transaction processing work in the daily educational administration work

© ICST Institute for Computer Sciences, Social Informatics and Telecommunications Engineering 2023
Published by Springer Nature Switzerland AG 2023. All Rights Reserved
M. A. Jan and F. Khan (Eds.): BigIoT-EDU 2022, LNICST 466, pp. 232–242, 2023.
https://doi.org/10.1007/978-3-031-23947-2_25

[1]. For example, with the help of Microsoft FoxPro's Microcomputer version database system technology, some simple and single function data storage and query systems have been established. This situation determines that the data storage and operation of their educational administration management system are scattered, and the system data is often inconsistent, and data loss and system infection are easy to occur [2].

At present, most of the educational management information systems of domestic universities are still in this mode. This makes it difficult for the semi manual management of student information to meet the new requirements, and because of the large amount of information and frequent updates, it brings many difficulties to the information management staff. In a sense, this kind of management not only brings inconvenience to students' management, but also easily leads to the loss of information [3].

The employment competition of college graduates is becoming increasingly fierce, and college students are facing greater employment pressure. Colleges and universities generally offer employment guidance courses, but most of them adopt classroom teaching, and students generally feel that they have not gained much. At present, the employment management data of colleges and universities are divided into two parts: one part is the personal information of students' foreign language training methods and majors reported by the college employment office to the province, and the other part is the employment information of students reported by various departments. Among them, the deployment information of each department basically belongs to manual management and is recorded at any time, which will inevitably lead to data loss in management; In addition, when the employment office knows the student employment data, it needs to be calculated and reported by each system. Therefore, the employment data cannot be unified in time and the data cannot be shared [4]. In order to standardize, systematize and informatization the employment work of our college, the Department of software engineering and the Employment Department of our college have formed a project team to develop the "employment information management system" suitable for higher vocational colleges. The system can support the college employment office and the employment managers of various departments to complete the management of student employment data. Its objectives are as follows: to support the standardized management of secondary employment data of colleges and departments; Support the data sharing between the college employment office and all departments to facilitate modification, output and query. Accurately grasping the employment confidence of college students is helpful to timely grasp the ideological trends of college students, and provides scientific basis for colleges and universities to formulate talent training programs and measures to deal with employment problems. It has strong practical significance. According to the latest statistical data of the Ministry of human resources and social security, the employment scale of university graduates will reach 8.74 million in 2020, an increase of 400000 over 2019 and a new high. Using scientific methods to predict college students' Employment Confidence in time is particularly important for the development of College Students' work. Therefore, in order to make the student management work efficiently and orderly, fully save resources, and achieve the purpose of data sharing, it is necessary to establish a practical and stable college student management system [5]. This paper proposes the design of the student employment module of the higher education management system based on genetic algorithm. Through this system, the communication and information release platform in the campus network can be established, the electronic management of student information and the paperless management of documents can be realized, and all kinds of information can be stored in an orderly manner for convenient management and inquiry, so as to comprehensively and effectively improve the efficiency and effect of student management in Colleges and universities.

2 Genetic Algorithm

2.1 Overview of Genetic Algorithm

Genetic algorithm is a kind of adaptive probabilistic randomized iterative search algorithm evolved from the evolutionary law of Biology (survival of the fittest, survival of the fittest genetic mechanism). In 1975, when engaged in machine learning.

In fact, genetic algorithm refers to the idea of "survival of the fittest and survival of the fittest" in Darwin's theory of evolution, and uses the evolution process similar to biology to provide ideas for solving practical problems. Professor John H. Holland of the University of Michigan in the United States began to put forward his own opinions on the idea of genetic algorithm in 1962. In the face of the complex and changeable living environment, organisms need to constantly change their own conditions and living habits without trying to adapt, and retain the "essence" to discard the "dross". Only when they become strong enough and have more conditions that can meet the living conditions can the population continue to survive. This is the process of biological evolution [6]. The evolution of organisms is not the evolution of individuals, but the evolution of the whole population. The survival of a group should not only stand the test of the environment, but also the competition between individuals among groups is very cruel. The individual competition is mainly manifested in the competition for food. The strong individual can get more food and improve the chances of survival, while the weak individual may lose his life because he cannot get food in the peer competition. A group through the competition between individuals is the process of survival of the fittest.

When using genetic algorithm for system development, follow the following steps:

(1) The system parameters are coded in an appropriate way, and the relatively optimized solution set is transformed into chromosomes for expression;
(2) Determine the initial population of the system;
(3) Define the adaptation function;
(4) Design the genetic operation of the system;
(5) Setting parameters such as controlling population size and probability of genetic operation;
(6) It is determined whether the generated population meets a specified indicator. If it does, the calculation will be exited. If it does not, the operation of calculating the fitness function value will be returned. See Fig. 1 for the specific flow chart.

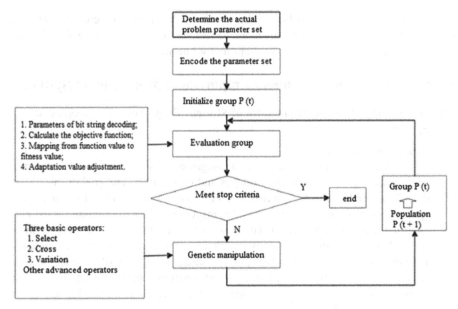

Fig. 1. Flow chart of simple genetic algorithm

2.2 Characteristics of Genetic Algorithm

Genetic algorithm uses the idea of biological evolution and heredity, which is different from the traditional optimization methods such as enumeration method, heuristic algorithm and search algorithm.

Genetic algorithm uses probability search technology. The selection, crossover, mutation and other operations of genetic algorithm are carried out in a probabilistic way, so the search process of genetic algorithm has good flexibility. With the evolution process, the new population of genetic algorithm will produce more new and excellent individuals.

When using genetic algorithm to solve the problem, we can transform it with the process of biological evolution. For example, when we encounter various urgent problems in the algorithm, we can look like the complex environment faced by biological survival; The method used in solving the problem can be regarded as every individual in the evolution process; There are many methods to solve problems in the process of solving, and the fastest and best method to solve problems is the "individual" with the strongest vitality and the best ability to adapt to the environment [7]. The process of solving problems and seeking the best method is actually the process of the environment to eliminate the fittest in evolution. We can gradually find the best way to solve the problem through the selective admission of individuals. The characteristics of genetic algorithm are as follows: Intelligence: it can organize, adapt and learn by itself; Robustness: generally, robust individuals are selected for operation, with certain fault tolerance space; The fitness function is used as the reference condition to solve the problem without adding other auxiliary conditions; When searching for the optimal solution, it does not specify which principle to use; It can be used to solve complex problems with huge data. The disadvantages of genetic algorithm are that the fitness function is difficult to determine, the convergence speed will slow down due to various factors, and the results obtained in the search process may only be local optimal solutions.

3   Analysis of College Student Employment Management System

3.1   Design Objectives and Principles of Student Employment Management System

(1) System design objectives

Student employment information management system is an important part of the information construction in Colleges and universities. The goal of the system should fully reflect the characteristics of the school's strategic objectives and development direction, and serve the school management. With the continuous increase of the number of students enrolled in the school and the huge amount of information, the student management system is required to have high management efficiency. Through such a system, the information of students can be easily queried, statistically modified, and the standardization of information management can be realized, so as to reduce the workload of management and avoid data omission and errors caused by human factors [8].

The goal of this system is to establish an integrated student information database for use by all school offices, make full use of the existing campus network, form a management network covering the whole school among the departments, departments and work departments, form a distributed student management system, realize the query and management of the basic information and management information of students in the whole school, share student information to the maximum extent, reduce expenses, and realize the networking and informatization of student management, Make the student management work flow in the whole school, and improve the management quality and efficiency [9].

(2) System design principles

The system should be uniformly planned, distributed and implemented to meet the informatization requirements of student employment management. The following principles should be followed:

1) Principle of practicality and progressiveness

The system should be based on the long-term goal, so as to adapt to the management objectives of various departments for a long time in the future, make full use of the resources of the existing campus network, and build an advanced distributed management system.

2) Modularization principle

The system adopts modular design and is divided into relatively independent functional modules according to different business functions. Each module completes its own required tasks, so that the system has high coupling and low cohesion. The impact of the change of a single module on other modules is controlled at a low level, so as to minimize the data transfer between modules, eliminate unnecessary dependencies, facilitate the design and development of programs and provide convenience for future system maintenance.

3) Safety principle

The system design shall fully consider the security principle, so that it has the function of identity authentication and authorization management for front-end users, prevent illegal users from entering the system and illegally using the database, prevent data leakage and damage, have good stability, safe and reliable operation, and easy to manage and maintain.

3.2 Design of Student Employment Module in Higher Education Management System Based on Genetic Algorithm

The employment management system software is designed according to the actual work needs of the employment information of a university. By using the employment management system, users can input, query and output the employment situation of students in various departments of the college, avoid many disadvantages of manual management, realize the sharing of employment data and improve work efficiency. The system mainly includes several modules: authentication, data operation, basic data and system maintenance [10]. Authentication mainly completes the authentication of secondary administrators and divides the permissions of different users to use the software; The data operation module mainly completes the input, query and printout of employment student information, employment tracking and data reporting; The basic data module mainly completes the setting of disciplines of each department and the setting of operators of the system. The system maintenance module includes data backup and recovery.

The key of building the combined prediction model is how to reasonably determine the weight value w (I) of each single model. In fact, it is a nonlinear optimization problem.

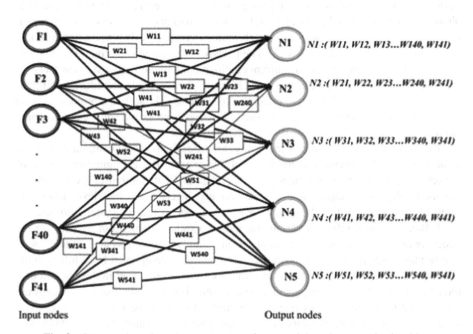

Fig. 2. Construction of employment system framework based on genetic algorithm

Genetic algorithm is especially suitable for solving this kind of problem. For example, the weight value of the text is {0.160,0.004,0.836}, and the prediction performance depends on the prediction results of the third model, which is not conducive to the comprehensive utilization of other model information, resulting in poor applicability of the combined model. In fact, the weight value series is a undetermined probability density function cluster. According to the information entropy theory, under the existing information constraints, the density function with the largest entropy value should be selected from the function cluster, and the density function determined based on this is more objective.

$$C + \sum D_i x_i (W_i + M) \leq R \qquad (1)$$

$$(D_i x_i) \bullet t \geq Q_i \qquad (2)$$

Through the design of the middle school students' employment module of the education management system, the genetic algorithm is used to predict the students' employment rate. The employment rate of a professional student reflects the effect of running a professional school. As shown in Fig. 2 above, the employment system framework under genetic algorithm is built.

At present, the provincial recruitment office counts and tracks the employment rate of students in various majors in Colleges and universities to determine the number of students enrolled in this major in the next year. How do colleges and departments track students' employment? Because once students leave the campus, it becomes very difficult to contact. When the system inputs the student's employment data, it includes the student's home address, contact telephone, student's own e-mail, QQ number, mobile phone, unit telephone and counselor's telephone, e-mail and QQ number. It locks each student's employment destination through multiple groups of data to facilitate timely communication, contact and tracking. The purpose of tracking is to count the employment rate; Second, understand the current employment direction and level of students to feed back to the teaching and professional reform; Third, provide recruitment information and employment assistance to unemployed students. The software provides a good contact platform for students, parents, counselors, departments and college employment offices.

The system configuration design mainly describes the physical configuration composition mode of software and hardware in the system. The configuration design of the educational administration management system is divided into user level, business module level, public component level, data exchange level and database level. User level refers to the user group that the system faces, and users operate the system through this level; Business level refers to various business operations carried out by users in the educational administration management system, mainly including system management, course management and other businesses; The common component level refers to the common components at the bottom of each clock commonly used in the operation of the educational administration management system. For example, the log center is the carrier used to record the daily operation records of users in the system; The database level refers to the storage of various data in the system, and is also used for data backup and restore. The specific system configuration design diagram is shown in Fig. 3.

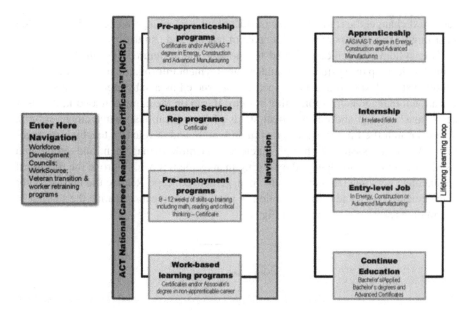

Fig. 3. The structure of college student employment management system

4 Description of Employment Module

The main functions are user data, student information and teacher information. It is divided into three files: password.txt, teacher.txt and student.txt.

The operation of password mainly includes three functional modules of the system: 1. User login module: before starting the system, completely read the password (a user name and password are stored in each line) file, put it into memory, close the file, obtain two strings from standard input, convert the characters into paired characters, and then encrypt them through MD5, Finally, match the data in memory one by one. 2. When the administrator manages teachers and students, after modifying students' student number and password, deleting or adding students successfully, the administrator shall write the password.txt file, mainly including user data, student information and teacher information. It is divided into three files: password.txt, teacher.txt and student.txt. The operation of password mainly includes three functional modules of the system: 1. User login module: before starting the system, completely read the password (a user name and password are stored in each line) file, put it into memory, close the file, obtain two strings from standard input, convert the characters into paired characters, and then encrypt them through MD5, Finally, match the data in memory one by one. 2. When administrators manage teachers and students, they should write the password.txt file after modifying the student number and password, deleting or adding students successfully. 3. When teachers and students modify their own passwords, the password reflects the changes of teachers' or students' passwords.

The operations of teacher.txt and student.txt are the same, so they are explained together. The data stored in these two files are in text file format. If the student scores in teacher.txt change, the student scores in student.txt in mapping number will be updated accordingly. The scores are the public data of teacher and l student.

This system uses object-oriented technology and structured system development method to develop the system. The student employment information management information system designed and developed is constructed as a subsystem of the school's educational management information system. Based on the campus network, it grasps the current research and development status of the educational management system, breaks through the limitations of previous research, and develops a teaching management information system with high efficiency, scientific management and simple and easy to use. In order to change the existing management mode, improve the quality of management personnel and change the management concept; Realize the innovation of management system and informatization of management means; Realize the sharing of information resources, as shown in Fig. 4.

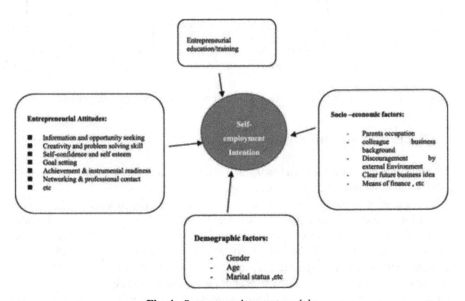

Fig. 4. System employment module

(1) Overall management and sharing of information resources

This application system reasonably classifies and manages information resources (mainly classroom resources and course information) to prevent the situation that some resources are idle and some resources are relatively tight; Realize the rational and efficient application of resources; Based on the campus network, the teaching information is fully shared at a high level in the whole school, which is convenient for the use of teachers and students in the whole school and improves the utilization rate of information resource sharing.

(2) Inclusiveness and scalability

The system shall have good scalability and inclusiveness. For example, it shall be able to accept the existing system and effectively protect the existing investment when the system software and hardware are expanded in the future. The system is easy to expand and upgrade, which can not only meet the current business needs, but also leave room for future expansion.

(3) The system is simple, easy to use, easy to maintain and suitable for non computer personnel

The application system is designed to meet the needs of daily office operation, with complete and practical functions, simple and easy to learn, friendly and clear interface, and easy to expand. The network structure is simple and clear, with clear levels, easy to manage and easy to expand.

(4) Provide good information services for teachers and students

The system has a reasonable layout of information. While providing high-quality and efficient business management and transaction processing, the teachers and students of the school can query the teaching information of the school on any platform to understand the course situation and classroom use. The leaders of the Department can understand the teaching level of the teachers and the teaching effect of the courses.

(5) Adopt advanced and mature technology to establish a practical and reliable system

Whether the construction goal of the system can be realized and whether the whole investment of the system can play its due role will ultimately depend on whether the system is reliable and practical. Therefore, the system should adopt mature and reliable technology, and implement the product design principle and implementation method. At the same time, the starting point of the system should be high, not based on obsolete technologies. The establishment of the system should adapt to the trend of future technology development.

5 Conclusion

Through the design of the student employment module in the higher education management system under the genetic algorithm, this paper solves the problem that the traditional manual management is to calculate the graduate data in each system and report it to the Employment Department of the college. The data of graduates are dynamic, and the data mastered by the employment department can not be updated in time, which brings difficulties to the statistics and reporting work of the employment department. The data sharing of employment offices of departments and colleges has been realized. The computers of all departments are clients, and the server is placed in the Employment Department of the college. All departments input, delete, modify and other information of graduate data at any time are carried out on an employment database. Therefore, the update is synchronous. The power-builder8.0 of Sybase company used in the client provides a special interface with SQL Server database management system in Pb, which is convenient and fast to access the database. Foreign keys are used between related data tables to ensure the legitimacy and consistency of input data.

Acknowledgements. Exploration and Practice on Personalized Employment Education Pattern Based on "4P Career Planning", Program No. 2020XGJPF2007.

References

1. Amar, G.I, Sajidan, S.: The use of creative problem solving based genetic mutation module in higher education. Int. J. High. Educ. **10** (2021)
2. García-Vélez, R., et al.: Automating the generation of study teams through genetic algorithms based on learning styles in higher education (2021)
3. Li, J., et al.: Design of higher education system based on artificial intelligence technology. Discr. Dynam. Nat. Soc. **2021** (2021)
4. Liu, J., Wang, C., Wu, Y.: Construction and optimization of higher education management system based on internet video online technology. Sci. Program. **2021** (2021)
5. Dewi, P., et al.: Technology-enhanced learning research in higher education: a recommendation system for creating courses using the management systems in the e-Learning 5.0. J. Phys. Conf. Ser. **1933**(1), 012125 (5pp) (2021)
6. Zhang, Y.: Optimization of computer teaching strategy based on genetic algorithm. In: CONF-CDS 2021: The 2nd International Conference on Computing and Data Science (2021)
7. Nur, R., et al.: The Integration Model of the Development of Student Religious Character Education Based on Integrative Morals in Higher Education. J. Etika Demokrasi. **6**(1) (2021)
8. Boatman, A., Callender, C., Evans, B.: Comparing high school students' attitudes towards borrowing for higher education in England and the United States: Who are the most loan averse? Eur. J. Educ. **57**(2), 199–217 (2022)
9. Mingoranceestrada, C., et al.: Validation of a questionnaire on the use of Interactive Response System in Higher Education. Rev. Lat. Am. Enfermagem. **29**, e3418 (2021)
10. Wu, J.: The design of project work based on the multiple intelligences in junior high school. J. High. Educ. Res. **3**(2), 160–162 (2022)

Discussion and Practice of Online and Offline Mixed Teaching of Track and Field Course Based on OBE Concept

Xiaoyu Shi[1,2] and Jianxin Zhang[1,2](✉)

[1] Physical Culture Institute, Yili Normal University, Xinjiang 835000, Yining, China
tyfy_zjx@ylnu.edu.cn
[2] Key Laboratory of College Student Physique Monitoring Center, Yili Normal University, Xinjiang 835000, Yining, China

Abstract. The emergence of the "Internet plus education" program has provided an opportunity. In recent years, the government has issued relevant documents in succession, so as to create a new mode of training talents that is suitable for the times and share high-quality educational resources. Especially during the epidemic period of New Coronavirus pneumonia, the online and offline teaching mode plays a vital role in the teaching process of colleges and universities. However, the development of online and offline hybrid teaching is not perfect, which needs further research and continuous improvement by scholars. In response to the implementation of the national "Internet plus education" program, reforming the traditional physical education teaching mode, improving the learning efficiency of students and promoting the development of students' personality, this paper, based on the OBE concept, takes the construction of online and offline blended teaching mode in track and field as the research object. Through the investigation and analysis of the current situation of traditional physical education teaching and the feasibility of online and offline mixed teaching mode of track and field course, this paper provides a basis for the construction and application strategy of online and offline mixed teaching mode of track and field course.

Keywords: OBE concept · Online and offline · Mixed teaching · Track and field course

1 Introduction

The Internet plus plan is proposed by Premier Li Keqiang in the government work report. It is a new form of education, which combines the network and education. Through this form, we share the excellent educational resources and achieve the fairness of education. The development of Internet plus education has played a positive role in the network, and has enhanced the students' ability of learning online. Learn to acquire network information, have the ability to distinguish favorable information and obtain the required knowledge. Students' self-esteem, self-confidence and competitiveness have

M. A. Jan and F. Khan (Eds.): BigIoT-EDU 2022, LNICST 466, pp. 243–253, 2023.
https://doi.org/10.1007/978-3-031-23947-2_26

been increased. Students can exchange learning methods with each other, mobilize students' enthusiasm and initiative, improve learning efficiency, let students really learn to use the network, and play the role of learning knowledge and educating morality [1].

In 2018, the Ministry of Education issued the "2 action plan for education informatization", which proposed the construction of the Internet plus education platform, education of large resources, and the upgrading of information literacy of teachers and students. The new mode of talent cultivation under the condition of "Internet plus" is developed, and the development of new mode of educational service based on Internet is also explored. China's educational modernization 2035 was put forward by the CPC Central Committee and the State Council in 2019, and pointed out that the reform of talent training mode should be promoted by modern technology, so as to realize the combination of large-scale education and personalized training, and improve the three systems of interest distribution, intellectual property protection and new educational service supervision, Digital education resources are jointly built and shared.

According to the data, in recent years, the decline of national students' physique has become a prominent problem, and the myopia rate of teenagers in China has reached 36.5% Obesity also affects the health of teenagers in China. These problems have a certain relationship with exam oriented education, but they are also inseparable from school physical education [2]. Although the traditional physical education teaching model has certain advantages, there are also many problems, which need to be reformed and innovated on the basis of the advantages of the traditional physical education teaching model. With the continuous development of network technology, many researchers combine the advantages of online teaching and offline teaching, The formation of online and offline mixed teaching mode, which has gradually attracted people's attention. This mode is still in the primary stage of development in physical education, and all aspects of development are not very mature, which needs further research.

On June 27, 2017, the world mobile conference was held in Shanghai. China Mobile held a sub Forum on "5g enabled education · wisdom lights up the future" at the conference. The white paper on 5g smart campus was released at the forum, proposing six smart education application scenarios, including education and teaching, education management, campus life, bright campus, education evaluation and 5g characteristic applications. It claims to fully enable the construction of smart campus, marking the opening of the application of 5g technology in education by using 5g, cloud computing, big data, artificial intelligence and other information technology means. In short, with the advent of the Internet era, the state has paid more and more attention to the combination of education and the Internet. From the beginning of the "Internet plus education" plan, the release of education to information policy, and the realization of modernization goals, all countries fully demonstrate the support of the state for blended teaching, and blended teaching will definitely be applied more widely in physical education [3].

By investigating the current situation of traditional teaching of track and field courses, this study finds out the problems existing in the current traditional teaching of track and field courses, analyzes the feasibility of online and offline mixed teaching mode of track and field courses, constructs an online and offline mixed teaching mode framework of track and field courses based on OBE concept, and puts forward application strategies, hoping to improve the problems existing in traditional physical education teaching, Improve students' enthusiasm and initiative in participating in physical education, improve students' learning efficiency, promote students' personalized development, enhance students' health, form the habit of lifelong exercise, improve teachers' teaching effect, improve teaching quality and promote teaching reform.

2   Related Work

2.1   Online and Offline Mixed Teaching Mode of Track and Field Course

The teaching mode is generally composed of five elements: theoretical basis, teaching objectives, realization conditions, operation procedures and teaching evaluation. Teaching models are established on the basis of theoretical basis. Different theories produce different teaching models and play a guiding role in the teaching model: any teaching model points to and completes certain teaching objectives. In the structure of the teaching model, the teaching objectives are in the core position, and the teaching objectives affect the operation procedures and the combination of teachers and students in teaching activities, Feedback on the realization of teaching objectives and improve the implementation process of teaching mode; If the teaching mode wants to achieve the best effect, it needs certain conditions for assistance, such as teachers, students and teaching environment. The realization conditions provide a guarantee for the smooth progress of teaching activities; Each teaching mode has its specific logical steps and operating procedures. It stipulates what teachers and students should do first and then do in teaching activities, and the tasks that should be completed in each step; Teaching evaluation is the evaluation method and standard for the completion of teaching tasks and teaching objectives [4]. Due to the different teaching tasks and teaching objectives, the evaluation methods and standards also change.

The teaching mode has directivity. Each teaching mode is designed around a certain teaching goal. The conditions and concerns of different teaching modes are different. We should pay attention to the directivity of the teaching mode. The teaching model is operational. The teaching model reflects the abstract teaching theory in a simplified form, formulates the activity program framework of teachers and students, stipulates the behavior of teachers and students, and allows teachers and students to have rules to follow and better enter the teaching. The teaching mode has integrity. The teaching mode combines practical teaching with theory. It has a set of complete structure and corresponding completion standards. The teaching mode is stable. The teaching mode is put forward after a lot of practice under a certain background of the times. It reveals the teaching law to a certain extent and has a certain stability. The teaching mode is flexible. The teaching subjects and teaching contents are different, and the details of the operation of the teaching mode will also be changed [5]. The teaching mode can be used flexibly to meet the needs of teaching.

Offline teaching is the traditional face-to-face teaching. Teachers systematically impart knowledge to students and students passively receive knowledge, which mainly reflects the dominant position of teachers. Offline teaching teachers can always supervise students, which is conducive to mastering students' learning status. During offline teaching, teachers communicate with students through body language and facial expressions, which is conducive to emotional communication between teachers and students, and is of great significance to the formation of students' emotional attitudes and values.

Online is a network word, which refers to the combination of physical education and network to form physical education online teaching. Physical education online teaching is a teaching activity in which teachers integrate and optimize physical education teaching resources based on online tools and platforms, and communicate and interact between teachers and students through various forms such as live broadcasting, video broadcasting, class worship, text plus audio, online interactive discussion and so on, so that students can master the learning content. There are four types of online teaching tools and platforms [6]. The first is the course network management platform, which can generally upload, download and use files online, send and receive homework, course data statistics, audio and video real-time interactive functions, such as Mu class, rain class, learning link, etc. The second category is audio and video real-time interactive tools, such as nailing, Tencent conference and other network conference software. The third type is the file upload platform, which can upload, download and play audio and video files online, such as Youku, online disk, email, etc. The fourth category is instant messaging tools, such as wechat group, QQ group, etc. From a practical perspective, online teaching crosses the constraints of time and space through webcast, is no longer limited to the constraints of traditional offline teaching methods, and breaks the barriers of traditional teaching, as shown in Fig. 1. Let students have more choices and choose the courses they are interested in [7]. At the same time, they can also choose the online courses of well-known scholars and experts. Students can use autonomous learning to better develop their subjective enthusiasm and initiative.

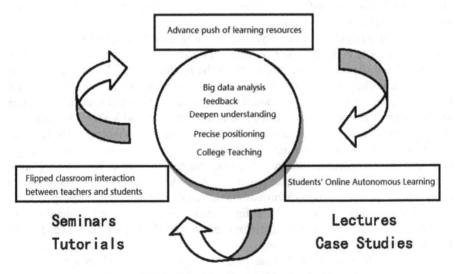

Fig. 1. Internet online teaching mode

To sum up, the online and offline hybrid teaching mode of track and field course is to better achieve the teaching objectives. Under the guidance of humanistic learning theory and constructivist learning theory, based on online tools and platforms, it mainly includes course network management platform, audio and video real-time interaction tool, file upload platform and instant messaging tool, and takes information technology as the means, Integrate and optimize teaching resources, mix online and offline teaching environment, teaching time, teaching space, teaching methods and teaching evaluation, and communicate and interact between teachers and students through various forms such as online live broadcasting, video broadcasting, class worship, text plus audio, online interactive discussion and offline opposite classroom teaching, The teaching activity program that enables students to master the learning content [8]. It has the characteristics of directivity, operability, integrity, stability and flexibility.

2.2 OBE Concept

OBE (outcome based education), also known as outcome oriented education or goal oriented education, is an educational concept put forward by American scholar W.G. Spady in his book "outcome oriented teaching management: from a sociological perspective" to improve the traditional "knowledge oriented" education model, It is defined as "result based education means clearly paying attention to and organizing everything in the education system, and always teaching around the tasks that all students can successfully complete at the end of their learning experience". OBE is an educational concept guided by the goal of expected results to reconstruct, implement and evaluate the teaching content, which shows that teachers need to clarify what is of great significance to students before organizing, implementing and evaluating teaching, and ensure that this learning can be realized finally, that is, taking the learning results as the starting point, reverse design the teaching process. The Education Department of Western Australia believes that the teaching integrated into the OBE concept must focus on the ability needs of students. If it cannot be met, it needs to be overthrown and reorganized. In the teaching process, syllabus and plan are tools to assist students in successful learning, not the ultimate educational purpose.

Although foreign scholars have different definitions of OBE concept, they have the same goal. Its core is to emphasize that teaching should focus on the expected learning results, reasonably design teaching links and optimize teaching activities, so as to ensure that students meet the graduation requirements and master the comprehensive skills they should have in employment. The main idea of OBE concept is a method of planning and evaluating teaching. Managers, teachers and students need to focus their attention and efforts on the expected educational results, and reflect the learning results through students' personal learning results. There are usually two common methods to describe the OBE concept: the first method focuses on students' mastery of relevant knowledge of traditional disciplines and the improvement of comprehensive practical ability, that is, the traditional OBE concept; The second method emphasizes long-term and interdisciplinary achievements, which are directly related to students' future life roles (such as doctors who save the lives and heal the wounded and knowledgeable scholars), that is, the concept of transformation OBE [9]. The OBE concept of this study is more inclined to the former. Firstly, teachers should clarify the abilities that learners should have when they graduate, and design appropriate teaching activities on this basis to ensure that the expected goals are achieved.

3 Teaching Analysis of Track and Field Course

3.1 Research and Development Trend of Track and Field Teaching Method in China

With the advent of the electronic and information age, scientific and technological means are gradually involved in track and field teaching, which has greatly enriched track and field teaching means. The outline of China's educational reform and development points out that the basic objectives of China's educational reform are to optimize the curriculum structure, reform the curriculum content and teaching methods, strengthen the construction of teaching materials, pay attention to the cultivation of students' quality and ability, and enhance students' adaptability to social needs. This points out the development direction for the teaching and research of modern track and field course. The research and development trend of track and field teaching method in China is as follows:

(1) Use modern teaching methods to constantly study and develop new feasible teaching methods. Such as slide projector, video camera, video recorder, tape recorder, electronic computer and other modern teaching means, constantly intervene in path teaching, which can intuitively show students various technical actions and extend students' vision. This is the focus of the research on the teaching method of using path in the future. At present, some scholars have used these modern teaching methods to create "six stage feedback teaching method", "guidance practice questioning interactive teaching method", "three-dimensional animation assisted teaching method", "see, think, discuss and practice" teaching methods.

(2) Pay more attention to the study of students' ability, especially the cultivation of students' automatic ability. Students' ability to find problems, language expression, organization, creation and adaptability, induction and deduction, and self-study are not only the urgent needs of the future society, but also the basis of students' future development. In particular, self-study ability, it has been predicted that in the 21st century, people who will not use computer retrieval and will not self-study will become "illiterate", which is enough to illustrate the importance of ability.

(3) Compatible with the humanities and Social Sciences, the research on the cultivation of students' comprehensive quality has been further developed. Strengthening the humanistic education atmosphere of physical education, enriching the spiritual connotation of students, cultivating students' sentiment, stimulating inspiration and making them have both morality and ability are not only the problems that physical education teaching should face in the future, but also an effective way to cultivate students' comprehensive quality and improve civilization.

(4) Teaching research on the combination of multiple methods and modes. Facing the complex physical education teaching system and the multi-objective and multi-functional characteristics of physical education, it is impossible to solve all the problems only by using one or several teaching modes. Therefore, the future teaching methods must be diverse, which can be used alone or in combination.

3.2   The Main Problems Existing in the Research of Track and Field Classroom Teaching in China

1) "Soviet style" teaching thought. China's physical education system is greatly influenced by the educational thought of the former Soviet Union. The only goal of teaching is to teach sports skills, which is still the thought of some teachers. Reflected in the track classroom teaching, it mainly takes competitive events as the main content, takes teaching sports technology and improving sports technology level as the only teaching purpose, and trains students majoring in Physical Education in the mode of training athletes. Under the guidance of this teaching thought, in order to enable students to form superb sports skills, large amount of sports teaching is generally adopted. The teaching method is a passing on teaching method, emphasizing the control of teachers over students. It should be said that under the guidance of "Soviet style" thought, China's physical education has trained a large number of excellent sports talents. Its main advantages are as follows: (1) strong controllability. This face-to-face teaching method enables teachers to control the teaching rhythm and emphasize teachers' authority according to students' characteristics, teaching materials, information feedback and other specific situations. (2) Intuitive and convenient. Teachers can transfer a lot of knowledge and information in a limited time according to students' acceptance ability and the difficulty of teaching materials.

But its disadvantages are also obvious, mainly in: (1) students practice more physically and think less. Students rely more on teachers and form the habit of only imitating rather than studying. Due to students' less participation in cognitive factors in technology learning, unclear orientation of activities, great blindness of practice and relatively low teaching efficiency, this phenomenon can be made up by relying on a large number of physical exercises under the condition of more technical class hours in the past. However, under the condition of reducing the current technical class hours, students' practice quantity is less and their mastery effect of technology is relatively poor, Technology teachers generally feel that the class is difficult, which makes this problem prominent. (2) It is not conducive to give full play to students' learning enthusiasm and initiative. In order to complete the teaching task and achieve the teaching goal, all teaching activities are under the control of teachers. Teachers and students are in an unequal personality relationship, and students' initiative can not be brought into play; At the same time, a large number of physical exercises make many students afraid of track and field technology courses. Moreover, there are many and boring repeated exercises with track events, students' interest in learning is not high, their awareness of active participation is not strong, their learning motivation is reduced, the quality of practice is not high, and the learning effect is relatively low [10].

In addition, students' interest in track and field and even sports is not high, and their awareness of participation is not strong. Even if they go to society, their attitude will be influenced by other social factors, resulting in low enthusiasm for physical education teaching and management. (3) Due to the reduction of technical class hours, teachers spend most of their time on practice, and students' practical ability can not be exercised. At the same time, due to the lack of depth and breadth of cognitive thinking participation in technical learning, students' cognitive thinking ability can not be exercised, which is not conducive to the development of thinking ability and originality.

2) There are many comparative studies. There are many studies that analyze that one teaching method is better than another. Typically, modern teaching is superior to traditional teaching methods and unilaterally negates traditional teaching methods. Traditional teaching methods, at present and even in the future, are still a teaching means used by teachers, such as explanation, demonstration and so on. The same teaching method has different effects due to the different application skills of the users. "In the teacher's knowledge structure, the teaching guiding ideology determines that he can find the students' psychological preparation in time and adopt corresponding methods and means for regulation, rather than traditional or modern teaching methods and means. Experienced teachers will generally give full play to their organizational ability and teach according to the actual level and psychological state of students.

3) There are few "three-dimensional" research results. That is, there are relatively few research results from the three dimensions of society, psychology and biology". There are relatively many researches on technology teaching from the perspective of psychology. However, many researches only stay at the level of experience, and the introduction speed of the latest achievements in the development of current teaching psychology is slow. On the one hand, because of the implicit psychological activities, it is difficult for researchers or teachers to accurately grasp the students' psychological state, which leads to the fact that the students' psychological state still stays at the level of experience in teaching. At the same time, with the development of sports psychology and physical education teaching psychology, the research on sports skill learning has changed from taking Pavlov's conditioned reflex theory of neuropsychology as the teaching guiding ideology to using sociology, psychology and physiology to comprehensively guide physical education teaching.

Looking at the traditional sports technology teaching and the current track and field technology teaching research, in the research of sports teaching method, the learning of sports skills stays at the biological level, and the research from the three-dimensional aspects of society, psychology and biology is relatively few, The learning mechanism of sports skills abroad has been "three-dimensional" "comprehensive research", which is very inconsistent with the requirements of vigorously promoting quality education and innovative education, advocating respect for teaching subjects and making students develop in an all-round way.

4 Online and Offline Mixed Teaching of Track and Field Courses Based on OBE Concept

The teaching model was first proposed by Joyce and Weill of the United States. They summarized the structure of the teaching model into five elements: theoretical basis, teaching objectives, realization conditions, operation procedures and teaching evaluation. These five elements are not independent of each other, but they operate together,

This study constructs the online and offline hybrid teaching model of junior middle school physical education from these five elements, as shown in Fig. 2.

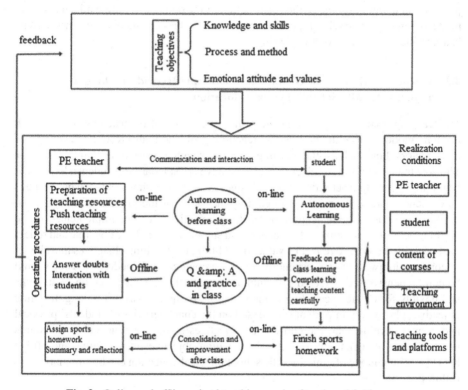

Fig. 2. Online and offline mixed teaching mode of track and field course

4.1   Junior High School Sports Line Theoretical Basis of On-Line and Off-Line Hybrid Teaching Mode

Teaching theory is of great significance to the standardization of teaching behavior. Different theoretical bases form different teaching modes. The online and offline hybrid teaching mode of junior middle school physical education is based on humanistic learning theory and constructivism theory, It is fully seen that these two theories provide theoretical guidance for the construction of online and offline hybrid teaching mode of junior middle school physical education.

The learning view and teaching view in humanistic learning theory emphasize that students' learning is not passive acceptance, but students' independent learning and active participation in learning. The teaching view emphasizes that teachers are only the guides of students' learning, and students are the main body of learning. The idea of constructivist learning theory is not mechanical. Teachers teach students to follow suit. It emphasizes that students take the initiative to learn, use the existing knowledge, actively explore the learned knowledge and construct new knowledge. This study emphasizes that under the guidance of teachers, students need to learn independently and explore new knowledge. These are the needs of the online and offline mixed teaching design of junior middle school sports, so the construction of the online and offline mixed teaching model of junior middle school sports needs humanistic learning theory and constructivist learning theory as the theoretical basis.

4.2   Teaching Objectives of On-Line and Off-Line Hybrid Teaching Model of Junior Middle School Physical Education

The teaching goal is in the core position in the structure of the teaching model. Each teaching model is to complete a certain teaching goal, and it also restricts the design of other factors. For teachers, the teaching goal is through a series of teaching behaviors. The goal that teachers themselves expect to achieve is a standard for students. Before the beginning of teaching activities, physical education teachers should know what changes may occur in students' emotion, cognition and skills in the process of carrying out teaching activities. The realization of teaching objectives must be implemented in the teaching activities participated by teachers and students. It should be concrete and reflect the feasibility in order to reflect its value. In addition, the teaching objectives must be set in combination with the corresponding teaching contents and conditions. They should be comprehensively considered in combination with the specific situation of students and flexibly formulated according to the situation. In the process of teaching, teaching objectives play a very important role. Based on the characteristics of students' physical and mental development, the curriculum objectives of the new curriculum standards and the needs of social development, the teaching objectives of the online and offline hybrid teaching mode of junior middle school physical education can be summarized as follows:

(1)   Knowledge and skill objectives

Form a good awareness of sports, and be able to more consciously and actively participate in sports activities; Master the basic knowledge of sports and health, and understand the simple technical and tactical knowledge and competition rules of the learned items; Master basic skills and the ability to use techniques and tactics.

(2)   Process and method objectives

Under the guidance of physical education teachers, build knowledge through inquiry learning and autonomous learning, promote students' personalized development, flexibly use learning methods, develop students' physical qualities such as speed, endurance and strength, and improve students' physical health.

(3)   Emotion, attitude and value goals

Learn to regulate your emotions by yourself, establish self-esteem and self-confidence by participating in sports practice activities, and enhance the spirit of unity, cooperation, mutual assistance and fraternity; Fully understand and try different roles, so as to form noble sports moral behavior; Cultivate lifelong sports awareness.

5 Conclusion

Through the analysis of the research history and progress of physical education teaching method and the current situation and development trend of track and field teaching, we find that the traditional physical education teaching method generally adopts the control and learning teaching method, takes technology as the center, pays attention to the strong production of external factors, ignores the excavation of students' internal factors, and in order to complete the teaching task, Exaggerating the leading role of teachers can effectively control the teaching process and rhythm, but it is not conducive to the cultivation of students' personality, independent thinking and creative ability. The "online" + "offline" teaching mode based on OBE concept is a student-centered teaching method. By giving full play to the dominant position of students in the classroom, Comprehensively integrate the advantages of traditional teaching mode and "Internet+" to change the original classroom problems, so as to comprehensively improve the teaching effect, and give full play to the important role of result oriented teaching mode in the teaching system of colleges and universities by selecting platforms, looking for online course resources, designing teaching methods, etc.

References

1. Huang, S., et al.: Teaching reform of obstetrics and gynecology nursing course in higher vocational colleges based on OBE education concept from the perspective of big data. Biomed. J. Sci. Tech. Res. **37** (2021)
2. Jiang, X.: Human tracking of track and field athletes based on FPGA and computer vision. Microprocess. Microsyst. **83**(4), 104020 (2021)
3. Jiang, Z.: Real-time monitoring of track and field teaching based on internet of things and sensors - sciencedirect. Microprocess. Microsyst. (2021)
4. Huang, A., Wang, J.: Wearable device in college track and field training application and motion image sensor recognition. J. Ambient. Intell. Humaniz. Comput. 1–14 (2021)
5. Shi, Y.: Teaching reform of database course based on the concept of outcome-based education. J. Contemp. Educ. Res. **5**(3), 5 (2021)
6. Zhang, X., et al.: Application of design based learning and outcome based education in basic industrial engineering teaching a new teaching method. Sustainability. **13**(5), 2632 (2021)
7. Akyon, F.C., et al.: Track Boosting and Synthetic Data Aided Drone Detection (2021)
8. Zhao, Y., et al.: Track-etch membranes as tools for template synthesis of highly sensitive pressure sensors. ACS Appl. Mater. Inter. **14**(1) (2021)
9. Aea, B., Jkb, C., Jjab, D.: Training in spikes and number of training hours correlate to injury incidence in youth athletics (track and field): a prospective 52-week study. J. Sci. Med. Sport. **25**(2), 122–128 (2022)
10. Thirumoorthy, K., Muneeswaran, K.: An application of text mining techniques and outcome based education: student recruitment system. J. Ambient Intell. Humaniz. Comput. (1) (2021)

Research and Application of Software Testing Method Improvement Based on Big Data Information

Peng Gao[1], GuoXing Chi[1], YuLing Liu[2], and WeiPeng Sun[1(✉)]

[1] College of Mathematics and Data Science (Software College), Minjiang University, Fuzhou 350108, Fujian, China
3197102140@stu.mju.edu.cn

[2] New Huadu Business School, Minjiang University, Fuzhou 350108, Fujian, China

Abstract. In order to improve traditional software testing methods, this paper will study from the perspective of big data information. Firstly, it discusses the necessity of improving software testing methods, then analyzes the application requirements of big data information, and finally puts forward the improvement strategies of software testing methods. Adopting the strategy in this paper can give full play to the role of big data information and improve the software testing method. The improved testing method is more effective, which indicates that the improved strategy in this paper is effective.

Keywords: Big data information · Software testing method · Methods to improve

1 Introduction

With the development of the network, information technology and popularization, people live, work and other places full of all kinds of software, people also need a variety of software to an activity, so the software on the quality of life of modern people, work efficiency has a great influence, such as in this case the software itself at least to do not make a mistake, can according to the standard process running smoothly, Therefore, in order to ensure this, every software needs to accept software testing before it is put into market application, and the test results determine whether the software can be put into influence. However, in view of the current situation, the software testing methods mainly adopted in China are relatively traditional, and the test results inevitably have the problem of insufficient accuracy, which is also the main reason why many software often need maintenance after being put into market application, and may cause serious impact. Therefore, in order to change the status quo, software testing methods must be improved. The current hot big data technology is the main way to achieve method improvement. How to give full play to the role of big data information to carry out improvement work is a problem worth thinking, and it is necessary to carry out relevant research.

M. A. Jan and F. Khan (Eds.): BigIoT-EDU 2022, LNICST 466, pp. 254–261, 2023.
https://doi.org/10.1007/978-3-031-23947-2_27

2 The Necessity of Improving Software Testing Methods

Software as an important tool in modern life and work, often the quality problems or errors, is bound to cause many inconvenience to people, so in order to avoid problems, software design need to be after completion of software testing, software according to the result, whether there is a problem, if there is a problem is to adjust, otherwise can into practical application. This background, the software test result must have higher accuracy, but the defect of traditional software testing method, testing various parameter Settings in the lack of mathematical basis, is dependent on subjective experience, at the same time, the test algorithm efficiency is generally low, and explain the process of traditional methods in the accuracy of the results and efficiency of two aspects flaws, It is impossible to guarantee that software can be used smoothly after it is put into practical application, and problems are still easy to occur in actual situations. From this point of view, traditional software testing methods must be improved, which is also the goal that related fields have been pursuing for years, and this goal can finally be realized under the background of big data. Taking the program P as an example, z is the self-variable vector and T is the input function based on the big data information, when $T = T1$, $T2,..., Tn(n > 1)$, the output expected value is $T' = T'1, T'2, ..., T'n$, o are program specifications s at $T = T1, T2,....$ When Tn, the actual output value is expressed as $o' = O'1, O'2, ..., o'n$, if $o' = o'1, o'2, ...o'n$, o and $T = T1, 2, T..., T'n$ is the same, or the difference is not big, then it shows that the software test is correct, this test logic finds the actual relationship between the software test, can output accurate test results [1–3]. Figure 1 shows the

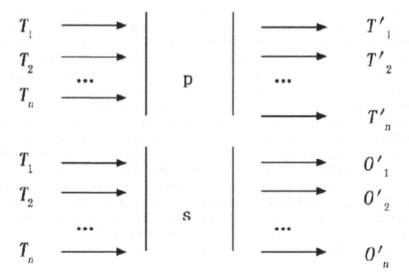

Fig. 1. The relationship between input and output in big data software testing

It is worth noting that the big data information of software testing the basic logic of basic logic and traditional software testing method has no evident difference in form, but they cannot confuse STH with STH else in the parameter, the traditional software testing methods lack the support of mathematical theory can't set the scope of o, o have no restrictions in the process of calculation, therefore, This kind of software test does not have normative, natural falloff test results, but the big data information based on software process model is based on the reality of the data of feedback, which involves various physical and chemical reaction, namely physical reaction is to point to in the case of no loss of test conditions reduce the amount of test data, Then without changing data on the basis of data collection, sampling and filtering operation method and so on, it can generate data, more clear understanding of the software on the "physical" whether can operation stability, and chemical reaction is to point to in no loss test conditions on the basis of the data extraction, and then to environmental testing of software data logic, Test whether it can operate in different environments, and each environment should be as close as possible to the environment when people use the software, so as to successfully teach and research whether the software has applicability. In the physical and chemical reactions based on big data information, o in the test has a clear range of values, test standardization is improved, and the accuracy of test results can be guaranteed naturally [4–6].

Big data information application requirements.

To transform software testing through big data information, it is necessary to master the basic application requirements of big data information in software testing. Therefore, relevant discussions will be carried out below.

2.1 Application of Big Data Information Mining Technology

Big data information in the main function of software testing is to provide the powerful data support, according to the data to deeply analyze the software running mode, find out the problem, but the big data information itself is just pure data integration of body, does not have the ability to actively play a role, so you need to solve the external means to mining, However, the huge amount of data information inside the big data information and the intricate relationship between the data information make it impossible to be mined by ordinary means, let alone effectively processed by manual, so special mining technology must be used, which is called the big data information mining technology. So-called data mining technology, in the modern theory will be classified as a kind of intelligent technology, this technology has a unique intelligent logic, can according to the known condition of the human input from huge data information extraction all eligible data in the body, after preprocessing will dig deep for extracting data from information, clarify the relationship between the data and information, This technology is the foundation of big data information application because it can be used to know how the software behaves in various data logic to detect problems [7]. Figure 2 shows the application flow of big data information mining technology.

2.2 Application of Big Data Information Storage

The most important feature of big data information is its huge amount of data, which can even reach hundreds of millions of levels, and its growth and update speed is extremely

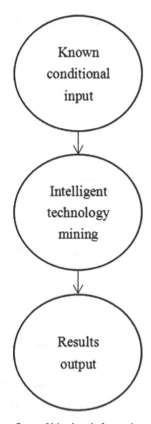

Fig. 2. Application flow of big data information mining technology

fast. Therefore, in order to play its role in improving the traditional software testing methods, it must meet the storage requirements of its huge amount of data. Based on this, common database storage capacity is limited, and the expansion has the certain difficulty, also can bring some cost, even if will meet the demand of storage, the short term will be in the big data information level growth reached its limits, illustrate common database does not meet the demand of large data storage, result in large data information application could satisfy the requirement of storage must be found in the database. According to this requirement, can satisfy the current big data information storage requirements of the database is cloud database, the database is the total storage capacity of the infinite (because of the cloud data is the data stored in the network environment, so the total capacity is infinite), and the expansion operation is very convenient in practical application, also won't bring too much cost, cloud database is a good choice to large data storage, It should be widely used. In addition, the cloud data under the unlimited storage capacity expansion is needed for operation, because the original cloud database data storage environment with openness, which may lead to data were leaked, it must be conducted on the basis of the original environment application in the enclosed storage, to ensure the security of data, for the current expansion of the reentry after storage capacity limits [8]. Figure 3 shows the basic application flow of cloud database.

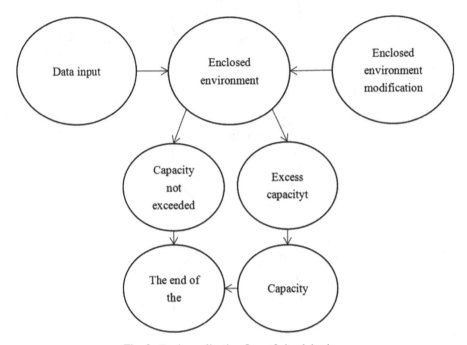

Fig. 3. Basic application flow of cloud database

3   Improvement Strategy of Software Testing Method Under Big Data Information

There are many improvement strategies for software testing methods under big data information, among which there are three representative ones, as follows.

3.1   Improvement of Particle Swarm Optimization and Ant Colony Algorithm

Using big data information to software testing is the purpose of the improvement in order to enhance the test method of intelligent, so that more accurate results, according to this purpose can use particle swarm - ant colony algorithm to improve, the method is mainly to provide mathematical logic to the software testing, data generated can be more accurate test software. The method steps are as follows: First, establish the basic framework of particle swarm optimization (pso), play a particle swarm can be found in the global optimal solution of advantage in preliminary tests, namely particle swarm optimization (pso) algorithm is a mimic the behavior of birds for food and create the algorithm, each particle in the algorithm is the equivalent of a bird in the flock, every bird know the general direction of food, so know the range of foods, too, Thus formed the global, but every bird doesn't know the location of the food, so it will be through the search for the way to the surrounding area in search of food, food represents the optimal solution, and when a bird confirm food after the general location of all the birds can to the bird and the nearest food, and in the search area, eventually find food, algorithm and get the optimal solution, Therefore, particle swarm optimization algorithm can effectively obtain the test index standard, according to the software data results and the comparison of the standard, the basic situation of the software; Second, ant colony algorithm is a typical probability algorithm, the main role is random optimization, in software testing can be further optimized particle swarm optimization results, in order to get better results. As the name implies, ant colony algorithm is an algorithm designed to imitate the collective behavior of ants. Logically, it is assumed that each ant in the ant colony has its own trajectory, according to which it can roughly infer the direction that the ant may go next (the direction is complex) and the probability that the ant enters each direction next. Which is based on the ant's current location and the target location in the distance, the distance between all sorts of unpredictable factors, and ants are social creatures, so when an ant current direction faster close to food, other ants would have to close here, this process will continue to cycle, until touch the food, with unpredictable factors during the period of change, The direction of the ant's movement will also change randomly, so that the optimal path can be obtained, so that the result is constantly optimized [9, 10].

3.2 Improvement of Modeling Processing

By big data information to test software, test personnel shall realize that big data information under the software testing can commence from multi-azimuth, is no longer a single test process, namely the past testers also tried different azimuth of software testing, but which involves the calculation of the amount is too big, can't get accurate data test results, The relationship between input data and output data cannot be well judged, and the process will be limited by various factors. However, the software testing under big data information has strong data support and can also be mined by technical means, so the multi-directional testing can be realized. Under the concept of multi-directional testing, modeling processing strategy can be adopted to improve the software testing method. See Fig. 4 for the specific operation process.

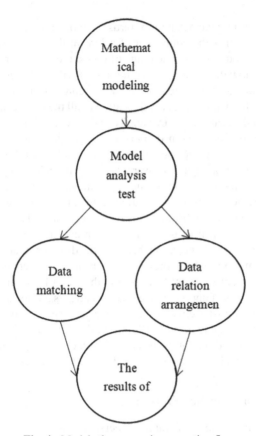

Fig. 4. Models the processing operation flow

According to Fig. 4, the software testing foundation is firstly established through data modeling, then data matching and data relation sorting and calculation are carried out on the model, and finally the results are obtained. According to the results, it can be known whether the actual software testing data matches the standard data of the model. The higher the matching degree, the better the software testing results. At the same time, the software performance level and software error rate can be judged according to the data relationship. The test results are not only of high accuracy, but also involve a wide range of areas.

3.3   Improvement Strategy of Big Data Simulation Test

Simulation software is a kind of general-purpose tools, the main function is based on user needs and the original data to create a virtual simulation environment, highly, the environment can testing various programming model, so long as the process model can basically normal operation in the simulation environment, so it can be put into use, shows that the simulation software is better software testing tools. From this point of view, the original data needed for simulation can be mined in the database by mining technology, and then the software model can be imported into the database, and the decision can be made according to the results. This method is simple to use, accurate results, and worth popularizing.

4   Conclusion

To sum up, big data technology is obviously helpful to basketball teaching in colleges and universities. Using this technology to establish an online platform can improve the theoretical teaching of basketball, develop students' interests through theoretical teaching, give full play to the role of physical education, and improve students' physical fitness. At the same time, the platform can also improve the teaching efficiency, promote the basketball teaching can be more smoothly.

References

1. Garousi, V., Felderer, M., Hacaloğlu, T.: Software test maturity assessment and test process improvement: a multivocal literature review. Inf. Softw. Technol. **85**, 16–42 (2017)
2. Garousi, V., Felderer, M., Hacaloglu, T.: What we know about software test maturity and test process improvement. IEEE Softw. **35**(1), 84–92 (2017)
3. Lawanna, A.: An effective test case selection for software testing improvement. In: Computer Science & Engineering Conference. IEEE (2016)
4. Onishi, K., Yumoto, T.: Introduction to software test processes and test process improvement (hot topics on software testing). IPSJ Mag. **49**, 133–139 (2008)
5. Belli, F., Güler, N., Linschulte, M.: IEEE 2010 Fourth International Conference on Secure Software Integration and Reliability Improvement Companion (SSIRI-C), Singapore, Singapore, 9 June 2010–11 June 2010. 2010 Fourth International Conference on Secure Software Integration and Reliability Imp, pp. 78–85 (2010)
6. Bo, J., Tse, T.H., Grieskamp, W., et al.: Regression testing process improvement for specification evolution of real-world protocol software. In: International Conference on Quality Software. IEEE Computer Society (2010)
7. Zhilo, N.M., Rudenko, P.A., Zhigaylo, A.N.: Development of hardware-software test bench for optical non-invasive glucometer improvement. In: Young Researchers in Electrical & Electronic Engineering. IEEE (2017)
8. Sato, M., Kanechika, H., Yoshizaki, R., et al.: The improvement of the analytical method of software test quality in consideration of effect factors: the proposal of the evolved "zone analysis method". In: National Conferences of the Society of Project Management. The Society of Project Management (2012)
9. Vock, S., Schmid, M., Staudt, H.: Test software generation productivity and code quality improvement by applying software engineering techniques. In: 2006 IEEE International Test Conference, ITC 2006, Santa Clara, CA, USA, 22–27 October 2006. IEEE (2006)
10. Lawanna, A.: Test case design based technique for the improvement of test case selection in software maintenance. In: Society of Instrument & Control Engineers of Japan. IEEE (2016)

Establishment and Application of Quality Evaluation System of College Students' Psychological Education Based on Genetic Algorithm

Xiaozhen Zhao and Bo Chen[✉]

China University of Geosciences, Wuhan 430074, China
cug_zhaoxiaozhen@163.com

Abstract. In this paper, the establishment and application of the quality evaluation system of College Students' Psychological Education Based on genetic algorithm, the increasingly fierce social competition and the accelerating pace of life, and the mental health problems of contemporary college students are related not only to the personal growth of a series of college students, but also to the future development of the whole society and nation. Therefore, paying attention to the psychological development process of college students, understanding their mental health status, correctly guiding college students to eliminate psychological obstacles, eliminate psychological shadow and prevent mental diseases should be the primary task of College Students' mental health education. Through the genetic algorithm of induction and deduction, comparative analysis, expert interview and questionnaire analysis, this paper constructs a set of evaluation system suitable for the quality of College Students' Psychological Education in China. Based on the typical situation of college students in China, this paper summarizes the weight evaluation system of College Students' psychological education at home and abroad, and puts forward a set of weight evaluation system suitable for college students' psychological education at home and abroad. It is of great significance for colleges and universities to make full use of the advantages of resources, effectively carry out the mental health education of all students, and improve the psychological quality and self-care consciousness of college students.

Keywords: Genetic algorithm · Mental health education · Evaluation system

1 Introduction

College Students' mental health education is a scientific, normative and operational work. It not only requires employees to have good psychological quality, but also has high requirements for the overall quality of employees, including knowledge, moral quality, sense of professional responsibility, accumulation of life experience, social experience and so on. In foreign countries, only those who have received professional training and special training can be competent. For example, the British Psychological Association

M. A. Jan and F. Khan (Eds.): BigIoT-EDU 2022, LNICST 466, pp. 262–274, 2023.
https://doi.org/10.1007/978-3-031-23947-2_28

stipulates the minimum qualifications for workers: graduate degree or above, teacher qualification certificate, more than two years of teaching experience for children and adolescents, at least two years of educational psychology training after graduate degree (at present, it is generally a one-year full-time Master's course and one-year practice under guidance), etc. Requirements for mental health educators in France: two years of major in psychology in universities, at least three years of teacher training and five years of primary school or pre-school work experience [1]. The American Psychological Association (APA) insists that school mental health educators should obtain a doctorate and pass the qualification examination before they can obtain the qualification recognized by APA; The qualification of the New York Association school psychological (NASP) is relatively broad. In addition to doctors, non doctors can also become school mental health educators. Non doctoral degrees include masters and professional workers. Professional workers usually refer to those who receive 5–6 years of education and training after completing undergraduate education. However, at present, most of the personnel engaged in psychological counseling and counseling in Colleges and universities in China are part-time. Some of them are not from psychology major and lack psychological education background and professional training. There are few people who really have psychological counseling qualification certificates. Many staff work only after short-term training and lack systematic professional training, This has affected the quality and effect of mental health education to a certain extent. Dr. Liu Keju of the Psychological Counseling Department of Peking University Shenzhen Hospital believes that students' psychological problems need professional medical psychologists. Obviously, at present, most colleges and universities do not have such conditions.

Throughout the historical development of College Students' mental health education, basically the research at each stage emphasizes the necessity and urgency of Strengthening College Students' mental health education, which reflects a problem that can not be ignored - although college students' mental health education and related research are carried out continuously, it does not play a good role in predicting and controlling college students' mental health problems. Therefore, it is necessary for us to further explore and seek an effective way to better apply the theoretical results of College Students' mental health education research to practical education. For example, Dr. Yue Xiaodong of City University of Hong Kong put forward the view that we should focus on Cultivating College Students' "pressure bomb" quality, which points out a new direction for the cultivation of College Students' psychological quality [2]; Also, Kate, an internationally famous master of psychodrama, has advocated a trauma treatment model called "psychodrama spiral therapy" for many years. These two cases have certain reference value for the research of the combination of theoretical results and practice of mental health education research. In addition, the ways of implementing mental health education in schools should also be diversified.

The basic purpose of China's higher education is to train qualified talents for socialist construction. A qualified college student should not only have solid professional knowledge and progressive ideology, but also have strong physique and healthy psychology. However, for a long time, colleges and universities have paid one-sided attention to the professional knowledge and skill education of college students, that is, professional quality education, but the closely related psychological quality education has not been paid

264 X. Zhao and B. Chen

enough attention. The defects in educational theory and practice affect the improvement of contemporary college students' psychological quality to a certain extent, and then affect their study, life, interpersonal communication Adapt to society and other aspects.

This paper needs to pay special attention to two points when constructing the quality evaluation index system of College Students' Psychological Education: first, the index system can accurately reflect the quality evaluation results of College Students' psychological education; Second, through the results of the evaluation of the quality of College Students' psychological education, we can promote the implementation of the technical means of the quality of College Students' psychological education, so as to promote the sustainable development of psychological education [3]. Therefore, under the basic principles of scientificity and rationality, representativeness and comprehensiveness, hierarchy and operability, we should build an effective evaluation index system for the quality of College Students' psychological education.

2 Related Work

2.1 Genetic Algorithm

Genetic algorithm is an intelligent optimization algorithm that simulates the process of natural selection and biological evolution. In nature, since Darwin put forward the species evolution theory of "survival of the fittest and survival of the fittest", researchers have conducted a long and far-reaching study on the process of biological evolution. Species form a new generation of individuals through the reproduction of the mother generation. In the new generation of individuals, most individuals will be similar to the mother generation due to chromosome crossing, and a few individuals will be different from the mother generation due to variation. As the executor of natural selection, nature keeps the individuals with strong adaptability and eliminates the individuals with poor adaptability in the process of changes in living resources and external environment and continuous competition among individuals. This process of natural selection provides a new way to solve problems for mankind. Its advantages include but are not limited to: genetic algorithm does not have much mathematical requirements for the optimization problem to be solved. Due to its evolutionary characteristics, the internal properties of the problem are not required in the search process [4]. For any form of objective functions and constraints, whether linear or nonlinear, discrete or continuous, it can be handled.

The ergodicity (ergodicity of States) of the evolutionary operator makes the genetic algorithm very effective in the global search of probability significance. Genetic algorithm can provide great flexibility for various special problems to mix and construct domain specific heuristics, so as to ensure the effectiveness of the algorithm. Do you feel that genetic algorithm is very powerful after reading it?

In fact, genetic algorithm has appeared in our previous tweets. You can learn about genetic algorithm in the detailed java code and comments of genetic algorithm and genetic algorithm.

Genetic algorithm solves the hybrid flow shop scheduling problem. Floating point coding can better meet the requirements of precision and space. This paper solves the discrete optimization problem. Using binary coding and floating-point coding will have accuracy errors, and using symbolic coding is a better choice. Symbolic coding means that the gene value in the individual chromosome coding string is taken from a symbol set with no numerical meaning but only code meaning, such as {a, B, C..} {1, 2, 3..} (numbers are represented as symbols only), {A1, A2, A3........} Wait. This paper adopts digital symbol coding in symbol coding.

The characteristics of intelligent optimization algorithms: they all start from any solution and explore the optimal solution in the whole solution space with a certain probability according to a certain mechanism. Because they can expand the search space to the whole problem space, they have global optimization performance.

Search mechanism of genetic algorithm: genetic algorithm simulates the phenomena of reproduction, crossover and gene mutation in the process of natural selection and natural heredity, retains a group of candidate solutions in each iteration, selects better individuals from the solution group according to some index, and combines these individuals with genetic operators (selection, crossover and mutation) to produce a new generation of candidate solution group, Repeat this process until some convergence index is met.

Simple genetic algorithms (SGA, also known as simple genetic algorithm or standard genetic algorithm) is the most basic genetic algorithm summarized by Goldberg. Its genetic evolution operation process is simple and easy to understand. It is the prototype and foundation of some other genetic algorithms [5].

Coding: GA abstracts objects into strings of specific symbols in a certain order through some coding mechanism. Just as the study of biological genetics starts with chromosomes, which are strings of genes. SGA uses binary strings for encoding.

Find the maximum value of the following unary function:

$$J(\Pi, W) = \sum_{k=1}^{K} \sum_{x \in \pi} \sum_{d=1}^{D} (x_{id} - v_{kd})^2 \qquad (1)$$

Since the interval length is 3 and the solution result is accurate to 6 decimal places, the interval defined by the independent variable can be divided into 3×106 equal parts. And because $221 < 3 \times 106 < 222$, so the binary encoding length of this example needs at least 22 bits. The encoding process of this example is essentially to convert the corresponding real value in the interval $[-1, 2]$ into a binary string (B21, B20 ... B0).

Initial population: SGA uses the random method to generate a set of several individuals, which is called the initial population. The number of individuals in the initial population is called population size.

Fitness function: the quality of an individual (solution) by genetic algorithm is evaluated by the value of fitness function.

Selection operator: genetic algorithm uses selection operation to realize the operation of survival of the fittest for individuals in the population: individuals with high fitness are more likely to be inherited into the next generation of population; Individuals with low fitness are less likely to be inherited into the next generation. The task of selection operation is to select some individuals from the parent population and inherit them to the next generation population. The selection operator in SGA adopts roulette selection method.

Roulette selection method: roulette selection is also called proportional selection operator. Its basic idea is that the probability of each individual being selected is directly proportional to the value of its fitness function [6]. If the population size is n and the fitness of individual I is fi, the probability that individual I is selected to be inherited to the next generation population is:

$$P_i = F_i / \sum_{i=1}^{n} F_i \tag{2}$$

Implementation steps of roulette selection method

(1) Calculate the fitness function value of all individuals in the population (decoding is required);
(2) Using the formula of proportional selection operator, the probability that each individual is selected to inherit to the next generation population is calculated;
(3) The simulated roulette operation (i.e. generating a random number between 0 and 1 to match the probability of each individual inheriting to the next generation population) is used to determine whether each individual inherits to the next generation population. Figure 1 below describes a simple genetic algorithm process:

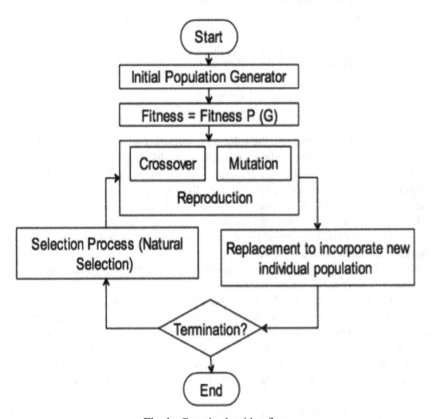

Fig. 1. Genetic algorithm flow

Crossover operator: the so-called crossover operation refers to the exchange of some genes between two paired chromosomes in some way according to the crossover probability PC, so as to form two new individuals. Crossover operation is an important feature that distinguishes genetic algorithm from other evolutionary algorithms. It plays a key role in genetic algorithm and is the main method to generate new individuals. The crossover operator in SGA adopts single point crossover operator.

2.2 Evaluation System of Psychological Teaching

The whole process of psychological education will involve planning and control. All personnel in the psychological education organization are engaged in planning and control to a certain extent and within a certain range. They perform their functions through planning and control to make the psychological education operate effectively. As the evaluation system of psychological education is an organic part of the management control system, it should also be organically linked with the strategic planning of psychological education. Therefore, when formulating strategic objectives, we should consider how to convert these indicators into measurable psychological education evaluation indicators, so as to effectively control the implementation of the strategy. Therefore, the design of psychological education evaluation system should also be based on clear strategic objectives [7]. The more clear, comprehensive and complete the goal is, the more the evaluation index of psychological education can reflect the requirements of the goal and the more effective the evaluation is.

Organizational behavior is an applied psychological education theory that systematically studies the behavior and attitude of people in the organization. Organizational behavior studies behavior problems in organizations from three levels: organization, team and individual. Among them, the core problem is how to make the goals of individuals, teams and organizations consistent, and finally achieve the goals of the organization. Generally speaking, organizational behavior is a systematic study of the behavior of all members in the organizational environment.

The theory of organizational behavior requires that the evaluation standard of psychological education should be incentive and operable. Incentive refers to the ability to drive the enthusiasm and creativity of employees; Operability refers to making the evaluated feel that their behavior can meet the standards set by the evaluation indicators. Therefore, the design of psychological education evaluation system should put how to stimulate employees' initiative in the first place. In this way, the goal of the organization can carry out extensive communication and exchange within psychological education, and then decompose the goal of the organization into the goal of students. Classification system is a computer self-learning system with certain artificial intelligence. The system contains a set of system evolution rules. Whenever some existing information meets the conditions of the rules, the system takes special actions. Through the organic combination of rules and information system, reliability distribution and genetic algorithm, we can obtain new rules that adapt to each other, so as to achieve the evolution of the whole large system.

In the rules and information system of the classification system, GUI Qing and ordinary The form of "if" then action * is the same, but different from the traditional expert system, the classification system limits the rules to the fixed length string representation. This has two advantages. One is that all applications can interpret the exact meaning after the permitted rules are assembled. The other is conducive to the string operation of gene mode, which provides a way for genetic algorithm to search for effective rules Then. In a given matching cycle, the classification system allows parallel rules to participate in and coordinate multiple activities at the same time [8]. When the number of matched rule sets must be determined in mutually exclusive activities or must be adjusted to accommodate a fixed length of information flow, the decision is delayed to the last moment and completed in a competitive manner. Competition urges rules to compete for control of system actions. Any rule that meets the conditions must compete with other rules that meet the conditions. And the most powerful or beneficial rules determine the action of the system in a certain situation. If the action of the system is successful, the winning rule will be strengthened. Otherwise, it will be weakened. This internal reliability circulation exchange and accumulation provides a good and bad evaluation index for the application of genetic algorithm, so as to facilitate the reproduction, exchange and variation of rules, so that the system can not only judge the existing rules, but also find new and better rules through the combination of old rules and wealth.

3   Establishment and Application of College Students' Psychological Education Quality Evaluation System Based on Genetic Algorithm

The premise of evaluating the quality of College Students' psychological education is to establish the corresponding evaluation index system of College Students' psychological education. Under this system, the quality evaluation results of College Students' psychological education can be accurately reflected through various evaluation indexes. Therefore, the construction of this system is very important. It needs to be comprehensive and hierarchical.

When constructing the quality evaluation index system of College Students' psychological education, we need to pay special attention to two points: first, the index system can accurately reflect the quality evaluation results of College Students' psychological education; Second, through the results of the evaluation of the quality of College Students' psychological education, we can promote the implementation of the technical means of the quality of College Students' psychological education, so as to promote the sustainable development of psychological education. Therefore, under the basic principles of scientificity and rationality [9], representativeness and comprehensiveness, hierarchy and operability, an effective evaluation index system for the quality of College Students' psychological education is constructed, as shown in Fig. 2 below.

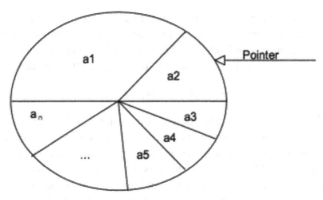

Fig. 2. Roulette of evaluation index system for the quality of College Students' Psychological Education

In the scientific research of comprehensive evaluation, the index system is an important aspect, and another important factor is the determination of index weight. To some extent, for various indicators, weight is the way to quantify the importance of various indicators. It depends on the existence of objective indicators and the existence of objective indicators. Therefore, the process of determining the weight can also be understood as the process of quantifying the subjective view. Generally speaking, if the weighting is based on the objective existence of indicators, it is called objective weighting method. The commonly used methods include factor analysis method, multi-objective programming method, principal component analysis method, coefficient of variation method, average weight method, etc. different weighting methods have different application conditions. Generally speaking, the objective weighting method is not affected by the subjective will of decision-makers, but depends on the actual business field, Lack of generality. If the weight is given according to the decision-maker's subjective view, it is called subjective weight method. The common methods include analytic hierarchy process, grey clustering, fuzzy clustering and so on. The common feature of these methods is that they need to rely on the experience of decision-makers to judge the actual situation, so they are easy to be affected by the subjective bias of experts, and compared with the objective weighting method, this method is cumbersome in calculation and weak in operability. More scholars combine the two, called the comprehensive weighting method. Due to the particularity of the quality evaluation of College Students' psychological education, the existing research mostly adopts the subjective weighting method to determine its weight. In recent years, with the rise of machine learning, a new method of determining weight began to emerge, that is, the method of determining index weight based on machine learning [10]. Using the strong fault tolerance of machine learning, this method can deal with the evaluation of complex systems, and is very suitable for the determination of index weight of various complex systems with large sample data, wide coverage and relatively independent indexes. At present, the methods based on machine learning mostly use BP neural network to determine the weight. In fact, there are many excellent and widely used algorithms to determine the weight, such as genetic algorithm.

Educational psychology focuses on how students learn and develop. In practice, it pays special attention to students with special educational needs (whether gifted children or children with emotional and behavioral problems). The quality evaluation system of psychological education can be calculated by the following theoretical formula:

$$\|y - \theta_i\| = \min(\|y - \theta_i\|) \tag{3}$$

College Students' mental health education has the tendency of formalization and simplification, which is obviously manifested in the following three points: first, pay attention to the opening of psychological courses and ignore the development of psychological training activities [11]. Mental health course is not a simple knowledge transfer, but a practical application course. Some colleges and universities are keen to set up courses of psychological knowledge. They simply equate psychological knowledge education with mental health education, and despise the training of psychological activities. For example, some colleges and universities believe that since college students' mental health education plays an important role in the growth of college students, it should be included in the teaching plan as a course. As a public compulsory course or elective course for students, it should be given certain class hours and credits. Teachers teach step by step, students learn section by section, and take an examination after learning. This approach seems to pay attention to this work. In fact, it leads the mental health education of college students to a dead end from concept to concept and from theory to theory. Teachers say that students can remember and cope with the exam. It is difficult to achieve the effectiveness of mental health education. The second is to emphasize psychological testing and ignore scientific analysis. Psychological testing is widely used in Colleges and universities, but some colleges and universities simply equate mental health education with psychological testing and spend all their efforts on psychological testing In fact, mental health education is formalized and simplified, and the scientific analysis of psychological problems is not enough. "Third, in psychological counseling, we should pay more attention to obstacle counseling than development counseling [12]." W at present, many college students think of psychological counseling only when they have psychological obstacles. For developmental problems in their life path, they rarely think of psychological counseling, and psychological counseling institutions rarely carry out activities for these problems. Figure 3 below shows the process of tournament selection with n = 3:

4   Establishment of Evaluation System

What is studied is all the comprehensive evaluation in the quality evaluation system of College Students' psychological education. As long as it involves multiple evaluation objects, it can be indicated by saism model.

When establishing the evaluation index system of College Students' mental health, the following principles should be taken into account:

(1) The principle of purpose. Any comprehensive evaluation has obvious purpose. Therefore, the evaluation index system as the basis of comprehensive evaluation must reflect the purpose of comprehensive evaluation and meet the requirements of comprehensive evaluation.

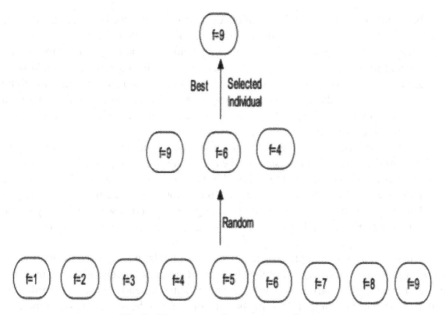

Fig. 3. The process of tournament selection

(2) Systematic principle. The systematic principle means that in the establishment of the comprehensive evaluation index system, the organic relationship between various indexes should be fully considered, and all aspects of the evaluated object are an inseparable organic whole.

(3) Principle of consistency. It refers to the selection number and statistical caliber of each evaluation index of the comprehensive evaluation index system, which should ensure the consistency of time (comparable year and month) on each element of the index.

(4) Independence principle. Minimize the overlap and statistical correlation of evaluation indicators in concept and extension, and select fewer evaluation indicator groups with strong independence, representativeness and greatest contribution.

(5) Principle of isotropy. Isotropy refers to that when each index reflects the characteristics and degree of the research object, its value is the same as the evaluation method of its characteristics and degree. Generally speaking, in the specific selection, it is required to form positive index, inverse index or neutral index, so as to avoid the offset of indicators in different directions in the application of the same problem due to different directions [13], It confuses the reflection of the essential characteristics of things. Even if positive, negative and neutral indicators appear in an evaluation index system at the same time in practice, we should convert them into indicators in the same direction for evaluation.

(6) The principle of comprehensiveness. In order to ensure the objectivity and accuracy of the comprehensive evaluation results, when initially establishing the index system, we should select as many evaluation indexes that can generally reflect the

basic characteristics of all levels of the evaluated things as possible, so that there is room for screening when finally determining the index system.

(7) Principle of comparability. When selecting evaluation indicators, attention should be paid to the caliber range of indicators and the principles of vertical and horizontal comparability of accounting methods. In the evaluation of the same thing in different periods, we should pay attention to vertical comparability, while in the evaluation of different things in the same period, we should pay attention to horizontal comparability.

(8) Principle of operability. The selection of indicators should not only meet the purpose of evaluation, but also support the comprehensive evaluation. In other words, the data of evaluation indicators should be easy to obtain, otherwise the established index system can only be put on hold and can not achieve the purpose of comprehensive evaluation, which will not help to guide the actual work [14]. At present, this is not fully noticed in some domestic research cases of index system.

Genetic algorithm is applied to many scientific fields, mainly because the overall search and optimization strategy of the algorithm itself does not rely on search information and external auxiliary information during calculation, and the algorithm rules are very flexible. The most important thing is that it only needs the help of "fitness function" to form a reference framework for solving complex problems, as shown in Fig. 4 below, It can be applied in many scientific fields.

```
class GASelection(metaclass=SelectionMeta):
    '''
    Class for providing an interface to easily extend the behavior of selection
    operation.
    '''

    def select(self, population, fitness):
        '''
        Called when we need to select parents from a population to later breeding.
        :param population: The current population.
        :type population: GAPopulation
        :return parents: Two selected individuals for crossover.
        :type parents: Tuple of tow GAIndividual objects.
        '''

        raise NotImplementedError
```

Fig. 4. Reference frame code for solving complex problems

5 Conclusion

This paper mostly studies the establishment and application of the quality evaluation system of College Students' mental health education based on genetic algorithm. From a theoretical perspective, this paper describes and preliminarily considers the research status of College Students' mental health education in China, and then analyzes the development trend of College Students' mental health education research. After a brief analysis of the relationship between mental health education and ideological and political education, this paper puts forward the problems existing in college students' mental health education in China and analyzes the reasons. To realize the standardization, scientization and effectiveness of College Students' mental health education is not a matter of one day. There are many fields that can be explored. Limited to time and writing power, this paper only makes a superficial exploration on several aspects of College Students' mental health education, which can not be comprehensive and thorough from theory and practice, I just hope it can play a role in attracting jade, so that schools and society can pay more extensive and in-depth attention to mental health education.

Acknowledgements. Fundamental research Funds for the central universities "Research Startup Fund for new Young Teachers"——Study burnout of college students and study support countermeasures.

References

1. Hossain, M.J., Ahmmed, F., Rahman, S., et al.: Impact of online education on fear of academic delay and psychological distress among university students following one year of COVID-19 outbreak in Bangladesh. Heliyon **7**, e07388 (2021)
2. Beltrán-Velasco, A.I., Donoso-González, M., Clemente-Suárez, V.J.: Analysis of perceptual, psychological, and behavioral factors that affect the academic performance of education university students. Physiol. Behav. **238**(3), 113497 (2021)
3. Novi, C.D., Leporatti, L., Montefiori, M.: The role of education in psychological response to adverse health shocks. Health Policy **125**(9464), 643–650 (2021)
4. Alshahir, A., Molyet, R.: Improving the reconfiguration of hybrid power networks by combining Genetic Algorithm (GA) with Particle Swarm Optimization (PSO). Am. J. Electr. Power Energy Syst. **10**(1), 6 (2021)
5. Liu, L., Weng, C., Li, S., et al.: Passive remote sensing of ice cloud properties at terahertz wavelengths based on genetic algorithm. Remote Sens. **13**(4), 735 (2021)
6. Shi, R., Zhao, Z., Huang, X., et al.: Ground-state structures of hydrated calcium ion clusters from comprehensive genetic algorithm search. Front. Chem. **9**, 637750 (2021)
7. Gharekhani, M., Nadiri, A., Moghaddam, A.A., et al.: Investigation of contamination risk using optimized DRASTIC-L method with genetic algorithm in Salmas plain aquifer (2021)
8. Gao, Z., Suo, Z., Liu, J., et al.: Construction practice of student evaluation system based on JFinal + webix integrated framework and Baidu AI platform. MATEC Web Conf. **336**, 05016 (2021)
9. A tentative study of translation evaluation system of Chinese classical poetry form: from the perspective of functional linguistics. 海外英语 (9), 4 (2021)
10. Hammond, K.C., Laggner, F.M., Diallo, A., et al.: Initial operation of a real-time Thomson scattering evaluation system on the Large Helical Device (2021)
11. Laar, R.A., Ashraf, M.A., Ning, J., et al.: Performance, health, and psychological challenges faced by students of physical education in online learning during COVID-19 epidemic: a qualitative study in China. In: Healthcare (2021)
12. Antonio, B., Sarmiento, P.: Philosophical, psychological and religio-cultural roots: contemporary challenges to religious education. Int. J. Res. Stud. Educ. **10**(2), 77–86 (2021)

13. Islyamov, B., Tolegenuly, N.: Psychological and pedagogical activity of a physical education teacher in strengthening the health of students (2021)
14. Sant'Anna, A., Vogel, L.O.: What about the diversity of psychological types? A study with emerging economy executive education alumni (2021)

Research on Coordination Between Power Information Security System and Environment Based on Fusion Mechanism

Hong Zhang Xiong[(⊠)] and Xiaokun Yang

State Grid Jibei Marketing Service Center, Fund Intensive Control Center and Metrology Center, Beijing 100045, China
18101172428@163.com.cn, betime@yeah.net

Abstract. The development of electric power is the guarantee of the whole social and economic development. With the development of national economy, the growth of total energy consumption will gradually slow down, but the growth of electric power consumption will maintain a relatively high speed. The strategic position of electric power will become more and more important. In the future, the energy consumption of China's power generation sector will inevitably increase greatly. Coal is the main primary energy for power generation in China, and its extensive use will cause serious harm to the ecological environment. Therefore, the most important thing for the coordinated development of China's power and environment is to reduce the environmental pollution caused by coal combustion, strengthen various measures to improve the utilization rate of coal for power generation and minimize coal-fired pollution emissions, develop non fossil fuel power generation and promote renewable energy power generation according to local conditions.

Keywords: Power information · Safety system · Environmental coordination analysis

1 Introduction

At present, the conflict between electric energy development and environmental protection in China is becoming more and more serious. As an energy sector, the power industry plays a fundamental supporting role in the development of the whole national economy, but at the same time, the environmental pollution caused by the power industry itself also brings a series of problems to the society [1]. Therefore, how to deal with the relationship between power economy and environment is an important issue for power to achieve sustainable development. In order to make rational use and allocate resources, it is necessary to ensure the coordinated development of power and economic environment from the perspective of government supervision. Therefore, this paper uses regulatory economics to study the problem of developing power economy and ensuring that power generation enterprises can try their best to reduce environmental pollution. Figure 1 below shows the current situation of power consumption under power information security.

© ICST Institute for Computer Sciences, Social Informatics and Telecommunications Engineering 2023
Published by Springer Nature Switzerland AG 2023. All Rights Reserved
M. A. Jan and F. Khan (Eds.): BigIoT-EDU 2022, LNICST 466, pp. 275–285, 2023.
https://doi.org/10.1007/978-3-031-23947-2_29

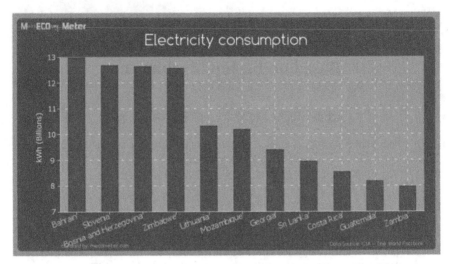

Fig. 1. Current situation of power consumption under power information security

Environmental pollution has a strong negative externality. Due to the existence of negative externalities, the output determined by perfectly competitive manufacturers according to the principle of profit maximization deviates seriously from that determined by the principle of social welfare maximization. This deviation is the inefficient output of over utilization of resources, over emission of pollutants and over production of polluting products [2]. This is neither in line with the principle of optimal efficiency nor the principle of social equity. In short, when there is negative externality, the profit maximization behavior of competitive manufacturers can not automatically lead to Pareto optimization of resource allocation. This leads to the failure of environmental policy, which is mainly reflected in the price distortion caused by the lack of sufficient attention to ecology and environment in the formulation of current sectoral policies and macroeconomic policies. With the increasingly prominent environmental problems, the environmental supervision of the power industry has attracted extensive attention of scholars at home and abroad. Banzhaf, burtraw, Palmer studied the pollution charge in the American power market; Mrozek and Keeler studied the emission trading model under the uncertainty of power plant emission. In China, with the implementation of power market-oriented reform, the power supervision system is also in the process of gradual improvement. Some scholars have actively explored many aspects of power supervision in combination with the characteristics of China's transitional economy [3]. Xia Qing and Li canbing analyzed and summarized the regulatory analysis methods, regulatory indicators, key regulatory speculation and regulatory means of foreign power market; Fan Jin added environmental protection factor into consumer utility function, and studied economic growth under sustainable development from the perspective of neoclassical economics; However, how to coordinate and supervise the economy and environment of the power industry remains to be further studied.

2 Related Work

2.1 Positive Impact of Electricity on the Environment

As a basic industry to develop a national economy and improve people's living standards, power industry plays a key role in national economic development and social progress. While energy consumption brings people economic benefits and life efficiency, it also brings people increasingly serious environmental problems. Especially the use of fossil energy. Electric energy is a clean secondary energy. Increasing the proportion of electric energy in terminal energy consumption will alleviate the contradiction between energy, economy and environment to a certain extent. It is conducive to the realization of sustainable development. At present, the proportion of primary energy converted into electric energy and the proportion of electric energy in terminal energy have become an important symbol to measure a country's economic development level, energy efficiency and even the whole economic efficiency and environmental protection [4]. According to statistics, according to the fuel structure and energy efficiency in 1990, the carbon dioxide emission of China's power generation industry increased by 283mt in 1994. However, due to the higher efficiency of electric energy than the direct use of fossil energy, the energy efficiency in 1994 increased by 6% compared with 1990. In this sense, the carbon dioxide emission in 1994 not only did not increase, but also decreased by 48mt If it is predicted that the power generation will quadruple by 2020, and all Chinese power plants can operate at the best level in China, that is, the energy utilization can reach the current level of power generation efficiency of large units, the carbon dioxide emission can be reduced by about 20%, about 600Mt At present, the task of increasing the proportion of electric energy in terminal energy in China is still arduous. By 2000, the proportion of electric energy in terminal energy consumption was only 11.2%.

$$\Delta w(i, y) = -\eta \frac{\partial e}{\partial w(i, y)} \tag{1}$$

$$\arg \min_{SC} \sum_{i=1}^{k} \sum_{x \in C_i} |X - \mu_i|^2 \tag{2}$$

The power generation side is the part that has the greatest impact on the environment. The power generation side in China is composed of thermal power generation, hydropower generation, nuclear power generation and new energy power generation. Hydropower, nuclear power and new energy power generation have little impact on the environment. Therefore, the positive effect of this part of power on the environment is more prominent. If the proportion of non fossil energy power generation is increased from 20% to 40%, the total carbon dioxide emission will be reduced by almost 40%, about 1200mt However, China's power generation side is dominated by thermal power, and coal power is dominated in thermal power. This power supply structure is not conducive to environmental protection. Therefore, it is very necessary to improve the power supply structure to play a positive role in the environmental system [2]. As shown in Fig. 2 below, power production: impact on climate and climate.

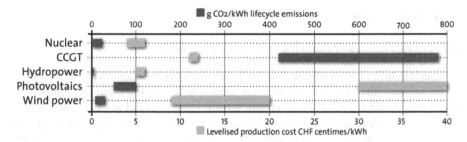

Fig. 2. Electricity production: impacts on climate and climate

2.2 Multimodal Fusion Mechanism

Due to the strong randomness of the composition of multimodal information in the real world, there is a certain imbalance in the distribution of each mode, both in the quantity and quality of information, resulting in the uncertainty of modal information.

Just take video as an example. In online video services with rich text information (such as bullet screen information), a relatively unpopular video is usually accompanied by a small amount of user comments. In this case, the information of text mode will be sparse or even missing. At the same time, users' comments tend to be more arbitrary and subjective. In this case, noise will be introduced into the text mode, thereby reducing the quality of the text [5].

Therefore, aiming at the uncertainty of modal information, this paper subdivides it into two sub problems: the lack of modal information and the high noise of modal information, and expounds these two problems respectively.

Neural networks enable the most advanced methods to achieve incredible results in computer vision tasks such as target detection. However, such success largely depends on expensive computing resources, which prevents people with cheap equipment from appreciating advanced technology. In this paper, we propose a cross stage partial network (cspnet) to alleviate the problem that previous work requires a lot of reasoning and calculation from the perspective of network architecture. We attribute the problem to the repeated gradient information in network optimization. The proposed network respects the variability of the gradient by integrating the characteristic graphs of the beginning and end of the network stage. In our experiment, this reduces the amount of calculation by 20% with the same or even higher accuracy on the Imagenet data set, and is significantly better than the state-of-the-art method in terms of ap50 on the MS coco target detection data set. Cspnet is easy to implement and universal enough to cope with the architecture based on RESNET, resnext and densenet [6].

When neural networks become deeper [and wider, neural networks have been proved to be particularly powerful. However, expanding the architecture of neural networks usually brings more computation, which makes the tasks with large computation such as target detection unaffordable to most people. Lightweight computing has gradually attracted more and more attention, because real-world applications usually require short reasoning time on small devices, which poses a serious challenge to computer vision algorithms A daunting challenge. Although some methods are specially designed for mobile CPU, the deep separable convolution technology they use is incompatible with industrial IC design, such as application specific integrated circuit (ASIC) edge computing system. In this work, we studied the computational burden of the most advanced methods such as RESNET, resnext and densenet.

$$J_c = \sum_{i=1}^{k} \sum_{p \in C_1} \|p - M_i\|^2 \tag{3}$$

$$J\left(\prod, W\right) = \sum_{k=1}^{K} \sum_{x \in \pi} \sum_{d=1}^{D} (x_{id} - v_{kd})^2 \tag{4}$$

We further develop components with high computational efficiency, so that the above networks can be deployed on CPUs and mobile GPUs without sacrificing performance [7].

In this study, we introduced the cross stage partial network (cspnet). The main purpose of designing cspnet is to reduce the amount of computation and realize richer gradient combination. This goal is achieved by dividing the feature map of the foundation layer into two parts, and then merging them through the proposed cross stage hierarchy. Our main concept is to make the gradient flow propagate through different network paths by splitting the gradient flow. We have confirmed that the gradient information propagated can have a large correlation difference through the concatenation and transition steps. In addition, cspnet can greatly reduce the amount of calculation and improve the speed and accuracy of reasoning, as shown in Fig. 3.

3 Negative Impact of Power Industry on Environment

The environment mentioned here refers to the space around people and the overall of various natural factors that can directly and indirectly affect human life and development. Environment is the foundation of human survival. The development of human society and economy will inevitably have an impact on the environment. The impact of modern mass production on the environment is particularly serious, and the development of power industry is no exception. Environmental protection is to take administrative, legal, economic, scientific and technological measures to make rational use of natural resources and prevent environmental pollution and destruction, so as to maintain and develop ecological balance and maintain the development of human society. Electric power environmental protection refers to the protection and treatment of the environmental impact of power generation, transmission and distribution. At the end of 1983, The State Council clearly stipulates that "environmental protection is a basic guarantee condition and strategic task in the modernization drive and a basic national policy" [8]. The development of the power industry must implement this basic national policy to make the coordinated development of power production and construction and environmental protection. In order to reduce the impact of the power industry on the environment, it is necessary to understand how the power industry causes damage to the environment. The production mode process of power industry is shown in Fig. 4 below.

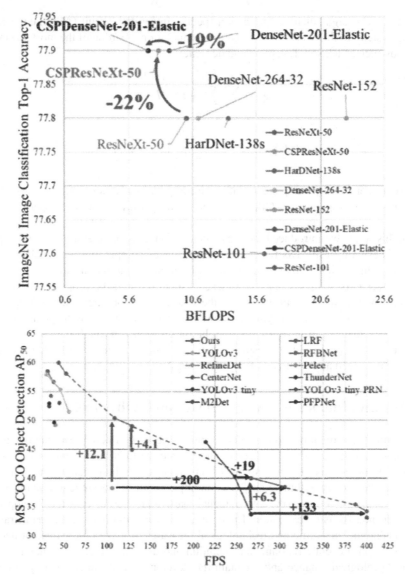

Fig. 3. Characteristics division of electric power environment sales network framework

1) Thermal power generation and environment.

Compared with thermal power, hydropower and nuclear power generation, thermal power production has the greatest environmental pollution and the most serious treatment work. The pollution caused by thermal power can be summarized into five basic pollution forms: wastewater, waste gas, waste residue (the above three items are commonly known as "three wastes"), waste heat and noise. The pollution sources are as follows: the waste

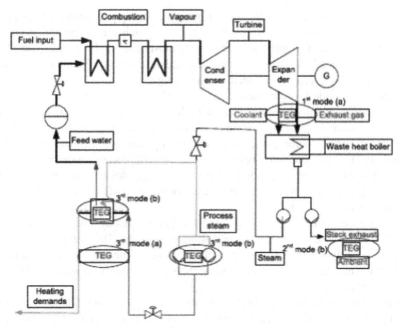

Fig. 4. Production mode flow of power industry

gas is mainly composed of dust, sulfur dioxide and nitrogen oxides, The information security framework of power system is shown in Fig. 5 below.

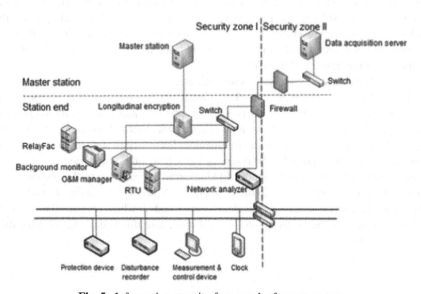

Fig. 5. Information security framework of power system

(1) Dust. It is a small solid pollutant that enters the atmosphere with flue gas, including fly ash after fuel combustion and unburned carbon particles. It is divided into floating dust and falling dust, of which floating dust is the most harmful. The treatment method is to use various dust reducers to eliminate smoke and dust. The installation of electrostatic precipitator is the development direction in the future.

(2) Sulfur dioxide It is a pollutant generated after the combustion of sulfur in fuel, which is discharged into the atmosphere with flue gas. It is one of the main substances forming acid rain. At present, SO2 emission from thermal power plants in China has become an important factor restricting power development [9]. The measures to prevent SO2 include fuel desulfurization before combustion, desulfurization during combustion and desulfurization after combustion. At present, flue gas desulfurization after combustion is widely used in the world. However, many power plants in China have not installed desulfurization equipment.

(3) Nitrogen oxides are also one of the substances causing acid rain, and nitrogen oxides can also cause damage to human respiratory system. The method to control this pollution is catalytic reduction, which reduces NOx in flue gas to nitrogen and H2O However, the new low no burner is mainly used to reduce the generation of NOx during furnace combustion.

Waste slag mainly refers to the fly ash produced by the power plant. It includes the burned coal ash, slag and collected fly ash. It is a solid pollutant with the largest emission from the power plant. At present, fly ash is mainly stored in the ash yard, which not only wastes land resources, but also affects the environment. Resource reuse is the way to solve waste slag pollution [10].

Waste water refers to ash flushing water. It is characterized by large discharge, high pH value and excessive turbidity, fluorine ion and arsenic, which are the main pollution problems of ash flushing water. Ash flushing water treatment is a prominent problem, which focuses on solving the problems of excessive pH, pipeline scaling and large discharge. The recycling of ash flushing water with water saving and less pollution is the development direction to be improved. In addition, the power plant will also produce thermal pollution, noise pollution, etc.

2) Hydropower development and environment.

Hydropower is considered as a clean power energy, because it does not release pollutants and heat pollution in its production process, and it uses renewable water resources, which is its biggest advantage compared with thermal power. However, it also has some potential impacts on the environment and ecosystem, such as land subsidence caused by reservoir impoundment, reservoir bank landslide, inundation of large areas of land, and earthquake can be induced [11]; Large evaporation in the reservoir area changes the microclimate; Change the downstream hydrological conditions and reduce the groundwater level; Large biological areas are flooded, which changes the water and land environment of the upstream and downstream, and affects the migration habits of fish in the downstream.

4 Power Information Security System and Environment Coordination Analysis

4.1 Environmental System

Environmental system is another important part of the sustainable development system. In the sustainable development system, the environment plays three major roles: (1) providing various natural resources indispensable to human activities. (2) Contain and purify the waste discharged by human activities. (3) Provide comfortable space for human survival.

For a long time, mankind has only paid attention to the first two functions of the environment, extracted a large number of resources from the environmental system to develop the economy, and discharged a large amount of waste to the environmental system. However, resources are limited in a certain period of time [12]. The consequence of excessive exploitation of natural resources is resource depletion. The consequence of excessive discharge of waste to the environmental system is an increasingly serious global environmental pollution problem. Human activities are not conducive to the realization of sustainable development strategy. Therefore, it is necessary to analyze the environmental system and study the methods to ensure the sustainable development of the environmental system. Pigou, an economist, proposed internalizing the cost of the environment in the way of Taxation, so that human beings can pay for the use of the environment. Coase also proposed to solve the problem of environmental externality by defining the property right of environmental resources [13]. Based on these theories, people put forward various policies for environmental management, such as levying environmental tax, implementing environmental subsidies, establishing emission trading system, etc. These measures have achieved certain results in practice, but there are also many problems, such as the formulation of tax rate and the distribution of emission right, which need to be based on information, and the information is asymmetric in practice, It is difficult for environmental regulators to accurately understand the specific information of polluters and establish accurate quantitative indicators. Therefore, through the analysis of environmental system, to measure the value of environment and establish environmental management system has become an important research content of environmental economics.

4.2 Power and Environment

Figure 6 reflects the relationship between power system and environmental system. Electric energy is a kind of secondary energy, which is transformed from primary energy. Environmental system provides the basis for the transformation of electric energy. In the process of converting primary energy into electric energy, many wastes will be generated, which will be absorbed and purified by the environmental system. The provision of primary energy is directly related to the development of power system [14]. With the improvement of environmental policy, the impact of power on environmental protection will also be related to the development of power system. The role of power system in environmental protection can be analyzed from both positive and negative aspects.

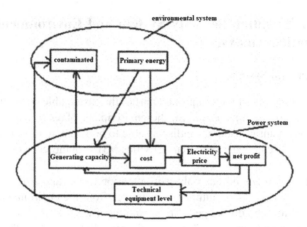

Fig. 6. Relationship between power system and environmental system

5 Conclusion

Electric energy is a kind of secondary energy. Compared with other energy sources, electric energy consumption has little impact on the environment and high utilization efficiency. According to statistics, due to the increase of the proportion of electric energy in the energy consumption structure, China's energy efficiency has also been comprehensively improved, which has greatly reduced the energy consumption of 10000 yuan GDP. From 1348t / 10000 yuan in 1980, it has decreased to 143t / 10000 yuan. Therefore, electric power plays an important role in promoting the balance between energy, economy and environment, so as to realize sustainable development. The conversion of coal into electricity and the percentage of electricity in total energy consumption can be used as an important indicator to measure a country's energy utilization efficiency, economic development level and environmental protection. This paper analyzes and studies the coordination between power information security system and environment based on fusion mechanism, which makes a new contribution to promoting the coordinated development of power and environment.

References

1. Ahlport, S.F., Stauffenberg, A.V.: System and method for collection of radio environment information using a limited datalink. US10700943B2 (2020)
2. Mu, L., Wang, L., Wang, M.: Research of integrated marine environment information support and forecast system (2020)
3. Savina, A., Malyavkina, L., Baturina, N., et al.: Information and technological support of the system of food quality and safety management in the digital economical environment (2020)
4. Botirov, S.R., Kh, D.R.: Analysis of information security evaluation models in the cloud computing environment. In: 2020 International Conference on Information Science and Communications Technologies (ICISCT) (2020)
5. Eba, A., Fa, B., Fa, C., et al.: Application of weighted linear combination approach in a geographical information system environment for nuclear power plant site selection: the case of Ghana. Ann. Nuc. Energy (2021)

6. Sarkar, D., Brahmachary, R., Barma, S.D.: Transient stability controlling and assessment of a congested power system in a deregulated environment (2020)
7. Ahmad, A.B., Othman, Z.B., Arshah, R.A., et al.: The suitability of technology, organization and environment (TOE) and socio technical system (STS) for assessing IT hardware support services (ITHS) model. J. Phys.: Conf. Ser. 2021, **1874**(1), 012040
8. Song, X., Hao, C., Zhang, X., et al.: Research on power environment monitoring system of information room. IOP Conf. Ser. Earth Environ. Sci. **680**(1), 012024 (2021)
9. Qi, L., Zhao, C., Yu, G., et al.: Application of Network Security Situational Awareness in Power Information System Security. IOP Publishing Ltd (2022)
10. Wang D, Dash D, Golomb G. System and method for identifying security entities in a computing environment. US11108796B1 (2021)
11. Markowska, K., Flizikowski, J., Bieliński, K., et al.: The comparative assessment of effects on the power system and environment of selected electric transport means in Poland. Materials **14**(16), 4556 (2021)
12. Kumar, S., Satyala, B., Santhi, N., et al. Title of Invention: A System and the Method for Efficient Communication Between Iot Devices in Heterogeneous Iot Environment Using ML Name of Inventor(s) (2021)
13. Казанчук, В., Яценко, П: Peculiarities of legal regulation of activities of the National Police of Ukraine in the field of ensuring information security in Ukraine. Law Safety **79**(4), 32–38 (2020)
14. Xiao, Y., Wang, R., Wang, F., et al.: Investigation on spatial and temporal variation of coupling coordination between socioeconomic and ecological environment: A case study of the Loess Plateau. China. Ecol. Indicat. **136**, 108667 (2022)

Research on Economic Management Experiment Teaching Management System Based on Computer

Xiaosu Feng$^{(\boxtimes)}$, Weiwei Miao, Pengcheng Cao, and Wenguo Zhao

Jingdezhen Vocational University of Arts, Jiangxi 333000, China
luolitian83@126.com

Abstract. In view of the current laboratory requirements for online experiment and online teaching, combined with the current direction of education and teaching reform in Colleges and universities and the rapid development of modern network technology, it provides an online experimental teaching and communication platform for teachers and students, and realizes the functions of students' online submission of homework, viewing materials, teachers' online correction of homework, and online real-time Q & A, It meets the needs of experimental teaching reform and innovation, and applies the convenience, real-time and accuracy of the network to the traditional experimental teaching. Therefore, the construction of experimental teaching management system based on network technology can not only solve the problems of professional experimental teaching, but also comply with the development direction of modern science and technology and experimental technology. It will effectively promote the profound reform of experimental teaching content and experimental teaching methods.

Keywords: Computer · Economic management · Experimental teaching · Management system

1 Introduction

"Economics" is an experimental science. With the continuous development of science and technology, economics and management majors are no longer pure liberal arts majors, but subjects that can carry out experiments and design. Since the 1990s, with the acceleration of the information process, the economic management laboratory with computer as the main medium has played a more and more important role in the simulation experiment of economic management specialty, and has become an indispensable basic condition for the construction of economic management specialty and the cultivation of students' practical ability and innovation ability, It has been widely valued by the majority of colleges and universities. Especially with the continuous development of Internet technology, the economic management professional laboratory based on BS architecture supported by network technology has become the mainstream of laboratory construction and development. At present, in order to cultivate a large number of

M. A. Jan and F. Khan (Eds.): BigIoT-EDU 2022, LNICST 466, pp. 286–291, 2023.
https://doi.org/10.1007/978-3-031-23947-2_30

economic management professionals with certain innovative spirit and practical ability, relevant colleges and universities have established a number of economic management professional laboratories in various ways, including those built separately, funded and jointly built with the society [1]. Either way, it has played a positive supporting role for the experimental teaching of economic management specialty, effectively promoted the construction of economic management specialty in these colleges and universities, and trained a large number of economic management professionals with strong practical ability for China's modernization.

Because the laboratory of economic management specialty started in the 1990s, there is a big gap in both teachers and management compared with the laboratory of science and engineering. However, after years of efforts, many schools have explored the successful experience of the construction of economic management professional laboratories. Especially since 2005, the Ministry of education has launched the evaluation of national experimental teaching demonstration centers, and all provinces have also launched the evaluation standards of provincial experimental teaching demonstration centers. These measures have effectively promoted the scientization, standardization and informatization of laboratory construction in Colleges and universities, especially for the construction of computer-based economic management specialty laboratories, And there have been some successful examples. For example, the economic management experimental center of Guangdong business school and the school of management of Shanghai University of technology, after evaluation, has become the only two national experimental teaching demonstration centers in China, providing many successful experiences for the construction and development of many economic management laboratories in China. Even in some western underdeveloped areas, because they are limited by teachers and students in theoretical teaching, they can't compare with colleges and universities in central and eastern developed areas. They put more emphasis on experimental teaching to improve the quality of training talents, and there are some successful models.

2 Related Work

2.1 Overview of System Structure

According to the requirements of the current laboratory for the reform and innovation of experimental teaching, this system refers to the functions of the current mainstream online teaching system, uses B/S (Browser/server) architecture, uses asp3.0 script to build the middle layer business processing component, completes the processing of most transactions, and uses VBScript/JavaScript and HTML to realize the interface display and user interaction functions, In the middle, mature application server products are used to support the operation environment of business processing components, with excellent data processing capacity. At the same time, the unified website template is used for function development, and the teaching functions suitable for the needs of fluid transmission and control laboratory are compiled to create convenience for experimental teaching.

In the process of system development, the program will reserve important fields for system administrator to change and maintain, so as to facilitate system transplantation and later function expansion. Achieve code compatibility, robustness and scalability.

Optimize the code structure, modularize the program as much as possible according to the object-oriented design idea, so that the functions of each module are relatively clear and independent. The management model of experimental teaching management system is shown in Fig. 1.

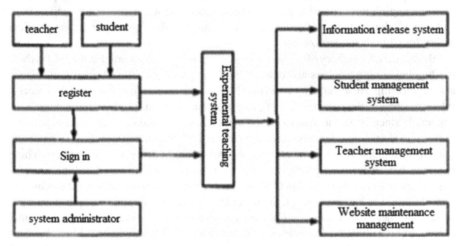

Fig. 1. Management model of experimental teaching management system

2.2 Design and Implementation of System Database Structure

The experimental teaching management system can be divided into two parts: the background management system of database and website and the front-end users' browsing, viewing, searching, uploading and downloading. After demand analysis and conceptual structure design, the logical structure of the experimental teaching management system database and the program structure of the system are designed. Then, the database is created and uploaded to the web directory of the server. Both SQL Server 2000 database server and Access2003 have a set of powerful application tools, which are perfect enough to meet the needs of professional developers. The following article mainly introduces the whole process of database file creation [2].

(1) Create database file

Through database creation, you can see the database object manager. It can manage all kinds of database objects, such as tables, queries, forms and reports, including new, modify and delete operations. The following takes the message record database of the online Q & A system as an example. Click the "empty database" option in the task window to open a dialog box. Select the database file to save to this directory, create the database "MSJ", enter "MSJ" in the file name input box, and click the "create (c)" button. Access will create a database named "MSJ. MDB" Database files. Tables are used to store data, so they are the basic components of all databases. In the database, each main topic (such as equipment details, bench instruments, large equipment use records, teacher information or user information) should have an independent table. The data in multiple tables should not be repeated. Each table contains rows called records and columns called fields.

(2) Establish relationships between tables

When a row in one table is associated with a row in another table, you can create a relationship between two tables. In the Database window, click database chart under objects, click the database chart you want to open, and then click design on the Database window toolbar. in the database chart, click the row selector for the database column or combination of columns that you want to associate with a column in another table. In the create relationship dialog box, ensure that the columns you want to associate appear in the primary key table and foreign key table lists. Select OK To create a relationship. In the chart, the primary key Party of the relationship is indicated by the key symbol. In the one-to-one relationship, the primary key party is determined by the table initializing the relationship. The experimental teaching management system has a total of 9 data tables, including 4 tables in edu database, which are interrelated.

3 Research on Economic Management Experiment Teaching Management System Based on Computer

3.1 Main Problems of Economic and Management Laboratories

Economic management laboratories are a new thing for many colleges and universities. Most of them have been established with the development of information network technology in recent years. Therefore, there are still deficiencies in many aspects, mainly as follows:

(1) There is no overall planning for laboratory construction and lack of systematicness. Many universities' economic management laboratories do not have laboratory construction planning. They often build several when they have money this year and none when they have no money next year. Due to the different location and design of the laboratories built before and after, coupled with some possible administrative affiliation, it is difficult to integrate them in the future.
(2) The management means of laboratory and experimental teaching are backward. Many economic management laboratories have not built corresponding laboratory management systems during construction, or even if they are built, they are mainly laboratory management systems, which are divorced from the teaching management system and do not support the management of experimental teaching [3].
(3) The laboratory structure is backward, and resources cannot be shared. Many economic and management laboratories are single LAN, and there is no connection between laboratories, so resources cannot be shared.
(4) There is no unified resource center, resulting in a waste of resources. The economic management laboratory supported by BS architecture should have a unified teaching resource center, so as to maximize resource sharing and avoid repeated work and inconsistent information.

3.2 Functional Design of Economic Management Experiment Teaching Management System

Based on the above reasons, how to design the economic management experimental teaching management system is the key to realize the learning and automation of experimental teaching management.

The experimental teaching management system automatically manages all links in the experimental process, and mainly realizes the following functions:

(1) Automatic management of students' experimental information. That is, the RF card number of each student is used as the information storage of this student. Query and modify the ID of the management. Students' experimental information is managed by the online laboratory system.

(2) Realize the connection with some functions of the online laboratory. Write the experimental reservation, experimental report submission, online counseling, experimental report submission and other modules into the same database management system for unified management.

(3) Realize the automatic management of each equipment in the laboratory, comprehensively improve the laboratory management level, optimize the allocation of laboratory resources, improve the utilization efficiency of experimental equipment, and lay a solid foundation for all-round and all-weather open teaching in the laboratory.

(4) All experimental computers are managed automatically. When students select the experimental computer through identity authentication, the power of the experimental computer will be turned on automatically, and the power of the experimental computer will be turned off when they leave.

(5) The failure of the experimental equipment is registered automatically. In case of failure, the students will automatically send it to the host computer of the laboratory management system for archiving by using the computer keyboard.

(6) When the experimental students leave the corresponding experimental computer during the experiment, they will automatically register and record and archive the departure and return time. The single chip microcomputer of each experimental platform designs an infrared monitor. When the students are in position to leave and from leave to position, they will send a signal to the single chip microcomputer, transfer it to the computer and store it in this student record.

(7) The experimental computer alarms and records. Manage the movement of experimental equipment. When students are found to change other experimental computers or bring out the experimental equipment.

   Send warning signal when the laboratory is, notify the laboratory management personnel to deal with it, and store and record it in this student record at the same time.

(8) The online laboratory realizes the functions of "experiment reservation", "experiment report submission", "online counseling", "online experiment" and so on.

(9) Teachers' attendance in class. Teachers sign in by computer during class and monitor by computer after class, and transfer this record to the educational administration management information system

3.3 Provide Supporting Software and Hardware Resources for Extracurricular Experimental Teaching

In addition to classroom teaching, experimental teaching also includes extracurricular practice. Extracurricular practice includes: Open Laboratory (or open experimental project), teacher training and serving the local heart. The experimental teaching object of open laboratory is students. In order to cultivate students' scientific style, innovative thinking and teamwork spirit, and improve their practical ability and engineering practice ability, open laboratory (or open experimental project) is an effective way. Laboratory opening is a new practical teaching mode different from the traditional teaching mode, which is conducive to the realization of professional talent training objectives; it can provide greater freedom and flexibility and make full use of laboratory resources.

The experimental teaching object of teacher training is teachers. On the one hand, we can use advanced equipment and environment to carry out various cutting-edge technology research and application system development or set up training courses to improve teachers' professional and technical level; on the other hand, we can combine the subject or research results with experimental teaching to transform the cutting-edge and latest research results into experimental teaching content, so as to improve teaching efficiency The scientific research level and teaching quality of teachers. The experimental teaching object of serving the local is the computer talents outside the school [4]. Make full use of the advantages of schools and laboratories, widely carry out socialized services such as training, certification and assessment, expand its influence, and make due contributions to the development of local economy and the training of talents.

4 Conclusion

Enabling students to realize independent learning and independent experiment through the network is the development direction of economic management specialty laboratories. Building a fully functional experimental teaching management system is conducive to improving the utilization rate and management efficiency of equipment. This paper studies and puts forward some ideas based on this purpose. It should be noted that with the rapid development of information technology, new technologies With the emergence of new equipment, the computer-based economic management experimental teaching management system should also be continuously improved and improved in order to meet the needs of experimental teaching in the information age.

References

1. Gong, Q.: Discussion on the new management mode of computer laboratory with multi teaching tasks. Comput. Educ., 9 (2006)
2. Yang, X.: Implementation of network system based on experimental teaching of economic management specialty. Lab. Res. Explor. 25(1), 1 (2006)
3. Peng, Y., Zhang, J., Yuan, T.: Design of experimental information management system based on C/s and B/s combination mode. Microelectron. Comput. 23(8) (2006)
4. Luo, L., Zhang, C., Huang, Y., et al.: Exploration on strengthening the teaching quality management of experimental courses. J. Hefei Univ. Technol. Du Ke Ed. 19(1), 16–18 (2005)

Research on the Design of Psychological Quality Education of Violin Course in Colleges and Universities Under Virtual Technology

Juanjuan Zhang[✉]

Faculty of Music and Dance, Hulunbuir University, Hulunbuir 021008, Inner Mongolia, China
zhangjuanjuan@hlbec.edu.cn

Abstract. Violin is a Western musical instrument, which emphasizes skills and practicality, which puts forward high requirements for the teaching of violin specialty, and also leads to a profound discussion on the teaching mode of violin specialty in Colleges and universities. In the past, in the practice of music education, colleges and universities mainly adopted the apprenticeship model. Although it can let teachers control the teaching process and grasp the teaching direction, the teaching effect is not ideal due to the limitation of teaching resources. This requires the reform of the past teaching mode of violin specialty. This paper studies the design of psychological quality education of violin curriculum in Colleges and Universities Based on virtual technology, and innovatively uses diversified education modes and teaching means to promote the cultivation of professional talents.

Keywords: Violin courses in Colleges and universities · Psychological quality education · Virtual technology

1 Introduction

With the development of national music industry, the demand for music talents has become more and more urgent. In the teaching of violin specialty in Colleges and universities, it is necessary to change the traditional thought and traditional mode, focus on cultivating compound music talents, and promote the innovative development of violin specialty teaching. Psychological quality is one of the basic qualities that each of us must have. It accompanies almost everyone's life and directly affects everyone's study, work, life and career success or failure. It can be said that a person with high IQ will not succeed if he lacks good psychological quality. Psychological quality is so important to one's life, so strengthening psychological quality education is of great significance. Especially the students in the adolescent stage, because of their physical development, social temptation, life twists and turns and learning pressure, they will often be troubled by bad emotions such as isolation, depression, anxiety and pessimism. If we strengthen the cultivation and education of their good psychological quality at this time, we can not only solve their problems in time, but also benefit them for life [1].

M. A. Jan and F. Khan (Eds.): BigIoT-EDU 2022, LNICST 466, pp. 292–297, 2023.
https://doi.org/10.1007/978-3-031-23947-2_31

This paper studies the design of psychological quality education in violin courses in Colleges and Universities Based on virtual technology. In the specific teaching practice of violin specialty, we should comprehensively use diversified and innovative education modes to change the status of students' passive learning, arouse students' interest in professional learning, and provide necessary support for the cultivation of students' comprehensive quality.

2 Virtualization Technology

2.1 Definition of Virtualization

In the early 1960s, the concept of computer virtualization technology first appeared in the United States. In 1959, Christopher Strachey published an academic report entitled time sharing in large high-speed computers. In this article, he put forward the concept of virtualization for the first time, which is also the earliest discussion of virtualization technology. It can be said that the concept of virtualization technology was formally proposed from this time.

Virtualization refers to the virtualization of a computer into multiple logical computers through virtualization technology. Each logical computer can run different operating systems, and the applications in the logical computer can run independently. Just like in a building, all walls are opened to form an open and transparent office environment. Users can build walls according to their own needs and corresponding rules to build a more independent and appropriate office space, which not only saves costs, but also greatly improves the utilization of space. The same is true of virtualization technology. On the premise of fixed hardware resources, according to different needs of customers, computing resources and storage resources are reallocated reasonably, which saves costs for customers and improves resource utilization.

Virtualization infrastructure plays an important role in virtualization technology. It can not only provide one physical machine resource to multiple virtual machines, but also enable all virtual machines in the virtualization architecture to share the physical resources of multiple physical computers, so as to greatly improve the resource utilization. Virtualization technology makes the physical hardware resources and application running environment transparent to each other. In this way, the characteristics of physical devices will not be exposed to upper layer applications [2]. Servers, storage devices and physical networks are integrated to form an IT resource pool, which can dynamically allocate resources for application software. This way of resource optimization can improve the flexibility of resource allocation, and is beneficial to the reduction of capital cost and operation cost.

2.2 Server Virtualization

Server virtualization technology can not only provide one physical machine resource to multiple virtual machines, but also integrate multiple physical servers. The original independent IT resources, such as CPU, memory, disk, etc., are gathered into a resource pool, which not only improves the resource utilization, but also reduces the software and hardware maintenance cost, makes it easier for it resources to adapt to the needs of application software, and realizes the dynamic management of resources. In x86 architecture, in order to protect the operation of instructions, four different ring level privileged instruction levels are implemented. Ring 0 is the instruction level with the highest permission level in the operating system, which is used to run privileged instructions. The virtualization layer runs on top of the physical layer and can allocate physical resources to guestos. Therefore, guestos cannot run at ring0 level. In this case, if the privileged instruction in guestos cannot run at the originally planned instruction level, a running error will be generated. Therefore, the industry has proposed two methods to solve the problem of privileged instructions in x86 architecture, namely full virtualization and para virtualization. Then, hardware assisted virtualization technology is proposed to process privileged instructions through processor hardware, as shown in Fig. 1.

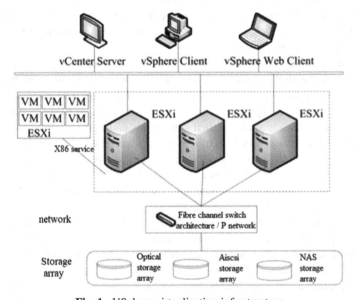

Fig. 1. VSphere virtualization infrastructure

3 Research on Teaching Mode of Violin Specialty in Colleges and Universities Based on Virtual Technology

3.1 Teaching Mode of Group Cooperation Specialty

Nowadays, the enrollment expansion of colleges and universities is carried out like tea, which also greatly increases the enrollment of violin majors in Colleges and universities, which virtually increases the difficulty of teachers' professional teaching. However, from the overall point of view, affected by many factors, the number and quality of professional teachers in Colleges and universities have not been significantly improved, which has brought great obstacles to the development of professional teaching. This is very obvious in the practice of music teaching in Colleges and universities, because the implementation of music education usually needs to carry out one-to-one teaching, and the lack of teachers will make teachers unable to meet the diversified learning and development needs of students in limited time and energy, let alone achieve ideal teaching results. In addition, the past teacher apprenticeship teaching model is relatively closed, which can not effectively broaden students' horizons, but also lead to the students' classroom learning environment is too boring. In the face of this situation, actively introducing the group cooperation professional education model can greatly change the above situation. Group cooperation mode is to divide students into multiple learning groups according to their abilities, personality characteristics, interests and hobbies, and carry out learning activities in groups [3]. This way not only reduces the collective class, but also enlarges the one-to-one education mode, integrates the advantages of the two modes, and greatly reduces the teaching pressure. In order to ensure the application effect of the teaching mode of group cooperation specialty, on the one hand, teachers should pay attention to scientific grouping of students to highlight complementarity and cooperation; On the other hand, we should pay attention to the development of students' comprehensive quality and provide students with a good atmosphere of benign interaction and active competition.

3.2 Teaching Mode of School Enterprise Cooperation Specialty

School enterprise cooperation is widely used in the field of music education. It is also an important achievement of education reform. It has played an important role in solving the employment difficulties of college students. Cultivating practical and applied talents is not only an important goal of music education in Colleges and universities, but also an important direction of violin professional education in Colleges and universities. To ensure the implementation of this goal, strengthen the communication and cooperation between schools and enterprises, let enterprises participate in school education and teaching, or let students enter enterprises for practice is an important teaching way. In the implementation of school enterprise cooperation, students can get effective exercise, improve professional quality and meet social needs. In order to better implement school enterprise cooperation in the practice of violin professional education, first of all, we need to do a good job in school enterprise consultation and mutual assistance in the process of professional construction. Both schools and enterprises should have an accurate positioning and in-depth understanding of the cultivation of violin professionals, and thus formulate a detailed talent cultivation plan. Secondly, we should do a good job in the selection and application of implementation methods to avoid making school enterprise cooperation empty talk. In the specific implementation process, enterprises need to appoint professionals to enter the school as the second tutor, and do a good job of professional guidance to students from the perspective of industry; Provide students with opportunities to enter enterprise practice and training, and provide a practice platform. Colleges and universities can also let violin teachers get practical training in enterprises and build a team of double qualified teachers. In addition, schools and enterprises also need to work together to create performance projects and provide students with opportunities for Violin professional training.

4 Ways to Cultivate the Psychological Quality of Violin Course

(1) The organic infiltration of classroom teaching combined with subject courses is the main position of quality education. The cultivation of psychological quality is also inseparable from the teaching activities of various subjects. We should base on subject teaching and carry out organic infiltration, especially intellectual factors, such as observation, memory, imagination, thinking, attention and other cognitive abilities, which are mainly formed through subject education. The cultivation of some non intellectual factors, including emotion, will and personality, is also inseparable from subject teaching, such as cultivating students' good moral sentiment in politics; Physical education training students strong will, exercise endurance and perseverance; Geography class carries out environmental awareness education for students and so on. This penetration is subtle, frequent and effective.

(2) Combined with the extracurricular position to carry out environmental education, which mainly refers to the extracurricular environment. In addition to classroom teaching, a very important way to cultivate students' psychological quality is extracurricular environment, including campus environment, family environment, social environment, interpersonal environment, cultural atmosphere and so on. In addition to genetic factors, human development is mainly affected by the environment. Therefore, creating a good educational environment is particularly important to cultivate students' psychological quality. The campus environment is very important. Students contact and edify every day. The beautiful campus environment, such as a unique cultural corridor at the entrance of the school, lifelike vertical carvings and relief carvings, green trees and flowers, makes students feel particularly comfortable, and one-man school has a good mood and interest. This beautification, greening, purification, fresh and harmonious campus environment plays a subtle role in cultivating students' sentiment and purifying students' soul. The family environment can not be ignored. Family education plays an important role in the growth of students, especially in the cultivation of students' personality. Correct family education can enable students to form good psychological qualities such as diligence, frugality, hard work, tolerance and openness, and distinguish right from wrong. Social environment is also an important factor affecting students' growth [4]. In today's colorful society impacted by the economic tide, it is not easy to distinguish what students want to accept and abandon, and they need to be guided correctly. In addition to the guidance of public opinion, there should also be the positive guidance of school education to enable students to eliminate the psychological interference of social and cultural environment and the interference of unhealthy social behavior. It is a special role of the social environment to organize students to purposefully carry out rich, colorful and educational social practice activities, deepen factories, villages and troops, encourage students with positive typical heroic deeds, establish a correct outlook on life and world outlook, cultivate materialistic and Dialectical Views and beliefs, and form correct moral concepts.

5 Conclusion

Colleges and universities are a solid position for cultivating high-quality violin professionals, and the achievements obtained in the long-term reform process of music education in Colleges and universities are becoming more and more abundant. However, nowadays, the society puts forward higher and higher requirements for Violin professionals, especially under the background of increasing employment pressure, colleges and universities are required to adjust and reform the teaching mode from the perspective of the market. Specifically, in the process of analyzing and constructing the violin teaching mode, colleges and universities should highlight students' professional advantages, guide students to apply what they have learned, and build a platform for the integration of students' theory and practice.

Acknowledgements. The 8th Teaching and Research Project of Hulunbuir University "Research and Practice on the Ideological and Political Construction of Violin Courses in an Omnimedia Media Environment" No: JYZC2021001.

References:

1. Zhao, X.: On the teaching method and practice of violin major in Colleges and universities. Music Forum **31**(8), 90–91 (2017)
2. Hu, X. (chief ed.): Virtual Reality Technology and Application. Higher Education Press, Beijing (2004)
3. Zhou, M.: Problems and reflections on violin teaching in colleges and universities. Contemp. Music **19**(9), 39–40 (2018)
4. Wang, H.: College physical education is a way to promote college students' mental health. J. Guangdong Norm. Univ. Technol. **28**(6), 1024–1039 (2003)

Study on Corrosion Wear and Protection of Coal Preparation Equipment Based on PLC Centralized Control System

Wenjuan Sun[1] and Guozhi Liang[2(✉)]

[1] Anhui Vocational and Technical College, Hefei 230011, Anhui, China
[2] Anhui Academy of Coal Science, Hefei 230001, Anhui, China
wjsungzliang@163.com

Abstract. This paper introduces the composition structure, system function and implementation method of the centralized control system of coal preparation production based on PLC, and discusses the application of PLC in the system, the function of each control module and the design method of communication network. According to the working principle and structural characteristics of beneficiation equipment, this paper studies the corrosion wear and protection of coal preparation equipment based on PLC centralized control system. The typical corrosion cases of mineral processing equipment are analyzed, the main products of rust layer on the surface of vulnerable parts of mineral processing equipment are determined, the main corrosion types, failure causes and corrosion mechanism are analyzed, and the corresponding protection countermeasures are put forward. The main purpose of this study is to design a new protective coating for coal preparation equipment by using PLC centralized control system. The results show that the protective coating has good corrosion resistance and wear resistance.

Keywords: PLC · Centralized control system · Corrosion · Wear and protection · Coal preparation equipment

1 Introduction

The total amount of coal in China ranks first in the world. Industrial development has an increasing demand for energy, in which the proportion of coal in energy production and consumption has been around 70%. It can be seen that China's energy will adhere to the long-term development strategy of taking coal as the basic energy source and the common development of various energy sources.

With the enhancement of everyone's awareness of environmental protection and the continuous progress of economic foundation, everyone's demand for high-quality coal is increasing. As the source of clean coal technology, coal preparation technology has received more attention. People use advanced technology, physics, chemistry and other methods to reduce ash, gangue and other impurities [1]. Use heavy medium washing and other processes to improve the quality of commercial coal from the source, reduce manual

M. A. Jan and F. Khan (Eds.): BigIoT-EDU 2022, LNICST 466, pp. 298–308, 2023.
https://doi.org/10.1007/978-3-031-23947-2_32

use, increase benefits, improve the utilization rate of raw coal, and reduce transportation costs. Improving automatic coal preparation technology in line with made in China 2025 has increasingly become the only way for China's coal industry to transform and upgrade and structural adjustment, and improve economic and social benefits.

With the development of computer network, communication, control technology and electrical technology, the traditional centralized control system of coal preparation plant has been fundamentally changed. The construction and transformation of coal preparation plant are developing in the direction of network and intelligence. The popularization and application of integrated automation system is a prominent feature of modern large coal preparation plants in China in recent years [2]. In recent years, the trend of large-scale production of coal preparation plants in China is obvious, and the requirements of coal preparation plants for the automation level of control system are becoming higher and higher.

In the process of metal mineral processing, due to the influence of geographical and climatic environment and surrounding chemical media, mechanical equipment inevitably has corrosion problems. The material, service time and environmental adaptability of parts of beneficiation equipment directly affect the service performance of the equipment. Field investigation is carried out for vulnerable parts, perishable parts and working conditions of mineral processing machinery and equipment, to understand the corrosion behavior and corrosion influencing factors of mineral processing equipment components, and to deeply understand the environmental adaptability of mineral machinery and equipment is the key to improve the material level of vulnerable parts and perishable parts of mineral machinery and equipment, prolong the service life and enhance the reliability of equipment [3]. At present, most of the existing studies focus on the exploration and efficient mining of metal mineral resources, and pay less attention to the corrosion behavior and failure mechanism of metal parts of mineral machinery and equipment. In this work, a typical corrosion case of beneficiation equipment in a mine in China is preliminarily analyzed by combining field investigation and sampling laboratory analysis. The rust layers of four main corrosion prone equipment, cone crusher, vibrating screen, ball mill and flotation machine, are analyzed by X-ray diffraction (XRD). Combined with the working principle and structural characteristics of the equipment, the main corrosion types of vulnerable parts of beneficiation equipment are determined, their failure mechanism is analyzed, and the corresponding protection countermeasures are put forward.

With the continuous innovation of industrial control technology, great progress has been made in basic disciplines, which makes the information obtained by measurement and control more reliable and fundamentally changes the control form. The centralized control system in the new era is a highly integrated system that includes over control, real-time parameter control, local automation, and digital analog integration. With the proposal of intelligent manufacturing and made in China 2025, centralized control automation technology has entered a new stage [4]. PLC module can realize logic control, process control, floating-point operation and data processing. At present, with the maturity of technology, the centralized control system has been popularized, in which the PLC control layer includes local, remote and on-site detection and control. It realizes the automatic control of equipment parameters and the automatic operation state of equipment monitoring.

2 Coal Preparation Equipment of PLC Centralized Control System

2.1 Overall Design Scheme of PLC Centralized Control System in Coal Preparation Plant

The overall design of centralized control system of coal preparation plant includes four subsystems: Production centralized control, safety monitoring, dispatching communication and emergency alarm. The functions of modules are not completely independent, and each module coordinates with each other to complete the overall functions of the system.

The production centralized control system needs to meet the status monitoring of all production equipment. Production equipment includes crushing equipment, screening equipment, sorting equipment, dehydration equipment, water spraying equipment, demineralization equipment, fluid equipment, clarified water equipment, etc. In order to meet the status monitoring of all production equipment by the production centralized control system, the video monitoring information at each production equipment needs to be transmitted to the monitoring host through the communication transmission line with the help of the safety monitoring system, and the emergency alarm system needs to transmit the detected production equipment status information to the communication substation at the nearest production equipment through the CAN bus, The communication substation transmits the information to the monitoring host in the production centralized control system through the communication transmission line. The purpose of setting two monitoring hosts at the production centralized control system is to process and backup the video monitoring information and classify, manage and process and backup the detected production equipment status information.

In addition, the production centralized control system needs to meet the remote control of production equipment [5]. A master control station is set up at each production equipment, which can control the work of production equipment manually or automatically. Through the monitoring host in the production centralized control system and the public address telephone in the dispatching communication system, the production equipment can be manually controlled through the main control station at each production equipment, or the direct connection between the monitoring host of the production centralized control system and the communication substation in the dispatching communication system can be established, Send control instructions to the master control station at each equipment through automatic control to realize the automatic control of each production equipment.

The control equipment involved in the operation process includes coal feeder, centrifuge, dewatering screen, conveying belt, crusher, jig, coal bucket elevator, oil pump and filter. Each module of PLC controls different types of motor equipment. The controlled equipment is required to realize local and remote control, and the upper computer system is required to monitor the state of the controlled equipment in real time. Take Fig. 1 as an example to make a simple analysis of the schematic diagram. As shown in the figure, when the three-phase switch is in automatic gear, the centralized control signal sends a high level to control the start and stop of the motor [6]. When the output is high, the relay is powered on, the contact is pulled in, the chain reaction, the main contact is pulled in, the motor starts, and then the auxiliary contact is pulled in.

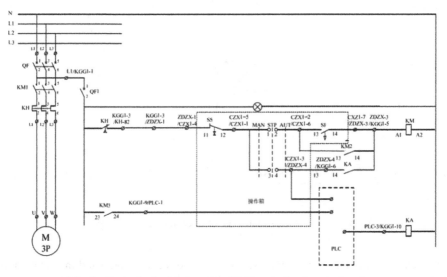

Fig. 1. Control principle based on PLC centralized control system

2.2 Hardware Platform Design and Implementation

(1) Production centralized control system

The production centralized control system relies on the safety monitoring, dispatching communication and emergency alarm subsystems. Therefore, the hardware design of the production centralized control system needs to establish a ring network structure with the production centralized control system as the core and the safety monitoring, dispatching communication and emergency alarm subsystems as the branches. The internal hardware organization of the production centralized control system needs to meet the functions of visual management, production equipment status monitoring and remote control of production equipment. The hardware organization is shown in Fig. 2.

Two monitoring hosts are set in the production centralized control system. The monitoring host 1 is responsible for processing the analog video monitoring information transmitted by the safety monitoring system, classifying the video monitoring information according to each production area and displaying it on the large screen display. At the same time, the monitoring host 1 stores and backs up the classified video monitoring information. The large screen display adopts 55 inch ultra narrow edge LCD splicing screen of Hikvision, the main body is 3 * 3, a total of 9 55 inch LCD splicing screens, and the splicing seam is only 3.5 mm. The monitoring host 2 is responsible for receiving the detection status information transmitted by the emergency alarm system through the

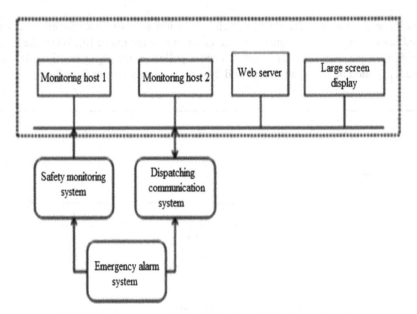

Fig. 2. Hardware organization chart of centralized control system

dispatching communication system, sending voice or control command information to the dispatching communication system, realizing manual or automatic control of production equipment, and backing up the above information [7]. A web server is set in the production centralized control system to realize the secondary storage of the information stored by the monitoring host 1 and the monitoring host 2, so as to clean the space of the two monitoring hosts regularly to meet the subsequent data storage management.

(2) Safety monitoring system

The hardware part of the safety monitoring system consists of 16 monitors, network hard disk camera and large screen display. The hardware organization logic is shown in Fig. 3.

The safety monitoring system adopts 16 monitors deployed around the production equipment of the coal preparation plant. The monitor adopts kdm2121 infrared waterproof network monitor, and the network hard disk camera adopts nvr2820e. Four SATA hard disks are built in, and each hard disk supports 1000 g at most. The video monitoring information of the network hard disk camera is classified and processed by the monitoring host 1 in the production centralized control system, On the one hand, it is used for the display of large screen display, which is the 3 * 3 splicing screen large screen display in the production centralized control system. On the other hand, it backs up the video monitoring information to the web server.

Under the centralized control mode, it is divided into automatic mode and manual mode. Under the centralized control automatic mode, the centralized control room sends the start-up warning signal to the site. After the delay, all equipment of the system will start automatically according to the locking relationship and linkage relationship. During the start-up process, the central control room can terminate the start-up process

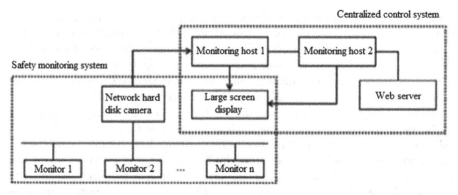

Fig. 3. Hardware organization chart of safety monitoring system

by revoking the instruction and setting a prohibit start on site. All posts are connected by telephone rings and instructions, and the main posts are accompanied by telephones. When starting up, all equipment participating in centralized control shall be started up first in the downstream than in the upstream to prevent the occurrence of stacking, and must be started up against the coal flow. During normal shutdown, each equipment participating in centralized control will stop first if it is located in the upstream than in the downstream, so as to ensure that no new material is added to the system during shutdown. In case of failure of coal preparation equipment, the system shall have the ability to solve the failure [8]. For example, when the equipment stops abnormally, the upstream equipment stops urgently to prevent stacking, and the downstream equipment stops late to prevent greater failure.

To sum up, the centralized control system of heavy medium coal preparation is divided into automatic and manual modes. In automatic mode, the reverse generation of faults can be monitored. Automatic and manual control modes are summarized as follows:

Under the automatic mode of the system, according to the production process, PLC controls the sequential start and stop of each equipment. There should be a locking function between the equipment. In case of equipment failure, it has the ability to solve it, prevent stacking and ensure the safe operation of production. And the important data parameters are transmitted to the upper computer in real time, so that the personnel in the central control room can grasp the on-site production situation in real time. In the manual mode, the system can remotely start and stop a single equipment in the centralized control room, and control the actuator such as valves, so as to complete the commissioning and maintenance of field equipment.

3 Study on Corrosion Wear and Protection of Coal Preparation Equipment

3.1 Application and Development of Coal Preparation Equipment

Before the design of PLC cabinet, the coal preparation process is briefly introduced and popularized. The basic principle of coal preparation is to use different density and surface characteristics of different substances to reduce ash, sulfur and grinding impurities through physical and chemical methods, and divide into different types of coal products according to actual needs. According to the basic principles of rational utilization of coal and resource conservation. There are roughly three coal preparation methods: 1. Gravity coal preparation; 2. Floating coal preparation (flotation); 3. Special coal preparation. Among them, the heavy medium coal preparation technology has been continuously improved due to its relevance to China's coal conditions, so we choose the heavy medium coal preparation technology for research. Coal is a mixture of many substances. The mainstream idea is to integrate Archimedes' principle, gravity settlement principle and fluid mechanics principle. The density of gangue is quite different from that of clean coal because it contains impurities such as sediment. According to the research, the density of coal is about 12 to 15 kg/m^3, and the density of gangue is about 3000 kg/m^3. The basic process is to divide the product into two different density layers through two kinds of dense media: low-density clean coal and high-density grindstone [9]. The high-density ones are on the surface, and the high-density ones sink at the bottom and are discharged through the overflow port respectively. The particle size and shape of raw coal are not studied. According to dense separation, it is necessary to configure liquid with density greater than water, that is, heavy medium suspension. Now because of the magnetic separator.

(1) Heavy medium cyclone

The coal preparation equipment has the advantages of simple structure, convenient operation, high separation efficiency and no moving parts. Since the hydrocyclone itself has no moving parts, the separation execution process depends on the structural parameters of the equipment itself and external operation to achieve the best separation results. There are many structures of dense medium cyclone, which can be divided into three product dense medium cyclone and two Product Dense Medium Cyclone according to the type of coal separation; According to the feeding mode of sorted coal, it can be divided into non pressure and pressure. Due to the advantages of dense medium coal preparation, it has a wide range of applications and can be applied to the separation of different coal qualities. Compared with other coal preparation methods, it has high separation accuracy for coal with large slime content or difficult to separate coal.

(2) Moving screen jig

The moving screen jig, also known as the single end jig, is currently mainly used to pre select the gangue in the lump coal. During the operation of the moving screen, the tank needs to be filled with a certain amount of water. The moving screen in the water, driven by the external power transmission, needs the pin shaft to move up and down repeatedly. When the raw material sorting coal is fed into the moving screen system, a bed with a certain thickness will be formed on the screen plate. During the upward movement of the moving screen, the water phase moves downward for the coal particles. During the downward movement of the moving screen, the water phase moves upward for the coal particles, and the coal particles are stratified by density after a certain repeated movement. At present, there are two types of oil injection for the moving screen jig: mechanical and hydraulic. The probability of failure of the hydraulic jig is relatively high. The mechanical jig has relatively simple structure and reliable function. At present, it is suitable for the operation and management of coal separation in China. However, the equipment has some problems, such as large mechanical noise and troublesome on-line adjustment. We need to improve this problem, improve the efficiency and quality of coal preparation, and realize the factor of environmental protection.

(3) Dry separator

The technology of dry separator is relatively primitive, which is suitable for the simple or medium degree of coal washability, as well as the separation of power coal gangue and coal gangue, the upgrading of inferior coal, the separation of easily argillaceous coal in case of water, and the separation of coal in cold and water shortage areas. At present, there are two types of dry separators: air heavy medium dry separators and composite dry separators. FX series wind dry separator and FGX compound dry separator are most used in China. These two types of equipment make full use of the advantages of wind and shaking table, and have the advantages of less investment, strong practicability and low coal separation cost. After separation, the coal ash content is obviously reduced, and the effect is good.

3.2 Various Factors Causing Wear of Beneficiation Equipment

When mining mineral resources, mineral processing equipment caused by metal materials is usually used. When processing high hardness mineral materials, these mineral processing equipment are often used directly to process the mineral materials. When the beneficiation equipment works, the workload is very large and the working time is relatively long. It is for this reason that it is easy to wear the beneficiation equipment and seriously reduce the service life of the beneficiation equipment. In the mining process of ore materials, it is a very common situation that the beneficiation equipment is worn [10]. If you want to fundamentally solve these problems, you should first find the causes of these problems and formulate a set of reasonable maintenance measures. The design, structure and personnel operation of beneficiation equipment are directly related to the wear of beneficiation equipment.

4   Maintenance Measures for Beneficiation Equipment

4.1   Reduce Resonance of Equipment

(1) In order to effectively reduce the resonance of beneficiation equipment, various aspects should be considered when manufacturing beneficiation equipment, and materials with more uniform texture should be selected. Reduce the possible errors in manufacturing, minimize the error value as far as possible, and ensure the basic rigidity of beneficiation equipment. Speed limit the beneficiation equipment so that it cannot reach the critical speed, which can effectively avoid resonance of beneficiation equipment due to too fast speed.

(2) Extend the eccentricity of beneficiation equipment and effectively reduce oil film oscillation. At the same time, properly adjust the oil supply temperature and the viscosity of lubricating oil, increase the oil supply pressure, and select the bearing structure with good vibration control performance to ensure its firmness during installation. Taking such measures can effectively prevent the abrasion of beneficiation equipment due to

oscillation and prolong its service life. In addition to the above methods, during the maintenance process, the management personnel shall also strengthen the observation of the beneficiation equipment, take notes of the parts, time, devices, symptoms and other conditions of the beneficiation equipment with wear or problems, and constantly summarize and summarize to improve the maintenance experience.

4.2   The Parts of Beneficiation Equipment Prone to Wear Shall Be Strengthened with High Wear-Resistant Materials

If the materials of the beneficiation equipment are poor, when the beneficiation equipment is working, the easily worn parts will often be damaged or faulty, delaying the project progress, and the staff also need to often replace the parts of these easily damaged parts, which will increase the investment of maintenance funds and manpower. Therefore, more wear-resistant materials need to be used for those parts in the beneficiation equipment that are extremely prone to wear or damage, so as to fundamentally prolong the service life of the beneficiation equipment, reduce the replacement times and quantity, and save maintenance funds. In recent years, foreign countries usually use reinforced high or and Ni or cast iron toothed plates in the selection of materials for beneficiation equipment. The wear resistance of this cast iron toothed plate is far higher than that of high manganese steel structure toothed plate. In the use of this reinforced high resistance material, even if there is cracking, it is rarely easy to break. This kind of equipment is worthy of our reference.

The corrosion, wear and protection system of coal preparation equipment based on PLC centralized control system is the production command center, and all monitoring and control commands are transmitted in the centralized control room.

(1) The flow chart is used on the display to display the operation status, parameter changes and historical curves of the process system equipment; The picture uses dynamic graphics to display real-time working condition information of the whole plant, and the picture displays PID loop status and analog signal monitoring; Automatic recording system and various alarm systems; When abnormal conditions occur, it is the correct alarm prompt for the operator. Each point can be assigned an alarm priority and automatically recorded, and displayed in the special alarm bar and alarm screen on the operator screen;

(2) Calculate and record the production data of the system: operation time, annual operation time and annual operation time. (3) The parameters of the system and the given values of process parameters can be adjusted at any time; Provide stable control.

(4) Provide the security level from operation function to multiple permissions that can complete the configuration function.

(5) Provide Chinese display screen to ensure that the operator can operate simply; Pull rope switch, deviation switch, stall switch, chute blockage switch, longitudinal tear protection switch. The centrifuge is equipped with an oil pressure switch; The scraper is equipped with chain breaking protection; The crusher is equipped with stall protection; The switching value signal is uploaded to the control system.

(6) Connect the low-voltage comprehensive protection device of each workshop by means of communication (RS485), upload the control and frequency setting of high-voltage and low-voltage converters in the central control room, adopt IO control mode,

and connect the system by means of communication to monitor the process parameters in a full range.

4.3 The Key Parts of Beneficiation Equipment Shall Be Tested in Time

With the rapid development of computer and network communication technology, information exchange technology has been widely used in automatic control, factory management, product quality management and other fields. The combination of Ethernet and Fieldbus can truly realize the integration of monitoring, control, management and decision-making in the production process of coal washing plant. SIMATIC NET is the general name of Siemens' industrial communication network solutions and an important part of Siemens' fully integrated automation. The typical factory automation system provided by Siemens mainly includes field equipment layer, workshop monitoring layer and factory management layer. The field device layer mainly realizes the field device control and the interlocking control between devices, and connects the distributed IO, sensors, drivers, actuators and other field devices. The master station is responsible for bus communication management and slave station communication. The workshop monitoring layer, also known as the unit layer, is used to complete the connection between the main production equipment in the workshop and realize the monitoring of workshop level equipment. Workshop level monitoring includes online monitoring of production equipment status, equipment fault alarm and maintenance, etc. The factory management usually adopts Ethernet conforming to iec802.3 standard and tcp/ip standard.

In the process of daily maintenance of beneficiation equipment, it is also necessary to detect the key parts irregularly. Once problems are found, relevant staff must evaluate and analyze these faults. If the situation is serious, stop production immediately for maintenance to avoid more serious damage to the safety threat of the whole project. In addition, while purchasing equipment, it is also necessary to adjust measures to local conditions and vary from mine to mine, and select high and new technologies or emerging technologies with a high degree of automation.

5   Conclusion

The design of the centralized control system of the coal preparation plant pays attention to the data linkage between various systems. The design of the centralized control system of the coal preparation plant includes the production centralized control system and safety monitoring system, realizes the equipment status monitoring and manual automatic control of the whole coal preparation plant, and ensures the safety of production. In the process of mining mineral resources, a variety of beneficiation equipment must be used. It is precisely because the working environment of beneficiation equipment is relatively special, coupled with its own working reasons, it is easy to wear the beneficiation equipment and lead to failure. The reasons for these problems are not only the unreasonable design of beneficiation equipment, but also the unreasonable and nonstandard operation of operators in the process of use. During the daily use of beneficiation equipment, attention must be paid to the maintenance and repair of beneficiation equipment. Once the equipment is worn, the causes leading to the wear of beneficiation equipment should be found at the first time and effective maintenance measures should be taken.

Acknowledgements. 1. Natural Science research project of Universities in Anhui:Study on corrosion effect of high salt wastewater as coal preparation recharge water on coal preparation equipment and countermeasures (KJ2020A1036). 2. 2021 Domestic Visiting and Training Program for Outstanding Young Backbone Teachers of Colleges and Universities (gxgnfx2021177)
.

References

1. Liu J, Chen T, Yuan C, et al. Effect of Corrosion on Cavitation Erosion Behavior of HVOF Sprayed Cobalt-Based Coatings. IOP Publishing Ltd, 2022
2. Lu, P., Wu, M., Liu, X., et al.: Study on corrosion resistance and bio-tribological behavior of porous structure based on the SLM manufactured medical Ti6Al4V. Met. Mater. Int. **26**(8), 1182–1191 (2020)
3. Liu, X., Wang, P., Zhang, D., et al.: Atmospheric corrosion protection performance and mechanism of superhydrophobic surface based on coalescence-induced droplet self-jumping behavior. ACS Appl. Mater. Interf. **13**, 13 (2021)
4. Modibane, K.D., Pesha, T., Maponya, T.C., et al.: Electrochemical Studies on the Corrosion Protection of Aluminum Metal in Acid Media by Unsubstituted and 4-Tetranitro Substituted Nickel(II) Phthalocyanine Inhibitors for Hydrogen Fuel Cells. BIBLIO-GLOBUS Publishing House2 (021)
5. Zhang, X., Wang, H., Shang, Z., et al.: Experimental study on the preparation method of coal-like materials based on similarity of material properties and drilling parameters. Powder Technol. **395**, 26–42 (2022)
6. Volkov, R., Valiullin, T., Vysokomornaya, O.: Spraying of composite liquid fuels based on types of coal preparation waste: current problems and achievements: Review. Energies **14** (2021)
7. Guo, R., Huang, S., Liu, F.: Study on preparation and simple calibration system of acoustic emission sensor based on epoxy resin. J. Mater. Sci. Mater. Electron. (2022)
8. Ma, X., Zhang, Z., Ma, X., et al.: Study on corrosion failure characteristics of silicone rubber in acidic environment. In: 2021 International Conference on Electrical Materials and Power Equipment (ICEMPE) (2021)
9. Jie, H.: Research on port ship pollution prevention and control system based on the background of marine environmental protection. IOP Conference Series: Earth and Environmental Science **781**(3), 032059 (2021)
10. Prasetya, A.D., Rifai, M., As'Ari, A.H., et al.: Electrochemistry study on the relationship between grain boundary state and corrosion behavior of ultrafine grained iron chromium alloy (2020)

Summary of Research on Learning Analysis Based on Educational Big Data

Weijuan Wang[✉]

Zibo Normal College, Zibo 255130, Shandong, China
wangwj62@163.com

Abstract. This paper is based on the log data of the computer basic information guidance platform developed by our institute and has been widely used. Firstly, collect and preprocess the data related to the students' login and resource browsing in the platform; then conduct statistical analysis on the students' login behavior and resource browsing situation; on this basis, the influencing factors of students' login behavior and resource browsing behavior are obtained by using decision tree algorithm. According to the results of the analysis, it is possible for educators to organize teaching content and construct teaching mode based on learners' learning situation.

Keywords: Big data · Information guidance platform · Education data mining · Landing behavior · Resource browsing behavior

1 Educational Data Mining and Its Value

Educational data mining is a process of transforming original data from various educational systems into useful information, which can be used by teachers, students and their parents, educational researchers and developers of educational software systems. "Education data mining can also be seen as a new module embedded in the existing education system, and it can interact with various elements in the education system, and ultimately achieve the purpose of improving teaching." For our educators, the role of education data mining is to provide us with more objective feedback information, so that we can better adjust and optimize teaching strategies, improve teaching process, complete curriculum development, and realize the organization, innovation and construction of teaching mode of teaching content based on learners' learning situation [1]. According to the application fields of data mining, educational data mining can be divided into three categories: ε Lear η ing (Teaching) data mining, ε Ma η Agee η t (Management) data mining and E-research (Scientific Research) data mining. In the field of e-learning (Teaching) data mining. 3 this paper, mainly from the e-learning (Teaching) data mining application, based on our college's information guidance platform log data, to analyze students' learning behavior.

M. A. Jan and F. Khan (Eds.): BigIoT-EDU 2022, LNICST 466, pp. 309–313, 2023.
https://doi.org/10.1007/978-3-031-23947-2_33

2 Data Mining Algorithm

In the practice of data mining, the common clustering algorithms based on map reduce include som clustering algorithm, FCM clustering algorithm, kmea η s algorithm and hierarchical clustering algorithm. This section takes κ means as an example [2]. K-means takes distance as the unique evaluation index of similarity shape, which is one of the clustering algorithms based on distance. Its goal is to find independent subsets (clusters) composed of objects which are close to each other. The basic process of the algorithm is as follows:

(1) Select training sample $Z = \{z^{(1)}, z^{(2)}, \ldots z^{(n)}\}$, where $Z^{(i)} \in R(i \in [1, n])$.
(2) The centroid point $u^{(1)}, u^{(2)}, \ldots u^{(k)}$ is selected randomly, where $u^{(k)} \in R(i \in [1, k])$.
(3) For any sample $z^{(i)}(i \in [1, n])$, according to the distance formula $d^{(i)} = \min(\|z^{(i)} - u^{(j)}\|2), j \in [1, k]$, map task calculates the classification of the sample, reduce
(4) The task is calculated according to formula (1)

$$u_j = \frac{\sum_i^n 1\{d^{(i)} = j\}\alpha^{(i)}}{\sum_i^n 1\{d^{(i)} = f\}} \tag{1}$$

(5) Iteration termination in the process of iteration, if the centroid does not change any more, it will terminate and output the centroid.

The time complexity of K-means algorithm is O (MKT), where m is the size of data set, K is the number of clusters and t is the number of iterations. Therefore, the overall efficiency of the algorithm can be improved by reducing the number of iterations or improving the efficiency of each iteration.

3 Construction of Educational Data Mining Model for Students' Online Learning Behavior Analysis

The online learning behavior analysis of learners is mainly based on the recorded data of the learning process of teachers and students based on the network teaching platform. It makes statistics, visualization and various kinds of mining on the behavior mode (landing, browsing resources, online communication, etc.) of behavior subjects (teachers and students), the usage of behavior objects (various resources, online course modules, etc.), and the occurrence time of behaviors, Combined with the characteristic data of teachers and students, this paper explores the factors that affect online learning behavior.

Educational data mining pattern is built to complete specific mining tasks, which is an integrated application of various data mining tools and algorithms.

Educational data mining mode is composed of "data mining tools and algorithms" and "data".}Tools and algorithms provide support for data mining and generate corresponding "data", as shown in Fig. 1. The expansion of these three elements in time will form data mining workflow, tool and algorithm flow and data flow respectively [3].

Data mining workflow includes data collection, data preprocessing, data mining, pattern interpretation evaluation and application. Among them, the learning process data mining pattern is used for learning process and learning behavior analysis, and its mining mode is shown in Fig. 1.

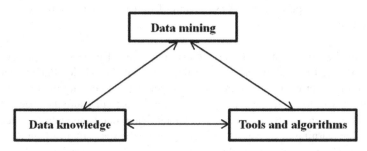

Fig. 1. Elements of educational data mining pattern

Among them, in the core link of data mining workflow, the main data mining tasks include the analysis of learners' login behavior, the analysis of the browsing mode of learning resources, and the analysis of influencing factors of students' behavior.

4   Analysis on the Influencing Factors of Students' Learning Behavior Based on the Information Guidance Platform

4.1   Basic Principle of Ant Colony Algorithm

Based on level 15 students, this paper selects the basic information data of students, log data of landing, resource browsing, learning experience and other log data generated when using the information-based learning guidance platform, as well as the test data generated by the students when using the formative examination platform. These data are imported into the database to form four data tables. The association of the four data tables is established through the "student number" field. After the joint query, the intersection operation of the four data tables is carried out, and 1265 students are obtained in the four tables. Then, the basic information data, landing data, resource browsing data and formative test data of these 1265 students are taken as the analysis objects, and statistical analysis and data mining are carried out.

4.2   Description of Students' Learning Landing Behavior and Analysis of Influencing Factors

In the data table of login behavior, student number and login time are two main fields. This paper does not take the number of students landing as the counting unit, but counts the number of landing people in a certain time unit. If the number of landing statistics may be due to the repeated landing of individual students, resulting in the illusion of strong learning. Therefore, this paper mainly uses the "week" as the classification field to count the students' login rate (the number of people landing on the platform divided by the total number of students); the field of student number is used to count the number of days each student has logged in. This paper takes the week of the opening day of the course on October 11, 2015 as the first week, and the duration of the course is 15 weeks.

(1) Taking the time period "week" as the unit of statistics, we found the learning cycle of students

For individual learners, the learning cycle is uncertain. But from the perspective of teaching, we need to understand the learning cycle of the whole student group, that is, through the records of the landing platform, analyze and count how long the whole student group will log in to participate in learning, so as to measure the speed of online learning. As a teacher, it is necessary to understand how many students no longer come to learn as the learning time goes on, so as to measure the speed of group online learning termination. Through the statistical analysis of the weekly cumulative landing rate, the learning cycle of the students is obtained.

(2) Analysis on the influencing factors of students' landing behavior

Microsoft/decision tree algorithm is a classification and regression algorithm provided by Microsoft SQL Server Analysis Services for predictive modeling of discrete and continuous attributes. For discrete attributes, the algorithm predicts the relationship between input columns in the dataset [4]. The decision tree makes predictions based on the trend toward a particular outcome. For continuous attributes, the algorithm uses linear regression to determine the split position of the decision tree. The principle of the algorithm is to create a series of splits in the tree to generate the data mining model. These splits are represented as "nodes.". When the input column is found to be closely related to the predictable column, the algorithm will add a node to the model. The algorithm determines the splitting method differently, which mainly depends on whether it predicts continuous columns or discrete columns. In order to improve the efficiency, Microsoft Decision Tree adopts a two-tier structure, and directly sets up data mining Middleware in tree building algorithm and database.

5 Conclusion

In this paper, through the statistics, mining and analysis of the login data and resource browsing data generated by the online learning of the 15 level students based on the computer basic information guidance platform, some basic characteristics and influencing factors of the students' online learning behavior are found. From the perspective of group, online learning behavior is relatively balanced in time distribution, with weeks as the time period, the highest login rate of students in the sixth and seventh weeks; from the individual perspective, the online learning time of students is relatively small; the internal factors influencing students' online learning time include level, specialty and gender, among which the level factor is the most important factor. For the same level of students, the main influencing factor of students' online learning investment between different majors is their major, which has a great relationship with their professional characteristics and the student management team they belong to; the difference of students' learning level of different resources mainly depends on the distribution of resources on the course page, the characteristics of learning resources and the students' own needs, If you want a certain type of resources to attract enough attention of students, you can first put it in a prominent position on the course home page, and at the same time, improve the characteristics of resources based on students' interests.

References

1. Hong, X.: Analysis of learning effect under educational data mining. J. Changsha Railw. Univ. Soc. Sci. Ed. **26**(5), 196–198 (2014)
2. Gong, X., Li, B., Chai, X., G, M.: Overview of big data platform technology. J. Syst. Simul. **42**(03), 1125–1136 (2014)
3. Ge, D., Zhang, S.: Methods and Applications of Educational Data Mining, p. 9. Science Press, Beijing (2012)
4. Wang, Q., Wang, C., Feng, Z., Ye, J.: Review of K-means clustering algorithm. Electron. Des. Eng. **38**(07), 2514–2523 (2012)

Research on the Influencing Factors of the Endangered Inheritance of Folk Intangible Cultural Heritage and the Educational Protection Based on Big Data Technology

Yafang He[✉]

Lanzhou Resources and Environment Voc-Tech University, Lanzhou 730010, Gansu, China
631093457@qq.com

Abstract. The traditional mode of intangible cultural heritage communication is mainly offline activities, such as market fairs, temple fairs, sacrificial activities or physical or text and picture display of scenic area museums. With the popularity of the Internet and mobile terminal devices, the traditional offline display methods obviously can not meet the needs of the audience. Communication through digital technology can truly realize the "living communication" of intangible cultural heritage. In the era of rapid development of mobile Internet, video and video have become popular communication methods for the audience. Intangible cultural heritage uses digital means to achieve more detailed and diversified communication, and substitutes the audience into its scene to have all-round contact with intangible cultural heritage. With the rapid development of economic construction, the construction of social spiritual civilization has also accelerated its own pace. We need to use big data technology to give modern attributes to the traditional intangible cultural heritage and make these unfamiliar information full of vitality. Therefore, this paper studies the influencing factors and protection of folk intangible cultural heritage endangered inheritance based on big data technology.

Keywords: Big data technology · Folk intangible cultural heritage · Endangered heritage · Intangible cultural heritage protection

1 Introduction

In recent years, the project of disseminating and protecting intangible cultural heritage through various new digital technologies is an important way to inherit intangible cultural heritage. Internationally, the digital dissemination and protection project of intangible cultural heritage has been carried out since the end of the last century. China's digital communication and protection should not only conform to the influence of advanced ideas and technologies, but also to the awakening of spiritual culture after economic development [1]. On march26,2005, the general office of the State Council issued the opinions on strengthening the protection of China's intangible cultural heritage, which

M. A. Jan and F. Khan (Eds.): BigIoT-EDU 2022, LNICST 466, pp. 314–324, 2023.
https://doi.org/10.1007/978-3-031-23947-2_34

clearly pointed out that "we should make a true, systematic and comprehensive record of intangible cultural heritage and establish archives and databases by means of text, audio, video and digital multimedia". It can be seen that in the digital protection of intangible cultural heritage, the overall planning, management and application of various digital information resources need the support of literature database to improve work efficiency and optimize work arrangement [2].

Intangible cultural heritage is the foundation and soul of a nation and the crystallization of the wisdom of people of all ethnic groups. It is urgent to protect intangible cultural heritage. Taking "Hua'er" as an example, the cultural accumulation is very deep, the songs are gentle and the tunes are ups and downs, but China's traditional protection methods can not guarantee the preservation and dissemination of cultural treasures [3]. The traditional word of mouth, the aging of film and tape, and the incompleteness of preservation lead to the loss of intangible cultural heritage. Based on this situation, the digital protection mode of intangible cultural heritage came into being, which combines the intangible cultural heritage with the market in a sustainable way, and has a relaxed grasp by means of contemporary science and technology. Therefore, the best way to inherit intangible cultural heritage is through digital activation.

Intangible cultural heritage is gradually integrated into our daily life through digitalization. Under the principle of mutual benefit, intangible cultural heritage not only reflects the economic characteristics, but also reflects the characteristics of communication value. However, in the process of digital communication of intangible cultural heritage, there will be corresponding problems of copyright protection. The definition of the subject of works produced after the digitalization of intangible cultural heritage is the foundation and foundation of the category of copyright under the digitalization protection of intangible cultural heritage; The definition of whether the photographic content of intangible cultural heritage is creative and constitutes photographic works should not be generalized, but should be analyzed according to specific circumstances [4]; Data belongs to the object of copyright protection, so the database composed of data can be regarded as a compilation work according to the minimum originality; The external authorization of intangible cultural heritage digital content enables it to enter the market, combines intangible cultural heritage with the market, and drives industrial development.

The construction of intangible cultural heritage digital resources database is not achieved overnight. It takes time to accumulate. With the continuous support of new research achievements such as digital image technology, digital video technology, three-dimensional scanning technology, virtual reality technology, augmented reality technology and document retrieval technology, a distributed resource database with document research function has been formed to achieve the purpose of recording, preservation and dissemination, develop and inherit the information symbols of intangible cultural heritage projects, and enhance the soft power of Chinese culture.

2 Related Work

2.1 Concept of Intangible Cultural Heritage

Intangible cultural heritage exists in the rich and colorful long-term life created by the people of all ethnic groups in China, and constitutes a cultural symbol of mutual recognition and mutual recognition in China. Intangible cultural heritage has subjectivity and is the main symbol of understanding different subjects of different nationalities. The educational inheritance of intangible cultural heritage is an effective way to reflect the subjectivity of the national culture, and the establishment of the subjectivity of the national culture is the basic premise to realize the great rejuvenation of the Chinese nation. Intangible cultural heritage can be divided into: folk literature, such as the legend of the White Snake and the legend of the butterfly lovers; Traditional music, such as "Hua'er", Mongolian Humai, etc.; Traditional dances, such as Yangko and dragon dance; Traditional dramas, such as Kunqu Opera and Liyuan opera; Quyi: such as Suzhou Pingtan, Yangzhou Pinghua, Shandong drum playing, Northern Shaanxi storytelling, etc. [5]; Traditional art: for example, Yangliuqing woodblock New Year pictures, Taohuawu woodblock New Year pictures, Gaomi Puhui New Year pictures, etc.; Traditional skills: such as Shiwan ceramic art, Jingdezhen handmade ceramic art, etc.; Traditional medicine: such as TCM diagnosis and treatment; Folk customs: such as Spring Festival, Tomb Sweeping Day, Dragon Boat Festival and other festivals. The characteristics of intangible cultural heritage are as follows:

First, it has specific national characteristics. Intangible cultural heritage reflects the different characteristics, different lifestyles and different cultural deposits of each nation. In the process of historical formation, each nation has its own different language, different regional conditions, different economic life and different psychological activities. Only the differences of nations can constitute a stable and diverse community of the whole Chinese nation. Each nation has formed its own unique culture in the process of historical evolution, which is a way for a nation to distinguish itself from other nations. For example, each nation has its own unique way of expression, or oral expression, or song and dance performances, or ritual activities and festival activities [6]. Although each nation has its own characteristics and different cultural forms, it inherits Chinese culture in its own way, shows the inheritance of history, and reflects the rich and interesting cultural symbols of the Chinese nation.

Second, it has the characteristics of living heritage. Immaterial culture is the wisdom of ancestors, the spiritual culture left over to future generations through historical evolution, and also the manifestation of culture in historical evolution. One side, He emphasized that the characteristic of intangible culture is "old". Even though social development has incorporated new things into the content of "old", the essence is still the "old" traditional culture. As the core part of intangible cultural heritage, it not only shows the accumulation of different ethnic ancestors in history, but also shows the unique cultural information of the region where the nation is located. On the other hand, intangible culture has the necessity of inheriting from generation to generation and cannot To "die without change", we should constantly adapt to the current society and "build a new place from the old". Therefore, intangible cultural heritage has the characteristics of living heritage, which reveals the reason why people call it cultural heritage.

Third, it is passed down by word of mouth or by word of mouth. For example, non-material cultures such as paper cutting and folk songs can not express their internal meaning in the form of words. They need to be spread, interpreted and developed collectively through the joint action of people's vision and hearing in the form of word-of-mouth and body teaching [7]. Therefore, oral and physical transmission is an important way to spread and inherit intangible culture. However, the way of communication depends on the way of oral and physical transmission, which has great subjectivity and limits the preservation, dissemination and development of intangible cultural heritage.

Fourth, the individuality of non-material culture. For the related performing arts, oral narration, process inheritance, etc., individuals bear the responsibility of inheritance and play an indispensable role in the inheritance. Individuals or groups organize words, graphics, models and other intangible cultures. Before the government set foot in the protection of intangible culture, individuals or groups have formed the materials of intangible culture. The law protects such people through copyright and other means; The instruments, tools, objects and works of art needed for the inheritance of intangible cultural heritage can be interpreted and protected through the property right in the category of private law.

2.2 Reasons for Endangered Intangible Cultural Heritage Projects

(1) Intangible cultural heritage has lost its original environment. Most intangible cultural heritage projects come from the clothing, food, housing, transportation, sacrificial rites, etc. with the changes of the times and the development of society, social and cultural customs are constantly evolving. Many projects play a very important role in the original cultural exchanges and religious ceremonies, but due to the change of the original environment Instead, it removes the role of the self itself. The national intangible cultural heritage project "Xi'an drum music" has a history of at least 600 years. It has played a role in the "God welcoming competition" of folk temple fairs, the "rain praying" of folk activities, weddings and funerals, etc. In 1954, the former president of the Hungarian Music Association, schapolch, visited and enjoyed the drum music. After that, he said with emotion: "this is the symphonic music of ancient China". Since the 1950s, relevant departments in Xi'an have carried out the rescue and protection of Xi'an drum music. However, with the gradual decline of folk temple fairs and the change of Customs of folk activities, "Xi'an drum music" has lost its original environment, and now it can only exist in the exhibition hall as daily entertainment of music art clubs or as image materials, If we cannot develop a protection method suitable for the redevelopment of intangible cultural heritage projects and adapt to the social rhythm, "Xi'an drum music", a traditional folk custom, is likely to face the dilemma of disappearing in the long river of history. Another example is the national intangible cultural heritage "Chengcheng embroidery" in this region. It is said that it is a fabric art since the Ming and Qing Dynasties. Although it has high historical and artistic value, due to the rapid development of light industry, there are more and more machine embroidery instead of folk manual embroidery. In addition, manual production has high cost and low benefit [8]. From our field investigation, even though the government is vigorously spreading and protecting, due to the change of the original environment, people no longer need inefficient manual embroidery, which can only exist as displayed works of art.

(2) The economic benefit is low or has lost its economic value. The spread of many intangible cultural heritage projects is inseparable from the general needs of the social population in the early years, such as tiger head shoes, tiger head hats, belly bags and other handicrafts. When the commodity economy is not so developed, they still have a good market and can exist as a job to support the family. According to the national plan, by 2020, China's urbanization water supply will increase Ping will reach more than 60%. When today's rural areas gradually develop into cities, there will be great changes in values and lifestyles. The dissemination and protection of endangered intangible cultural heritage in Shaanxi will face more severe challenges. The Intangible Cultural Heritage Representative project "paper making technology" has been inherited for more than 1000 years. Manual paper making requires a lot of human resources, and the practice is also complex and cumbersome. Due to the development of industrialized paper making industry, the manual paper making industry has been impacted [9]. Ma Songsheng, a representative inheritor in his 60s, has not found anyone who can inherit this craft. He is very eager and eager to continue to pass on this craft, but few people are willing to learn this craft because of low economic benefits. There are also traditional folk arts such as traditional shadow play, which was originally the product of the local people's daytime recreation and fun. However, due to the maturity of digital photography technology, shadow play has lost its audience, making it in a worrying situation.

(3) Alienation of social reasons and environmental conditions. Most intangible cultural heritage projects are inherited by the way of oral instruction from masters and apprentices. Some inheritors can no longer carry out Intangible Cultural Heritage Inheritance activities due to physical reasons. During our investigation in Chang'an District, an elderly inheritor was even ill and bedridden all year round. He was also worried about the impossibility of inheritance Very sorry; Some inheritors believe that the project itself has been divorced from social development, and their attitude towards inheritance is not very positive; Some old masters of inheritors are very resistant to the inheritance itself due to the setbacks of the cultural revolution and other social reasons; However, the most important thing is that the original environment of the project itself has been destroyed, resulting in many reasons leading to difficulties in inheritance.

(4) The problem of protective destruction. Due to the unsatisfactory and biased understanding of intangible cultural heritage dissemination and protection by relevant departments, the more protection, the more destruction. The unique customs are closely related to the unique local customs. Some destroy the carrier carrying historical and cultural memory because of rural demolition and resettlement. Others are because the protectors lack professional protection knowledge, the protection of cultural heritage is shoddy and has no aesthetics. This situation mostly occurs in rural areas. Taking the 18th Mausoleum of the Tang Dynasty as an example, the mausoleum sculptures are scattered in the fields. The sculptures are damaged due to wind, sun and man-made damage. Local governments and organizations lack corresponding historical knowledge, aesthetic knowledge and sculpture knowledge in the restoration work, In the process of repair, only cement was casually stacked, which further "destroyed" the damaged sculpture. There are also some intangible cultural heritage projects that, after being determined by experts to have great economic value, are one-sided and blindly developing their

economic value. This imposed business logic is also a kind of damage to intangible cultural heritage projects.

3 Inheritance and Protection of Folk Intangible Cultural Heritage Based on Big Data Technology

3.1 Digital Communication of Intangible Cultural Heritage

Communication is the flow process of information carrier in the channel. Communicators need to convert information into symbols and use the media as the material carrier to spread it between communicators and receivers. From the perspective of intangible cultural heritage communication mode, communication first needs to reinterpret a series of internal cultural symbols, geographical symbols, historical symbols and environmental symbols contained in intangible cultural heritage, and then deal with them through different technical means to become the information needed for communication. The choice of media should also comply with certain rules. The audience can receive symbols by re converting specific media information into symbols. The audience can understand the information about intangible cultural heritage in symbols according to their own cultural system through the interpretation of the re transformed symbols.

The technological revolution led by information technology has not only greatly impacted the development of the cultural industry, but also brought opportunities for the transformation and upgrading of the cultural industry. With the support of high and new technology, intangible cultural heritage protection began to use digital technology. According to the definition of digital protection, digital protection fully adopts digital acquisition, digital storage, digital processing, digital display, digital communication and other technologies, which need to rely on many new technologies and means, such as text scanning, holography, database, digital animation, virtual reality, etc. Especially in the 1990s, the further improvement and application of virtual reality theory expanded the development space of cultural heritage and enhanced the feasibility of cultural space protection of cultural heritage. Combined with the virtual reality of network technology, the spatial information of cultural heritage can be copied in three dimensions, and the cultural heritage information can be scientifically and permanently preserved by creating a resource database. In addition, on the basis of not changing the original appearance of intangible cultural heritage, virtual reality technology can carry out digital display and digital communication, and greatly enhance the economic and social value of intangible cultural heritage.

"Intangible" in intangible cultural heritage emphasizes "intangible, invisible and intangible". For example, in the folk intangible cultural heritage: Although the Dragon Boat Race of the Dragon Boat Festival custom can be seen and felt, it is difficult to touch the customs and taboos here. The traditional protection mode focuses on the development and protection of the forms and results of intangible cultural heritage. The main body of protection is "people". Therefore, in the process of protection and development, it is easy to cause the destruction of the original environment of intangible cultural heritage and the distortion of intangible cultural heritage. On the basis of ensuring the quality of information input, the digital protection by using information technology reproduces the display environment of intangible cultural heritage, ensuring that the presentation and perception effects of intangible cultural heritage are not affected by the audience.

The existing form of intangible cultural heritage is an information form, but different from general information, the original form of intangible cultural heritage needs the support of a large number of regional cultural customs, that is, only when the original environment is mature to a certain stage can intangible cultural heritage projects be born, such as social fire performance, Xi'an drum music, etc. From the perspective of information transmission, the information form of intangible cultural heritage must be produced in the inefficient original communication environment. Once the environmental factors change and the information communication efficiency is improved, the intangible cultural heritage information must change with the change of environmental factors [10]. When using digital information technology to disseminate intangible cultural heritage information, it is necessary to create characteristics similar to its original environment in the digital environment, because the intangible cultural heritage in the original environment can show its cultural value to the greatest extent.

For the endangered material cultural heritage, the basis of digital information technology intervention in protection is to change the existence form of self information. (as shown in Fig. 1) describes the way of centralized environmental existence in the protection of intangible cultural heritage, evaluates the feasibility of various protection forms, and the premise of effective involvement of digital information technology in protection.

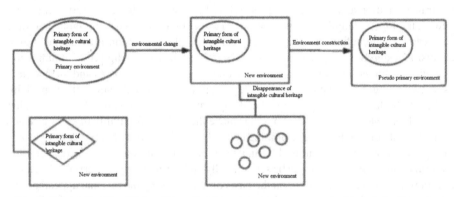

Fig. 1. Dissemination of intangible cultural heritage picture source / self made by the author

3.2 Significance of Folk Intangible Cultural Heritage Dissemination of Big Data Technology

In the dissemination and protection of intangible cultural heritage, how to use digital information technology and Internet is a very worthy problem. It can be seen that China is now in a period of rapid economic development, system reform and improvement. In such a period of rapid development, we should avoid the damage to China's precious intangible cultural heritage due to large-scale social construction, so that it can be reasonably and sustainable spread and development on the premise of effective protection.

Digital technology enables the traditional intangible cultural heritage to be presented, preserved and spread in a new form, showing its unique cultural heritage and style. Therefore, the digital processing of intangible cultural heritage information is to extract intangible cultural heritage projects from the original environment and give them a platform for inheritance and dissemination in the current digital form. While developing and expanding their own cultural soft power, it can enhance China's cultural self-confidence and give the cultural industry enough information to cope with the increasingly powerful cultural invasion.

A wide range of dissemination. Intangible cultural heritage projects in digital form can be widely disseminated through the Internet for interested people to enjoy and study, so as to realize resource sharing. Secondly, by establishing a digital virtual Intangible Cultural Heritage Museum, it is convenient for the long-term preservation of these social memories. The construction of intangible cultural heritage database through digital museum can drive the collection, preservation, dissemination and display of intangible cultural heritage data in our country and region. Digitizing intangible cultural heritage information can make social memory sorted and systematized, so as to improve its protection level. Thirdly, the dissemination of intangible cultural heritage in digital way can give full play to the important role of the national traditional excellent culture in the construction of social spiritual civilization. The core significance of the dissemination of intangible cultural heritage lies in the protection of traditional culture and cultural diversity. For example, the construction of digital museum, digital library stores and manages all aspects of intangible cultural heritage information in digital form, and provides digital display, education and research services for the audience through the Internet.

4   Build a Digital Protection Technology System for Folk Intangible Cultural Heritage

The digitalization of intangible cultural heritage is to overcome the abnormal playing caused by the aging of audio tapes, the image distortion caused by the duplication of video recorders and the difficulty of searching caused by paper records by means of artificial intelligence, computers, multimedia, big data, etc. under the background of the network, and to provide a new way of protection for intangible cultural heritage.

First, it is easy to preserve. In the past, the recording of intangible cultural heritage by means of tapes, video recorders, paper, etc. could not overcome the abnormal playback caused by the aging of tapes, the image distortion caused by the duplication of video recorders, and the difficulty of searching caused by paper recording. Therefore, digital protection is more conducive to the protection of the existing intangible cultural heritage. Digitalization makes use of the media's convenience to preserve and consult at any time, combines pictures with pictures, and fully transmits intangible cultural heritage through audio-visual and scene.

Second, the times. In the 1990s, intangible cultural heritage has begun to combine with digitalization, but the form is relatively single. So far, the combination of intangible cultural heritage and digitalization has been more diversified, such as the use of digital collection methods, digital storage means, digital display technology, digital communication channels, etc., so that the intangible cultural heritage "takes on a new look" and presents the diversity of digitalization. The traditional preservation mode of intangible cultural heritage has gradually disappeared. Instead, it is a digital ecological mode that can be transformed, copied and regenerated. Digitalization interprets intangible culture in combination with the new era. Digitalization preserves culture in a new way in the new era. Digitalization reproduces, utilizes and spreads culture in accordance with the new needs of the new era. Therefore, the digitalization of intangible cultural heritage is an inevitable trend and a necessary product in the new era. In today's information-based society, digitalization combines with intangible cultural heritage with the characteristics of process, stability and rapidity. The increasingly mature digital technology overcomes the challenges and difficulties brought about by traditional protection methods, and uses Internet technology to protect intangible cultural heritage.

Intangible cultural heritage is an important part of cultural heritage and an important source of nurturing human civilized life. It is widely rooted in people's civilized life and social life; It has witnessed the history of human development and is also an indispensable spiritual civilization for social development. Therefore, the protection of intangible cultural heritage is of special significance to maintain the sustainability and diversity of society. Many legal issues have arisen in the process of digitalization. What we need to pay attention to is that digitalization should always prevent possible copyright problems, and attention should also be paid to the digital database of intangible cultural heritage. Because digital content is an important part of public interest for the public, it must be actively protected and orderly managed.

The construction of digital protection technology system of folk intangible cultural heritage is the excavation and application of digital technology from simple to deep. Relying on computers and using binary numbers "0" and "1", digital technology is mainly used to collect and store the pictures, pictures and audio-visual images of the traditional cultural manifestations of intangible cultural heritage. It is a shallow technology in digital protection. The multimedia presentation of intangible cultural heritage forms and the virtual representation of cultural space require the integration of digital technology, database management and services, scene modeling, visualization and other technologies (see Fig. 2). In order to ensure the integrity of the construction of the digital protection technology system of folk intangible cultural heritage, the digital protection technology system of folk intangible cultural heritage should include the relevant technologies involved in four digital protection means: digital collection and processing, digital restoration and reproduction, digital storage and management, and digital display and dissemination (see Fig. 2). Scene modeling is a technology that focuses on the interpretation of folk intangible cultural space. It is used to construct three-dimensional scenes and roles to achieve three-dimensional knowledge expression and human-computer interaction; Database management and service technology refers to the use of mass storage, semantic retrieval and other technologies to achieve unified standard storage, description, management, release, retrieval and browsing of folk intangible cultural heritage resources; Visualization refers to the use of virtual reality, 3D animation and other technologies to build models for intangible cultural heritage. Based on the interpretation of intangible cultural heritage knowledge ontology, it extends to the visual expression and display of the decomposition of knowledge points, the connection between knowledge ontologies, knowledge sharing and other aspects.

The purpose of building a digital protection technology system for folk intangible cultural heritage and creating a more perfect virtual environment is to improve the attraction of intangible cultural heritage and increase the number of visitors to physical museums and scenic spots. Therefore, while using the complete digital technology, we should pay attention to the true interpretation of cultural heritage and guide tourists to visit the entity.

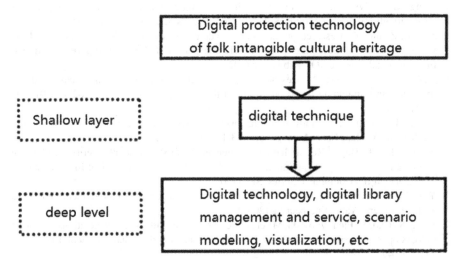

Fig. 2. Digital protection of intangible cultural heritage

5 Conclusion

Based on big data technology, establishing a reasonable and effective information perspective compatible with research in the field of culture and digital technology is the key point for digital technology to intervene in the dissemination and protection of intangible cultural heritage, and it is also a channel to promote communication between ordinary audiences, professional researchers and inheritors of intangible cultural heritage projects.

The Chinese nation has a long and splendid traditional culture, and intangible cultural heritage is a dazzling pearl in the long river of history and culture. We use modern means such as digital image technology, digital video technology and three-dimensional scanning to record, disseminate and protect intangible cultural heritage. We hope that this long-standing culture can have its own position in the modern society of information explosion. We should make use of the new thinking, new perspective and new environment in the information age to endow these traditional cultures with modern attributes, so as to revitalize these excellent folk cultures.

Acknowledgements. Innovation Fund Project for colleges and universities in Gansu Province in 2021: 2021A-258. On innovative practice of mounting calligraphies and paintings and restorating under the background of intangible cultural heritage.

References

1. Huang, J.: Research on the Influencing Factors of the Audience's Purchase Intention in Head Specialized Livestreamers' Live Streaming: Based on the Comparison of Two Platforms (2021)
2. Yin, C., Zhou, Y., He, P., et al.: Research on the influencing factors of the switching behavior of Chinese social media users: QQ transfer to WeChat. Library Hi Tech. (2021)
3. Wang, X.: Analysis and evaluation research on the influencing factors of the development of local agricultural products. In: E3S Web of Conferences. EDP Sciences (2021)
4. Xie, Y., Zhang, Z.: Research on the foreign trade efficiency and influencing factors of the yangtze river delta under high-quality development. In: IOP Conference Series: Earth and Environmental Science. IOP Publishing (2021)
5. Yang, S., Lv, X., Yang, Y.: Research on the influencing factors of manufacturing transformation and upgrading based on grounded theory. J. Phys: Conf. Ser. **1827**(1), 012103 (2021)
6. Li, X.: Research on the influencing factors of internet financial risk and its prevention mechanism. Modern Econ. Manag. Forum **3**(1), 20–24 (2022)
7. Ma, H., Guo, T., He, L.: Research on the influencing factors of accident severity based on the optimization of density clustering algorithm. In: Society of Photo-Optical Instrumentation Engineers (SPIE) Conference Series. SPIE (2022)
8. Yuan-Yuan, L.U., Tong, Y.: Research on the Influencing Factors of Reemployment for Retired Younger Elderly Value Engineering (2020)
9. Wang, S., Cao, Y., Pietrzykowski, M., et al.: Research on the influence of vegetation restoration in loess open-pit coal mines of China: Influencing factors and mechanism. Ecol. Eng. 2022, **177**:106549-
10. Mhlanga, D., Hassan, A.: An investigation of the factors influencing the choice of healthcare facility in South Africa. Int. J. Res. Bus. Soc. Sci. **11**, 2147–4478 (2022)

Teaching Practice and Research of Recognition System in Art Teaching Based on Visual Communication

Guiping Li[✉]

Lanzhou Modern Vocational College, Gansu 730300, China
1937083261@qq.com

Abstract. With the continuous progress of science and technology and economy, the innovation of recognition system in the process of art teaching has attracted the attention of all sectors of society. All visual communication work needs to be transmitted by the corresponding media. Today, China has entered the new media era, people's life and reading style have undergone new changes, but also brought new opportunities and challenges to Chinese traditional folk art. This paper expounds the main significance of visual communication, and the teaching practice and research of recognition system in the process of art teaching based on visual communication.

Keywords: Visual communication · Art teaching · Teaching practice

1 Introduction

With the development of Multimedia Internet, the development information of visual communication design industry changes. As the front line of education, design teachers need to reflect on teaching behavior and form their own education and teaching ideas and styles. While completing the teaching workload, think about how to improve the teaching quality and transform the teaching concept, so that college graduates can have a skill after four years of professional study, seamlessly connect with the needs of relevant enterprises, and improve the employment rate of students majoring in visual communication design. With the development of China's economic and cultural construction and the increasing demand for talents in art design, the enrollment scale of art candidates is also expanding year by year. Colleges and universities have set up majors such as packaging design, art design, fashion design and so on [1].

Design sketch and color are basic art courses. Through the study of these courses, students can cultivate their painting expressiveness and reproducibility, and lay a foundation for senior professional learning and deeper artistic creativity in the future. However, the art foundation of students entering colleges and universities is relatively weak. Students can be divided into two types. One part has participated in the pre examination art class before entering the school. These students have a certain art foundation, but their basic skills are not very solid; After entering the school, we should carry out systematic

M. A. Jan and F. Khan (Eds.): BigIoT-EDU 2022, LNICST 466, pp. 325–330, 2023.
https://doi.org/10.1007/978-3-031-23947-2_35

teaching for them, and make up for the parts that we have learned before but have not learned well, so as to lay a foundation for future learning. Another part of students study arts and Sciences in Colleges and universities without art foundation. For these students, they need to cultivate their painting ability from scratch, start training from basic sketch and color, cultivate their interest in art first, and then carry out the next professional study after mastering a certain foundation. Teachers can do more demonstrations step by step in the teaching process, When students encounter difficulties, teachers give guidance in time. In addition, these students should spend more time on painting training after class. After a period of practice, they will keep up with the overall progress of the class.

2 Relevant Overview

2.1 Visual Communication Design

Visual communication design mainly refers to the use of relevant visual symbols to convey information. Among them, the designer is the sender of information, and the transmission object is the receiver of information resources. From the literal meaning, visual communication design mainly refers to relying on graphics and images to complete the communication work. There are many types of visual communication. If it is classified simply in the form of media, the early paper media can be divided into advertising design, packaging design, brand design and book binding. Multimedia design belongs to the design method of the new era, mainly including web page design, UI design and advertising production.

Visual communication course is a comprehensive course, and its teaching focus is on visual expression. In the information age, the early expression of words is gradually replaced by images. These two ways of information can fully reflect the actual situation of social development. With the development of the times, the manifestations of visual communication have more diversified characteristics, and the overall influence is also increasing [2].

Visual design is usually closely related to media communication. At present, the emergence and development of new media and we media not only change people's daily living habits and reading methods, but also bring new opportunities to the popularization of folk art in China. In addition, wechat, web advertising, we media and big data platform have injected new vitality into folk art. Combined with different media forms, the effect is more expressive, the acceptance of the audience is more accurate, and the efficiency of information transmission will naturally be improved.

2.2 Current Situation of Visual Communication Design Teaching

Visual communication design refers to the process of analyzing and summarizing information according to specific design purposes, and designing and creating through basic elements such as text, graphics, color and modeling. It is a process of transmitting visual information to the audience and influencing the audience. In short, visual communication design is a design that conveys to the audience through visual media. The birth of a design idea is often closely related to many factors, such as brand positioning, preferences of target customer groups, market mainstream, communication ability with customers, team spirit and so on. If the design works are only done from the perspective of the designer, it may not be the best design. Only the design that improves the brand value and brings economic benefits is a good design. The characteristics of visual communication design determine its unique application-oriented and practicality. Therefore, visual communication design education is mainly to cultivate application-oriented professional design talents guided by social needs. The talent training goal of visual communication design specialty is to cultivate the all-round development of morality, intelligence, physique and beauty, meet the needs of modern social and economic construction, be able to pay attention to life, express the times and serve the society, have good cultural literacy, strong practical ability and innovative consciousness, and be able to engage in enterprise and product image planning, graphic design Senior application-oriented professionals working in new media art design and other fields. College Art and design students, although they have many advantages, such as curiosity about new things, strong acceptance ability, like beautiful things, many ideas, sensitivity to design and certain innovation ability. But at the same time, in the classroom teaching, it is found that they are easy to lose concentration in class, have unclear learning objectives, have high eyes and low hands, lack of execution, answer questions, lack of clear language expression, lack of logic and organization, and do not take the initiative to pay attention to industry information. In view of the current situation of students, I hope that through comprehensive design teaching, students can clarify goals, apply what they have learned, master professional technology, pay attention to industry information, and become senior application-oriented professionals who understand design and can express.

3   Research on Art Teaching Based on Visual Communication

In college art teaching, the teaching of visual communication design method is one of the important teaching contents. In teaching, teachers should pay attention to cultivating students' imagination and creativity, helping students better understand and master knowledge, so as to improve the teaching effect of visual communication design. Imagination and creativity are the necessary abilities for students to master the relationship between things [3]. Things that seem to have nothing to do with life are often inextricably linked. At this time, students need to exert their imagination, expand their thinking depth and try to find the relationship between things, which is very helpful for students to understand the visual communication design method. Therefore, in art teaching in Colleges and universities, teachers should guide students to give full play to their imagination and design unrestrained graphics. On this basis, teach students the creative design methods of graphics, such as: ① replacement refers to the integration of different materials in graphics, which requires us to find the integration point of these materials, give play to our imagination, and creatively integrate these materials together to form a unique and novel graphics; ② Variation refers to the natural transition from one thing to another. After skillfully constructing graphics, it deeply reveals the internal relationship between things; ③ Positive and negative shapes refer to a visual communication design method to create contradictory points of graphics. People often only pay attention to the positive shape and ignore other parts. The positive and negative shapes share a contour line and rely on each other to reflect two different objects (as shown in Fig. 1); ④

The contradictory space can mislead our vision and lead to visual illusion. In the image reading era where images can be seen everywhere, people have higher visual requirements for pictures, and new and unique images can effectively attract people's attention. Therefore, visual illusion is a graphic creative design method widely used at present.

Fig. 1. Visual communication design picture

In short, in the teaching of art visual communication design in Colleges and universities, teachers should consciously create imagination space for students, such as displaying some imaginative images, teaching students the necessary visual communication design methods, encouraging students to imagine boldly, creatively use these methods and design highly creative graphics. In this way, students' imagination and creativity can be effectively cultivated, At the same time, improve students' visual communication design level.

4 Teaching Practice

Homework is not only an indispensable part of teaching, but also an important tool for teachers to test the effect of classroom teaching and understand students' learning. By arranging practical homework, students' practical ability can be cultivated. Taking the teaching of "graphic creative design" as an example, teachers can arrange homework, that is, students are required to analyze and discuss the graphic composition forms mentioned above, learn from the creative design ideas of these graphics, and complete the graphic creative design based on things in life. Such as people, cars, fruits, plants, animals, etc. Through homework, let students use the learned theoretical knowledge for practical operation, and gradually make flexible use of visual communication design methods to design works. In the process of students completing their homework, teachers should pay attention to understand the completion of students' homework and give timely guidance, so as to effectively improve students' visual communication design ability [4].

Guide Students to Appreciate Works and Cultivate Students' Creativity

In the process of cultivating students' visual communication design ability, in addition to letting students master the necessary visual communication design methods, they should also guide students to learn to appreciate art works, so as to improve students' aesthetic ability and promote students' innovation ability. For example, teachers can organize students to appreciate Rodin's work omiel (as shown in Fig. 2) and guide students to feel the extraordinary beauty in the work. The work presents an old man with a bent back and dry breasts. Although this is not the beauty in our traditional sense, the years precipitated on him can bring people different visual feelings and reach the depths of people's hearts, This is the visual communication design creativity of the work. Teachers can ask students to learn from the visual communication design method of the work, select life things for general or exaggerated design creation, and cultivate students' creativity in this process.

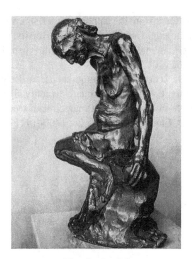

Fig. 2. Omiel

Confucius said, "if a worker wants to do well, he must first sharpen his tools.". To do education and teaching, we need a sharpening stone of "not mistaking firewood cutting" and not fighting unprepared battles. Teachers echo what the books say, and they can not read the text, but they need to extract the essence from all kinds of professional reference books, and complete the courseware handouts with the design hot spots and the new cases. They should pay attention to the design sense of PPT courseware and keep the freshness of the course content. Clarify the ability and cultivation of visual communication designers, and help students find ways to accumulate information without reading dead books. When arranging teaching tasks, we should take the market as the guide and complete the actual projects with students, so that students can do each homework as a work and make a systematic and research-based in-depth design. Closing homework should not just stay at the stage of copying and reference. We should pay attention to the design process, think about the basis of design form, and summarize the graphic information, so as to make students realize that there is a complete structural line behind the mature design and improve the comprehensive quality of design students.

5 Conclusion

Visual communication design is an important part of art teaching in Colleges and universities. High school art teachers should closely follow the trend of the times, carry out teaching in combination with life, create problem situations, guide students to master graphic creative design methods, give play to their personal imagination, and design highly creative works. In this process, they should broaden students' horizons and cultivate students' creative thinking and artistic quality.

References

1. Yanpin, W., Leyu, Q.: Research on the application of innovative thinking in Art Visual Communication Design Teaching. Guangxi Normal University, Guilin (2015)
2. Du, Y.: Research on visual communication design curriculum in primary and secondary schools. Educ. Ref. 46(3), 2251–2262 (2017)
3. Du, Y.: Research on middle school visual communication design curriculum and teaching under Constructivism Theory. East China Normal University, Shanghai (2016)
4. Peng, J., Leng, F.: Research on traditional art image reconstruction method based on visual communication effect. Mod. Electron. Technol. 24, 1400–1421 (2017)

Research on the Integration Design of Algorithm Teaching and Mathematics Curriculum Under Information Technology

Guomin Fang[✉]

College of Humanities, Qujing Medical College, Qujing 655011, Yunnan, China
1299193524@qq.com

Abstract. With the reform and innovative development of education, the proportion of information technology in education reform is becoming more and more important, and more and more people begin to pay attention to the integration and development of information technology and other disciplines. This paper analyzes the current situation of international and domestic teaching design of information technology and curriculum integration, studies the current teaching design process of information technology and new curriculum integration, and studies the teaching design mode of information technology applied to different teaching methods and teaching processes, which fully embodies the concept of independent learning and independent exploration advocated by the new curriculum, This paper explores how to use information technology to optimize the teaching process and improve the teaching methods under the new curriculum, obtains and establishes its own teaching design process on this basis, starts with the guiding theory and practice of the integration of information technology and curriculum, and expounds the important position of information technology teaching in primary school education through cases in the actual teaching process, And the problems in the integration of information technology and other courses. In order to help front-line teachers improve the teaching design level of integrating information technology into teaching.

Keywords: Information technology · Algorithm teaching · Curriculum integration

1 Introduction

In the storm of world education reform, the integration of information technology and curriculum has become the most important issue. China attaches great importance to the integration of information technology and curriculum, and defines the objectives and contents of the integration of information technology and curriculum in the new curriculum. In the outline of basic education curriculum reform (Trial Implementation) issued by the Ministry of education in July 2001, it was proposed that: "Vigorously promote the universal application of information technology in the teaching process, promote the

M. A. Jan and F. Khan (Eds.): BigIoT-EDU 2022, LNICST 466, pp. 331–343, 2023.
https://doi.org/10.1007/978-3-031-23947-2_36

integration of information technology and subject courses, gradually realize the transformation of the presentation mode of teaching content, students' learning mode, teachers' teaching mode and teacher-student interaction mode, give full play to the advantages of information technology, and provide a rich and colorful educational environment and powerful learning tools for students' learning and development." In particular, the new curriculum adopted in the past two years has more clearly defined the requirements for the integration of information technology and curriculum. How to integrate information technology and subject teaching, so as to improve the traditional teaching mode, improve the efficiency of teaching and learning, improve the effect of teaching and learning, and then promote the qualitative changes in Teachers' lesson preparation, classroom teaching, knowledge structure, curriculum arrangement, ability evaluation, collaborative learning, teacher-student relationship, etc., This puts forward higher requirements for the integration of information technology and subject courses [1].

Information technology curriculum is an important part of information technology education in primary and secondary schools. It is included in the compulsory curriculum of primary and secondary schools, and promotes the combination of information technology and curriculum teaching in turn, so as to promote the reform of teaching methods [2]. In the study of each course, we should organically combine information technology as a tool with subject education, fundamentally change the traditional teaching concepts, teaching modes and teaching methods, as well as the corresponding learning methods and evaluation means, so as to improve the new form of curriculum, and then integrate information culture with people's study and life into an organic continuum and unity. The integration of information technology and curriculum has the characteristics of "integration of knowledge", "integration of experience", "integration of value" and "integration of curriculum development" [3]. In terms of a case in teaching, the best teaching method of mathematics "translation and rotation" in the past was to use teaching aids to demonstrate translation or rotation for students. It is lack of image and vividness, which is often easy to mislead students. Now we use the animation made by information technology to enable students to perceive what is translation, rotation and related knowledge vividly, vividly and stereoscopically. Students can also do these animations by themselves. For students, the combination of theory and practice can get twice the result with half the effort. In the teaching of this lesson, the role of teachers is only a provider of learning resources, a guide for students' learning, an organizer of students' group cooperative learning, a promoter of students' loose knowledge and an evaluator of learning [4].

The concept of mathematics education is a more systematic and rational understanding of the phenomenon of mathematics education. Whether the concept of mathematics education is correct or not is directly related to the direction and success or failure of the reform and development of mathematics education. The role of contemporary information technology in the concept of mathematics education is the most direct and obvious. It has changed the form, content, dissemination and reception of knowledge. Mathematics curriculum is the overall arrangement and preliminary design of the content, standard and progress of all mathematical cultural knowledge studied by students in school. It is the means and medium to achieve mathematics teaching objectives and complete mathematics teaching tasks [5]. It must be constantly changed with the development of the times. Due to the rapid development of contemporary information technology and the accelerated obsolescence rate of knowledge, great changes will take place in the hierarchy, relative importance and manifestation of mathematical knowledge in the knowledge system. The importance of operation emphasized by mathematics in the 1960s and 1970s will be relatively weakened due to the development of computers, and the beauty of symmetry and structure of mathematics, Because of the intervention of computer, it presents more recursive beauty and structural beauty; Mathematics has changed from overemphasizing reasoning and demonstration to paying equal attention to reasoning and demonstration and mathematical experiment. Some new mathematical ideas and concepts will gradually penetrate into the content system of mathematics teaching materials; The inherent textbook arrangement mode of "introduction, examples, formulas, theorems, rules, examples and practice" will be broken, and diversified textbooks will make students love reading and learning and be more beneficial to teaching [6].

The impact of contemporary information technology on the process of mathematics teaching may be the most essential, because its impact on the concept of mathematics education and the content of mathematics teaching should be reflected in the process of mathematics teaching [7].

Academician Zhang Jingzhong talked about the role of "information technology" in the educational technology training course for middle school mathematics teachers of Capital Normal University, and also mentioned these three points:

(1) Tools to improve teaching efficiency and learning efficiency: many things in the teaching process used to be done by teachers and students. When the computer and Z + Z platform are used, it becomes faster and easier and improves efficiency.

(2) Observation of phenomena enlightens the knowledge expression environment of thinking: there are many phenomena and processes of quantitative relations, spatial transformation and movement in mathematics. In the teaching environment provided by blackboard, paper and pen, teachers can only talk and students can only think. With the computer and Z + Z platform, many things that were thought of but could not be done in the past can now be demonstrated and operated.

(3) New teaching resources and creative platform for student activity topics. With the computer and Z + Z platform as tools and teaching environment, the innovative potential of teachers and students will be more encouraged to make courseware and learning pieces that may not have been thought of or dare not be thought of in the past. These courseware contents may be directly related to the deepening of the course and the extension of the course contents. They can be appreciated, operated, researched and developed by students.

The above is the theoretical description of the integration effect of information technology and middle school mathematics curriculum by relevant educators. In practical operation, there must be some factors affecting the integration effect, which requires us to summarize these problems with teaching practice, so as to effectively control relevant factors and make the integration effect move towards our expected goal.

2 Related Work

2.1 The Influence of Information Technology on Mathematics Education

Information technology is not only the object of learning, but also the tool of learning. Information technology is mainly used as the following tools in the integration of mathematics curriculum:

(1) Information technology as a demonstration tool

The use of information technology for demonstration in mathematics teaching is an aspect of the integration of information technology and mathematics curriculum. The traditional presentation methods of teaching content are mainly sound (teacher language), text and image, which are mainly recorded and transmitted through books and paper. Information technology can provide a variety of media stimulation, which is conducive to the acquisition and maintenance of knowledge. The external stimulus provided by multimedia computer is not a single stimulus, but a comprehensive stimulus of multiple senses, which is very important for the acquisition and maintenance of knowledge [8]. The psychologists obtained a large amount of information from human vision and hearing experiments. Multimedia technology can be seen, heard, operated by hand, discussed and communicated, and expressed in their own language. In this way, the information obtained through the stimulation of multiple senses is more than that obtained by listening to the teacher alone. Information is closely related to knowledge. If you get a lot of information, you can master more knowledge. Although abstract thinking plays a major role in mathematics, it does not rule out the help of image thinking to abstract

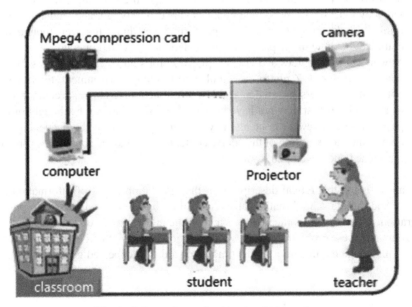

Fig. 1. Information technology teaching mode

thinking in the process of concrete practice. In teaching, there are some dynamic and three-dimensional concepts that are not easy to be explained clearly by traditional teaching methods [9]. Teachers use geometric sketchpad, PowerPoint, Authorware, flash and other multimedia production tools to make teaching courseware by comprehensive use of various teaching materials, so as to give students an intuitive image, which is easy for them to understand and contribute to the deepening of teaching. Through reasonable design and selection, information technology can develop multimedia electronic teaching materials and teaching materials, organically integrate text, sound, image and animation, and make them into CDs such as CD-ROM for long-term and large-capacity storage, as shown in Fig. 1.

(2) Information technology as an exploration tool

In the process of cultivating students' exploration ability, the ability to find and solve problems, and creative ability, information technology plays the role of exploration tool. Information technology can be used as an important tool for students' autonomous learning. Information technology can be used from improving the basic learning efficiency (reading, writing and calculation) to completing more complex research tasks, so as to help students improve the quality and efficiency of learning. Students use network technology to find, evaluate and collect information from different resources; Students use data processing technology to analyze experimental data, draw charts and report research results; Students use virtual technology to simulate and study real problems, and put forward solutions and schemes. Some teaching software, such as "Geometer's Sketchpad", can help students dynamically observe phenomena, estimate data, explore and discover the quantitative change relationship between research objects: "2 + 2 intelligent education platform" can help students discover and summarize some mathematical laws and phenomena through experiments, and also verify the assumptions and reasoning put forward by students themselves. In addition, various commonly used software can also provide good support for mathematics inquiry learning. For example, word can sort out various materials and write research reports; Excel can analyze data and make statistical charts; PowerPoint can make presentations for report exchange; Frontpage can make websites for learning achievements, experience exchange, professional discussion, and so on.

(3) Information technology as a communication tool

The communication between teachers and students is not only one of the important links of teaching, but also one of the important factors for the success or failure of teaching. Introducing information technology into the field of teaching and creating certain communication opportunities for students and teachers, students and students, teachers and teachers in class or after class is conducive to promoting the cultivation of teachers' and students' feelings, strengthening the discussion and cooperation between teachers and students, and promoting the transformation of the relationship between teachers and students. Information technology changes the relationship between teachers and students from initiative to equality and harmony. The transmission of information has the characteristics of fast, hidden and flexible. It can enrich the traditional way of interaction between teachers and students and enable teachers and students to communicate more widely, democratically and targeted. Through Explorer browser, e-mail, BBS, online forum, chat room, etc., the interaction between a teacher and multiple students can be realized. Students can ask teachers questions at any time, and teachers can provide individual guidance according to the characteristics of each student. Information technology can also realize long-distance interaction between teachers and students and strengthen cross time and space exchanges and cooperation.

(4) Information technology provides resources and environment

The information society needs new talents with information ability. Using information technology to provide resource environment is to break through the restrictions of taking books as the main source of knowledge in the past, and enrich classroom teaching with various relevant resources, so that students can learn not only the contents of textbooks, but also network resources or other electronic resources. Information technology uses multimedia and network development tools to transform learning contents into digital learning resources in the form of multimedia, hypertext and friendly interaction, including digital library, electronic reading room, online newspapers and periodicals, etc. It can provide learners with a rich and colorful interactive man-machine interface with pictures, audio and video, and can provide learners with a large-scale knowledge base and information base organized according to the hypertext structure in line with the characteristics of human thinking and memory. Therefore, it can broaden the learning vision of teachers and students, stimulate learners' interest, and create powerful conditions for learners to carry out inquiry learning.

2.2 The Connotation of Information Technology and Curriculum Integration

Traditional classroom education and teaching is often criticized for its inherent weaknesses. However, in the foreseeable future, classroom teaching will still be the main way of school teaching activities. Practice has also proved that the idea and practice of completely replacing classroom teaching with technology, especially in the field of basic education, is not desirable. Because the direct face-to-face communication between teachers and students in classroom teaching still has its advantages in many aspects compared with the indirect communication mode of teachers teaching completely through modern media and students learning through media. How to use technology reasonably and effectively in the classroom, especially modern information technology to improve classroom teaching, has become a major topic in school education research. Therefore, the concept of "integration" appears.

"Integration" is a term widely used in the current teaching reform. Its basic meaning is to integrate the related different things or subject contents in order to produce good results. There may be several ways to integrate information technology: the integration of information technology education and curriculum, the integration of information technology and curriculum, the integration of information technology and subject teaching, etc. The integration of information technology education and curriculum is to have clear and unified standards for the application of information technology in the curriculum of each school, and no information technology curriculum is set in the same school segment. The integration of information technology and curriculum has clear requirements for the application of information technology in the curriculum of each school segment, but there are still information technology courses in the same school segment. The integration of information technology and subject teaching is that there are no clear and unified standards and requirements for the application of information technology in the curriculum of each learning stage, but the application of information technology in the process of subject teaching in an integrated way [10].

In China, many experts and scholars have defined the concept of information technology and curriculum integration from different angles. Nanguonong, a famous audio-visual education expert in China, said that it is necessary to integrate information technology into all elements of the curriculum teaching system, so as to make it become a teaching tool for teachers, a cognitive tool for students, an important form of teaching materials and a main teaching media; Become both the object of learning and the means of learning, so as to promote learning.

Professor he Kekang of Beijing Normal University pointed out that the essence and connotation of the integration of information technology and curriculum requires the integration of computers and networks under the guidance of advanced educational ideas and theories, especially under the guidance of the leading subject teaching theory! As a cognitive tool and emotional incentive tool to promote students' autonomous learning and a tool to create a rich teaching environment, information technology with network as the core, and comprehensively applies these tools to the teaching process of various disciplines, so that various teaching resources, various teaching elements and teaching links can produce aggregation effect on the basis of overall optimization through sorting, combination and mutual integration, So as to promote the fundamental reform of traditional teaching methods, that is, to promote the reform of teacher-centered teaching structure and teaching mode, so as to achieve the goal of cultivating students' innovative spirit and practical ability.

Professor Li Kedong of South China Normal University pointed out in the article "objectives and methods of information technology and curriculum integration", that information technology and curriculum integration is a new teaching method that organically combines information technology, information resources, information methods, human resources and curriculum content in the process of curriculum teaching, and jointly completes the curriculum teaching task. The integration is positioned as a teaching type, and the importance of information environment and digital learning resources (a wide range of curriculum learning contents) is emphasized. Positioning the goal as the attitude and ability of lifelong learning, good information literacy and mastering the learning mode in the information age, that is, digital learning, highlighting student-centered problem and theme centered personalized learning, negotiation and cooperation quality. Its basic idea includes three basic points: to implement curriculum teaching activities in the information environment based on multimedia and network; After the course teaching content is informationized, it becomes the learning resource of learners; Use information processing tools to reconstruct students' knowledge.

3 Research on the Integration of Information Technology and Mathematics Curriculum

3.1 Theoretical Basis

(1) Behaviorism learning theory

Behaviorism learning theory is a learning theory gradually formed since the beginning of the 20th century. Its representatives include Thorndike, Pavlov, Skinner and so on. Behaviorist learning theory holds that it is impossible to observe human thinking activities or psychological processes directly, and the stimulating information of the environment will make learners produce certain response behavior. By studying what kind of stimulus information produces what kind of response behavior, we can find and summarize the general law of learning. Therefore, the study of learners' learning psychology should pay attention to the relationship between their visible external behavior and environmental stimulation. Behaviorism also believes that complex behaviors can be decomposed into a series of simple behaviors. The above view of behaviorism holds that learning is to form a certain "stimulus response" connection, This connection is mainly established through "trial and error". That is, in repeated attempts, the wrong response is gradually eliminated, and the correct response is continuously strengthened until a fixed "stimulus response" connection is finally formed. In the learning process of "trial and error", the correct "stimulus response" The connection can only be formed under the action of strengthening conditions. The main idea of sanddike's connectionist learning theory can be summarized as follows: the essence of learning lies in the formation of stimulus response connection (without concept as the medium); People and animals follow the same learning rules; The process of learning is a gradual process of blind attempt and error: learning should abide by three principles - the law of preparation, the law of practice and the law of effect; The stimulus response connection that individuals learn in a stimulus situation has a transfer effect in other similar situations.

(2) Cognitive learning theory

Cognitive psychology holds that the learning individual itself acts on the environment, and the activity process of human brain can be transformed into a specific information processing process. Since people living in the world want to survive, they must exchange information with their environment; As cognitive subjects, people will constantly exchange information with each other. People always appear as information seekers, transmitters and even information formers. People's cognitive process is actually a process of information processing. People are transforming and processing information. Its basic viewpoints are as follows: ① it is the characteristic of human learning to respond to the environment subjectively and actively; Cognitive psychology believes that human behavior can be divided into two different types: low-level behavior and high-level behavior. The former is shared by humans and animals, but the latter is unique to humans. According to this view, cognitive psychology divides learning into "habitual learning" and "intelligent learning". In habitual learning, behavior is strengthened after some consequences. For this kind of learning, learning occurs after action and what is learned is a fixed response to external stimuli; In intelligent learning, people's actions are determined by goals (or expectations), not by stimuli. People use variable action plans to adapt to different new environments, and plans are established before actions and can be adjusted at any time in action. This kind of subjective and dynamic response to the environment and purposefully control and regulate their own response is a unique learning style of human beings. ② Learning is a process of information processing: cognitive psychology believes that learning must pass through the internal psychological process, and compares this process with the process of computer information processing. It believes that human cognition is carried out through the mechanism of receiving information, coding and storing in memory, making decisions using memory materials and guiding external behavior. The information processing model is shown in Fig. 2.

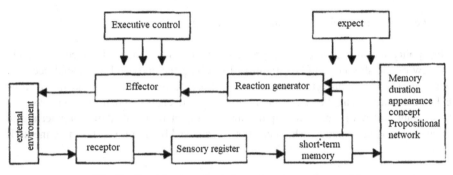

Fig. 2. Cognitive learning information processing model

3.2 Implementation Principles of the Integration of Information Technology and Mathematics Curriculum

(1) Principles of promoting students' understanding of mathematics learning content

Mathematics science is a discipline integrating rigor, logic, creativity and imagination, which is also considered difficult to learn. Therefore, the introduction of information technology into mathematics teaching should strive to promote students' effective and direct cognition of abstract mathematical concepts and rigorous mathematical proof. The use of information technology in mathematics class should not only pursue the vividness of the surface and the beauty of the interface, but also pay more attention to whether it is enlightening and guide students to think deeply. Some contents only rely on Teachers' language description, which is difficult for students to understand. Now we use information technology to help teachers organically combine abstraction and intuition, which can not only make students easy to understand and impressive, but also better attract students to conduct in-depth exploration.

(2) The principle of complementary advantages between information technology and teachers

In the process of integrating information technology and mathematics curriculum, the problem often encountered is how to treat the role of information technology and teachers. There are two completely opposite opinions: one is to exaggerate the explanation of teachers in traditional teaching, which is actually an exclusive attitude towards information technology; the other is to exaggerate the role of information technology, which actually negates teachers. The former is not familiar with the advantages of information technology, but is very familiar with traditional teaching; The latter does not fully consider the complexity of mathematical activities, and does not correctly understand that whenever the computer is just a tool for human use, and the current level of computer intelligence is far from meeting the expectations of mathematics teaching. Therefore, we should adopt the principle of complementary advantages, give full play to both the advantages of computers and the role of teachers, and combine the two perfectly.

(3) Pertinence principle of information technology

The application of computer should be appropriate, and it should be used reasonably in view of the shortcomings of traditional teaching methods and the actual needs of teaching. Computer has great advantages in track formation, measurement, accurate calculation and dynamic expression of arbitrariness to enable students to find laws. The processing ability of data and graphics and the interaction ability of computer are of great value to mathematics, which can not be achieved by traditional teaching methods in many cases.

(4) Principles conducive to student participation

Firstly, the introduction of information technology into teaching should not be satisfied with demonstration tools, but more importantly, change the way students acquire mathematical knowledge. Students are the subjects of cognitive activities and the active constructors of knowledge meaning. Therefore, we should let students participate in the activities of doing mathematics, give better play to students' initiative and better promote cognition. Taking information technology as a tool and environment to understand mathematics can improve students' mathematical activities, cultivate students' discovery and innovation ability, practical ability, and enhance students' self-confidence in learning.

4 Integrated Design of Algorithm Teaching and Mathematics Curriculum Under Information Technology

Information technology can not reflect its advantages everywhere in mathematics curriculum. As a special subject, mathematics does not exclude vividness on the one hand, but on the other - hand, it pays special attention to logical thinking. We mainly choose the content that is difficult to explain clearly in the traditional teaching methods, and the facts that are difficult to explain in language or general teaching aids. We use information technology tools to help students establish appearances and understand new knowledge. By analyzing the middle school textbooks, it is considered that the following aspects can be used as the integration point of information technology and mathematics curriculum:

(1)   Problems with dynamic changes

In traditional mathematics teaching, problems with dynamic changes can only be described by teachers' language, and students think abstractly according to some static graphics. In this way of learning, it is difficult for students to form a deep understanding of mathematical objects. The introduction of information technology in teaching will help students get a comprehensive understanding of mathematical objects. In geometry teaching, the effect of using graphics with language is better than using language alone. With animation, it is easier for students to understand and form a comprehensive understanding. For example, in the teaching of "trajectory", the trajectory function of geometric sketchpad or graphic calculator can be used to make animation effects and explore the trajectory of graphics. When describing the nature of a circle, you can introduce a set of animation: rolling tires, rotating waterwheel, rotating windmill and other real-life scenes to guide students to observe and think, and finally get the properties of central symmetry and rotation invariance of the circle. For another example, some fixed point or fixed point problems can be discussed by using information technology.

(2)   From constant to variable

The transition from constant to variable is a difficulty for students. We can use information technology to help students break through this difficulty. For example, the function in algebra can be taught by using Mathematica, maple, Mathcad, geometric sketchpad and other software or graphic calculator to obtain the corresponding function image.

(3)   Transformation of space graphics and plane graphics

The problem of transforming spatial graphics into plane graphics is more difficult for students with poor spatial imagination. Using information technology to show this process intuitively and vividly will help these students learn, and for students with better spatial imagination, it will also help to deepen their understanding of the problem. For example, the section problem and the expansion problem of three-dimensional graphics can dynamically demonstrate the formation process through software such as Geometric Sketchpad to explain the relationship between points, lines and surfaces of spatial graphics.

(4)   The combination of logical thinking and image thinking

For some abstract problems, making corresponding graphics accurately and quickly is helpful to solve the problem. For example, the conical curve in analytic geometry can effectively reveal the internal relationship between number and shape by using the rapid processing and vivid graphic transformation of computer.

(5)   Exploratory questions

For some exploratory questions, we often get different answers according to different conditions. You can use the drawing function of the Geometric Sketchpad to make function images and explore the relevant properties of functions. For these problems, the use of information technology to solve, can do not repeat, do not leak, and deepen understanding. For example, when teaching "quadratic function image", we need to discuss the relationship between function image and coefficient. Teachers can let students operate on the computer in person, or after drawing the function image in advance, let students change the coefficient, observe the image change and explore the conclusion of the problem.

(6)   Transition from finite to infinite

In mathematics teaching, from the perception of action to representation, and then from abstract concept to rational understanding, this is the law of students' understanding of things. People often develop students' abstract thinking through concrete image thinking. Concrete image thinking plays an important role in the establishment of abstract concepts and the composition of the special nature of mathematical thinking. Because of this, some mathematics involves the transition from finite to infinite, such as iterative problem, tangent and secant, asymptote, multiple roots of quadratic equation, etc., and the volume problem of cylinder, cone and circular platform can be described intuitively by the method of gradual approximation. The bottleneck of students' thinking can be broken through the simulation and demonstration of computer.

(7)   Complex graphics rendering and complicated calculation

Some complex graphics, such as the visual images of various geometry (column, cone, billiards, ball crown, ball defect and other visual images), if drawn on the blackboard, it will waste time and can not achieve the effect of accurate drawing. At the same time, it lacks universality and flexibility, and can not be changed once drawn. The use of information technology can solve the above problems and make various changes. Some complicated calculations, such as the expansion of binomial and the data generated in some practical problems, are more time-consuming and laborious if they are calculated only with paper and pen, while using the fast computing power of computer can improve the classroom efficiency.

(8)   Summary of a large number of mathematics teaching materials

When there are many words or pictures involved in mathematics teaching, the use of information technology can help to express these contents vividly, quickly and accurately. For example, in the teaching of mathematics history, we can use computers to synthesize pictures, sounds, words and images to make mathematics feature films, enrich teaching forms and improve classroom teaching efficiency. Students can be informed of the topics to be taught in advance, so that they can use their spare time to find relevant materials through the Internet, and then make a situation report in class.

5 Conclusion

The integration of information technology and subject curriculum is the hot spot and focus of the current education and teaching reform. Through the research and practice at all levels and aspects of the education sector in recent years, many achievements have been made and some valuable experience has been accumulated, but the problems and misunderstandings are also serious, which hinders and restricts the development and promotion of curriculum integration to a certain extent. In view of these problems and misunderstandings, we should take corresponding countermeasures for the research and development of information technology and curriculum integration, and make deep thinking in combination with practice. The influencing factors in the process of information technology and middle school mathematics curriculum integration include teachers' factors, students' factors, information tool factors and external factors. This conclusion theoretically summarizes the educational experience for the integration of this new educational problem and lays a foundation for the follow-up research; In practice, it can guide educators to control these factors in teaching and achieve the optimal integration effect, so as to promote the better development of integration.

References

1. Chen, J., Kan, J., Gao, Z.: Research on multi-sensor integration algorithm based on the multi-source data of smart-phone. In: Yang, C., Xie, J. (eds.) CSNC 2021. LNEE, vol. 772, pp. 333–342. Springer, Singapore (2021). https://doi.org/10.1007/978-981-16-3138-2_32
2. Xing, Y., Sheng, Y.: Research on theoretical innovation and design method of the integration of highway and toruism. E3S Web Conf. **233**(1), 01112 (2021)
3. Wang, Y., Wang, Y.: Research on the integration of bim technology in prefabricated buildings. World J. Eng. Technol. **9**(3), 10 (2021)
4. Song, Q.: Research on the teaching reform of tourism vocational education based on the idea of "Integration of Teaching and Doing"—taking the handicraft course of batik dyeing as an example. J. Contemp. Educ. Res. **5**(1), 5 (2021)
5. Li, J., Chen, Z., Chen, S.: Practical research on the integration of curriculum ideology and politics into the teaching reform of nursing specialty. J. Contemp. Educ. Res. **5**(11), 6 (2021)
6. Zhang, T., Zhang, W., Shao, X.L, et al. Research on optimization sparse method for capacitive micromachined ultrasonic transducer array: heuristic algorithm. Sens. Rev. (2021, ahead-of-print)
7. Sen, T., Kawajiri, Y., Realff, M.J.: Integration of material and process design for kinetic adsorption separation. Ind. Eng. Chem. Res. **60**(6), 2536–2546 (2021)
8. Massa, A., Salucci, M.: On the design of complex EM devices and systems through the system-by-design paradigm – a framework for dealing with the computational complexity (2021)
9. Ma, C., Wang, W., Zhao, X., et al.: The design of a time-interleaved analog-digital conversion modulator based on FPGA-TDC for PET application (2022)
10. Lu, Q.: Algorithm research on manufacturing agglomeration under the background of regional integration based on GMM model. J. Phys. Conf. Ser. **1995**(1), 012043 (2021)

The Application Design of Modern Educational Information Technology in Kindergarten Teaching

Linjiao Liu[1]([✉]) and Chao Gong[2]

[1] Ganzhou Teachers College, Ganzhou 3410000, Jiangxi, China
llj208@163.com
[2] Gannan Health Vocational College, Ganzhou 3410000, China

Abstract. With the rapid development and popularization of information science and technology, higher and newer requirements are put forward for modern early childhood education. Information technology teaching has become the main body of audio-visual education and plays an increasingly significant role. With its unique advantages, information technology plays an important role in education and teaching. Especially, the use of information technology in kindergarten teaching can effectively stimulate children's interest in learning, promote children's understanding of teaching content, and resolve the key and difficult points of teaching Enrich children's emotion; The application of advanced educational information technology in kindergarten teaching can fundamentally change the traditional concept of teaching and learning, teaching methods and evaluation means, optimize the teaching process and promote the comprehensive and coordinated development of children.

Keywords: Kindergarten teaching · Information technology · Modern education

1 Introduction

In the history of human civilization, the development of technology has experienced three stages: manual technology stage, machine technology stage and information technology stage. At present, we are in the stage of information technology. In this way, the development of educational technology is also divided into three stages: Educational traditional technology, educational media technology and educational information technology. In the philosophy of technology, some scholars "divide the type characteristics of technology into pre-modern technology, modern technology and post-modern technology around the modernity of technology or modern technology".

The concept of educational information technology is a compound concept, which can be decomposed into "education information technology", and its meaning can be simply understood as "information technology in education" or "Application of information technology in education". The "information technology" here refers to the information technology marked by computer and network gradually formed since the 1960s. In

M. A. Jan and F. Khan (Eds.): BigIoT-EDU 2022, LNICST 466, pp. 344–349, 2023.
https://doi.org/10.1007/978-3-031-23947-2_37

September 1993, the Clinton administration of the United States formally put forward the national "information superhighway" plan, which was followed by many countries. As a result, an information tide sweeping the world has formed, and the term "information technology" has been widely quoted and disseminated by people [1]. At the same time, a series of new concepts and terms marking the development of educational information technology are also emerging rapidly in the field of education, such as "network-based education", "it in education", "online education", etc. it can be seen that educational information technology (it in Education), with the advent of information technology, refers to the application of information technology in the field of education. This is also the specific technical connotation of educational technology in the development of information society. The application of advanced educational information technology in kindergarten teaching can fundamentally change the traditional concepts of teaching and learning, teaching methods and evaluation means, optimize the teaching process and promote children's overall development Coordinated development.

2 Research on the Application of Modern Educational Information Technology in Kindergarten Teaching

2.1 Research on the Implementation Strategy of Early Childhood Teaching Under the Environment of Information Technology

The development of kindergarten teaching in the information technology environment should not only skillfully integrate the content and form of books with information technology, but also use appropriate strategies for specific implementation. The use of teaching strategies should fully consider the characteristics of preschool children's physical and mental development, the content of books and the environment of preschool children. The appropriate and ingenious use of teaching strategies is very important for effective organization This content plays a good role in promoting the efficient development of picture book teaching. In "on the effective strategies of kindergarten teaching", Yuan Qiuping discusses the effective development of teaching methods from four aspects: selecting reading materials, developing effective questions, cultivating reading interest and creating situations. He Ping's research on the strategies of picture book reading teaching for children under the environment of information technology" In addition, in 2019, Xu Xiying elaborated on the strategies of teaching from the perspective of children, so as to provide guidance for the effective implementation of teaching For reference.

2.2 Research on the Impact of the Integration of Information Technology and Teaching on Children

In 2012, the Ministry of Education published the learning and Development Guide for children aged 3–6 It puts forward clear requirements for children's learning and development in the five fields of health, language, society, science and art, so as to guide and ensure children's healthy development. The integration of information technology and teaching provides more extensive choices for children's development in these fields [2]. Hu Chunchun points out that in the information environment, starting from the perspective of children's reading ability According to the characteristics of children's development, with the help of early reading materials and corresponding information equipment, it has promoted the cultivation of children's reading ability, and put forward the strategies and methods of cultivating children's reading ability under the information environment. Zhu Shunli expounded in detail the methods of improving children's critical thinking ability by combining information technology and teaching, and proved through experiments In the picture book teaching in a standardized environment, children's critical thinking can be effectively improved with the help of the cultivation strategy of problem consciousness, the cultivation strategy of distinguishing facts from views and the expression of views. In addition, Shen duanning also proposed in his research that the application of information technology in teaching not only improves children's language expression ability, but also helps to stimulate children's romantic feelings and enrich children's emotional experience in daily life.

3   Application of Modern Educational Information Technology in Kindergarten Teaching

Einstein said, "interest is the best teacher." Interest plays an extremely important role in children's learning process, because only when interest is generated can children form learning motivation, as shown in Fig. 1. Information multimedia technology teaching organically combines sound, image and other information, creates various vivid teaching situations, makes teaching vivid and interesting, and can fully mobilize children's vision and hearing And other senses to stimulate children's interest in learning [3]. For example, in the appreciation of prose poetry in big class "autumn rain", after using multimedia, the static and flat picture is transformed into a dynamic and vivid scene, and the background music gently sounds "whispers of autumn", raindrops patter down from the sky, the door of autumn opens slowly, chrysanthemums bloom, ginkgo turns yellow, maple leaves turn red, and fruits mature. In this poetic and picturesque atmosphere, children pay attention and have strong interest, and actively tell everyone what they hear and see about autumn.

3.1   Information Technology Can Effectively Promote Children's Understanding of Teaching Content, Break Through Key and Difficult Points and Optimize the Teaching Process

Children's cognition has specific and vivid characteristics. It is easy to understand specific, intuitive and vivid things. Using multimedia technology for dynamic demonstration can make abstract things and phenomena that can not be expressed in previous teaching become vivid, vivid, specific and intuitive, show the teaching content vividly, vividly and vividly, and analyze the key points and difficulties of teaching, It can also effectively support and guide children to find, explore and solve problems, so that children can use a variety of senses to find laws and understand relationships in their sound, shape and environment, so as to achieve twice the result with half the effort. Visualizing abstract knowledge makes children easy to understand and remember, which can effectively promote children's understanding.

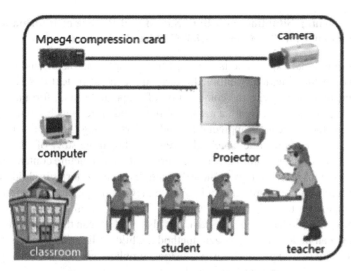

Fig. 1. Multimedia information teaching mode

For example, in the art activity "lovely turtle", the picture layout is a problem that children are difficult to master. In order to solve this problem, the teacher made a courseware to help with the difficulties of layout. At the same time, he used anthropomorphic techniques and sound effects that are easy for children to accept, so that children can feel the feeling of the picture and the feeling of the turtle living in different places in the sea, let the turtle speak, and help children understand the importance of picture layout, which is easy for children to accept. With the help of the advantages of multimedia pictures and texts and the combination of audio and video, teachers change the static wall chart into a dynamic picture and preach into an image visual stimulation, so as to fully mobilize the synergy of children's hearing, vision and feeling, so as to make children feel like they are on the scene and easily break through the key and difficult points of teaching. It also gives children an opportunity to enjoy happy learning, fully mobilizes children's enthusiasm and desire for exploration, and optimizes the teaching process.

For another example, in the activity of "understanding the cuboid", the multimedia courseware is used to flash the faces, edges and vertices of the cuboid in turn, so that children can understand the names of various parts of the cuboid, then remove the physical image of the cuboid and abstract the plan to help children transition from image thinking to abstract thinking, and then through a series of demonstrations such as the movement and combination of faces and edges, Help children understand the law of cuboid "equal relative faces and equal length of relative edges". Through this clear and dynamic picture display, children can easily and happily perceive the characteristics of cuboids. It can be seen that multimedia image demonstration can effectively solve the key and difficult points of teaching and realize the optimization of teaching process.

3.2 The Learning Situation with Both Sound and Picture of Information Technology Can Effectively Enrich Children's Emotion

Children's emotional experience is more specific, simple and direct, and has a strong dependence on the situation. Multimedia turns the content of text description into a three-dimensional scene with the combination of shape and sound, forming emotional radiation, tapping the soul, creating a state of mind, and enriching children's emotional experience in the process of appreciating and understanding things. For example, in the activity of "photos of little mice", children have heard the story of "the journey of little mice" before and are familiar with the story content and picture content. Therefore, teachers use scanning technology to show the pictures of small stories in children's books to the big screen. Children are very excited when they see the pictures in their own books suddenly appear on the "big TV". In this way, the enthusiasm of children's activities has been mobilized. In addition, the scanner is also used to scan the puzzle materials, so that children can understand the puzzle method... Children like this teaching form very much, which not only expands children's vision, stimulates children's curiosity, but also cultivates children's interest in learning [4].

For another example, in the activity of "protecting the Tibetan antelope", teachers let children watch the cartoon of "Tibetan antelope", so that children can feel that animals are our friends and cherish their feelings. When the children saw that groups of lovely Tibetan antelopes were suddenly knocked down by shotguns, the blood stained the grassland, and the surviving Tibetan antelopes shed sad tears, they were deeply moved by the realistic picture, and had a strong resentment against those who did not love the Tibetan antelopes. It can be seen that children not only have sympathy for the Tibetan antelope, but also sublimate the noble emotion of loving animals and caring for others. This specific, vivid and real environment shocked the children's hearts and stimulated their deep sympathy. Inspired by this emotion, they launched a conscious publicity campaign to protect Tibetan antelopes in the whole park.

Practice shows that multimedia technology, with its unique means of expression, enhances the intuitive image of teaching, makes children feel immersive, and can actively discover, question and explore in the context of sound, color and light created by multimedia technology, so as to obtain useful knowledge and experience. These advantages are beyond the reach of traditional teaching methods.

4   Conclusion

Use courseware or media demonstration to flexibly break through key and difficult points and optimize the teaching process. With the help of the advantages of multimedia information technology, both pictures and texts and the combination of sound and image, teachers change the static wall chart into a dynamic picture, and preach into an image visual stimulation, so as to fully mobilize the synergy of children's hearing, vision and feeling, so as to make children feel like they are on the scene and easily break through the key points and difficulties of teaching. It also gives children an opportunity to enjoy happy learning, fully mobilizes children's enthusiasm and desire for exploration, and optimizes the teaching process.

Acknowledgements. Comparative study on rural and urban kindergarten teachers input: SZUG-GYJ2020–1048.

References

1. Xu, L.: Philosophy of Technology. Fudan University Press, Shanghai (2004)
2. Zhou, Z.: E-Learning and Educational Reform. Zhejiang University Press, Hangzhou (2006)
3. Li, B., Wang, Y., Ju, H.: Application of information technology in Education. People's Posts and Telecommunications Press, Beijing (2004)
4. Hehui: Information Education Technology. Science Press, Beijing (2008)

Research on the Management System of an Internet Big Data Analysis Platform Based on Machine Learning

LinHao Liu[✉]

Institute of Management, Shenyang University of Technology, Shenyang 110000, China
L78930363@163.com

Abstract. In recent years, the Internet has become an important source of information, especially in the area of big data, which has led to the explosive growth of the number of network services and the gradual increase of Internet traffic data. The operation and maintenance environment of the analysis platform becomes more complex, and puts forward new requirements for the operation ability of the platform. At present, the common servers used in big data analysis platforms are prone to failure in terms of performance stability, so there is a risk of business data loss. The research on the management system of Internet big data analysis platform based on machine learning aims to provide comprehensive research suggestions for the development of new and improved intelligent management systems. The solution will be applied to the data analysis platform developed using artificial intelligence technology. This project is divided into three parts: (1) analysis and design; (2) Implementation; (3) Evaluation and verification. Therefore, this study will also analyze the construction mode of the Internet big data analysis platform management system supported by machine learning from the perspective of security, so as to reduce the operation and maintenance cost and ensure the operation and maintenance efficiency.

Keywords: Machine learning · Internet big data · Analytics platforms · Management systems

1 Introduction

In the current era, mobile phones with mobile networks, scanning sensors everywhere in life, smart homes and other intelligent and non intelligent terminals are constantly producing data. All aspects of life in society are recorded and stored in the form of data all the time. Society has entered the era of big data, and all levels of people's lives are closely related to data (Zhao Guodong, 2013) [1].

Big data is undoubtedly a decisive and epoch-making disruptive innovation after cloud computing and the Internet of things (Victor Mayer Schoenberg et al., 2013). Cloud computing provides a place for big data storage, computing and access, and the real value is big data (Zhang Lanting, 2014). In enterprises, cloud computing without

M. A. Jan and F. Khan (Eds.): BigIoT-EDU 2022, LNICST 466, pp. 350–360, 2023.
https://doi.org/10.1007/978-3-031-23947-2_38

big data is a foam. The operation data of enterprises, the people collected by the Internet of things, the data of logistics, the communication and interaction of the public in the Internet, and the life data have exceeded the carrying capacity of the current information technology architecture. Nowadays, how to properly and efficiently manage and apply these data assets so that they can serve national governance, enterprise development and personal convenient life is the focus of big data related personnel and the development direction of cloud computing (TU zipei, 2012) [2].

Since the concept of "big data" first appeared in the government work report in 2014, the executive meeting of the State Council has mentioned the use of big data six times in a year (C news, 2015). As a new productive force, computer technology infiltrates and transforms social life. Blowout data, like oil in the industrial age, has become a strategic resource for the country and society. The application of big data in the whole society is the inevitable choice to realize modernization. Big data platform is a powerful tool to deal with big data challenges and give full play to the value of big data. This paper mainly studies the construction of big data platforms in the Internet industry, and provides references for the big data practice of various organizations (Guo Hui, 2014) [3].

The cluster of big data analysis platform is composed of large general-purpose servers. The stability difference of general-purpose servers makes the whole platform possible to produce exceptions. Once an abnormality occurs, it is difficult to rely only on manual monitoring, so an automatic monitoring system is needed to complete comprehensive predictive monitoring, timely report the abnormal conditions or potential risk status to the operation and maintenance department, and quickly find the cause of the failure and take treatment measures. With the support of machine learning clustering algorithm, the monitoring index information of big data platform can be fitted and predicted, and the monitoring index can be judged by comparing the real value with the predicted value, so as to optimize the overall system performance.

2 Machine Learning Based Internet Big Data Platform Management System

At present, the purposes of the Internet industry data platform are: to integrate all business data of the company and establish a unified data center; Various reports of various businesses provided to senior management; Provide operational data support for application operation, and let the operation know the operation effect in time through data; Provide online or offline data support for various businesses, and become a unified data exchange and provision platform for the company; Analyze user behavior data, reduce investment cost and improve investment effect through data mining, such as targeted and accurate advertising, user personalized recommendation, etc.; Develop data products to directly or indirectly make profits for the company [4]; Build an open data platform and open company data; Not only offline batch processing, but also various real-time and near real-time query calculations.

The above requirements look similar to the use of traditional data warehouse, and all require the data platform to have good stability and reliability, but in the Internet industry:

(1) In addition to the large amount of data, more and more businesses require timeliness, and many even require real-time.
(2) Business changes quickly, which requires new businesses to be integrated into the data platform soon. Businesses that will be offline at the end of their life cycle can be easily offline from the existing data platform.

In fact, the data platform of the Internet industry can be regarded as the so-called agile data warehouse, which requires not only rapid response to data, but also rapid response to business; Not only static data, but also dynamic data.

Data collection system. All experimental and algorithmic processes are based around an internet big data analysis platform, with a focus on clustering and analysing data traffic from network devices [5]. The platform's operations and maintenance system uses supervised learning to make predictions about indicators, thus helping the platform to avoid potential risks. The current architecture of the platform's network traffic collection system is shown in Fig. 1.

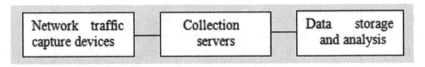

Fig. 1. Network traffic collection system architecture

One feature of big data is the sparsity of value. Therefore, the core of applying big data value is to analyze and mine big data to perceive the present, predict the future and assist in decision-making.

With hardware, we can't give full play to the value of data. We also need systems and software. With systems and software, we still need data analysis methods to give full play to the value of big data. It's not enough to only analyze correlation, but also have intelligent data analysis methods to gain insight into the real laws behind data. To mine data through the method of "facing practical problems", the integration of data disciplines and specific fields is the key to realize the value of big data. However, it is a step-by-step process for enterprises to convert data into their own competitive advantages, and they need to gradually move from exploration to orderly planning [6].

Data analysis is where the whole system directly affects the business. Here, we will use data mining algorithms to support the decision-making of the whole enterprise for all static and dynamic data collected and stored by users. Research the methods of establishing user portraits, and other data analysis methods that make big data valuable. A big data business analysis tool should be able to connect PC and mobile terminals across the screen, calculate massive data such as user behavior and attributes based on cloud computing platform, analyze crowd characteristics, and synthesize consumer user portraits, so as to establish a solid foundation for consumer insight and assist business decision-making. In addition, the big data platform also launched multi-dimensional analysis reports, including market pattern research, consumer attribute analysis, consumer preference analysis, industry marketing dynamics, etc.

The user-side based acquisition module is the original data input module that monitors user traffic and reports logs and information to the data platform as soon as access is recorded. The intermediate collection module is the equivalent of an information transfer station collection server, where all information is processed and combined in different areas of the device and eventually transferred to the big data analysis platform [7]. It should be noted that existing traffic collection systems have two problems: firstly, there is no separate monitoring and analysis module for user-side network devices, which can only passively receive information; secondly, user-side network devices in the same area are likely to cause waves that affect server performance, leading to additional wasted resources [8]. The main anomaly detection methods we currently use are shown in Table 1 below.

Table 1. Anomaly detection methods

Anomaly detection methods	Description
Classification-based anomaly detection	Learn classifiers that distinguish between positive and negative samples within a specific space and find features that are strongly representative for application in real-time monitoring scenarios
Anomaly detection based on proximity	The unsupervised learning model involves only distance calculation and is simple to implement
Clustering-based anomaly detection	Faster model predictions and shorter test times allow for real-time monitoring requirements

Clustering-based detection is a frequently used anomaly detection solution today. In response to the usage of information resources, a user device traffic analysis module and a traffic balancing module can be added to the existing framework. The former aggregates device data to determine the traffic consumption of devices through differences in usage rates, while the latter clusters the historical data of normally used user network devices to ensure that peaks and valleys of the same server can be interleaved.

Intelligent operation and maintenance system. In the intelligent operation and maintenance system, business indicators and platform indicators need to be managed and monitored according to the type of equipment and traffic differences, with common monitoring content shown in Table 2 below.

Table 2. Server monitoring metrics

Type of test	Contents	Time frequency Time frequency
Host_cpu_used	CPU utilization	60 s
Host_mem_used	Memory utilisation	60 s
Host_network_UP	Network uplink	10 s
Host_network_down	Network downlink	10 s

In addition to such detection indicators, it also includes the monitoring of the overall performance status of the cluster, and different monitoring indicators differ in terms of the detection time, for example, the collection interval of network upstream and network downstream indicators is relatively short, and not timely processing may affect the whole big data cluster, while for some monitoring indicators with low time frequency requirements, the collection interval can be appropriately extended. The monitoring indicators are divided into periodic and non-periodic monitoring indicators. For non-periodic monitoring indicators, only the upper and lower thresholds need to be set to complete the monitoring process, whereas for periodic monitoring indicators, a judgement has to be made on the development trend first, and then anomaly detection is performed on each monitoring data, and the operation and maintenance management department is notified if there is anomaly. The entire model parameters are updated once a week, and the normal state of business operations is not affected when the model is updated [9].

3   Cluster Analysis Process for Big Data Analytics Platforms

Equipment traffic data processing. Based on the data sources of the data platform, these time series data can be clustered using static data processing solutions to discover patterns and regularities in them and to understand the distribution relationships of different data sources. If there are significant anomalies in some of the data, the device is judged to be anomalous. All the information in the big data platform represents the network traffic of a network device over a certain period of time, and a time series refers to the historical network traffic information of a network device. If the results of the spark operation are sampled, the sparsity characteristics of the data can be understood to determine which phase of network traffic is the largest, and the whole experiment can take an additive model. As shown in Fig. 2.

$$Yt = Tt + St + Rt \tag{1}$$

Tt refers to the trend of the curve, Rt is the residual and St is the cycle period. When analysing the network traffic data, an inverse ranking method is chosen, where the devices with the highest traffic and the devices with the lowest traffic are ranked together to determine which network devices account for the majority of traffic consumption. After communicating with the operations and maintenance department, it was found that some devices had little traffic access for a short period of time due to a significant drop in usage of existing devices following the installation of new devices. In order to ensure the accuracy of the data, you can remove all the data information of some devices with low usage rate, and keep the data content of some devices with usage rate greater than a certain threshold (for example, the data information of devices with usage rate over 50% can be kept), so as to ensure the accuracy of the data flow analysis [10].

Application of clustering evaluation algorithms. In the application of the clustering evaluation algorithm, the first thing to determine is the contour coefficient, as the contour coefficient evaluation metric combines two evaluation factors, separation and cohesion, to analyse the impact of different parameters on the same raw data. The higher the cohesion and separation, the better the clustering effect. For a given clustering result, a number of sample points can be taken from all the samples and the distance and

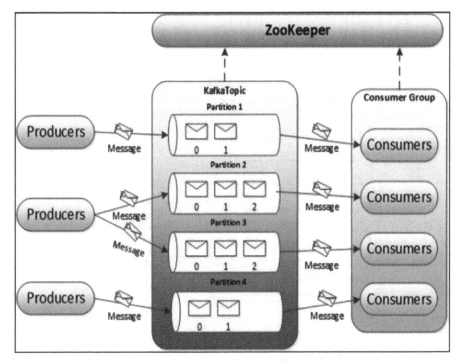

Fig. 2. Big data analysis platform management system

mean of the centre of the category to which they belong can be found. In the actual data process, considering the differences in the size of the traffic data generated by each device, in order to facilitate the clustering and calculation, all the data can be normalised and then compressed to a certain range according to the time series curve for equal proportional calculation. Different application scenarios have different calculation methods. To guarantee the displacement characteristics of the time series, it is necessary to use the dynamic programming idea to determine the similarity of the time series curves with sufficient similarity and smaller distance between them.

K-means algorithm optimisation. K-means is essentially a vector quantization algorithm and the most classical clustering algorithm, which divides all the training sample points into K categories, with the distance of each sample point being the closest to the centre of the category to which it belongs, in order to quickly obtain a locally optimal solution using a heuristic algorithm. After calculating the distance between each sample point and the cluster centre vector, the sample mean in each cluster can be used as the new cluster core. After repeating these steps, K clustering results are obtained. It can be seen that the most important aspect of this work is to determine the value of the parameter K. Once the optimum K value has been chosen, the equipment flow curve can be evaluated in clusters, and the sample points and curve profiles can be determined from the resulting clusters. As shown in Fig. 3.

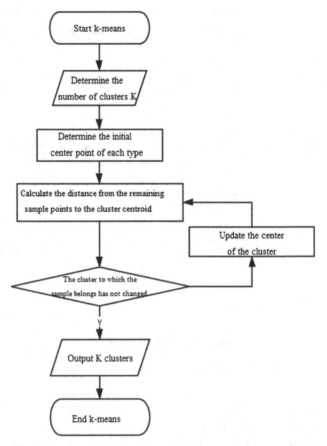

Fig. 3. K-means algorithm flow of platform management system

If the sample points and curves show a trough in the early morning hours and a peak in the daytime, then the curve fits well with the working hours of the general workforce; conversely, if the daytime work period is in a trough and the evening traffic is in a peak, two curves of this type fit with places such as nightclubs or bars; if the golden hours of midday and evening are in a peak and the rest of the curve is in a smoother state If the curve is at the peak at noon and in the evening, the rest of the curve is in a smoother state. Clustering the different K values based on these patterns reveals underlying patterns and regularities, indicating that samples within the same cluster have similar characteristics. The shape of the device traffic time series was evaluated. It has been learned that if the time series are more similar, the higher the likelihood that these flows come from the same application scenario. After judging the different devices according to the development patterns of the flows it is possible to determine the device flow profile and information feedback results to improve the operational efficiency in an integrated way. As an unsupervised learning mode, only the number of centres of clustering needs to be set manually before clustering, and the K-value can be adjusted according to the actual business needs to get the desired clustering results. Although the method is not sensitive to noise and some samples are judged as unique classes in the experiments. Even so, it is possible to evaluate certain anomalous data through statistical methods and to identify the devices that produce anomalies. After clustering the traffic profiles of devices under the same customer, feedback of the anomaly information can reduce the frequency of device operation, using the wave and valley mechanism to achieve a balanced load operation of the server.

Indicator anomaly handling. In the field of operation and maintenance anomaly detection has certain rules requirements, but because there are more indicators to be monitored, anomaly detection should be completed in an unsupervised way. In order to solve the original work pressure, the algorithm can be considered to improve the sequence decomposition method, the sequence trend will be removed to get a smooth sequence without trend, and then according to the sliding time window to accurately predict the trend of the curve. For some of the more important monitoring core index data, the O&M team will spend more time and effort on this part to carry out the extraction and detection of anomaly information, and the method of conducting feature extraction, mainly contains three types, as shown in Table 2.

Customer satisfaction surveys. The purpose of customer satisfaction surveys is to reach the target group and consolidate core customer relationships. In this respect, user data and information can be counted in the form of questionnaires, for example asking customers what factors influence their desire to buy. The questionnaire is also designed to analyse the final marketing process of the product according to the different conditions of the customer, such as gender or occupation, and the basic questionnaire content is included in Table 3.

Table 3. Time series feature extraction

Extraction method	Contents
Extraction of statistical features within sliding windows	Mean, median, variance
Extraction of current characteristics in comparison with the previous moment	Strongest feature
Difference between the current window and the previous window	Statistical characteristics

For most monitoring data, it is difficult to label each piece of data. Once the unsupervised approach to anomaly detection has been developed, historical data can be obtained based on time series, and the variance of the change corresponding to each point can be obtained. After importing the trained model to obtain the predicted value, the comparison between the predicted value and the historical data is used to derive information on the upper and lower thresholds of the data to determine the actual Whether this threshold is exceeded or not, so as to determine whether an anomaly has arisen. After importing the abnormal sample oversampling method, the data imbalance phenomenon can be effectively avoided, and then the statistical value and the result of mining the abnormal feature information can be obtained to meet the operation and maintenance monitoring requirements of the management platform.

   In the field of industrial big data, although data sources are extensive, data acquisition means are rich, and the total amount of data is large, the quality of available data is low and the value density is not high due to the low conditional probability of most high-quality data, high acquisition cost, sample duplication and other problems. The incomplete, insufficient and low quality of high-value data samples will limit the accuracy and accuracy of industrial big data analysis. Therefore, data simulation generation methods can be used to solve the problems related to data samples and improve the accuracy and accuracy of industrial big data analysis. In the data analysis and processing link, appropriate data processing methods should be selected according to the data distribution, main characteristics of the data and application scenarios. However, it is difficult to observe the data distribution characteristics of a large number of high-dimensional industrial data, and there are a large number of low value data in the high-dimensional data, which affects the selection of data processing methods and the accuracy of big data analysis. Therefore, it is necessary to reduce the dimension of the data, Then select the appropriate data processing methods to improve the usability, value and accuracy of the analysis results. The main scenarios of industrial big data processing applications are equipment fault prediction, health management, process decision-making and control monitoring. In the actual data processing process, it can be divided into clustering, classification, correlation and other analysis. Due to the large variety and volume of big data in the industrial Internet, the large-scale data volume will greatly reduce the efficiency of big data processing and analysis. Therefore, the algorithm can be parallelized to improve the efficiency of industrial big data analysis.

   The amount of big data is large, the data noise is large, and the value density is low. Only through the analysis and modeling technology of big data can we obtain the value of big data. The whole process includes data collection, storage, computing, application and other stages, which need the support of infrastructure provided by cloud computing technology, so that big data related personnel can focus on data processing. Cloud computing with virtualization technology as the core (baun, 2011) is the infrastructure of Internet big data system. The agile infrastructure and other ideas contained in cloud native are also in line with the trend that many companies are moving to cloud platforms. On the basis of cloud computing, the cloud platform integrated with the data platform is now the first choice for enterprises with data as their strategy.

   In the process of industrial big data analysis, there are problems of incomplete and unbalanced data information. Although the amount of data is huge and some data are continuous, there are still gaps between many data points, resulting in incomplete and unbalanced data information, which makes it impossible to fully realize the value of data. The scarcity and imbalance of high-quality data have become a major problem in industrial data processing and analysis. The uncertainty of the time and location of data collection, the high cost of sample data acquisition, and the low conditional probability of data occurrence can all lead to the problems of industrial data samples. High quality data is the premise of intelligent analysis. Therefore, in order to improve the accuracy, accuracy and applicability of industrial big data analysis, effective data needs to be generated to meet big data analysis. There are many typical data generation algorithms, such as bootstrap data generation algorithm and smote data generation algorithm, but there are some problems. There is no new data in the data generated by bootstrap algorithm.

Its working principle will be to simply copy the original data, resulting in the continuous analysis of duplicate data in the subsequent industrial Internet big data analysis, which is inefficient. When smote algorithm generates data, if there is abnormal data (such as noise), it will generate some new abnormal data, which will affect the distribution of real data samples, resulting in the decline of big data analysis accuracy and analysis accuracy. The data generation based on the generated countermeasure network will not cause the above problems. The new data generated based on the generated countermeasure network is different from the original data, and can avoid the interference of noise abnormal data to a large extent. This chapter will use the generation confrontation network algorithm to realize the simulation generation of industrial big data, so as to improve the data quality and further improve the accuracy and accuracy of big data analysis.

There are three ways to implement Cloud Computing: cloud, private cloud and hybrid cloud. The major manufacturers of shared cloud mainly include Alibaba cloud, Amazon's AWS, Microsoft's aure, etc. For the cloud architecture of enterprises, the main difference between public cloud and private cloud is the degree of openness to users of cloud services. At present, cloudstack, openstack and other cloud computing platforms in the open source community are flexible to use, can avoid being locked by manufacturers, and have low costs. They have open standards and programming interfaces, which facilitate companies and manufacturers outside the cloud computing giant to use cloud computing technology. Many companies rent public cloud resources as a supplement to form a hybrid cloud in the presence of their own private cloud.

4   Conclusion

In the era of increasing number of clusters and physical devices, an effective management system can ensure the intelligent operation and maintenance needs of the big data platform, so that all kinds of abnormal monitoring indicators can be supervised and abnormality detection can be started from understanding the distribution law. This research is based on time series and clustering analysis, and future work will need to be optimised in terms of model fitting and extraction of anomaly information features to help the platform collect raw and intelligent data and update and upgrade the O&M system.

References

1. Li, M.: Research on Financial Management Algorithm Based on Machine Learning in Big Data Era (2021)
2. Zhao, Y., Mu, R., Li, X., et al.: SAT0647-HPR Develop a Machine Learning Model and Algorithm Based on Smart System of Disease Management (SSDM) Big Data for RA Flare Prediction. BMJ Publishing Group Ltd. (2020)
3. Ning S . Analysis of College Students' Behavior Based on Machine Learning and Big Data Technology[J]. 2022.
4. Wang W . Online Machine Learning System of Power Quality Information Technology Based on Big Data. Journal of Physics: Conference Series, 2021, 1952(2):022057-.
5. Vo, A., Zr, A., Fy, B., et al.: Big Data Analysis Methods Based on Machine Learning to Ensure Information Security (2021)

6. Zhang, H., Meng, F., Wang, G., et al.: Research on the automation integration terminal of the education management platform based on big data analysis. Adv. Data Sci. Adapt. Anal. **14**(01n02) (2022)

7. Gao, L., Yang, Q., Zou, B., et al.: Research on data asset management system of graph database based on Internet of Things. In: Journal of Physics: Conference Series, vol. 1802, no. 3, p. 032134 (7pp) (2021)

8. El-Alfy, E.S.M., Mohammed, S.A.: A review of machine learning for big data analytics: bibliometric approach. Technol. Anal. Strat. Manag. **32**(7), 1–22 (2020)

9. Shivaprakash, K.N., Swami, N., Mysorekar, S., et al.: Potential for Artificial Intelligence (AI) and Machine Learning (ML) applications in biodiversity conservation, managing forests, and related services in India. Sustainability **14** (2022)

10. Luo, B.: A method for enterprise network innovation performance management based on deep learning and Internet of Things. Math. Probl. Eng. (2022)

Construction of Maker Education Resource Sharing Platform Based on Web Technology

Kan Wang[(✉)]

Henan University, Kaifeng 475000, China
2056955435@qq.com

Abstract. At present, what maker education lacks is not a certain software or hardware, but a system. This platform should connect students, teachers and education authorities in series. This series is not a series of products, but a series of data. Now the exam oriented education industry is very concerned about the construction of three links and two platforms, and the same is true of maker education. Considering the practicability and economy, building a network teaching platform based on Web technology is an important task and development direction of the current construction of educational resource sharing platform. The summary of the construction of maker education platform may have some enlightenment.

Keywords: Web technology · Maker · Educational resource sharing · Platform construction

1 Introduction

It should be the construction of the learning resource integration system of famous teachers and courses of maker education. Maker education is still in the primary stage. At present, many companies are developing and integrating maker education products, but they are not the main body of maker education. The main body of maker education is teachers and students. Only teachers take out their own courses can bring out real campus makers, Therefore, the primary task of the maker education platform should be the construction of the famous teachers and courses sharing system that has carried out maker education. This can also be said to be the establishment of an online teaching system, so that famous maker teachers across the country can present their maker education courseware indirectly or directly in front of teachers and students all over the country, so that school teachers who have not yet carried out maker education can also participate in and form a self-training system, so as to cultivate more famous teachers and classes to form a circular system [1]. Of course, these famous teachers' famous courses are only the beginning, and the next step is to form a series of courses or serial courseware, because what the current maker education really lacks is not a courseware, but a series of courseware supporting a semester or an academic year, so the construction of the platform should also provide those famous teachers with a mechanism incentive system that may serial courseware, For example, these serial courseware can be connected

M. A. Jan and F. Khan (Eds.): BigIoT-EDU 2022, LNICST 466, pp. 361–367, 2023.
https://doi.org/10.1007/978-3-031-23947-2_39

with the publishing house in the future, so that these excellent courseware can have the opportunity to publish, so as to encourage more famous teachers to form their own courseware series, which is the foundation of platform construction.

2 Maker Education

2.1 Maker Connotation

(1) Definition of maker

Maker is an innovative entrepreneurial model that draws lessons from the American stem education model and combines the current situation of China's economic development to promote China's economic take-off and revitalize the world economy. The concept of maker is a new innovation and Entrepreneurship Model rising in recent years. Taking universities, companies and enterprises as the carrier, it came into being for the vigorous development of innovative industry. The government formulates maker related policies, provides human resources guarantee and carrier guarantee for makers, and promotes maker movement in the new era. Colleges and universities establish maker spaces, provide them with supporting maker venues, maker courses and maker teachers, and guide college students to know, get familiar with and become makers.

(2) Definition of maker Education

Maker education is a new innovation and entrepreneurship education model to adapt to the rapid development of China's economy, solve the problem of insufficient innovation and entrepreneurship ability in China, and promote the revival of the global economy. Maker education is a new educational model originated from the community innovation and entrepreneurship education in the United States. On the basis of learning from the spatial experience of American community maker education and combined with the reality of entrepreneurship education in China. The government has formulated a maker education policy to widely disseminate maker education and attract more members of society to become makers. As the main position of maker education, colleges and universities strictly implement the spirit of the central document, cooperate with the government to create maker centers, set up maker courses and establish maker education colleges.

2.2 Problems and Causes of Maker Education in Colleges and Universities

(1) Insufficient investment in maker Education

In order to adapt to the development of socialist market economy, China pays more and more attention to education, and the investment in education is increasing year by year, especially in vocational education. However, in terms of maker education, the funds invested by the state are not enough to comprehensively promote innovation and entrepreneurship education. In terms of publicity, guidance and investment, the state's public guidance for maker education is not enough, and it fails to continuously invest funds for long-term publicity. In terms of maker space investment, the funds allocated by the state can not allow all colleges and universities to establish special maker centers, so it can not provide necessary venues for makers. In terms of maker teacher investment, the introduction and training of maker mentors by the state or colleges and universities are far from enough.

(2) Insufficient guarantee of maker education site

Maker education site is the most basic educational facility, which is very important for the cultivation of makers. At present, most colleges and universities can not establish corresponding maker education sites or set up fixed maker education sites, resulting in the failure of maker education to form a centralized effect and create an innovation and entrepreneurship atmosphere. Coupled with the enrollment expansion year after year, the number of students is increasing. Colleges and universities use the only open space or applied land for the construction of teaching buildings and student dormitories, and it is impossible to build a special maker education and teaching building at all. On the basis of not affecting normal teaching, very few colleges and universities set some classrooms as flexible places for maker education activities, but they are not fixed.

(3) Maker education teachers are not strong

There are few tutors specializing in maker education in China, which is the current situation of maker education and an urgent problem to be solved. Maker education does not belong to any professional category of higher education, which leads to an unprecedented shortage of maker education tutors and rings an alarm for national higher education [2]. The state strongly advocates the transformation of teachers in economic and management colleges and universities into maker education tutors to supplement teachers. However, most college teachers fail to change their teaching ideas and are not familiar with the content of maker education, so they still need long-term training. In addition, most colleges and universities in China have not established innovative education colleges, set up maker courses, and have no plans to train or introduce maker education tutors.

(4) Weak support of maker education policy

The maker education support policy formulated by the state only stays at the outline level and fails to be implemented in detail, resulting in the public's lack of in-depth understanding of maker education, let alone the corresponding path of innovation and entrepreneurship. According to the guidance of national policies, most local governments only simply forwarded them and failed to combine them with local reality, resulting in the maker education policy becoming empty talk and failing to implement it. In addition, the maker education support policies of colleges and universities are guided by national and local policies, which only improve the current situation of maker education of the University, but fail to meet the national requirements. It can be seen that the policy support formulated by the state, local governments and colleges and universities is not enough.

(5) Incomplete maker education system

China's basic education and higher education are formulated by the Department of basic education and the Department of higher education of the Ministry of education, which is a very perfect educational mechanism. However, the new maker education can not be strongly supported by national policies, nor can it be vigorously reformed by local governments and universities, resulting in the incomplete maker education system. The Ministry of education failed to prepare the maker education program and teaching materials, and failed to give guidance to local governments and universities, resulting in maker education being just a slogan. In addition, as an important position of maker education, colleges and universities have failed to establish corresponding teacher teams and curriculum systems of maker education colleges.

3 Construction of Maker Education Resource Sharing Platform Based on Web Technology

In order to ensure the practicability of the system, windows 2003 server, web server IIS and Microsoft sol Server 2003 are selected as database servers, and ISAPI interactive programs are written with ASP, Java and VB to realize an intuitive Tibetan medicine information sharing platform with the functions of database collection, maintenance, management and retrieval based on Web.

3.1 System Architecture

The system adopts the architecture of B/S architecture based on Web. This structure includes three layers: Browser/Web server 1 database server, which is mainly used to realize information browsing and query. Windows 2003 ser began to integrate Web server IIS. IIS provides Web server, FTP server and gopher server at the same time. The server management program with windows and HTML interfaces has powerful and flexible management tools. IIS also provides Internet information server application program interface (ISAPI) to expand the functions of web server and realize the rapid development of Web programs through ASP. ASP realizes the interconnection diagram of maker education resource sharing platform based on Web, as shown in Fig. 1.

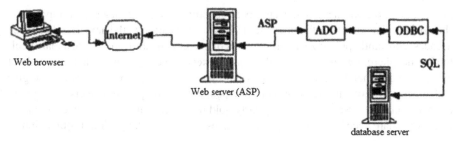

Fig. 1. ASP realizes the interconnection diagram of maker education resource sharing platform based on Web

3.2 Related Technologies

The network operating system adopts Windows 2003 server version, the database adopts MS SQL 2003, and the server adopts Internet information server 6.0 (IIS 6.0).

(1) ASP (active server pages) is a web application development technology launched by Microsoft. The main characteristic of ASP is that it can organically combine HTML, script and components to form an application that can run on the server, and send the standard HTML page specially made according to the user's requirements to the client browser. ASP runs in the same process of web server, which can process customer requests faster and more effectively; ASP provides a more convenient and simple method to access the database, which makes it easier to develop web applications based on database drive [3]. Therefore, ASP is selected to develop maker education resource sharing platform in the development of maker education information system.

(2) MS SQL Server 2003 SQL is an industry standard database sublanguage, which is especially suitable for designing, maintaining and controlling relational databases. SQL statements can be embedded into any language that can write application programs, so as to make use of its powerful data maintenance and query ability to make it have the function of database access. SQL is an interactive query language, which allows users to query and store data directly. Using this interactive feature, users can answer quite complex questions in a very short time. Maker education resource sharing platform uses mssqlserver2003 to establish and manage maker education database.

4 Research on the Construction Path Innovation of Maker Education Platform in Colleges and Universities

(1) Maker culture path

Culture is the inside information of a country and reflects the country's soft power. The construction of maker education platform is inseparable from the edification of creating a cultural atmosphere. On the one hand, continuously publicize maker education and improve public awareness. The state, local governments and colleges and universities should formulate plans for the promotion of maker education in the next decade or even decades, constantly publicize all the contents of maker education and create a maker cultural atmosphere. On the other hand, a maker exchange conference is held throughout the year to commend successful makers. The state should set up maker awards to give makers greater motivation and attract more people to participate in makers. Local governments and universities should regularly hold maker exchange conferences to enable makers to share successful or failed experiences and consolidate cultural foundation.

(2) Maker carrier path

National, local and universities are the three carriers and main positions of maker education. Deepening the three carriers of reform and broadening the carrier path are the key to the development of maker education. First, deepen the reform of the three carriers of the state, local governments and colleges and universities. Vigorously promote maker Education under the leadership of the national government; Formulate specific maker education development plans based on local governments; Take colleges and universities as the front line of reform and improve the maker education teachers and curriculum system. Second, broaden the path of maker carrier. On the basis of national, local and universities, attract the capital and strength of companies, enterprises and social organizations to jointly build a new situation of maker education.

(2) Maker technology path

Science and technology is the primary productive force and an important embodiment of a country's comprehensive national strength. In the information age, the development of maker technology is an important guarantee for national and social stability. First, set up more maker technology projects. In terms of project application, the state, local governments and universities should set up more maker science and technology projects to provide innovation direction for makers. Second, lower the threshold for the establishment of maker technology companies [4]. The lowering of the threshold provides convenience for makers and enables more people to participate in the innovation and technology industry. Third, gradually liberalize high and new technologies in military industry and carry out military civilian integration. Under the guidance of national policies, maker technology company should actively participate in the bidding of military science and technology projects and jointly build a military civilian integration platform.

5 Conclusion

The establishment of maker education is inseparable from the state, local governments and universities, and should integrate the support forces of society, at home and abroad. First, mobilize the whole society to establish a maker education system. Both social organizations and individuals should fully support maker education in terms of human and material resources. Second, introduce foreign capital and advanced educational ideas. Although maker education originates from the stem teaching model in the United

States, it still needs to absorb and learn from the advanced education methods of other countries. The state should actively introduce advanced foreign education groups to invest in running schools in China. Third, increase public opinion support. The state should actively guide makers to make positive comments through forums, wechat and QQ to provide public opinion support for maker education.

References

1. Li, Z.: My opinion on innovation and entrepreneurship education. China Univ. Educ. (4), 5–7 (2014)
2. Yang, X., Li, J.: Value potential of maker education and its controversy. Res. Mod. Distance Educ. (2) (2015)
3. Yan, H.: Research on learning support of information teaching. China Audio Vis. Educ. 18–21 (2003)
4. Gou, X.: Application of maker thinking in information technology teaching. Knowl. Libr. (20), 68 (2015)

The Application of Documentary New Media Communication Platform in Education and Teaching

Te Zhai[⊠]

Shandong Media Vocational College, Jinan 250003, Shandong, China
xiaobaoxixi6688@163.com

Abstract. Since the emergence of documentary film in China, it has a strange fate with TV media. Documentary has improved the cultural quality of TV media, and the recording has been widely spread with the help of TV media. However, at present, the media ecological environment in China has changed, the proportion of documentary in TV media is small, the viewing situation is poor, and the documentary has fallen into a communication dilemma. The rapid development of new media provides opportunities for the dissemination of documentary films. New media strategies such as setting the category of scientific documentaries, TV scientific documentaries for microblog, and micro scientific documentaries on mobile terminals in the network recording channel are conducive to the dissemination of documentaries.

Keywords: Documentary film · Television · New media

1 Introduction

In the development of science and technology, new technologies continue to enter people's vision. From the beginning of computer technology and Internet technology, to the mobile Internet technology represented by smart phones and mobile network terminals, and then to the emerging artificial intelligence technology in recent years, they are imperceptibly changing the social communication environment [1]. With the emergence of new media, the proportion of traditional media, mainly newspapers, radio and television, in social communication is decreasing. Specifically, the rapid development of network technology is destined to change people's way of production and life. Mobile Internet technology has released people's pace, making people's scope of activities more and more broad. Coupled with the continuous popularization of various mobile intelligent terminal devices, people can obtain a variety of information at any time and place [2]. More flexible, rapid and convenient communication conditions have broken people's previous regular life and learning time, and the fragmented living state has been continuously developed and popularized.

In February 2017, Hu Bo published a review on the broadcasting and viewing of documentary programs in 2016. According to the investigation on the viewing of different

M. A. Jan and F. Khan (Eds.): BigIoT-EDU 2022, LNICST 466, pp. 368–378, 2023.
https://doi.org/10.1007/978-3-031-23947-2_40

types of TV programs in 2016, TV documentaries were broadcast for 61000 h, an increase of about 10%, as shown in Fig. 1. The ratings of documentary programs ranked fifth, second only to interview programs and better than sports and TV dramas. It can be seen that although documentary, as the main type of programs, is not as high as entertainment variety, it also ranks in the forefront and has been recognized and loved by the audience. At the same time, the research report points out that in terms of the structure of the audience of the documentary, the proportion of men and women is basically the same, and the group aged 25–34 accounts for the highest [3]. On the whole, the audience structure is relatively young. Similarly, most of the Internet users of documentaries are between the ages of 20–34. In this way, the viewing group of documentary and the receiving group based on the network platform have reached a high degree of overlap at the age level. The middle-aged and young groups have become the main audience of documentary, and the network media platform has become an important position for the dissemination of documentary [4]. According to the statistics of documentary audiences in another Research Report on the development of Chinese documentaries in 2016, the top three objectives of audiences watching documentaries are to increase knowledge (65.2%), understand history and culture (60.6%) and broaden their horizons (49.8%). It is not difficult to see that these three belong to the needs of cognitive level. As a media product that truly reflects social reality and has high cultural added value, documentary can just meet the cognitive needs of young and middle-aged audiences and become a documentary type with good market development prospects.

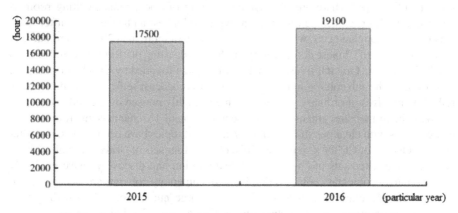

Fig. 1. Comparison of the output of column documentaries (2015–2016)

In recent years, documentaries have played a positive role in improving citizens' scientific literacy and the soft power of national science, technology and culture. Although the production level of Chinese TV documentaries is constantly improving, it should be noted that niche has always been an embarrassing situation for Chinese TV documentaries, and has also become one of the factors restricting the development of the whole Chinese documentary industry. A very important reason is that there are few public platforms for documentary broadcasting. Since its emergence, Chinese documentaries have an indissoluble bond with TV media, and TV media has become an important communication channel for documentaries [5]. However, at present, the development of documentary in China's TV media is facing many problems, which restricts the dissemination of scientific documentary. In the broadcasting period, documentaries are often far away from the viewing time of ordinary audiences. From the perspective of building the development of China's TV documentary industry, the scarcity of public broadcasting platforms directly affects the development speed of the documentary market, thus limiting the win-win benign interaction between producers, broadcasters and the market. The vigorous development of new media provides an opportunity for the wider dissemination of scientific documentaries.

2   Related Work

2.1   Current Situation of Public Broadcasting Platform of Documentary

TV columns constitute the main body of the current public broadcasting platform of Chinese TV documentaries. The documentary editing room of the former Shanghai TV station is considered to be the first to carry out the column operation of Chinese documentary in the industry. Since its launch in 1985, it has broadcast a large number of domestic documentaries in various styles with weekly broadcasting volume and stories mainly about people in different lives Under the background of ideological enlightenment and rediscovering its own ideological trend at that time, the documentary emphasizing non fiction can be regarded as an effective carrier for Chinese TV viewers to yearn for authenticity [6]. Therefore, the audience rating of documentary editing room is considerable. It once became the program with the highest audience rating after news network and Shanghai news, with the audience rating of more than 20%. A new stage in the development of Chinese documentary public broadcasting platform appeared in 1993 The TV magazine Oriental time and space, which was founded by CCTV for one year, was revised. The sub column living space turned to broadcast self-made documentaries reflecting the lives of ordinary people, which was highly praised by the audience.

With the further strengthening of the specialization of TV channels, many documentary columns with clear positioning and concentrated topics have been opened one after another. One set of CCTV's "journey of discovery", four sets of "travel through China", "record China", ten sets of "people" and "exploration and discovery" have gradually matured into documentary columns [7]. These documentary columns are clearly located in historical and cultural themes, resulting in a large number of excellent long-term theme documentaries such as "archaeological China" and "Forbidden City".

2.2   Problems in Public Broadcasting Platform of Documentary

Documentary film is a kind of image works that express objective things through sound and picture by means of non fictional artistic techniques and taking real life as the prototype. "Truth and art are the connotation and extension of documentary." Its own significance and charm lies in its presentation to the audience by means of artistic sound and painting through real and objective pictures and images. However, as the transmission of traditional media is greatly influenced by new media, the main means of transmission of documentary is television media. Therefore, in the new media environment, documentary creation has exposed more and more obvious problems in its emphasis on publicity rather than literature and art, single broadcast channel, audience demand and so on.

First, it pays more attention to propaganda than literature and art. Most documentaries are created by government agencies and related large-scale media. Due to the limitations of broadcast media, themes, scenes, duration, etc., the selected angles tend to be political ideals, natural landscapes, long history, social development, etc. relatively speaking, they pay more attention to publicity and ignore the literary and artistic value of documentaries themselves [8].

Second, the single broadcast channel. The traditional documentary broadcast channels are relatively concentrated on the theater lines, TV and other mainstream platforms, and the audience is in a passive acceptance state. Affected by the development of new media environment and the popularity of portable devices such as smart phones and tablet computers, people will use the Internet and mobile communication networks to find the film and television works they want to watch when watching movies. Moreover, the development of new media environment has improved the status of the audience in information transmission, which is not only passive acceptance, but also active communication, and there is more room to give play to their subjective initiative. Therefore, it is urgent to develop more diversified communication channels for traditional documentaries.

Third, it can not meet the needs of the audience. The audience of traditional documentaries are more intellectuals and elites from various industries. Compared with the elite class, ordinary people are relatively pragmatic in terms of life concept, consumption concept and thinking. Except for a few loyal fans of documentary, few ordinary people are willing to spend one or two hours watching a complete documentary [9]. Although Chinese documentaries have won awards on the international stage in recent years, they do not have an open exhibition platform and lack a broad mass base. Chinese documentaries have been in an awkward situation of being too high and too few in China.

Although, at present, CCTV and provincial and municipal TV stations have successively launched some documentary columns, especially in provinces with rich documentary resources such as Yunnan and Sichuan, documentary has become a significant feature in their TV production; However, there are many problems in the public broadcasting platform of documentary based on TV columns. These problems directly affect the formation and development of China's documentary industry chain, and the broadcasting platforms are decreasing day by day. At present, among more than 2000 TV channels in China, few columns are used for documentary broadcasting. Especially in the past four or five years, the broadcasting market of the whole TV documentary has been in a downturn. This situation can be said to run counter to the development of the whole TV market. First, in terms of the number of channels, among the more than 2000 channels, more than 20000 broadcasting hours a day (the total broadcasting time of all channels), the broadcasting time of Chinese self-made documentaries is very rare; Second, there are almost no special documentary channels, and the ratings of columns generally decline. Although some self-made documentaries such as archaeological China and the Forbidden City broadcast by CCTV 4 and 10 have achieved quite good ratings, these are only rare from the overall ratings statistics. The documentary columns set up by local TV stations in previous years have been gradually cancelled. Although some columns exist, there are many problems in the subject selection, narrative methods and expression methods of self-made documentaries, resulting in a significant decline in ratings. Private institutions are generally excluded from public broadcasting platforms. In the discussion on the public broadcasting platform of Chinese Documentaries held at the 2005 China (Guangzhou) International Documentary conference, private institutions attending the conference generally reflected that although there are many independent documentary producers and private production companies in China, their documentary films rarely get the opportunity to be broadcast in TV columns [10].

3 Communication Characteristics of Documentary Under the New Media Environment

The unique personality of new media is different from that of traditional media, which brings great test to the form of traditional media. The evolution of interaction theory and the development of interaction technology make the author realize that today's interaction is no longer the traditional media and audience, but involves the overall interaction of all levels or factors. In order to find and solve the survival problem of traditional science and education documentary, we must re understand and examine itself.

3.1 Diversification of Communication Subjects

In the traditional media communication mode in the past, whether it is the paper media communication represented by the news press or the radio communication represented by radio and television, in terms of communication status, there is an unequal status between the newspaper, radio and television as the initiator of information and the audience as the receiver. Communicators are often highly organized authoritative communication organizations represented by radio, television and news newspapers. The most obvious characteristic of their communication is the single communication route. The opinions and feelings of the audience cannot be fed back in time. The audience will accept what information is published in the newspaper; What is broadcast on TV, the audience will watch what, and the audience's first feelings and feedback are neglected.

In contrast, in the new media environment, due to the increasing development and popularization of network and information technology, the audience can give timely feedback while receiving information, and the communication mode is more free, blurring the boundary between the two. Specifically, it is the media to audience communication, audience to audience communication, audience to media communication and other ways, which realizes the interactivity of communication methods. In the new media environment, the audience is no longer just a passive receiver. Each audience may become a topic center endowed with information. While receiving a large amount of information, they can make more independent choices according to their personal preferences, which improves their status in the process of information dissemination and realizes the exchange of identities.

The diversification of communication methods and carriers leads to the diversification of communication content. The popularization of network technology has led to the popularization of mobile phones and clients. The audience can act as the source of information dissemination to initiate, receive and disseminate information. The interactivity of the communication mode is reflected all the time. While promoting the communication status, it has also achieved the goal of advertising personalization. As shown in Fig. 2.

Fig. 2. Diversified communication modes of new media

With the development of technology, the communication subject of science and education documentary is no longer single. In addition to professional documentary editors and directors in traditional media institutions and professional directors trained and trained, many amateurs have also joined the creative team. They use portable, low-cost and powerful digital imaging equipment to record the major and minor events around them, create and express their lives. College students are the outstanding representatives of this group. They have rich scientific knowledge, active creative thinking and positive creative enthusiasm, which has brought a new force and injected new vitality into the future of science and education documentaries.

The organization is also the main body of science and education documentary communication. Under the traditional media environment, there are mainly radio and television stations, film studios and professional educational media, such as science and education channel of CCTV and China Education Television. With their unique educational responsibilities and obligations, they undertake the important task of the dissemination of science, education, film and television in China. The integration of resource advantages of different media institutions, government departments, enterprises and institutions brought by the new media environment has formed a "joint production body", which cooperates from the whole industrial chain of capital, production and communication for mutual benefit, forming a diversified communication subject.

3.2 Personalized Communication Content

The diversification of subjects not only makes more ordinary people join the ranks of science and education documentary creation, but also enriches the content of communication. Scientific knowledge is everywhere. Compared with the officially released and produced scientific and educational documentary works, the contents created by the general public have more practical value in life, such as using scientific experiments to popularize the methods of identifying the food safety of agricultural products and explain some scientific phenomena questioned by people. Although these contents are not as scientific as the large-scale works, they are full of connotation, But it is enough to establish people's correct scientific concept and solve the personalized knowledge they are concerned about and interested in immediately and accurately.

Everyone's needs vary according to gender, educational background, occupation, interest, region and other factors. Just as Li Chao's survey on the reasons why undergraduate groups watch documentaries in the questionnaire survey on documentary audience needs and contact channels found that 48.3% of students can obtain knowledge in areas they don't know, 4.4% of the students thought that they chose documentaries because of their elegant behavior, and 13.6% chose documentaries for entertainment. 26.7% of the students are for the needs of study and work. Everyone chooses information according to their own needs. New media makes use of the technical advantages of mobile intelligent terminals to capture and meet the audience needs that change with the change of individual environment.

In today's new media environment, people receive information in more diverse and convenient ways. As mentioned above, the audience's participation in the information dissemination process in the new media environment is as the receiver of information and the initiator of the next information. Such a divergent dissemination environment will produce a large amount of fragmented information, which requires each audience to screen the information according to their own needs. The regular daily pace of reading newspapers during the day and watching TV at night may no longer meet the needs of the "post-80s" and "post-90s". The word "fragmentation" is not only reflected in information dissemination, but also in specific real life. The acceleration of the pace of life will promote the process of fragmentation and divide people's time into fragments. In the interval of walking, waiting for the bus, picking up meals and even friends' gatherings, the fragmented life needs a faster and more efficient way to receive information. Under this demand, mobile terminals such as mobile phones and tablets become more popular. Compared with long reading, people tend to take out their mobile phones to get information. This fast-food reading method can get a lot of information in a short time. Under such influence, the new media will inevitably reflect the characteristics of fragmentation in the communication content, making it more suitable for the needs of the times. The specific performance is that the information content is more concise, more immediate, more quantitative and more general.

3.3 Three Dimensional Communication Platform

In the new media era, it is not enough to meet the needs of the audience at any time and anywhere through a single platform. Today's science and education documentary has developed into an all media era dominated by TV media and integrating film media and new media. CCTV record channel established in 2011 is a highly recognized Documentary Channel in China. The documentary broadcasting and promotion of this channel is a three-dimensional platform for the integrated communication of traditional media and new media, such as CCTV, CCTV network, official microblog wechat, CCTV video client, iqiyi client and so on. Among them, the content broadcasting of TV channels can meet the viewing needs of stable viewing groups for a fixed time; Documentary website and mobile terminal platform can meet the needs of modern people to watch videos and social activities anytime and anywhere; The associated video client and record channel reprint can integrate the audience resources of the platform and expand the comprehensive influence. New media makes the communication platform more three-dimensional, which not only expands the influence of works, but also promotes the development of documentary art.

4   Ideas for Building a New Media Communication Platform for Documentaries

According to the above analysis of the current situation of documentary communication and development, and with the development of information technology, there are many novel and interesting apps and web pages with documentary as content and digital technology as carrier. The gradual emergence of such apps related to documentary can take advantage of the technical advantages of new media to assist the dissemination and inheritance of documentary. Since China has the largest mobile phone market in the world, operators, terminal manufacturers, software and Internet enterprises are competing. Tens of millions of applications are of mixed quality. We need to build a green and high-quality mobile app.

(1) The application object of documentary communication platform. The excellent documentary communication platform can first take young documentary lovers as the main audience, gradually expand the age group of the audience, and constantly launch new ideas to retain current users and attract potential users. The platform takes short video as the medium and random consumption as the way to consume according to personal preferences and temporary interests. Consumption habits start with the commodity itself, create the characteristics of the commodity itself, gradually improve the quality of the platform, and achieve the purpose of forming users' preference for this commodity.

(2) The overall structure of documentary communication platform. The platform is expected to be divided into three main parts: culture, communication and personal center. By pushing high-quality posts, such as videos, pictures and books, it will enrich cultural researchers' understanding of eastern Guangdong documentaries and understand the traditional customs, architecture, thought and literature and art

contained in the ancient eastern Guangdong region. Deepen teenagers' understanding of documentaries in a way loved by the public. At the same time, the platform will be equipped with excellent courses on documentaries, lectures by famous teachers, subject research, etc., and the comment function will be set in the exchange area to facilitate the interaction between schools.

In terms of project research, in order to close the cooperation between students and instructors and pay attention to the dynamics of students' project research and development, the software sets up a project discussion area, and the administrator can set the openness of the project. Students participating in the research project can interact with their instructor in the discussion area. The instructor can make periodic comments according to the phased harvest uploaded by students, so as to provide students with directional guidance in time. If the discussion area is open, other external members can participate in the discussion of the topic and collect friends' cultural activities when they encounter topics of interest.

(3) The significance of constructing documentary communication platform. The platform is a new communication mode of excellent documentary network communication platform under the situation of the prosperity and development of network new media, which is conducive to promoting the promotion and inheritance of excellent documentary. The popularization and development of new media provide more convenient life services for the society. We should face up to its impact and positive impact on documentaries, and use its positive role to promote the modern communication of documentaries. At the same time, we should pay more attention to the development of documentary and documentary communication, innovate the documentary, make the new media culture communication platform and documentary complement each other, cooperate and develop, build a beautiful picture of the future development and communication of documentary together, do not forget the root of the nation, and truly realize the great rejuvenation of the Chinese nation.

(4) Dissemination of micro scientific documentaries by mobile terminals

Mobile terminals include mobile phones, iPads, mobile TV, etc., which can make full use of these new media for the re dissemination or multiple dissemination of TV Science documentaries. The spread of new media such as mobile phones, iPads and other handheld terminals, and mobile TV on vehicles is different from the traditional TV media. Its program form, spread rhythm, content structure and expression methods should be changed. The traditional TV Science documentary should fully combine the characteristics and advantages of these new media to innovate the film.

With the popularity of "micro" movies and other "micro" video content on the Internet, we can try to launch micro TV Science documentaries. At present, Phoenix video has launched the new content product "micro documentary" for the first time. In addition to the authenticity, authority and artistic tension of the documentary itself, it is also more in line with the modern fast-paced information needs of the audience. This new type of "micro documentary" began to attract more and more people's attention. The reason why it is new is that the length of these works is extremely short. All the single episodes are 5 to 10 min, which is very different from the previous documentaries in terms of length; However, in terms of content creation means and narrative style, it is also a very sophisticated documentary operation method. Compared with traditional documentaries, micro documentaries focus more on conveying the most valuable information in a limited time, and then infiltrate and spread through rich output terminals. Information can spread more quickly to meet the fragmentation of current user needs. Original traditional TV Science and technology documentary.

This "micro" video mode can be used for reference for reform, innovation and re dissemination. But broadcast those.

TV sci-tech documentaries that have been produced for a long time are simplified into micro sci-tech documentaries, which use mobile phones and other mobile terminals to spread science and technology and popularize science in the form of diversity and continuous broadcasting. Taking the Forbidden City 100 as an example, it tells 100 space stories of the Forbidden City in the form of 6 min per episode and 100 episodes in total. Through the "visible" space, it interprets the practical and aesthetic values of the "invisible" Forbidden City Architecture, and creates an image Museum beyond time and space for the Forbidden City. Among them, the documentary reveals for the first time some traditional palace architectural techniques, as well as technologies such as fire prevention and cold storage. Compared with the documentary "the Forbidden City", which was shot on the same subject but lasted more than 40 min per episode, the series broadcast form of "the Forbidden City 100", which is a single episode of several minutes and multiple episodes, is more suitable for today's fast-paced modern audience information needs. For another example, documentaries such as "Expo year of science and technology" can also simplify the construction technology of each exhibition hall or a certain scientific and technological achievement into a single program of about a few minutes, which can be broadcast and transmitted anytime and anywhere by using mobile terminal carriers such as mobile phones and iPads.

5   Conclusion

With the return of new media, documentary will become the main content of its dissemination. The development of the new media environment has brought about a new communication environment. The acceleration of people's pace of life and the demand for fragmented information have prompted traditional documentaries to push through the old and bring forth the new under such an environment, resulting in a new form - micro documentaries to adapt to the new media environment. The concept of micro documentary has only been mentioned in recent years, and has quickly occupied a place in the network market with its own characteristics of objectivity, reality, populism, micro duration, micro narration and deep connotation. Phoenix video, Youku Tudou, ergeng platform and other video websites have special micro documentary channels. After adapting to the characteristics of new media communication, documentaries will make corresponding changes in form, which will once again glow its unique charm. New media has become the main force of China's media market, and its rise will have a great impact on traditional media. But what the market values more is complementarity. New media will let documentaries see new hopes and opportunities in this market.

References

1. Renshaw, C., Liew, C.L.: Descriptive standards and collection management software for documentary heritage management: attitudes and experiences of information professionals. Glob. Knowl. Mem. Commun. (2021), ahead-of-print(ahead-of-print).
2. Marin, A., Contreras, F.: The new research techniques in visual communication: a methodological proposal of videography (2020)
3. Maria, K., Peleshchyshyn, A.: Identification of patterns of the dysfunction of documentary information in social communication. Sci. J. "Library Science Record Studies Informology" (1) (2020)
4. Kovalska, L.: The concept of document in historical documentary studies. Sci. Her. Uzhhorod Univ. Ser. Hist., 1(44), 179–184 (2021)
5. Doyle, K., Desta, T.: An analysis of Common Security and Defence Policy's (CSDP) strategic communication (StratCom). J. Polit. Law (2) (2020)
6. Ganzha, A.: Linguosophical reception of decoding of documentary film text (on the example of films about Lesa Ukrainka. Cult. Word 93, 134–149 (2020)
7. Odunlami, D.: Agenda setting-inclusiveness in Nigeria: challenges of the new media (4) (2020)
8. Skopeteas, I.: Documentary genres. Criteria and dominant theories. In: International Conference on Cultural Informatics, Communication & Media Studies, vol. 1, no. 1 (2020)
9. Zafra, N.: Do-it-yourself interactive documentary (i-doc): a post-textual analysis. Media Pract. Educ. 1–5 (2020)
10. Ngong, P.A.: Music and sound in documentary film communication: an exploration of Une Affaire de Nègres and Chef! CINEJ Cinema J. 8(1), 156–184 (2020)

Research on the "Online and Offline" Operation Education and Teaching Mode of Cross-Border E-commerce Business Based on the Internet

Jihong Zhang[✉]

Big Data College, Haidu College of Qingdao Agricultural University,
Yantai 265200, Shandong, China
zhangjihong@hdxy.edu.cn

Abstract. As one of the carriers to bring in and go out, we should seize the opportunity, accelerate the integrated development of online and offline omni-channel retail, further improve the cross-border trade supply chain, and promote the steady expansion of the scale of the cross-border e-commerce industry. Taking "Omni channel retail" as the starting point, this paper integrates specific cases into problems and measures to provide reference for promoting the integrated development of online and offline Omni channel retail of cross-border e-commerce platforms.

Keywords: Cross border e-commerce · Online and offline integration · Internet

1 Introduction

The global trade of retail industry is booming day by day, and domestic consumers gradually turn their attention to the personalized and high-quality international commodity service market. With the upgrading of user demand, more and more e-commerce platforms have successively expanded overseas business, such as tmall global, Jingdong Haidun, Netease koala overseas shopping, Austrian buyers, xiaohongshu, etc. began to seek ways to integrate the development of online and offline omni-channel retail. The platform uses big data cloud computing to select popular products for offline physical store sales, make up for the lack of online experience, and is committed to the coordinated development of offline corporate image, reputation and convenient online sales and logistics. According to the Research Report on China's cross-border e-commerce market in the first half of 2019 by AI media consulting, 57.0% of the surveyed overseas Amoy users participated in the promotion and preferential activities of the cross-border e-commerce platform during the "618" period in 2019, while 12.3% of the users participated in the offline promotion activities of the platform, and 93.1% of the surveyed users were satisfied with the offline consumption experience during the "618" period.

M. A. Jan and F. Khan (Eds.): BigIoT-EDU 2022, LNICST 466, pp. 379–388, 2023.
https://doi.org/10.1007/978-3-031-23947-2_41

In the context of consumption upgrading, the integration of offline and online based on the Internet has become one of the trends of cross-border e-commerce. However, most platforms do not have enough understanding, experience and positioning for the integrated development of online and offline omni-channel retail, which is still in the exploration stage, so that the omni-channel sales model can not really enhance its advantages [1]. On the contrary, the offline business is due to high cost The uncoordinated supply chain has become a "chicken rib", or because of the uneven distribution of online and offline promotions, resulting in the development conflict between online stores and physical stores, serious interest friction, and affecting the image and performance. In order to solve the problems of cross-border e-commerce platforms, further meet the increasingly high-quality needs of consumers, expand the sales of cross-border e-commerce retailers, it is urgent to explore the development path of online and offline Omni channel retail integration. Figure 1 below shows the problem framework of cross-border e-commerce platforms.

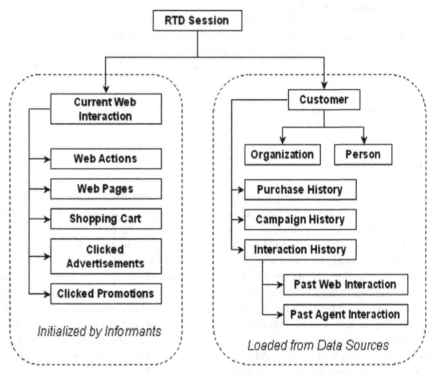

Fig. 1. Cross border e-commerce platform problem framework

As a new form of international trade, cross-border e-commerce is to network and electronize the traditional international trade, take electronic technology and logistics as the main means, take commerce as the core, move the traditional sales and shopping channels to the Internet, and break the tangible and intangible barriers of countries and regions. Because it can reduce intermediate links and save costs, it has developed rapidly all over the world.

The cross-border e-commerce diagram is shown in Fig. 2.

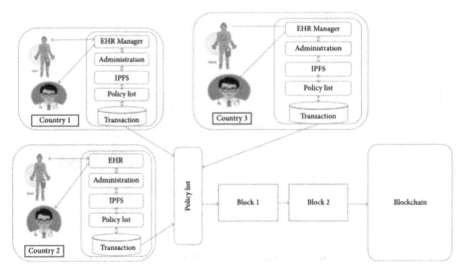

Fig. 2. Cross-border E-commerce diagram

2 Related Work

2.1 Concept of Cross-Border E-commerce

E-commerce starts from the initial B2C model (such as Amazon, eBay, express, Dunhuang, etc.), B2B model (such as Alibaba, global resources, made in China, etc.) and C2C user to user model. Later, due to the particularity of cross-border e-commerce, ABC model, namely agent, business and consumer model, is derived. As shown in Fig. 3 below, concept of cross border e-commerce.

It is jointly built by agents, businesses and consumers E-commerce platform integrating consumption. B2M mode is aimed at the seller of the enterprise or product, not the final consumer. M2C mode is an extended concept of B2M mode, and the manufacturer directly to the customer [2]. Another is the 020 model, which is suitable for a new e-commerce model to solicit customers online through offline services. However, the development of this model in the field of cross-border e-commerce is still in its infancy.

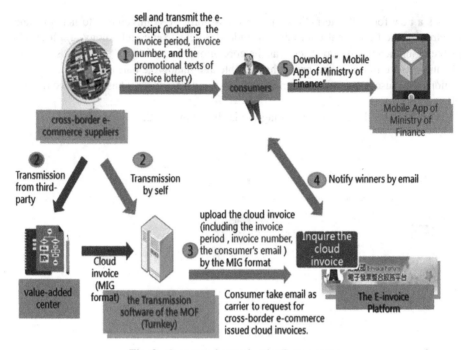

Fig. 3. Concept of cross-border E-commerce

2.2 Development Characteristics of Cross-Border E-commerce in China

This has obviously caused trouble for the tax authorities. The tax authorities cannot find out the identity and geographical location of the online traders who should pay taxes, so they cannot know the taxpayer's transactions and tax payable, let alone audit and verify. This part of the transaction and the taxpayer are invisible in the vision of the tax authorities, which is fatal to the tax authorities. Take eBay as an example. EBay is an online auction company in the United States that allows individuals and businesses to auction any item. By 2019, eBay has 30million users, auctioning tens of thousands of items every day, with a total turnover of more than 5billion US dollars. However, most eBay users do not accurately report their income to the tax authorities, and there are a lot of tax evasion, because they know that due to the anonymity of the network, the US Internal Revenue Service (IRS) has no way to identify them. See Fig. 4 below for the comparison of the import framework of direct procurement.

The anonymity of e-commerce transactions has led to the deterioration of tax avoidance. The development of the network has reduced the cost of tax avoidance and made e-commerce tax avoidance easier. The anonymity of e-commerce transactions makes it possible for taxpayers to use online financial institutions in tax havens to avoid tax supervision. The widespread use of electronic money and the "complete tax protection" provided by the Internet to customers by online banks in some tax havens enable taxpayers to directly remit their investment income from countries around the world to online banks in tax havens, thus avoiding the income tax payable. In its largest audit survey, the

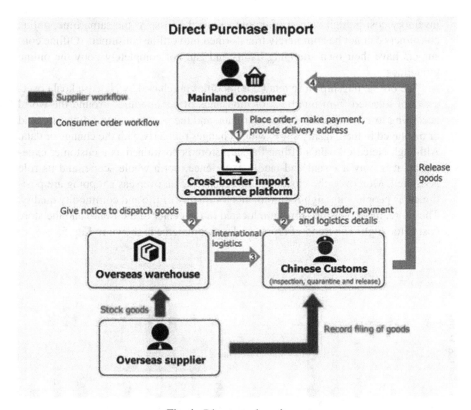

Fig. 4. Direct purchase import

US Internal Revenue Service (IRS) found that a large number of resident taxpayers hid a large amount of taxable income through financial institutions in offshore tax havens. The U.S. government estimates that about $3trillion of funds are hidden in tax havens because of the "full tax protection" of online banks in tax havens.

3   Problems in the Integrated Development of Online and Offline Omni Channel Retail of Cross-Border E-commerce Platform

Since 2015, the platform has begun to focus on offline physical stores. At present, it is still in the exploration stage and faces many problems.

(1)   Online and offline homogeneous operation

Even if selected online sales and popular models are placed in offline physical stores, homogeneous operation can not be avoided. Although it can increase consumers' confidence in the protection of genuine products on the platform to a certain extent, popular models are usually scattered, including makeup, personal care, mother and baby, electronic digital, home appliances, etc., as well as segmentation in different countries. The space of offline physical stores is limited and the inventory cost is high, which often outweighs the loss. At the same time, online consumers can not be completely transformed into offline consumers. Offline consumers have their own shopping habits and can not completely copy the online guidelines.

The offline flagship store retail commodities purchased by Netease koala overseas are selected from hundreds of thousands of commodities around the world according to the online Shanghai user data, and the popular commodities are sold or displayed in the flagship store, which changes regularly with the change of data. Although Netease koala's offline flagship store is positioned as a customer experience, it is only a visual and tactile experience, not a whole scene, and its role is limited. Moreover, the customers of Netease koala overseas shopping are positioned as people with high requirements for quality of life and commodity quality. Therefore, most flagship stores are located in the center of the trend, and the store cost is too high. The trend of cross-border e-commerce is shown in Fig. 5.

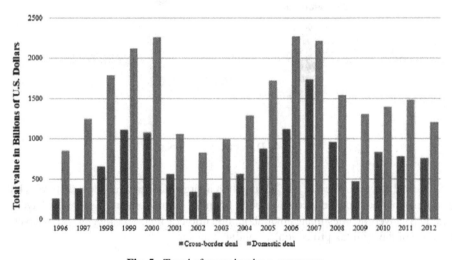

Fig. 5. Trend of cross-border e-commerce.

(2) Low efficiency of the cross-border e-commerce logistics chain

Cross-border e-commerce logistics have always been a pain point for cross-border e-commerce. From a macro perspective, the rise of trade protection policies in recent years has led to trade barriers. At the same time, different financial systems, such as interest rates, foreign exchange policies, different laws and regulations, the balance of payments, and other factors will directly or indirectly hinder commodity circulation. From a micro perspective, cross-border e-commerce commodities need to go through multiple links such as logistics in the exporting country, customs, commodity inspection, international transportation, customs, and logistics in the importing country, with long logistics time and opaque information. Once the goods are lost or damaged, the return and exchange procedure is cumbersome and the loss is large [3]. The online goods on the platform generally adopt the import mode of overseas direct mail + bonded import. Due to the slow speed of overseas direct mail, the platform mostly adopts the bonded import mode. However, some customers will be confused about the origin of the goods: they clearly buy imported goods. Why are the goods sent from Suzhou, Guangzhou and Hong Kong? They have low confidence in product quality and genuine product guarantee.

(3) Lack of funds to develop online and offline integrated development

Cross border e-commerce platforms such as tmall global, Haidun global, Austrian buyers and Netease koala overseas shopping all have strong group support, while second-class platforms such as xiaohongshu, foreign wharf and honey bud are not so lucky. Figure 6 below shows the online and offline integrated development process of foreign trade.

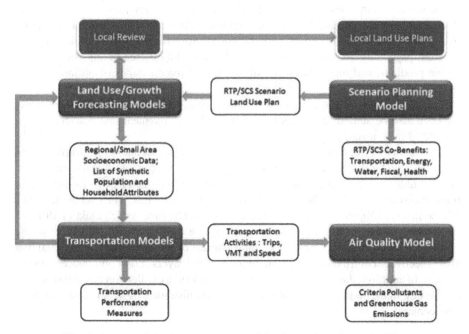

Fig. 6. Integrated development process of foreign trade online and offline

They not only don't have strong working capital, but also need to leverage the leading platform achievements in all aspects. It's really difficult to grab food at the mouth of a tiger. Although the platform carries out online and offline omni-channel integration, it is conducive to expanding the marketing scope of the platform, increasing sales and improving profits. However, in practice, for example, with the help of offline factories and stores, Netease koala Haigou selects manufacturers from all over the world and incubates its own high-quality brands. The consumption of human and material resources is huge, but the rate of return after investment is uncertain. If the early investment is insufficient and interrupted, it is very easy to destroy the balance of the enterprise and affect the future of the enterprise.

4 Exploration of Online and Offline Development Path of Cross-Border E-commerce Platform Based on Internet

4.1 Implement Differentiated Business Strategy for Different Psychology of Online and Offline Consumers

According to Nielsen Institute data in 2017, Consumers who prefer online shopping focus on "price concessions", which also includes the advantages of e-commerce such as "providing door-to-door service", "full discount and coupons", "selling unique featured goods", "saving time" and "social publicity". Consumers who like to shop in offline physical stores think "buy as soon as they arrive" It is the key factor of your choice. You can receive the goods when you buy them now. In other words, when formulating online and offline retail strategies, cross-border e-commerce platforms should grasp the different psychology of consumers, pay attention to the differentiation of online and offline products, and make the most efficient use of the resources of offline physical stores.

The transactions of some digital products (such as audio-visual products, software, etc.) can also be settled immediately, and the ordering, payment and delivery can be completed in an instant.

The immediacy of e-commerce transaction improves the efficiency of people's communication and transaction, eliminates the intermediary link in traditional transactions, but also hides the legal crisis. In the field of Taxation, the immediacy of e-commerce transactions often leads to the randomness of trading activities. The trading activities of e-commerce subjects may start, end and change at any time, which makes it difficult for the tax authorities to master the specific trading conditions of both parties to the transaction, which not only makes the control means of tax source withholding fail, but also objectively contributes to the randomness of taxpayers' non-compliance with the tax law, In addition, the serious lagging role of modern tax collection and management technology in the field of Taxation makes the administration of taxation according to law feeble.

4.2 Optimize the Online and Offline Cross-Border E-commerce Logistics Chain

The first step to optimize the cross-border e-commerce logistics chain is to optimize the customs clearance conditions of cross-border e-commerce commodities. Cross border e-commerce platforms should focus on "overseas direct mail" To increase the guarantee of genuine goods. JD Haidun launched an enabling plan around the world, which is committed to building the first stop for overseas brands in China and helping overseas brands open the Chinese market. It is also of great significance to build domestic and overseas warehouses for cross-border e-commerce logistics and improve the cross-border e-commerce logistics infrastructure. Goods stored in regional warehouses and border warehouses can effectively avoid the exchange rate change zone in the event of economic turmoil In order to stabilize commodity prices. Although jd.com, tmall.com and Austrian buyers have built a large number of smart warehouses at home and abroad, the time cost of warehousing is one of the most important costs of the platform. This requires the government to play a role in establishing a safe and green channel for cross-border e-commerce products [4]. It also requires the platform to establish good cooperation with overseas brands to ensure that goods can be delivered. In addition, we can use big data to improve the online and offline logistics operation system of cross-border e-commerce, transparent information during commodity packaging, coding, transportation and distribution, optimize commodity transportation routes and accurately locate cross-border e-commerce consumer groups. The integrated development of cross-border e-commerce and cross-border e-commerce logistics chain is the path to maximize their value.

4.3 Formulate Double Line Cooperation and Development Strategy

The higher the degree of online and offline integration, the better it can meet the needs of different consumers, with wide access channels and lower cost. In order to formulate a reasonable and effective online and offline Omni channel retail strategy and put it into action, one of the conditions for integrated development is to reconstruct the organizational cooperation mechanism. Investigate and analyze the internal and external conditions of the organization, such as the development status of cross-border e-commerce, the company's working capital, government policies, international law, the company's personnel relations, etc. We should break down barriers between different departments. Reposition online and offline to break barriers between different channels. Integration but not homogeneity, or complementarity, supplement and subsidy, the final result will be complementary.

(4) Establish "boundless" Omni channel retail

From an omni channel perspective, In order to avoid consumers feeling "bounded" in the shopping experience, the omni channel service blueprint is no longer "purchase" In this stage, it has expanded from the middle of sales to the early and late stage of sales. Extending forward can increase new customers, attract traffic and enhance popularity, which is very necessary in the increasingly crowded cross-border e-commerce platform. Backward extension can improve user stickiness, retain old customers and reduce unnecessary sales costs. Among them, the two-line shopping mode, which emphasizes the deep integration of online and offline Omni channels, has become a model of "boundless" Omni channel retail, which can effectively give play to the advantages of two-line shopping channels and enhance users' consumption experience The most widely defined and recognized business model is the business model of deep integration of online and offline channels based on offline retail physical stores and online e-commerce platforms, which is data-driven, connects users, goods, inventory, marketing and other links, and provides consumers with a sub connected shopping experience in the whole scenic spot, as shown in Fig. 7.

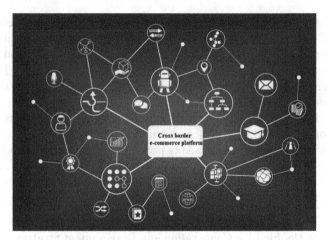

Fig. 7. Internet cross border e-commerce platform

5 Conclusion

For cross-border e-commerce platforms, online and offline omni-channel retail integration is a long-term development strategy. At present, China has strengthened its opening to the outside world and the state has strongly encouraged the development of foreign trade. Facing this huge development opportunity, as an emerging form of cross-border trade emerging in the mobile Internet era, cross-border e-commerce should seize the opportunity to further improve the cross-border trade supply chain and promote the steady expansion of the scale of cross-border e-commerce industry. In this context, this paper puts forward the implementation path for the integrated development of online and offline Omni channel retail of China's cross-border e-commerce platform: implement differentiated business strategy and optimize cross-border e-commerce lines according to the different psychology of online and offline consumers Online and offline logistics chain, formulate a two-line cooperative development mechanism, establish "boundless" omni-channel retail, and establish a good corporate image and reputation for different channels.

References

1. Ma, S., Guo, J., Zhang, H.: Trade cost reduction effect of cross-border e-commerce: mechanism and demonstration. Int. Econ. Trade Explor. **35**(5), 69–85
2. Zhao, P.: The development of online and offline integration has entered a substantive stage—review of China's circulation industry in 2015 and prospect in 2016. China's Circ. Econ. **29**(12), 24–29 (2015)
3. Liu J.: Exploration of retailers' online and offline Omni channel marketing path. Bus. Econ. Res. **34**(7), 65–67 (2017)
4. Zhang, W., Lu, X., Li, M.: Research on Influencing Factors of cross-border e-commerce development in China. J. Hainan Univ. (Humanities and Social Sciences Edition) **37**(3), 57–63 (2019)

Construction of Large-Scale Chinese-English Bilingual Corpus and Sentence Alignment

Sun Jie[⊠]

School of International Culture and Education, Heilongjiang University, Harbin 150088, Heilongjiang Province, China
2011011@hlju.edu.cn

Abstract. With the development of computer and Internet, applications based on bilingual (or multilingual) parallel corpora are increasing in the field of natural language processing. In addition to the application of machine translation, the construction of parallel corpus is also of great value for bilingual dictionary compilation, word meaning disambiguation and cross language information retrieval. At present, the bilingual corpus of word alignment and sentence alignment has a large scale, and the related alignment algorithms are also relatively mature. In contrast, the chunk level alignment algorithm remains to be studied, and the chunk level alignment corpus required by the alignment algorithm is quite lacking. The construction of bilingual corpus and its automatic alignment are of great significance to the development of computational linguistics. At present, the existing bilingual corpora at home and abroad, especially Chinese-English bilingual corpora, are not large, the processing standards are not unified, and there is no general bilingual corpus that can be used publicly. It has laid a solid foundation for the large-scale establishment of bilingual language information and knowledge base with unified standards and norms, multi fields, multi genres and sentence level alignment.

Keywords: Non restricted areas · Bilingual corpus · Sentence alignment

1 Introduction

Today's society is in the information age and the Internet is developing rapidly. There is an urgent need to eliminate the language barriers between people of different nationalities through machine translation (MT). However, natural language translation is one of human advanced intelligence activities, and the research of artificial intelligence (AI) has not yet reached the level of fully understanding natural language. Therefore, the research of machine translation (MT) is an important content in the research of computational linguistics and has great socio-economic value. Moreover, with the rapid increase of information and the increasingly frequent international exchanges, especially the gradual popularization of the Internet, the demand for machine translation is increasing.

© ICST Institute for Computer Sciences, Social Informatics and Telecommunications Engineering 2023
Published by Springer Nature Switzerland AG 2023. All Rights Reserved
M. A. Jan and F. Khan (Eds.): BigIoT-EDU 2022, LNICST 466, pp. 389–399, 2023.
https://doi.org/10.1007/978-3-031-23947-2_42

According to the different knowledge representation and processing methods, there are mainly two translation methods: rule-based machine translation method and corpus based machine translation method. The main characteristics of rule-based translation system are: through the understanding and understanding of language phenomena, constantly summarize their regularity, and form grammatical structure rules and semantic rules to express language knowledge. The analysis system uses these rules to analyze and understand the input language to form an unambiguous and definite internal expression form [1]. Then, according to these expression forms, they are transformed into the corresponding target language structure and form the translation. This rule-based approach is the most successful translation technology at present. However, because this method requires a large number of rule knowledge bases and dictionary bases that can represent the laws of language phenomena, most of these knowledge are obtained by manual methods with low intelligence. Therefore, knowledge acquisition has become a fundamental factor restricting the development of rule-based translation methods.

Many research institutions at home and abroad are committed to the construction of bilingual corpora, and use these corpora for extensive research. Canadian hansards is a very famous English French bilingual corpus. Many initial studies based on bilingual corpus are based on this corpus. With regard to the construction and research of Chinese foreign bilingual corpus, the Hong Kong University of science and technology has collected and processed the minutes of the meeting of the Hong Kong Legislative Council to form a Chinese English bilingual corpus. In addition, researchers from Peking University, Northeast University and Harbin Institute of technology have also established a large-scale Chinese-English bilingual corpus. However, at present, the scale of Chinese and foreign bilingual corpora is relatively small and the processing standards are not unified, which affects the research on knowledge acquisition of bilingual corpora. The realization of alignment at all levels is an important content of bilingual corpus construction. This paper mainly discusses the sentence level alignment technology of Chinese-English bilingual. Sentence alignment methods can be basically divided into three categories:

(1) Length based method: originally proposed by brown and gale, it is based on the fact that the length of the two language translations meets a certain proportional relationship. They have achieved good alignment results in the proceedings of the Canadian Parliament in both English and French; The researchers of Tsinghua University and Harbin University of technology applied the length based method to the Chinese-English bilingual sentence alignment of Microsoft NT 3.5 server installation guide and legal literature respectively, and obtained the experimental results. (2) Vocabulary based method: Kay and Chen align English German and English French bilingual sentences according to the distribution information of bilingual words and vocabulary translation model respectively. The bilingual dictionary is directly used to align the sentences in College English textbooks, and satisfactory results are obtained. (3) Hybrid method: the length based alignment method has simple model and is independent of language knowledge and other external resources, but it has poor robustness and is easy to cause error spread. The word based alignment method is relatively reliable and accurate, but the calculation is quite complex. The researchers tried to combine the two methods for sentence alignment. Wu of the University of Hong Kong improved the length based

method by creating a special thesaurus, and did an alignment test on the minutes of the Hong Kong Legislative Council, and achieved good results.

Most of the above alignment studies are carried out around the bilingual texts of a single field or a certain literature and manual. This work is oriented to multiple fields and genres, uses the sentence alignment method based on bilingual dictionary to align the texts, and makes further research and Discussion on how to improve the alignment accuracy. This method is different from Kay and Chen's method using the distribution correlation of translated words and vocabulary translation model. It is also different from the alignment method in the design of evaluation function and the arrangement of bilingual dictionary resources. Another driving force to promote the research of bilingual corpus comes from the research of statistical machine translation. The core of this method is to calculate various translation relations using statistical methods based on bilingual corpus. Since then, the potential value of bilingual corpus has been fully recognized. Researchers have done a lot of research on how to obtain bilingual knowledge from bilingual corpus more effectively, such as lexical alignment, structural alignment, bilingual dictionary construction and translation model.

2 Related Work

2.1 Corpus

In the modern sense, corpus can be defined as a collection of real language instances stored in machine-readable form, which may contain various forms of linguistic information annotations, text or speech. These corpora must take the computer as the carrier, usually the electronic documents in the computer. The language examples in the corpus must be the language materials that have appeared in the real language environment, which can be written in the form of text or spoken in the form of phonetics. In addition, these corpora may be analyzed, processed and processed to contain various forms of linguistic information annotation, such as part of speech tagging and so on [2].

Corpus (corpus or corpus) is a large-scale library with a certain capacity, which is built by collecting naturally occurring continuous language texts or discourse fragments according to certain linguistic principles and using random sampling method. In essence, corpus is actually a random sampling of natural language use, with a certain size of language samples to represent the overall language use determined in a study.

As a linguistic research method, corpus and index (concordance) was applied in Europe as early as the 18th century. At that time, most corpora were collected by hand, and the indexing and analysis process were also carried out by hand, which was very time-consuming and laborious. With the development of modern corpus and natural language processing, a new type of corpus bilingual (or multilingual) parallel corpus and some natural language processing methods and technologies based on Parallel Corpus began to appear in the early 1990s [3]. Research on bilingual (or multilingual) parallel corpora is emerging one after another, including the construction of bilingual parallel corpora, covering issues such as design, collection, coding, maintenance and management: different levels of alignment technology of Parallel Corpora: Research on various applications of bilingual parallel corpora in natural language processing and information retrieval.

Extracting language knowledge from corpus can be summarized as a two-step process: the first step is to establish an appropriate corpus; the second is to obtain the required language knowledge information from the established corpus. The establishment of corpus includes the collection, sorting and processing of corpus. The reason why we should process the corpus is self-evident: no matter how large a corpus is, if it is not processed, it is only a simple accumulation of some texts, and its research value and use value are extremely limited. In order to obtain relevant linguistic knowledge from the corpus, it is necessary to process the corpus and add the raw corpus to the mature corpus. The processing mode and degree of corpus vary with the types of corpus, application requirements and so on.

Corpus can be divided into monolingual corpus and multilingual corpus according to the number of language types it contains. Monolingual corpus only contains a single language text. Its processing is mainly multi-level processing of corpus, such as vocabulary, syntax, semantics and even pragmatics. Compared with monolingual corpora, multilingual corpora, that is, corpora containing multilingual texts translated to and from each other. Among them, the most typical multilingual corpus is the bilingual corpus containing two mutually translated language texts. Because bilingual corpus contains cross reference information between two different languages, it can provide direct and strong support for bilingual natural language research.

The so-called parallel corpus refers to a bilingual (or multilingual) corpus composed of the original text of one language and its translated text in another (or more) language. Figure 1 below shows an example of an English Chinese bilingual corpus (unprocessed):

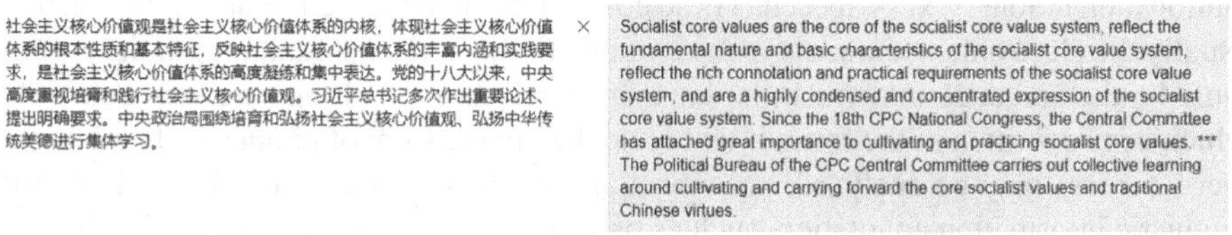
社会主义核心价值观是社会主义核心价值体系的内核，体现社会主义核心价值体系的根本性质和基本特征，反映社会主义核心价值体系的丰富内涵和实践要求，是社会主义核心价值体系的高度凝练和集中表达。党的十八大以来，中央高度重视培育和践行社会主义核心价值观。习近平总书记多次作出重要论述、提出明确要求。中央政治局围绕培育和弘扬社会主义核心价值观、弘扬中华传统美德进行集体学习。

×

Socialist core values are the core of the socialist core value system, reflect the fundamental nature and basic characteristics of the socialist core value system, reflect the rich connotation and practical requirements of the socialist core value system, and are a highly condensed and concentrated expression of the socialist core value system. Since the 18th CPC National Congress, the Central Committee has attached great importance to cultivating and practicing socialist core values. *** The Political Bureau of the CPC Central Committee carries out collective learning around cultivating and carrying forward the core socialist values and traditional Chinese virtues.

Fig. 1. Examples of English Chinese bilingual corpus (unprocessed)

2.2 Definition of Bilingual Chunks

Based on our extensive investigation and analysis, this paper proposes a chunk definition for Chinese-English bilingual alignment. Formula 1 gives the formal description of bilingual chunks. Where BC is the set of bilingual chunks. BS and BT are source language sub blocks and target language sub blocks respectively, which meet the syntactic requirements, low semantic ambiguity and the characteristics of mutual translation. WS and WT are source language words and target language words respectively, WSI is the center word of the source language sub block, and WtJ is the center word of the target language sub block [4]. RS and RT represent the tree roots (i.e. the syntactic structure types) of the source and target language subblocks, respectively. 1 and m are the lengths of the source language sub block and the target language sub block; NS and NT are the length of source and target sentences.

$$BC = \{< bs, bt > | bs = ws_o, \Lambda, ws_i = rs(ws_i), bt = wt_o\} \quad (1)$$

It can be seen that each bilingual chunk is composed of two parts: source sub chunk and target sub chunk. For example, "my baggage" and "my baggage" are the corresponding noun chunks, "in the room" and "in my room" are the corresponding prepositional chunks. Each sub block also includes a semantic core and several attached words around it. Empty sets, words, continuous strings and clauses may become sub blocks in bilingual chunks. Therefore, the sentence will be composed of sub blocks and words. Subblocks are unambiguous in sentences, and there is no intersection and nesting between subblocks. Formula 2 gives the bilingual chunk representation of parallel sentence pairs.

$$Q = \{< S, T > \mid < bs_k bt_k >, k \in [0, K]; \ bs_k \in S \} \tag{2}$$

where, q is a bilingual sentence pair; S and T are source language and target language sentences respectively; Is a sequence of bilingual chunks contained in sentence pairs; K is the number of bilingual chunks [5].

3 Construction of Large-Scale Chinese-English Bilingual Corpus in Unrestricted Fields and Research on Sentence Alignment

One of the most important and key technologies to build a bilingual corpus with practical application value is align. The so-called alignment is the process of finding out the translated fragments from the translated texts in different languages. Since the constituent units of text can be section, paragraph, sentence, phrase, word and byte, the aligned units are also divided into different levels such as chapter, paragraph, sentence, phrase, word and byte. Different natural language applications may require different levels of alignment. For example, the compilation of dictionaries often requires the alignment of bilingual texts at the lexical level.

Because of the important research and application value of bilingual corpus, so far, many scholars at home and abroad have made many attempts to align bilingual corpus and achieved some results. In general, because of the important research and application value of bilingual corpus, so far, many scholars at home and abroad have made many attempts to align bilingual corpus and achieved some results. Generally speaking, most of the current bilingual database alignment work is carried out around sentences or words. The main research work of sentence level alignment includes:

Brown and gale implemented a length based bilingual corpus sentence alignment method according to the length relationship between translated sentences. The difference between them is that the former takes the number of words in the sentence as the length unit of the sentence, while the latter takes the number of bytes in the sentence as the length unit of the sentence. The experiment of length based method on English French bilingual corpus has achieved satisfactory results. Gale believes that the length method is not suitable for sentence alignment between Asian Languages (especially Chinese and Japanese) and Western languages. However, Liu Xin of Tsinghua University and others have made a useful attempt to apply the length method to Chinese-English sentence alignment. The experimental results show that the length method can also be used for Chinese–English sentence alignment.

In recent years, there have also been many studies in this field in China. For example, Tai Yajuan and others first use the N-gram model to obtain the candidate translation units, then calculate the translation probability of the candidate equivalent pairs according to the statistics, and use the greedy strategy to realize the automatic extraction of translation equivalent pairs. Chang Baobao proposed a multi word combination unit recognition method based on word relevance, and used the hypothesis test method to extract translation equivalent units from Chinese–English bilingual corpora. Qu Gang et al. Pointed out that there are a lot of translation anomalies in the candidate syntactic analysis tree of Chinese-English sentences, To solve the problem that there is often no simple correspondence between the source language syntax tree and the target language syntax tree, a phrase alignment model based on the concept of "effective sentence pattern" and "relative invariance criterion in translation" is proposed, as shown in Fig. 2.

On the whole, these methods basically use the multi word unit recognition technology in monolingual, now process each language separately, and then use various statistical and rule methods to form bilingual multi word units. This method should achieve satisfactory results for the correspondence between European languages, but it is impossible to obtain ideal results because Chinese and English belong to two different language systems. However, for the methods that rely on syntactic analysis, the current use level is still relatively poor, and there is still a big gap between Chinese syntactic analysis and English syntactic analysis, so the effect of this method is not ideal.

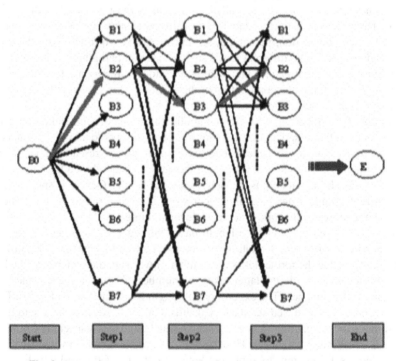

Fig. 2. Dynamic programming search of optimal sentence pair sequence

The construction of Chinese Uygur bilingual parallel corpus involves the collection, sorting, screening, processing and organization of bilingual original corpus. In order to better carry out this work, ensure the quality and scale of corpus, and reasonably and effectively promote corpus construction, we need a relatively complete and easy to operate corpus construction process t [6]. Therefore, we investigate the bilingual corpus itself and its sorting and processing, analyze the complexity of the problem, and form a model of the construction process of bilingual parallel corpus. According to this model, the construction of Chinese Uyghur bilingual parallel corpus is mainly carried out as shown in Fig. 3.

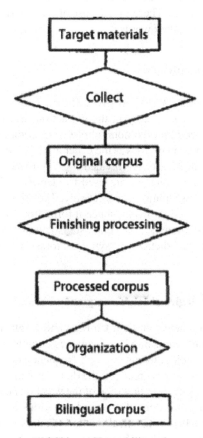

Fig. 3. Flow chart of Chinese Uygur bilingual corpus construction

Addition of corpus Work is an important part in the systematic construction of corpus. Since deep processing must be based on shallow processing And the shallow processed bilingual corpus will also have direct application value in machine translation research. With different processing depth, the accuracy of bilingual corpus will be different [7]. At present, the processing link is first positioned at the shallow level, that is, bilingual alignment at the level of chapter, paragraph and sentence.

It is considered that the content words in Chinese and English materials are divided into high-frequency content words and low-frequency content words and preprocessed respectively: the use of high-frequency content words is generally relatively flexible and the translation changes greatly. If the dictionary method is adopted, because the dictionary only provides the interpretation of the word in another language, but does not provide the translation equivalent of the word in various contexts, it will inevitably lead to the low recall rate [8]. If the statistical method is adopted, it is possible to obtain its translation equivalents in various forms from the real corpus; For low-frequency notional words, the use of statistical methods can not obtain the real corresponding information, but due to its less use, the translation equivalent is relatively fixed and may be covered by Chinese-English dictionaries. Therefore, the use of dictionaries will not lead to a very low recall rate like high-frequency words.

4   Notional Correspondence

Because Chinese and English belong to two different language systems, we should focus on the noun phrase of one party in the extraction. Because the English grammar is relatively standardized and the noun phrase extraction technology is relatively mature, we choose English noun phrases as the benchmark [9]. After identifying English noun phrases, English noun phrases are divided into high-frequency phrases and low-frequency phrases. Different strategies are used to identify Chinese phrases and correspond English and Chinese phrases respectively. For high-frequency phrases, we can obtain more accurate word correspondence information from the corpus: for low-frequency phrases, because there is no accurate statistical information to use, we make full use of the existing bilingual dictionary "synonym forest" to obtain the corresponding information.

4.1   Corresponding Strategies of High-Frequency Phrases

It is considered that the content words in Chinese and English materials are divided into high-frequency content words and low-frequency content words and preprocessed respectively. Generally speaking, the use of high-frequency content words is relatively flexible and the translation changes greatly. If the dictionary method is adopted, because the dictionary only provides the interpretation of the word in another language, but does not provide the translation equivalent of the word in various contexts, it will inevitably lead to the low recall rate. If the statistical method is adopted, it is possible to obtain various forms of translation equivalents from the real corpus. For low-frequency notional words, the statistical method can not obtain the real corresponding information, but because they are less used, the translation equivalents are relatively fixed and may be covered by Chinese-English dictionaries, Therefore, the use of dictionaries will not lead to a very low recall rate like high-frequency words.

For high-frequency phrases, firstly, the statistical method is used to obtain the Chinese words associated with each English noun phrase and the degree of association between them from the bilingual corpus; Then, according to the relevance information, the Chinese noun phrase corresponding to an English noun phrase is determined in the bilingual aligned sentences. The relevance learning algorithm between English phrases and Chinese words adopts an iterative reassessment algorithm. Compared with the statistical model based on mutual information, the statistical results obtained by the mutual information method are only related to the occurrence frequency and location of the corresponding words, but independent of other words, which leads to the isolated consideration of the related information: the iterative re evaluation algorithm can increase the corresponding probability of the corresponding correct Chinese words in each iteration, Since the sum of the corresponding probabilities of - English noun phrases to all Chinese words is 1, the corresponding probability of the wrong Chinese words must decrease, so the corresponding information can be considered as a whole.

The recognition and corresponding steps of high-frequency noun phrases are:

① Identify English noun phrases in corpus.
② The relevance information of English noun phrases and Chinese words is obtained from Chinese-English bilingual corpus.
③ Determine the corresponding Chinese noun phrase in the aligned sentence according to the English noun phrase and the above correlation information.

4.2   Corresponding Strategies of Low-Frequency Phrases

For low-frequency noun phrases, we make full use of the word correspondence information in the bilingual dictionary for phrase correspondence [10]. As the order of words may change when English phrases are translated into Chinese, we first obtain the first and last words in the corresponding Chinese word order with the - fixed rule, and then use the corresponding strategy of low number notional words in Chapter 3 to find the corresponding words from the corresponding Chinese sentences and obtain the corresponding results.

Because it is difficult to get the correct results of low-frequency notional words by statistics, we must rely on the corresponding information in the existing English-Chinese dictionaries. However, through experiments, it is found that in the current bilingual electronic dictionary, the translated words of English words can only be found in 30% of the real corpus, while the translated words dictionary in the real corpus can not be obtained. The main reason is that the information given in the dictionary is only to give a Chinese interpretation of the English word, not to give various translations of the word in the real language environment. In addition, such as the mismatch of specific meanings between words caused by the difference between the two languages, and the impossibility of listing all Synonyms in the dictionary.

In order to improve the coverage (the ratio of the number of corresponding notional words to the total number of notional words can be found), it is decided to use synonym forest to expand the Chinese words obtained from the English Chinese electronic dictionary, but the Chinese words obtained from the English Chinese electronic dictionary will certainly have some polysemy. If the synonyms corresponding to each word meaning of the polysemy are matched, It will inevitably lead to the increase of error rate. However, through the textual research of the English Chinese electronic dictionary, it is found that since the purpose of compiling the dictionary is to give a Chinese interpretation of English words, the Chinese words used in the dictionary should be some words whose meaning can be clear to people even when they are separated from the context, that is, if the Chinese word used to explain the English word is a polysemy, Then the meaning it expresses should also be the most familiar, that is, the meaning with the highest frequency of use. Therefore, we filter the synonym forest, so that all polysemy words only retain the most commonly used semantic categories, so as to become a "monosemy synonym forest", and then use it to expand the Chinese words obtained from the English Chinese electronic dictionary.

(1) Construction of prefix and suffix functions

Since the order of words in English phrases and Chinese phrases with the same meaning may not be the same, in order to find the corresponding phrase in the corresponding Chinese sentence, we look for the first word and the last word after each English noun phrase is translated into Chinese, that is, the first and last words, such as mainland of China, If Chinese should be "mainland China", then the first word should be China and the last word should exceed mainland. We can get an ideal function of the first and last words as long as we make a few simple rules for the structure of English phrases.

(2) The correspondence of low frequency phrases in Corpus

Scan the English Corpus sequentially. For each low-frequency English phrase, adjust the first and last word function, restore the first and last words, and then check the first and last words_ This chapter constructs an electronic dictionary of low-frequency notional words, so as to obtain the corresponding sequences of Chinese beginning and ending words. Match the words of these two sequences (first group and last group) into the corresponding Chinese sentence (they can only be matched if they are located in a block of start and end marks described in Sect. 3 above). If both words can be matched, extract the two words and mark the middle part of the Chinese sentence with corresponding marks, Otherwise, the similarity between each Chinese word and the first and last words is calculated according to the method described in Chapter 2, and the word with the greatest similarity is used as the corresponding matching. If such words cannot be found, ignore them.

5   Conclusion

This paper studies the construction of large-scale Chinese-English bilingual corpus and sentence alignment in unlimited fields. The existing chunk alignment algorithms do not use the corpus with manually labeled chunks for training, but are basically based on the word aligned bilingual corpus. The bilingual chunk database constructed in this paper lays a good foundation for proposing a new chunk alignment algorithm.

References

1. Berga, D., Moreno, B., Nicolò, A.: Undominated rules with three alternatives in an almost unrestricted domain. Soc. Choice Welfare. (2) (2021)
2. Mathew, S.M., et al.: Identification of potential natural inhibitors of the receptor-binding domain of the SARS-CoV-2 spike protein using a computational docking approach. Q. Med. J. **2021**(1) (2021)

3. Taylor, N.C., Johnson, J.H., Herd, R.A.: Making the most of the Mogi model: size matters. J. Volcanol. Geoth. Res. **419**(B7), 107380 (2021)
4. Liu, Z., et al.: DuRecDial 2.0: A Bilingual Parallel Corpus for Conversational Recommendation (2021)
5. Li, J., et al.: Are synthetic clinical notes useful for real natural language processing tasks: a case study on clinical entity recognition. J. Am. Med. Inform. Assoc. **28**(10), 2193–2201 (2021)
6. Chala, S., et al.: Crowdsourcing Parallel Corpus for English-Oromo Neural Machine Translation using Community Engagement Platform (2021)
7. Liang, Y., et al.: Modeling Bilingual Conversational Characteristics for Neural Chat Translation (2021)
8. Jia, H., et al.: Bilingual Terminology Extraction from Non-Parallel E-Commerce Corpora (2021)
9. Duan, G., Yang, H., Qin, K., Huang, T.: Improving neural machine translation model with deep encoding information. Cogn. Comput. **13**(4), 972–980 (2021). https://doi.org/10.1007/s12559-021-09860-7
10. Lu, X., et al.: An Unsupervised Method for Building Sentence Simplification Corpora in Multiple Languages (2021)

The Application of Graphic Composition Design in Computer Vision Art Teaching

Chunyuan Wu[✉]

City College of Dalian University of Technology, Dalian 116600, Liaoning, China
w.yuan.niu@163.com

Abstract. The application of plane composition design in computer visual art teaching can be divided into two aspects: the first is to help students learn how to use computers and software tools; The second is to teach them how to make effective use of their artistic skills. In this course, we mainly focus on the former aspect. In order to make students have a deep understanding of computer graphics and its applications, they should first understand what a computer is. They must know that computers are not magical machines, but devices and systems that can perform certain functions by using various programs or algorithms as instructions. In modern society, graphic composition design has gradually become the mainstream demand of people. Designers began to have more diversified contents and elements for the design of plane composition. However, the main elements of design are inseparable from graphics, text and color. This paper analyzes the graphic composition design and its constituent elements. Taking the color and artistic modeling of the graphic composition design as the starting point, this paper makes a more reasonable research on the aesthetic thinking and visual expression techniques in the art design, in order to play a certain role in enlightening the modern visual art design.

Keywords: Plane composition design · Visual arts · Computer

1 Introduction

In the teaching of art design in recent decades, the teaching content of the three components has changed little, and little attention has been paid to the source and development of the composition theory. The three components are the compulsory basic courses for all majors of modern design. Among them, plane composition is paid more attention in the field of plane advertising design, and is closer to three-dimensional composition in the fields of environment, architecture, visual art and so on. In the discipline of architecture and visual art, because the class hours of the three components are relatively limited, the understanding of the components is also limited and superficial. Especially for the plane composition, most people think that it is only a problem that needs to be concerned in the field of plane design, and we should pay more attention to other composition forms in the three-dimensional and four-dimensional space [1].

M. A. Jan and F. Khan (Eds.): BigIoT-EDU 2022, LNICST 466, pp. 400–411, 2023.
https://doi.org/10.1007/978-3-031-23947-2_43

In fact, plane composition is the basis of other composition. It is a form of simplifying many design elements to the limit, that is, it is expressed on the two-dimensional plane, in order to understand the composition law more conveniently and clearly. Just because it is easier to understand and apply this model in the fields of print advertising design, the print composition is more applicable, but this extremely simplified form of composition and the expressed design law can be concrete and three-dimensional [2]. They can be applied to the specific computer vision art through theory and practice, abstract and concrete transformation. Here, this paper attempts to find some design elements in the excellent works of computer vision art to correspond to the well-known law of plane composition, and preliminarily explore the appearance and existence mode that the law of abstract plane should have when it is put into the concrete three-dimensional computer vision art.

Graphic thinking is that designers use different thinking orientations to create creative graphics in the process of graphic creativity, and finally produce graphics with visual impact and new visual enjoyment. Figure 1 below shows the creative thinking process of random vector images.

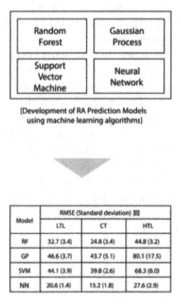

Fig. 1. Random vector image creative thinking processZ

The forms of graphic thinking include convergent thinking and divergent thinking. Divergent thinking is the core of graphic thinking, and convergent thinking is the top priority of graphic thinking. First of all, the concept of divergent thinking can be understood literally. It emphasizes the radiation and diffusion of thinking. Taking the design theme as the origin, a number of relevant elements radiate around, and then the relevant elements continue to radiate around as the origin, leading to more creative points. The creative points obtained by divergent thinking cover a wide range, because there is no certain connection between the elements radiated around the design theme, Therefore, the elements obtained from the continued divergence of design elements will be multi-faceted. The reason why it is the core of graphic thinking is that the foundation of any creative graphics is the breadth and uniqueness of thinking. Only when thinking can spread smoothly in all aspects, can we get more possibilities and innovation [3]. The process of convergent thinking can be vividly compared to the process of closing the network. It is a thinking process that closely focuses on the design theme and looks for the best creative point in the design elements obtained by divergent thinking. It is very important for graphic thinking, because designers can't only focus on creativity and aesthetics when carrying out design activities, but also need to consider the market and audience. Therefore, convergent thinking can summarize and extract the evaluation criteria of different topics. Divergent thinking and convergent thinking seem to have no connection on the surface, but in fact, they restrict and complement each other in the process of graphic creativity, which can not only meet the ductility of thinking, but also meet the feasibility of thinking. If we blindly use divergent thinking and pursue creativity in the process of graphic creativity, the resulting graphics are likely to be thousands of miles away from the design theme. At this time, we need convergent thinking to partic-ipate in it. The role of convergent thinking is like a rule by rule, which plays a general role in the creative process. It grasps the overall direction of graphic creativity, so that divergent thinking can play a proper role.

Divergent thinking and convergent thinking must interact in the process of graphic creativity. Although the meaning is very different from the literal point of view, in fact, they are like the right arm, which is indispensable. In the creative process of graphic creativity, the divergent thinking of the design theme to the convergent thinking of deter-mining the creative point, and then divergent and convergent from the creative point, and the process of continuous divergence and convergence finally forms creative graphics. In the whole process, divergent thinking and convergent thinking cycle alternately [4]. Only in this case can we form thinking activities, form a kind of thinking innovation, and achieve design innovation. In this creative process, we can clearly draw a conclusion that the creative source of graphic creativity starts from divergent thinking. With the continuous divergence of divergent thinking, it is easy to get off the topic. At this time, convergent thinking plays a key role.

2   Related Work

2.1 Plane Composition

Plane refers to the difference from three-dimensional. It mainly solves the modeling problems in the two dimensions of length and width. Composition, that is, many elements needed in graphic design, like machine parts, are combined according to the formal law of beauty to form a new figure that meets the needs [5].

Plane composition is also a composition of visual image. Its research object is mainly how to create images in graphic design, how to deal with the relationship between images, how to master the formal law of beauty, and arrange the graphics required for design according to the formal law of beauty, so as to improve the ability of designers to create "abstract forms" and deal with combination relations.

At the same time, from another point of view, plane composition is a revolutionary art form. Its most basic form of expression is abstraction, and the most important way of expression is to express by virtue of the relationship between elements. The emergence of this art form is the inevitable result of social and historical development. Plane composition originated from Bauhaus's modern education curriculum. Some people will think that it only belongs to the basis of general modeling, is a means of training, and is aimed at beginners of modern design. But it is also a theory, its content is also related to quite high-level problems, and is also gradually deepening and developing The introduction of plane composition into computer vision art at the height of theory only hopes to develop this relatively abstract theory in the specific design field, and is more conducive to the improvement of the current level of this field in our country [2]. Figure 2 below shows the graphic design process.

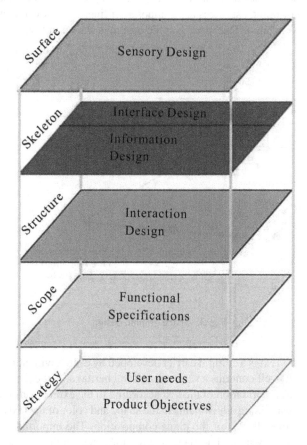

Fig. 2. Graphic design process

Computer vision art itself is an art, so it must also pay attention to the principles of art, the expression of beauty, the transmission of spiritual connotation and how to put it into form. Starting from this point, this paper attempts to use the principle of plane composition to interpret or create a beautiful image or form of landscape. To understand the plane composition, we should first understand the problems between modern design and composition [6].

2.2 Basic Element Analysis of Plane Composition

Before discussing the concept of Cenozoic plane composition, we need to understand the basic elements of plane composition.

First, graphics. Figure is the most important element in plane composition and the most direct element. The origin of art as a form of artistic expression began on the basis of graphics. This basic element is composed of points, lines and surfaces. The smallest element "point" in geometry can accurately express a detailed position and the beginning and end of lines and surfaces; lines are composed of points and express the change direction of points; surfaces are composed of lines and show the characteristics of points in a specific area. The space graphic design is shown in Fig. 3 below.

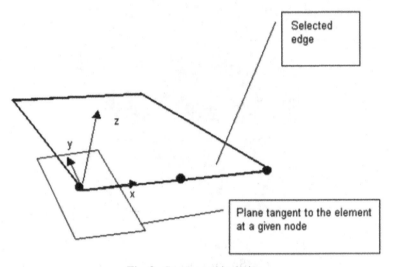

Fig. 3. Space graphic design.

Second, words. Text is a cultural carrier developed by every civilization. It is a sacred and great design. It itself contains a very rich cultural heritage. In the plane composition, in addition to the transformation of the text according to the expression content, we also need to make corresponding adjustments to the shape and color of the text, so as to make it conform to the overall idea of the plane composition. The important characteristics of the text can also play a good aesthetic expression effect in the text, not only let the public understand the meaning of the plane composition, Can make it move [7].

Third, color. In plane composition, color can also play an important role in expression, which is the basis of producing distinctive visual effects At the same time, it creates a perceptual atmosphere, such as bringing surging visual impact, or creating dark nostalgic scenes. These are the color charm reflected from people's sensitivity to different emotional expressions brought by different colors, which greatly gives play to the effect of graphic design, as shown in Fig. 4. In the different applications of hue, lightness and saturation, the emotional image can make people appreciate the moral of graphic design expression. Therefore, the expression of color in plane composition can not be ignored. It is people's continuous precipitation of aesthetics and understanding of culture in the long river of history, which also makes color have good plasticity. Enhancing the plasticity of color also has certain significance for plane composition.

Fig. 4. Visual art of color composition

3   Application of Graphic Composition Design in Computer Vision Art

3.1   Principles of Computer Vision

Computer vision is also known as the optical recognition system of computer imitating human beings. It needs the help of light source sensor, computer control system, etc. to study the positioning, judgment and action of objects. At present, it has been more than 30 years, and this technology is mostly used in engineering. Although it is different from the human visual system, it can work completely and accurately by computer under a certain environment and mode background, Complete the work that human beings cannot do and complete some tasks with large workload instead of human beings. Image processing is the main content of computer vision, which mainly includes ten technologies, such as digital image processing, analog signal input, analysis, sampling and so on [8]. The specific process is to enhance the image after ingestion, remove noise and compress it, compare the samples in the database, make analysis and judgment by the program, and complete the command [3]. As shown in Fig. 5 below, the visual principle framework is shown.

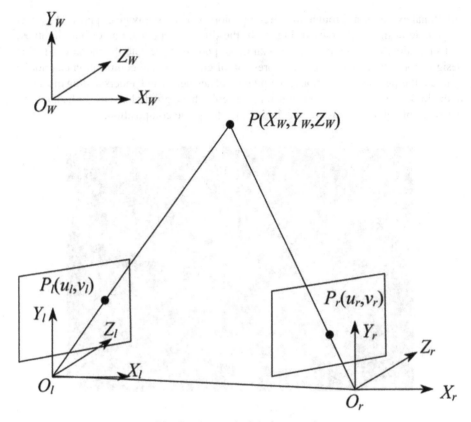

Fig. 5. Visual principle framework

From the concept analysis of visual art, art, including visual art, refers to the intuitive artistic modeling based on specific materials and materials. The modeling of visual art has two-dimensional and three-dimensional, which plays an important role in film and television, sculpture, architecture and so on. Digital art can convey information through visual display. It can use images, graphics and other forms to express content. Computer visual art, also known as mechanical art, is an optical recognition system created by machines according to people's vision. The system has the characteristics of object positioning, action tracking and perspective analysis. Computer visual art is a visual information created in a digital way based on the theory of computer vision [9], We can show the characteristics of computer vision through artistic means, so that people can be moved by this artistic atmosphere. It can be said that computer vision and computer vision art are produced at the same time. Computer vision originated in the 1960s, and has been using abstract things to describe the essential structure of objects. With the development of computer vision, people have been studying images, words and audio, and then computer vision art has been understood by people, and its formal changes have also been widely concerned by the public. In order to enrich games and movies, they gradually began to use some words, sounds and images. Now this factor has become a part of people's daily life.

Digital art is an artistic creation produced by exponential digitization. Compared with traditional art, it mainly uses digital technology, not the spiritual connotation of the work itself. All art can be expressed by digital methods and other scientific and technological means. This is digital art. Some researchers believe that the common ground of digital media art is the direct interaction between users and works, participate in changing the image, form and even the meaning of works, and trigger the transformation of works through different forms. It can be said that interaction is not only an important feature of digital art, but also a new feature of digital art.

3.2 Characteristics of Computer Vision Art

(1) Virtualization. Many computer visual arts are expressed by digital information imitated by computers. They do not exist independently and are generated by computers. Although this phenomenon is common, people virtualize things in real life and use computers to express them. This can show that computer visual art does not really exist in people's daily life, It uses a form of virtualization to display a variety of physical objects [10].

(2) Spatiotemporal. As a free form, computer vision art exists in life. It is not limited by time and space. Although many things do not really exist, it can also create a virtual image world through relevant materials and people's imagination.

(3) Versatility. Different national cultures will have great differences, but in terms of computer vision art, it is the same. People can use its universal characteristics to use it in the display form of the same information, mainly because there is no difference in computer vision art for any national language. Art is free and not controlled by foreign objects, It has a great impact on the expression of some emotions and things [4].

3.3 Application of Graphic Composition Design in Computer Vision Art Design

Plane composition modeling is divided into practical modeling, perfect modeling, symbolic modeling, general modeling, random modeling, abstract modeling and programmatic modeling. Its overview comes from Chinese traditional culture. The modeling consciousness of Chinese graphic composers is deeply affected by the cultural background of the Chinese nation, the philosophical thought of previous dynasties, the traditional Chinese aesthetic standard, the level of economic development and so on. Its shape comes from people's daily life and reflects people's good wishes. It is directly drawn from daily life. For example, bamboo, chrysanthemum and plum, which represent firm friendship, mean jujube, longan and lotus seeds. The most profound perception of graphic composition teachers on modeling consciousness is to reflect the authenticity of things, such as characters, animals, mountains, plains, rivers, flowers and trees. This coincides with the purpose of "people-oriented and returning to nature" in modern art design, and it is also the perfect combination point of plane composition applied to modern design art, so as to further promote the long-term development of computer vision art design [11]. The modeling implication of plane composition mainly comes from its abstraction. Plane composition designers use abstract points, lines and surfaces to successfully shape without ostentation, showing the original face of nature. For example, through the belly of an animal, you can see the son in the belly. This shape is countless in plane composition works. The modeling consciousness in plane composition is not limited to life. In order to express the aesthetic realm of harmony and unity, the modeling consciousness can sometimes be whimsical, not for the purpose of reproducing objective reality, but completely focus on subjective imagination, so that the modeling of plane composition is simple and vivid.

In the picture thinking of plane composition, there are also many phenomena passing through time and space. The scenes inside and outside the house, in the water and mountains, in the sky and underground in the plane composition modeling appear in the same picture, which not only does not appear awkward, but also appears reasonable, harmonious and unified. Not only that, it also combines the perspective and composition ideas of the West. Chinese graphic composition is extremely imaginative, and its aesthetic value has a far-reaching impact on modern visual design, real life and other arts. It can supplement their imagination, provide materials for their creation, and further carry forward Chinese traditional folk culture.

4   Basic Methods of Graphic Design

Art is human aesthetics. Artistic creation makes life boring, like water, like clouds, like steaming air, and makes life meaningful. In the online world, the goddess of art is graphic design. The vitality of design is always the most attractive in boring network construction projects.

Graphic design takes "vision" as the means of communication and expression, and creates and combines symbols, pictures and words in various ways to make visual expression, so as to express ideas or information. Graphic design is the art of communication, communication, style, and problem-solving with words and images.

In life, graphic design is everywhere, such as brand logo, poster making, magazine typesetting, photo decoration and so on, which are all used to decorate our life. And we always only see its surface, but we don't know how to construct it under its gorgeous appearance [12]. In fact, it is a perfect combination of aesthetics and computer science:

1. Making the first sign is not easy. First, understand the purpose of the developed logo and determine its style. Then, the main introduction of graphic design, creative inspiration comes from ideas, new ideas are particularly important, in the design of the use of color, you can achieve a direct visual impact!

In the production process of logo, artistic conception is required to form a sketch on paper, and computer technologies such as Ali and PS must be mastered to complete it. Logo is a brand's Facebook, and graphic design is the craftsmanship on this Facebook.

2. Secondly, the production of posters also needs to go through multi-level processes to achieve the final effect. Graphic designers use font layout Professional technical cases in visual art, layout, computer software, etc.

The charm of graphic design is very infectious. A good graphic design work must also cover many aspects of technical combination. A good graphic designer must also have professional skills. The basic skills of painting, image optimization and professional typesetting are also essential. Figure 6 below shows the graphic design image design process.

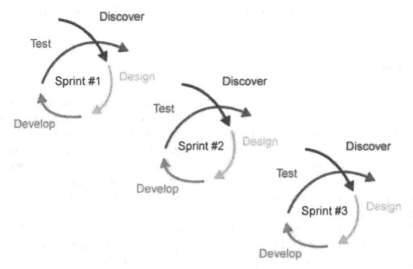

Fig. 6. Graphic design image design process.

Graphic design skillfully conceives the basic elements of the plane to convey the purpose, and creates a new image with bright colors and unique shapes. The formal beauty of graphic design makes graphic design produce artistic charm and give people the enjoyment of beauty. The beauty of graphic design is worth doing seriously, feeling and reaching the power of resonance.

The so-called "graphic design" refers to the design activities in the plane space. Its design content is mainly the design of various elements in the two-dimensional space and the layout design of the combination of these elements, including the use of font design, layout design, illustrations, photography, and the core of all these contents is to convey information, guidance, persuasion, etc., while its expression is achieved by modern printing technology" [13].

Graphic design is not flat -- Thinking about graphic design should be multidimensional

Although the business scope of graphic art design ° is limited to two-dimensional space, from the perspective of its picture composition, graphics, text, color, layout and other constituent factors, on the basis of serving the theme concept together, not only have distinct symbolic information dissemination function, but also include deep-seated thematic culture. The thinking of graphic design should be multidimensional. After entering the information age, human beings began to transform from the technology that can be seen by the naked eye to the technology that cannot be seen by the naked eye. All this has led to a fundamental revolution in the theory of graphic design.

Graphic design is infinitely extended -- the comprehensive effect it expresses is three-dimensional

Although graphic design is the conception and expression of graphic language in two-dimensional space, its concept focuses on modeling activities, so the comprehensive effect it expresses is indeed three-dimensional and infinitely extended. Its specific ideas and forms make graphic design not only have distinct information transmission function, but also include deep-seated social significance and cultural value, which is the so-called "graphic design is not flat" [14].

5 Conclusion

The application of graphic composition design in computer vision art can make art vividly expressed through digital technology. Using this digital technology in art and practical art can create personal vision, transform art into visual products and obtain benefits. The public can obtain visual art by copying and cutting, and transform art resources into the basis of personal artistic creation. With the public's higher and higher requirements for art, the evaluation standard of data art is further improved. The application of graphic composition design in computer vision art brings aesthetic enjoyment to the public, so that the public can maintain a happy and comfortable mood when appreciating art works, and can also obtain corresponding aesthetic evaluation, which imperceptibly affects people's spiritual level without doping other factors, Reflect the essence of art to the greatest extent. Graphic composition design itself has the character of beauty. After being organically combined with computer vision art, it not only reflects the beauty, but also reflects the sense of reality. Therefore, the application of graphic composition design in computer visual art improves the public's aesthetic concept and aesthetic value, so that the public can experience visual art through feeling.

References

1. Zhang, R.Z., Yang, L., Lan, L.I.: Art design teaching in Colleges and universities from the perspective of traditional culture. J. Cangzhou Norm. Univ. 36, 254–258 (2018)
2. Wu, G., et al.: The advantages of micro-class platform in architectural design technology teaching. J. Hanjiang Norm. Univ. 28, 1120–1130 (2018)
3. Zhao M . an study on the practice teaching of art design specialty in colleges on the basis of red culture on campus——taking Guilin normal college as an example. J. Guilin Norm. Coll. 19, 2254–2265 (2018)
4. Zhang, M.: The idea of "symbolic-graphic combination" in mathematics teaching in primary schools and its application. Res. Modern Basic Educ. 69, 25–38 (2018)
5. Guo, W.: Study on teaching reform of art design in colleges and universities under the background of "internet +". Guide Sci. Educ. 54, 3357–3368 (2018)
6. Liu, L.L.: Research on the training mode of integration of innovation and entrepreneurship education in art design teaching. J. Heilongjiang Coll. Educ. 92, 518–529 (2018)
7. Chen, R., University C.: Research on the practical teaching mode of art design education in the system of "internet + cluster studio". In: The Theory and Practice of Innovation and Entrepreneurship (2019)

8. Chen, F.: Research on the teaching reform of environmental art design major in Guangxi universities under the idea of innovation education. In: The Theory and Practice of Innovation and Entrepreneurship (2019)

9. Yan-Jun, H.E.: The application of information teaching design in the course of "business negotiation": taking "effective communication skills in business negotiation" as an example. Comput. Know. Technol. **25**, 678–692 (2019)

10. Sun, G.: Research on the course teaching of art and design specialty in higher vocational education under the background of informatization:taking the design of commercial space based on VR technology as an example. Wireless Inter. Technol. **37**, 452–463 (2019)

11. Cui, Y.: Problem-oriented teaching research in art design. Ind. Design. **46**, 881–895 (2019)

12. Zhang, X.M.: The analysis of graphic teaching method of verb of acceptance in Japanese. J. Qiqihar Univ. (Philosophy & Social Science Edition) **56**, 6127–6138 (2019)

13. Preprotic, S.P., Petkovi, G.: Learning and teaching of bookbinding in graphic technology thro. Lib. Inf. Sci. Res. **55**, 1024–1036 (2018)

14. Xingli, L.I.: Exploration and practice of "Chinese traditional art" course teaching in art design specialty. Design. **39**, 2258–2269 (2018)

Research on the Quality Evaluation of College Students' Innovation and Entrepreneurship Education Based on Ant Colony Algorithm

XingRong Zhang[✉]

Entrepreneurship College of Chengdu Polytechnic, Chengdu 610041, China
rr20220106@126.com

Abstract. This document studied the quality of news and entrepreneurial education of students based on a column algorithm. The current news and entrepreneurial education in college and universities refer to the education of culture and improvement of basic entrepreneurial quality and entrepreneurial capacity of students so that students can have the knowledge, ability and psychological quality required for entrepreneurial practice and adapt to the current social environment. Because of the current problems of innovation and entrepreneurship of college students, this document studies the application and advances of previous column algorithms in optimization problems, and uses algorithm of previous columns to solve the problems of innovation and entrepreneurship of college students. The main search content includes: the new ability of skills to improve continuously. It's an effective new way to solve the problem of working well in the conduct of news and entrepreneurship of college students. This paper analyzes the current situation of news and entrepreneurship and shows that innovation and entrepreneurship education for college students is a complex project. Colleagues and universities need to coordinate forces in different fields within and outside schools, build a system of innovation and entrepreneurial education platform, and try a comprehensive and high-quality education system for innovation and entrepreneurial talents. Per la antaŭa kolonio forigas konduton, la baza principo de antaŭa kolonio-algoritmo estas eksplodita, la vojelekto, feromona liberigo kaj aktualiso de antaŭa kolonio-metodo estas analizita, kaj la avantaj de antaŭa kolonio-metodo por solvi tiujn problemojn estas resumita.

Keywords: Ant colony Innovation and entrepreneurship · Education quality evaluation

1 Introduction

At present, innovation and entrepreneurship education in Colleges and universities refers to the education of developing and improving students' basic entrepreneurial quality and entrepreneurial ability, so that students can have the knowledge, ability and psychological quality needed to engage in entrepreneurial practice, so as to adapt to the current social environment.

M. A. Jan and F. Khan (Eds.): BigIoT-EDU 2022, LNICST 466, pp. 412–423, 2023.
https://doi.org/10.1007/978-3-031-23947-2_44

In the outline of the national action plan for scientific quality (2021–2035), "implement the action of improving vocational skills [1]. Further highlight the relevant contents of scientific quality and safe production in pre service education and vocational training, and build a lifelong skill formation system for industrial workers integrating vocational education, employment training and skill improvement." It can be seen that we need to pay attention to the cultivation of College Students' vocational skills, scientific quality and ability to improve their skills.

It is the practicality, openness and professionalism of the teaching process. Innovation and entrepreneurship education is the key to cultivate high-quality technical and skilled talents.

At present, the world has entered a new era of high-tech led and innovation driven development. What kind of innovation and entrepreneurship education do college students need and how to make them avoid detours in the process of entrepreneurship? The teaching purpose of vocational colleges is "promoting teaching, learning and reform through competition". Therefore, how to study the integration mechanism of "ant colony algorithm" has become the primary issue of innovation and entrepreneurship education in Colleges and universities.

Vocational education and higher vocational education in developed countries in the world have a long history of more than 100 years. With the economic and social development of developed countries, the existing teaching mode of cultivating applied talents has formed a relatively mature mode. The main training modes are BTEC mode in Britain, TAFE mode in Australia, CBE Mode in Canada and the United States and dual system mode in Germany.

The countries with better development of vocational education are Germany, South Korea, Japan and Switzerland, which attach great importance to vocational skill competition. Students trained in these countries have achieved very good results in participating in vocational skills competitions [2]. Therefore, they take vocational skills competitions as an important means and method to test the achievements of vocational education and promote the development of vocational education. In 1972, medley, director of the German Institute of labor market and vocational research, put forward the concept of "key ability" and began to cultivate students' ability to adapt to vocational changes. "Cultivating vocational ability" is an important research topic of vocational education curriculum and education reform in various countries.

Entering the new era, China is facing many challenges in economic structure adjustment and industrial upgrading. From the perspective of the overall situation, the party and the state have designed a series of top-level policies to support college students' innovation and entrepreneurship, which reflects that the Chinese government attaches great importance to the employment of college students. College students are the main body of employment. Scientifically adjusting and guiding the employment direction of college students. At the same time, it can also provide strong financial and policy support for college students with entrepreneurial passion and ideas. Government policy support and private capital investment have objectively helped college students' innovation and entrepreneurship, and the achievements of innovation and entrepreneurship in Colleges and universities have begun to take shape. However, there are still some problems in college.

2 Related work

2.1 Principle of Ant Colony Algorithm

The algorithm is developed by simulating the behavior that ant colony will eventually find the shortest route from ant nest to food when foraging in nature. In the real nature, the foraging behavior of ants is not a simple random behavior. Although food may exist in any direction of the ant colony, and the distance is not fixed, over a period of time, all ants in the ant colony will focus on the same route, and the distance from the ant colony to the food is the shortest.

Although ants do not have developed limbs and brains, each individual in the whole ant colony can complete many complex behaviors by cooperating with each other. Among them, the behavior of ant colony finding the shortest path from ant nest to food through mutual cooperation in the process of foraging may be only one of the complex behaviors. Observing the real ant colony in nature, it can be found that the path formed between the ant nest and the food is approximately a straight line, as shown in Fig. 1.

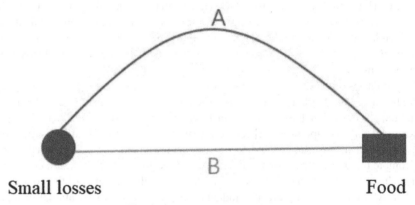

Fig. 1. Ant colony foraging process

Suppose that the surrounding environment changes when the ant colony is foraging, and there is a sudden obstacle on the known shortest path. At the beginning of the change, each ant colony will reselect the route. Although the distance of each route is not equal, the probability of each route being selected by the ant is equal [3].

In the process of foraging, ants will release pheromones on the routes they pass through. Ants communicate information through pheromones. Ants can identify whether pheromones exist and choose routes with higher pheromone content. When there are multiple routes for ants to choose, the ants will release pheromones while randomly choosing a route. Because the pheromone will volatilize, the longer the route, the lower the pheromone content, and the shorter the route, the higher the pheromone content. When later ants face the same choice in the process of traveling, the probability of moving in the direction with high pheromone content is greater, that is, ants will guide their own direction through pheromone. Therefore, on the premise of the same time, the shorter the distance, the more times the ants walk, the more pheromones the ants release on the route, and the greater the probability of the ants choosing the route again [4].

(1) The environment is changed by insects in the form of non synchronous communication;
(2) The information in this form has the attribute of localization, that is, it can only be found by insects passing through the path of the information. For example, in many ant species, workers go out to find food and release pheromones on the road. Other workers perceive the existence of pheromones and tend to follow the path with high pheromone concentration. Ants can significantly and efficiently transport food to the nest, as shown in Fig. 2 below.

Ants can find food through either bridge, and each ant releases pheromones on the passing bridge. On this premise, ants begin to explore the surrounding areas and reach the food source. At first, ants will randomly choose a bridge. Over time, the pheromone concentration of a bridge is higher, so it attracts more ants, and finally makes the whole ant colony choose the same bridge.

In another, the random fluctuation effect of the initial selection is smaller than before, and the ants who choose the short bridge always return to the nest (or food source) first. The pheromone release on the short bridge is earlier than that on the long bridge, so ants tend to choose the short bridge.

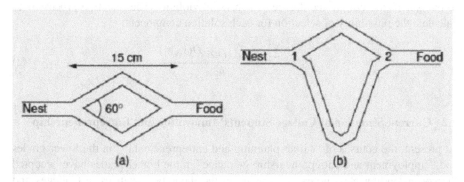

Fig. 2. Ant double bridge experiment equidistant double bridge (a) non equidistant double bridge (b)

It not only uses pheromones, but also heuristic factors:

$$W(C_h) = \sum_{e \in C_h} w(e) = \min\{eachHamilton\} \tag{1}$$

Pheromone heuristic factor α: Indicates the influence degree of the amount of information on whether to select the current path. α The size of reflects the strength of random factors in ant colony path search [5]. The general value is [1, 4] expected heuristic factor β: indicates the guidance of pheromones in the search path when they know that ants choose the path. Expected heuristic factor β The greater the value of, the greater the possibility of selecting the local shortest path at the local point, β General value range [3, 5], a, β It is a set of parameters with strong correlation.

The pheromone evaporation coefficient P: is too small, which means that the previously searched path is too likely to be selected again. Too large P can improve the random search ability and global search ability of the algorithm, but too many useless searches will reduce the convergence speed of the algorithm.

Ant number m pheromone strength Q: the influence of total information Q on the algorithm depends on α, B. The selection of P and the selection of algorithm model. Relevant research shows that the total information Q has no significant impact on the performance of ant cycle model ant colony algorithm, and can be selected arbitrarily.

Start with solver components. These components allow you to construct a structure diagram, a list of structures to consider and parameters used in the algorithm.

On the first page, set all parameters, treat the structure diagram and assign the first information element value to each variable (edge). In the rescue phase, the M Ali group starts group by group and rescues from the calendar. Every song maintains its own solution, moves according to the graph and updates [6].

In the early stage, all walls start with an empty solution. Select the node where you want to show software components in each structural page and then expand the current solution.

Ideally, the choice of components and some solutions is to preserve the solution viable. If it is impossible or difficult to maintain, part of the solution can be deleted or punished according to the degree of constraint violation.The selection process is to calculate the possibility of selection for each solution component:

$$D_r = \frac{\sum_{x_j \in Z_r} \sum_{x_j \in Z_r} D(x_i, x_j)}{n_r^2} \tag{2}$$

2.2 Current Situation of College Students' Innovation and Entrepreneurship

At present, the courses of "career planning and entrepreneurship" in the lower grades and "employment and entrepreneurship guidance" in the higher grades have occupied the corresponding class hours and credits in the theoretical courses in Colleges and universities. The curriculum system of online and offline education and the combination of theory and practice is basically mature. However, the education of entrepreneurship ideas of college students in China is seriously backward, and it is difficult for newly graduated college students. Therefore, entrepreneurship education of college students in China also needs to be correctly guided in the concept of entrepreneurship.

The innovation and entrepreneurship education of college students has gradually become a "prominent learning". Many colleges and universities have carried out a lot of exploration and Research on the innovation and entrepreneurship education of college students, accumulated a lot of valuable experience and achieved gratifying results. "However, because China's higher education at this stage is still affected by traditional ideas, the mode of carrying out college students' innovation and entrepreneurship education is still relatively single. College students' innovation and entrepreneurship education is often carried out in the form of interesting activity groups or extracurricular activities, not in the form of training or non curriculum, so it is still at a low level of non systematic and non planned In the state of low-level management, the traditional single method obviously can not meet the training needs of innovative and entrepreneurial talents in the new situation [7]. Therefore, we must build a perfect and systematic integrated management education mode combining entrepreneurship and innovation of college students, promote entrepreneurship with college students' innovative activities, drive innovative education with entrepreneurial activities, make them complement each other, and gradually improve the new education mode, so as to promote the cultivation of innovative and entrepreneurial talents.

1. Awareness education

    College Students' innovation and entrepreneurship education is first of all a kind of spirit and concept education, but its essence is quality education. The purpose of College Students' innovation and entrepreneurship education is to carry out comprehensive and systematic education on students' innovation and entrepreneurship psychological quality, personality quality and team management ability, so as to cultivate college students with innovative and entrepreneurial spirit.

2. Knowledge and ability education

    In today's society, having the awareness of innovation and entrepreneurship may not be successful. Another necessary condition is to have strong innovation and entrepreneurship skills, skills, communication and management skills. Only with these skills can the road of innovation and entrepreneurship be smooth. The direction of College Students' innovation and entrepreneurship should be high-tech industry, so they must have continuous innovation ability and certain core technology, because only with advanced core technology, college students' entrepreneurship can be competitive and their team can gradually develop and grow [8]. As a challenging and difficult system project, innovation and entrepreneurship is difficult to be strong and big by one person alone. Therefore, the key to the success of innovation and entrepreneurship is to establish a coordinated team with clear division of labor and cooperation.

3. Practical education

    Therefore, it is a very important activity to combine the education of entrepreneurship with the education of practice. For example, we can open laboratories and reference rooms, create practice bases, set up online simulation laboratories, and establish practice bases with enterprises and institutions, so as to enable college students to obtain more practice opportunities; We should also arrange experienced instructors for guidance, focusing on Cultivating College Students' practical ability and improving their practical ability.

3   Research on the Quality Evaluation of College Students' Innovation and Entrepreneurship Education Based on Ant Colony Algorithm

The evaluation index system is one of the elements of evaluation activities and the basis for carrying out evaluation activities and ensuring the objectivity and accuracy of evaluation. The essence of a set of scientific, objective and feasible index system is the technical reproduction of the decomposition, concretization and quantification of evaluation standards. It is not only the key to the success of evaluation activities, but also the key to improve the efficiency of evaluation. The consistency of scientificity and operability is the essential requirement of the evaluation index system, and completeness and testability are the technical characteristics of the evaluation index system. Entrepreneurship needs the support of many conditions, such as entrepreneurial knowledge, entrepreneurial ability, Entrepreneurial Capital and personal quality. Venture capital is the material premise of entrepreneurship, entrepreneurial knowledge provides a powerful knowledge system guarantee for entrepreneurship, and entrepreneurial ability makes it possible to increase the value of venture capital. The demand of College Students' innovation and entrepreneurship ability determines the talent training orientation and development mode of innovation and entrepreneurship education,, the teaching method and training mode of innovation and entrepreneurship education.

Innovation consciousness, entrepreneurship and creativity are inseparable, which are jointly reflected in the innovation and entrepreneurship practice of college students. Innovation and entrepreneurship education is an education with the basic value orientation of cultivating through educational activities [9]. In comparison, innovation consciousness is a subjective cognition, entrepreneurship is a psychological personality, and creativity is more a process of combining innovation and entrepreneurship knowledge with social material conditions, which is finally reflected in innovation and entrepreneurship achievements.

To investigate and analyze the whole process of the formation entrepreneurship education quality, this paper mainly makes further quantitative analysis through the evaluation system established by him. Because there are non quantifiable indicators in his evaluation indicators, we select quantifiable indicators for analysis. This paper makes a quantitative analysis through quantifiable evaluation indexes.

The school should guide students to pay attention to improving their personal comprehensive ability, encourage students to actively study entrepreneurship knowledge theory, pay attention to the dynamics of entrepreneurship circles at home and abroad, learn relevant basic professional knowledge, management knowledge, marketing theory, entrepreneurship related laws and regulations, national support policies for college students' entrepreneurship, etc. This paper studies the ant colony algorithm to solve the optimization problem. The key is to make the ant colony algorithm search more solution intervals with optimal solutions when solving the quality problem of College Students' innovation and entrepreneurship education. However, in order to improve the solution efficiency, it is required to give full play to the advantages of ant colony algorithm, combined with the effective information currently mastered by ant colony, and focus the search on the area where the optimal solution is more likely to appear. Only in this way can we ensure that has a greater probability to converge to the global optimal solution with fewer iterations. From the basic principle of ant colony algorithm, we can know that ant colonies mainly exchange information through pheromones and cooperate with each other to complete complex behavior. The search for the optimal route of ant colony foraging behavior is to constantly repeat the process of pheromone positive feedback [10]. The advantage of positive feedback is that it can continuously strengthen the current optimal solution; However, the disadvantage is also obvious. If it falls into local optimization, the solution process will stagnate and no better solution can be obtained.

Since each student's innovation and entrepreneurship data is different in the original data, we must integrate the original data according to the evaluation indicators. We use the weighted average method to integrate the data. The weighted average is similar to the arithmetic average. The difference is that the contribution of each number in the data to the average is not equal, and some points are more important than others.

Algorithm representation, assuming that the original data is $x_1 \sim x_n$, Respectively $[x_1, x_2, ..., x_m]$, Each value has a weight W, which is $[w_1, w_2, ..., w_m]$, The weighted average of these values is:

$$\bar{x} = \frac{w_1 x_1 + w_2 x_2 + \cdots + w_m x_m}{w_1 + w_2 + \cdots + w_m} \tag{3}$$

If all weights are equal, the weighted average is equal to the arithmetic average. In this paper, when calculating the weighted average, the weight of each is determined by the innovation and entrepreneurship data.

Since cluster analysis divides the categories according to the similarity between things, we must first determine the meaning of similarity, that is, determine the similarity index. The measure of similarity is to calculate a non negative number for any two sample points in the input space, which measures the similarity between the two sample points.

The samples are clustered according to the differences between sample data, so that the samples in each category contain similar information, while the categories contain different information. In the experiment, we use an unsupervised learning method - k-means method to cluster the samples [11]. The clustering criterion function used here is the sum of squares of the distance from each sample point in the cluster set to the cluster center of this kind. The purpose of K-means clustering is to gather the sample data together, and the common method of similarity measurement is to calculate the "distance" between samples. What kind of method to calculate the distance is very particular, and even related to the rationality of classification.

Creativity is the ability of innovation and entrepreneurship, which can also be simplified as creativity. It is the ability to systematically and scientifically process the learned knowledge on the basis of knowledge learning and experience accumulation, so as to generate new ideas, new concepts, new knowledge and new methods, and apply them to creatively solve new problems. It is the ability of strategy, planning, implementation, finance, project Time and other management capabilities. The creativity of college students is a deep-seated feature hidden behind the appearance of College Students' innovation and entrepreneurship. It is the realistic embodiment of innovation consciousness, entrepreneurship and innovation and entrepreneurship knowledge. It is the ability of college students to use known information and knowledge to produce some novel, unique and socially valuable products and services.

4 Evaluation Process of Innovative Education

The process evaluation. Relevant research points out that through the implementation of the process evaluation of entrepreneurship education in Colleges and universities, we can timely find the internal deep-seated problems and causes, especially comprehensively monitor the factors that have a key impact on the quality results, and then timely prevent and accurately "treat" the existing problems. The researcher evaluates the implementation status and impact of innovation entrepreneurship associations. Some researchers have also used analytic hierarchy process to construct the quality evaluation system of innovation and entrepreneurship education in Colleges and universities. The evaluation indicators include curriculum, teacher background, teaching methods, practice platform, organizational leadership, financial support, social coordination and so on. Other researchers advocate the modular design of evaluation indicators for the implementation process of innovation, teaching, practice, curriculum, project and special topic [12]. According to the characteristics, based on CIPP model, the researchers constructed an evaluation model of innovation and entrepreneurship education elements in Colleges and universities, including practice platform, teacher construction, curriculum teaching, guidance service, practical activities, innovation achievements, social benefits and other dimensions. In addition, relevant studies also believe that teachers' scientific research achievements in entrepreneurship, such as entrepreneurial enterprise life cycle management and technological innovation, can promote innovation and entrepreneurship education. Teachers and students can greatly deepen the connotation development of innovation and entrepreneurship education by using scientific and technological achievements. In recent years, joint innovation and entrepreneurship projects between teachers and students are gradually rising in Colleges and universities in China. Joint innovation between teachers and students has also become an important element in the evaluation of innovation and entrepreneurship education process. This view of quality evaluation based on the process of innovation and entrepreneurship education reflects the trend of returning to the standard of education quality evaluation, and avoids the disadvantages of relying too much on result evaluation, as shown in Table 1.

Table 1. Dimension and reliability analysis of the quality evaluation questionnaire of innovation and entrepreneurship education in Colleges and Universities

Dimension	Problem example	Explained variance %	Reliability coefficient
Classroom teaching	There are various types of innovation and entrepreneurship education courses, and teachers have rich teaching experience in innovation and entrepreneurship education	18.435	.940

(*continued*)

Table 1. (*continued*)

Dimension	Problem example	Explained variance %	Reliability coefficient
Government support	Local governments strongly support college students to register as enterprises, and the society often provides entrepreneurship guidance and training free of charge	16.325	.952
Co creation between teachers and students	Co creation between teachers and students helps to improve professional knowledge and ability, and co creation between teachers and students helps to understand the frontier of subject knowledge	12.039	.955
Entrepreneurship Competition	Entrepreneurship competition is of great help to real entrepreneurship, and the combination of entrepreneurship competition projects and majors is high	11.954	.955
Educational effectiveness	Innovation and entrepreneurship education helps to enrich entrepreneurial knowledge and improve entrepreneurial skills	11.954	.956
Entrepreneurial practice	The special entrepreneurship practice base outside the school is rich in resources, and the combination of entrepreneurship practice projects and professional learning is high	7.738	.950

On the whole, but a scientific and reasonable quality evaluation system has not been formed [13]. Moreover, the existing, and the literature using empirical methods is insufficient. Students' cognition of the elements and effectiveness of innovation and entrepreneurship education is lack of evidence support from empirical research. Empirical research often needs normative research, which needs empirical research to verify [14]. The evaluation of innovation and entrepreneurship education process can be carried out from the dimensions of personal resources, classroom teaching, entrepreneurship competition, entrepreneurship practice, government support, joint creation of teachers and students and so on; The evaluation of the results of innovation and entrepreneurship education should focus on entrepreneurial knowledge and skills, entrepreneurial will and spirit.

5   Conclusion

Students' cognitive evaluation of educational process elements and educational effectiveness. The evaluation of innovation and entrepreneurship education quality in Colleges and universities is generally at the upper middle level, but the score in the dimension of personal resources is low, indicating that college students are at a disadvantage in owning personal entrepreneurship resources. This result reveals two facts: first, after more than 20 years of exploration and development, innovation and entrepreneurship education in Colleges and universities in China has achieved great success, and has met the needs of educatees and society in terms of the coverage and effect of innovation and entrepreneurship education; Second, the disadvantage of college students having personal entrepreneurial resources is closely related to the source of students. Most college students come from rural areas, and their family, social status and social resources are not enough to support their entrepreneurial activities. In addition, innovation and entrepreneurship education in Colleges and universities is better at cultivating students' entrepreneurial spirit and stimulating students' entrepreneurial will, but it is relatively insufficient to improve students' entrepreneurial skills. This urgently requires colleges and universities to change the phenomenon of "learning innovation and entrepreneurship in books and watching innovation and entrepreneurship in videos", and improve the innovation and entrepreneurship education mode based on school enterprise cooperation.

References

1. Tukimin, R., Mohd, N., Yusoff, R.N., et al.: Source of ideas of teacher-generated innovation in teaching Arabic language in primary schools. Int. J. Acad. Res. Prog. Educ. Dev. 9(2), 2226–6348 (2021)
2. Research on the innovation of college students' ideological and political education under the new media. Adv. Educ. 11(4), 1131–1135 (2021)
3. Monge, C.B., Chaturvedi, A., Delanoe-Gueguen, S., et al.: Innovation in global entrepreneurship education: Babson collaborative and international comparison. Acad. Manag. Ann. Meet. Proc. 2021(1), 13331 (2021)
4. Ertekin, A.B.: The relationship between innovation skill and entrepreneurship on bachelor students of sports education. J. Educ. Issues 7(1), 324 (2021)

 5. Nalluri, P., Gn Anadhas, J.B.: A cognitive knowledged energy-efficient path selection using centroid and ant-colony optimized hybrid protocol for WSN-assisted IoT (2021)
 6. Jaganathan, R.: Prostate image segmentation using ant colony optimization-boundary complete recurrent neural network (ACO-BCRNN) (2021)
 7. Bai, L.: Reconfiguration performance of the urban power distribution system based on the genetic-ant colony fusion algorithm. In: E3S Web of Conferences, vol. 257, no. 4, 02062 (2021)
 8. Sun, L., Zhai, H., Zhai, Q., et al.: Fast update method of new equipment status in IMS network based on ant colony optimization algorithm. J. Phys. Conf. Ser. **1948**(1), 012049 (2021)
 9. Hakala, S.M., Meurville, M.P., Stumpe, M., et al.: Dynamic variation in a socially exchanged fluid indicates a role in the regulation of ant colony development and maturation (2021)
10. Li, L.: Practical exploration of integrating practical teaching into innovation and entrepreneurship education in colleges and universities (2021)
11. Chen, C.: Effective integration strategy of professional education and innovation and entrepreneurship education under the background of "double first-class". In: CIPAE 2021: 2021 2nd International Conference on Computers, Information Processing and Advanced Education (2021)
12. Dang, T.T.: Certification of extension master's education program: technology entrepreneurship and business management and innovation (2021)
13. Cui, Y., He, F., Feng, X.: Research on teaching reform of design-oriented majors in colleges and universities based on innovation and entrepreneurship education. In: 2020 3rd International Seminar on Education Research and Social Science (ISERSS 2020) (2021)
14. Prasad, S., Bhat, R.S.: India industry-university collaboration - a novel approach combining technology, innovation, and entrepreneurship. In: 2021 IEEE Global Engineering Education Conference (EDUCON). IEEE (2021)

The Application of Hierarchical Teaching Mode Based on Hybrid Criterion Fuzzy Algorithm in Higher Vocational English Education

Chuanwei Zhang$^{(\boxtimes)}$

Ganzhou Teachers College, Ganzhou 341000, Jiangxi, China
zcwteacher@163.com

Abstract. This paper studies the English Teaching in Higher Vocational Colleges Based on the hybrid criterion fuzzy algorithm, which must adapt to the current new situation and actively carry out the teaching reform. In English teaching, the hierarchical teaching strategy is adopted, that is, teachers teach students according to their aptitude, teaching should be targeted, different teaching objectives should be formulated according to the individual differences of students, and different teaching requirements should be put forward, It can make students have a strong interest in learning, enhance their learning confidence and sense of achievement, and promote their healthy development.

Keywords: Fuzzy algorithm · Hierarchical teaching · English education

1 Introduction

Layered teaching refers to the teaching mode that teachers divide students into several levels according to the difference of students' learning ability and knowledge mastery, then formulate corresponding teaching objectives, select appropriate teaching contents and teaching methods, so as to make students get the best learning effect.

As the main base of the supply of applied and skilled talents in society, higher vocational colleges, the state and society attach more and more importance to their education. For most vocational colleges, students in school often have obvious differences in learning in various subjects, and the teaching effect will often show a significant polarization, especially in English teaching, the teaching effect of "the excellent students are not satisfied, the secondary students are difficult to improve, and the students with difficulty cannot keep up with each other" [1].

Facing the problems in education, English Teaching in higher vocational colleges must adapt to the current new situation, keep pace with the times and actively carry out teaching reform. For the above phenomenon of students' learning effect differentiation, we can adopt the strategy of layered teaching in English teaching, that is, teachers teach according to their aptitude and aim at teaching, Different teaching objectives are set according to the individual differences of students, different teaching requirements are

M. A. Jan and F. Khan (Eds.): BigIoT-EDU 2022, LNICST 466, pp. 424–430, 2023.
https://doi.org/10.1007/978-3-031-23947-2_45

put forward. Different teaching methods are adopted in classroom teaching, which can maximize the enthusiasm of each student, including superior students and poor students, so that students have strong interest in learning, enhance their learning confidence and sense of achievement and promote their healthy development.

2   The Characteristics and Current Situation of English Teaching in Higher Vocational Colleges

There are great differences in the English base of students in higher vocational colleges. Generally speaking, the average English level of secondary vocational students is the worst, followed by vocational college students, and the best is general high school students. The traditional English teaching system in higher vocational colleges does not distinguish the three major students, namely, secondary vocational school, vocational college and general high school. The teaching system adopted is still unified, that is, the same teaching materials, the same teaching objectives and the same teaching mode, often ignore the differences of students, which not only leads to the difficulty of organizing classroom teaching and poor teaching effect, At the same time, it makes the scale of the post-english examination difficult to grasp, which makes the students who have poor foundation study hard but fail to pass the exam, and lose their confidence in learning; The students who have good foundation can pass the examination easily and relax their study without taking seriously the study [2].

At present, most vocational colleges usually compress their hours into one year when they are in the first year of their entrance, which means 135–145 class hours. The assessment standard is whether they pass the English level 3 (i.e. the English competence test of colleges and universities). Because the CET-3 focuses on the assessment of English application ability, grammar and question type are very simple, even less than college entrance examination English, so it leads to the passing of CET-3 by some students with better basic English learning before entering school, This results in many English teachers in Higher Vocational Colleges and universities in the second semester of the English classroom teaching found that many students with good results do not study seriously. At the same time, teachers in higher vocational colleges also found that there are students who are not familiar with English in every class, even their English level is not even higher than that of junior high school students. As far as English textbooks in vocational colleges are concerned, students' views are also polarized: students with poor English foundation feel that textbooks are like "Tianshu", they can not understand in class, and they don't know words that are difficult to read; Students with good English foundation feel too simple, even less difficult than high school. Therefore, limited to the teaching materials and classes in higher vocational colleges, teachers have to take the average value. The teaching plan and difficulty are mainly for the students who are based on the Middle English.

3   Decision Model of Mixed Criteria Fuzzy Algorithm

The English Teaching in higher vocational colleges should be reformed to adapt to the new situation. Teachers teach students according to their aptitude, and set different teaching objectives according to the individual differences of students. They put forward different teaching requirements for the superior students, middle-level students and difficult students respectively. In the database module, a mixed criteria fuzzy decision model is built to analyze the user preferences, and the most recommended English Education information is extracted to users according to the user preferences.

1) Weight of educational information

Set the English education information set to $Y = \{Y_1, Y_2, \ldots, Y_m\}$, and set different weights according to different information types.

2) Fuzzy interest set construction

Before the database management module selects English information to recommend to users, it sets two kinds of criteria: ideal criterion and dissatisfaction criterion according to user preference, and set multiple compromise criteria between the two criteria. Then the decision criteria set is $A = \{A_j | j = 1, 2 \ldots, J\}$. In practice, the user's choice criteria for English education information are cross related to the factors of English information.

3) Construction of recommendation expression

① Simulation relation matrix

The candidate English information recommended by the system is set as the whole field $V = \{V_m | m = 1, 2 \ldots, M\}$. The evaluation results are Y-V simulation matrix

$$Q = (q_m) = \begin{bmatrix} Q_1 \\ Q_2 \\ \vdots \\ Q_5 \end{bmatrix} \tag{1}$$

In the simulation relation matrix Q, fuzzy likelihood inference is implemented according to the decision criteria, and the fuzzy subset a of decision criteria in the domain V can be obtained A_j.

② Fuzzy decision matrix

Through fuzzy subset A_j can obtain the fuzzy relation matrix from V to u:

$$E_j = (e_j(m, e)) \tag{2}$$

where: e_j represents the fuzzy decision-making factor of English information; M is the number word. Fuzzy relation matrix $(e_j(m, e))$ represents the likelihood distance between each kind of candidate English information and fuzzy subset a of decision criteria [3].

In order to calculate the recommendation degree of M candidate education information at one time, the mean value of cut set is set as follows:

$$G(F_{c,m}) = \frac{1}{M} \sum_{m-1}^{M} H_n(c) \tag{3}$$

Students are divided into several levels, then corresponding teaching objectives are formulated, and appropriate teaching content and teaching methods are selected to make students get the best learning effect. Therefore, layered teaching means that in classroom teaching, students are recognized to be different. Teachers should set up different learning objectives according to different levels of students. Whether they are poor or good-level students, teachers should adopt teaching materials and teaching methods that can adapt to their abilities to carry out targeted teaching, To achieve the maximum effect of each student can achieve the set goal set by the teacher under the teacher's instruction. Based on the teaching practice, layered teaching requires teachers to face all students, including the students with good foundation and poor foundation, so that teaching can be suitable for each student's "Recent Development Zone", so that students can obtain their own success and confidence, thus stimulating their learning enthusiasm, promoting their mental health and healthy development.

According to the basic requirements of English Course Teaching in higher vocational colleges, English teaching can be divided into three levels according to the actual situation that the enrollment level of students in vocational colleges is uneven. The implementation of hierarchical guidance and corresponding English ability requirements, which further puts forward the reform direction and goal for the higher vocational English teaching.

4   Hierarchical Teaching Mode

4.1   Requirements for Higher Vocational English Teachers

1. Improve the quality of teachers

In the process of hierarchical teaching, teachers are the direct executors. Teachers' behavior and language have a subtle impact on students. Therefore, English teachers in higher vocational colleges should not only master English knowledge skillfully, but also study effective teaching methods to effectively improve English teaching effect. In addition, higher vocational English teachers should fully understand each student's learning situation and actual needs, pay more attention to students in life, provide them with help in learning and life, strengthen communication with students, and shorten the distance between them.

2. Take incentive measures

In hierarchical teaching, teachers should encourage students to improve their self-confidence. Due to the serious polarization of higher vocational students in English learning, there are differences in the mastery of basic English knowledge and learning ability. Therefore, teachers should start from the actual situation of students, take reasonable incentive measures, praise and encourage the students with good English learning performance, and pay attention to those with weak English foundation and poor English learning ability Students with poor acceptance ability should be encouraged to help them build up their self-confidence in English learning.

3. Carry out teaching seminar activities

In the use of hierarchical teaching mode, teachers should strengthen the communication with other English teachers, participate in some English teaching seminars, exchange teaching experience and teaching experience, learn from other teachers' experience or lessons, and explore more effective hierarchical teaching methods. Carry out English teaching research activities regularly to make teachers aware of their own shortcomings, so as to improve their own quality and improve the effect of English teaching. Figure 1 below shows the requirements for English teachers.

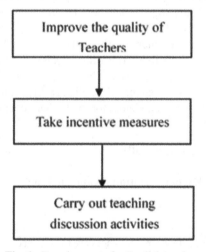

Fig. 1. Requirements for English teachers

4.2 The Implementation of the Layered Teaching Mode

1. Prepare for the implementation of layered teaching. First, the preliminary investigation of teaching content. Before the implementation of layered teaching, we should first consider whether the content of the layered teaching that should be prepared can arouse students' interest in learning, so as to stimulate the students' internal motivation and help them to establish their confidence and enthusiasm for learning English.

Second, ideological preparation. The layered teaching of students in Higher Vocational Colleges means that students should be studied in different classes according to their learning achievements. In other words, they should concentrate the students with good grades and those with poor grades together.

2. Specific implementation measures. First, teaching in different classes. Taking the branch of higher vocational colleges as the unit, the students of the same grade are given the bottom examination, and then according to the results of the bottom test, they are divided into three different levels of classes.

Second, the teaching objectives are layered. Class a students belong to relatively solid groups, and their English ability basically meets the requirements of ordinary high school graduates. Therefore, for class a students, we should pay attention to the teaching depth. The teaching materials can use the 21st Century College English textbook to ensure the teaching content is extensive, deep and good expansibility. The specific teaching objectives are to broaden the knowledge of students' English [4], On the basis of training its ability to use basic English, we should strengthen the training of its comprehensive language application skills. Therefore, the students in class B should pay attention to the broadening of knowledge and strengthen the cultivation of their language application ability. The textbook can use "new starting point College English", which is very difficult and convenient for the improvement of students' ability. The basic English level of class C students can only reach junior high school level, and they are not familiar with the common college English and lack of interest in English learning. Therefore, the cultivation of class C students mainly focuses on the establishment of students' confidence and the cultivation of learning habits. The cultivation of learning interest can be made of the new general college English textbook, which is relatively easy and involves a wide range of knowledge, which is conducive to the cultivation of students' interest.

5   Conclusion

Nowadays, the demand for English talents is increasing, which puts forward higher requirements for English education in higher vocational colleges. The application of the layered teaching model based on mixed criteria fuzzy algorithm in Higher Vocational English education is that the students' English level is different and their learning ability is different. The traditional English teaching model can not meet the actual needs of students. The emergence of the layered teaching mode has achieved good results in the improvement of this problem. Therefore, the English teachers in higher vocational colleges should recognize the important value of the layered teaching mode, apply it reasonably to English teaching, improve the students' English level and learning ability in different levels, and effectively improve the effect of English teaching.

References

1. Xing, Y.: Research on the application of hierarchical teaching mode in Higher Vocational English education. Educ. Occup. (24) (2012)

2. Hei, Y., Liu, L., Huang, Y.: Research on the effectiveness of Higher Vocational English Education under the hierarchical teaching mode – taking Xingtai vocational and technical college as an example. J. Xingtai Vocat. Techn. Coll. (2013)
3. Xu, H., Teng, G., Wang, D., et al.: Tag elastic recommendation based on modular clustering. Mod. Intell. **38**(4), 58–64 (2018)
4. Hu, H.: The necessity of introducing hierarchical teaching into higher Vocational English Education. J. Changchong Inst. Educ. (14) (2013)

Research on the System Design of Primary School Science Multimedia Teaching

Yanmei Zhao[(✉)]

Xianyang Normal University, Xianyang 712000, Shaanxi, China
zifan_2001@163.com

Abstract. Primary school science classroom can endow students with more scientific literacy and expand students' knowledge and scientific vision through self exploration. With the continuous advancement of teaching reform, the current science teaching reform in primary schools has also received extensive attention from relevant scholars. Multimedia technology has mobilized primary school students' curiosity, improved students' interest in learning, and cultivated students' excellent scientific perception. Multimedia has increased teaching resources and led students to explore deeply, Through the combination of sound and form, multimedia technology makes primary school science teaching difficult and easy, and provides powerful help for the effect of primary school science classroom teaching.

Keywords: Multimedia teaching · Primary school science · System design

1 Introduction

Multimedia is a special teaching method with the development of science and technology. It is also used in the process of teaching. It is a good auxiliary teaching method. Multimedia is intuitive, vivid and colorful. It can help students learn with multiple senses, stimulate students' interest in learning and inspire students' wisdom. It can also help complete the tasks of teaching management and teacher-student communication that cannot be completed by other teaching equipment. In teaching, multimedia can use the functions of animation, graphics and image transformation to make the static graphics in teaching materials dynamic, so as to reveal the rich connotation of graphics and images and help students understand the essence of things comprehensively and deeply; We can also create teaching situations according to the needs of teaching, guide students into artistic conception and guide teaching in-depth.

From the discipline characteristics of primary school science, primary school science classroom can endow children with more scientific literacy, expand students' knowledge and scientific vision through self exploration, fully stimulate students' noble quality of loving and advocating science, and greatly promote students' lifelong development. Today, with the rapid development of science and technology, in the face of primary school students who have been frequently exposed to various electronic products, the traditional teaching mode is no longer enough to attract students' interest and meet the

M. A. Jan and F. Khan (Eds.): BigIoT-EDU 2022, LNICST 466, pp. 431–442, 2023.
https://doi.org/10.1007/978-3-031-23947-2_46

requirements of modern education. Rigid exposition will only keep scientific knowledge in a simple and rigid state, and can not reveal a rich and colorful scientific world for students, Multimedia teaching can make up for these shortcomings. Through multimedia technology to show various scientific phenomena, the application of video, text and animation in primary school science classroom can create an "immersive" atmosphere for students, make scientific knowledge more clear and complete, and is conducive to the cultivation of students' scientific support [1]. Therefore, aiming at the problems existing in primary school science teaching, this paper puts forward countermeasures, hoping to introduce multimedia teaching technology into primary school science classroom and comprehensively improve students' learning efficiency.

In the application of multimedia courseware, there are many sounds, images and words, which can meet the sensory needs of students' visual and listening. Therefore, some teachers make articles in this regard and concentrate a large amount of sound and image information in the courseware, resulting in invalid information, which not only distracts students' attention, but also affects the realization of teaching objectives. At the same time, it also reduces students' speaking time in class, and English class has become a courseware display class [1].

Multimedia assisted instruction has obvious advantages. Therefore, some teachers unilaterally pursue courseware assisted teaching, and even form an open class without courseware, while some teachers' courseware is only the accumulation of simple words and pictures, which can be realized only by projection and pictures, which leads to a waste of resources. Therefore, our teachers should also appropriately choose multimedia and effectively combine multimedia with conventional means.

As teachers, they should first grasp their leading position and role in teaching. Multimedia teaching is only an auxiliary teaching means and can not replace teachers' basic responsibilities of "preaching, teaching and dispelling doubts". Making noise can only backfire and can not reflect the charm of multimedia teaching means. Teachers are always the soul of teaching, Using multimedia teaching is a basic skill of teachers. Necessary multimedia technology should be used in teaching to make multimedia really play an auxiliary role in teaching.

2   Related work

2.1   Current Situation of Science Teaching in Primary School

In the current rapidly developing society, education has become a multifaceted problem. In addition to the shortage of education funds, teachers can not be supplemented in time, and there are new contradictions in the implementation of curriculum education in primary and secondary schools. The emergence of new contradictions is intertwined with unresolved problems, which restricts and affects the effective implementation of curriculum teaching in primary and secondary schools. Relevant investigation and research shows that the problems existing in the current curriculum teaching situation in primary and secondary schools roughly include the following three points:

1. course teaching management lags behind

Scientific teaching management can effectively promote teaching development. Due to the lack of educational funds, some conventional teaching and research activities can not be carried out efficiently and normally. In addition, the insufficient allocation of teachers and the low overall level also restrict the innovative development of curriculum teaching. In addition, the quality of educational managers is not high, the management of the school is too loose, and there is no scientific planning, which leads to curriculum teaching becoming a kind of teachers' coping style and completing tasks at will.

2. The teaching efficiency of the course is not high

There are two main reasons for the low efficiency. First, the teaching methods are backward. Some senior "old teachers" stick to the rules and are unwilling to change their "old ways", which leads to the lack of students' learning motivation, rigid learning methods, single training methods and teachers' own evaluation means. The fundamental reason for this phenomenon is that the high workload makes teachers have no time and energy to study the means of curriculum teaching. They can only do the mechanical repetition of "speaking" and "Practicing", which can not give full play to the creativity of teachers' own curriculum teaching. What is more ridiculous is that teachers' work intensity is not rewarded. Second, schools and parents do not pay enough attention to nurturance education. On the one hand, the school pursues the enrollment rate and militarized management to win a better social reputation. On the other hand, the parents are too utilitarian and have little control over the children's education. They blindly pursue the children's scores, but ignore the children's growth, and completely ignore the importance of family education. What's more, they ask the school: "isn't education your school?"?

3. The concept of curriculum teaching is old L

The main reasons for this situation are: first, many teachers are not equipped with teaching facilities in most primary and secondary schools due to their weak cultural foundation and limited conditions, and teachers are used to implementing curriculum teaching with a piece of chalk and a book [2]. How can such teaching means adapt to the modern scientific and technological society? Second, teachers' learning initiative is insufficient. In addition to teaching materials and lesson preparation manuals, teachers basically have no learning materials to help teachers change their educational ideas and improve their professional ability.

Education is the foundation of the country. If the youth is strong, the country is strong. Facing the current severe situation, I summarize the following points in combination with relevant literature:

1. renewal of teachers' ideas and improvement of professional quality

The role of teachers has changed from a single curriculum executor in the past to an executor, a researcher and a participant in curriculum development. In curriculum leadership, teachers' various curriculum roles put forward higher requirements for teachers' professional knowledge and ability. Teachers can do this from the following two points. 1. Strengthen self reflection. 2. Strengthen the cooperation among teachers.

2. Always follow the law of curriculum teaching management

The law is inviolable. The reason why the law is formed is mainly because the law guides the process of people's cognition of something. However, the law of curriculum teaching management mainly includes its own education, timeliness, cooperation, standardization, systematicness, self-organization and integrity. In the process of management course teaching, these laws will always run through it, which will naturally achieve a certain effect. The multimedia information system is shown in Fig. 1 below.

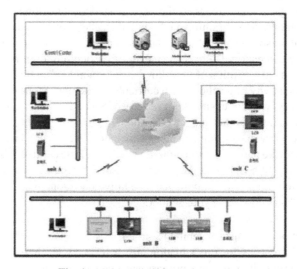

Fig. 1. Multimedia information system

2.2   The Coverage of Multimedia Technology Is Not Wide

Multimedia technology has been introduced into primary school science classroom for some time, and teachers and students have benefited a lot. Multimedia technology not only helps teachers reduce the teaching pressure, but also makes teachers' classroom more attractive. At the same time, it also effectively mobilizes students' enthusiasm and stimulates students' thirst for knowledge. However, from the overall science classroom teaching, the coverage of multimedia technology is not comprehensive enough, which is mainly reflected in two aspects. First, some rural primary schools in remote areas do not have advanced teaching equipment, which is the so-called "a clever woman can't cook without rice". Second, teachers need more professional training to use multimedia technology [3].

Primary school science is an abstract subject. Some scientific phenomena are difficult for students to feel the charm of science by observing the pictures in textbooks, and the descriptive words in science books are difficult for primary school students to really understand the true meaning. If only relying on the traditional classroom teaching mode, students will find it difficult to learn, and the subsequent problem is to reduce their interest in learning. Therefore, teachers need to make science teaching more specific with the help of external teaching tools.

Science is an all inclusive subject. It is novel and interesting. The traditional "oral teaching" teaching method can not better reflect this novelty and interest On the contrary, it will backfire and make it dull, so the classroom atmosphere and students' interest in learning can be expected. Therefore, there is an urgent need for multimedia technology to enter the classroom to enrich teaching methods.

2.3   Advantages of Multimedia Technology in Primary School Science Teaching

Multimedia is intuitive, vivid, rich and colorful, and can store a large amount of data and information, which not only creates more situations for us, but also plays the main role of students, creates a relaxed, pleasant and moderately tense learning atmosphere, and improves the quality and effect of teaching.

1.   Before class: adjust the atmosphere and introduce new knowledge

In each English class, teachers will play some English songs with multimedia and start a class with greetings. There are many interesting English songs in our English textbooks. These songs can interest students and attract their attention. Let the students sing a happy English song a few minutes before class, so that the students will quickly concentrate and transfer their emotions to their study [4].

For example, 1A unit 4 learning supplies, the teacher can take the students to sing the song a pencil a few minutes before class, and the students can quickly concentrate and turn their attention to English learning. At the same time, the purpose of the teacher's selection of this song is also to pave the way for the next learning of the content of school supplies.

2.   In class: fade the boredom and solve the difficulties

At the same time, we can use a variety of media to help our teaching, make textbooks live and move, and turn the teaching content into audible, visual and perceptible knowledge. For example, teaching a simple English song Hello, as far as this song is concerned, the lyrics are few and the content is very simple. If it is just a teacher's performance and then teaching students to sing, it will be a little boring, and students will not concentrate on German teachers' teaching. Therefore, with the help of computer and TV, music and animation will stimulate students' interest, and let animation interact with students at the same time, Learn this song in a pleasant and relaxed atmosphere. When the computer was turned on and the music sounded, many students had become interested in the song.

3. End of class: assist teaching and consolidate knowledge

A class lasts for 40 min. Towards the end, most children can't sit still and are impetuous. They think they have mastered all the knowledge they have learned in a class. At this time, teachers should use multimedia to design some activities to suppress the children's impetuosity. Students learn by playing and play by learning. In this process, students are the main body of learning. Teachers should fully stimulate students' interest and let students have the courage to explore and practice.

(1) Stimulate students' interest in learning

Multimedia technology is applied to primary school science The first advantage is that it can stimulate students' interest in learning, and the art of teaching is also here. Using multimedia technology in teaching can attract students' curiosity to a great extent [5]. At this time, as long as teachers give a little guidance, they can turn curiosity into a strong thirst for knowledge, so as to trigger positive learning behavior. For example, in the class of "is there life outside the earth" in the first volume of grade 6, in the guidance link, you can first play a clip of UFO film, tell students that this is only a lens of science fiction film, and then ask, do you believe there is life outside the earth? Students will rush to express their views. In this way, the classroom atmosphere can be mobilized, so as to attract students' curiosity and pave the way for the next study.

(2) Strengthen key points, break through difficulties and improve teaching efficiency

In primary school science teaching, multimedia technology is used to design science teaching courseware. The auxiliary teaching with both sound and emotion, graphics and text and dynamic and static combination not only optimizes the original teaching means, but also improves the teaching efficiency. For example, when teaching the "solar system family" in Volume 1 of grade 6, when exploring the relationship between the distance between planets and the sun and the planetary revolution cycle, students can observe and explore in combination with the solar system simulation software, so as to find the law. Because many cognitive objects in the universe are too empty and far away for students, and the demonstration experiment is limited by environmental conditions and can not be well implemented, it is also very difficult for students to understand [6]. With the help of multimedia technology and tool software, creating a virtual simulation environment can provide conditions for students to explore and experience, so that students can observe phenomena in dynamic situations. Students observe more comprehensively and carefully, so that students can not only intuitively and accurately understand the details, but also obtain the intuitive experience of process and method, so as to better enhance the teaching effect.

(3) Broaden students' learning horizons

The content of Science in primary school science textbooks is often difficult to meet students' desire and pursuit of knowledge. The emergence of multimedia technology improves the classroom efficiency. At the same time, teachers can better liberate themselves from the classroom and explain more contents outside the textbooks to students. At the same time, they can use relevant software to show these contents to everyone in the form of text, pictures, video or audio. In this way, students' classroom experience is improved and it is convenient for them to learn more fields of knowledge.

3   System Design of Primary School Science Multimedia Teaching

3.1   Overview of Overall System Functions

The system consists of two-level control systems: remote control system and field control system. The field control system is composed of multimedia centralized controller as the core and multimedia teaching equipment as the controlled object. It can be operated by the user when the remote control system does not work or is paralyzed for various reasons Use the relevant buttons on the or the operation interface of the teacher's computer to make the multimedia teaching system enter the normal working state [7]; The remote control system takes the special computer as the remote central control host, takes dozens or even hundreds of multimedia classrooms distributed in different teaching buildings as the controlled object, and is connected to the network through the campus network as a bridge The purpose of controlling multimedia teaching equipment is achieved by the teacher's computer on the; The field control system can be turned off through relevant operations, the multimedia teaching system can enter the normal working state through relevant operations, and the operation status of relevant equipment in the multimedia classroom can be displayed on the display screen of the remote central control host [8].

The development of multimedia teaching software needs to do a good job in teaching design, system structure model design, navigation strategy design and interactive interface design under the guidance of modern educational thought and educational theory, and use and modify it repeatedly in teaching practice, so as to make the developed multimedia teaching software conform to the teaching law and achieve good teaching and learning results. The design and production process generally includes: requirements analysis, script writing, software structure design, material collection and production, sample production, testing, evaluation and other steps.

The design of multimedia teaching software includes two parts: software teaching design and software system design.

The preset and storage functions of multimedia are suitable to meet the presentation requirements of special experimental phenomena of time delay and acceleration in science teaching. The duration of different physical processes varies from long to short, such as the evolution of the universe and the decay of some atomic nuclei, which are often billions of years, far beyond human life. Short like lightning, the action between light and matter is fleeting. Through the multimedia system, we can speed up or slow down a process that cannot be changed in nature, so as to help students form perceptual knowledge better.

There seems to be no doubt about the repeatability of scientific phenomena. Scientific laws will not be recognized if they cannot be repeated and verified under different conditions and places. At present, the conditions of primary school laboratory have some difficulties to meet these repeatability. The multimedia system can play a step in the experiment repeatedly to strengthen the emphasis on this step.

A very important method in scientific research is approximation, so there are many idealized models. There are many such words in science teaching: smooth (no friction), regardless of air resistance, uniform linear motion, but our science teachers understand that these words can not find completely consistent examples in practice. Of course, many phenomena can be approximated almost perfectly by ingenious design, such as air cushion, magnetic levitation, vacuum, etc. in order to reduce friction, but real idealization will never appear in reality, and some phenomena can not even be approximated easily [9]. Multimedia system can exclude these interference factors in advance through programming, so that students can observe the real ideal physical phenomena.

3.2   System Working Principle

The system is composed of controlled object (multimedia teaching equipment) - centralized controller - classroom computer - campus local area - central computer; The basic working principle is as follows: 1) the classroom computer simulates the equipment control interface through software programming, and encodes the relevant control information. The user clicks the desktop operation software panel, the control software reads the control information and communicates with the centralized controller through the serial port [10]. The centralized controller receives the control code through the serial port and analyzes it, and controls the operation of the corresponding peripheral circuit according to the analyzed control command; At the same time, the classroom computer records the status information of equipment operation and provides it to the central computer for query and statistics. 2) "Network management platform software system based on C / s remote control system" is installed on the central control computer and teacher computer, and the function of central computer controlling classroom computer is realized through mutual access of web pages; At the same time, the central computer counts the use time of classroom equipment according to the collected client status information.

3.3   System Input and Output

The main inputs of the system include video signal, audio signal, VGA signal (computer display signal) and serial communication data. The video signal mainly comes from the DVD player; The audio signal mainly comes from the sound signal of classroom computer, DVD player, etc.; VGA signal mainly comes from the input signal of classroom computer and classroom notebook computer; Serial data communication mainly comes from the signal sent by the classroom computer to the centralized controller. The output signals of the system include switching value signal and serial communication signal [11]. The switching value signal output mainly includes video signal, audio signal and VGA selected signal; The serial signal is mainly used to output to the projector and return to the running state of the equipment.

3.4   Overall System Design

Build a remote control system with a special computer as the remote central control host. The overall design of the system is:

(1) In the central control room, a special remote control host (industrial computer or special server) is connected with the campus network through the network cable to realize the remote control of the campus multimedia classroom;

(2) The transmission of system control signal uses the existing campus network, which can be extended to each multimedia classroom without special wiring for the control system. The specific method is to introduce a network cable into each multimedia classroom and connect it to the multimedia centralized controller through the computer of the multimedia classroom for remote control [12];

(3) A multimedia equipment centralized controller is installed in each multimedia classroom. It has a variety of interfaces, which can be connected with multimedia projectors, electric control screens, multimedia computers, VGA distributors, digital (video) physical booths, wireless sound amplification systems and other equipment, and control their various functions.

The overall design diagram of system hardware is shown in Fig. 2.

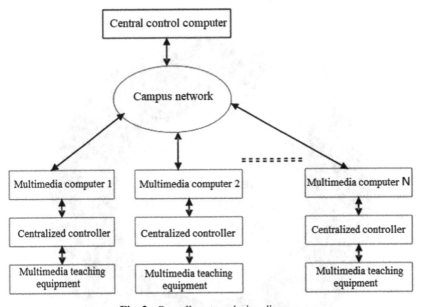

Fig. 2. Overall system design diagram

4   Multimedia System Benefits

Multimedia teaching refers to that in the teaching process, according to the characteristics of teaching objectives and teaching objects (students), teachers reasonably select and use modern teaching media through teaching design, and organically combine with traditional teaching means to participate in the whole teaching process, act on students with a variety of media information, form a reasonable teaching process structure and achieve the optimal teaching effect [13].

1. Convenient, fast and efficient. Through courseware and material demonstration, multimedia teaching makes the teaching method convenient, fast, large amount of information and large capacity, greatly saves space, blackboard writing time and description time, and improves teaching efficiency.
2. Three dimensional teaching, visual and intuitive. Multiple indexes, links, mutual calls, and human-computer interaction between users and computers; The comprehensive application of text, pictures, animation, video and other materials to carry out teaching activities [14]. There are pictures, text, sound and even moving images. However, the application of ordinary teaching means is difficult to explain clearly, or even the key points and difficulties of knowledge, which makes some abstract and difficult knowledge intuitive and vivid. Especially with pictures, animations and videos, it is more intuitive and more vivid. The flow of multimedia courseware is shown in Fig. 3 below.

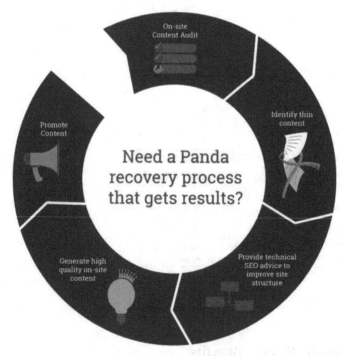

Fig. 3. Multimedia courseware flow

3. Rich cases, materials and information stars. Comprehensively process and control symbols, language, text, sound, graphics, images, images and other media information, and organically combine various elements of multimedia according to teaching requirements. By using a variety of multimedia materials and making full use of network materials (cloud materials), teachers can bring a lot of information to students and update rich cutting-edge materials through the Internet.

4. Simulation, virtual reality, interactivity. The expansion of ordinary experiments is realized through multimedia experiments, and students' exploration and creativity are cultivated through the reproduction and Simulation of real scenes. Students have more participation, learn more actively, and create a reflective environment, which is conducive to students to form a new cognitive structure [15].

5. Novel and lively, stimulate interest. Making classroom teaching activities lively, interesting, enlightening and authentic can fundamentally change the traditional monotonous teaching mode, so as to activate students' thinking, stimulate students' learning interest and cultivate students' creative thinking.

5   Conclusion

Multimedia teaching and traditional teaching have their own advantages and disadvantages. In primary school science classroom, it is more important to cultivate students' scientific support and inquiry ability. Teachers should take multimedia as an auxiliary means of traditional teaching. Primary school science multimedia technology teaching not only comprehensively improves the current teaching quality, but also is of great help to both teachers and students. For teachers, learning new skills can improve their professional quality; For students, they can integrate themselves into the classroom and improve the learning efficiency of the classroom. Therefore, multimedia technology into the primary school classroom It plays an important role in the construction of the whole teaching atmosphere and the improvement of teaching quality.

References

1. Tian, G., Darcy, O.: Study on the design of interactive distance multimedia teaching system based on VR technology. Int. J. Contin. Eng. Educ. Life-Long Learn. **31**(1), 1 (2021)
2. Wu, J.: Design of traditional drama multimedia network teaching system. In: The 6th International Conference on Arts, Design and Contemporary Education (ICADCE 2020) (2021)
3. Liu, R.: Design of ideological and political multimedia network teaching resources integration system based on wireless network. Sci. Program. **2021**(3), 1–15 (2021)
4. Han, Y., Yin, W.: The effect of multimedia teaching platform based on virtual technology on students' English learning motivation. Int. J. Electr. Eng. Educ. 002072092098849 (2021)
5. Liu, T., Ning, L.: Deep convolutional neural network and weighted Bayesian model for evaluation of college foreign language multimedia teaching. Wireless Communications and Mobile Computing, (3, article e3080), 1–7 (2021)
6. Li, W.: Multimedia teaching of college musical education based on deep learning. Mob. Inf. Syst. **2021**(2), 1–10 (2021)

7. Hjy, A., Xl, B., Mz, C., et al.: Child neglect and eating habits in primary schoolchildren: a prospective study in Wuhan, China - ScienceDirect (2021)
8. Corni, F., Fuchs, H.U.: Primary physical science for student teachers at kindergarten and primary school levels: Part II—implementation and evaluation of a course. Interchange **52**(2), 203–236 (2021). https://doi.org/10.1007/s10780-021-09424-6
9. Kwok, K.O., et al.: Likelihood of COVID-19 vaccination among primary school students in Hong Kong - ScienceDirect (2021)
10. Wood, L.: Wallington C. ASE Primary Science Lessons for Home (and School) Learning: A Response to COVID-19. Primary Science (2021)
11. Communications P. Correction: Primary and secondary school teachers 鈥perceptions of their social science training needs (2021)
12. Sánchez-Ibáez, R., Guerrero-Romera, C., Miralles-Martínez, P.: Correction: primary and secondary school teachers' perceptions of their social science training needs. Palgrave Communications **8**, 1–11 (2021)
13. Assemie, M.A., Shitu, D., Hune, Y., et al.: Prevalence of intestinal parasitic infection and its associated factors among primary school students in Ethiopia: A systematic review and meta-analysis. PLOS Neglected Trop. Dis. **15**, e0009379 (2021)
14. Siouli, S., Stefa, E., Dratsiou, I., et al.: The effects of creative use of Technology and Drama on primary school students' attitude towards science and science careers. In: International Conference "STEAM Approach in Science Education" (2021)
15. Saputri, H.S., Retnowati, H., Mustadi, A., et al.: Group investigation to improve science at primary school. In: 6th International Seminar on Science Education (ISSE 2020) (2021)

Research on the Teaching Application of the Improved Genetic Algorithm in E-commerce

Sisi Zhang[✉]

SiChuan TOP IT Vocational Institute, Chengdu 611743, Sichuan, China
zss850324@163.com

Abstract. Facing the backward traffic conditions in the western rural areas, based on the analysis of the actual situation of agricultural e-commerce in the western region, the vehicle routing optimization model of agricultural e-commerce is scientifically established. The fitness function and improved selection operation, crossover operation and mutation operation are reasonably selected, the improved genetic algorithm is proposed, and the application value of the proposed algorithm in agricultural product e-commerce is introduced. The simulation results show that compared with genetic algorithm, the improved genetic algorithm uses less iterative steps and has better optimal solution. The model provides the optimal vehicle distribution path for agricultural product e-commerce enterprises or farmers in western rural areas, and improves the service quality of agricultural product e-commerce in western rural areas.

Keywords: E-commerce of agricultural products · Genetic algorithm · Improved genetic algorithm

1 Introduction

With the rapid development of modern information technology, the gradual improvement of e-commerce technology and the popularization and application of network, the development level of e-commerce of agricultural products has been continuously improved with the innovation of cloud computing, information engineering and artificial intelligence. At the same time, e-commerce has also broadened the "last mile" channel for the sales of agricultural products in western rural areas, and provided intellectual support for boosting the targeted poverty alleviation in western rural areas.

In recent years, many scholars have studied and analyzed the development of e-commerce of agricultural products. Chen Jinsong and others analyzed the current situation, existing problems and reasons of e-commerce development of new agricultural business entities in Guizhou, and put forward targeted policy suggestions for the development of e-commerce of agricultural products in Guizhou. On the basis of expounding the development status of rural e-commerce platform, Zhang Daohua and others put forward the construction strategy and development ideas of targeted poverty alleviation

© ICST Institute for Computer Sciences, Social Informatics and Telecommunications Engineering 2023
Published by Springer Nature Switzerland AG 2023. All Rights Reserved
M. A. Jan and F. Khan (Eds.): BigIoT-EDU 2022, LNICST 466, pp. 443–453, 2023.
https://doi.org/10.1007/978-3-031-23947-2_47

e-commerce platform, and analyzed the key technologies of building the platform, in order to achieve high efficiency and high benefit of agricultural production and increase farmers' income [1]. Pei bin uses China's provincial panel data to empirically analyze the impact of e-commerce on rural poverty alleviation and regional differences. These documents mainly analyze the current situation of E - commerce of agricultural products Existing problems and causes Development countermeasures and suggestions, and there are few literatures analyzing the vehicle routing optimization of agricultural e-commerce logistics distribution in Western China. Due to the limited traffic conditions in the western region, the development of e-commerce of agricultural products is restricted, resulting in problems such as untimely vehicle distribution, low efficiency and inadequate connection in the sales of agricultural products in the western rural areas of China. These problems not only increase the transportation cost and time cost of agricultural products sales, but also aggravate the price fluctuation of agricultural products, and directly affect the income of farmers and agricultural e-commerce enterprises. Solving the bottleneck of e-commerce vehicle distribution path of agricultural products has become a livelihood engineering problem related to the people in western rural areas. Therefore, selecting the optimal distribution route of agricultural e-commerce vehicles through intelligent optimization algorithm is one of the important means for farmers and agricultural e-commerce enterprises to save costs, improve service quality and improve revenue -.

2 Related Work

2.1 Overview of Genetic Algorithm

Genetic algorithm is a kind of adaptive global optimization probabilistic search algorithm based on the natural selection and natural genetic mechanism of biology. It was first proposed by Holland of the University of Michigan in the 1970s. The main characteristics of genetic algorithm are that the population search strategy and the information exchange and search between individuals in the population do not depend on gradient information, It is especially suitable for dealing with complex and nonlinear problems that are difficult to be solved by traditional search methods. As a global optimization search algorithm, it is widely used in the fields of combinatorial optimization, machine learning, adaptive control, planning and design and artificial life because of its simplicity, universality, strong adaptability and robustness, and suitable for parallel processing. It is one of the key technologies in Intelligent Computing in the 21st century.

$$\|\Delta x_{k+1}(t)\| \le \| \int_0^t e^{(pk_f+m_2+m_3)(t-\tau)}(m_1\|\Delta u_k(\tau)\| + pd)d\tau \tag{1}$$

Compared with other optimization algorithms, it has the following main characteristics:

(1) Genetic algorithm takes the coding of decision variables as the operation object. Traditional optimization algorithms often directly use the actual value of the decision variable itself for optimization calculation, but genetic algorithm does not

directly take the value of the decision variable, but takes some form of coding of the decision variable as the operation object. Thus, we can learn from the concepts of chromosome and gene in biology and imitate the mechanism of biological genetic and evolutionary mechanism in nature. For some optimization problems without numerical concept or difficult to have numerical concept, but only code concept, such as various combinatorial optimization problems, the coding processing method shows its unique advantages [2].

(2) Genetic algorithm directly takes the value of objective function as search information. Traditional optimization algorithms need not only the value information of the objective function, but also some other auxiliary information such as the derivative information of the objective function to determine the search direction. The genetic algorithm only uses the information of the fitness function value transformed by the objective function value to determine the further search direction and search range, without other auxiliary means such as the derivative information of the objective function.

(3) Genetic algorithm uses the search information of multiple search points at the same time. Traditional optimization algorithms often start the iterative search process of the optimal solution from an initial point in the solution space, but the search information provided by each search point is not much after all, so the search efficiency is not high, and sometimes the search process is even stuck in the local optimal solution. The operation object of genetic algorithm is a group of feasible solutions, not a single feasible solution: there are many search tracks, not one search

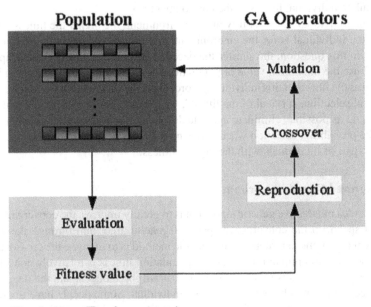

Fig. 1. Genetic algorithm evolution process

track. Therefore, genetic algorithm has good parallelism. The evolution process of genetic algorithm is shown in Fig. 1 below.

The construction of the objective function is usually calculated by the corresponding value of the individual after decoding, and the process of single point crossover, in which the male parent and the female parent reproduce to produce a new individual is called crossover. The offspring obtain the DNA of some male parents and some female parents. In this process, the offspring inherit the excellent characteristics of the previous generation, and finally obtain the optimal solution of the problem in the continuous crossover and mutation.

Usually, the crossover rate is 0.8–1. The specific operation is to randomly select an intersection. One offspring gets the gene of the male parent before the intersection and the gene of the female parent after the intersection, and the other offspring gets the gene of the female parent before the intersection and the gene of the male parent after the intersection.

For example, select the male parent [0.22,0.98,0.34,0.42,0.17] and the female parent [0.55,0.32,0.76,0.23,0.01]

Select the intersection after the second point

The offspring are [0.22,0.98,0.76,0.23,0.01] and [0.55,0.32,0.34,0.42,0.17] respectively. Finally, the offspring are added to the population, and three positions $u < v < w$ are randomly selected from the sequence. After the parts between u and V are removed and inserted into W, this is a means to achieve population diversity and a guarantee to achieve global optimization [2].

Calculate individual fitness in the environment

For the individual's adaptability in the environment, the higher the fitness, the more suitable the individual is for the environment, and the greater the probability of being selected. In this question, the shorter the decoded path is, the stronger the adaptability will be. I use the maximum value of population decoding minus the value of individual decoding as the fitness of this individual. In order to reflect Darwin's natural selection law of "natural selection, survival of the fittest", we should choose individuals with higher fitness as far as possible, eliminate individuals that are not suitable for the environment, and make probability selection when choosing a new population, You can also directly select the part of individuals with the highest fitness.

2.2 Improved Genetic Algorithm

The basic idea of adaptive genetic algorithm is to greatly improve the convergence accuracy and speed up the convergence speed of genetic algorithm through the adaptive adjustment of genetic parameters. The specific method is to increase the crossover probability and mutation probability when the population fitness is relatively concentrated; When the group fitness is relatively scattered, it will be reduced, and the degree of fitness concentration will be measured by the individual. Some people have improved to use the variables of maximum fitness, minimum fitness and average fitness to measure the concentration of group fitness. Based on the above genetic algorithm, an improved genetic algorithm is proposed by reasonably selecting the fitness function and improving the selection, crossover and mutation operations. The proposed algorithm obtains the optimal distribution path between the vehicle distribution center point and the customer demand point of agricultural product e-commerce, and provides the best scheme of vehicle distribution path for agricultural product e-commerce enterprises [3]. The specific steps of the algorithm are as follows:

(1) Information collection. Collect all orders that need to be delivered by e-commerce enterprises of agricultural products in the study area, analyze and sort out customers' distribution needs, and calculate the transportation distance from customers to vehicle distribution center.

(2) Code. According to the characteristics of vehicle distribution related problems, all distribution demand customers are coded according to natural numbers, where 0 represents vehicle distribution center, 1, 2, L represents the customer with distribution demand. Because there are N distribution vehicles in the distribution center, it is assumed that there will be at most 1 distribution paths. Consider adding $n - 1$ virtual vehicle distribution − centers, numbered $L + 1, L + 2, L + n - 1$, together with the distribution center, forms the corresponding N distribution paths.

$$P(t) = E(t) + B(t)L(t)C(t) \tag{2}$$

(3) Initialize the population. An individual from 1 to $L + n - 1$ and other complementary individuals appear randomly. If the population size is m, m individuals are randomly generated, which is the initial population [3].

(4) Fitness function. Firstly, determine whether the vehicle distribution path can meet the constraints. If not, the path is infeasible; Otherwise, it is feasible, and the corresponding objective function value is calculated.

$$\Delta F_{k+1}(t) = \int_0^t Q^{-1}(f(t, x_d(\tau)) - Q^{-1}f(t, x_{k+1}(\tau)))d\tau \tag{3}$$

(5) Select the action. In order to ensure that some individuals with large fitness function can enter the next generation population smoothly, deterministic sampling selection operation is used [4].

(6) Mutation operation. In order to preserve the diversity of individuals in the population, the continuous exchange mutation method is adopted to ensure that the position of each individual in the ranking changes significantly. The process is as follows:

Step 1: select the mutated individuals in the population with the mutation probability, that is, if the mutation probability p occurs, carry out the mutation operation;

Step 2: obtain the corresponding exchange number r by random method;

Step 3: exchange the individuals requiring mutation for R times to obtain new individuals.

(7) The flow of the improved genetic algorithm is shown in Fig. 2.

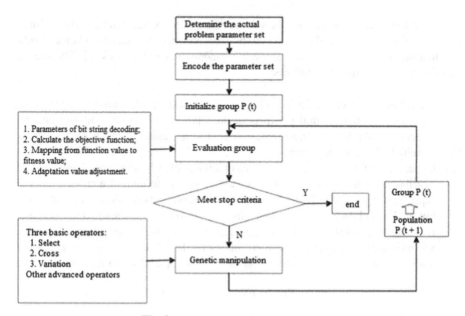

Fig. 2. Improved genetic algorithm flow

3 Research on the Teaching Application of the Improved Genetic Algorithm in E-commerce

What kinds of e-commerce logistics can be divided into? Logistics can be divided into four types: production logistics, sales logistics, procurement logistics and recycling logistics. Retail stores sell goods to customers, which is called sales. So what happens when you look at sales from the standpoint of customers? Customers go to the store to pay for goods, which is not sales, but "purchase" [5].

"Selling" and "buying" these two economic behaviors are carried out at the same time, which is actually the same thing. It also exists in logistics to say the same thing in different languages from different angles. Such as "sales logistics" and "procurement logistics". From the perspective of retail stores, the logistics of the part where the purchased goods are transported from the place of purchase through the company's commodity center or directly to the store belongs to procurement logistics, while from the perspective of manufacturers and wholesalers, because they are shipped to retail stores, they belong to sales logistics. There is also the term "recycling logistics", such as recycling pallets and containers for transportation, accepting customer returns, collecting containers, commodity waste of raw materials and other usual sales flow and reverse logistics ", which is called recycling logistics [6]. But for container recycling operators, this belongs to purchasing logistics and sales logistics.

The logistics distribution route optimization problem can refer to the classic problem in operations research: vehicle routing problem. The iterative process of SGA is shown in Fig. 3 below.

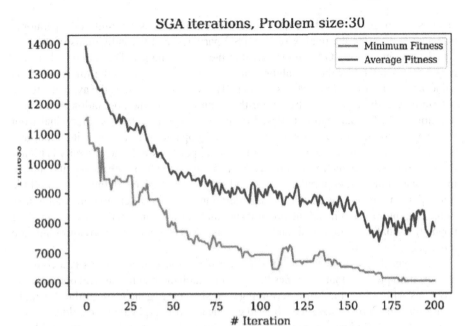

Fig. 3. Iterative process of SGA

Problem, VRP) given a set of vehicles with capacity constraints. A logistics center (or place of supply) · several customers with supply needs, organize appropriate driving routes so that vehicles can pass through all customers in an orderly manner, and meet certain constraints (such as demand, service time limit, vehicle capacity limit, mileage limit, etc.), Achieve certain goals (such as the shortest distance, minimal cost, as little time as possible, as few vehicles as possible, etc.) [7].

2. The vehicle routing problem has been proved to be NP hard, so it is difficult to solve. The existing solutions include heuristic methods such as mileage saving method and scanning method, and intelligent algorithms such as genetic algorithm and particle swarm optimization algorithm.

3. As a classical intelligent algorithm, genetic algorithm has several advantages, such as wide application, strong adaptability, easy to understand the solution idea, easy programming and so on. There are many related research materials, and it is often used in vehicle routing problems;

4. It is suggested to understand the idea of genetic algorithm first, and then choose a programming language (such as MATLAB) to write the solution program in combination with the specific situation of the problem. There are also relevant reference programs on the Internet that can be used for reference. It is best to improve the genetic algorithm from the problem to adapt to the problem and improve the solution quality and accuracy of the algorithm.

The PSO method of e-commerce logistics path based on parallel hybrid genetic algorithm based on dynamic rules, that is, the individuals in the population are regarded as the individuals of GA and PSO at the same time, and PSO is used to update the speed and position of particles. At the same time, the selection crossover mutation operator is executed to evaluate the quality of new PSO particles, and the individuals of the new population obtained by GA are evaluated at the same time [8]. The individuals of the population obtained by the two algorithms are sorted according to the fitness function value, and the average fitness MQ is calculated respectively Based on the average fitness, determine the shares that the two algorithms can obtain in the population in the next iteration, good 0.6 and bad 0.4. Based on the shares, select the best individual from the two new population results to fill the initial population in the next iteration, and use variance to evaluate the diversity of the initial population. If the diversity is higher than the minimum diversity threshold, enter the next iteration, Otherwise, the unique individuals in the parent population are randomly selected based on the share to fill the initial population, and then enter the next iteration. After each iteration, the individuals of the current population and the previous populations are compared to see whether the population quality is improved, and the relevant parameters of the two algorithms are moderately modified.

The hybrid genetic algorithm (nhga) with inexact search conditions is a complex optimization problem that combines the inexact search method in classical optimization problems with the method of determining step size under genetic algorithm for multi peak value [9]; Combined with the hybrid genetic algorithm (ghga) of the golden section method, that is, the local search operation of the golden section is combined with the e-commerce logistics path under the genetic algorithm to construct a new e-commerce logistics path under the hybrid genetic algorithm, so as to solve the unconstrained high-dimensional optimization problem; The hybrid genetic algorithm (fhga) combined with screening method is used to solve constrained optimization problems [10]. The basic idea is to combine the screening method in classical optimization problems with genetic algorithm to solve complex optimization problems with constraints.

4   Experimental Simulation

Under the traditional logistics pattern, inventory and orders are one-way, and there is no communication between the buyer and the seller. In B2C e-commerce logistics, inventory and orders are interactive, and customers can monitor and even modify inventory and orders in real time. Manufacturers and retailers can also adjust inventory and orders at any time according to the different requirements of customers, so as to optimize logistics performance.

For the traditional logistics model, it is often unable to match the cargo displacement information at the first time, especially the information of scattered customers, plus the lack of differentiated personalized service function. Under the traditional logistics mode, due to the lack of information, it is impossible to obtain the information of commodity flow process in time, especially the information of scattered customers, and the lack of personalized service function matching, so it can only provide centralized batch distribution and non differentiated services [11].

However, B2C e-commerce logistics is to carry out the flow of goods according to the personalized needs of customers. It not only needs to achieve the lowest transportation cost through centralized transportation, but also relies on differentiated distribution to improve the quality of logistics services. Because of the above points, its distribution destinations are also decentralized.The simulation experiment is carried out in Windows 7 0 Intel (R) Celeron (R) CPU g1820 2.70 ghz memory (RAM) 4.00 GB and MAT-LAB 2014a platform [12]. Assuming that there is only one e-commerce vehicle distribution center for agricultural products in a rural area in the west, within a certain period of time, the vehicle distribution demand orders of 20 customers, 40 customers, 80 customers and 200 customers are received respectively. The population crossover rate is 0.95, the variation rate is 0.05, the maximum driving distance of vehicles at one time is 60km, the maximum number of iterations is 200, and the penalty coefficient is w = 1000.

The improved genetic algorithm uses fewer iterations than the genetic algorithm, and the average optimal value and optimal result are better than the genetic algorithm, which shows that the improved genetic algorithm can reduce the vehicle distribution distance, reduce the transportation cost, increase the income of e-commerce of agricultural products and improve the service quality of e-commerce [13]. Therefore, the improved genetic algorithm can obtain the satisfactory solution of the vehicle distribution path optimization problem of agricultural products e-commerce in a certain region, that is, the improved genetic algorithm can effectively realize the vehicle distribution path optimization [14].

Figure 4 shows that compared with genetic algorithm, the improved genetic algorithm not only has less convergence time and average iteration times, but also the improved algorithm is more stable. Figure 5 shows that the improved genetic algorithm not only has better optimal value than genetic algorithm, but also has better convergence effect. Therefore, the improved genetic algorithm can make the vehicle distribution path of agricultural e-commerce in this area more reasonable, reduce the transportation cost and increase the income of agricultural e-commerce enterprises or farmers.

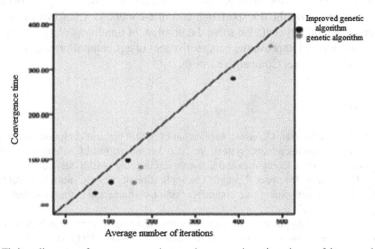

Fig. 4. Fitting diagram of convergence time and average iteration times of improved genetic algorithm and genetic algorithm

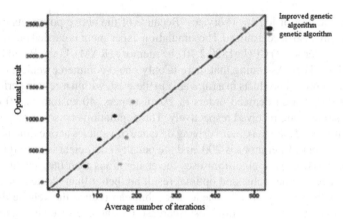

Fig. 5. Fitting diagram of optimal results and average iteration times of improved genetic algorithm and genetic algorithm

5 Conclusion

Vehicle distribution route optimization is not only the key problem to solve the timeliness of e-commerce transportation of agricultural products, but also a difficult problem to realize. According to the actual situation of western rural areas, the author establishes a simple mathematical model, combined with the improved genetic algorithm, studies the vehicle logistics distribution problem of agricultural product e-commerce in a certain - region, and obtains a more feasible and effective optimal solution than the traditional algorithm. The simulation experiments show that the improved genetic algorithm is an algorithm with stable performance and strong search ability. The application of this algorithm can not only save the transportation cost of e-commerce enterprises and improve customer service quality, but also solve the problem of timeliness of agricultural product transportation and improve the competitiveness of agricultural product e-commerce enterprises in the market Competitiveness in.

References

1. Huang, S., Liu, J., Zhu, D., et al.: Application of multi-objective evolutionary algorithm in E-commerce recommendation system. In: 2020 3rd International Conference on Advanced Electronic Materials, Computers and Software Engineering (AEMCSE) (2020)
2. Edy, I.C., Riyanto, Marsono, S., et al.: The application of the ABC attitude model to online purchasing decisions (Study on e-commerce fashion consumers in Indonesia). Tech. Soc. Sci. J. **26**, 616–635 (2021)
3. Oh, K., Lee, S.H.: Application of home economics teaching-learning plan in the clothing for teenager's empowerment. J. Korean Home Econ. Educ. Assoc. **33**(1), 169–185 (2021)
4. Zhang, Y.: Research on the application of micro-classes in higher vocational English teaching. Adv. High. Educ. **4**(8) (2020)
5. Fu, S., Wang, L., Du, Y, et al.: Application of improved NSGA-II algorithm in matching optimization for tractor powertrain. In: 2020 ASABE Annual International Virtual Meeting (July 13–15, 2020)

6. Wulan, E., Apriani, N.: The application of genetic algorithm in solving traveling sales-man problem. In: Proceedings of the 1st International Conference on Islam, Science and Technology, ICONISTECH 2019, 11–12 July 2019, Bandung, Indonesia (2020)
7. Ma, Z.: Application of information-based education technology to physics teaching in the internet era. J. Phys.: Conf. Ser. 1648:042016- (2020)
8. Yuliana, A.S., Parno, Taufiq, A.: Application of teaching materials based on 7E-STEM learning cycle to improve student's problem solving skills. In: 28th Russian Conference on Mathematical Modelling in Natural Sciences (2020)
9. Bobobekov, S.R.: About teaching students an improved method of applying a block-based encryption algorithm based on the feistel network. ACADEMICIA Int. Multidiscip. Res. J. **10**(5), 1398 (2020)
10. Ding, H, Wang, Z., Li, B., et al.: The application and improvement of S-P chart method in teaching evaluation. In: 2020 International Conference on Social Science, Economics and Education Research (SSEER 2020) (2020)
11. Kaddour, B., Bensikaddour, H.: The Application of some Modern Teaching Strategies as a Guide for the Detection of Excellent 9–10 Years Old Students in the Psychomotor Domain (2020)
12. Pu, Y.X., Feng, Y.J., Yu, Q.: Research on the application of a high-dimensional Bayesian net-work in the evaluation of Ethnic-Chinese bilingual teaching. In: 2020 IEEE 2nd International Conference on Computer Science and Educational Informatization (CSEI). IEEE (2020)
13. Zhang, H., Zhang, M., Meng, F.C., et al.: Application of the online judge technology in programming experimental teaching. In: 2020 5th International Conference on Modern Management and Education Technology (MMET 2020) (2020)
14. Huang, F., Lu, Q.: An application study of the implicit hierarchy interactive and self-inquired mode in English reading teaching in inland ethnic mixed class. Educ. Study **2**(4), 225–240 (2020)

Construction of a Mathematical Model Based on the Big Data Information Platform

Lei Huang(✉), Yan Wang, and Li Zhang

School of Zhenjiang, Jiangsu Union Technical Institute, Zhenjiang 212016, Jiangsu, China
appleflowercici@126.com

Abstract. The improved genetic algorithm is designed for the problem of data redundancy in genetic algorithms, and is combined with the least squares method to construct a computer mathematical model to cope with real-time changes in data. The results show that the improved genetic algorithm has high recognition ability and the ability to find the optimal solution, and improves the efficiency and quality of operation to a certain extent. The simulation results show that the computer mathematical model based on the improved genetic algorithm and the least square method greatly expands the search space and improves the operation efficiency.

Keywords: Improved genetic algorithm · Least squares · Mathematical model

1 Introduction

With the rapid development of computer science, mathematical methods and methods, they are widely used in natural science and play an important role in social science. Mathematical technology is also an important part of high technology from basic mathematics. In many mathematical analytical methods, mathematical models are often closely related to practical problems [1]. In general, mathematics models are not direct copies of real problems, but deep observation and analysis of problems, using a large range of mathematical theory and knowledge. In this process, we first built systems models and experimented with familiar models in most cases. Fakte, la model a solvo estas bazita sur la konata sistemmodela strukturo per matematika teorio kaj teknologio por konstrui funkcionalan rilaton kaj estimi la modelan parametrojn laux la enigi kaj eligi datumoj de la sistemo. Estimating the model of parameters relative to data and curves [2]. The experimental error is closely related to the analysis. The key here is the application of the smallest square method. The least square method is the most commonly used method for synthesizing data and the main method for observation data research. It can observe multiple iterations of two variables to ensure the accuracy of data [3].

Genetic algorithms, on the other hand, are evolutionary algorithms that select populations by mimicking the doctrine of species selection and Darwin's laws of evolution in order to optimise them by random search. Genetic algorithms, are more robust and have

M. A. Jan and F. Khan (Eds.): BigIoT-EDU 2022, LNICST 466, pp. 454–462, 2023.
https://doi.org/10.1007/978-3-031-23947-2_48

general-purpose models, which have been widely used in many fields such as function optimisation, and have achieved significant results [4].

We build a big data information platform, as shown in Fig. 1. We take Huawei cloud as an example.

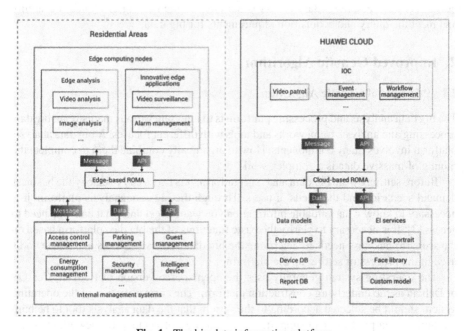

Fig. 1. The big data information platform

Big data information platform is a network platform that provides services through content sharing, resource sharing, channel co constrco-construction sharing. Build a basic data center for the enterprise, build a unified data storage system for the enterprise, conduct unified data modeling, and lay a foundation for the value presentation of data. At the same time, the data processing capacity sinks, and a centralized data processing center is built to provide strong data processing capacity; Ensure thEnsuringle operation of the system through a unified data management and monitoring system. With a data basedatabase unified BI application center to meet business needs and reflect data value [5].

When you mention big data, you will mention Hadoop. Big data is not the same as Hadoop, but Hadoop is indeed the most popular big data technology.

As the message management layer of the unified collection platform, Kafka can flexibly connect and adapt various data source collections (such as integrated flume), providing flexible and configurable data collection capabilities.

Using spark and Hadoop technology, build the storage and processing capacity center of basic data, which is the core of the big data platform, to provide strong data processing capacity and meet the data interaction needs. At the same time, spark streaming can effectively meet the requirements of enterprise real-time data and build a real-time index system for enterprise development [6].

At the same time, in order to better meet the data acquisition needs of enterprises, RDBMS provides highly summarized statistical data of enterprises, meets the regular statistical report needs of enterprises, and reduces the use threshold. For big data detail query requirements, the HBase cluster is built to provide fast big data query capability and meet the query and acquisition requirements for big data.

2 Improved Genetic Algorithm

2.1 Principle of Genetic Algorithm

The big data analysis and processing platform is to integrate various mainstream big data processing and analysis frameworks and tools with different focuses. A big data analysis platform involves many components. How to organically combine them to complete the mining of massive data is a complex work.

Before setting up the big data analysis platform, it is necessary to clarify the business demand scenarios and the needs of users. Through the big data analysis platform, it is necessary to know what valuable information you want to get and what data you need to access [7]. It is necessary to clarify the basic functions of the big data platform based on the scenario business needs to determine the big data processing tools and frameworks used in the process of setting up the platform.

The operating system generally uses the open source version of RedHat, CentOS or Debian as the underlying construction platform. The correct version of the operating system should be selected according to the system that the data analysis tool to be built on the big data platform can support.The core design of Hadoop framework is HDFS and MapReduce:

HDFS is a highly fault-tolerant system, which is suitable for deployment on cheap machines and can provide high-throughput data access. It is suitable for applications with large data sets.

MapReduce is a programming model that can extract data from a large amount of data and finally return the result set.

In production practice, Hadoop is very suitable for big data storage and big data analysis applications. It is suitable for cluster operation serving thousands to tens of thousands of large servers, and supports Pb level storage capacity.

The Hadoop family also includes various open source components, such as Yan, zookeeper, HBase, hive, sqoop, impala, spark, etc. The advantages of using open source components are obvious. Active communities will constantly update component versions iteratively, and many people will use them. Problems will be easier to solve. At the same time, the code is open source, and high-level data development engineers can modify the code in combination with their own project needs to better serve the project.

As an important part of an evolutionary computer, genetic algorithm has been very interested in students over the past few years and is enjoyable in January. Unlike traditional search algorithm, genetic algorithm begins the search process of randomly created original solution (called population). Ĉiu individuo en la populacio estas nomata chromosomo kaj estas la solvo de la problemo. These chromosomes evolve in the following substitutions called genetics. The general algorithm is considered to be transversal, mutation and selection. The next generation of chromosomes created by cross or mutation is called offspring. This is used to evaluate chromosome's advances. After many generations, algorithm converses to the optimal chromosome. This may be the optimal or next optimal solution of the problem [8]. The concept of convenience in genetic algorithm is used to assess the possibility of all individuals in the population to get the best results in the calculation of optimization. The function measuring individual compatibility is called compatibility. The definition of the convention function is generally related to the concrete solution to the problem. The basic genetic algorithm pages are shown in Fig. 2.

Aiming at the premature convergence problem of IAGA adaptive genetic algorithm, an improved adaptive genetic algorithm (niaga algorithm) is proposed. According to the user-defined discriminant, it can judge whether the population has the trend of premature convergence. According to different situations, two methods, macro-control and micro processing, are used to set the crossover probability PC and mutation probability PM, so as to make the algorithm get rid of premature convergence Simulation results show that the new algorithm effectively improves the premature convergence of IAGA algorithm and shows stronger global convergence.

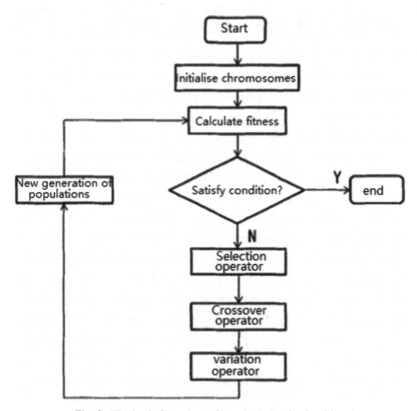

Fig. 2. The basic flow chart of standard genetic algorithm

2.2 Analysis of Improved Genetic Algorithms

Genetic algorithm through the principle of genetics, following the biological genetic evolutionary variation and crossover mechanism, global search for practical problems to obtain the basic genetic algorithm, that is, to improve the important premise of into the transmission algorithm, the specific process is shown in Fig. 3.

Randomness is a key property of genetic algorithms, in which crossover and variation probabilities are set reasonably important and closely related to genetic algorithm performance. Therefore, improving the genetic algorithm can lead to a faster convergence rate. Function optimisation is an important component of genetic algorithms. Given an objective function, the optimal value is sought through the solution space, based on unconstrained conditions. The Rastrigin function is used as a test vehicle to analyse in detail the mechanisms influencing the convergence of crossover and variation probabilities. As the algorithm runs, the crossover and variation moderately expand the search area [9]. At the end of the run, the search area needs to be strictly controlled based on the protection of the specific position of the individuals, and the optimal value can be obtained if the cluster with relatively high mean fitness can be sought during the initial run of the algorithm. In order to maximise the preservation of the optimal individuals, it is necessary to increase the speed of convergence during the iterations to ensure that the optimal solution is found before the maximum value of the mean fitness is obtained.

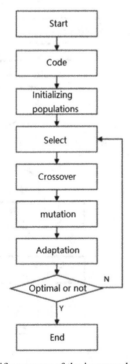

Fig. 3. The specific process of the improved genetic algorithm

3   Improved Genetic Algorithm and Least Squares

3.1   Least Squares Analysis

Least squares is a mathematical optimisation technique that is a fundamental machine learning algorithm, i.e. the least square method, which seeks the best matching function for known data by minimising the sum of squares of errors, facilitating access to unknown data, and minimising the sum of squares of errors between the data and the measured data. In addition, least squares can be transferred from a linear fit to a curve fit, i.e. linear regression to non-linear regression.

Suppose there are m data points, $(x_w,y_v)(w = 1,2,3...,m)$ roughly in line with the linear function, then you can set the linear function that: $y = fx + g$. f and g represent the constant term to be determined, in the coordinate chart tracing out the data points, generally they are not exactly in the same line, this expectation can be found a straight line, to ensure that its deviation from all data points The deviation from all data points is very small. For this purpose, a reasonable choice of the appropriate constant terms f and g can be considered in order to achieve the minimum state.

The method of selecting the constant terms in this way is based on the condition that the sum of the squared deviations of the m terms is minimised, i.e. the least square method, i.e. the least squares method.

In practice, the deviations cancel each other out if the sums are not squared but are one-time squares [10]. If absolute values are added, and there is a correlation between how absolute values are turned on, then the sum of squares of the deviations of the data points from the line is chosen as the result of the comparison. In terms of geometric intuition, after plotting the data points in the coordinates, a number of lines close to the data points can be drawn correspondingly, where the criteria for assessing the best line, i.e. based on the previous analysis, are refined by calculus.

3.2   Improved Genetic Algorithms Combined with Least Squares

Help with the problem of data redundancy in the basic genetic algorithm is an improved genetic algorithm. The algorithm combines the smallest quadratic method to build a computer mathematical model to better handle data changes. The results show that the improved genetic algorithm has a certain ability to recognize it, can find the best result and improve the work efficiency. Use atlas software to solve the equation, determine the use range of parameters, and solve the problem of parameter value range and identification. The results of the simulation show that the improved genetic algorithm and the smaller square method are combined to build a mathematical model. Compared to the basic genetic algorithm, the individual search space is large and the operation increases by 90%.

The combination of improved genetic algorithms and least squares is in fact a combination of improved genetic algorithms and discrimination methods which, when combined, results in relatively more effective new methods for solving discrimination problems, which play a key role in the implementation of industrial processes and in the design of industrial control systems. The improved part of the Improved Genetic Algorithm is oriented towards optimising the genetic coding operation, which improves operability, facilitates crossover, is relatively simple and convenient, and not only reduces the length of the matrix coding to a certain extent, but also reduces it moderately, thus speeding up the operation. The matrix coding of the improved genetic algorithm is more closely integrated with the Matlab language, which facilitates the implementation of simulation and programming. In short, the matrix coding genetic algorithm is already a major breakthrough in genetic algorithms in terms of content and role transformation.

4   Mathematical Model Construction Based on Improved Genetic Algorithms

4.1   Problem Formulation

An improved genetic algorithm is based on the search for an optimal solution, which is based on the discriminatory ability to obtain the relevant parameters. The discriminative model is specifically:

$$y(t) = -f_1 y(t-1) - \ldots - f_m y(t-1) + g_1 k(t-1) + \ldots + g_m k(t-1) + \gamma(t) \quad (1)$$

By combining the most improved genetic algorithm with the least squares method to solve the parameters, the improved genetic algorithm is one of the most commonly used methods for solving the discrimination.

4.2   Building the Model and Simulation Analysis

First, define the quality of the matrix, then define the matrix by the number of parameters. If the number of parameters is greater than 6, the matrix distribution model is defined and the corresponding parameters are defined by several elements. When the specific search interval is defined, the search interval is defined according to the improved genetic algorithm, the used interval is defined for the actual problem, and the estimate interval and the discrimination problem are defined according to the specific circumstances of the measurement date. And again, the fitness of the individuals is assessed, Based on the least squares method, it was found that:

$$L = \sum \left[y(t) - \lambda^K(t)\beta \right]^2 \quad (2)$$

L reprezentas la diferencon inter la eksperimenta estima valoro kaj la mezurita valoro, kaj la plej malgranda grupo estas elektita per la eligaj kvalitajn datumoj.

In combination with the improved genetic algorithm, the difference between the value of the parameter and the measured value can be effectively solved on the basis of the genetic algorithm, and the key to open the function of the genetic algorithm can be solved. Its:

$$u(x) = \frac{1}{L} = \frac{1}{\sum \left[y(t) - \lambda^K(t)\beta \right]^2} \quad (3)$$

Finally, in order to avoid the loss of mutation and the change of the parent column, we can directly enter the child in place of the transition and mutation, and use the improved genetic algorithm to quickly and precisely reach the global optimal solution, but we need to build the transversal function and the probability of mutation.

Because there are too many parameters in the calculation, problem identification will generate growth codes and use intersections of the intersections of the intersections of the search space sections. Tio povas kalkuli per du aŭ pli da intersekcioj. The whole process needs to be acquired based on genetic algorithm. The circle and the mutated population have a huge range of searches for individuals who can achieve maximum optimisation.

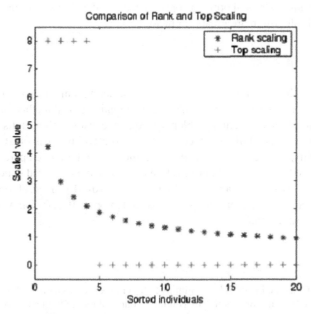

Fig. 4. The companison of rank and top scaling

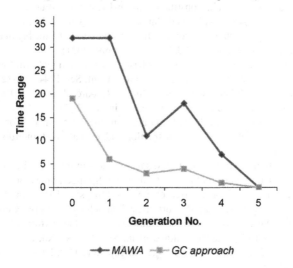

Fig. 5. Compare analysis

Through Figs. 4 and 5, we can see that the traditional genetic algorithm is prone to problems such as low search efficiency, falling into local extremum, instability, etc. in the process of computer mathematical modeling. This paper proposes an improved genetic algorithm in computer mathematical modeling The improved algorithm can use the fitness of an evolutionary population to disperse the values of nonlinear adaptive operation flow, mutation probability and crossover probability, so as to generate a new individual to search for the global optimal solution without local extreme value, and use the optimal preservation strategy to ensure the convergence of the improved adaptive genetic algorithm The global optimal convergence speed, solution accuracy and optimal solution of this algorithm are greatly improved.

5   Conclusion

In summary, mathematical modelling means constructing a mathematical model based on a specific problem, solving the model through mathematical methods and computer tools, and then solving the actual problem based on the results. The results show that the improved genetic algorithm, as a modern advanced algorithm, has outstanding global search capability, simple and clear coding techniques and heritable operation methods, and is less limited at the level of optimization problems; the improved genetic algorithm has a strong discriminatory ability and can The improved genetic algorithm is more discriminative and can seek optimal solutions, and improve the efficiency and quality of operations to a large extent.

References

1. Cheng, J.: Construction of School Administration Platform Based on SAAS Model (2022)
2. Wang, J., Li, W.: The construction of a digital resource library of English for higher education based on a cloud platform. Sci. Program. **2021**, 1–12 (2021)
3. Zhang, K., Gao, J., Li, S., et al.: Construction of a pH-responsive drug delivery platform based on the hybrid of mesoporous silica and chitosan. J. Saudi Chem. Soc. **25**(1), 101174 (2021)
4. Ma, Q., Yang, Y.: Research on the construction of smart cities by the big data platform of the blockchain. J. Phys.: Conf. Ser. **1883**(1), 012144 (6pp) (2021)
5. Guo, S.: On the construction of a computer-based examination platform for the introduction of basic principles of marxism in colleges. J. Phys: Conf. Ser. **1744**(3), 032225 (2021)
6. Wang, J., Li, W.: The Construction of a Digital Resource Library of English for Higher Education Based on a Cloud Platform. Hindawi Limited (2021)
7. Sundar, N., Arulalan, A.S.A., Priya, R., et al.: A mathematical model for cost budget optimization in the early stage of house construction budget analysis. J. Interdiscip. Math. **25**(3), 839–849 (2022)
8. Ba, Y.: Construction of clothing pattern database platform based on digital color matching. In: International Conference on Frontier Computing. Springer, Singapore (2021)
9. Xiaoying, F., Xiaoli, X.: Construction of a Multi-dimensional Dynamic College Students' Innovation and Entrepreneurship Platform Based on School-Enterprise Cooperation (2022)
10. Luo, Y., Wan, J., She, S.: The construction and research of the platform of intelligent sharing laboratory based on big data. In: Atiquzzaman, M., Yen, N., Xu, Z. (eds.) BDCPS 2021. LNDECT, vol. 102, pp. 587–594. Springer, Singapore (2022). https://doi.org/10.1007/978-981-16-7466-2_65

Construction and Development of Chemistry Teaching Platform in Higher Vocational Colleges Under the Background of Artificial Intelligence

Yiping Wang[✉] and Wei Li

Yichun Vocational Technical College, Yichun 3336000, Jiangxi, China
yxjcb888@163.com

Abstract. Artificial intelligence technology has set off a wave of industrial clusters in digital economy, accelerated the evolution of social industries and occupations, and promoted the transformation and upgrading of higher vocational colleges. Under the background of artificial intelligence, the teaching of chemistry teaching platform in higher vocational colleges, as a new teaching form, has become a hot issue of network teaching. Starting with the characteristics of network teaching in higher vocational colleges, this paper gives a construction and system management mode of chemistry teaching resource platform in higher vocational colleges; This paper analyzes how teachers and students share teaching and learning through this platform; Try to solve the double problems of teaching resource construction and management of chemistry teaching platform software.

Keywords: Artificial intelligence · Higher vocational colleges · Chemistry teaching platform

1 Introduction

The era of artificial intelligence information technology driven by big data has triggered sudden changes in economic industries. The construction of digital economy industrial clusters such as Internet of things, big data and artificial intelligence has boosted the high-quality development of electronic information, equipment manufacturing, biomedicine and other industries. There is no doubt that artificial intelligence is accelerating the challenge of our production, life, learning and other fields, and education is naturally impossible to stay out. In July 2017, the State Council issued the development plan for a new generation of artificial intelligence, which clearly proposed that colleges and universities should improve the artificial intelligence education system. As higher vocational colleges cultivating high-quality skilled professionals, they must improve the new construction of practical teaching platform as soon as possible, strengthen practical teaching, innovate talent training mode and improve talent training quality, Take on the important task of talent training entrusted by modern vocational education.

With the development of network technology and the popularization of computer education, network teaching is more and more widely used. Using the network can

M. A. Jan and F. Khan (Eds.): BigIoT-EDU 2022, LNICST 466, pp. 463–471, 2023.
https://doi.org/10.1007/978-3-031-23947-2_49

easily obtain multi-channel information, communicate with pictures and texts across space, and share resources conveniently and effectively. The network teaching platform makes full use of the latest research results in the field of modern it and organically integrates advanced education and teaching ideas with computer network technology [1]. Building an advanced, characteristic and open intelligent education and teaching information resource platform, enhancing students' interest in learning, and strengthening the communication between teachers and students will play a positive role in promoting the sustainable development of the school, the overall improvement of students' comprehensive quality and the cultivation of students' innovative ability.

Under the background of the new curriculum reform, the educational goal of our country has become to cultivate talents with all-round development, so teaching innovation is very important. The important task of higher vocational colleges is to train new workers and builders needed by the country. The traditional teaching mode has been unable to achieve the above tasks and objectives. The innovation of Chemistry Teaching in higher vocational colleges is an innovation aimed at students, which can ensure the subjectivity of students. In addition to paying attention to the teaching of basic knowledge, it also pays attention to students' interest in learning and future employment, which has a far-reaching impact on their long-term development.

There are some differences between general education and higher vocational education. Their training directions are different. The former pays more attention to the training of academic talents, while the latter pays more attention to the training of applied talents. However, in practice teaching, chemistry teachers in higher vocational colleges only pay attention to the academic needs of the school, ignoring the sustainable development of students. In addition, chemistry is inseparable from experiment and exploration, especially for the chemistry major in higher vocational colleges, it needs the support of experiment. However, many teachers do not pay much attention to the experimental classroom and ignore the students' dominant position in the classroom, which makes it difficult for many students to effectively acquire the corresponding chemical knowledge and ability.

2   Importance of Chemistry Teaching Platform in Higher Vocational Colleges

2.1   Improving the Chemistry Teaching Platform is a Prerequisite for Cultivating High-Quality Skilled Professionals

The transformation and upgrading of China's economy, especially the adjustment of industrial structure, has greatly increased the demand for high-quality workers with applied technology and skills. They are required to have high skills and high quality required by the front line of production, construction, service and management in various industries or fields. Relying on traditional teaching methods, means and approaches, students can only understand the technologies in various industries or fields, and most of these technologies stay at the theoretical level and can not be converted into productive forces; To really cultivate high-quality skilled professionals needed by various industries or fields of society, we must also rely on a perfect practical teaching platform. Only a perfect chemistry teaching platform can enable students to put the learned technical knowledge into practice, test and test in experimental training, repeatedly train, experience and improve in production training and social practice, truly transform technology into skills, improve professional quality and cultivate creative innovation ability.

2.2   A Perfect Practical Teaching Platform is the Cornerstone of the Survival and Development of Higher Vocational Colleges

As a new type of education, the orientation of vocational education has brought great attention to the development of modern vocational education and the development spring of higher vocational education. Whether higher vocational colleges can shoulder the historical mission entrusted by modern vocational education, cultivate high-quality workers with applied technology and skills needed by the production line of various industries in social development, and stand out in many higher vocational colleges, in addition to the basic school running concept and school running mode, they must have a practical teaching platform to adapt to the development of modern vocational education. A perfect practical teaching platform is a training platform for students' professional quality and a training stage for professional ability. It is an important measure for higher vocational colleges to highlight their school running characteristics and improve teaching quality. Whether the professional quality and professional ability of students trained by a higher vocational college are high or not depends on the perfection of the school's practical teaching platform and the situation of practical teaching, which is also the key to whether the school can let students choose to accept, industry recognition and social approval, and is the cornerstone of the survival and development of higher vocational schools.

2.3   The Perfect Practical Teaching Platform is the Booster for Higher Vocational College Teachers to Improve Their Educational Skills

The core of talent training in higher vocational colleges is to vigorously promote the combination of work and study, highlight the cultivation of students' practical ability, and improve students' professional quality and professional ability. A perfect practical teaching platform can urge teachers to strengthen the idea of cultivating students' professional ability and professional quality, so as to cultivate students' professional quality, train students' professional skills and let students create innovation in practice. A perfect practical teaching platform can help teachers strengthen their professional skills and professional quality, promote teachers to train repeatedly in operation, process and production practice, improve their professional skills, especially systematic skills and innovation skills in the industry field, and further improve their professional quality. A perfect practical teaching platform is the guarantee for teachers to improve their professional teaching skills, Teachers can experience it in practice, understand it in operation, and understand the relationship and skills of doing, learning and teaching, so that teachers can be familiar with teaching, improvement and innovation in production, so as to realize education in practice and service industry in production [2].

In order to undertake the historical mission entrusted by modern vocational education, promote the reform of talent training mode, realize the practicality, openness and professionalism of teaching process, and truly integrate "teaching, learning and doing", higher vocational colleges must improve the new construction of practical teaching platform.

3 Construction of Chemistry Teaching Platform System in Higher Vocational Colleges

The main goal of this platform is to facilitate teachers' teaching work, meet students' learning needs, and strengthen the communication between teachers and students. The key point of the design is that the platform is required to have strong flexibility, and the module and function layout can be easily adjusted according to the change of demand. This adjustment should be as simple and easy as possible, which is completely separated from the underlying code. Platform managers can adjust the functions of the platform without holding the database and programming language.

3.1 System Structure Design

At present, the framework of many domestic teaching systems is fixed after they are designed and implemented. When the requirements change and the functional modules of the system need to be expanded or the system framework needs to be modified, professional programmers are often required to make a lot of modifications to the program code and database, and further debugging and testing are required after modification. The whole process is time-consuming, labor-consuming and money consuming. The biggest feature of this platform is that it breaks through the limitations of the functional modules of the previous network teaching platform and the operation complexity when modifying the platform, gets rid of the traditional bottom code modification system, and instead establishes the management platform of the network teaching system, and directly uses the management platform as a tool to modify the functions and framework of the application platform safely and quickly [3]. The whole process does not need to understand the program code, and the functions and modules of the application platform can be modified through the multi-layer dialog mode of the management platform.

As shown in Fig. 1, the system is divided into two parts: management platform and application platform. The management platform is the bottom control mechanism of the other two platforms. Entering the management platform, you can adjust the basic function modules, frameworks, service parameters and user permissions of the application platform. Application platform is divided into teacher work platform and student learning platform. The two platforms are closely related and contain the transmission of a variety of information flows. The application platform is a space for users to work and learn. It pays attention to the analysis of teaching objectives and teaching contents, the design of various resources, the use of various resources to support "learning" and the day of "learning". It should pay attention to the design of collaborative learning environment and the design of network-based teaching strategies. The organization of content is based on Web pages with good navigation structure, and according to the cognitive law of students. Organize and describe the content.

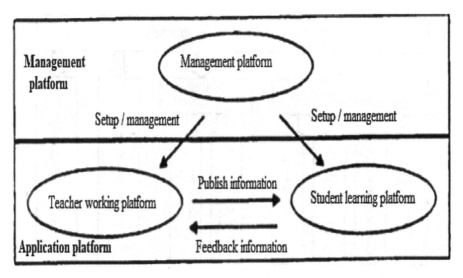

Fig. 1. Structure diagram of network teaching platform

3.2 System Function Requirement Analysis

Since the users of the platform are teachers and students, and the management platform is a tool for system maintenance personnel to manage the application platform, the demand analyst of the system function should analyze the application platform. The main functions are as follows:

(1) When there is a network, you can enter the system anytime and anywhere for work and learning.
(2) There are different user interfaces. After logging in, the teacher user enters the classroom working platform to add, delete, modify and check the courseware and exercise library. After logging in, the student user enters the student space to browse the courseware and solve the exercises.
(3) Teachers can add, modify or delete the teaching student table columns, and set students' browsing permissions.
(4) Teachers can select test questions to form test papers in the system or generate test papers intelligently by the system and publish them to students within a certain time limit.
(5) Students can ask questions about this course on the network platform and teachers can answer them.
(6) Students can evaluate and grade teachers' teaching and leave comments and suggestions.

The system structure is shown in Fig. 2.

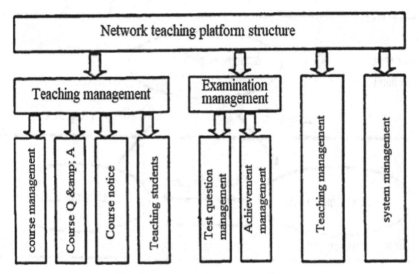

Fig. 2. System design structure diagram

4   Improve the Practical Teaching Platform

In order to meet the needs of the development of modern vocational education and undertake the training of a large number of high-quality workers with applied technology and skills required by various industries of the society in economic transformation and upgrading, higher vocational colleges must rebuild a perfect practical teaching platform.

4.1   Clean Up the Existing Practical Teaching Platform

According to the needs of economic transformation and upgrading, higher vocational colleges should revise the training plan of professional talents, clarify the applied technologies and skills that high-quality workers in various professional fields must master, and formulate a practical training platform for these technical skills, so as to ensure the training of teachers and students' professional quality and practical training of technical skills. On this basis, higher vocational colleges should clean up the existing practical teaching conditions, make clear what professional and technical skills can be trained in the on campus training room and training base, and what professional and technical skills can be trained in the off campus training base, and make clear what technical skills can not be trained or can not be trained in place at present, Clear the shortcomings of the existing practical teaching conditions, so as to strengthen the new construction of the practical teaching platform.

4.2   Some Notes on the Construction of Practical Teaching Platform in Higher Vocational Colleges

When constructing the practical teaching platform, higher vocational colleges should adhere to the principles of economy, efficiency and full coverage. First, based on the existing practice and training conditions, higher vocational colleges should strengthen the new construction of practical teaching platform, so as to fully cover the practical training of professional and technical skills. The second is to strengthen the breadth and depth of school enterprise cooperation, such as through joint technology development between schools and enterprises, joint application for scientific research topics, allowing professional backbone teachers to work as part-time production technology consultants for industrial enterprises, so as to improve the tightness of school enterprise cooperation, give full play to the role of enterprises in the cultivation of highly skilled talents, benefit enterprises and form a win-win model between schools and enterprises. Third, we should pay attention to the complementarity of the construction of practical teaching platform inside and outside the school [4]. The basic skills and system operation skills of production processes with strong universality, high frequency of use and low operation cost of each specialty are guaranteed by a perfect on-campus practical teaching platform, and the practical training of production facilities and equipment necessary for large, heavy, poor universality and industrial enterprises is guaranteed by establishing off-campus practical training bases, Ensure that the professional technical skills and professional quality required by industrial enterprises are comprehensively cultivated and systematically trained, and ensure the training quality of high-quality workers with applied technology and skills.

The biggest difference between cooperative teaching and ordinary teaching mode is that it changes the situation of students' "fighting alone", makes a scene of "group English communication" in the classroom, and is conducive to the accumulation of students' wisdom. No matter in the theoretical class or the experimental class, the chemistry teachers in higher vocational colleges can use the method of group cooperation to carry out teaching activities, so as to encourage students to fully show themselves through cooperative methods, cultivate their learning self-confidence, and lay a solid foundation for their future study and life.

For example, when teaching the "buffer solution" section, the chemistry teachers in Higher Vocational Colleges first dropped dilute hydrochloric acid and sodium hydroxide into dilute hydrochloric acid of a certain concentration, and the students observed that the pH value of the solution changed greatly. Then, the teacher replaced diluted hydrochloric acid with acetic acid of the same concentration and volume to conduct the experiment again. At this time, the students observed that the pH value of the solution did not change much. At this time, the teacher divides the students into groups to carry out discussion activities, and carefully analyzes the reasons for the two different phenomena. After the students' discussion, the teacher can introduce the concept, composition and principle of buffer solution. After explaining the buffer mechanism, teachers can encourage students to discuss the solution concentration of ammonia and ammonium chloride in groups, and encourage students to use the formula just obtained to answer questions, so as to enhance their learning self-confidence. After the improvement of self-confidence, students will get better development in both study and life.

5   Conclusion

Network teaching platform teaching is a teaching form between traditional classroom teaching and distance network teaching. It relies on the Internet. More precisely, it depends on the campus network. Through the network teaching platform. It is a synchronous teaching method in the multimedia classroom. For the management of this teaching form, from the domestic point of view, most scholars in the educational field pay attention to the development of teaching resources. Application of teaching technology. Discussion on teaching mode. The realization of network technology, and few people pay attention to teaching management. Under the new teaching mode. How teachers manage knowledge. How to manage students. Evaluation. And so on are all new problems caused by the new teaching model. Obviously. The solution of these problems requires us to rethink in order to improve the teaching management under the new situation, and the network teaching platform education is a systematic project. It is by teachers. Network education media. Students and other factors constitute an organic whole with teaching function, and the constituent factors are not isolated. Surfaces are interactions. Mutually restrictive. Only a high level of teaching management. Through careful planning, organization and coordination, all factors can be optimized and combined into an organic whole. So as to ensure the teaching quality.

The future competition is the competition of education quality, so teachers should pay attention to the all-round development of students. The history of chemistry is to study the history of chemical development. It can help students understand the process of chemical knowledge and the process of sparks when scientists' thinking collides. It is of great significance. Higher vocational chemistry teachers can introduce chemical historical materials at the right time, stimulate students' enthusiasm for learning chemical knowledge, and improve students' cultural quality through the analysis and research of chemical historical materials.

For example, when teaching "transition metals", the chemistry teachers in Higher Vocational Colleges first display the periodic table of elements with the help of multimedia in class, encouraging students to say the elements they are familiar with or interested in. At this time, students speak freely. Some students express the properties of metal elements or non-metal elements and other knowledge points they have learned before; Some students are interested in some transition metals that have not been studied. At this time, teachers use the hyperlink function of the Internet to show the knowledge points of these elements according to the students' statements, so as to achieve the effect of expanding teaching. After students gradually enter the learning state, teachers can use network resources and environment to explain transition metal elements, so as to encourage students to understand and acquire relevant knowledge points from atomic radius, ionization energy, physical properties, chemical properties, oxidation state and color, so as to improve students' classroom learning efficiency. In this process, teachers can also use electronic whiteboards or virtual laboratories to assist teaching, so that students can actively participate in classroom learning and efficiently acquire chemical knowledge. In a word, under the background of the new curriculum reform, chemical teachers in higher vocational colleges can try to present chemical knowledge points in the form of excitement by means of life, cooperation, history, greening and networking, so as to attract students' attention and promote students to acquire chemical knowledge points efficiently.

References

1. Lamare, R.: Massive MIMO systems: signal processing challenges and research trends. URSI Radio Sci. Bull. **86**(4), 8–20 (2017)
2. Butterfield, J.D., Krynkin, A., Collins, R.P., Beck, S.B.M.: Experimental investigation into vibro-acoustic emission signal processing techniques to quantify leak flow rate in plastic water distribution pipes. Appl. Acoust. **119**, 146–155 (2017)
3. Luo, G., Qi, K., Xiong, X.: A RGB LED driving structure and signal processing based on tone-to-color conversion. Wuhan Univ. J. Nat. Sci. **22**(3), 252–256 (2017)
4. Sainath, T.N., Weiss, R.J., Wilson, K.W., et al.: Multichannel signal processing with deep neural networks for automatic speech recognition. IEEE/ACM Trans. Audio Speech Lang. Process. **25**(5), 965–979 (2017)

Construction and Application of Computer Network Experimental Teaching Platform Based on Big Data

Zhangsheng Zhong[⊠]

Nanchang Institute of Technology, Nanchang 330044, Jiangxi, China
z13576003643@126.com

Abstract. With the development of computer science and the popularization of computer application, the social demand for computer talents is increasing day by day. This paper takes "wisdom" as the teaching material as the carrier, we should focus on serving teachers and students in higher vocational colleges. We should not only give play to the leading role of teachers in guiding, enlightening and monitoring the teaching process, but also fully reflect the initiative, creativity and enthusiasm of students as the main body of the learning process. Colleges and universities have successively set up computer related majors, and even training institutions have participated in the training of computer professionals. However, with the enrollment regulations in recent years With the continuous expansion of the model, the construction speed of some school laboratories is far from keeping up with the expansion of enrollment scale. Combined with the reality of our school, this paper analyzes that when the conditions of computer network laboratory can not meet the computer network experimental teaching temporarily, the computer network experimental teaching platform is constructed by using packet tracer, VMware, pdffactory and other virtualization software to ensure the computer network The experimental course went smoothly.

Keywords: Big data · Computer · Teaching experiment platform · Platform construction

1 Introduction

The advent of the big data era has a significant impact on the field of education and promotes the reform of traditional education. In March 2012, the US government put forward the "big data research and development proposal", which clearly proposed to improve the application ability of big data in the field of education. In China, based on data mining technology, GE Daokai and others have carried out learner feature recognition, learner online learning behavior analysis and teacher-student interaction analysis in e-learning data mining.

In recent years, data-based learning analysis has become the focus of research and practice in the field of education. In the process of network-based teaching, the technology platform has accumulated a large amount of log data. Mining and analyzing these

M. A. Jan and F. Khan (Eds.): BigIoT-EDU 2022, LNICST 466, pp. 472–480, 2023.
https://doi.org/10.1007/978-3-031-23947-2_50

data will provide more and more accurate basis for teaching intervention, so as to promote learning, teaching and management more effectively. At the same time, data-driven analysis and mining also provide a new paradigm for educational research. The rapid development of learning analysis in recent years shows the consensus of researchers and practitioners on its importance. However, so far, learning analysis still can not form a unified model, so it is necessary to deeply study the learning analysis model of specific situation. This paper focuses on the teaching situation based on the network teaching platform, tries to build the corresponding learning analysis model, discusses its core elements and data processing process, and verifies and expands it through the application of the model [1].

The computer network experiment course of this college will basically include the following contents: the production of network cable, the installation and sharing of printers, the basic operation of switches and routers, the server related configuration based on Windows Server 2003 operating system, the server related configuration based on Linux operating system, etc. When the professional computer network laboratory can not guarantee the normal experimental teaching, we can consider using virtualization software to ensure the smooth progress of computer network experimental course. For example, use pdffactory virtual printer software to simulate real printers and provide printer sharing, so that students can master how to share printers; Use the virtual network equipment provided by packet tracker to simulate the real network environment for students to configure and debug, so that students can master the basic operation of switches and routers; Based on VMware virtual machine software, multiple operating systems are virtualized on a PC for students to learn the relevant configuration of various server operating systems. Through the above virtualization software, the smooth development of the computer network experiment course of the college can be basically guaranteed in the public computer room.

Computer network refers to a computer system that connects multiple computers and their external devices with independent functions in different geographical locations through communication lines and realizes resource sharing and information transmission under the management and coordination of network operating system, network management software and network communication protocol. Teachers need to place computers on the comprehensive experimental platform of computer network practice teaching when conducting computer teaching, However, the current computer network practice teaching comprehensive experimental platform can not adjust the height of the experimental platform. The height of students is different, and the height they need to use is also different. The unified height will reduce the comfort of most students, reduce the learning efficiency of students, and make it inconvenient to use.

Technical realization elements:

(1) Technical problems solved

In view of the shortcomings of the existing technology, the utility model provides a comprehensive experimental platform for computer network practice teaching, which has the advantages of being able to adjust the height of the experimental platform, and solves the problem that the current comprehensive experimental platform for computer network practice teaching can not adjust the height of the experimental platform, and the height of students is different, so the unified height will reduce the comfort of most students and their learning efficiency, Inconvenient to use.

(2) Technical proposal

In order to realize the purpose of the above computer network practice teaching comprehensive experimental platform, the utility model provides the following technical scheme: a computer network practice teaching comprehensive experimental platform, including a test platform, both sides of the bottom of the test platform are fixedly connected with lifting rods, both sides of the bottom of the test platform are provided with adjustment boxes, and the top of the adjustment box is provided with through holes, The bottom of the lifting rod passes through the through hole and extends to the inside of the adjustment box, and is fixedly connected with a connecting rod I, the bottom of the connecting rod I is movably connected with a connecting rod II through a pin shaft, the bottom of the inner wall of the adjustment box is fixedly installed with a mounting plate, the front surface of the mounting plate is fixedly connected with a motor, the output end of the motor is fixedly connected with a disc, and the bottom of the connecting rod II is movably connected with the bottom of the front surface of the disc through a pin shaft.

Preferably, the top of the regulating box is fixedly connected with the limit cylinder I, and the top of the lifting rod extends through the limit cylinder to the outside of the limit cylinder I and is fixedly connected with the bottom of the test bench.

Preferably, the bottom of both sides of the lifting rod is fixedly connected with a sliding rod, the top of both sides of the inner wall of the adjusting box is provided with a sliding groove, and the sliding rod is sliding connected with the sliding groove.

Preferably, a limit cylinder 2 is arranged inside the adjusting box and at the position of the connecting rod 1, the bottom of the connecting rod 1 passes through the limit cylinder 2 and extends to the outside of the limit cylinder 2 and is movably connected with the connecting rod 2 through a pin shaft, both sides of the limit cylinder 2 are fixedly connected with the limit rod, and the side of the limit rod close to the inner wall of the adjusting box is fixedly connected with the inner wall of the adjusting box.

Preferably, the bottom of the regulating box is fixedly connected with a bracket, and the bottom of the bracket is movably connected with a roller through a rotating shaft.

Preferably, the bottom of the adjusting box and one side of the roller is fixedly connected with an electric telescopic rod, and the bottom of the electric telescopic rod is fixedly connected with a friction plate.

(3) Beneficial effects

Compared with the prior art, the utility model provides a comprehensive experimental platform for computer network practical teaching, which has the following beneficial effects:

1) The computer network practical teaching comprehensive experimental platform can adjust the height of the experimental platform, improve the comfort and learning efficiency of students, and facilitate the use of the platform by setting the lifting rod,

adjusting box, through hole, connecting rod I, connecting rod II, mounting plate, motor and disc.

2) The computer network practical teaching comprehensive experimental platform can improve the stability of the lifting rod when moving by setting the limit cylinder I, prevent the lifting rod from shaking when moving, and make the lifting rod more stable when lifting by setting the sliding rod and chute. By setting the limit cylinder II and the limit rod, it can limit the moving track of the connecting rod I, and improve the stability of the connecting rod I when moving. By setting the bracket and roller, It can move the test-bed and bring convenience to people in handling. By setting the friction plate and electric telescopic rod, students can make the roller stationary when using the computer and prevent the test-bed from shaking.

2 Related Research Review

2.1 Significance of Teaching Platform Construction

"Smart teaching material" refers to the achievement of reconstructing the existing teaching materials creatively by teachers with the help of mobile teaching mode, on the basis of traditional paper teaching materials, based on big data learning and analysis technology, students as the core, guided by the cultivation of thinking mode, and using new generation information technologies such as big data, cloud computing and Internet of things.

"Smart textbook teaching platform" is a teaching support system based on wireless communication technology. It covers a variety of functions such as teaching, counseling, self-study, teacher-student communication, homework, testing and quality evaluation. It can provide real-time and non real-time teaching interactive support for teachers and students. It is a new one-stop teaching platform to customize teaching tasks for teachers and students, let teachers teach students according to their aptitude and let students apply what they have learned. The educational resources in smart textbooks are prepared, recorded and designed by professional authoritative experts and teachers in higher vocational colleges, and presented systematically and logically in front of teachers and students with characteristic contents such as micro class, animation and virtual simulation.

At present, the information construction of colleges and universities is also developing from the traditional web service based on PC to mobile intelligent terminal. Based on JavaWeb and PHP server and Android 4.4 mobile client, Wu Kaicheng designed and implemented a set of mobile teaching assistant system integrating teacher-student communication, teaching management and student ability test [2]. Based on the new wechat public service platform and its API interface, Yang Qing and others have built a micro teaching service platform by using java development technology and MySQL as the local database of the platform. They have developed an operating system mobile learning platform based on J2E and SSH framework, and verified by teaching experience that this method has good teaching effect. As shown in Fig. 1 below.

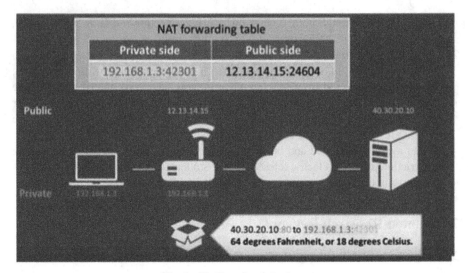

Fig. 1. Platform local database

Throughout the relevant research at home and abroad, blended learning has received more and more attention. It is another peak of teaching development. It will become the mainstream mode of teaching. The hybrid teaching platform based on mobile platform will also be more widely used.

2.2 Application Status in Big Data Environment

Research status of big data application in Education
The advent of the big data era has a significant impact on the field of education and promotes the reform of traditional education. In March 2012, the U.S. government put forward the "big data research and development proposal", which clearly proposed to improve the application ability of big data in the field of education. In China, based on data mining technology, GE Daokai and others carried out learner feature recognition, learner online learning behavior analysis and teacher-student interaction analysis in the big data environment in e-learning data mining.

Research status of Blended Learning
According to the statistics of the American survey report, half of the four-year university education and two-thirds of the three-year education in the United States are mixed learning forms. At the same time, most training institutions, university education institutions and K-12 schools in the United States use mixed learning forms. Since 2009, when the United States emphasized that blended learning is the most effective teaching form in its report on big data environment, blended learning has attracted much attention in the United States. According to the data in 2015, blended learning and flipped classroom in the United States account for 60% of American education [3].

Guo Ying of Fudan University found that blended learning can effectively improve learning effect and meet individual learning needs compared with conventional classroom learning after implementing physiology teaching based on e-learning platform. After comparing traditional education with blended learning mode, Ma Guoqing found that in Higher Vocational English teaching, blended learning mode has higher student satisfaction, interest and outstanding achievements. Kong Weijun et al. Combined with the NC programming course in higher vocational colleges, it is proved that the application of hybrid learning mode is conducive to cultivating students' lifelong learning habits and improving their autonomous learning ability.

3 Construction and Implementation of Computer Network Teaching Platform

The two basic network courses in computer specialty are computer network and network engineering. Computer network is the previous course, which describes the basic principle and architecture of network, and pays special attention to the relevant protocols at all levels, such as TCP protocol and IP protocol, and network engineering After learning the basic concept and principle of network, learn how to build a simple LAN, how to simulate Wan, generic cabling and other technologies, involving not only theoretical principles, but also some hardware devices such as switches, routers and firewalls. As shown in Fig. 2, the computer network teaching platform.

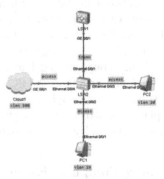

Fig. 2. Computer network teaching platform

Therefore, when designing the computer network experimental teaching platform, we should consider the following aspects:

1) Considering the implementation function, this experimental teaching platform should provide a protocol simulation experiment environment for students to observe and verify, so that students can master the protocols at all levels when learning the basic courses of computer network, and get in-depth experience through the practical process of sending data and analyzing data. In addition, it should also have the mainstream hardware equipment on the Internet Students build various networks and are familiar with the actual operation of various hardware devices.

2) In terms of teaching management, the experimental teaching platform must have the most mainstream and core network technology for today's networked information management, which can provide help for students' employment and provide advanced hardware platform for teachers' scientific research. The whole network platform must be efficient, smooth, stable and reliable; the whole network platform must provide a simple and convenient network management system; the whole network platform must be It must be able to provide flexible and rich network authentication system.

3) Considering the investment, in order to save the cost, the author suggests that the network engineering hardware experiment platform can be built first, and the protocol simulation software and necessary hardware can be installed on this basis. The two experimental systems share a PC, do not interfere with each other and switch conveniently.

Switches and routers are the two most important devices in the Internet. Switches are the most used devices in LAN. Switches are divided into two layers and three layers. Among them, layer three devices can link different subnets and have routing function. Routers are undoubtedly important devices connecting different networks. In addition, firewalls, wireless LAN, VOIP voice, etc. are the most popular devices on the Internet Popular technology, after learning the basic knowledge about the network, mastering the more important mainstream network hardware equipment is also the requirement of the society for college students.

We mainly rely on Ruijie's network university to build a network hardware configuration practice platform. The built experimental platform can not only carry out network experiments in the local laboratory, but also enter the laboratory for network experiments through remote login authentication; the existing PC can be used as the network terminal (the PC is shared with the network protocol analysis and simulation platform built earlier, saving resources) At the same time, the PC also retains the performance of entering the Intermet network, and can complete the verification of all experiments internally; the experimental platform can meet 40 people to carry out experiments at the same time. Topology diagram of network hardware configuration practice platform.

4 Significance of Building Computer Experiment Platform in Colleges and Universities

4.1 The Construction of Computer Network Experimental Teaching Platform in Colleges and Universities Can Improve the Teaching Level of Network Courses

For computer majors, learning network courses not only needs to learn theory, but also has a certain practical ability in line with the times. However, due to the lack of experimental conditions, the teaching of network courses is limited to theoretical teaching, and the effect is not ideal [4]. Therefore, the construction of experimental teaching platform can greatly improve the effect of network teaching. On the other hand, experimental teaching is flat The construction of the platform can improve the teaching level of teachers. First of all, through training, teachers can be exposed to many cutting-edge network knowledge and technologies, improve their own network technology literacy, and improve the teaching level of network theory and application. At the same time, through the construction of network laboratory, they can maintain close technical contact with first-class network equipment manufacturers, so as to follow up China in time The latest and most popular network technology in the world to improve the teaching level.

The effect comparison is shown in Fig. 3.

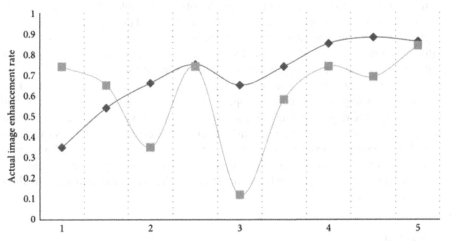

Fig. 3. The effect comparison

4.2 The Construction of Computer Network Experimental Teaching Platform in Colleges and Universities Can Improve Students' Employment Competitiveness

Colleges and universities are the place to cultivate talents in the 21st century. According to the demand point of view of society, real talents should not only have knowledge, but also have ability. Especially in T industry, more and more attention is paid to the practical experience and hands-on operation ability of technicians, and the cultivation of ability needs the combination of classroom education and experimental practice. The computer network experimental teaching platform in Colleges and universities we have built can be put into practice On the combination of education and practice, provide a real network environment, let students intuitively and comprehensively understand all kinds of network equipment and application environment, really deepen their understanding of network principles, protocols and standards, truly improve students' network skills and practical ability, and let them have obvious competitive advantages in future employment competition.

5 Conclusion

By building a college computer network experimental teaching platform integrating teaching, research and experimental functions, on the one hand, it is conducive to the cultivation of students' practical ability and independent thinking and innovation ability; on the other hand, it also provides a good platform for College Teachers' self-development and teaching and scientific research.

To sum up, the computer network practice teaching comprehensive experimental platform, by setting the lifting rod, adjusting box, through hole, connecting rod I, connecting rod II, mounting plate, motor and disc 9, solves the problem that the current computer network practice teaching comprehensive experimental platform can not adjust the height of the experimental platform, and the height of students is different due to their different heights. The unified height will reduce the comfort of most students when using it, It reduces students' learning efficiency and inconvenient use.

It should be noted that in this article, relational terms such as first and second are only used to distinguish one entity or operation from another entity or operation, and do not necessarily require or imply any such actual relationship or order between these entities or operations. Moreover, the term "including", "including" or any other variation thereof is intended to cover non exclusive inclusion, so that a process, method, article or equipment that includes a series of elements includes not only those elements, but also other elements not explicitly listed, or elements inherent in such a process, method, article or equipment.

References

1. Da, W.J., Hu, J.: Gan Hong in big data environment: research and design of cookie based web platform identity authentication mechanism. Jiangxi Sci. (2), 21–26 (2018)
2. Li, C., Gan, H.: Cross platform application and development of Mu Dong based on MVP architecture. Sci. Technol. Plaza (5), 35–39 (2017)
3. Li, Y., Ma, S., Huang, R.: Learning analysis technology: service learning process design and optimization. Open Educ. Res. 18(5), 18–24 (2012)
4. Yu, X., Gu, X.: Learning activity flow: a behavior model for learning analysis. J. Distance Educ. (4), 20–28 (2013)
5. Liu, Y., Yu, Q., Li, S.: Research on intelligent detection method of multi-model fusion images based on deep learning. Electron. Meas. Technol. 44(20), 7 (2021)
6. Zhang, F., Zhang, C., Yang, H.: Color compensation method for projected images based on deep learning in combat assistance systems. J. Mil. Eng. 42(11), 6 (2021)
7. Lian, X., Liu, Z., Zhang, L.: An image recognition method for retinopathy based on deep learning. Comput. Appl. Softw. 38(1), 7 (2021)
8. Cao, Y., Liu, H., Jia, X., Li, X.: Review of image quality evaluation methods based on deep learning. Comput. Eng. Appl. 57(23), 10 (2021)
9. Wang, Y., Sun, W., Zhou, X.: Research on image recognition method of Chinese herbal medicine plants based on deep learning. Chin. Med. Inf. 37(6), 5 (2020)
10. Hao, S., Liu, Y.: Overview of image intrinsic attribute prediction methods based on deep learning. J. Graph. 42(3), 13 (2021)
11. Xu, Z., Chen, S.: Recognition and localization of key target points in weak texture images based on deep learning. Comput. Meas. Control 30(2), 7 (2022)

Computer Ability Education and Training of Tourism Talents in the Era of "Internet + Tourism Big Data"

Li Xing[1(✉)] and Yanhong Dong[2]

[1] Tourism College of Mount Tai University, Taian 271000, Shandong, China
xingli0910@163.com
[2] Shandong Zhigu Big Data Co., Ltd., Taian 271000, Shandong, China

Abstract. Internet plus tourism big data "Under the environment of the information age, the development of the tourism industry has entered the information age, and the lack of compound tourism talents is prominent, especially the employees skilled in computer skills. In view of the weak pertinence and practicability of the computer curriculum in the current tourism talent training, this paper puts forward a new mode of tourism talent computer ability training based on the CBE teaching mode, starting from the setting of modularization Curriculum, adjustment of specialized teaching content and practical role-based projects, combined with examples, this paper gives relevant construction ideas and implementation schemes.

Keywords: Tourism talent training · Computer skills · Modular courses · Specialized content

1 Introduction

With the goal of building a well-off society in an all-round way, people's living standards are improving day by day, and tourism is booming and developing rapidly. The tourism industry is a comprehensive industry. According to the data of the Ministry of culture and tourism, the number of domestic tourists in 2018 was 5.539 billion, an increase of 10.8% over the same period of last year; The total number of outbound tourists was 291 million, a year-on-year increase of 7.8%; In the whole year, the total tourism revenue was 5.97 trillion yuan, a year-on-year increase of 10.5%. The comprehensive contribution of national tourism to GDP is 9.94 trillion yuan, accounting for 11.04% of the total GDP. 28.26 million people were directly employed in tourism, and 79.91 million were directly and indirectly employed in tourism, It accounts for 10.29% of the total employed population in China. It can be seen from the above data that China's tourism industry has developed rapidly and occupies an irreplaceable important position in the growth of the national economy. It is worth studying how to do a good job in talent training for such a large industry. According to the data of the Ministry of culture and tourism, tourism management undergraduate majors were opened in 2017 608 ordinary colleges and

M. A. Jan and F. Khan (Eds.): BigIoT-EDU 2022, LNICST 466, pp. 481–487, 2023.
https://doi.org/10.1007/978-3-031-23947-2_51

universities (mainly including tourism management, hotel management and exhibition economy and management), with a total enrollment of 59000 people [1]. With such a large enrollment scale, educators need to make continuous exploration and efforts on how to do a good job in the professional training of students during school, transport a continuous new force for the development of the tourism industry and promote the development of the whole industry.

A trend which cannot be halted is Internet plus and big data change rapidly. In the face of this new economic normal, under the situation of a large gap of compound tourism talents, the cultivation of tourism talents' computer ability has also become an urgent task. How to change the current situation of serious homogenization of "Da Wen and Da Li" in computer curriculum in talent training, weak professional pertinence and weak practicability, and explore the way of innovation of relevant curriculum and reform of training mode in the process of computer ability training of tourism talents is a topic worthy of deep discussion. Our higher education should actively think about how to help future tourism practitioners master the computer business ability of using Internet tools and big data analysis, so as to better boost the development of the tourism industry.

2   Demand Analysis and Feasibility

Facing the development of Internet plus Internet, the construction of tourism talent team needs to deepen the supply side reform, in order to solve the deficiencies and shortcomings in the construction of tourism talents. Only the training goal facing the needs of the market and employers is reasonable. If we want to effectively solve the problem of insufficient computer ability in the current tourism talent training process, we need to clarify the market demand and further formulate effective reform plans, so as to truly cultivate students' ability and satisfy students and society.

2.1   Demand for Computer Ability of Tourism Talents

In view of the demand of the tourism industry for the computer application ability of employees, Ma Wei et al. Conducted a survey in the form of a questionnaire on the tourism market. Through the statistics and analysis of the results, they believe that employers usually tend to choose compound graduates with strong computer operation ability and plasticity. 96.52% of managers think that the demand for computer skills in their posts is more than important. In the recruitment process, most people will consider the candidate's computer ability. Through investigation, analysis and empirical research, Qin Zhaoxiang pointed out that foreign language and computer ability are the constituent factors of the core competitiveness of Undergraduate Tourism Management students. It can be seen that computer application ability has become a necessary quality for tourism practitioners, which has formed a consensus at all levels. Whether they have good computer application ability directly affects the employment and career of tourism students [2].

The demand of employers is the direction of our education and teaching contents. At present, the survey shows that the requirements for the computer skills of the employees in the tourism industry are mainly focused on the use of office software, the use of software in the industry, the simple maintenance of computers, the use and management of networks, the management of databases and the application of analysis. The requirements are shown in Fig. 1. Since the "Internet plus Internet" plan and the "515 strategy", the industry has further enhanced the skills of practitioners and Internet plus Internet applications and the ability to collect and process large data.

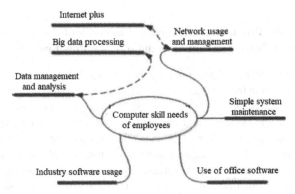

Fig. 1. Demand for computer skills of tourism practitioners

2.2 Current Situation of Computer Ability Training of Tourism Talents

At present, the problems of school computer education are as follows: the specialty is not targeted enough, and there is a lack of optimization and adjustment for the specialty in the relevant curriculum; The teaching content is not closely combined with practical application, and it is easy to talk about knowledge points in isolation; The teaching method is relatively monotonous, mainly traditional teaching and demonstration, and the main role of students is not prominent. The result is that students have no use in learning, can not use computers to solve practical application problems, and can not use the Internet and big data platform to collect and analyze effective information. The main reasons for these problems are as follows: when the professional teaching plan is formulated, it is large, because it is not a professional course, but only proposes to set up a computer course, and does not optimize the specialty and application; Due to the limitation of class hours, professional courses are emphasized. Computer courses have less class hours, and teaching is a mere formality. When students learn, they "skim the water", which can not really achieve the effect of flexible learning and application; Teachers lack industry knowledge and experience, the differentiation of teaching methods and contents is not obvious, and the knowledge points are overemphasized in the teaching process, but the personalization of specialty and application scene is ignored.

3 Tourism Talents Training Mode in the Era of Internet Plus

China is vast and rich in natural resources. In recent years, China's tourism economy has developed rapidly, and more and more regions are promoting tourism to enter the track of nationalization. China's tourism development needs the promotion of tourism talents, especially the tourism industry should focus on the development of local culture and the promotion of national culture It is necessary for tourism talents to bear the responsibility of tourism culture publicity We should also have professional operation of tourism, that is, we should have high political literacy We should also focus on improving our professional ethics according to the needs of the future development of tourism.

3.1 Increasing the Proportion of Training Courses and Focusing on Training New Tourism Talents in Line with the Internet Plus Era

Tourism has ushered in new development opportunities, but tourism talents do not conform to tourism ethics in their work, which has a negative impact on the tourism industry. With the strategic development of tourism, the excavation and creation of tourism elements that tend to be localized and nationalized need to focus on the cultivation of political quality and pay attention to the education of traditional culture in the cultivation of tourism talents. Therefore, we should guide tourism talents with correct values and pay attention to improving the cultural soft power of tourism talents. China's mainstream values are socialist core values. In the cultivation of tourism talents, we should take this as the core, pay attention to the moral cultivation of tourism talents, guide tourism talents to love the country, devote themselves to tourism, and establish the concept of integrity, so that tourism talents can serve tourists with an honest attitude in their professional posts and transmit positive energy to tourists, Contribute to building a harmonious society. The cultural soft power of cultivating tourism talents is to take the publicity of traditional culture as the starting point, so that tourism talents can realize that their imagination represents the image of the country. With the development of tourism economy, the international comprehensive strength will be enhanced. Therefore, vocational schools should break the traditional single teaching mode in the training of tourism professionals, but pay attention to the tradition of tourism culture, and guide students to continuously tap the local cultural characteristics in order to give full play to their professional value [3]. This requires vocational schools to set up tourism professional courses and incorporate the courses related to tourism profession into the teaching of tourism professional courses, including literature and art, information communication and design, which can be set up as elective courses. Students can choose elective courses according to their own needs to broaden their horizons. To improve teaching quality, practical teaching is an indispensable part. The purpose of practical teaching is to improve students' professional operation ability. Situational training is usually used to introduce work examples in the tourism industry into practical teaching, and set up situations for students to participate in it. Situational teaching should pay attention to cultural guidance and the cultivation of students' innovative ability, but also to the cultivation of students' foreign language application ability. Teachers can create tourism situations for students to simulate tour guides and communicate with foreign tourists in foreign languages, which can not only guide students' professional ability, but also cultivate students' foreign language ability, so as to facilitate students to enter professional posts and give full play to their professional ability.

3.2 Construction of a Tourism Compound Talent Training Base Suitable for the Internet Plus Era

The construction of a compound talent training base is to train the compound tourism talents in order to adapt to the "Internet plus" era. The training mode takes the occupation ability of tourism talents as the main training content. In the training of tourism professionals, vocational schools should not only establish on campus training bases, but also establish off campus training bases. From the perspective of the development of tourism industry, the training label of compound talents is formulated so that the trained talents have solid theoretical knowledge and high professional operation technology, as well as professional operation ability, that is, they will face various problems in tourism professional posts, which require tourism talents with high comprehensive quality to be able to deal with them freely, And solve all kinds of problems well. This requires vocational schools to cooperate with the local tourism industry to establish an off campus practice base. Students are no longer limited to participating in situational teaching in the on campus training class, but enter the tourism enterprise and feel the post environment. In such an environment, students will consciously abide by the norms of enterprises. As students integrate into the post environment of tourism enterprises, they will shape themselves according to the quality requirements of tourism enterprises for tourism talents Perfect yourself. Tourism Majors in vocational schools can also establish cooperative relations with local scenic spots, and invite tourism experts as instructors of the school's training base To guide students' learning in the training base, we should also participate in the construction of tourism professional talent training mode, so as to make the tourism professional talent training mode more in line with the requirements of tourism compound talent training. For example, tourism majors in vocational schools can establish cooperative relations with Maotai distillery. On the one hand, experts from Maotai distillery can be hired to teach students Maotai culture and introduce the industrial tourism projects established by Maotai distillery; On the other hand, students can participate in the industrial tourism development of Maotai distillery, so that students' professional thinking is no longer limited to the tourism industry itself, but pay more attention to the excavation of tourism cultural elements, which is conducive to the cultivation of students' tourism innovation ability.

3.3 Pay Attention to the New Requirements of the Quality of the Internet Plus Talents in the Training of Tourism Talents

Tourism itself is a real economy, so it has certain quality requirements for tourism talents. Tourism itself is showing industrial development. Therefore, while giving full play to the role of tourism, we should also play a talent strategy In order to improve the quality of talents, stimulate the economic pull of tourism, the inclusiveness of multiple resources and the openness of economy and culture, start the strategic development strategy to build tourism into a landmark industry in regional economic development. In the era of Internet plus, the quality of tourism talents must be created in order to achieve sustainable development in tourism.

(1) Carry out professional knowledge training for tourism talents. With the increasingly fierce competition in the tourism industry, tourism talents are the spokesperson of

the tourism industry and the window image of the tourism industry. The mastery of tourism knowledge by tourism talents is directly related to the tourism quality, and whether tourism talents have service awareness can prove whether they can provide high-quality services for tourists. The improvement of people's living standards Improve, more and more advocate tourism, which has brought good development prospects for the tourism industry. While giving full play to its resource advantages, the tourism industry should also give full play to the talent advantages, and shape talents according to the needs of tourists, so as to meet the high-quality service requirements of tourists. In the era of Internet plus, in the training of tourism talents, we should pay attention to the service consciousness of tourism talents from the perspective of tourism, so as to enable them to provide tourism services for tourists, not only to guide tourists to travel and sightseeing, but to exchange cultural exchanges with tourists more often, and to guide tourists to understand the culture contained in tourist attractions. Thus, it plays a role in spreading cultural traditions [4]. Then, tourism talents should constantly improve their knowledge and cultivation, start from the reality of tourism development, shape their own tourism image according to the quality needs of tourists for tourism talents, and provide humanized services for tourists. Only when tourism talents have service awareness can they improve tourism service level and make tourists satisfied.

(2) training occupation ethics for tourism talents. Internet plus In the new era, tourism talents are the guides of knowledge So that visitors can feel the humanistic culture of the region where the scenic spot is located. Therefore, it is very important to cultivate the professional ethics of tourism talents in order to give full play to the publicity role of tourism resources. At the same time, we should also cultivate the international awareness and traditional ceremony of tourism talents, and have the ability to publicize the national culture and national culture to tourists in a correct way. Tourism talents are the representative image of the tourism industry. To raise the cultural level and reflect it from the professional image, good professional ethics is the key. In particular, tourists from all over the world began to be keen on traveling to China To feel Chinese culture, tourism talents need to have good political and ideological quality and constantly improve their professional ethics In order to establish a good image of China in front of foreign friends, it will also indirectly enhance China's position in the world.

4 Conclusion

Facing the new situation of "Internet plus tourism big data", the development of tourism industry change rapidly, and the computer ability of tourism talents becomes the necessary skill. Teaching reform is not a proposition that can be achieved overnight. It needs to be analyzed in the process of practice in combination with the situation of majors and students, and teach students according to their aptitude due to professional reform. In the future, we should constantly think about new teaching contents related to the majors taught and adapt to the teaching methods of students of corresponding majors according to different majors, so as to achieve the training effect required by the training objectives and satisfy the students and social employers.

Acknowledgements. The Social Science Program in Tai'an:Research on the mechanism of Tai'an Research Travel Education based on the promotion of core literacy (Item number: 21-ZX-017).

References

1. Ma, W., Liu, R.: Investigation, analysis and Reflection on the demand for computer application skills of employees in tourism industry. SME Manag. Technol. **21**(1), 193–194 (2012)
2. Qin, Z.: Empirical Study on the cultivation mechanism of core competitiveness of undergraduate students majoring in Tourism Management. J. Inner Mongolia Normal Univ. (Educ. Sci. Ed.) **25**(5), 95–98 (2012)
3. Hu, F., Fang, L.: analysis of education and teaching mode based on big data thinking. J. Hunan Univ. Adm. **18**(5), 25–29 (2018)
4. Liu, R.: Research on the cultivation of computer application skills highlighting the characteristics of industry demand. Comput. Knowl. Technol. **8**(24), 5845–5847 (2012)

Comparison Between American Restorative Justice and Chinese People's Mediation System in the Era of Big Data Intelligence

Yang Xiao[1(✉)], Yanhong Gan[2], and Leihan Yu[3]

[1] Mianyang Teachers' College, Mianyang City 621000, Sichuan Province, China
yyyxxx1@163.com
[2] Jilin University, Changchun 130012, Jilin Province, China
[3] Shanghai Normal University, Shanghai 200030, China

Abstract. With the continuous expansion of the application scope of Internet technology, the application of big data technology and the development of artificial intelligence have become the focus of attention of groups at all levels of society. The research work on big data and artificial intelligence has never stopped. To a large extent, there is a close relationship between big data and artificial intelligence. The arrival of the era of artificial intelligence shows a strong dependence on big data technology. This paper compares American restorative justice in the era of big data intelligence with China's people's mediation system.

Keywords: Big data · Restorative justice · People's mediation system

1 Introduction

Since the upsurge of restorative justice in the 1970s has been widely concerned by scholars all over the world, restorative justice has become a new criminal justice procedure implemented by the international criminal justice community. Retributive justice and corrective justice have been the mainstream of criminal justice for a long time. However, with the deepening of people's understanding of crime and criminal justice, people have found many disadvantages of traditional criminal justice. In the process of exploring how to eliminate disadvantages and solve problems, people have established a new model from a new perspective, So the theory and practice of restorative justice came into being. Restorative justice emphasizes that in the process of dealing with criminals and criminal acts, we must fully consider the needs of victims and communities, pay attention to the role of victims and communities, pay attention to the confession and confession of perpetrators, encourage them to sincerely assume the responsibility for the repair of victims and communities caused by criminal acts, and give full play to the role of communities in preventing recidivism and rebuilding harmonious communities, Instead of punitive measures taken by the family against the offender. The judicial practice of various countries has achieved good social results, realized social justice, saved social costs and judicial resources, and improved the effectiveness of criminal justice.

© ICST Institute for Computer Sciences, Social Informatics and Telecommunications Engineering 2023
Published by Springer Nature Switzerland AG 2023. All Rights Reserved
M. A. Jan and F. Khan (Eds.): BigIoT-EDU 2022, LNICST 466, pp. 488–496, 2023.
https://doi.org/10.1007/978-3-031-23947-2_52

With the development of market economy and the continuous adjustment of social interest pattern, today's social contradictions and disputes in China have new manifestations. According to the characteristics of current social disputes in China, it is an inevitable requirement to study a set of dispute resolution mechanism suitable for the current actual situation to promote social stability and the development of a harmonious society. Therefore, in the era of big data intelligence, this paper makes a comparative analysis of restorative justice in the United States and people's mediation system in China.

In fact, there are great differences in court mediation methods between China and the United States. China applies the system of mediation and trial in one and a single mediation subject. The parties' admission and concession in mediation have a great impact on the trial, which increases the parties' preparedness and easily leads to the failure of mediation. The mediation system attached to the U.S. court is independent of the court trial. It is clearly carried out in a private way. The mediation procedure is separated from the trial procedure, and the negative impact of mediation on the trial is avoided as far as possible. The court mediation in our country runs through the whole process of civil litigation, and the scope of mediation is very wide. Except for some non litigation cases, all other civil and economic cases are within the mediation scope of the court. However, our law also stipulates that court mediation is not the pre procedure of trial. Except for cases that must be preceded by mediation, such as divorce proceedings, if the parties are unwilling to mediate or have no mediation conditions, the court may directly try them. Some states in the United States have limited the scope of application of the court attached mediation system. For example, the mediation law of Dakota in 1921 stipulates that mediation is applicable to cases below US $200.

To learn from the experience of foreign systems, it is bound to find the similarities with similar systems in China. Only in this way can we learn from them. In essence, the court mediation system in China and the United States has similarities: court mediation is an indispensable trial substitute tool in both countries. The court mediation system of China and the United States both originated from the surge of civil litigation.

During this period, the practical circles all welcomed the court mediation system, and even there was an extreme demand for 100% mediation in China. The settlement rate of court affiliated mediation in the United States accounts for more than 90% of all civil litigation cases. Although the court mediation in our country has various shortcomings, we can not deny its important role in judicial practice. Compared with the trial procedure, the court mediation in our country is more efficient and flexible. The court mediation system of China and the United States also has many shortcomings, and the author has made a comparison in the previous article. The differences in these systems are what we need to compare and learn from. Although they are not completely copied, the advantages of these systems need us to transplant and learn from the court mediation in our country to improve and solve various problems in the system design and judicial practice of court mediation in our country.

2 Facing the Era of Big Data Intelligence

2.1 Big Data

Big data is also called massive data. In essence, it is to obtain batch information assets with strong insight, accurate decision-making ability and high-quality procedures, with great growth space and diversified information assets with the help of emerging models" The concept of "big data" was originally mentioned in the book "the age of big data" compiled by Victor Mayer Schoenberg and Kenneth: cook. It can be understood as a convenient method of applying all data for analytical processing instead of random analysis (sampling survey). The characteristics of big data can be summarized as follows: large scale, diversity, fast analysis speed, high authenticity of data information and great practical value of data. To fully understand the connotation of big data, we need to take systematic decomposition measures from the following three aspects: ① Theory: theory is not only a necessary channel for cognitive improvement, but also a baseline for affirmation and transmission. Analyze the overall outline and characterization of big data in various industries from the characteristic definition of big data: deeply analyze its value from the value level of big data; Insight into the development trend of big data; Examine the relationship between individuals and data information from the unique and important perspective of big data privacy. ② Technology: technology can be regarded as the embodiment of the value of big data and the basis of sustainable development. Big data technology mainly focuses on cloud computing, distributed processing technology, storage technology and perception technology, which can explain the whole process of big data from collection, processing, storage to result formation. ③ Practice: practice is the ultimate way to reflect the value of big data. At present, the Internet, government agencies, enterprises and individuals have made corresponding practices on big data and outlined a beautiful scene and a blueprint to be realized.

Chinese traditional judicial system culture has a long history, of which two systems have attracted the attention of later generations: one is the death penalty review system, and the other is the long-standing mediation system. The traditional mediation system plays an important role in the dispute resolution mechanism in China's feudal society for more than 2000 years, and has a far-reaching impact on the dispute resolution and social governance in contemporary China. This topic is also to study the mediation system, but what is different from the past is that the research scope of this paper is selected as the early days of the founding of new China, on the one hand, because the mediation system has an important impact on the political power construction in the transition stage of the early days of the founding of new China, on the other hand, because the special historical period of the early days of the founding of the people's Republic of China has given the mediation system its unique ideological basis and form of expression – which is different from any previous period in China. Through comparative analysis and investigation of historical materials, this paper focuses on the innovation of mediation system in this period, which has two main purposes: first, to better understand the modernization of Chinese traditional legal culture; Second, objectively understand and understand the concept of governance and the characteristics of the judicial environment at the beginning of the founding of new China.

2.2 Relationship Between Big Data and Artificial Intelligence

In recent years, there have been a lot of research work on big data and artificial intelligence, which promote each other and develop a lot of new methods, applications and values. At present, human beings have many abilities such as preservation, extraction, retrieval, classification and integration for big data with large data scale, various data types, rapid data flow and high data authenticity. The development and progress of big data technology play different roles in it. Moreover, some theories and methods developed in the era of artificial intelligence have been applied in big data analysis and achieved relatively good results.

Domestic studies have found that dealing with the practical problems of the expansibility and growth of artificial intelligence must need the assistance and support of big data technology. In the past, artificial intelligence technology did not have the learning and research ability similar to human beings. The main reason is that artificial intelligence is similar and simple. In fact, it is a kind of complicated things. The two necessary conditions of artificial intelligence are the support of massive data and the strong processing ability of this kind of data. The machinery used in the past did not meet the above two conditions.

From a certain level, artificial intelligence has many similarities with human beings. It should hold a large number of knowledge and sufficient experience, and behind these knowledge and experience, there should be a large amount of data as the "background". The development and progress of big data technology functions provide certain technical support for the storage and analysis of a large amount of data information, and promote the machine to obtain sufficient data and hold the corresponding processing capacity, which is consistent with the data required in the development of artificial intelligence era and the demand for data processing capacity, as shown in Fig. 1.

Mediation is a kind of dispute resolution with the development of society, and it develops continuously with the development of society. China's mediation system is now in a renaissance period after experiencing a period of prosperity and decline. The revival at this time is not a simple revival, but a revival process of removing the dross and taking the essence from the previous mediation system in China. The case filing mediation system is an important system produced in this revival process. At this stage, local courts have implemented the case filing mediation system to reform and improve the court mediation system, and achieved great results. However, in practice, due to the lack of unified legal provisions, the case filing mediation system produces some confusion in the process of understanding and application. Based on the above situation, this paper clearly defines the concept of the case filing mediation system, demonstrates the necessity and feasibility of establishing the case filing mediation system in China, and affirms that the case filing mediation system is a major innovation in China's judicial practice. Finally, this paper puts forward some suggestions on the establishment of the case filing mediation system in our country in order to expect the successful development of the case filing mediation system in our practice.

Only under such circumstances can the goal of sustainable development be achieved in the era of artificial intelligence. The arrival of the era of artificial intelligence also reverses the big data technology and promotes the development and progress of data. It can be seen that there is a benign interactive relationship between big data technology

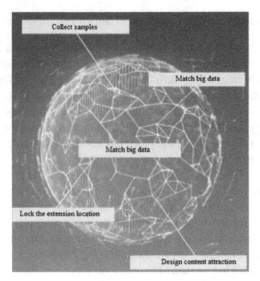

Fig. 1. Big data intelligent analysis technology

and the development of artificial intelligence era. If the relationship between big data and the era of artificial intelligence is regarded as a dependency, it is better to say that big data technology is the "golden key" to the era of artificial intelligence. Some theories and methods in the era of artificial intelligence can promote the "value-added" of big data technology in a great sense. At the same time, the development of big data provides a greater power source for the development of artificial intelligence era.

3   People's Mediation System in China

People's mediation is an activity of mediating, persuading, persuading and educating the parties to civil disputes under the auspices of the people's mediation committee and on the basis of laws, regulations and social ethics, so as to promote mutual understanding, equal consultation, voluntarily reach an agreement and eliminate disputes. People's mediation has a long history of thousands of years in China. It is known as "a flower of the East" and is widely praised by the judicial circles at home and abroad.

Since the 1970s, with the rise and development of restorative justice in the world, Chinese scholars have advocated the introduction of dialogue mechanism in criminal proceedings to improve litigation efficiency, improve the subject status of the parties and promote social harmony. With the deepening of the concept of harmonious society, mediation system has been widely used in the settlement of disputes between the parties. Criminal mediation is widely used to solve minor criminal cases in order to improve litigation efficiency, respect the subject status of the parties and help build a harmonious society. Criminal mediation refers to the activity of determining a series of solutions after the occurrence of criminal acts through voluntary and equal negotiation between the perpetrator and the victim under the auspices of a neutral third party as the moderator of mediation when criminal facts occur and criminal responsibility needs to be investigated. However, there are some problems in the criminal mediation system in both legislation and judicial practice, which need to be reformed and improved. Based on the current criminal mediation system in China, combined with the problems existing in legislation and judicial practice, this paper uses comparative methods, appropriately draws lessons from foreign experience, and puts forward some suggestions on the reform and improvement of the criminal mediation system, in order to have a deeper understanding of the criminal mediation system.

3.1 People's Mediation

People's mediation is an out of litigation mediation, which is presided over by the people's mediation committee and conducted in accordance with laws, regulations and social ethics. The parties negotiate on an equal footing, distinguish right from wrong, make mutual understanding and compromise, and reach an agreement. This way promotes unity and maintains stability. It is an organizational form of people's self-education, self-management and self-service. People's mediation is an act of mass autonomy, A mediation agreement has the effect of a civil contract. People's mediation is free, convenient and fast. It is the "first line of defense" to resolve contradictions and disputes and maintain social stability.

With the profound changes in society and economy, contradictions and disputes are becoming more and more complex, diversified, comprehensive and mass. Under this background, the party and government and other relevant departments, many experts and scholars have proposed to establish a large mediation system of people's mediation, administrative mediation and judicial mediation, which cooperate with each other and coordinate combined transport. Of course, this also requires the legislative department to consider the role of the three in the design of the legal system, guide the three to complement each other, establish a large mediation system and play a role together. In practice, some localities have engaged in the linkage of three adjustments, coordination and cooperation, complementary resources and information, and comprehensively used legal, policy, administrative and other means, as well as dredging, education, consultation and other methods to resolve contradictions at the grass-roots level and in the bud. The establishment of a large mediation system and the implementation of three mediation linkage are conducive to the integration of mediation resources, complementary advantages, saving judicial costs, resolving contradictions as soon as possible and achieving the unity of legal and social effects.

3.2 Legal System of People's Mediation

The people's mediation system is an important part of the socialist legal system ≪ Article 111 of the Constitution stipulates that residents' committees and villagers' committees shall establish people's mediation committees to mediate civil disputes. This is a clear provision on the constitutional status of the people's mediation system. The regulations on the organization of people's mediation committees in May 1989 further defines the status and role of people's mediation organizations. Article 16 of the civil procedure law stipulates that people's mediation committees are mass organizations that mediate civil disputes under the guidance of grass-roots people's governments and basic people's courts, The provisions of the Supreme People's Court on the trial of civil cases involving people's mediation agreements in September 2002 and the people's Mediation Law of the people's Republic of China adopted in 2010 have clarified the nature and legal binding force of people's mediation agreements, enhanced the credibility and authority of people's mediation work, and further expanded the field of people's mediation work, It has standardized the procedures of people's mediation and strengthened the guidance of judicial administrative organs on people's mediation.

4   American Restorative Justice and Chinese People's Mediation System

4.1   Overview of Restorative Justice

Restorative justice mode is a diversified exploration of dispute resolution mode. It refers to a dispute resolution scheme under the auspices of mediation, in which the offender, the victim and other people affected by the crime and the community participate together, negotiate and determine how to make up for the losses caused by the crime in order to restore the interpersonal relationship and normal social order before the crime. Under the restorative justice model, crime is not only a violation of the law, a violation of the state, but also an injury to the victim, society and even the offender himself. It especially emphasizes the status and role of the victim in the process of case handling, and takes the sincere repentance and apology of the offender and the consent of the victim as the preconditions for starting the restorative justice program, Emphasize the important role of community in the process of case handling, and regard it as the party whose legitimate rights and interests have been infringed. In this way, under the restorative justice model, all people affected by crime can openly exchange their feelings, put forward their own opinions and negotiate to solve criminal disputes. As a supplementary form of the traditional criminal justice system, restorative justice is an expansion of the original litigation rights of the offender and the victim. To a certain extent, it gives the victim the right to deal with disputes and helps to meet their psychological and spiritual needs. The voluntary reconciliation between the victim and the offender helps to completely solve the contradiction between them and help the offender repent, Social reintegration.

4.2   Analysis of American Restorative Justice and Chinese People's Mediation System

A socialist harmonious society is a society of democracy and rule of law, fairness and justice, honesty and fraternity, vitality, stability and order, and harmony between man and nature. Therefore, preventing and coordinating conflicts has become the due meaning of building a socialist harmonious society. Restorative justice is an effective way to solve criminal conflicts and achieve harmony. The goal of restorative justice is to restore the social relations damaged by criminal acts, pay full attention to and comfort the victims, give full play to the active role of the victims in the judicial process, reflect the judicial purpose of the law respecting the victims' personality rights, actively resolve the original contradictions and conflicts, and effectively restore the normal order of social life. Through the dialogue and coordination between the perpetrator and the victim, we can give full play to the ability of the community to eliminate contradictions, greatly reduce the frequency of the use of free punishment, effectively alleviate the contradiction of prison overcrowding, reverse the sharp rise in the execution cost, and effectively realize the purpose of criminal law to prevent and control crimes. Therefore, people's mediation should be regarded as the pre procedure for bringing a lawsuit to the court for some specific subject matter or less than a certain amount of subject matter, with little dispute and little impact. These civil cases should be diverted from the court to alleviate the litigation pressure of the court. The judicial resources saved should handle cases with great influence and controversy, and better safeguard the judicial authority. Give play to the advantages of convenient and timely people's mediation organizations.

5 Conclusion

With the development of big data technology, cloud computing, computer and other technologies and the arrival of the era of artificial intelligence, the basic ideas of artificial intelligence have been applied in many fields. Facing the era of big data intelligence, in order to make people's mediation better play its function and effectiveness, whether it is the judicial response in the United States or the people's mediation system in China, it is necessary to improve the organization network, team quality, legal effect of the agreement and how to connect with other mediation through legislation, and guide It is suggested that all forces should jointly participate in resolving contradictions and disputes, and establish a large mediation pattern integrating people's mediation, administrative mediation and litigation mediation. Through the law to further standardize people's mediation, increase its authority, improve the trust of the masses, make it summon vitality and vitality again, and play its due role in a harmonious and stable society.

At present, China is in a period of rapid transformation, with rapid economic growth, major changes in social structure, and frequent occurrence of various political and social problems. It is urgent to solve them in a timely and effective manner through appropriate means. There are contradictions and conflicts between the limited judicial resources and the expansion of social disputes. The unity of litigation confrontation can no longer meet the requirements of diversified social relations. It is in this opportunity that entrusted mediation came into being. It does not break away from the mediation tradition of our country, but also draws lessons from the judicial ADR system in the judicial reform of various countries. It is a non litigation dispute resolution method developed on the local resources of our country. Since the people's Court of Changning District of Shanghai implemented the entrusted mediation mode of "people's mediation window" in 2003, the people's courts of at least 17 provinces, autonomous regions and municipalities directly under the central government are exploring entrusted mediation. However, due to the lack of legislation, there are many factors restricting the development of entrusted mediation in practice. Therefore, it is necessary to study the nature and actual situation of entrusted mediation to provide theoretical support for improving entrusted mediation. The first part of this paper analyzes the basic theory of entrusted mediation, introduces the concept and characteristics of entrusted mediation, makes a qualitative analysis of entrusted mediation, and makes a comparative study with the concepts of people's mediation, court mediation and assisted mediation, in order to better understand entrusted mediation.

Evaluation Method of English Teaching Quality Based on SOFM Neural Network

Jing Sheng[✉]

Wuchang University of Technology, Wuhan 430070, Hubei, China
wclgxyxf@sina.com

Abstract. With the globalization of world economy, culture, science and technology, international cooperation and exchanges are becoming more and more frequent, and English will occupy a more and more important position. As a public compulsory basic course for Non-English Majors in Colleges and universities in China, College English plays a very important role in Expanding College Students' knowledge, improving foreign language comprehensive quality and cultivating language application ability. Therefore, the quality of College English teaching is also included in one of the important indicators of college curriculum construction evaluation. This paper analyzes four problems existing in College English teaching, and points out that emphasizing summative assessment and neglecting formative assessment are the main reasons affecting the quality of English teaching. Therefore, this paper proposes an English teaching quality evaluation method based on SOFM neural network to strengthen the monitoring of the formation process of teaching quality, so as to improve teaching quality.

Keywords: SOFM neural network · English teaching · Quality Assurance

1 Introduction

The reform of College English teaching began in early 2004. After two years of pilot, a new teaching model has been implemented in most colleges and universities in China. The new question type reflecting the College English Curriculum Requirements (Trial) (hereinafter referred to as the "curriculum requirements") has also appeared in CET4 in June 2006. We have conducted a comparative study on the curriculum requirements with reference to the College English Syllabus (Revised), which has deepened our understanding of the differences in the objectives of the College English teaching reform. Implement the new In the course requirements, we must pay attention to: (1) the teaching requirements are different, and put forward the requirements of "especially listening and speaking ability"; (2) This paper puts forward a new teaching model, namely "English multimedia teaching model based on computer and classroom"; (3) It emphasizes the importance of a "comprehensive, objective, scientific and accurate evaluation system", and points out that "teaching evaluation should be divided into formative evaluation and summative evaluation"; (4) It is clear that the process method is the method of teaching

© ICST Institute for Computer Sciences, Social Informatics and Telecommunications Engineering 2023
Published by Springer Nature Switzerland AG 2023. All Rights Reserved
M. A. Jan and F. Khan (Eds.): BigIoT-EDU 2022, LNICST 466, pp. 497–502, 2023.
https://doi.org/10.1007/978-3-031-23947-2_53

management, that is, "College English teaching management should run through the whole process of College English teaching. By strengthening the guidance, supervision and inspection of the teaching process, we can ensure that college English teaching can achieve the established teaching objectives." Next, this paper studies the evaluation method of English teaching quality based on SOFM neural network, focusing on the quality management of College English teaching and our ideas, hoping to attract jade, so as to attract the attention of many peers to the in-depth development of College English teaching reform [1].

2 SOFM Neural Network

Artificial neural network (ANN) is a widely parallel interconnected network composed of simple computing units, which can simulate the structure and function of biological nervous system. The single neuron of neural network has simple structure and limited function, but the network system composed of a large number of neurons can realize powerful function. So far, the artificial neural network system has some characteristics similar to the human brain. It is very similar to the human brain in the distributed storage of information, parallel processing of data and the ability to use external information for self-learning Pattern recognition and other fields have played an important role and have broad application prospects.

Artificial neural network model is a new intelligent computing model. It can imitate the structure and some working mechanism of human brain neural network, so it has very important research value. This intelligent computing model has the characteristics of using a large number of simple computing neural units to connect into a network to realize large-scale parallel computing, and has the working mechanism of changing the connection strength between neurons through learning.

2.1 SOFM Network Structure

According to its mapping characteristics and good topology preservation, self-organizing feature mapping neural network can transform the input signal of any dimension into one-dimensional or two-dimensional discrete grid, and maintain the original features of the image. SOFM network is a two-layer network, which is composed of input layer and output layer, as shown in Fig. 1. The Euclidean distance between the input pattern vector and the weight vector is calculated at the input layer, which is the matching degree mentioned in this paper; The best winning neuron is selected in the output layer. They compete according to the matching degree. The neuron with the largest matching degree and the smallest distance wins [2]. According to the principle of lateral inhibition, after repeated competition and updating, neurons will eventually learn the pattern vector and save it in the form of weight vector, so as to realize the cluster analysis of pattern vector.

2.2 SOFM Algorithm

The basic algorithm process of SOFM has been given earlier. It mainly includes three processes: competition, cooperation and adaptive adjustment:

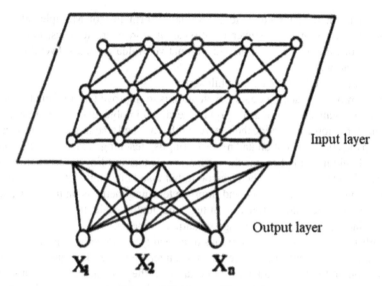

Fig. 1. SOFM network model

(1) The small random number in (0,1) assigns an initial value to each weight vector, that is, the initialization operation of the weight;

(2) Automatically select a sample x from the sample set as the input of the network, and then start self-organizing training;

(3) At time n, the best matching winning unit is selected according to the given rules, which is the competition process;

(4) Determine the neighborhood function of the network, which is the cooperation process;

(5) The weights are adjusted adaptively according to the given weight modification formula, which is an adaptive adjustment process;

(6) $N \leftarrow n + 1$ returns to (2) and continues training until a meaningful map is formed.

3 Principles to be Followed in the Evaluation of English Teaching Quality

During the implementation of English teaching quality evaluation, the following principles should be adhered to:

(1) Diversified principle of teaching evaluation.
    Under the new situation, English teaching evaluation is a process of integration of teaching and learning. Traditionally, the teaching evaluation of students is only determined by the final evaluation of test scores or grade passing scores at a single level, while the new teaching evaluation is a developmental dynamic evaluation carried out in many aspects, which not only involves the test scores, but also the students' pragmatic skills, learning attitude This teaching evaluation feature

is consistent with the educational evaluation principle of Multiple Intelligences Theory: development and diversification are its core characteristics, and the combination of formative evaluation and summative evaluation is its diversified method of evaluation.

(2) Guiding principles of teaching philosophy.

The purpose of teaching quality evaluation is to improve teaching quality and promote the realization of teaching quality evaluation objectives. The premise is that educators should first guide themselves with advanced teaching ideas and accurately grasp the current situation and needs of English teaching. Teaching quality evaluation should not only become the evaluation standard of English teachers' teaching effect inside and outside the classroom, but also help English teachers clarify the direction of teaching efforts, and improve teaching methods on this basis, so as to fully reflect the guiding function of teaching quality evaluation.

(3) Prominent principles of teaching evaluation elements.

English teaching course has obvious universality and development in connotation. In terms of content, the course has a stronger integrated learning of knowledge, emotion and meaning, attaches importance to the cultivation of students' overall quality, and pays particular attention to the cultivation of innovative skilled talents. English has obvious differences from other courses in teaching characteristics, such as the multi factors restricting teaching, the complexity of teaching environment, the differences of students' foundation, the systematicness of teaching process and the practicality of teaching effect [3]. These uniqueness require us to fully understand its generation process and implementation process in teaching evaluation to form a systematic Dynamic curriculum view. When improving the evaluation of English teaching quality, we should build a scientific and reasonable evaluation system according to its elements and characteristics. Carefully analyze the relationship between the elements, and focus on the elements that play a leading role in teaching quality, so as to ensure the essential improvement of English teaching quality.

(4) Effective feedback principle of teaching evaluation.

The fundamental purpose of teaching quality evaluation is to promote teaching development, improve teaching quality and ensure the smooth operation of teaching. Teachers can find their own teaching deficiencies in time and strive to improve from the set teaching feedback process of receiving feedback information, finding deficiencies, serious reflection and improving teaching level. Similarly, for teaching managers, feedback information can help them formulate the strategies and directions of teaching reform and teaching innovation, and improve the level of decision-making and management. The feedback system also needs to have a certain timeliness, timely find problems, solve problems, find highlights and promote highlights, so as to really promote teaching and realize a virtuous circle. In the process of evaluation, the communication between supervising teachers and teachers is not in place, and the feedback is not timely, which can easily lead to teachers' resistance.

4   English Teaching Quality Evaluation Method Based on SOFM Neural Network

Generally speaking, the standard used for performance evaluation is the standard used by students for behavior decision-making and learning, "what gets measured gets done". Assessment of achievement is not only a tool for evaluating completed teaching activities, but also can be used to stimulate learners' specific behavior, so future results can be formulated in advance. In the past, in our semester's overall evaluation results, the midterm and final examination results accounted for 70%, so students ignored the daily learning process, and there were phenomena such as absence from class and failure to hand in homework; Due to problems in the quality formation process of classroom teaching and after-school practice, it is bound to be reflected in the results of mid-term and final exams (the output of the process). For example, in three of the four semesters, we did not take oral ability as part of the overall evaluation results, so students did not pay attention to the improvement of oral ability for a long time. As a result, the passing rate of oral ability was only 28%. Therefore, we must change students' learning concept and behavior route by reforming the standard of general evaluation of semester results.

(1)   Five language skills: the curriculum requirements puts forward five requirements for English ability at each level, namely listening comprehension ability, oral expression ability, reading comprehension ability, written expression ability and translation ability. Therefore, it is necessary for us to include each skill in the scope of teaching process and performance evaluation. It should be noted that listening comprehension and oral expression rank first and second respectively. In particular, the curriculum requirements emphasizes that "no matter what form is adopted, students' actual language communication ability, especially their oral and written expression ability, should be fully assessed". Therefore, after dividing the five skills into three major teaching processes (reading, writing and translation teaching, audio-visual self-study and group oral practice), we should not only score the oral examination, but also score the usual class attendance rate, classroom question answering and written expression homework completion rate, and include these scores into the total evaluation score of the semester.

(2)   Three teaching forms: we should take three forms of classroom centralized teaching, network autonomous learning and learning group activities as the teaching mode to cultivate the five English abilities. Although the computer network provides the teaching modules of audio-visual oral and reading, writing and translation respectively, according to the questionnaire survey we conducted in October 2005, about 90% of teachers and students are satisfied and more satisfied with learning audio-visual oral through computer network multimedia, Only about 10% of teachers and students are satisfied with learning the course of reading, writing and translation through the computer network interface. Obviously, the traditional classroom teaching and written expression exercises still have certain advantages in the teaching process of reading, writing and translation. Therefore, we advocate that the teaching of reading, writing and translation should continue to adopt the traditional classroom centralized teaching method, and the advantages of computer multimedia should be mainly used in the learning process of listening [4]. As for

college oral English teaching, due to the limitation of teachers, it is feasible to adopt the form of learning group. The main tasks of teachers are to design group activities, urge students to carry out oral activities in group form, interview in turns, check and evaluate the achievements of the learning group in completing the tasks. In order to promote the development of learning group activities, students must bear in mind that oral English is a skill and is practiced. Practice makes perfect. In addition, in order to create a language learning environment, the school should take specific measures to support and encourage students to participate in English extracurricular activities (for example, in addition to English speech competition, there are English vocabulary challenge competition, English drama performance competition, English story competition, English recitation competition, etc.).

5 Conclusion

Under the new situation determined by the Ministry of education, the focus of talent training in Colleges and universities has been determined to strengthen practical, applied and skilled abilities. After employment, graduates give full play to their professional ability in various service, production and sales industries. Among all the public basic courses in Colleges and universities, English has always been a language and culture course of great concern. The model of English education and teaching has its uniqueness and non replicability, and its role in improving students' English level and language ability is continuous and irreplaceable. To improve the quality of English teaching and meet the needs of the new era for the compound talents under the educational system is the fundamental purpose of College English teaching quality evaluation.

References

1. Dai, W.: Research on diversification of English teaching evaluation in Higher Vocational Colleges. Comp. Study Cult. Innov. **5**, 115–116 (2017)
2. Hu, Y.: On the evaluation system of English teaching quality in Higher Vocational Colleges. Econ. Trade Pract. **1**, 248 (2016)
3. Xing, D.: On the evaluation system of English teaching quality in Higher Vocational Colleges. Heilongjiang High. Educ. Res. **11**, 125–127 (2016)
4. Huang, Y., Chen, L.: A star pattern recognition algorithm based on SOFM clustering. Opt. Precis. Eng. **12**(6), 346–351 (2004)

Communication Path and Influence Analysis of Drama, Film and Television Performance of Data Technology

Yan Zhang[✉]

Wuchang University of Technology, Wuhan 430223, Hubei, China
6612358@qq.com

Abstract. With the development of China's economy, great changes have taken place in various fields. Drama, film and television performing arts have also been richly presented on the TV screen, which has greatly enriched people's spiritual life. In this development process, the research on the theory of drama, film and television performance art can also promote the actual development. Based on this, this paper analyzes the communication path and impact of drama, film and television performance in the era of big data, and analyzes the artistic differences between them in detail, hoping to play a guiding role in the development of this field.

Keywords: Big data · Drama · film and television performance · Feature analysis

1 Introduction

The origin of the concept of "big data" first appeared in Alvin Toffler's book the impact of the future. The book predicts a large amount of data, unstructured data, information channel and information overload, and believes that a large amount of "manually encoded information" will replace natural information in the future. In 2013, we ushered in the so-called first year of big data. Almost all domestic Internet companies have expanded their business scope to the field of big data. Today, big data has not only penetrated all walks of life, but also gradually entered all aspects of our life. When we travel, the electronic map based on big data technology can help us accurately locate and find the most suitable travel path; When we shop, the price comparison website based on big data analysis can accurately help us distinguish the price of goods; When we read mobile news, personalized recommendation based on big data technology can accurately help us find the information we need.

Performing art is closely related to the development of human civilization history. Since the emergence of human consciousness, there has been the beginning of performing art, and performing art has become the most primitive form of expressing human emotions and expressing their minds [1]. Based on the analysis of the communication path and impact of drama, film and television performance in the era of big data, this

M. A. Jan and F. Khan (Eds.): BigIoT-EDU 2022, LNICST 466, pp. 503–511, 2023.
https://doi.org/10.1007/978-3-031-23947-2_54

paper strengthens the theoretical analysis of the characteristics of drama, film and television performance art, which is helpful to further understand and spread drama, film and television performance.

Film and television performance can only be presented to the audience through the TV screen or movie screen after script, shooting and editing. It needs a certain period to produce social value. There is a lot of room for regulating the requirements of actors. If this section is not shot well, you can shoot another one. You can adjust the film and television effect through post production.

Stage performance is a real live stage performance, which can directly communicate with the audience face to face, and has more performance value. However, drama performance tests the actors' on-the-spot adaptability and stage expressiveness. It is highly consistent in performance and no big mistakes are allowed.

Film and television performances are not limited by time. As long as the team and actors cooperate with each other before and after the film and television, they can complete the film and television performances, and can reasonably allocate the performance time according to the shooting needs. In many cases, a shot needs to be shot many times, or it is found that there are few shots in the later production, and then it is taken again.

The time requirements for stage performance are very strict. Because drama performance belongs to stage drama and directly faces the audience, the time arrangement is more compact. All scripts have a time sequence and the characters have continuity. Actors need to combine the characteristics of the characters in the play to reasonably connect different periods of time.

Film and television performance requires that the performance of actors should be as true and natural as possible, and should not be too exaggerated or exaggerated. For stage effect, stage performance will deliberately use exaggerated or exaggerated ways of expression to shape the role.

2   Related Work

2.1   Big Data Era

Today, the industry does not have a completely unified definition of the concept of big data. McKinsey, a world-renowned consulting firm, was the first to put forward the term "big data" in the world. In its report big data: the next frontier of innovation, competition and productivity released in 2011, McKinsey claimed that "big data refers to a data set whose size exceeds the acquisition, storage, management and analysis capabilities of conventional database tools.". In Schoenberg's big data age, he believes that "at first, the concept of big data means that the amount of information to be processed is too large, which has exceeded the amount of memory used by ordinary computers when processing data."

Through the above analysis of the concept of big data, it is not difficult to see that the so-called big data, as the name suggests, mainly refers to a kind of massive data, which exceeds the range that our current conventional computers can store and bear. The big data mentioned in this paper not only includes the traditional Shanghai data set, but also includes the related technologies based on these big data, including the collection, analysis and processing of massive data, as shown in Fig. 1.

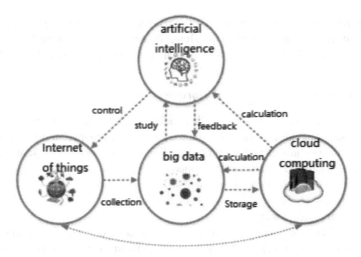

Fig. 1. Big data technology analysis

In order to better understand big data, we should first clarify the characteristics of big data. At present, the statement recognized by the academic and industry is put forward by IBM. They believe that big data has four characteristics in general, also known as "4 V", namely: first, large volume, which mainly means that the amount of data to be collected and analyzed by big data is very large, which has become the original TB level and has risen to the Pb level; The second is variety, which mainly refers to the diversification of data sources, and the types and formats of data are very rich; Third, speed, which mainly means that big data technology needs to analyze and collect data in real time and quickly, which is faster than traditional data collection. Fourth, high accuracy, which mainly means that the information collected through big data is very real and objective, which is closely related to the real world.

In order to make a good movie, I think an actor should have certain character characteristics and detail control ability, such as the silly root played by wangbaoqiang. He has the character characteristics, because wangbaoqiang originally came from the countryside, his speech has a strong flavor of local dialect, and he is also very stupid and quiet, so Feng Xiaogang fell in love with Wang Baoqiang at a glance. Only he can meet all the requirements of the role of silly root! But not everyone can master the control ability of details. For example, superstar Chow Yun fat's films are really unrivalled in the handling of details. This is the ability of good actors! So it is an unchangeable fact that a good film must have a group of good actors.

I think TV dramas are less than movies, but from the actor's point of view, they are lower in the details of the role. The TV play highlights the dialogue and has high requirements for lines. My understanding is that it is similar to a radio drama. You can know the plot by just listening to the sound with your eyes closed.

In my opinion, compared with film and television, stage drama has the highest and most stringent requirements for actors. No matter from the actor's role control, the detailed expression of the characters, the on-the-spot play of the lines, etc., there can be no mistakes, otherwise the performance will be ruined! The most important point is that they face the audience live. The actors in movies and TV dramas are not perfect. The director can let them never do it again. However, actors are not allowed to perform on stage. They have only one chance. They have no choice whether to perform well or fail.

2.2   Drama, Film and Television Performance

In our country, performance major can be divided into broad sense and narrow sense. In a broad sense, it includes music performance, dance performance, sports performance, opera performance, model and clothing modeling performance, etc. "Drama, film and television performance" includes two concepts, one is "drama performance" and the other is "film and television performance".

(1)   Theatrical performance
Drama takes people as the object of expression and uses "action" A comprehensive art as a means of expression. Dramatic actors perform on the stage and communicate directly with the audience. The performance of actors is the final image accepted by the audience [2]. According to different classification standards, drama can be divided into different types: according to the size of capacity, drama literature can be divided into multi act drama, single act drama and sketch; according to the form of expression, it can be divided into drama, opera, dance drama and drama According to the theme, it can be divided into myth drama, historical drama, legend drama, citizen drama, social drama, family drama, etc.; according to the nature and effect of drama conflict, it can be divided into tragedy, comedy and drama. The drama concept discussed in this paper takes drama as an example. The analysis of drama and film for ligula are shown in Fig. 2.

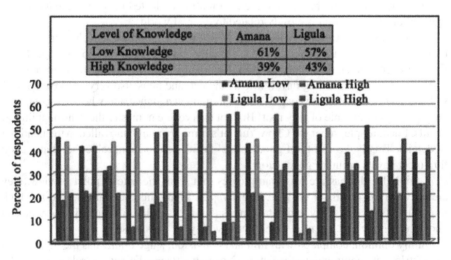

Fig. 2. The analysis of drama and film for ligula

(2) Film and television performance

Film and television performance is an art in which actors play roles and perform the plot in front of the camera. The performance of film actors is indirectly communicated with the audience through the screen, and the final image on the screen can be completed only after photographic art processing and artistic re creation by the director using montage means. Up to now, film and television performance is also based on Stanislav's basic theory of performance Department and other drama systems. Drama performance and film and television performance belong to the category of performing arts and have common basic laws. In essence, they are the display of skills, but the display methods are slightly different. In terms of performance concept, the performance of drama, film and TV drama should be consistent. In the inner and outer skills of character creation, in the internal and external skills of character depiction In terms of Zhibu's character, understanding, understanding and analysis of tasks, today's effective teaching methods of performance specialty do not violate the principles and requirements of film and television performance. The main methods and means of role creation are the same in drama and film, and the main difference is the difference between the sense of lens and the sense of stage [3]. Because drama performance is the basis of all performing arts, Because the theoretical basis of drama and film and television performance is the same, this paper combs and expounds the theoretical basis and historical development of drama performance with drama as an example.

The stage actors perform in front of the audience in the theater. The performance is dramatic and has a lot of body language. They had to train their voices so that the audience in the last row of the theatre could hear them. The stage actor should also attract and guide the audience's attention. Film and television actors are relatively more "static", and their performances are closer to the daily life of the audience.

Drama is the expression of stories in many ways. It is usually performed on the stage. For example, TV dramas such as dance dramas and operas are performed in advance and then broadcast. Generally speaking, drama, including drama and TV dramas, is definitely different. Actors' performance belongs to film and television.

3   Analysis on the Characteristics of Drama Performance and Film and Television Performance

3.1   Analysis of Main Characteristics of Drama Performance

The analysis of the performance characteristics of drama should be carried out from multiple levels. Firstly, from the perspective of role characteristics, drama actors should be able to perform truthfully in front of the audience, and each stage is also the actor's reshaping of the role. Therefore, drama performers make progress in the performance art in the continuous performance process, and only by constantly breaking through the performance form in the performance Moreover, the dramatic actors should be able to break the limitations of time and space on the stage, and make a perfect combination of practicality and timeliness. Because the image of stage character art is intuitive, it can have an impact on the audience's vision, and the actors' secondary creation is also their own performance instrumentalization and creative materials Materialization.

The most basic feature of dramatic performance art is that actors create stage role images. Dramatic actors are secondary creation according to the playwright's script. Dramatic actors must be able to perform in front of the audience in person, and their role images are gradually displayed in the stage time and space.

Although there are many similarities between film performance and drama performance in the methods of creating characters, there are great differences in the forms of creation.

1. fidelity - hypothetical
   The film performance meets the audience through the screen with the help of scientific media, and indirectly communicates with the audience after shooting and recording. Continuous camera shooting and montage processing bring great freedom to use time and space, enabling actors to perform in the real exterior environment or the real interior environment.

   Theatrical performance is in the form of stage, and the actor himself meets the audience directly. It requires certain exaggeration and virtual techniques, and stylized performance.
2. distance from the audience: variable - constant

The camera's changeable orientation, cutting shooting and montage are important means of expression of film art. It changes the distance between the audience and the actors, thus producing close-up, close-up, mid shot, long-range and other shots.

On the stage, the distance between the audience and the actors is unchangeable. They are always in a "panoramic" position, and the audience will always watch the performance from a certain perspective.

3.2 Main Features of Film and Television Performance

For film and television performance, the most basic feature of film and television performance is that actors create the image of screen roles. Specifically, film and television actors should be able to create with the basis provided by the playwright. As film and television actors, they should not only read the literary script, but also study the director's lens book in detail, so as to go deep into the director's shooting intention The preparation before the performance is complete. Moreover, film and television actors have strict restrictions in front of the camera. When film and television actors see the director's split shot script, they should be able to accurately find the close-up, medium shot and close-up positions, and know the motion position of the camera and the relationship between motion perspective, etc.

In addition, film and television actors perform disorderly. Due to financial constraints and restrictions on the shooting site, they can't shoot according to the sequence of the script, mainly in combination with the schedule. In addition, film and television performance is a one-time recording moment, delicate and real performance, and film and television performance is mainly through editing and re structure table The complete performance is created from the original performance arranged under the camera in the editing room.

Film emphasis - stage emphasis.

Although actors occupy an important position in film art, film is a comprehensive art with rich means of expression. The director has many ways to emphasize: through the change of camera orientation, the change of scene and different lenses, the use of different techniques of music, the description of the details of the scene through the empty lens, and so on.

Although there are lights, effects and music on the stage, the drama largely depends on the performance of the actors, especially the lines. The director mainly depends on the performance art and the scheduling of actors on the stage.

Sense of lens - sense of stage.

The so-called sense of shot includes three points: the specific feeling of the camera lens, the sense of different scenes, and the adaptation to the scene scheduling of the film. The acting area of film actors seems to be infinite, but this infinite space is reflected through the limited screen. Film actors are restricted by the camera lens when performing.

Theater actors should be familiar with the stage, master the formal rules and scheduling rhythm of the stage, and have a sense of stage.

Discontinuity – all at once.

Film actors create intermittently in front of the camera, and the scenes they shoot are not coherent, or even are shot in reverse classification. Actors must adapt to this situation, which requires actors to quickly enter and leave the image.

Drama performance requires actors to shape characters from beginning to end on the stage.

Special creative conditions.

Film actors need more attention. Not only the role play, but also pay attention to the tasks proposed by the director, the angles determined by the cameraman, and the limitations of actors' activities on the drawing grid.

4 Commonalities Between Drama Performance and Film and Television Performance

(1) Both are performing arts. Drama performance and film and television performance are both performing arts, which are designed to add fun and color to people's life. They both need scripts, plots and creation, and they must also have their own creation room, including the full cooperation of various departments such as sound, lighting, photography and make-up, but film and television art needs to be improved in the end Editing, sorting and so on, but on the whole, these two belong to a comprehensive art, which is created to meet the spiritual needs of the audience.

(2) The purpose of actors' performance is the same. As performing artists, they all have a common purpose, that is to create fresh and powerful characters for the people, give everyone a sense of relaxation after intense work, and let everyone enjoy unique excellent works. Therefore, the performances of actors are aesthetic, and they will create roles in various ways Make, or make-up, or unkempt, use their own body language and image depiction to interpret life and interpret roles, so that the audience can feel deeply and unforgettable through watching.

(3) The training requirements of actors are unified. Three minutes on stage and three years off stage, whether drama actors or film and television actors, their performance training process is the same, acting as a "Trinity" It can be said that actors are the most important in the whole performance process. They are not only the main body of creation, but also the props of creation, but also the objects of creation through their performance [4]. In order to make the plot move the audience and win the hearts of people, actors must use their unique plastic arts to activate the image, conquer the audience, and treat the audience with the results of their high-intensity training and slender emotions Each character is reasonably shaped, and each character evolves into flesh and blood and spirituality, leaving a deep impression on the audience.

(4) The expression methods of actors are consistent. Although the performance methods of actors are rich and colorful, the ideas expressed in the end are consistent, that is to say, no matter what methods are used to depict and perform characters, they should aim at authenticity and life, so that people can feel life and understand life from the performance, because since ancient times, the most real performance is the most moving and most beautiful Natural performance is the most breath of life. If you are separated from life, you are separated from the masses. Without the support of the masses, the performing art has no value and significance. Therefore, the actors who can be sought after by the audience must be closer to life and people's hearts in the Performing Art, which is consistent and meaningful for both drama performance and film and television performance Only actors who can give life to their works are qualified actors.

5 Conclusion

In a word, drama performance and film and television performance have gone deep into people's daily life and become a way for people to find a little spiritual relaxation and liberation after dinner. Although the two are very different, in a fundamental sense, they are interconnected, interrelated, serve the majority of the audience, and want to give people happiness through realistic and life-oriented art performance The rhythmic life can relieve the pressure, let everyone get the decompression of mood and enjoy the beauty. As long as these performing artists try their best to shape and depict each character, they will become powerful actors, have more fans and bring more happiness and moving to people.

In terms of the degree of difficulty in achieving success and the expectation of the audience, actors need to spend more time on stage drama than on film, and film is higher than television. Stage drama has the highest requirements. It faces the audience directly, without ng opportunities, special effects, and dubbing. It is an all-round test of actors' basic skills such as lines and body shape. Most stage drama actors are allowed to stage after years of hard training. It is a true portrayal of "ten minutes on stage and ten years off stage". The length of the film is shorter than that of the TV, which requires a higher expressiveness of the actors; The number of actors is limited, and the requirements for each major actor are very high. A major actor's poor performance is likely to lead to the quality of the whole film. TV is relatively less demanding among the three, because it takes a long time to compare the stage drama with the film, and one episode has loopholes that can be corrected or whitewashed in the follow-up broadcast; Compared with the stage drama, the technology of dubbing can be used to improve the later stage; There are a large number of actors participating in the performance. If one person has poor performance, more other actors can make up for it. For example, the TV with poor performance of the female host in the TV can still be a good work.

Stage drama is equivalent to a microscope. The performance of the actors is displayed in front of the audience in all directions and from all angles. It is easy to enlarge the advantages. A movie is like a magnifying glass. For a limited time, you can't fast forward. All the performances will be noticed. The TV is equivalent to a flat mirror. The next floor has no amplification effect and is not demanding.

Finally, I often see new people or passers-by without any experience making movies and TV, but I rarely hear people without any foundation on the stage. This also shows that film, television and stage drama have different requirements for actors in performance.

References

1. Zhu, D.: Understanding and analysis of drama performance and film and television performance. Orient. Corp. Cult. **16**, 262–263 (2011)
2. Zhong, M.: Field investigation and analysis of folk drama, song and dance, film and television performance. Drama Art **03**, 60–69 (2005)
3. Cao, J.: On the "separation" and "combination" of film and television performance and drama performance. J. Jilin Inst. Educ. (late) **04**, 147–148 (2015)
4. Liu, S.: Exploration on the application of multiple thinking in drama, film and television performance teaching in colleges and universities. Popular Lit. Art **02**, 244 (2016)
5. Dyn, N., Levin, D.: Subdivision schemes in geometric modelling. Acta Numer. **11**, 73–144, (2002)
6. Conti, C., Hormann, K.: Polynomial reproduction for univariate subdivision schemes of any arity. J. Approx. Theory **163**(4), 413–437 (2011)
7. Hameed, R., Mustafa, G.: "Family of a -point b -ary subdivision schemes with bell-shaped mask. Appl. Math. Comput. **309**, 289–302 (2017)
8. Feng, Y., Yu, X., Wang, G.G.: A novel monarch butterfly optimization with global position updating operator for large-scale 0-1 knapsack problems. Mathematics **7**(11), 1056 (2019)
9. Sun, L., Chen, S., Xu, J., Tian, Y.: Improved monarch butterfly optimization algorithm based on opposition-based learning and random local perturbation. Complexity **2019**, Article ID 4182148 (2019)
10. Pasupuleti, V., Balaswamy, C.: Performance analysis of fractional earthworm optimization algorithm for optimal routing in wireless sensor networks. ICST Trans. Scalable Inf. Syst. **8**(32), Article ID 169419 (2018)
11. Li, J., Lei, H., Alavi, A.H., Wang, G.-G.: Elephant herding optimization: variants, hybrids, and applications. Mathematics **8**(9), 1415 (2020)
12. Li, Y., Zhu, X., Liu, J.: An improved moth-flame optimization algorithm for engineering problems. Symmetry **12**(8), 1234 (2020)
13. Liu, H., Tang, A.D., Tang, S.Q., Han, T., Zhou, H., Xie, L.: A Modified slime mould algorithm for global optimization. Comput. Intell. Neurosci. **2021**, Article ID 2298215 (2021)
14. Yang, Y., Chen, H., Heidari, A.A., Gandomi, A.H.: Hunger games search: visions, conception, implementation, deep analysis, perspectives, and towards performance shifts. Expert Syst. Appl. **177**, Article ID 114864 (2021)

Evaluation Model of College English Teaching Effect Based on Big Data Platform

Suyun Gan[(✉)]

Jiangxi Industry Polytechnic College, Nanchan 330002, Jiangxi, China
871645721@qq.com

Abstract. At present, there are many methods for teaching assessment in different universities. As we know, now each university has different assess system for English teaching. Firstly, as a compulsory course, teachers and students pay great attention to English learning, but there are also many problems. At present, there are still relatively few high-quality English teachers, especially in rural universities. There are serious deficiencies in teacher resources and teaching equipment, which can not meet the urgent needs of College English teaching. The teaching method of teachers is relatively simple, and the teaching method is mostly used. In teaching, face-to-face is used to instill knowledge into students. In the teaching process, the Chinese teaching method takes a long time, and the translation teaching method is used too much. There are many grammatical errors in the teaching process, which is difficult for students to understand: in the teaching process, the passive teaching is mainly used, and the teachers teach the students to listen to the notes. There is a kind of "dumb English"; Teachers do not have enough time to interact with students. At present, most of the teaching tasks of College English substitute teachers are heavy. Under the existing education system, the goal of English education is mainly exam oriented, and the practical application is lack. As a result, many students' interest in learning English decreases. Students with good academic performance and some interest in English often neglect their listening ability. For students with poor grades, their interest in learning is very low, and their opportunities to actually use English are also very limited. Therefore, how to improve the efficiency of College English teaching and improve the comprehensive quality of students on the basis of meeting the existing teaching and examination requirements is the key to teaching research. In view of this, this paper proposes a wide area database based College English teaching performance evaluation model.

Keywords: Teaching effect · Big data · College English · Evaluation model

1 Introduction

With the rapid development of the Internet in the new era of information, digitization and globalization, English has become more and more important. English is not a language and a means of communication, but a necessary skill. As one of the most important

M. A. Jan and F. Khan (Eds.): BigIoT-EDU 2022, LNICST 466, pp. 512–522, 2023.
https://doi.org/10.1007/978-3-031-23947-2_55

international languages in the world, English is widely used in all fields of human life. At present, in many countries in the world, English education is considered as an important subject and is included in the school curriculum of basic education [1]. English education has become an important part of civic quality education. In China, English is one of the compulsory courses in middle schools, universities and postgraduate courses. In the advanced level examination and CET-4 and CET-6, the passing rate of the English Department is very high. So English learning becomes more and more important.

As a part of College English teaching, teachers teach students English through the online English platform, so that they can listen, speak, read and write in English, making students' learning more convenient and effective.

Teaching effect evaluation has become one of the focuses of teaching work at home and abroad. Especially at the university level, the school fully recognizes that the effectiveness of teacher education is the core of survival and development. The evaluation standard of teaching effect has great subjectivity, but it also has quite objective regularity. Therefore, more scientific methods and calculations can obtain more reliable results.

The performance evaluation of College English teaching is also helpful for school administrators to have a comprehensive understanding of middle school English teaching. For example, middle school English teachers improve their teaching methods, promote the new curriculum, emphasize interaction with students, and use modern teaching methods to improve teaching efficiency. It is an arduous task with important scientific research value to comprehensively evaluate the effect of English Teaching in middle schools, accurately define and formulate the school's subject development direction and teacher training plan [2]. In recent years, more and more attention has been paid to

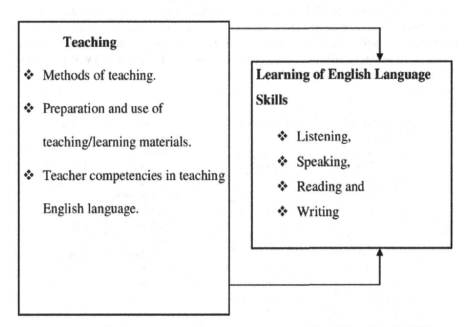

Fig. 1. The relationship for teaching effect.

the evaluation of middle school English teaching effect, the development of evaluation system and methods, and the improvement of middle school English teachers' political quality, noble character and experience. However, the evaluation of classroom teaching effect of middle school English teachers involves many aspects and factors. Participants' knowledge level, cognitive ability and personal orientation directly affect the evaluation indicators. It is difficult to exclude the influence of individual factors, and the fuzziness of evaluation indicators makes the work of evaluators more difficult [3]. The following relationships should be understood about the English learning achievements of some universities: As shown in Fig. 1.

2   Related Work

Nowadays, the value orientation of the evaluation of English classroom teaching effect in middle schools is that the author evaluates in advance, modifies the index system, and the pre established index system provides "what" and "how to evaluate". The core of this kind of evaluation method is the guidance and inspection between superiors and subordinates [4]. It is difficult to exchange and test the objects that actually participate in the evaluation and improve teaching through evaluation. Although the school attaches great importance to the evaluation of those participants, there is a lack of cognition and attention to the actual ideas and intentions of the evaluation objects, and there is a great deal of ambiguity. The evaluation results are difficult to reflect the authenticity of English classroom teaching in middle schools [5].

The China Conference on data mining (CCDM) was jointly sponsored by the Chinese computer society and the Chinese society of artificial intelligence, and jointly directed by the Special Committee on machine learning of the Chinese society of artificial intelligence. It was held in Beijing for the first time in 2005, has been held for six times, and was held in Guilin in 2016. In China, there are many big data platforms with education, the structure is as follows that is shown in Fig. 2.

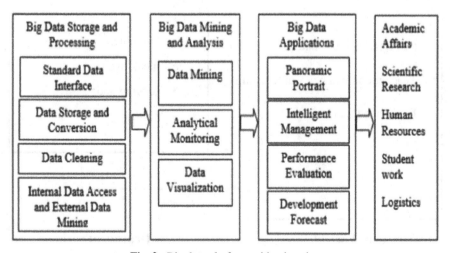

Fig. 2. Big data platform with education

Educational data mining is an emerging research field, which comprehensively uses the technologies and methods of statistics, machine learning and data mining, trains the data through the machine learning model, mines and analyzes the educational big data, and finds the correlation between learners' learning results and variables such as learning content, learning resources and teaching behavior, To predict learners' future learning trends and learning related laws. Since 2005, AAAI, aied, its, um and other international conferences related to computer applications have held theme seminars on "educational data mining" for many times. In June 2008, the first international academic conference on educational data mining was held in [6].

It was held in Montreal, Canada. Since then, it has been held once a year, sponsored by the international educational data mining Society (IEDMS). So far, it has been successfully held for 9 times, mainly discussing the application of data mining in education. In July 2011, the fourth EDM international conference successfully founded the Journal of educational data mining (jemd). In 2009, Beijing Normal University held the Fifth International Conference on advanced data mining and application, which put forward the theme of "Application of data mining in education" for the first time. At present, it has successfully held eight sessions [7].

The role of each individual in the Big Data platform in higher education is shown in Fig. 3.

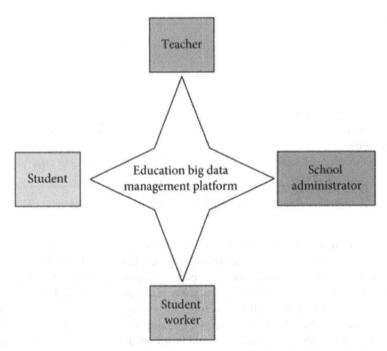

Fig. 3. The role of each individual in the Big Data platform in higher education

3   Research on the Evaluation Index System of Middle School English Classroom Teaching

In the past few years, the subjective understanding of hearing professionals and teachers on the English teaching process, but the results are often different from the actual situation. In view of this, researchers have proposed a series of classroom teaching evaluation indicators. At the same time, most of the current researches on the evaluation index system of English Teaching in middle schools lack a clear evaluation of the effect of English Teaching in other schools. According to the practical experience of middle school teaching and the opinions of other English teachers and experts, the author has designed an index system that is consistent with the new English teaching evaluation of grade five, so as to facilitate the evaluation in the future [8]. Therefore, this chapter will elaborate on the principle of index selection and index screening of English classroom teaching evaluation system which is shown in Fig. 4.

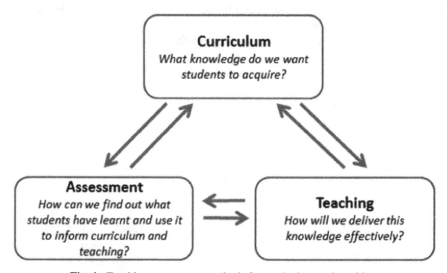

Fig. 4. Teaching assessment methods for curriculum and teaching.

After the principle of constructing the evaluation index system is determined, the next step is to construct a scientific evaluation index system to clarify the primary indicators, primary indicators and the critical value of observation points, that is, the grade judgment standard. Referring to the research results at home and abroad, through the analysis of the key elements of English teachers' teaching, and through the reference to the literature related [9], The middle school English experts (mainly teachers of Xinjian No. 5 middle school, English teachers of Xinjian No. 6 middle school and students engaged in English teaching) were investigated [10]. The specific index system is given in Table 1, and we preset all the evaluation indexes according to the experts' and teachers' years of teaching experience.

Table 1. English teaching evaluation index system

Index			Standard				
Primary index	Serial number	Secondary finger	Weight	Excellent	Good	Commonly	Poor
Teaching attitude	1	Lectures are energetic and infectious, can attract students' attention, and teachers can treat all students equally	0.1	≥ 3	≥ 2	≥ 1	Other
		Carefully and timely arrange and correct homework and papers, and patiently guide and answer questions	0.1	≥ 20	≥ 15	≥ 10	Other
Content of courses	2	The content is rich and informative, which can reflect or contact the new ideas, new concepts and new achievements of discipline development	0.15	≥ 4	≥ 3	≥ 2	Other
		The explanation of the problem is concise, accurate, simple and enlightening; Highlight the key points, have clear ideas, be proficient in the course content and use it freely	0.15	3	2	1	Other
Teaching method	3	It can give students the Enlightenment of thinking, association and innovation, and make effective use of various teaching media	0.15	≤ 24	≤ 48	≤ 72	Other
		It can mobilize students' emotions, activate the classroom atmosphere, make effective use of classroom time, properly organize and manage the classroom, and have a good classroom order	0.1	≥ 90	≥ 80	≥ 60	Other
Teaching effectiveness	4	Student completion rate	0.1	90%	75%	50%	Other
		Student learning effect (one-time pass rate)	0.15	$\geq 85\%$	$\geq 70\%$	$\geq 60\%$	Other

4 Evaluation Model of College English Teaching Effect Based on Big Data Platform

The traditional teaching evaluation lacks the support of advanced educational ideas, and the concept of evaluation is often confused with examination and testing. Therefore, the evaluation only focuses on the learning results of students, and the object of evaluation is only directed to students, while the development of curriculum, the research of students' learning process and the participation of students' subjects are placed outside the evaluation [11]. The result is: the knowledge structure and content of the course lag behind the development of society and the progress of science and technology, and cannot meet the needs of students; Students' learning is only passive acceptance and mechanical rote, and their active development and self-directed learning are seriously restricted.

With the comprehensive and in-depth implementation of quality education and the introduction of the new curriculum concept, the evaluation concept is gradually updating and changing. People begin to realize that we must use the modern concept of quality education to guide and evaluate English teaching and students' learning [12]. The evaluation should be based on the lifelong development of students, pay attention to the comparison between the past and present of individual students, strive to find their own flash point, and strive to show their personality and tap their potential in the process of students' English learning, so as to make them grow harmoniously in all-round development [13]. The evaluation model of College English teaching effect based on big data platform is shown in Figs. 5 and 6

① Collection of evaluation data. To evaluate teachers' teaching, we must first try to get the original data of evaluation. We can mine two kinds of data in the e-learning platform: one is to mine the web log by using the data mining method based on statistics. In addition to mining the web log, we should also mine the data in the background database to obtain the data in the relevant evaluation index system. The method of mining is to use database management software, such as Oracle, SQL server and other data mining functions [14].

② Integration of evaluation data. The integration of evaluation data refers to the consolidation of data in several databases.

③ Selection of evaluation data. According to the evaluation index system, select relevant data and delete some strange data, so as to improve the quality of data mining.

④ Cleaning of evaluation data. The cleaning of evaluation data means that in order to solve the problem of semantic ambiguity, it is realized by cleaning the dirty data and dealing with the missing data in the data. If an option data in a log is wrong, it can be filled after averaging according to other log conditions. For example, when some data in a log is unreadable or wrong, it can be discarded to reduce the capacity of the database and improve the processing efficiency of the database.

⑤ Conversion of evaluation data. The conversion of evaluation data refers to the conversion of different values in the database into data coding form. For example, in order to facilitate processing, The grades "excellent", "good", "average" and "poor" are converted into 1, 0.75, 0.6 and 0.3 respectively. In addition, the data conversion converts the collected original data of teachers' teaching evaluation in e-learning into

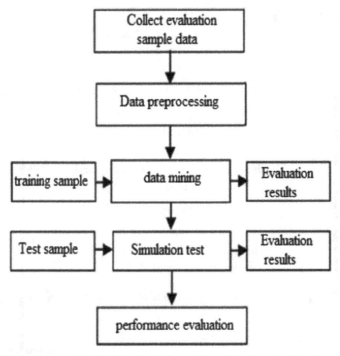

Fig. 5 Evaluation model of College English teaching effect based on big data platform

the grade of each index according to the standards of the evaluation index system, and saves the relevant index values.

⑥ Analysis and processing of evaluation data. There are many processing methods for evaluation data, such as neural network, fuzzy concept, etc. here, in order to simplify the aura processing process, the weighted linear average is selected to calculate the quantitative results of teachers' network teaching evaluation, and then the quantitative results are transformed into grades.

⑦ Expression and interpretation of evaluation results. According to the purpose of English teachers' teaching evaluation, extract and express the useful information for necessary explanation and explanation.

⑧ Feedback of evaluation results. Feedback the evaluation results to teachers and teaching managers in appropriate ways and forms.

Teaching evaluation is an important part of the teaching process. It takes the teaching objectives as the basis, formulates scientific evaluation standards, uses all effective technical means to measure the process and results of teaching and learning activities, and gives value judgment [15]. The commonly used types of teaching evaluation include diagnostic evaluation, formative evaluation and summative evaluation. Diagnostic evaluation is carried out at the same time of course teaching design, and its results are reflected in the column of "student characteristic analysis"; Formative evaluation is carried out in the process of teaching practice and filled in the column of "formative evaluation"

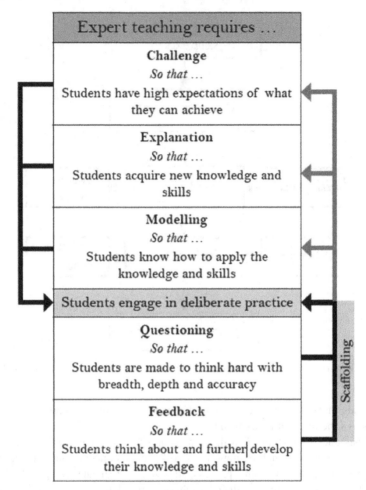

Fig. 6. Expert teaching system.

in the classroom teaching design form at any time. If necessary, it can organize class attendance evaluation and classroom teaching evaluation; The summative evaluation is carried out after the end of the whole course, and the teaching effect is analyzed and evaluated according to the test results. In the process of autonomous learning, learning effect evaluation is often used. It not only attaches importance to the evaluation of learning results, but also attaches more importance to the evaluation of learning process. Classroom teaching evaluation is the most important and specific content we must face first. Classroom teaching is the most important and key link in the whole educational process. Its quality determines the quality of the whole teaching. Therefore, the classroom teaching should be evaluated scientifically frequently, so as to affirm the advantages, find the deficiencies, give feedback in time and facilitate improvement.

5 Conclusion

Teaching evaluation is also a regular work to be carried out by education and teaching management departments at all levels. But for a long time, there have been misunderstandings about what is evaluation, the function of evaluation, the difference between formative evaluation and summative evaluation, and the relationship between evaluation and testing. Due to various reasons, there is a phenomenon that examination is regarded as the ultimate goal of language learning in English teaching. Using examination instead of multiple teaching evaluation purposes, evaluation strategies and evaluation means makes test equal to evaluation, resulting in many negative effects. The English curriculum standard puts forward new evaluation concepts and requirements, and emphasizes that the English teaching evaluation system, so as to achieve the harmony and unity of the evaluation of learning process and learning results. This undoubtedly puts forward new challenges and requirements for English teaching evaluation. Therefore, we should seriously study and understand the spiritual essence of English curriculum standards, change the concept of evaluation, clarify the principles of evaluation, master the evaluation methods, and comprehensively and scientifically implement teaching evaluation according to English curriculum standards. Through the evaluation, students can constantly understand the progress and achievements of English learning, understand themselves, build confidence, and develop comprehensive language skills. Let teachers get the information of English teaching and properly reflect and adjust their teaching behavior. Promote the continuous improvement of teachers' teaching level, timely understand the school's compliance with the curriculum standards, improve teaching management, and promote the continuous development and improvement of English courses.

References

1. Yan, X., Tian, J.: Evaluation model of college students' entrepreneurship success rate based on grey relational theory. E3S Web Conf. **235**(25), 03019 (2021)
2. Zhang, Z.: Evaluation model of college students' mental health based on neural network. J. Phys. Conf. Ser. **1744**(4), 042116 (2021)
3. Tan, L., Guan, Y.: Talent Evaluation Model of College Students Based on Big Data Technology (2021)
4. Li, N.: A fuzzy evaluation model of college english teaching quality based on analytic hierarchy process. Int. J. Emerg. Technol. Learn. (iJET) **16**(2), 17 (2021)
5. Yuan, X.: Construction of moral education evaluation model based on quality cultivation of college students. Sci. Program. **2022**(8), 1–11 (2022)
6. Tang, J.: Training model and quality of college students in English major. Int. J. Emerg. Technol. Learn. (iJET) **16**(4), 152 (2021)
7. Guan, A.: Research on blended teaching model in college English based on mobile learning app. J. Contemp. Educ. Res. **5**(1), 4 (2021)
8. Zhang, M., Yuan, X.: Application Research of the Current Situation of College English Online Teaching Model in the Big Data Era (2021)
9. Zhao, X., Zheng, C.: Fuzzy evaluation of physical education teaching quality in colleges based on analytic hierarchy process. Int. J. Emerg. Technol. Learn. (iJET) **16**(6), 217 (2021)
10. Dereje, R., Hassen, K., Gizaw, G.: Evaluation of anthropometric indices for screening hypertension among employees of Mizan Tepi University, Southwestern Ethiopia. Integr. Blood Pressure Control **14**, 99–111 (2021)

11. Chang, H.: College English flipped classroom teaching model based on big data and deep neural networks. Sci. Prog. **2021**, 1–10 (2021)
12. Luo, G.: Integration and Optimization of College English Teaching Information Resources in the Context of Big Data (2021)
13. Zeng, Y.: Application of flipped classroom model driven by big data and neural network in oral English teaching. Wirel. Commun. Mob. Comput. **2021**(1), 1–7 (2021)
14. Ye, Y.: English Teaching Ability Evaluation Algorithm Based on Big Data Fuzzy K-means Clustering (2021)
15. Wang, L.: Construction of English network teaching platform relying on computer big data. J. Phys. Conf. Ser. **1744**(3), 032142 (2021)

Based on C4 Design and Implementation of College Health Sports System Based on 5 Algorithm

Shaorong Lin[✉]

Hankou University, Hubei 430212, China
whgacedu@126.com

Abstract. With the advent of the era of big data, it is particularly important to obtain the knowledge behind massive data through data mining. Spatial data is the basis of big data, which makes the significance of spatial data mining more prominent. Spatial classification is an active branch of spatial data mining in recent years. College students are the main force of China's socialist modernization. In the process of investigating the physique of college students, we found that the physique of college students showed an obvious downward trend. The reason for the decline of College Students' physique is not only the relationship between schools, but also a serious social problem. This paper is based on C4 The system separates the data layer, business layer and user interface, and uses a structured relational database to provide different forms of user interfaces for the staff and members of the health and sports center. By modularizing the program design, the system meets the design requirements of high cohesion and low coupling, so as to provide efficient basic support for different applications of members and health and Sports Center staff. It is of great significance to guide the use of structured data in the operation of sqlserver, so as to help the operators to find the rules of structured data management.

Keywords: C4. 5 algorithm · System design · College physical education

1 Introduction

The constitution of college students is the physical health quality of college students. It includes both congenital factors and the influence of acquired exercise. It is a comprehensive sports index. The current definition of health is no longer limited to the absence of physical disease, but also includes sports health, interpersonal health, moral health and so on. It is a comprehensive performance index. Although health is not equal to physique, they are an interrelated organic whole. Only a healthy body can guarantee a good physique, but the physical health is not only affected by its own conditions, but also restricted by the environment, health, diet, habits and many other aspects.

© ICST Institute for Computer Sciences, Social Informatics and Telecommunications Engineering 2023
Published by Springer Nature Switzerland AG 2023. All Rights Reserved
M. A. Jan and F. Khan (Eds.): BigIoT-EDU 2022, LNICST 466, pp. 523–534, 2023.
https://doi.org/10.1007/978-3-031-23947-2_56

People think that the decline of College Students' physique is always a serious problem because of the decline of College Students' physique. But in fact, it is not. With China's excellent achievements in international competitions in recent years, there are fewer and fewer voices of doubt. However, there is a widespread problem of emphasizing competition and neglecting physique in China. Some experts believe that we should reduce the awareness of gold medals and improve the physique of college students. This view holds that the poor physique of college students is caused by unscientific sports health [1]. The national fitness proposed by China cannot meet the needs of national fitness, which leads to the continuous decline of College Students' physique. On the contrary, China has made outstanding achievements in international events in recent years. They believe that this is due to the problems of China's sports strategy. The reason for this doubt is that people simply regard the decline of College Students' physique as a sports problem. Although it is said that increasing physical exercise can improve the physique of college students, we should also consider what causes the decline of College Students' physique and why college students lack physical exercise.

For the declining trend of College Students' physique, universities should take some responsibility. Therefore, China has been carrying out the reform of college physical education. Because college physical education in China is generally only available for freshmen and sophomores, and there is only one class per week, which seriously affects the requirements of College Students' physical exercise. Moreover, since the implementation of College Students' physique standards, there has never been a situation that college students' physique does not meet the standards. All these have aroused the voice of the society that universities should be responsible for the decline of College Students' physique. However, for the decline of College Students' physique, it cannot be paid by the University, because the decline of College Students' physique is a social problem. If all the blame is on the sports level of the University, it will be biased. College students are the backbone of a society. They represent the intellectual class of the society. If the physique of college students decreases, it is bound to affect the international competitiveness of the whole country [2]. Therefore, the society must attach great importance to the decline of College Students' physique. We should start with family education. At present, because parents only unilaterally emphasize their children's academic achievements and ignore the cultivation of their children's physical exercise habits, college students lack the motivation of independent exercise and have a resistance to physical education.

For improving the physique of college students, colleges and universities shoulder important responsibilities. Due to the low desire of college students to exercise independently, colleges and universities should strengthen the intervention of physical education for college students. The purpose of physical education intervention is to improve the physical health of every college student, so that college students have a strong physique, can bear all kinds of social pressure and effectively realize their own value after entering the society in the future. The intervention of physical education in Colleges and universities should start from the following points: first, we should change the traditional education mode, focus on quality education, and bring physical education into the evaluation system of college students. Second, we should reduce the burden of college students, give college students enough time for physical exercise, and reasonably arrange the time allocation between cultural courses and physical education. We should not emphasize knowledge and ignore physical education. Third, for the current physical problems of college students, carry out targeted physical education intervention, so that college students can develop good physical exercise habits and form the consciousness of independent physical exercise. Fourth, strengthen the publicity of health education, make college students aware of the importance of health, pay more attention to diet matching, and reasonably arrange their work and rest time. Fifth, actively improve the sports facilities in Colleges and universities, replace the old facilities, and add some sports equipment that meet the physical exercise needs of contemporary college students, increase the flexibility of physical education courses, and inject vitality into the physical education courses in Colleges and universities. Through the intervention of physical education in Colleges and universities, strive to get rid of sub-health and improve students' physique.

2 Related Work

2.1 C4. 5 Algorithm

First, C4 5 is a kind of decision tree algorithm. As a classification algorithm, the goal of decision tree algorithm is to divide n samples with p-dimensional characteristics into C categories. It is equivalent to making a projection, $C = f(n)$, and assigning the sample to a category label after a transformation. In order to achieve this goal, the decision tree can represent the classification process as a tree and fork by selecting a feature PIP each time.

So how to choose the characteristics of bifurcation? Which feature is selected for each bifurcation to divide the samples, which can classify the samples fastest and most accurately? Different decision tree algorithms have different feature selection schemes. Information gain for ID3, C4 5 information gain rate and Gini coefficient 8 for cart.

Decision tree algorithm is the main algorithm used for classification and prediction. It usually infers the classification rules expressed in the form of decision tree from a group of irregular cases, uses the top-down recursive method to constantly compare the attribute values at the internal nodes of the decision tree, and judges whether to branch down from the node according to different attributes, The conclusion is obtained at the leaf node of the decision tree [3]. Therefore, there is a classification rule from root node to leaf node, and a whole tree corresponds to a set of expression rules. One of the biggest advantages of decision tree algorithm is that it does not need to obtain a lot of background knowledge in the learning process. As long as the training samples can be expressed in the way of attribute and conclusion, it can be learned by decision tree algorithm.

C4. 5 algorithm is the most commonly used decision tree algorithm because it inherits all the advantages of ID3 algorithm and improves and supplements ID3 algorithm. C4. The algorithm adopts the information gain rate as the standard for selecting branch attributes, which overcomes the deficiency that the information gain in ID3 algorithm prefers to select attributes with more values, and can complete the discretization of continuous attributes and incomplete data. C4. 5 algorithm belongs to the method based on information theory. It is based on information theory and takes information entropy and information gain degree as the measurement standard, so as to realize the induction and classification of data.

C5. 0 algorithm and C4 5 algorithm is also constructed based on gain rate, which is also an extension of ID3 algorithm. The difference is C5 0 algorithm as C4 The revised version of 5 algorithm has made some improvements, which makes it more efficient, occupies less computer memory, and is more suitable for processing large data sets.

Cart algorithm is a kind of decision tree algorithm. Its basic theory is the same as C4 5 algorithm, which is also a classic decision tree algorithm. It uses binary recursive segmentation technology to divide the sample into two subsets, which are carried out in turn, so that each non leaf node of the decision tree derives two branches. The final decision tree generated by cart algorithm is a simple binary tree structure.

C4. 5 the classification algorithm classifies the decision tree with the information gain rate as the index. The total information value of a group of sample data is defined as formula (1):

$$I(s_1, s_2, \ldots, s_m) = -\sum_{i=1}^{m} p_1 \bullet \log_2 p_1 \tag{1}$$

Then the direct value of the subset divided according to attribute a can be expressed by formula (2):

$$E(A) = \sum_{j=1}^{Y} \frac{S_{ij} + \cdots + S_m}{S_i} * I\left(S_{ij} + \cdots + S_m\right) \tag{2}$$

Calculate the information gain rate of all attributes in sequence according to the above process, then take the attribute with the largest information gain rate as the root node to divide the attribute and derive the branch downward, and then successively calculate the attribute with the largest information gain rate among the remaining attributes as the division attribute of the next round of derived branches of the node, Until all the samples in the current node belong to the same class, a complete decision tree is obtained and the iterative calculation is terminated [4].

Decision tree is a tree structure that classifies samples by classifying characteristic attributes, including directed edges and three types of nodes:

Root node, which represents the first characteristic attribute, has only out edge but no in edge;

Internal node, which represents characteristic attributes, has one in edge and at least two out edges;

Leaf node refers to the category. There is only one in edge but no out edge. Figure 1 below shows an example of a decision tree.

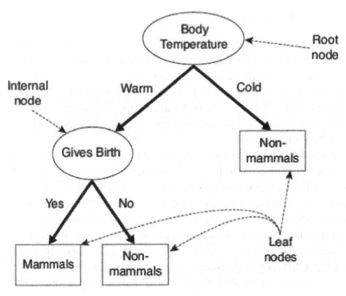

Fig. 1. Decision tree example

For binary decision tree, it can be regarded as a set of if then rules, which corresponds to a classification rule from the root node to the leaf node of the decision tree;

Classification rules are mutually exclusive and complete. The so-called mutual exclusion means that each sample record will not match the previous two classification rules at the same time. The so-called complete means that each sample record can match the previous rule in the decision tree [5].

The essence of classification is the division of feature space, as shown in Fig. 2 below.

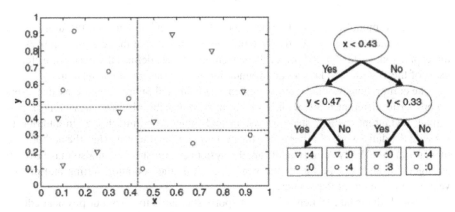

Fig. 2. The essence of classification is the division of feature space

2.2 Development Environment

Software developers develop software in the hope that their products will be used by more people. In order to do this, developers will try their best to explain how to install and configure the software in the official documents.

The software worthy of your special study must have been recognized and widely used in a certain field. Behind such software, many people are constantly providing feedback and improvement. Its documents are relatively mature and perfect, and common problems can be found in it [6].

.net framework4 is a coding model produced by Microsoft for Windows programming Net framework can be used for windows form application design (ADO.Net) and web project development based on B/S architecture (ASP.Net). The framework uses Net control provides user interface design, adopts c# language for background coding, and encapsulates complex program functions such as database access, network communication, file storage, data verification and encryption Net framework effectively solves the technical details of the system in the process of project development, greatly improves the development efficiency and ensures the quality of software.

ASP. Net is a script embedded in web pages and running on the server side. ASP. Net responds to browser events by adding JavaScript to the web page, and completes the communication from the client to the server in the way of "post", so as to realize the process that the client sends requests to the server through the web page. ASP. Net also provides developers with many ASP. Net that can be embedded into web pages Net controls. These controls are compiled into standard HTML controls that can be recognized by the browser through the server-side program, and their style attributes and functions are encapsulated in CSS and JavaScript. Then the page is compiled into HTML script by the server and sent to the client browser.

3 Based on C4 Design and Implementation of College Health Sports System Based on 5 Algorithm

The use case model of the system describes the relationship between the user role of the system and the use case of the system function, points out the relationship between the expansion, inclusion and use of the system use cases, defines the needs of different users of the system, and lays a good foundation for the design of the system.

The comprehensive management system of health and Sports Center classifies users according to different roles, mainly including system administrator, service desk personnel, restaurant cashier, stadium cashier and financial administrator. In addition to viewing the daily work of other users, the system administrator also has the authority to manage and set the system. In addition, the system administrator can also make overall arrangement and scheduling for the venues, such as the operation setting and private venue management of the venues.

Through the establishment of certain sports standards to carry out physical education intervention for college students. China has issued the physical health standard for college students, which has passed this evaluation standard; Let college students realize that only certain physical exercise can reach the standard, promote the improvement of their physique and reach a healthy level. At the same time, we should change the singleness of sports evaluation in China. In China, sports evaluation is only to assess the sports skills of college students, which will make some students with poor physique fear physical education and fear physical education because their skills are not up to standard. Therefore, the sports intervention in Colleges and universities should change the evaluation system and make a comprehensive evaluation from four aspects: sports skills, physical quality, sports participation degree and theoretical knowledge [7]. Of course, this should take the physical quality of college students as the main assessment content, improve the attention of college students to physical quality, and force students to take physical exercise. In addition, we should also establish a file of physical quality for college students, measure the star of physical quality for college students at the beginning of each semester, and measure the physical quality of college students after a semester of physical exercise; Compare the data before and after the two times, and evaluate the score according to the improvement of body and body quality.

The intervention of colleges and universities in college students' physical education should focus on improving the physique of college students, supplemented by the realization of comprehensive quality education. Physical education in Colleges and universities has multiple functions, such as physical fitness, emotional catharsis, quality education and so on. The focus of physical education intervention activities for college students is to improve the awareness of College Students' independent physical exercise, so that college students can come out of a static state of life and enter a dynamic state of life. In order to promote the physical health of college students as the ultimate goal, we should actively change the educational concept, and change the simple completion of physical education tasks into the awareness of helping college students establish health awareness and lifelong physical exercise.

The intervention of physical education should take the subjective initiative of college students as the starting point, and actively set up a variety of teaching modes, so that college students can choose the mode they are interested in, so as to like physical exercise. At present, due to the long-term lack of physical exercise, college students in China have poor physique. In view of such problems, physical intervention should be carried out pertinently, arrange physical education courses according to the actual situation, and gradually cultivate college students' physical awareness and sports skills. When carrying out educational intervention, we can start with the interests of college students and set up more courses that college students like, such as aerobics, yoga and other courses that girls prefer, so as to attract college students to the physical education classroom first. For the teaching content, we should try our best to choose the teaching content with certain confrontation and strength practice, so as to improve the sports competition consciousness of college students, such as more football games and basketball games, and enhance the team spirit of college students. These intervention activities have a certain effect on enhancing the physique of college students.

As a relational database, the data logical structure of the relational model is a two-dimensional table. The data structure is stored by transforming the data entity into a data table with the nature of the relational model. When using relational database as data storage, we should pay attention to the integrity of the relationship, meet the basic principles of database design of 3NF, make rational use of data dependence, and establish a standardized relational model.

When the system is put into use, the system administrator needs to set the user account and user role of the system, and assign corresponding permissions. The design of this system allows administrators to dynamically add users and roles of the system, and dynamically configure the use permissions of different roles, which enhances the operability of system management (Table 1).

Table 1. Main data sheet of system management module

Field name	Data type	Can it be blank	Explain
UserID	INT	No	Primary key user ID
UserName	VARCHAR(20)	No	User login
PassWord	VARCHAR(20)		Password
Name	VARCHAR(20)		User's real name
Telephone	VARCHAR(11)		Telephone
RoleID	INT		Role foreign key ID

There are three different and powerful software components designed by the open source software framework. Each function of these components is different. This component mainly has an interception function for customers, so that the controller can make better judgment and know what's going on. Most of these components are owned by users themselves, so they can help users deal with problems very quickly. After finding out the problem, they can tell users quickly.

In the model part, the components are mainly the beginning part of the object-oriented programming language [8]. The action form mainly depends on the user's feeling and how the assembly is. The assembly is done according to the request. At this time, the user's request will be ignored. If it can't pass, it will become a system object, and then the object will be sent and transmitted by the device and processed according to different requests, Each processing method is different, so the action will happen by itself, and the action is coherent.

The so-called sports data access essentially refers to the system framework of object-oriented programming language. You don't have to swipe your card when you use it. At the beginning, this framework is for enterprises. There are many program problems that need to be solved in enterprises. The program development of enterprises is relatively difficult. It's not so difficult to solve problems with sports data access framework, and it can save a lot of time. The solution is mainly layered architecture, so that system developers can choose the appropriate components according to their needs [9].

The model of sports data access framework is shown in the figure below. From here, we can see that the core part of the framework has seven parts. These seven parts are more important, including website and other core texts and core.

Among the seven components, the most important component is the core, and other components are studied on the basis of this core (Fig. 3).

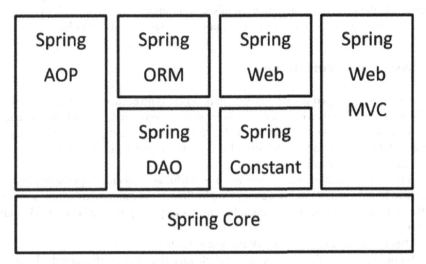

Fig. 3. Structure diagram of sports data access framework

The basic structure of the whole sports data access framework is the sports data access core. It is based on this module that various functions are used. These functions are the program processing plant, where the model is operated and changed, and then some codes are used under the program. When writing, some programs are used to divide the codes into two categories, The operation is also different.

From the perspective of configuration files, sports data access context is typical. Its main function is to process context messages. It can also do service work in enterprise programs.

The system management code is AOP for sports data access. The main function is to focus the underlying code on this framework. System developers can manage AOP. This work is very simple and supports any object. In addition, the system can provide better methods when dealing with things. Some components in the work do not need to participate in life, and all things can be released here.

Sports data access template and callback are abstract layer modules, and their basic function is to provide the management function of exception hierarchy. If this method is used for operation, the error information in different layers can be detected and then changed. Exception level is to solve the problem by comparing the previous methods, so that the abnormal results of system processing can be corrected and the rewriting of exception code can be avoided.

There are many sports data access object modules in the sports data access framework, and there are also tools for mapping object relationships. These need to be carried out according to the transaction rules of sports data access, so that the hierarchy of template and callback exceptions can be solved [10].

Based on the application context module is the sports data access web page module, which aims at the web page program service and provides corresponding help. Therefore, based on the sports data access framework, it can be integrated with Jakarta open source software in the process of operation. In this way, multiple requests can be processed at the same time, and these requests can be put into the work of domain objects.

4   System Implementation

The system is developed with B/S architecture. There is no need to install any plug-ins or tools on the client. Only a browser that can browse the web can run flexibly on any client. On the server side, you only need to deploy the project to a computer with Framework version 2.0 or above and IIS 6.0 installed 0 or above and SQL Server 2008 database server, the system can run normally.

In terms of operation, the system has a beautiful and generous operation platform, and most functional operations are very simple. Simple operation steps are encapsulated in the user presentation layer, and complex business logic is processed in the background server.

After the above analysis, the system is feasible in operation.

According to the different personality characteristics of each individual student, accurately analyze and grasp the sports change state of college students at different levels and stages, carry out sports health counseling for college students, and reflect interactivity in the counseling process. Establish college students' Sports files, track the learning status in real time and dynamically, improve the crisis mechanism, timely and effective intervention, and find college students with sports obstacles for effective control. By teaching students in accordance with their aptitude, standardize the guidance of physical health education, and explore the model of physical health evaluation training plan and physical health evaluation system. Respect the subject status of college students, promote their individual potential and individual development, make them achieve the goal of all-round growth through physical health education, and realize a harmonious and perfect physical health teaching mode [11]. Publicize sports health care and sports health knowledge to college students, make college students understand and master their own sports situation through various means such as online Q & A, testing and consultation, especially the students with sports obstacles, and realize their self-management and self-healing ability through the sports health evaluation system.

The open source object mapping framework of the framework provides a simple level of driver encapsulation, which avoids the details of the connection between many drivers and the database, so that the system developers will not be distracted and can devote all their energy to the system instead of looking at these data, so the development efficiency is also very high.

As can be seen from Fig. 4 below, the open source object mapping framework has six core interfaces, including session, session factory, transaction, query, condition and configuration interfaces.

```
import pybaobabdt
import pandas as pd
from scipy.io import arff
from sklearn.tree import DecisionTreeClassifier
from matplotlib.colors import LinearSegmentedColormap
from matplotlib.colors import ListedColormap
from colour import Color
import matplotlib.pyplot as plt
import numpy as np

data = arff.loadarff('vehicle.arff')
df   = pd.DataFrame(data[0])
y = list(df['class'])
features = list(df.columns)
```

Fig. 4. Open source object mapping framework

Especially in today's society, many students lack exercise and unhealthy eating habits, resulting in premature physical development, overweight, thin and so on. Looking at the increasingly unhealthy physical state of the child day by day, I deeply reflected that I attached great importance to the child's achievements, but I was short of physical training. However, the enjoyment of learning and life that students should enjoy, such as physical exercise, scientific and technological activities and other quality education, can only become students' extravagant expectations.

The system adopts B/S structure. Under this structure, the user interface is completely realized through the browser, and part of the transaction logic is realized at the front end, but the main transaction logic is realized at the server end, forming the so-called 3-tier structure (B/S structure), which mainly uses the constantly mature browser technology and combines the browser's multiple script languages (VBScript, JavaScript...) And ActiveX technology, through buffer and other mechanisms, effectively manage various resources of the system and access to the background through API interface [12]. The client is easier to be maintained and developed. It is not affected by changes in background programs. With a general browser, the powerful functions that originally needed complex special software can be realized, and the development cost is saved, to a great extent, it is convenient for business expansion and system maintenance.

5 Conclusion

In recent years, many facts have also proved that sports activities can promote the improvement of students' academic performance and learning efficiency. This paper is based on C4 In the daily management of the school, school sports health is particularly key and indispensable. Moreover, school sports health management is also the top priority of physical education teaching. We must strengthen the management in order to effectively improve the management quality. Through the analysis of "sports health management", it can be found that it is based on organization, coordination and control to promote the management activities to present a better state, order and conditions. The paper also introduces the relevant professional technology of system development and application, such as Net framework, SQL Server database, etc., and analyzes the development status of similar products in the domestic industry, and puts forward the idea of meeting the needs of the times for the design of the system. Physical exercise can promote the growth and development of human body and the development of function.

References

1. Swadesi, I., Kanca, I.N., Wijaya, M.A.: Analysis of problems and challenges in teaching sports, health and physical education to students with disabilities. In: 5th Asian Education Symposium 2020 (AES 2020) (2021)
2. Yao, C.M., Poovendran, P., Kirubakaran, S.S.: Internet of things-based energy-efficient optimized heuristic framework to monitor sportsperson's health. Technol. Health Care: Off. J. Eur. Soc. Eng. Med. 1, 1–14 (2021)
3. Badilla, P., Herrera-Valenzuela, T., Ramirez-Campillo, R., et al.: Effects of Olympic combat sports on older adults' health status: a systematic review. Int. J. Environ. Res. Public Health (2021)
4. Li, F., Martínez, O.S., Aiswarya, R.S.: Internet of things-based smart wearable system to monitor sports person health. Technol. Health Care: Off. J. Eur. Soc. Eng. Med. 2021(8), 1–14 (2021)
5. Meech, J.T., Stanley-Marbell, P.: An algorithm for sensor data uncertainty quantification (2021)
6. Irawan, Y.: Penerapan algoritma decision tree C4.5 Untuk Memprediksi Kelayakan Calon Pendonor Melakukan Donor Darah Dengan Klasifikasi Data Mining. JTIM Jurnal Teknologi Informasi dan Multimedia 2(4), 181–189 (2021)
7. Yang, Y.: The evaluation of online education course performance using decision tree mining algorithm. Complexity 2021 (2021)
8. Zhang, T.: Analysis and design of university financial management system based on decision tree classification algorithm. In: 2021 IEEE Asia-Pacific Conference on Image Processing, Electronics and Computers (IPEC). IEEE (2021)
9. Adhikari, S.: Data mining: a bagged decision tree classifier algorithm for ids intrusion detection system based attacks classification. Design Eng. (Toronto) 2021, 1826–1839 (2021)
10. Lightfoot, J.T., Roth, S.M., Hubal, M.J.: Systems exercise genetics research design standards. Med. Sci. Sports Exerc. 53, 883–887 (2021)
11. Siddiqui, S., Verma, A.: Designing of WSN based embedded system using wearable sports sensors: a theoretical approach (2021)
12. Kaya, D.G.: Views of sports sciences students about distance education during Covid-19: SWOT Analysis (2021)

Evaluation Model of College Students' Psychological Education Quality Based on Data Technology

Bo Chen[✉] and Xiaozhen Zhao

China University of Geosciences, Wuhan 430074, China
chenbo1801@126.com

Abstract. With the advent of the era of big data, it is urgent to use information technology to help the comprehensive reform of students' psychological education. This paper expounds from the perspective of comprehensive evaluation of students' psychological education quality. By formulating national unified data standards, this paper constructs a comprehensive evaluation platform of students' psychological education quality, provides interfaces for provinces, cities and counties, and forms an integrated comprehensive system of students' psychological education quality to serve the country At the same time, it also provides services for students' psychological education decision-making by students' psychological education institutions at all levels, so as to promote the process of comprehensive reform of students' Psychological Education in China. The course of College Students' mental health and students' psychological education is close to life, which provides us with a good ideological guidance, consolidates the positive, healthy and upward spiritual bond of college students, stimulates our spiritual motivation of self-improvement, helps us maintain the spiritual motivation of hitting the water in the middle stream, and makes me think more about myself, Use big data to provide opportunities for multi participation in education evaluation. Tablet computers and other devices can be used to carry out data processing on learning data, so as to realize the data information collection of teachers on students' learning process, and provide data basis for the development of informatization in the field of education. From the perspective of comprehensive evaluation of students' psychological education quality, this paper briefly analyzes and discusses the help of big data in education.

Keywords: Data technology · College students · Psychological education · Promotion of information technology

1 Introduction

The establishment and management of mental health archives began when children went to school. At present, the world attaches great importance to mental health education. The country of origin of mental health is the United States. Mental health education in the United States is a management system carried out by the whole society. Most universities

M. A. Jan and F. Khan (Eds.): BigIoT-EDU 2022, LNICST 466, pp. 535–545, 2023.
https://doi.org/10.1007/978-3-031-23947-2_57

in the United States have set up mental health and consulting institutions, all equipped with psychological counselors. In addition to general psychological education and counseling, American students also attach importance to the development of various forms of psychological group training, such as psychological flexibility training, psychotherapy and making friends, and carry out psychological diagnosis, consultation, evaluation and counseling for ordinary and special types of college students [1]. The main purpose of introducing psychological counseling into American colleges and universities is to establish detailed files for each student by recording characteristics, achievements, interests, family background, intelligence and health. The advantages of the mental health system of foreign colleges and universities are as follows: (1) the mental health system has diversified archives storage. The college students' archives are kept on the Internet. For a long time, the college students can query themselves or keep them in the school archives. Everyone follows the principle of confidentiality. (2) Keep psychological files for a long time. Each student's file is established and saved since childhood, and the original file will not be deleted due to their own reasons, such as changing schools and occupations. After the file is established, it will be preserved for life, and the file materials will be updated in different periods. (3) Centralized management. All materials about archives are managed by special personnel. Usually, foreign psychologists are multifunctional scholars and are very familiar with psychological counseling and education. (4) Standardized management. After the establishment of students' psychological archives, they can be inquired through the corresponding authority and can not be consulted casually. There is a principle of confidentiality for these. If some people want to publish students' archives, they must obtain the consent of the parties and be anonymous. Foreign mental health system management system has a certain systematicness and comprehensiveness in these aspects.

The report of the 18th CPC National Congress proposed that deepening the comprehensive reform in the field of students' psychological education is a new requirement for the reform of students' psychological education. In order to thoroughly implement the requirements and deployment of the 18th CPC National Congress on deepening the comprehensive reform in the field of students' psychological education, the Ministry of students' psychological education put forward relevant opinions, pointing out that it is necessary to fully understand the urgency of deepening the comprehensive reform in the field of students' Psychological education and focus on the key points of the reform [2]. Among them, the quality evaluation of students' psychological education is the key link of the comprehensive reform of students' psychological education, which plays an important guiding role. With the implementation of the curriculum reform of students' psychological education, all localities have actively explored and made some progress in improving the evaluation of the quality of primary and secondary school students' psychological education, but the current situation based on students' academic achievements has not been fundamentally reversed, and the comprehensive evaluation of students' Psychological Education quality lacks a national unified evaluation standard and evaluation platform.

The comprehensive evaluation of students' psychological education quality relies on big data from various sources. Rational planning, storage and utilization of big data has become an essential element of development and reform. Using information technology to improve the evaluation method of students' psychological education quality can reduce the workload on the one hand; On the other hand, using unified standards for evaluation can improve the accuracy of evaluation to a certain extent. Using information means to monitor and evaluate the comprehensive data of students' psychological education quality is of great significance to improve the quality of students' psychological education, and finally achieve the purpose of promoting the comprehensive reform in the field of students' psychological education.

The concept of "health" in modern society has gone beyond the traditional medical point of view. It should not only physical and physical health, but also mental and mental health. Today's fierce social competition has caused heavy psychological pressure on people. Middle school students in school survive in such a social environment and face the pressure of entering a higher school [3]. They are psychologically fragile and their psychological depression can not be vented to a certain extent. If we only pay attention to the education of students' physical health and do not pay attention to the education of mental health, it will be extremely unfavorable to the healthy growth of students. As far as the current situation is concerned, it is particularly important to carry out mental health education for students.

2 Related Work

2.1 Data Technology

The concept of "big data" has been popular for a long time, but it is not easy to make it clear (otherwise? How can it be a single digit answer). It may be more fragrant to buy a book at this time. Let's start with the conclusion - big data technology is actually a complete set of "data + business + demand" solutions. It is actually a very broad concept, involving five fields: 1 Business analysis; 2. Data analysis; 3. Data mining; 4. Machine learning; 5. Artificial intelligence.

From 1 to 5, there is an increasing need for technical background; From 5 to 1, it is closer and closer to specific business. In fact, in addition to products that rely on data technology such as search engines, most Internet products do not particularly need big data technology in their lifetime, that is, the stage of a product from 0 to 1. In the development period of products, that is, from "1" to "infinity", the role of "big data technology" on products will be gradually reflected. The main reason is that there are few functions and services of the initial products, and there is no "accumulated user data" for model research and development [4]. Therefore, we often hear of "barriers to building big data", in which "data technology" is a small barrier and "big data" itself is a big barrier. Let's start with "big data".

Theory is a necessary way to understand big data and a baseline widely recognized and disseminated; Here, we can understand the overall description and characterization of big data by the industry from the definition of the characteristics of big data, and deeply analyze the precious variety of big data from the discussion of the value of big data;

Insight into the development trend of big data; Examine the long-term game between people and data from the characteristic and important perspective of big data privacy;

Technology is the means and cornerstone of big data. Here, the whole process of big data collection, processing, storage and analysis results is explained from the development of cloud computing, distributed processing technology, storage technology and perception technology;

Practice is the ultimate value of big data. Here, we describe the beautiful scene and blueprint of big data from four aspects: big data of the Internet, big data of the government, big data of enterprises and big data of individuals;

Next, let's talk about the development status of big data: in recent years, China's big data industry has developed from scratch and developed big data all over the country. The enthusiasm of big data is high, the industrial application has been popularized rapidly, and the market scale has increased significantly; China's big data industry is still in a period of rapid development, and the market will continue to expand in the future; Big data technology is spreading to all industries. The combination of big data with cloud computing, AI, finance, medical treatment, Internet and government public services has created many new jobs. The wave of big data has not only begun to sweep the whole bank, but also government functions, urban planning and security law enforcement will need the support of big data. Therefore, big data is an all inclusive skill in all industries, There is basically no need to worry about employment;

Data collection: This is the first step of big data processing. There are two main types of data sources. The first type is the relationship data of each business system, which can be extracted regularly or synchronized in real time through tools such as sqoop or cannal; The second type is various buried point logs, which are collected in real time through flume [5].

Data storage: after collecting the data, the next step is to store the data in HDFS. In case of real-time log flow, it will be output to the subsequent streaming computing engine through Kafka.

Data analysis: this step is the core of data processing, including offline processing and stream processing. The corresponding computing engines include MapReduce, spark, Flink, etc. the processed results will be saved to the data warehouse designed in advance, or various storage systems such as HBase, redis, RDBMS, etc.

Data application: including various data application scenarios such as visual presentation of data, business decision-making, or AI.

Through the above contents, we may have a preliminary understanding of big data, and then the core part, because any learning process needs a scientific and reasonable learning route to complete our learning objectives in an orderly manner. The content of big data needs to be learned is complex and difficult. It is particularly necessary to have a reasonable big data technology learning roadmap to help clarify ideas.

Data warehouse is a form of data organization from the perspective of business. It is the foundation of big data application and data center. The data warehouse system generally adopts the hierarchical structure shown in Fig. 1 below.

According to this layered method, our development focus is on the DWD layer, that is, the detailed data layer. Here are mainly some wide tables, which store detailed data; When we arrive at the DWS layer, we will aggregate the data for different dimensions. In

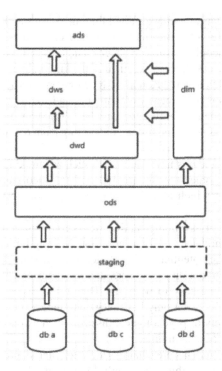

Fig. 1. Data technology hierarchy

principle, the DWS layer is the market layer, which is generally divided according to the theme and belongs to the category of dimension modeling; Ads is the partial application layer, the output of various reports [6].

2.2 Quality Evaluation Mode

The main psychological problems of students are shown in the following aspects:

1. Tired of learning. It shows that some students are not interested in learning, distracted, don't listen carefully in class, slow thinking, negative complex, delayed and perfunctory homework, low learning efficiency and high error rate in exams and homework. 2、 Rebellious. Some students often have psychological reactions contrary to normal to external stimuli, adopt a non cooperative attitude in communication with others, get bored with teacher education and contradict the persuasion of their families.
2. Irritable. When such students are stimulated generally or slightly, their complex is easy to fluctuate, such as anger, impatience, anger, etc.; Such students have a strong sense of revenge and sometimes shout loudly for no reason. They often have the impulse to do thousands of dangerous or stupid things, and then calm down and regret later.

3. Social panic. Students are often afraid of finding excuses and avoiding social behavior, even if they are not comfortable with their classmates. Such students are too sensitive to other people's words and deeds, and they will fall into pain if they have something unpleasant [7]. He is skeptical of the kind help of his classmates, wary of the teacher's education, and has normal reactions in interpersonal communication, such as shyness, embarrassment, awkwardness and so on.

4. Jealousy. Some students feel resentment when they see that their academic performance is not as good as others. Instead of learning from others' strengths, they make sarcasm.

5. Bad habits. Some students have bad habits such as smoking, drinking and playing video games, and some students are addicted to video games, resulting in many problem behaviors, which affect the normal education and teaching order of the school.

6. Anxiety. This kind of psychological disorder is common in middle school students. Most of them are mild and last for a short time. Mild and transient anxiety is helpful to mobilize learning potential. A few students are anxious for a long time and are sensitive to the stimulation of the surrounding environment. They have difficulty falling asleep and are easy to wake up. They often experience inexplicable fear, tension and upset. This not only has a negative impact on learning, but also easily evolves into a variety of psychological diseases such as phobia and conjecture if it is not dredged and treated in time.

7. Depression. Some students are usually sad, lonely and depressed emotionally, have negative self-evaluation, think they can't do anything, lack confidence in learning, have a tendency to fear what they have done, and are pessimistic about changing their situation. This kind of students are often unobtrusive. They do not affect the order inside and outside the class, and do not hinder teaching and various activities. However, with the development of their bad emotions and the aggravation of their inner tension, they will become increasingly depressed, which may seriously develop into depressive mental diseases, and some will make self injuring behaviors or even commit suicide.

The evaluation of students' psychological education quality can be divided into two parts: Students' comprehensive quality evaluation and teachers' teaching evaluation. The main body of students' comprehensive quality evaluation is students. Students' comprehensive quality evaluation is divided into five aspects: Ideological and moral character, academic level, physical and mental health, artistic quality and social practice. According to different stages of students' psychological education, different contents of students' comprehensive quality evaluation system are adopted to make students' comprehensive quality not only pay attention to students' academic achievements, but also pay attention to comprehensive quality, so as to reflect students' growth from the side. The main body of teachers' teaching evaluation is teachers. Because of the different teaching levels in different places, the teaching evaluation of teachers is also different. We should establish a national unified evaluation index, carry out different evaluations for different learning stages, and form a complete description of teachers' teaching according to the data of teachers' daily activities [8].

When building the quality evaluation platform, we should follow the systematic principle, so that various indicators can be connected with each other and have a certain logical relationship. It is also convenient for data collection and sorting, so that the teaching quality evaluation platform can better serve students' psychological education.

3   Evaluation Model of College Students' Educational Quality Based on Psychological Data

Data is a physical symbol arranged and combined according to certain rules. It can be expressed in the form of symbol, text, number, voice, image, video and so on. It is the expression form and carrier of information. The data explosion of human society starts from three dimensions: first, the amount of the same type of data is increasing rapidly, second, the speed of data growth is accelerating, and third, the sources and new types of data are increasing [9].

Big data refers to data sets that cannot be acquired, managed and processed within a certain time using traditional software technologies and tools. The focus of big data not only lies in the definition of data scale, but also represents that the development of information technology has entered a new era, represents the technical challenges and difficulties brought by explosive data information to traditional computing technology and information technology, represents the new technologies and methods required for big data processing, and also represents the new inventions brought by big data analysis and application New services and new development opportunities.

According to the data source analysis and daily work practice, the collected mental health data roughly include: the basic personal information of freshmen entering the school, the relevant data information generated during the mental health evaluation, and the consultation materials sorted out by the psychological counselor during the psycho-logical consultation [10]. This kind of data records the causes of students' psychological problems; There are also crisis assessment, counselor interview, students' psychologi-cal course scores, data of participating in mental health education activities, etc. These contents reflect the psychological state of students from different angles and degrees, but often rely on students' active participation. Therefore, it is inevitable that the infor-mation is untrue or refuses to participate, resulting in the untrue and incomplete data collected. And this kind of data is obtained through subjective conjecture, so it is difficult to scientifically reflect the real mental health state of students, which affects the accuracy and reliability of post-secondary dynamic evaluation.

At present, college students' mental health data come from different collection sub-jects and are kept by different collection subjects. Students' mental health data is in a fragmented state and has not been integrated. At the same time, the mental health data obtained by psychological census and psychological interview is static. It can only reflect the mental health status of students in the recent period, and can not predict the mental health status of students in the future. This "breakpoint" data is difficult to repre-sent the changing level of students' mental health, and it is more difficult to realize the dynamic tracking and management of students' mental health. Therefore, colleges and universities should build a dynamic evaluation system of students' mental health, so as to dynamically reflect students' mental health in different periods of time (Fig. 2).

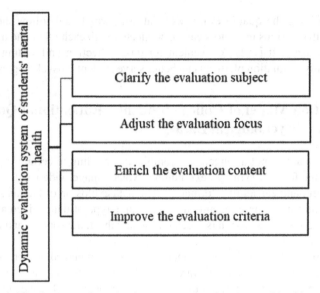

Fig. 2. Dynamic evaluation system of students' mental health

Clarifying the evaluation subject is the basis and premise of building a big data student evaluation model. Colleges and universities must change their evaluation ideas and keep pace with the times. In the information age, the relevant data of students are gradually becoming transparent and information-based, and the evaluation activities become simpler from the operational level. The use of big data foundation can realize diversified evaluation methods such as parent participation, peer evaluation and student self-evaluation in student evaluation. Therefore, colleges and universities must clarify the evaluation subject and improve the scientificity and accuracy of evaluation.

In the process of evaluating students, colleges and universities should adjust the focus of evaluation, change the evaluation method that only paid attention to achievements in the past, collect data from all aspects of students through big data, and then form a comprehensive evaluation. At the same time, colleges and universities should also pay attention to the dynamic evaluation of students' learning process, use big data technology to record students' learning trajectory, and then make developmental and dynamic evaluation.

The evaluation standard of college students in China is single, which is not conducive to making a comprehensive evaluation of students' school performance and future development. In the information age, the use of big data technology can enrich the evaluation content and give targeted and specific suggestions to students according to their shortcomings and advantages [11]. Through big data, we can enrich the evaluation content of students, and then carry out comprehensive evaluation on students, for example.

For example, by using big data, we can observe the students' actual activities on the word I you, and then understand the students' actual learning situation. Observe students' practical activities,

Then understand the students' learning burden and interest, and make a reasonable analysis of the students through the data, so as to turn the students' learning behavior and learning trajectory into visual evaluation content.

Formulating scientific and reasonable evaluation standards is an important part of student evaluation. At present, in the process of formulating evaluation standards, colleges and universities do not pay enough attention to the differences of different teaching objectives and different classrooms, but use unified standards to evaluate students. In the case of big data, colleges and universities should formulate evaluation standards according to the differences in different evaluation fields, and comprehensively consider the actual situation of students to improve the evaluation standards.

For the evaluation of students' psychological education level, at present, the evaluation indicators of various regions and schools are different, which is also related to the different concerns of various regions. The evaluation of teachers' teaching level is usually divided into two aspects [12]. The first is teachers' personal attributes, which can also be called hard indicators, such as teachers' professional title, teaching age, award-winning achievements and so on. The second is the indicators of students' psychological education, such as students' psychological education content, teaching methods, teaching attitude, teaching effect and so on. Among them, the teaching content includes the scientificity of the teaching content, the amount of information, the teaching schedule, etc.; Teaching method refers to the method that teachers organize teaching, including classroom interaction, blackboard writing, whether the teaching ideas are clear, etc.; Teaching attitude mainly refers to teachers' mental state, speech and behavior; Teaching effect refers to students' acceptance of knowledge, which can be combined with students' comprehensive evaluation results. According to these aspects, build a national unified evaluation index system of students' psychological education level in different sections, and form a complete description of students' psychological education by inputting teachers' basic information, students' evaluation data of teachers and teachers' daily activity data in the system.

In the process of designing students' quality, we can follow the logical and comprehensive principles, which can reflect the students' psychological level from top to bottom. In addition, we should follow the principles of comparability, operability and quantification, and select indicators that are simple, clear, micro, easy to collect, operable and comparable to facilitate later data collection and ensure the effectiveness of the evaluation.

4   Evaluation System

The dynamic evaluation system of College Students' mental health based on big data technology aims to provide new research methods and theoretical practice for colleges and universities in the follow-up mental health education, and ensure the scientific and reasonable development of college mental health education and the realization of dynamic monitoring of students' mental health.

Focus on building a mental health data platform to realize the comprehensive monitoring content. At this stage, big data realizes the sharing and transmission of data with its massive data resources and intelligent cloud computing technology, and improves the work efficiency of all social subjects. Therefore, under the background of big data, the construction of college mental health network data platform can not only realize the accuracy and diversity of student data collection, but also detect students' mental health in an all-round and three-dimensional way. Firstly, build a data evaluation system related to students' mental health education. In the network information age, students often publish their daily life behavior records and emotions on relevant social media, which is more convenient for relevant staff to understand students' mental health. Students' psychological information is collected through social media, and students' psychological information is input into the system. Secondly, colleges and universities can set up online mental health confidential chat rooms [13]. On the one hand, it can ensure students' privacy, better understand students' mental health, and then take corresponding measures to avoid students hurting their own and others' rights and interests due to psychological problems. Finally, with the help of the construction of smart campus, new technologies such as data monitoring, equipment monitoring and Internet of things are used to build a mental health data platform. Therefore, colleges and universities should break the closed "island" state of data, realize data information sharing, and establish a set of all staff, whole process and all-round health education mode.

Improve the dynamic evaluation mechanism of College Students' mental health and realize the scientific evaluation content.

As the data varies with the subject, time and space, new data information will continue to appear. Therefore, colleges and universities should constantly improve the dynamic evaluation and detection system of students' mental health to ensure that the information is updated and accurate at any time. Firstly, construct the early warning mechanism of College Students' mental health. By analyzing and evaluating the situation of students' psychological crisis, clean up and extract effective data, so as to predict students' psychological crisis early. Secondly, add other indicators to the dynamic evaluation system of College Students' mental health to expand the scope of evaluating students' mental health. Focusing on the internal and external environment and characteristics of college students, the internal level increases the internal indicators of College Students' personality characteristics, cognitive style of stimulating events, coping styles of stress and frustration, crisis experience and personal physical and mental health [14]; At the external environment level, increase the indicators of College Students' interpersonal relationship, social support, family environment, campus environment and so on. Finally, set the threshold standard line of College Students' mental health crisis. According to the data related to college students' mental health collected by big data, set the threshold standard. When there are students who exceed the normal threshold standard data, the staff should take relevant measures in time to avoid the distortion of students' psychology.

5   Conclusion

This paper studies the quality evaluation model of College Students' Psychological Education Based on data technology. In the face of massive data, students' psychological education should not only regard big data as an information technology of data mining and data analysis, but also as a strategic resource, Give full play to the development advantages brought by big data to students' psychological education, and make all-round deployment in strategic planning, business model and human capital. In the big data on students' psychological education, what decision-making role does big data technology play. Applying the mature operation platform or establishing your own operation platform for data analysis can give full play to the advantages of big data, and use professional analysis tools to effectively process the collected structured and unstructured data, so as to find some problems existing in the enterprise. Therefore, the application of big data technology can fully improve the effectiveness of work. In addition, the big data analysis platform can monitor the follow-up management of students' mental health.

Acknowledgements. Fundamental research Funds for the central universities "Research Start-up Fund for new Young Teachers"—Exploration and Practice of Evaluation Mechanism of Curriculum-based Ideological and Political Education: Taking College of Marin Science and Technology as an Example.

References

1. Xie, W.: Big data analysis on the management content of college students' mental health education. In: 2021 13th International Conference on Measuring Technology and Mechatronics Automation (ICMTMA) (2021)
2. Pottinger, A.M., Passard, N., Stair, A.G.: Using faith-based organisations to promote mental health education to underserved populations in Jamaica. Health Educ. J. **80**(5), 001789692098803 (2021)
3. Liu, Q., Liao, X.: Research on university mental health education based on computer big data statistical analysis. In: 2021 2nd International Conference on Big Data and Informatization Education (ICBDIE) (2021)
4. Emerging Trends in Mental Health Education – An Empirical Investigation (2021)
5. Wang, X.: Construction of civil engineering teaching system based on data mining algorithm and big data technology. J. Phys.: Conf. Ser. **1852**(3), 032022 (2021)
6. Denisova, O.A.: Big data technology: assessing the quality of the educational environment. J. Phys. Conf. Ser. **2001**(1), 012027 (2021)
7. Ran, Y., Feng, Z.: An image recognition algorithm based on big data technology. J. Phys. Conf. Ser. **1952**(2), 022044 (2021)
8. Rahman, N., Daim, T., Basoglu, N.: Exploring the factors influencing big data technology acceptance. IEEE Trans. Eng. Manage., 1–16 (2021)
9. Zhi, M.L.: Analysis of operation reliability of distribution network based on big data technology (2021)
10. Bardon, J.I.: Mental health education: a framework for psychological services in the schools. J. Sch. Psychol. **1**(1), 20–27 (1963)
11. Hong, C., Song, Y.: Positive Psychology——A new perspective of college student's mental health education. China J. Health Psychol. (2007)
12. Jia, X.Z., Zhao, D.F.: On the construction of mental health education system under the new situation in college. J. North Univ. China (Social Science Edition) (2006)
13. Zhuravlev, V.A., Sukhorukov, V.P., Zakharishcheva, T.P.: How to understand the mental health education in the curriculum standards of physical education and health. Curriculum, Teaching Material and Method **28**(3), 33–37 (2004)
14. Dong, L.X.: On the confliction in values of mental health education and moral education. J. Henan Normal Univ. (Philosophy and Social Sciences Edition) (2002)

Classification Method of Educational Discourse Power Imbalance Data Set Based on Mixed Big Data Analysis

Jinzhi Teng[✉]

Yiwu Technical College of Industry and Commerce, Zhejiang University, Yiwu 322000,
Zhejiang, China
tengjinzhi2008@163.com

Abstract. Discourse power is a tool to express social ideology, which controls the
direction of public opinion in the whole society, and the competition for discourse
power is the concrete manifestation of ideological struggle. With the development
of artificial intelligence, the trend of information globalization is becoming more
and more obvious. In the field of ideology, a hundred flowers bloom and a hundred
schools of thought contend. At present, China's socialist mainstream ideology is
Sinicized Marxism - it is Mao Zedong Thought and socialist ideological system
with Chinese characteristics guided by Marxism. However, with the influx and
flood of Western discourse thoughts, our ideological education discourse has also
been impacted to a certain extent. *** Therefore, this paper proposes an effective
classification method for unbalanced data sets. The core idea of the classification
of educational discourse unbalanced data sets based on mixed big data analysis is
to provide a comprehensive solution for the classification of unbalanced data sets
from two aspects: sample preprocessing and classifier improvement.

Keywords: Educational discourse · Big data analysis · Data sets · Classification
method

1 Introduction

Realize the whole process and all-round education, and strive to create a new situation
in the development of China's higher education. At the same time, the 19th National
Congress also proposed to strengthen cultural self-confidence, firmly grasp the leadership
in the field of ideology, pay attention to ideological and moral construction, and pay
attention to the development of higher education, which undoubtedly highlights the
importance China attaches to the discourse power of higher education.

Ideological and political education in Colleges and universities is an important position to spread the mainstream ideology and an important guarantee for the ideological
security of our country. Educational discourse power is an important link for colleges and
universities to carry out ideological and political education. It shoulders the important
task of disseminating the core values of socialism with Chinese characteristics and helps

M. A. Jan and F. Khan (Eds.): BigIoT-EDU 2022, LNICST 466, pp. 546–557, 2023.
https://doi.org/10.1007/978-3-031-23947-2_58

colleges and universities undertake the great mission of cultivating qualified socialist successors [1]. In the context of the new era, China's ideological and political education is facing a situation of diversified ideas and values, and the ideological and cultural exchange is gradually deepened, which will interfere with the majority of young students to establish a correct outlook on life, world outlook and values. Therefore, in order to master the field of ideology, China's colleges and universities should actively educate and guide students to objectively understand the general trend of world and China's development, understand the regularity of human social development, and grasp the inevitable trend of the development of socialism with Chinese characteristics.

The current classification technology has been able to solve most of the problems and applications with the characteristics of relatively small amount of data, relatively complete annotation and relatively uniform data distribution However, the development and large-scale application of classification technology are still plagued by many problems, such as massive data, data set imbalance, annotation bottleneck and data aliasing [2]. Among them, the classification of unbalanced data sets is one of the most challenging difficulties in the research of classification technology, which has been paid great attention by the majority of researchers.

Many studies have shown that some standard classification models are directly applied to unbalanced data, such as neural network, support vector machine and C4 5, etc., can not get satisfactory classification effect. At present, there are two main strategies to solve the problem of data imbalance: one is resampling, which can appropriately shield the amount of information of large classes or increase the cost of classification errors of small classes; The second is to improve the classification strategy according to the characteristics of the new algorithm. However, at present, the classification accuracy of all methods in rare categories is very low, which can not improve the overall recognition level of rare categories to a practical and acceptable level [3]. Relevant research still needs to be further deepened, and researchers are facing great challenges.

This method realizes the organic combination of sample resampling and classifier improvement. It creatively adopts the resampling method of unsupervised clustering and k-nearest neighbor rule to select and prune the samples of unbalanced data sets, which not only effectively balances the skew state of data, but also greatly reduces the number of support vectors This sampling method overcomes the shortcomings of traditional sampling methods, such as lack of theoretical basis, strong randomness, human subjective interference and information loss. At the same time, it solves the aliasing phenomenon in the data, and significantly improves the generalization performance of the subsequent SVM classifier. In order to adapt to the state of sample imbalance, we also improve the SVM classification model. The equiangular transformation of the kernel function is used to achieve the purpose of class boundary calibration [4]. It is worth noting that the method in this paper has been applied to the answer extraction technology and obtained satisfactory results, which has been objectively and fully evaluated in the international trec6006 QA evaluation task.

Research on the classification method of educational discourse power imbalance data set based on mixed big data analysis: first, it is conducive to promoting the development of Sinicization of Marxism. *** We should unswervingly spread Marxist scientific theory, do a good job in Marxist theoretical education, and lay a scientific ideological foundation for the growth of students. Therefore, analyzing the current situation of the discourse power of higher education is the requirement of the development of the times. Through the analysis of the current situation of the discourse power of higher education, this paper analyzes the opportunities and challenges of its development, and explores the new path to strengthen the effect of the discourse power, so as to promote the development of the Sinicization of Marxism with the times. Second, it is conducive to enrich and develop the theoretical system of Ideological and political discourse power in Colleges and universities. As an important link of Ideological and political education in Colleges and universities, the right of discourse is an important carrier to convey the content of Ideological and political education and spread the mainstream values of society [5]. To do a good job of Ideological and political work in Colleges and universities, we must firmly hold the position of educational discourse power in Colleges and universities, innovate the system of Ideological and political discourse power, and pay attention to humanistic and ideological education. Third, it is conducive to ensuring the security of China's social ideology. Our colleges and universities are colleges and Universities under the leadership of the party. It is an important position for the dissemination of mainstream ideology in our society. In order to master the voice and leadership of social ideology, China should improve the ideological and political awareness of colleges and universities, adhere to the correct political direction, strengthen ideological and cultural construction, adhere to the guidance of the thought of a new era of socialism with Chinese characteristics, and fully implement the spirit of the 19th national Congress and the spirit of the national ideological and political work conference [6]. In the era of fast information, our mainstream ideology will inevitably not be challenged. The key lies in our colleges and universities to firmly grasp the initiative of ideological discourse power and give full play to the function of educational discourse power in Colleges and universities. Therefore, studying the path to strengthen the effect of the discourse power of higher education can ensure the security of China's social ideology.

2   Related Work

2.1   Discourse and Discourse Power

For the definition of "discourse and discourse power", scholars pay attention to different objects due to different research perspectives. So far, a unified definition has not been formed in the academic community, and there are still many disputes. At present, there are many definitions of discourse and discourse power at home and abroad:

Discourse is interpreted as "speech, speech" in modern Chinese dictionary, and as a language in practical application in Cihai, which is composed of components larger than or similar to sentences. Roland Barthes once said a similar explanation. He believes that discourse has its own unit, rules and grammar, and its organization goes beyond the scope of sentences. Todorov, a western scholar, explains discourse more specifically [7]. He points out that discourse is produced in a certain social context, and points out that sentences produced by languages with certain vocabulary and grammar are only the starting point of discourse activities. From the perspective of the origin of the thought of "Discourse", there are two main sources: first, in the field of linguistics, the discourse analysis published by the American structuralist linguist Harris first proposed to take discourse as the research object. He pointed out that these discourses refer to coherent sentences, that is, oral or written language fragments with internal relevance; Second, in the field of philosophy and sociology, taking Foucault, a typical representative of postmodern thinkers, as an example, he clearly put forward that the concept of discourse has two meanings: one is that discourse is composed of symbols, and the other is that people can hear and see discourse.

With the change of communication mode, discourse has gone beyond the scope of interpersonal communication, and the concept of discourse has also changed greatly, which is reflected in: first, it has gone beyond the instrumental cognition of discourse; The second is the diversification of research perspectives. After absorbing the theory of speech act, the relevant factors of discourse production, such as social, cultural and contextual factors, begin to be related to discourse products. Discourse is no longer an isolated combination of language symbols, but a specific social background and production conditions; After absorbing the thoughts of the critical school on discourse and power, discourse and ideological control, discourse and hegemonism, discourse began to expand to the field of social order and social control [8]. The discourse studied in this paper is a speech act carried out by people in a specific social context and production conditions. It mainly includes certain elements such as speaker, receiver, text, communication, context and so on.

The theoretical source of discourse power is the 1920s. From the perspective of discourse criticism, Gramsci's theory of cultural hegemony reveals how the state realizes the emergence of social "consensus" in ideology, culture and morality; In the 1970s, Baudrillard, a master of semiotics, took "imitation" as the logical starting point and proposed that in the era of digital technology, the "surreality" constructed by self reference gradually replaced reality. As a part of symbols, discourse is also included in the construction of "surreality"; In the 1990s, Habermas, a German sociologist, published a series of works, such as the theory of communicative behavior and between facts and norms. He hoped to rebuild the public sphere eroded by power and commerce through the rational interaction of discourse, so as to promote the formation of modern democracy. In fact, the right of discourse was first put forward by French philosopher Foucault. He believes that the right of discourse is an independent concept. The power here is different from the top-down control in politics. The discourse power emphasized by Foucault is dispersive and structural in practical application. The individual is not only the owner of the discourse power, but also the receiver of the discourse power. This kind of power is omnipresent. So what is the right to speak? In fact, the right of discourse is the right of people to speak in order to express their thoughts and conduct verbal communication. The right to speak is equal to every citizen. For a country, discourse sovereignty is the right to speak. Like national sovereignty, territorial sovereignty and territorial sovereignty, it is a symbol of national independence. Therefore, the discourse power actually has the characteristics of the field. In the political field, the discourse power is subject to the political authority; In the academic field, discourse power is subject to academic authority.

The distribution of discourse power in real society is mainly divided into four types: one is the inverted pyramid. That is, within a country, from the perspective of government led system, the distribution of discourse power is an inverted pyramid, and the size of national government functions corresponds to the size of discourse power; Second, umbrella type. This is mainly because in the United Nations, the distribution of discourse power is open, that is, around the discourse focus, every country has the discourse power of equal dialogue; Third, oral type. In other words, language exchanges between countries and between countries and nations, such as dealing with various affairs between countries and nations. The distribution of discourse power is verbal. Both sides generally exercise the right to speak, discuss and negotiate around an established topic. The fourth is reverse equivalence. In the verbal communication between people, the distribution of discourse power is reverse equivalence, because the verbal communication between people is two-way communication.

2.2   Discourse Power of Higher Education

The discourse power of higher education is not the mechanical addition of higher education, ideological and political education and discourse power, but the organic interaction of the three. Ideological and political education in Colleges and universities refers to "within the scope of colleges and universities, colleges and universities or college educators use certain ideological concepts, political views and moral norms to carry out planned, purposeful and organized education for college students, so as to make them form educational practice activities that meet the requirements of social development." The development of educational activities depends on the construction, development and application of discourse. Without the education or application of discourse power, teaching practice cannot be carried out. Therefore, the problem of discourse power is always hidden in the ideological and political education activities in Colleges and universities.

The discourse power of higher education mainly includes three levels: first, the discourse power, understood from the perspective of the subject of Ideological and political education, refers to that in the ideological and political education activities of colleges and universities, educators use discourse construction to publicize the mainstream values of society, guide the thoughts and behaviors of College students, and control the dominant power of campus ideological and public opinion according to national policies and social development requirements. The second is the discourse right, which is understood from the perspective of the object of Ideological and political education. It means that the educatee has the right to receive education in the process of Ideological and political education and the right to freely express his views on the teaching content of Ideological and political education, school management, national events and social phenomena. The third is the effect of discourse power. From the essential understanding of Ideological and political education, it refers to the ideological and political education in Colleges and Universities Based on the social mainstream ideology, giving full play to its leading power, cohesion, regulation and persuasion, indicating that the ideological and political education "how to be a man and act with words", so as to ensure that the ideological development of college students conforms to the national consciousness and achieves the expected goal. In short, the discourse power of higher education is the unity of discourse power, discourse power and discourse power effect.

3   Unbalanced Data Set Classification Method Based on Mixed Big Data Analysis

3.1   Analysis on the Influence of Unbalanced Data Set Sampling on SVM Classification

There are two internal factors in unbalanced data, namely, skew slope and lack of information. Skew rate refers to the ratio of large category to small category, which represents the degree of data imbalance. Lack of information refers to the data volume of small category samples, which represents the information volume of small categories in the data set This paper only discusses the most widely used binary classification problem in the classification of unbalanced data sets, and the order of magnitude of the default counterexample is much larger than that of the positive example.

Support vector machine has been successfully applied in many fields such as information retrieval, image recognition and text classification. However, when faced with unbalanced data sets, its performance also decreases significantly. The main reason is that the imbalance of training data makes the ratio of positive and negative examples of support vectors obviously unbalanced, and the negative examples play a dominant role and drown the positive examples, Finally, the decision function inclines the classification results to counterexamples too much.

We analyze the influence of data imbalance and sampling on SVM classification through the linearly separable imbalance data set [9]. From the training process in Fig. 1 (a), we can see that the classification hyperplane obtained by actual learning is basically consistent with the ideal hyperplane in direction due to the imbalance between positive and negative examples, but it is far away from the negative example and close to the positive example, which is the result of data inundation. As shown in Fig. 1 (b), such a classification hyperplane will have a strong tendency to counter examples during testing, so that some positive examples are wrongly divided into counter examples.

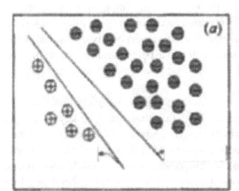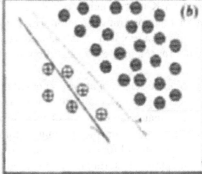

Fig. 1. Data inundation

We randomly select the same number of samples from the counterexample as the positive example to make the data reach a balanced state. Figure 2 (a) is the training result after resampling. Although the distance between the learned classification hyperplane and the positive and negative examples basically reaches the ideal state, it deviates greatly from the direction of the ideal hyperplane, which is the result of information loss after sampling. As shown in Fig. 2 (b), such classification hyperplane will also have misclassification during testing.

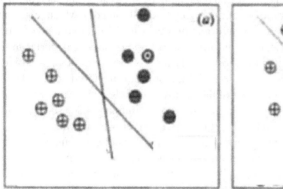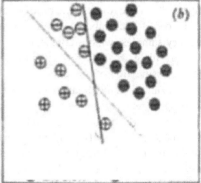

Fig. 2. Information loss phenomenon

Therefore, how to reduce the skew slope and minimize the loss of information is a problem that must be considered when using resampling method to solve the classification of unbalanced data sets.

3.2   Unbalanced Data Classification Algorithm Based on Mixed Big Data Analysis

The classification method in this paper consists of three sub algorithms: sample selection algorithm based on dynamic self-organizing map clustering, sample pruning algorithm based on K-nearest neighbor rule and class boundary calibration algorithm based on kernel function transformation The algorithm gives a comprehensive solution to the classification problem of unbalanced data sets from two aspects: sample resampling and the improvement of SVM algorithm itself.

(1)   Sample selection algorithm based on dynamic self-organizing map clustering.
Resampling is an effective way to solve the data imbalance. The key is how to eliminate a large amount of noise information, significantly reduce the degree of data skew, and ensure the minimum information loss to retain the vast majority of sample points useful for classification learning In this paper, the dynamic self - organizing mapping clustering method is used to solve this paradoxical and difficult problem The original large-scale imbalance data is divided into n clusters by clustering method, and the clusters whose sample points are counter examples are deleted, and other clusters are taken as the selected sample set.
    The clustering method of dynamic self-organizing map (v-som, variable SOM) is used to avoid the underutilization of neurons due to the expansion of neurons, and

can also overcome the boundary effect caused by rectangular structure and other structures. The weight adjustment of neurons adopts the following formula:

$$\Delta u_{k+1}(t) = \Delta u_k(t) - \Gamma_{p1} C(\dot{x}_d(t) - \dot{x}_{k-1}(t)) \tag{1}$$

(2) Sample pruning algorithm based on K-nearest neighbor rule.
In the real unbalanced data set, there will be data aliasing in the sample set This data aliasing not only increases the difficulty of training, but also causes over learning, which greatly reduces the generalization ability of SVM and the classification performance. In this paper, a sample pruning algorithm based on K-nearest neighbor rule is proposed to solve this difficulty in practical application The basic idea of the algorithm is to investigate the category attributes of each sample point in the new sample set and its nearest k nearest neighbor samples, and judge whether the calculated attributes of the query samples are consistent with their real attributes by calculating the predicted values of the current query sample points. In practical application, the control threshold of the positive example is usually less than that of the negative example, This is because in the unbalanced data, the positive case resources themselves are relatively scarce, and the positive case information is more precious than the negative case information. Moreover, due to the imbalance of data, there are far more negative cases mixed in the positive case than in the negative case Therefore, through different control thresholds, pruning is more inclined to delete counterexample mixing points, so as to ensure that rare positive example information is not lost as much as possible [10].
The algorithm assumes that all sample instances correspond to points in n-dimensional space. More precisely, any instance x is represented as the following eigenvector, and the standard Euclidean distance is used as the distance between the two vectors.

$$x(t) \leq c + \int_0^t (ax(\tau) + by(\tau))d\tau \tag{2}$$

4 The Function of the Discourse Power of Higher Education

4.1 The Individual Function of Educational Discourse Power

The so-called individual function refers to the objective influence of educational discourse power on the individual of educational object. It is also the ontological function of Ideological and political education, which is mainly reflected in the following aspects:

(1) Individual survival function. It mainly refers to the positive influence of educational discourse power in guiding human individuals to seek a better living state on the basis of following the objective law and survival law. Marxism believes that the biggest difference between human survival activities and animal instinct activities lies in practice. Man is a dynamic social being, and practice is the way of human existence. In social practice, in order to survive, human beings must meet the most

basic material survival needs before they can pursue higher-level spiritual needs. Only when human beings have their own survival needs can they pursue the spiritual needs beyond the material. The same is true of the pursuit of the right to speak in education. Only by continuously improving people's living conditions and meeting people's growing needs for a better life to the greatest extent can the pursuit of the right to speak as a spiritual level develop by leaps and bounds.

(2) Individual development function. It refers to the role of educational discourse power in shaping individual morality and promoting people's all-round development, which is mainly reflected in four aspects: first, guiding the political direction, that is, guiding the educatees' thoughts and behaviors to the direction required by the core values of socialism through education, guidance and inspiration, That is, through rich and colorful activities to improve the ideological and moral quality of the educated and promote them to strengthen the correct political direction. The second is to regulate and restrict the behavior, which is the power effect of the right of educational discourse. By imparting laws, morality and other social norms to the educated, we can affirm and praise the behavior that conforms to the social norms, and deny and criticize the behavior that violates the social norms, so as to better restrict and regulate the behavior of the educated. The third function of discourse is to stimulate the spirit of education. Use various incentive means to fully mobilize the enthusiasm of educational objects and promote them to actively participate in the construction of the great project of socialism with Chinese characteristics. When using incentive means, we should adjust measures to local conditions, local conditions and personal conditions. According to the different situations of different objects, we should use some means alone or comprehensively use a variety of means to form a scientific and effective incentive mechanism to stimulate the enthusiasm of the educated to the greatest extent. Fourth, shaping individual personality, which is an important function of the right to speak of education, mainly promotes the educated to form a lofty spiritual realm and healthy psychological quality, become a qualified social successor in the future society, and participate in social life with a positive attitude.

4.2 The Social Function of Educational Discourse Power

The so-called "social function" refers to the objective role of educational discourse on social development, which is mainly reflected in economic function, political function, cultural function and ecological function, as follows:

(1) Economic function. It refers to the teaching of Ideological and political discourse to mobilize the enthusiasm of educational objects and promote them to actively participate in economic activities, so as to promote sustainable economic development, which is mainly reflected in the following three aspects: first, it can ensure the adherence to the essence and direction of socialism in economic construction. The ruling class of any society uses its ideological system and political theory to affect social material production and set the direction of economic development. Mao Zedong also pointed out: "ideological work and political work are the guarantee for the completion of economic and technical work. They serve the economic foundation.

Ideology and politics are the commander and soul". China's educational discourse system adheres to the guidance of Marxism and the theoretical system of socialism with Chinese characteristics, which ensures that China's economic construction always follows the road of socialism with Chinese characteristics. Second, actively promote the development of social productive forces. The development of educational discourse power can improve the ideological and moral quality of workers and mobilize the enthusiasm, initiative and initiative of educatees in work or production and life. Only those educated or workers with good ideological and moral quality will actively learn scientific and cultural knowledge, consciously improve labor skills, strive to improve production tools, adopt new processes and technologies, reduce labor intensity, change labor organization and innovate production management system, so as to promote the development of productivity. Third, create a friendly and harmonious environment for economic and social development. The smooth progress of material production requires people to establish some kind of connection or relationship. As Marx said: "in order to carry out production, people have certain connection and relationship with each other; only within the scope of these social connections and social relations can they have their influence on nature and production." The deepening of Ideological and political discourse can maintain this relationship between people. Carrying out ideological and political discourse work regularly is conducive to straightening out various relations between people and between people and society, resolving various social contradictions, creating a harmonious social environment for the economic development of socialism with Chinese characteristics, and promoting sound and rapid economic development.

(2) Political function. It refers to the promotion of political development through the education of the content of educational discourse and the cultivation of educatees with good ideological and political literacy. The specific manifestations are as follows: first, guide the social mainstream ideology and standardize the social spiritual production. "The ideology of the ruling class is the dominant ideology in every era". If the ruling class wants to make its thoughts dominant in society, it must strengthen the ideological and political education of social members and master the leading power of Ideological and political education, so as to standardize the spiritual production of society. By spreading the information of educational discourse power, unifying people's thoughts and integrating the elements of social spiritual production, we can realize the positioning and adjustment of educational discourse power to spiritual production. Second, spread the mainstream ideology and strengthen the political guidance of the audience. Thought is the forerunner of behavior. People's political behavior is always dominated by some thoughts. By transmitting China's socialist core values, laws, regulations and moral concepts to educational objects, educational discourse power helps educational objects strengthen the correct political direction, improve their political judgment, discrimination, choice and awareness of participating in political life, and form higher political literacy. Colleges and universities give full play to the political function of educational discourse power, use various educational means, systematically carry out theme education for educational objects, and take cultivating "Four Haves" new people as the educational goal, which has laid the foundation for the construction of socialist democracy and rule of law. Third, give full play to the function of information communication

and feedback to maintain social and political stability and development. From the perspective of the discourse power and discourse right of Ideological and political education, on the one hand, the discourse power of education publicizes Marxist theory, advanced socialist culture and the party's advanced principles, policies and lines, urges the educated to internalize these scientific theories, and fully implement the party's principles, policies and lines; On the other hand, we should listen to the voice of the educated, collect their opinions and suggestions on some social events, and feed them back to the relevant departments, so as to provide factual basis for the political decision-making of the leaders. In the complex interpersonal relationship, the right of educational discourse plays an important role in strengthening the relationship between the party and the people, coordinating interpersonal relations and resolving social contradictions.

5 Conclusion

In the new era, the discourse power of higher education has been given new connotation and put forward new requirements. Due to the long-standing historical inertia, the current situation of educational discourse power in Colleges and universities has been wandering within the scope stipulated in textbooks, and the educational discourse power has not played its due role. This paper systematically analyzes the current situation and reasons of discourse power, and holds that there are still four difficulties in the field of educational discourse power in Colleges and universities, such as the difference of global discourse, the lack of educators' own ability, the lag of discourse transformation and the new requirements put forward in the new era. The classification algorithm of unbalanced data set proposed in this paper provides a comprehensive solution to the classification problem of unbalanced data set from two aspects: the preprocessing of unbalanced data set samples and the improvement of support vector machine kernel function Through the sample selection algorithm based on dynamic self-organizing map clustering, a large amount of noise information in unbalanced data is filtered while preserving effective information to the greatest extent, which greatly reduces the number of support vectors and improves the classification accuracy and training speed of unbalanced data This sampling method effectively solves the disadvantages of traditional resampling methods, such as strong randomness, man-made subjective interference and information loss Through the sample pruning algorithm based on K-nearest neighbor rule, the resampled data are pruned to solve the actual problem of data aliasing, so as to improve the generalization ability and classification accuracy of SVM We propose a class boundary calibration algorithm based on kernel function transformation. The class boundary is calibrated by using kernel function equiangular transformation to adapt to the imbalance of sample data.

Acknowledgements. General topic of Zhejiang Federation of Social Sciences "analysis and Reflection on the competency characteristics of excellent ideological and political teachers in Colleges and universities" (No.: 2022N124)).

References

1. Jiang, D., He, J.: Text semantic classification of long discourses based on neural networks with improved focal loss. Comput. Intell. Neurosci. **2021**(1), 1–9 (2021)
2. Zhang, H., Hu, J., Zhang, Y.: Research on classification method of network resources based on modified SVM algorithm. Security and Communication Networks **2021**(69), 1–8 (2021)
3. Stoica, A.S., et al.: Classification of educational videos by using a semi-supervised learning method on transcripts and keywords. Neurocomputing **456**, 637–647 (2021)
4. Spangher, A., May, J., Shiang, S.R., et al.: Multitask Learning for Class-Imbalanced Discourse Classification (2021)
5. Lugini, L., Litman, D.: Contextual argument component classification for class discussions (2021)
6. Radyuk, A.V., Kozubenko, A.V.: Semantic classification of phraseological verbs in publicistic discourse of economic orientation. Revista Amazonia Investiga **10**(37), 107–115 (2021)
7. Poddenezhnyi, O.: Management of digital transformation in education: modern scientific discourse. Scientific Papers NaUKMA Economics **6**(1), 105–110 (2021)
8. Taniguchi, T.: Classification of educational skills for university students in computer programming classes. Int. J. Inf. Educ. Technol. **11**(7), 313–318 (2021)
9. Ismail, S.: Distribution of discourse markers elements or discourse particle as an entity relationship in discourse. Turkish J. Comput. Math. Educ. (TURCOMAT) **12**(3), 190–200 (2021)
10. Yankovskaya, T.: Mastering by students of the second grades of the universal educational action of classification. Primary Education, 35–39 (2021)

Evaluation of Business English Practical Teaching Based on Decision Tree

Xiaojia Lai[✉]

Guinlin College, Guangxi, Guinlin 541004, China
xiaojia899@tom.com

Abstract. Business English practical teaching evaluation based on decision tree is a tool to help teachers evaluate their teaching effect. This helps them identify and prioritize areas for improvement. Decision trees are used by many companies, educational institutions and governments as evaluation tools to improve the quality of education provided. The tool can be applied to any type of business environment that requires English skills, such as retail, banking or tourism. It can be applied to any type of educational institutions, such as schools and universities. The main purpose is to understand whether the students have mastered all the necessary skills for effective English communication during their college years. Since its first introduction in 2003, this method has been adopted by many institutions. The evaluation process includes three stages: pre-test, post test and analysis. In these three stages, students are required to complete the task of testing their specific knowledge. Based on the advantages of decision tree in data processing, this paper makes an effective evaluation of the problems existing in the current business English practice teaching in Colleges and universities, and improves the practice teaching strategies according to the evaluation results, so as to cultivate more qualified English talents for the society.

Keywords: Business English · Decision tree · Practical teaching · Effectiveness evaluation

1 Introduction

Since the 21st century, with China's higher education entering the stage of popularization, secondary vocational colleges and higher vocational colleges have emerged and gradually developed like the seeds of spring. Among these schools, nearly 100 secondary vocational colleges have business English majors. In terms of teaching methods, the vast majority of secondary vocational colleges have directly adopted the teaching mode of colleges and universities [1]. Therefore, we need to seriously consider the following issues: under the situation that most colleges and universities in China have set up business English majors, how to reform the teaching of business English Majors in secondary vocational colleges, improve the level of running schools and the quality of education, cultivate practical talents required by the society, and form the unique competitive advantages of business English Majors in secondary vocational colleges.

M. A. Jan and F. Khan (Eds.): BigIoT-EDU 2022, LNICST 466, pp. 558–568, 2023.
https://doi.org/10.1007/978-3-031-23947-2_59

With the deepening of China's reform and opening up and the market economy, the society has higher and higher requirements for application-oriented Business English talents. In the past, English graduates who could only speak fluent English and travel all over the world could hardly meet the needs of enterprises in the talent market [2]. However, the traditional business English courses based on import and export business and foreign trade English correspondence are too broad and do not highlight the specialty and practicality, so they do not have competitive advantages in society. In terms of talent training methods, secondary vocational colleges can not form their own characteristics in terms of professional training objectives, curriculum design, teaching material construction, teaching methods, teacher structure, especially professional practice teaching, and do not have their own competitive advantages. Therefore, it is often difficult to gain a foothold in the market competition.

At present, most business English Teaching in China is based on theoretical teaching, mainly explaining the basic knowledge of English, vocabulary, grammar and business English to students. There are few practical teaching aimed at students, which leads to the disconnection between students' theory and practice. Students are unable to apply theoretical knowledge to practice, which affects their enthusiasm for learning. Secondly, the business English teaching curriculum is unreasonable, most of which are mainly English courses, supplemented by business English courses. In addition, many colleges and universities have set professional business English courses as elective courses, which shortens the time for students to learn professional business English. Students cannot learn business English knowledge comprehensively and systematically, resulting in low business English level and unable to meet social needs [3]. Finally, business English majors include not only the knowledge of English majors, but also the knowledge of finance, law, trade, economic management and so on. It covers a wide range and requires high requirements for business English teachers. Business English teachers need not only professional English knowledge, but also other relevant professional knowledge. However, most business English teachers do not have these abilities and relevant business English practical teaching experience, which leads to students unable to learn more useful knowledge and students' practical business English ability cannot be improved [4].

With the gradual advancement of curriculum reform, modern higher education begins to pay attention to the practical ability of students. In formulating an education plan, a teacher set out to establish a practical education system. In practice, students combine theoretical knowledge with practice to help them fully develop. As a part of business English teaching, students should participate in practical work to improve their professional skills and English knowledge. However, there are still many problems in Business English education. According to the characteristics of College Business English practice teaching and the nature of College Business English teaching, a set of teaching performance evaluation system of College Business English is designed, and the current business English training is improved to increase human resources and meet social needs [5].

At present, the lack of application of modern scientific and technological methods and means, as well as the imperfect evaluation feedback and control mechanism, are important problems faced by the teaching quality evaluation system. In particular, the scientificity of the evaluation index establishment and the rationality of the index weight distribution will directly affect the correctness and public reliability of the evaluation results. Therefore, establishing and improving the teaching quality evaluation system is an important way to improve the teaching quality of teachers and an urgent requirement to improve the teaching management level of colleges and universities [6]. Data mining technology is an effective technology to extract or "mine" knowledge from a large amount of data. In the research of this paper, data mining technology can not only assist the construction of teaching evaluation system, but also realize the knowledge mining of teaching evaluation data. Therefore, the research of teaching quality evaluation system in Colleges and Universities Based on data mining technology will be an important trend in the future education science research and has great practical significance.

2 Related Work

2.1 Practical Teaching Meaning

Due to various reasons, the research on the practical training mode of business English Majors in China started late. Since the establishment of ESP, the research on the application of business English has been started, and the content of the research is only limited to the analysis of teaching methods and language characteristics, but the research on practical teaching mode is blank. So far, the applied research results of business English are not ideal. The reason is that there is no relevant paper on the Chinese Journal network that systematically studies and introduces the practical teaching mode of business English majors. The research on the practical teaching mode of business English Majors in China still puts forward the development direction of its mode on the basis of learning from other professional modes, which is not practical and operational [7].

After years of development, higher vocational colleges in China have a relatively deep understanding of practical teaching, and have formed a practical teaching content system with certain characteristics and an effective management mechanism. Highlighting the cultivation of students' practical ability is the most important and significant feature. Strengthening the theoretical research and practical exploration of the construction of practical teaching system and practical teaching base in Colleges and universities is conducive to the healthy development of higher education and the realization of the training objectives of applied professional and technical talents in higher vocational colleges.

Literally, practical teaching is first of all an educational term opposite to theoretical teaching. When the word "practical teaching" appeared is difficult to verify from the existing literature, but as a form of teaching, it is always related to education, especially vocational education. Vocational education, which originated from productive labor, is the oldest and most basic of all types of education. In the ancient society with under-developed productivity, vocational education mainly passed on skills through hand to mouth and simulated demonstration. This form can be said to be "practical teaching" in its original state. Although in the later development, only a very small part of the original productive vocational education has been absorbed by school education, paying attention to the practical color in the teaching process, that is, by guiding students to practice themselves, so as to master relevant craft or technical knowledge and skills, has always existed in educational behavior, especially in non school educational behavior, which is typical of the apprenticeship system in the Roman era [8]. It emphasizes the practicality and Simulation in the teaching process, and believes that letting students participate in production practice is the fastest and most effective means to master skills. Even in the West in the middle ages, the church monopolized education, and secular education was greatly destroyed. "Practical teaching" was still inexhaustible. Represented by the "apprenticeship" prevailing in Europe at that time, paying attention to the cultivation of students' practical ability and mastering vocational skills in production practice or simulated production practice is still the main way for human beings to inherit technology and craft. Vocational education, which has been divorced from formal school education for a long time, is the "physical practitioner" of practical teaching. Even in some famous classical universities, some courses also pay attention to the teaching method of learning in practice.

2.2 Generation Process of Decision Tree

The generation process of decision tree is the process of generating new decision tree, which is the most important part. The generation process will create a new decision tree based on the input data. This is a very simple process. The training algorithm (learning algorithm) obtains the input vector and generates the output vector, which is called "training set". If we use all possible inputs in the example, it will produce a large number of vectors. Therefore, the training set will be reduced to a certain size, but still large enough to represent all possible inputs in the problem domain. This step is called "reduction" or "partitioning". We need to use the generation process, because whenever we need different outputs of the model, it can help us generate a new decision tree [9]. We can also use this method to create multiple models with the same training data set but different outputs or predictions. If you have only one model and are using it for prediction, there is no need to carry out another step, namely cross validation. Figure 1 briefly describes the process of decision tree generation.

The core of ID3 algorithm is to use information gain as the selection criterion of attributes when selecting attributes on the nodes at all levels of the decision tree, so that the largest category information about the tested records can be obtained when each non leaf node is tested).

The specific method is to detect all the attributes, select the attribute with the largest information gain to generate a decision tree node, establish branches based on different values of the attribute, and then recursively call the method for subsets of each branch to establish branches of the decision tree node until all subsets contain only the same category of data. Finally, a decision tree is obtained, which can be used to classify new samples.

By calculating the information gain of each attribute and comparing their sizes, the attribute with the largest information gain can be obtained. Let s be a set of data samples. Assuming that the class label attribute has m different values, define m different classes C, (I = 1, 2, ..., m). Let s be the number of samples in class C. The expected information required to classify a given sample is given by the following formula:

$$Info(S) = -\sum_{i=1}^{m} p_i \log_2(p_i) \tag{1}$$

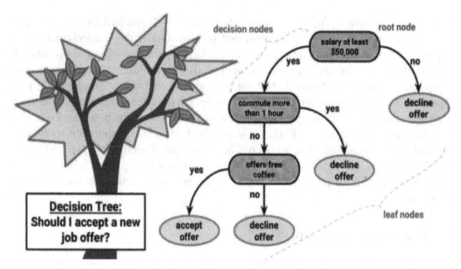

Fig. 1. Decision tree generation process

3   The Guiding Significance of Decision Tree Practical Teaching Effect Evaluation Model to Business English Practical Teaching

In recent years, there are many different views on the conceptual description of "business English". Many experts and scholars have such views on the definition and connotation of business English. The first point of view is that "business English" is a vague term. It refers to the English communication in the course of business activities. It has many common features with the English used in daily life. The second view is that business English is regarded as an interdisciplinary subject of literature, economics and management. The third point of view is that business English is the English used in the business environment. It is a variant of English for special purposes (ESP), which is the ESP learned or applied by professionals in the business industry. Although these views are different, they are not contradictory. It can be said that they are interrelated and complementary to each other. They are only understood and explained from different angles.

"Practical teaching" is a teaching form that is always closely connected with vocational education. The original form of "practical teaching" was in ancient society. People passed on skills through hand to mouth and simulated demonstration. From ancient society to today's folk people, they pay more attention to the practical color in the teaching process. Folk masters teach crafts through apprentices' follow-up practice and imitation. In essence, they master crafts and skills through apprentices' practice. This is an educational behavior of non school practical teaching, This kind of behavior was typical of the "apprenticeship system" in Roman times. This behavior emphasizes the simulation and operation in the teaching process, so that the apprentices can master the skills as soon as possible. This is also the fastest and most effective means, as shown in Fig. 2. The "apprenticeship system" prevailing in Europe attaches great importance to the cultivation of students' practical ability. It believes that the main way for human beings to inherit technology and craft is to master vocational skills in production practice or simulated production practice. Therefore, vocational education other than formal school education is regarded as a "physical practitioner" of practical teaching.

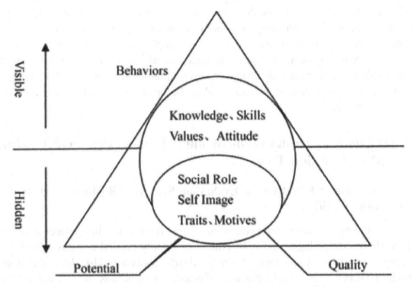

Fig. 2. Business English practical teaching model

First of all, it is conducive to the establishment and development of practical English teaching system. The decision tree evaluation model is conducive to the establishment and development of the company's talent training system. Decision tree evaluation model can make school decisions according to the characteristics of business English learners. When establishing the education system, schools should design education courses according to the characteristics of professional companies. The purpose of business English teaching is to cultivate students with professional knowledge and experience, so that students majoring in Business English have the opportunity to obtain professional guidance in education [10].

Second, promote teachers' practical training. The educational effect of decision tree evaluation model in practice is conducive to teachers' practical education. In practical business English teaching, teachers usually receive theoretical training. According to the learning level of each student, precision education can make students learn English better. Teachers can use decision trees to evaluate students so that they can complete English teaching. In English practice, teachers can reasonably arrange students' practical activities and improve the quality of practical training. The performance evaluation model of practical teaching is helpful for teachers to cultivate students in practice and stimulate their all-round development.

Third, promote the integration of practical education evaluation system and management system. Under the business English practical teaching system based on decision tree, teachers are conducive to combine the evaluation system of practical teaching with the management system. On this basis, effectively use the data provided by the decision tree to evaluate and integrate the whole management system, reasonably analyze the learning situation of each student, and manage them according to the amount of knowledge students master, so as to make the evaluation and management of students in the same data system and effectively carry out educational work for each student. The detailed division of levels in the evaluation system can evaluate students' learning situation and their ability to complete practical homework, so that students can clearly recognize their shortcomings. According to the samples provided by the decision tree, supervise students' learning and make rational use of the resources of the evaluation system. Such interaction not only promotes the complete operation of the whole practical teaching management system, but also makes the business English practical teaching system more perfect.

4   Effectiveness Evaluation of Business English Practical Teaching Based on Decision Tree

4.1   Composition of Effectiveness Evaluation System of Business English Practical Teaching

At present, the examination and evaluation of the practical teaching effect of business English Majors in Colleges and universities are mainly carried out through the practice reports submitted by students. This method still adopts the old-fashioned evaluation method, so it is necessary to establish a set of evaluation standards and methods that meet the needs of enterprises and can guide the practice teaching of schools. On the whole, the reform of practical assessment and evaluation of college students is relatively lagging behind. The main performance is that the assessment and evaluation system does not reflect the characteristics of colleges and universities, the assessment content is heavy on knowledge and light on ability, the assessment method is too simple, the emphasis is on summative and the process assessment is ignored, and the practical teaching evaluation system of business English Majors in Colleges and universities has not been fully established. In terms of the school's assessment and evaluation methods for students, college education should take the ability standard as the fundamental feature, and the teachers' teaching effect should take the students' employment ability and the employers' satisfaction as the standard. However, at present, the traditional single and rigid education evaluation method is still adopted, which hinders the in-depth development of the reform to a certain extent.

The construction of the evaluation system of business English practice teaching effect is to make statistics of business English majors. Collect the scores of business English majors. Assuming that C is a collection, it is the scores of business English majors. Arrange each of them according to their student number, in which the student number can be represented by A1 and A2, and set their expectations at the same time. As shown in Fig. 3. Teachers can evaluate each student's ability in English practice according to the data in the decision tree. The formula is

$$u_{k+1}(t) = u_k(t) + \Gamma_{l1}\dot{e}_k(t) + \Gamma_{l2}\dot{e}_{k+1}(t) + \Gamma_{p1}\Delta\dot{e}_k(t) + \Gamma_{p2}\Delta\dot{e}_{k+1}(t) \qquad (2)$$

However, in practical teaching, there are still some problems. For example, with the increase of business English practice content, the amount of calculation of the evaluation system will increase, and the decision tree will be difficult to bear a lot of data. As a result, when dealing with data, the decision tree needs to constantly establish a new decision tree, which brings some troubles to teachers in evaluation teaching.

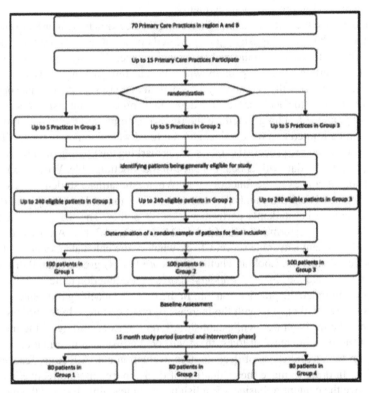

Fig. 3. Evaluation system of business English practical teaching effect

4.2 Improvement of Decision Tree Practical Teaching Effect Evaluation Model

The level of teaching quality is the external manifestation of the effectiveness of teaching activities. Good teaching evaluation has the functions of guiding, promoting, encouraging and regulating the teaching quality. It is an important part of school teaching management and the main means of evaluating the teaching performance. The school conducts classroom teaching evaluation survey every semester and accumulates a large amount of data. At present, the teaching evaluation is mainly based on numerical calculation, which summarizes the students' evaluation and reports the results to the teachers as the basis for promotion of professional titles and evaluation of excellence, without deep thinking. In this chapter, association rule mining is applied to the teaching quality evaluation system. According to the purpose and data characteristics of mining, the mining system is designed to find the relationship between the teaching effect and the overall quality of teachers by mining the relationship between the teaching effect and the teachers' age, professional title, education background and workload, and reasonably allocate the teachers of a class to enable students to maintain a good learning state, Thus, it provides decision-making support information for teaching departments, promotes better teaching work and improves teaching quality.

First, optimize the teaching data. When using the decision tree, in order to ensure the performance of business English majors, repeated operations are required, which brings a certain burden to teachers in the evaluation and reduces the efficiency of decision tree operation to a certain extent. Especially when the teaching data increases, the operation speed of decision tree will become very slow, which increases the cost of data operation. In order to optimize the decision tree, the data can be processed intensively according to the data in practical teaching to reduce the time consumption. During data processing, the data can be limited to a fixed value, and the fixed value interval is [C, D]. Teachers can use the computer to process the data, such as marking the floating of the current data. When $f(x) > 0$, the data will appear concave in the function table. When $f(x) < 0$, the data will appear convex in the function table. When estimating a student's performance, the teacher can select a value and bring it into the (C, d) range. For example, in Business English practice, the student's performance is 98 points. The teacher can bring the student's different performance into $f(x) = A0 + A1 + A2 + \ldots$ An divided by an to calculate the student's average score. Check whether the calculated value conforms to the value in the interval. Look at whether the score is $f(x)$ greater than 0 or $F(x)$ less than 0, and evaluate the shape of students' scores in the function table.

Second, optimize the practice content. In the practical teaching of business English, the decision tree will change with the increase of practice times. In the process of data processing, the decision tree will establish different trees according to the increase of content. Due to the increase of trees, there will be confusion in information exchange, resulting in the effectiveness of decision tree evaluation and Affecting Teachers' data processing. In order to make the evaluation of decision tree more effective, we should first improve the content of business English practical teaching. Expand the memory of the data processing system and comprehensively process the practical content. Evaluate each student's performance in Business English practice, and draw a table according to the students' practical ability. Decision tree is prone to instability in algorithm. In order to make it better meet the needs of teaching, it is improved accordingly. The practical teaching effectiveness evaluation system uses the decision tree, which can carry more practical content and take the data with the smallest change as the basis of evaluation. Teachers can evaluate students' grades according to the values given by the evaluation system, As shown in Fig. 4.

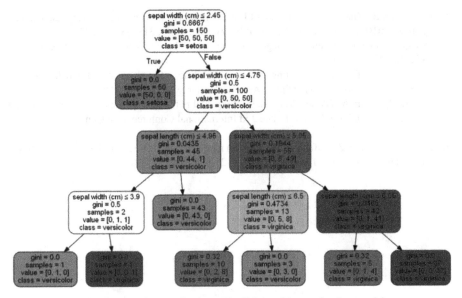

Fig. 4. Decision tree business English teaching evaluation model

5 Conclusion

In the practical business English training course, students can reasonably and effectively use the existing educational resources of specific institutions through decision-making analysis and improvement of the existing educational system. Prepare students for all-round development, organize theory and practice organically, and cultivate their professional and practical skills. This paper studies business English practice based on decision tree. Based on decision tree samples, students' learning can be controlled and the resources of the evaluation system can be effectively used. This interaction makes the practical education management system and business English teaching system fully implemented.

References

1. Wang, X.: Research on education evaluation of business English talents training in the new era. In: 2020 3rd International Seminar on Education Research and Social Science (ISERSS 2020) (2021)
2. Xu, T.: Immersion teaching method of business English based on virtual reality technology. J. Inf. Knowl. Manage. **21**(Supp02) (2022)
3. Yi, L.: Research on English Teaching Ability Evaluation Algorithm Based on Particle Swarm Optimization Algorithm (2021)
4. Ji, S., Tsai, S.B.: A study on the quality evaluation of English teaching based on the fuzzy comprehensive evaluation of bat algorithm and big data analysis. Math. Probl. Eng. **2021** (2021)
5. Wu, X.: Research on the reform of ideological and political teaching evaluation method of college English course based on "online and offline" teaching. J. High. Educ. Res. **3**(1), 87–90 (2022)

6. Lu, C., He, B., Zhang, R.: Evaluation of English interpretation teaching quality based on GA optimized RBF neural network. J. Intell. Fuzzy Syst. **40**(2), 3185–3192 (2021)

7. Tan, Q.: Evaluation system of college English teaching based on big data. J. Phys. Conf. Ser. **1852**(2), 022014 (2021)

8. Almutairi, B.: Towards estimating global probabilities of evaluation in English based on automatic extraction of least delicate Appraisal in large corpora (2021)

9. Gao, K.: Evaluation of college English teaching quality based on particle swarm optimization algorithm. In: CONF-CDS 2021: The 2nd International Conference on Computing and Data Science (2021)

10. Jing, Y., Mingfang, Z., Yafang, C.: Evaluation model of college English education effect based on big data analysis. J. Inf. Knowl. Manage. **21**(03), 2250046 (2022)

Application of VR Technology in Practical Courses of Preschool Education Specialty

Lijuan Liao[✉]

Baise University, Guangxi Zhuang Autonomous Region, Baise 533000, China
474818066@qq.com

Abstract. In recent years, with the rapid development of science and technology, VR (virtual reality) technology, as the most potential modern information technology, has been widely used in the fields of architecture, entertainment, manufacturing and education. Taking the practical course of preschool education as the teaching research object, this paper analyzes the teaching status and main problems of the course. Aiming at the problems existing in preschool education, such as general shortage of practical teaching resources, many teaching difficulties and difficult to solve, scattered resources and difficult to meet students' personalized learning needs, Using VR technology to develop "virtual factory", integrate relevant VR practical teaching resources, build a practical teaching environment with the combination of virtual and real, innovate the VR technology application mode of "training pre-school vocational skilled talents, combining virtual environment with real environment, and supporting practical teaching, innovating practical teaching and carrying out research", and realize "teaching + real training" The traditional practical teaching mode changes to the mixed practical teaching mode of "Online Autonomous Learning + virtual practical training + face-to-face teaching + real practical training", and studies the advantages and problems needing attention of the application of VR technology in the course, in order to provide a help for the application and promotion of VR technology in the course.

Keywords: Virtual technology · Preschool education professionals · Practical teaching

1 Introduction

VR technology is a new computer graphics technology rising from the U.S. military in the late 1980s. With the help of computers, it can generate realistic virtual worlds in the form of three-dimensional vision, hearing and touch. At present, VR technology has been widely used in aerospace, medical practice, architectural design, military training, entertainment and many other fields. As a new teaching technology, virtual technology plays a significant role in promoting the development of education.

The talent training goal of preschool education in Colleges and universities in China is mainly to meet the needs of preschool education talents. Practical teaching is the

© ICST Institute for Computer Sciences, Social Informatics and Telecommunications Engineering 2023
Published by Springer Nature Switzerland AG 2023. All Rights Reserved
M. A. Jan and F. Khan (Eds.): BigIoT-EDU 2022, LNICST 466, pp. 569–579, 2023.
https://doi.org/10.1007/978-3-031-23947-2_60

key to cultivate students' vocational skills and innovative quality. However, due to the limitations of construction funds, venues, resources and other conditions, building perfect practical training conditions has become an urgent problem to be solved in many colleges and universities [1]. Virtual reality technology creates an observable and interoperable three-dimensional virtual world for users in a highly simulated way, which reflects the internal structure, operation law, interaction process and state change of things, so as to realize the invisible and inaccessible in real life Immersive experience of things and phenomena that cannot be touched or moved. Therefore, it is of great significance to explore the application, exploration and practice of VR technology in preschool education courses.

2 Related Technologies

2.1 Realization Principle of VR Effect

How to ensure that the virtual object appears in the real scene I want it to appear. For example, the hero BR is displayed in the center of the stage. The principle is very clever. In fact, a large number of reflection points are covered on the dark walls on both sides of the finals. These reflection points only reflect the human eye and invisible infrared rays. The camera on the scene has been modified, When shooting with the camera, the photographer will transmit infrared through an additional infrared transmitting and receiving device.

Including the infrared ray will be reflected back and received by the device after reaching the reflection point. Then, by calculating the time difference between transmission and reception, we can know the distance between the camera and different reflection points. By calculating the included angle between different reflection points and the camera, we can calculate the current position of the camera and the shooting direction, Make the position and direction of the virtual camera completely consistent with the real camera, so that the virtual picture produced will completely match the real scene.

It mainly represents the maximum angle range of the image that the human eye can see. Generally speaking, our eyes are 200 degrees horizontally, and there will be 120 degrees of overlap. Binocular overlap is very important for human eyes to build stereo and depth of field, which we will talk about later, and the vertical angle of view is about 130 degrees, as shown in Fig. 1 below.

Full immersion
These are standard fully immersive virtual reality displays. These stereoscopic displays are combined with sensors to track position and direction. Like the book ready player one, they completely block the user's view of the outside world.

Optical perspective type
In "optical perspective glasses", users can view reality directly through optical elements, such as holographic waveguides and other systems that can overlay graphics in the real world. Microsoft's hololens, magic leap one and Google glass are recent examples of optical perspective through smart glasses [2].

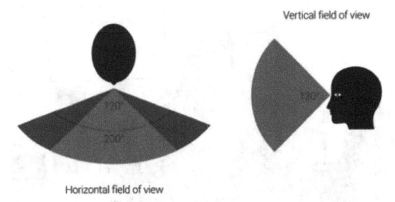

Fig. 1. Maximum angle range of image

Video Perspective

With these smart glasses, users can view the real image first captured by one or two cameras installed on the display. These camera views are then combined with computer-generated images for users to view. HTC vive VR head display has a built-in camera, which is usually used to create ar experience on the device, as shown in Fig. 2 below.

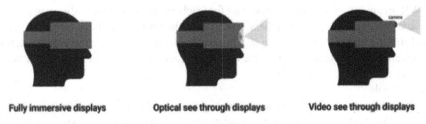

Fig. 2. Create ar experience on device

2.2 Application of VR Technology in Education Industry

1. For students.

The most direct advantage of VR technology is to present planar and monotonous information / images in a three-dimensional, vivid, interesting and interactive form. The change of presentation and interactive form can make the teaching content, teaching form, method of acquiring knowledge and learning efficiency have positive significance. Take a simple example: traditional students can only learn geography through plane textbooks or slides, and can only watch it through documentaries or 3D models. The application of VR technology not only brings three-dimensional display forms, but also students can interact with the scene in the courseware, such as climbing towering snow mountains and diving into trenches several kilometers deep, The enhancement of interaction is more conducive to stimulate students' interest in knowledge; As shown in Fig. 3 below.

Fig. 3. VR teaching application

2. To teachers.

VR technology is a powerful assistant for teachers. Thanks to the addition of AI, VR, AR and other technologies, teachers' teaching in the future will focus on the presentation form, rich courseware content and interactivity. Compared with the single teaching presentation form, the addition of VR and other Internet technologies can undoubtedly improve teachers' teaching level;

3. To schools.

The addition of VR and other technologies can solve the educational innovation problem that has plagued the school for many years. At present, there is a serious homogenization in school running in terms of form, hardware and courseware, which makes it difficult for most schools to build a distinctive campus [3]. The use of VR and other Internet technologies will enable customized course production, customized intelligent classroom and customized multi-functional smart laboratory, which undoubtedly adds wings to educational innovation!

In addition to the teaching innovation mentioned above, VR teaching has also brought more changes to the school in terms of school management! First of all, the operating cost of the school is reduced. If the traditional teaching form is used for teaching, the school needs to prepare a large number of teaching aids and teaching consumables, and a large part of these teaching supplies can not be reused. Secondly, reduce the cost of school management of teaching aids. The addition of VR technology not only saves the cost of purchasing a large number of teaching aids, but also saves the subsequent management of teaching aids. In addition, the risk of dangerous experimental supplies has been reduced. Previously, it has been reported that colleges and universities have lost or someone has used flammable, explosive, toxic and harmful chemical experimental supplies for other purposes. With the addition of VR courseware, the school can no longer worry about the management of dangerous goods. Finally, classroom resources are saved. Only one laboratory is needed. VR laboratory can meet the experimental courses of physics, chemistry, biology and other disciplines. For the school, the classroom can be used for more teaching work.

2.3 Application Significance of VR Technology in Professional Practice Courses

The application of VR technology in education is the direct embodiment of the rapid development of educational technology. It is a way for learners to realize the transmission and teaching of knowledge and skills with the help of the interaction of themselves and information environment. Its main applications are: virtual laboratory, virtual classroom; Virtual library, virtual campus, virtual studio and virtual distance teaching.

Virtual reality technology can truly simulate the corresponding things and environment [4]. At the same time, it can also provide diversified natural interaction ways and conversation methods, which can significantly improve students' learning enthusiasm and improve students' visual memory ability of learning content. In the teaching process of architecture courses, Especially in the teaching process of some preschool education teaching programs and teaching processes, teachers can use VR technology to play the real preschool teaching process to students, and let students really feel the construction process, so as to improve students' memory of this content and achieve the purpose of efficient teaching. In this regard, VR technology is highly feasible in education. At the same time, practical education is often limited by experimental equipment and teaching funds. At the same time, there may be some phenomena or difficulties that the teaching environment can not meet the standards. In such an environment, the introduction of VR technology for teaching must be based on the limited financial constraints, with the help of software and wisdom, carry out simulation teaching or simulation experiment teaching with significant teaching significance and pertinence. In addition, among the WBE sites in the field of education, the emerging educational forms such as virtual examination room and virtual teacher must also be reflected. At the same time, they must be closer to the real work, which is also one of the inevitable development directions in the field of education in the future. Therefore, the application value of VR technology in education and training can not be ignored.

With the advent of 5g era, vr virtual reality has gradually penetrated into our life. With the continuous development of social productivity and science and technology, the demand for VR technology in all walks of life is becoming stronger and stronger. In the long run [5], vr virtual reality education and teaching will have a profound impact on the future education and teaching methods. The future VR education and teaching provides humanized, efficient, diversified and customizable interactive teaching methods, so as to make learning simple, happy and efficient! As shown in Fig. 4, vr virtual reality teaching.

1. VR education and teaching enables students to have immersive interactive experience and bid farewell to brainless endorsement.

In terms of traditional teaching, the emergence of VR technology can make students get rid of the traditional boring and boring teaching. As long as students wear vr virtual reality equipment and relevant scenes in the classroom, they can easily realize it, completely replacing the traditional way of teachers' dictation and chalk blackboard

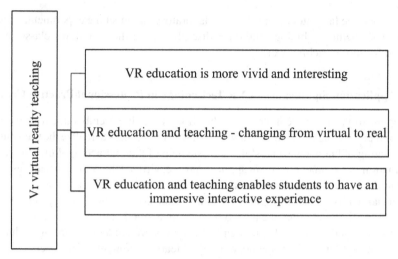

Fig. 4. VR virtual reality teaching.

writing. In addition, students' interest in VR teaching software and restrictions on wearable devices make them highly focused. This learning method can be said to be very efficient.

2. VR education and teaching - changing from virtual to real.

VR education class is especially suitable for solving complex and abstract knowledge difficulties. For example: Chemistry, celestial motion, human structure, etc.; After using vr virtual reality technology, abstract knowledge points can construct interactive examples by modeling in the virtual world, so that students can intuitively learn and understand these abstract knowledge [6]. Through VR teaching, we can simulate the operation and intuitive interactive learning experience that are difficult to realize in the real environment, so that students can deepen their understanding of knowledge.

3. VR education is more vivid and interesting.

Traditional classroom teaching is often boring, which is an important reason why many students don't like learning. VR education immersive experience gets rid of simple words and pictures. You can learn while playing and have fun. Truly experience the fun of learning, so as to improve the learning effect.

In the future, VR education industry will be an integrated solution based on customized head display, content, interactive equipment, service platform and so on. It can create a vivid, immersive, interactive and interesting way of learning. It will give more applications and significance to the field of digital education.

3   Application of VR Technology in Practical Courses of Preschool Education Specialty

With the advent of 5g era, vr virtual reality has gradually penetrated into our life. With the continuous development of social productivity and science and technology, the demand for VR technology in all walks of life is becoming stronger and stronger [7]. Vr virtual reality equipment is not only applied to games. VR technology has made great progress and is gradually becoming a new field of science and technology. The knowledge in books is only memorized by rote or only listened to the teacher's blackboard instruction. Students may not be easy to remember, understand or concentrate. With the rapid development of VR technology in recent two years, VR education has broken the rigid and single way of traditional teaching.

In terms of traditional teaching, the emergence of VR technology can make students get rid of the traditional boring and boring teaching. As long as students wear vr virtual reality equipment and relevant scenes in the classroom, they can easily realize it, completely replacing the traditional way of teachers' dictation and chalk blackboard writing. In addition, students' interest in VR teaching software and restrictions on wearable devices make them highly focused. This learning method can be said to be very efficient. In traditional teaching, some scenes may not be described by teachers in language. If these scenes can be displayed, the effect must be better than language, just like allowing students to see human organs directly, which is more vivid and intuitive than what teachers describe [8].

VR education, combined with games, scene conversion and other means, can effectively solve educational problems and stimulate students' interest. Using the immersion sense of VR technology to provide students with practical operation opportunities in virtual scenes, so that students can directly participate in interaction in a natural and realistic environment, which can increase their interest in learning and strengthen their memory of knowledge points. As shown in Fig. 5 below, VR teaching class is shown.

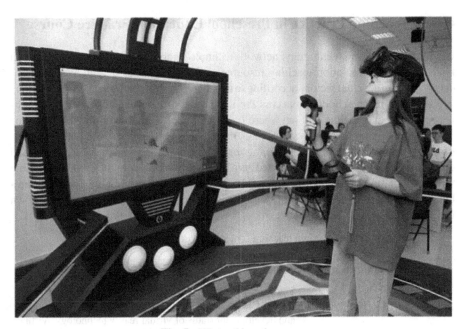

Fig. 5. VR teaching classroom

When people look at the world around them, due to the different positions of the two eyes, they get slightly different images. These images are fused in the brain to form an overall picture of the world around them, which includes the information of distance. Of course, distance information can also be obtained by other methods, such as the distance of eye focal length, the comparison of object size, etc. When people are used to the display screen, they suddenly accept this new visual mode, which is really amazing.

Binocular stereo vision plays an important role in VR system. Different images seen by the user's two eyes are generated separately and displayed on different displays. Some systems use a single display, but after users wear special glasses, one eye can only see odd frame images and the other eye can only see even frame images [9]. The difference between odd and even frames, that is, parallax, produces a three-dimensional sense.

Tracking of users (head and eyes): in the artificial environment, each object has a position and attitude relative to the coordinate system of the system, and so does the user. The scene seen by the user is determined by the user's position and the direction of the head (eye).

Virtual reality headgear for tracking head movement: in traditional computer graphics technology, the change of field of view is realized by mouse or keyboard. The user's visual system and motion perception system are separated. Using head tracking to change the perspective of image, the user's visual system and motion perception system can be connected and feel more realistic. Another advantage is that users can not only recognize the environment through binocular stereo vision, but also observe the environment through the movement of the head.

4   VR Teaching Practice in Preschool Education Practice Course

Use cloud computing technology, network technology and other means to integrate all kinds of virtual simulation teaching resources [10]. If possible, we can also independently develop a virtual factory according to the characteristics of the school. All teachers and students of the school can access the integrated virtual simulation training teaching resources at any time and anywhere by using the on-campus training room, office computer, VR equipment, off-campus PC, mobile terminal, etc., so as to make the multimedia classroom and computer training room, Teaching places such as on campus and off campus training bases have realized zero distance docking with the cloud computing virtual simulation training center to build a good practical teaching environment combining virtual and real. The main teaching contents of virtual reality course are shown in Table 1 below.

Table 1. Main teaching contents of virtual reality course

	Teaching module	Content of courses
Theory	Basic theory	The basic concept, characteristics and composition of virtual reality; Classification of virtual reality system; Application and development status of virtual reality technology; Virtual Reality Architecture

(continued)

Table 1. (*continued*)

	Teaching module	Content of courses
	Core technology	3D modeling technology Stereoscopic display technology, rendering technology, human-computer interaction technology Collision detection technology; Input and output equipment of virtual reality system
Practice	Application software	3D panoramic roaming (panoramic Master). 3ds max, unity 3D, augmented reality (vuforia SDK)
	System development	Children's 3D model production, puzzle game production, semester education augmented reality mobile app development

This paper sinnovates the application mode of VR technology in higher vocational practical teaching. The ultimate purpose of VR technology in education and teaching is to serve talent training. In the process of practical teaching, the application mode of VR technology in the practical teaching of talent training in preschool education has been formed [11].

Situational teaching theory holds that all learning should change with the situation. Learning needs to take place in a real situation, and the environment is an inevitable factor. In the process of situational teaching, teachers can truly show the teaching content with the help of VR technology. Assist teachers to carry out corresponding teaching activities to improve teaching effect. Teachers can teach according to the needs of teaching content, provide independent and real teaching content, and unify various teaching contents containing different media information. For example, in the teaching of preschool teachers, teachers can play corresponding teaching pictures with the help of VR technology, let students "enter" into the pictures with the help of VR technology, and use virtual teaching tools. At present, there are many VR technologies, and many businesses have also created many simulation software according to the characteristics of VR technology. These software can achieve the purpose of refraction, reflection and dynamic shadow with the help of shading technology [12], so as to realize realistic and high-quality real-time rendering of 3D image content, especially for the night scene which is difficult to be effectively represented by traditional VR, its scene performance ability is more realistic. In this regard, such an environment also promotes the wide popularization and application of this VR technology in education. We should improve the three dimensional scene teaching scene, adjust and set up various advanced material effects such as dynamic water body, reflection, mirror reflection and HDR, and publish it into a roaming 3D scene packet, which will make the situational teaching of preschool education courses more vivid and vivid.

Like all kinds of school system education, preschool education is a science with its own professional characteristics. Therefore, all preschool education institutions must ensure the safety of children's activity places according to children's physiological and psychological characteristics On the premise of necessary conditions such as food hygiene and safety, there is a purpose Organized to help children develop in a comprehensive and harmonious way in four aspects: body, intelligence, morality and beauty. However, people often do not pay enough attention to this educational law, and there are even universal misunderstandings. First, from the perspective of children in the old Chinese tradition, young children are "little yellow hairs" who are still wet behind the ears. They are childish and ignorant. Adults either ignore them and let them grow up, or use violence to discipline these children. Among the people, there is a saying that "nothing can be accomplished without beating"; Second, many people simply believe that early childhood education is nothing more than "taking care of children". There is no profound knowledge. As long as there is an activity place, it seems that no matter who can set up a kindergarten; Third, in the environment of exam oriented education, some people in society aim at making profits, Constantly clamoring that "don't let children lose at the starting line", and some parents often report to the Miao unrealistically with the psychology of "hate iron but don't become steel", and the phenomenon of "primary education" is common, inadvertently strangling children's pure childhood, childlike innocence and childlike fun, leading to diametrically opposed consequences.

In fact, as a science, early childhood education needs to study a wide range of contents. For example, in sports, young children are still in a weak, imperfect and immature growth stage, and their adaptability to the environment and ability to resist diseases are poor. In addition, they do not have rich life experience and weak self-control ability, which requires adults to create an appropriate environment, give careful care, guidance and education, promote children's normal physical development and coordinated development of functions, and enhance their physique, Cultivate good living habits, health habits and interest in participating in sports activities; In intellectual education, children have the characteristics of intuitive action thinking. They think through direct perception and concrete action. Therefore, only by making use of and creating a large number of opportunities to guide them to use a variety of senses and languages to contact things and people, can they enhance their understanding of the environment, cultivate beneficial interest, desire for knowledge and preliminary practical ability, so as to develop their intelligence; In terms of moral education, young children are young and have little experience. They can only guide and help them form a preliminary concept of right and wrong step by step according to the specific and tangible situations around them, starting with emotional education Germinate preliminary moral feelings, such as cultivating children's feelings for their parents, relatives, teachers and peers The love of neighbors begins, and then leads to the love for family, hometown and surrounding social life, so as to form love for the motherland and cultivate good morality Behaviors and habits; In terms of aesthetic education, as an art enlightenment education, we should focus on cultivating children's interest and ability to feel and express beauty, rather than emphasizing how many artistic skills children must master. Thus, early childhood education is a real science. No wonder some people sigh: university professors may not be able to teach kindergarten classes well! The reason is that "there are specialties in technology", their respective research fields and teaching objects and tasks are different.

5   Conclusion

In short, with the rapid development of virtual reality technology in modern society, its application scope is also growing. In the process of Higher Vocational architecture curriculum education, the rational application of VR technology can promote the communication between teachers and students in the teaching process to be more harmonious, and enable teachers to make students truly feel the recognition and analysis of architectural drawings with the help of VR technology, Promote students to have a more accurate understanding and mastery of construction equipment, so as to truly improve the teaching quality of preschool education courses.

References

1. Lin, C.: Research on the design of multicolored ceramic cultural creative products based on computer VR technology. J. Phys: Conf. Ser. **1744**(3), 032160 (2021)
2. Xiao-Bing, H.U., Zhang, L., Tong, F.: Research on green idea in modern ceramic products —— also discuss the construction of VR technology on ceramic product display E3S Web of Conf., 236, 04048 (2021)
3. Tong, Y., Cao, W., Sun, Q., et al.: The use of deep learning and VR technology in film and television production from the perspective of audience psychology. Front. Psychol. **12** (2021)
4. Tian, G., Darcy, O.: Study on the design of interactive distance multimedia teaching system based on VR technology. Int. J. Continuing Eng. Educ. Life-Long Learn. **31**(1), 1 (2021)
5. Yang, H.: Explore how artificial intelligence and VR technology will change the development of future education. J. Phys: Conf. Ser. **1744**(4), 042146 (2021)
6. Design and implementation of 3d visualization intelligent home decoration system based on VR technology. Comput. Sci. Appl. **11**(4), 814–820 (2021)
7. Kim, A.P.,Carollo, S.L., Stendell-Hollis, N.R., et al.: Outcomes of an interprofessional faculty development program on knowledge and value of interprofessional practice and education. Health Interprof. Pract. Educ. **4**(2), 2138 (2021)
8. Nikulina, I.A.: Rhetorical training in higher education as the basis of professional speech practice of a lawyer. Courier Kutafin Moscow State Law Univ. (MSAL) **11**, 133–140 (2021)
9. Ayish, M., Dahdal, S.: Going mobile in journalism education: how media students perceive mobile journalism as a professional practice. Int. J. Smart Educ. Urban Soc. **12**(2), 21–31 (2021)
10. Royce, M., Jariwala, J., Petzer, M., et al.: Perspectives of authentic assessment and professional practice interventions in teaching and learning. SHS Web Conf. **99**(5), 01033 (2021)
11. Molina, O.E., Cancell, D.: Results of the blended learning training for teachers and tutors of the professional practice (2021)
12. Kock, L., Mlezana, N.B., Frantz, J.M.: Perceptions, attitudes and understanding of health professionals of interprofessional practice at a selected community health centre. Afr. J. Prim. Health Care Fam. Med. **13**(1) (2021)

Evaluation of English Teaching Quality in Higher Vocational Colleges Based on Artificial Intelligence Optimization Network

Lingli Zhang[✉]

Hubei Three Gorges Polytechnic, Yichang 443000, China
lilyfy520@163.com

Abstract. English teaching evaluation is an important part of English evaluation. It is a process of measuring, analyzing and value judging the process and results of English teaching activities based on teaching objectives and using effective evaluation techniques and means. This study aims to evaluate the quality of English Teaching in Higher Vocational Colleges Based on artificial intelligence optimization network. The research method used in this study is descriptive analysis, which combines qualitative and quantitative analysis. This study was conducted in the form of a questionnaire survey, with a sample of 100 students from various vocational colleges. In addition, use the reliability coefficient (Cronbach α) Was 0.858, and the validity coefficient (Pearson correlation coefficient) was 0.923; Therefore, they are regarded as high values of reliability and validity respectively.

Keywords: Higher vocational English · Teaching evaluation · Network optimization · English language teaching

1 Introduction

By evaluating English classroom work and calculating the corresponding educational workload according to its expression form, we can reveal the aggressiveness of English classroom and English teaching, and improve the educational effect by using educational resources to improve teaching methods.

English teaching quality evaluation system is an effective tool to strengthen higher education. In principle, the evaluation standard is determined according to the evaluation method to establish the quality foundation. However, in practice, the quality evaluation system is difficult to achieve the desired effect. This problem involves deep-seated problems such as management culture, standard recognition and dynamic differentiation. The traditional education quality evaluation system should be one of the important goals of the reform. Therefore, schools should deepen the basic laws of educational activities and establish an English education quality evaluation and management system on the basis of improving the efficiency of English construction and management. In order to evaluate English education, two problems must be solved. On the one hand, establish an English ranking index system, on the other hand, collect and process ranking data [1].

© ICST Institute for Computer Sciences, Social Informatics and Telecommunications Engineering 2023
Published by Springer Nature Switzerland AG 2023. All Rights Reserved
M. A. Jan and F. Khan (Eds.): BigIoT-EDU 2022, LNICST 466, pp. 580–590, 2023.
https://doi.org/10.1007/978-3-031-23947-2_61

Large scale data analysis is one of the main applications of parallel distributed systems in the future. The era of big data has brought rapid development in various fields. Large scale data analysis technology mainly includes collecting and storing data in different fields, scientifically and effectively analyzing these data according to the needs of different industries, and improving the value and availability of data through data extraction, We can quickly select useful data from massive data and play an important role in the development of any leading city. Data extraction is one of the effective methods of data mining, which can effectively enhance the key role of information technology in data extraction. This study aims to identify English skills based on big data analysis technology.

It is very important for English teaching to establish and improve the evaluation system of English teaching quality. Implement the English education quality evaluation system to evaluate the quality of English education quantitatively, objectively, systematically and scientifically. At the same time, quality control and safety issues will be considered in school content, English teaching process, English teaching evaluation, etc. The integration that meets the needs of the reform and development of English higher education provides scientific management for the quality of English education.

To effectively implement the English education quality evaluation system, we must first clarify the level of using computers and networks at all levels to collect and obtain information that affects the quality of English education in real time, And collect the collected information in time to ensure the authenticity and credibility of the evaluation results We need to establish an assessment mechanism for the quality of English education. This system is usually composed of three levels: school, Department, department and Jingzi. Structure [2]. The structure of the network evaluation system mainly includes the following contents: (1) the quality assurance system of the English quality evaluation system. This subsystem mainly includes English teaching resources, English teaching process, English education information, English teaching accident information and English teaching evaluation. This study aims to standardize the management of English education, improve the institutional structure, and promote the improvement of the quality of English education, Restore the information and trends of the evaluation of English teaching quality outside school, and improve the evaluation system of English teaching quality in school. (2) Manage and maintain English teaching quality evaluation indicators. The main function of this subsystem is to ensure that Based on the English quality evaluation system, the subsystem ensures that the systems at all levels are in place, quantifies the indicators of each observation post, and timely maintains and quantifies each observation post according to the changes and adjustments of the system. (3) English education quality evaluation information management system. This subsystem mainly collects data from educational institutions and colleges and universities to assess the quality of English education and complete the design of relevant mechanisms. In addition, According to the English education quality evaluation indicators and the observed quantitative indicators of the service subsystem, the English education quality evaluation data are processed and processed [3], and a feedback platform for English education quality is provided for teachers, students and teachers, Study the problems and situations in the English curriculum, dynamically adjust the English curriculum, and ensure that many students and lecturers with noble morality become the real evaluators of the English curriculum. (4) Interactive education quality assessment system. The sub-system is evaluated by teachers, students and educational administrators. Experts and participants working in this field will assess the effectiveness and quality of English Teaching in the current English teaching process, and input the assessment results into the English quality assessment database as input to the preliminary assessment of English teaching quality.

2   Related Work

2.1   Research Status of English Teaching Quality Evaluation

In the era of big data, every industry in Japan has accumulated a large amount of data of great significance to the development of the whole industry, which puts forward higher requirements for data analysis. By applying big data analysis technology, we can collect and store data of any industry and analyze industry needs. In this way, useful data can be extracted from existing data to provide a good basis for industry development and decision-making.

Educational evaluation was born with human education. The earliest educational evaluation in China can be traced back to the Western Zhou Dynasty, when there was a relatively complete examination system. The imperial examination system was estab-lished in the Sui Dynasty, forming a complete national talent selection system. This should be the earliest talent knowledge evaluation system implemented by the gov-ernment. With the change of dynasties, the pace of educational development remained unchanged. The evaluation of teaching quality in modern sense should be traced back to the curriculum reform experiment in the United States in the 1930s. Nearly half a century later, with the reform and opening up and the restoration of the college entrance examina-tion system, in the 1980s, western teaching evaluation ideas were introduced into China, and higher education teaching entered a new journey [4]. However, in higher education, especially in higher vocational education, the scientific and professional teaching eval-uation, we are far behind western countries. In the HowNet, we have inquired about the literature on the evaluation of English teaching quality in Vocational Colleges for more than ten years. In the domestic mainstream foreign language journals and authoritative foreign language journals such as foreign language teaching, foreign language circles, foreign language teaching and research, not only are there rare articles on the evaluation of English teaching quality in higher vocational colleges, but also there are few teaching related articles signed and published by English teachers in Higher Vocational Colleges in various journals. In other relevant journals, there are few articles on the evaluation of Higher Vocational English teaching quality, and the influence of the articles is not great. Download and browse these articles and works, and find that the research topics mainly focus on the following aspects: 1. The concept and connotation of Higher Vocational English teaching quality evaluation. 2. The mode and content of English teaching quality evaluation in higher vocational colleges. 3. Problems and Countermeasures of English teaching quality evaluation in higher vocational colleges.

The research and Exploration on the professionalization and scientization of teach-ing evaluation in the United States are relatively mature, and there are also some more detailed minority teaching evaluation studies. American scholar Andy Senna Weber pointed out in his doctoral thesis that the impact of education on students is not determined by school management and curriculum reform, but triggered by changes in teaching methods and teaching evaluation, which really leads to changes in students' learning and the improvement of teaching quality. Foreign research on teaching evaluation also involves different ways of teaching evaluation, such as teacher self-evaluation and peer evaluation. American scholar Levine Debra In this paper, an discusses the promoting function of teachers' self-evaluation on teaching. The author agrees with self-evaluation, but his attitude towards peer evaluation is relatively negative. He believes that due to the light of peers, the teaching evaluation made is subjective and not objective and fair enough.

Many domestic scholars have also done in-depth research on foreign teaching evaluation. Zhao fengjuan pointed out that the third-party evaluation is the teaching quality evaluation method adopted by many western countries. The main body of this evaluation is generally social intermediary institutions. The evaluation process is open and transparent, and the results are not sorted. It is published to the public in the form of written reports, and the external evaluation and internal evaluation of the college are combined. Peng Weiqiang pointed out that the transformation of foreign teaching evaluation from language ability to pragmatic ability is the general trend, and the evaluation of students has also changed from general evaluation to personalized evaluation.

2.2 Big Data Analysis and Application Status

The platform includes five main stages of data processing: the selection of platform operating system, the creation of hadop cluster, data integration and preprocessing, data storage, data extraction and analysis, and the efficiency of wider application data.

(1) Select the platform operating system. In large-scale data analysis, we are faced with huge data sources. In order to improve the organization and management efficiency of these data resources, it is necessary to use a consistent operating system to provide the widest possible data access and hot data storage, and manage the physical planning and data resource configuration of large space. Common operating systems include RedHat CentOS and Debian systems, which can be used as underlying platforms and can be extended to support data processing. The platform operating system can also be virtualized, enhance the physical memory capacity of the system, share processors, and increase communication bandwidth [5].

(2) Build Hadoop cluster. Hadoop is a software platform that can run big data processing software. The core technology is MapReduce, which can form a cluster of a large number of computers to realize massive data distributed computing. Hadoop has attracted many commercial companies to develop and design, and has built various open source components, including sqoop and HBase And spark. Hadoop includes many constituent elements. The lowest constituent element is Hadoop Di distributed file system (HDFS), which can maintain all storage node files in Hadoop cluster platform. The upper layer of HDFS is a MapReduce engine, which includes two constituent components, jobtrackers and tasktrackers. Hadoop can be used to realize data processing and operation, Further meet the distributed data operation.

(3) Data integration and preprocessing. These have both structural and non structural data. Therefore, preprocessing is required when integrating the data together, so that the service bus can be used for communication transmission and improve the consistency and reliability of the data [6]. Data preprocessing can use impala Tools such as sparksql and hivesql.

(4) Data mining and analysis. There are many resources for big data storage. These resources are usually disordered and messy. Although certain organization principles are adopted, people's use of data is also very complex. Therefore, the introduction of data mining and analysis function can improve the timeliness of data utilization and shorten the time of data processing. Artificial intelligence technology is introduced into data mining and analysis, K-means algorithm. The data mining process is shown in Fig. 1.

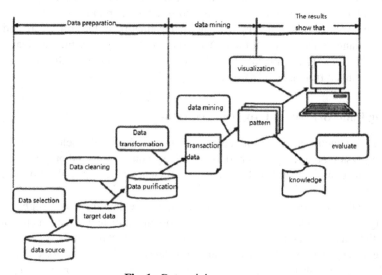

Fig. 1. Data mining process

3   Evaluation of English Teaching Quality in Higher Vocational Colleges Based on artificial Intelligence Optimization Network

(1) The evaluation project is separated from reality.

English teaching quality evaluation system will play a positive role in improving teaching quality. However, some English teaching quality evaluation systems have some problems, such as the evaluation items are divorced from the real environment and so on. If we adhere to this evaluation system, it will have a negative impact on teaching work. For example. The evaluation projects launched include multimedia teaching videos, the application of new teaching methods, etc. However, the real English teaching environment is not suitable for this kind of teaching means. Taking multimedia video as an example, the production and use of English will consume too much cost. In the absence of school support, most English can not bear the corresponding cost for a long time. This problem will lead to the decline of teaching video quality and the lack of teaching purpose [7]. The teaching method of encouraging students to participate is not suitable for our classroom. At present, some advanced teaching methods generally have problems such as long time-consuming, unsatisfactory effect and no guarantee of classroom discipline. The density of classroom knowledge in Colleges and universities in China is high. If such teaching methods are widely popularized, it will affect the teaching output and the teaching quality is difficult to be guaranteed.

(2) Excessive attention to procedural justice.

Procedural justice, also known as "visible justice", refers to the process and means of justice to achieve the goal of justice. This concept has been popularized in our society and has become an important part of the ethics of the rule of law. However, in the real environment, there are negative cultures such as bureaucracy in our society. If bureaucratism is deepened in procedural justice, it will inevitably lead to the alienation of procedural justice. For example, takes administrative instructions as the main basis for designing assessment items. In use, the innovation and adjustment of teaching work should be planned in strict accordance with the relevant design of the evaluation system, otherwise it will violate the procedural requirements. In response to such incidents, English will submit relevant applications to the regulatory authorities to maintain the normal development of teaching work. However, in practice, procedural justice has become an excuse to shirk responsibility and ignore the changes in reality. These problems will lead to the increasingly rigid management of teaching quality and the mere formality of supervision regulations. English enthusiasm will also be affected.

(3) Lack of humanistic care.

Therefore, a unified implementation standard should be adopted to bring all English into the scope of assessment. However, the evaluation items designed by some colleges and universities are too rigid and lack of humanistic care for English. This instruction comes down in one continuous line with the humanistic concept advocated since the 16th National Congress. The ideological core of humanistic concept is to take people's needs as the starting point of work and treat the limit of workers' ability scientifically. However, the teaching quality evaluation system proposed by some colleges and universities does not consider the expertise and shortcomings of English. So that the project design is too comprehensive, and the high-quality talents with professional expertise but obvious shortcomings will be affected. However, in the quality assessment system, high requirements will be put forward for students' participation, classroom atmosphere, examination results and other elements. The professional specialty of the English can not be highlighted in the quality evaluation system.

(4) Ignore growth value.

In essence, English teaching is an empirical science. With the accumulation of experience, English teaching ability will be gradually improved. This problem will have a negative impact on the construction of English team. First of all, Youth English will be used in this field The teaching evaluation system has been greatly impacted. Young people's English has just stepped into the education post, and their work enthusiasm and learning willingness are relatively strong [8]. However, the teaching quality evaluation system without growth consideration will make young English bear more pressure, and the efforts are difficult to show results in the short term. After a period of accumulation, self-confidence is very vulnerable. Youth English is the basis of English team construction, so the psychological feeling of Youth English should be considered in the evaluation of teaching quality. Moreover, some English that have reached the standard of teaching quality will gradually lose their learning motivation. English that meets this standard will no longer be assessed by the outside world, and the pursuit of teaching quality will gradually decline.

Through the research on the content of teaching evaluation, it is found that the content of English teaching evaluation is mainly the index system or elements of evaluation. At present, the specific content is still the focus, focus and difficulty of academic discussion. Therefore, in the process of constructing the teaching evaluation system, whether the index content is properly established is the key to whether the College English teaching evaluation can be scientific, standardized and democratic. At present, the content of English teaching evaluation mostly includes English teaching attitude, teaching content, teaching professional level, teaching effect and teaching methods. English teaching process is divided into many aspects, not just classroom teaching. In practice, there are also some college English teaching evaluation, including extracurricular guidance to students, teaching papers published in English, guiding students and various student work participated in by English.

The purpose of its evaluation determines that its evaluation has the following characteristics: on the one hand, the core of college teaching evaluation is to evaluate the quality of English teaching. The focus of the evaluation is the mental work of English - the teaching and research of professors and the quality evaluation of spiritual products - students and achievements [9]. This must start from the laws and characteristics of mental work, school education and special spiritual products - students and learning, and pay attention to the mutual connection and combination characteristics between them; On the other hand, unlike the fixed model of primary and secondary schools, College English teaching is flexible and diverse. At the same time, considering the limited time and energy of evaluators, the evaluation content is simple and easy. Although it can not be seen, it can still reflect the focus of evaluation and the evaluation objectives to be completed; Moreover, College English teaching evaluation is a multi factor, multi-level and crisscross network structure system. In the specific operation, teaching evaluation makes a complete and scientific evaluation in the relationship between the evaluation factors by investigating the relationship between the constituent teaching factors, is shown in Fig. 2.

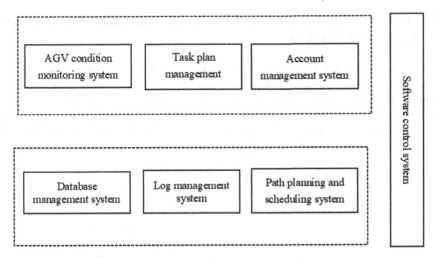

Fig. 2. Structure of English teaching evaluation system

The establishment of a scientific and reasonable English education evaluation system should follow the following four principles.

① Principle of unification. The evaluation index system should be retained for evaluation, that is, the evaluation index system should be retained. The purpose of English teaching evaluation is to promote the continuous improvement of English teaching resources, optimize teaching methods, and improve the attraction to students and the enthusiasm of English teaching. English education evaluation should be carried out from three aspects: educational attitude, learning process and educational influence.

② Scientific principles. According to the characteristics and laws of modern teaching, a set of evaluation index system is scientifically designed. We should also consider students' autonomy and the effectiveness of English teaching.

③ Principle of operability. Each evaluation index has clear classification and connotation, and there are observation points convenient for judgment. In addition, technically, it should also be able to collect the data of each evaluation index [10].

④ The principle of pertinence. The requirements of English teaching vary with different courses, student types and teaching modes, so the critical value in the evaluation grade standard should.

After clarifying the design principles of the evaluation index system, the next step will be to establish a scientific evaluation index system, determine the threshold, primary and primary observation points, that is, the index system of scientific evaluation. Evaluation criteria. Based on the analysis of English teaching elements, the evaluation system of English teaching plan is established through extensive research. The E-learning Evaluation Index System of other courses can be retained by adjusting the threshold in the "standard" to match the index system and aim at the specific situation of the learning object [11].

4 Collection and Processing of Evaluation Data Based on Big Data Analysis Technology

To evaluate English teaching activities according to the evaluation index system, the key is to obtain the evaluation data of English teaching activities according to the system network log, that is, the value and grade of each evaluation index. Because English teaching activities will be recorded in the network log, we can use web-based data mining technology to obtain the value of each index, and process the data to obtain the grade value of each index. Figure 3 English teaching evaluation model.

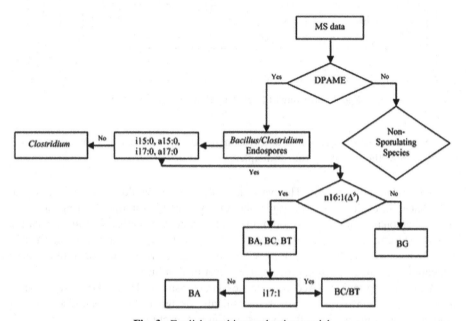

Fig. 3. English teaching evaluation model

① Evaluation of data collection. English learning assessment needs the first assessment data. The e-learning platform allows the use of two kinds of data mining logs based on statistical data. In the process of mutual relationship evaluation in dex system, it is not only necessary to mine logs, but also need to search the background database to obtain data. Mining method is to use database management software (such as Oracle and SQL Server) to extract data.

② Comprehensive data evaluation. Evaluating data integration involves integrating data into multiple databases.

③ Select the data to evaluate. Select data according to the scoring index system, delete abnormal data, and improve the quality of data retrieval.

④ Cleaning of evaluation data. The cleaning of evaluation data means that the problem of semantic ambiguity, it is realized by cleaning the dirty data and dealing with the missing data in the data. If an option data in a log is wrong, it can be filled after averaging according to other log conditions. For example, when some data in a log is unreadable or wrong, it can be discarded to reduce the capacity of the database and improve the processing efficiency of the database.

⑤ Conversion of evaluation data. The conversion of evaluation data refers to the conversion of different values in the database into data coding form. For example, in order to facilitate processing, The grades "excellent", "good", "average" and "poor" are converted into 1, 0.75, 0.6 and 0.3 respectively. In addition, the data conversion converts the collected original data of English teaching evaluation in e-learning into the grade of each index according to the standards of the evaluation index system, and saves the relevant index values [12].

⑥ Analysis and processing of evaluation data. Fuzzy concept, etc. here, in order to simplify the aura processing process, the weighted linear average is selected to calculate the quantitative results of English online teaching evaluation, and then the quantitative results are transformed into grades.

⑦ Expression and interpretation of evaluation results. Explain the necessary teaching information and extract the useful information according to the teaching purpose.

⑧ Feedback of evaluation results. Feedback the evaluation results to teachers and teaching managers in appropriate ways and forms.

Higher vocational education is an important part of higher education. The Ministry of education has determined that under the new situation, the focus of higher vocational education has been determined to strengthen practical, applied and skilled abilities. Graduates can play their professional abilities in various service, production and sales industries after employment. Among all the public basic courses in higher vocational colleges, English has always been a language and culture course of great concern. The mode of English education and teaching has its uniqueness and non replicability, and its role in improving students' English level and language ability is continuous and irreplaceable. To improve the quality of English teaching and meet the needs of the new era for the compound talents under the vocational education system is the fundamental purpose of Higher Vocational English teaching quality evaluation.

5 Conclusion

Under the background of the new curriculum reform, higher vocational education is facing new development opportunities and challenges. Higher vocational education has become a key link in cultivating talents for the society. With the in-depth development of economic integration, the social demand for high-quality international skilled talents is increasingly prominent. The essence of teaching quality evaluation is to promote the improvement of teaching quality. Most of the research on the evaluation of College English teaching quality is still focused on the evaluation of College English Teaching in Colleges and universities. This paper uses a variety of research methods, collects and integrates data, uses new methods, explores new highlights, and tries to explore new strategies to strengthen the evaluation of Higher Vocational English teaching quality combined with the analysis of examples of Higher Vocational English teaching quality evaluation.

References

1. Xie, Z., Su, Z.: Evaluation of college English classroom teaching quality dependent on triangular fuzzy number. Int. J. Elec. Eng. Educ. (2021). https://doi.org/10.1177/002072092110 02075
2. Huang, W.: Simulation of English teaching quality evaluation model based on gaussian process machine learning. J. Intell. Fuzzy Syst. **40**(2), 2373–2383 (2021)
3. Chen, Y.: College English teaching quality evaluation system based on information fusion and optimized rbf neural network decision algorithm. J. Sens. **2021**(5), 1–9 (2021)
4. Wang, Q.: Research on teaching quality evaluation of college english based on the CODAS method under interval-valued intuitionistic fuzzy information. J. Intell. Fuzzy Syst., 1–10 (2021)
5. Yildirim, K., Aslan, A.: Examination of the quality teaching in Turkish higher education based on the external evaluation reports from multiple perspectives. J. Qual. Res. Educ. **25**(1), 102–125 (2021)
6. Ge, D., Wang, X., Liu, J.: A teaching quality evaluation model for preschool teachers based on deep learning. Int. J. Emerg. Technol. Learn. (iJET) **16**(3), 127 (2021)
7. Li, Y., Zhou, L., Duan, Y., et al.: Establishment of evaluation index system of online classroom teaching quality for international students in universities and countermeasure research. In: 2021 International Conference on Diversified Education and Social Development (DESD 2021) (2021)
8. Yuan, K.Y., Wang, J.L., Jiang, J.W.: Construction and application of fuzzy evaluation index system for classroom teaching quality of applied undergraduate. DEStech Trans. Econ. Bus. Manage. 2021(eeim)
9. Qin, J., Zhou, S.: Constructing a scientific and multidimensional quality evaluation mechanism for ideological and political education in colleges and universities **5**(11), 5 (2021)
10. Koerniawaty, F.T., Nova, M.: Developing Industry 4.0-based English for hospitality business learning model. Premise J. English Educ. **10**(1), 1 (2021)
11. Padmini, K.B., Kumar, G.V., Babu, K.R.: Evaluation of quality assurance of activity against accreditation norms of the imaging services in a tertiary care teaching Hospital (2021)
12. Hong, D., Gao, Z., Luo, J., et al.: Emotion analysis of teaching evaluation system based on AI techno-logy towards Chinese texts. MATEC Web of Conferences 336 (2021). https://doi.org/10.1051/matecconf/202133605007

Application of Virtual Reality Technology in Environmental Art Design

Liao Wang[✉]

Wuchang University of Technology, Hubei 430223, China
Wliao@163.com

Abstract. The important application theory and algorithm of virtual reality technology in environmental art design simulation, and the new tools and methods of virtual reality development based on SGI graphics workstation. Firstly, in the aspect of acquisition and processing of environmental art design data, this paper discusses how to classify and process the existing data and establish the database needed for the virtual simulation of environmental art design. Virtual reality system is a high-tech system combining software, hardware and a variety of sensors, involving many basic and frontier disciplines. There are still a large number of unsolved problems and blind areas of theory and technology, which need to be further studied and solved. Based on this, this paper analyzes the characteristics of virtual reality technology and studies the application of virtual reality technology in environmental art design.

Keywords: Virtual technology · Environmental art · Application research

1 Introduction

Virtual reality technology is a new technology that uses computer to generate a realistic three-dimensional virtual environment and interacts with it through the use of sensing devices. It is completely different from the traditional simulation technology. It combines the simulation environment, visual system and simulation system, and connects the operator with the three-dimensional virtual environment generated by the computer by using sensor devices such as helmet mounted display, graphic glasses, data service, stereo headphones, data gloves and pedal. Through the interaction between the sensor device and the virtual environment, the operator can obtain a variety of senses such as vision, hearing and touch, and change the "unsatisfactory" virtual environment according to his own will. For example, the computer virtual environment is a building with various equipment and articles. The operator can walk in the house through various sensing devices to view, open and close the door and move articles; If you are not satisfied with the house design, you can change it at will. Obviously, it is much easier and cheaper to use this virtual reality technology to modify the design of buildings, machinery and weapons, and implement technical operation training and military exercises.

M. A. Jan and F. Khan (Eds.): BigIoT-EDU 2022, LNICST 466, pp. 591–601, 2023.
https://doi.org/10.1007/978-3-031-23947-2_62

The most important characteristics of virtual reality world are "realistic" and "interactive". Participants are in the virtual world. The environment and portraits are like in the real environment, in which various objects and phenomena are interacting. The objects and characteristics in the environment develop and change according to the laws of nature, in which people have the senses of vision, hearing, touch, motion, taste and smell. Virtual reality technology can create all kinds of mythical artificial reality environment. Its image is realistic and immersive, and can interact with the virtual environment to confuse the false with the real.

Virtual reality (VR) is a hot spot in the scientific and technological circles at home and abroad in recent years, and its development is also changing with each passing day. In the domestic scientific and technological circles, VR technology is being paid more and more attention. After more than 20 years of research and exploration, virtual reality technology went out of the laboratory and began to enter the practical stage in the late 1980s. At present, it has been applied in entertainment, medical treatment, engineering and architecture, education and training, military simulation, science and financial visualization, and achieved remarkable comprehensive benefits. In the 21st century, mankind will enter a new technological era of virtual reality. Figure 1 below shows the forecast of VR / AR expenditure scale in China from 2019 to 2024.

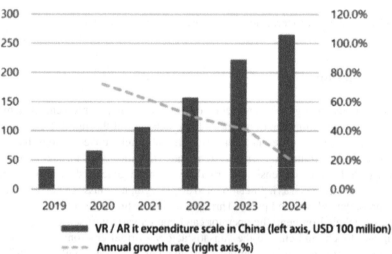

Fig. 1. Forecast of VR / AR expenditure scale in China from 2019 to 2024

Virtual reality technology takes the computer network system as the carrier, maps the real scenery in the network data model, and then presents it to people interactively with the virtual mapping carrier. In the virtual reality scene, people can change the parameter information to obtain a series of results consistent with their own design concept, and the isolation and interaction between the virtual environment and the real environment can more intuitively show the needs of designers [1]. Using virtual reality technology in environmental art design can map the environment to the data model, provide an implementation way for designers' sense of art and innovation, and then lay a foundation for the improvement of the quality of environmental art design.

2 Related Technologies

2.1 Characteristics of Virtual Reality System

Virtual reality system is to use all kinds of advanced hardware technology and software Tools to design reasonable hardware, software and interaction Means to enable participants to interactively observe and manipulate the virtual world generated by the system. Conceptually, any virtual reality system can use three "I" to describe its characteristics, namely "sinking", "interaction" and "imagination".

These three "I" reflect the key characteristics of virtual reality system, that is, the full interaction between the system and people. The design of virtual reality system shall meet the following self standards:

First, make participants have a "real" experience. This kind of experience is "immersion" or "input", that is, entering the whole body and mind, simply speaking, it is an illusion produced in the virtual world. Ideally, the virtual environment should make it difficult for users to distinguish between true and false, or even "true" than real. The significance of this immersion is to enable users to focus. In order to achieve this goal, we must provide the ability of multi perception. The ideal virtual reality system should provide all the perceptual abilities of human beings, including vision, hearing, touch, even taste and smell. As shown in Fig. 2 below, the principle of digital optical element of virtual reality technology is shown.

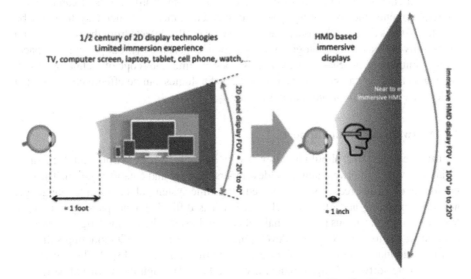

Fig. 2. Principle of digital optical element based on Virtual Reality Technology

Secondly, the system should provide convenient and rich human-computer interaction means mainly based on natural skills. These means enable participants to manipulate the virtual environment in real time, get feedback information from the virtual environment, and enable the system to understand the location, state, deformation and other data of key parts of participants that need to be known by the system. Real time is very important. If there is a large delay in interaction and is inconsistent with people's psychological experience, it is impossible to talk about the interaction of natural skills and it is difficult to obtain a sense of immersion. In order to achieve this goal, high-speed computing and processing are essential.

Finally, because virtual reality is not only a high-end interface of media or users, but also an application that aims at a specific field and solves some problems. In order to solve these problems, we need not only to understand the needs of the application and the ability of technology, but also to have rich imagination. As the creator of virtual world, imagination has become one of the most critical problems in the design of virtual reality system [2].

There are two forms of participants' activities or experiences in the virtual environment: one is subjective participation, the other is objective participation. In subjective participation, the participant is the center of the whole experience, and everything revolves around the participant; When participating objectively, participants can see their interaction with other objects in the virtual environment.

Interaction and immersion are two essential characteristics of any virtual reality system. Therefore, according to different applications of virtual reality, it can be divided into different categories. Early virtual reality may only have some characteristics of virtual reality, such as environment film, three-dimensional film and three-dimensional TV. Some applications do not require complete immersion and investment. In practical application, the emphasis and constraints of different virtual reality system design are different. For example, due to financial constraints, the most advanced hardware equipment cannot be equipped, or the performance of the hardware itself cannot meet the requirements, the computing speed and interaction means of such a system may be affected. At this time, we can only start to make up for the defects from the software, and many software-based technologies will be produced, such as virtual panoramic space, virtual simulation, etc. Since virtual reality does not limit the scope of technology used, as long as the goal can be achieved, various technologies can be effectively integrated to design a successful virtual reality system.

2.2 Software and Data Support

A virtual reality system should be supported by image software environment. Generally, it can be divided into two categories: developers Package and creation system. The programming of virtual reality software needs real-time system, object-oriented language, network, modeling and other knowledge, but it is difficult for people eager to apply VR technology in various professional fields to understand these knowledge. Therefore, the best way is to use VR system development Tools, including 3D modeling software, real-time simulation software and corresponding function library [3]. Authoring system is a complete software with graphical user interface. Through them, virtual world can be generated by simple programming. In the process of research, we adopt two software development methods. One is to use multigenii 3D modeling software package and Vega VR system development kit for faster development. The other is to develop the bottom layer of V fire R system with MultiGen II 3D modeling software package combined with performer and OpenGL. The following Fig. 3 shows the simulation in environmental art design.

Fig. 3. Simulation in environmental art design

At the same time, the support of geospatial database is particularly important in the development of virtual environment art design environment. Geospatial database, also known as map database, is one of the spatial information infrastructures in various countries. It is a national project with large investment and long-term establishment. It is an information resource. The map database is mainly spatial data, including 3D data of environmental art design, water system, residential area, traffic line and features, which is the basis for generating spatial positioning environmental art design images. Matched with it is the ground image database, which is digitized according to the located aerial photos and satellite photos. It is an important data source for 3D images of environmental art design. Environmental art is defined through the internal space and external space of the building, involving a variety of disciplines and a wide range, including all spatial elements inside and outside the building. The spatial combination design combining furnishings, furniture and indoor elements is the environmental art design inside the building, including landscape sketch, sculpture, water body, pavement The space combination design of greening, site, road and building refers to the design of the external environment of the building. Environmental art design is a systematic and complex project, which is very different from ordinary art design. It uses artistic and scientific methods to create and improve the environment on the basis of respecting realistic and environmental conditions, so that the building can finally meet people's needs for communication and activities such as leisure, work and life. People start cognitive activities from feeling. Through feeling, they can understand the attributes of different objective things, and then further understand psychological activities and consciousness, so as to meet people's needs for communication and life.

3 The Perfect Combination of Virtual Reality and Art Design

Virtual reality technology has the characteristics of conception, interactivity and multi perception. With the help of these characteristics of virtual reality technology, designers communicate and communicate with participants through demonstration in virtual environment. This virtual environment with three-dimensional sense of space can act on people's cognitive ability and perception ability, stimulate people to think deeply, and then make people feel immersive and realize the powerful advantages of virtual reality technology. The following Fig. 4 shows the virtual implementation system of pipeline engineering design.

Fig. 4. Virtual realization system of pipeline engineering design

Vr virtual reality technology is a kind of environment that can simulate three-dimensional and entity [4]. The application provided by VR fun network can perfectly support the current popular devices and VR game download content, and is committed to providing users with new VR resources. In the era of increasing popularity of VR, people in various industries are competing for a share in the virtual reality industry. Designers are also gradually participating in this feast. The combination of vr virtual reality and art design is perfect.

1. Graphic design
One of the biggest features of vr virtual reality is panoramic operation. Google recently developed a painting software called "tilt brush" [5]. The software requires designers to wear VR glasses, and then they can give full play to their imagination and create freely in the space. In the past, designers used to draw with pencils, erasers and triangular rulers at the edge of the table, which was not efficient. Later, I sat in the office, drawing with the software in the computer, facing the computer screen day and night. Then it is

possible to create in VR. At that time, designers can take VR equipment to model in the virtual reality world with VR version of PS, Al, sketch and other software, and send the design directly to the boss.

2. Interior design

Dirttenvironmental solutions, a company based in Calgary, Canada, has combined their interior design products with virtual reality technology. Barrie loberg, chief technology officer and co-founder of dirtt, developed the company's ice 3D design software, allowing users to interact through the use of the company's construction products. The application of virtual reality technology can perfectly represent the indoor environment and walk freely in the three-dimensional indoor space. At present, VR technology can be used for indoor 360 degree panoramic display, indoor roaming and pre decoration system in the industry. VR technology can also change the color of the wall in real time and dynamically according to the preferences of customers, and paste Wallpaper of different materials. The color and material of floor and ceramic tile can also be changed at will, which can move the placement of furniture and replace different decorations. All this will be perfectly represented under vr virtual reality technology.

3. Fashion design

In the United States, virtual reality technology has been integrated into fashion design. Consumers can bring a VR glasses at home and try clothes through online stores. Consumers can upload their body data to fashion designers. Designers can first select and set cloth parameters (gravity and wind force) in the virtual space to simulate and simulate human dynamic motion [6]. When people buy clothes, they can try on virtual clothes at home and then buy them, so that they will not be dissatisfied with the size or style of online shopping.

4 Practical Application

4.1 Intuitive Art Design

As an important symbol of urbanization, residential real estate projects indirectly drive the development of other industrial chains. Public environmental space is attached to real estate projects and has a certain value attribute. In the practical application of virtual reality technology, through the data model mapping of drawing files, the traditional paper design can be transferred to computer equipment. Through three-dimensional and four-dimensional display, the three-dimensional presentation of environmental art in the design process can be effectively guaranteed. Through the construction of hardware platform, the software system is accurately connected with the hardware system, and then supplemented with visual, auditory and other sensory effects, which can effectively combine reality and virtual. When viewing, users can browse the mapped image of the data model through interconnection settings, and all details can also be adjusted by scaling [7], To accurately present the information nodes. In this way, the content can be set and displayed to the greatest extent through virtual reality technology, so as to create an immersive feeling of being in the scene for users, so as to visually present the environmental structure.

In the understanding of art design, we should first clarify the fact that art design is not a traditional art category. Different from pure art, art design can not be imagined and expressed at will like painting. Art design needs the perfect combination of material function and spiritual function. The existence of art design must solve the problems existing in human life and meet the needs of human beings. Therefore, art design is more like a service, a "dance in shackles". Art design comes from the beautiful planning of human life, from various human needs, and is the crystallization of social development. Thus, we can find the civilization of human progress and the pace of scientific and Technological Development in art design. Art design comes from life, parallel to life, and guides and affects life.

Furthermore, when we explore art design, we can find that art design and the development of science and technology have always been inseparable. As mentioned earlier, the beginning of the first industrial revolution brought qualitative changes to art and design. Here we can find that the emergence of new production technology and the development of new science and technology play a great role in promoting art design. The invention of new technology naturally brings new products. With products and technology, artistic design is inevitable, which reflects the inevitability of artistic design. In 1955, Teague cooperated with Boeing to jointly complete the design of Boeing 707 jumbo jet, which not only made the Boeing aircraft have a very concise and modern appearance, but also created the classic interior design of modern airliner. Therefore, science and technology are like philosophical guidance to art design. Art design is the embodiment and application of science and technology, and the two complement each other.

Since the understanding of art and design is mentioned, it is necessary to affirm the relationship between commerce and art and design. Business is the largest demand and investment in art design, and art design in business is also the most abundant. In the era of commodity economy, in order to open the market and cater to consumers, we must study the market to produce products that meet the market demand. After a long period of capital accumulation, enterprises have entered a new stage - innovation stage. Innovation is not only the first productivity, but also the soul of enterprises. In the increasingly competitive market, in order to find a foothold, it is necessary to process and deal with art design.

4.2   Accurate Art Design

The application of virtual reality technology takes computer equipment as the carrier, through the accurate check of internal data information, and then through the established program for logical operation, it can effectively set the cost target and construction target of the whole spatial structure. Confirmation of operation and maintenance objectives. At the same time, the scope confirmation of data information makes the virtual reality technology have the art design of large environment space [8]. Through the simulation and amplification of virtual scene, the whole design process is no longer limited to the fixed space framework, and the statistics and confirmation of different time nodes can be realized, so as to make a macro layout of the overall environment and coordinate the distribution of work, The independent integration of various architectural details is realized to improve the accuracy of environmental design. As shown in Fig. 5 below, the independent integration of architectural details improves the accuracy of environmental design.

Fig. 5. Independent integration of architectural details based on Virtual Reality Technology

Fun, harmony and beauty in nature have always been pursued. Beauty has almost become one of the criteria for scientists to test themselves. Scientists think they are seeking beauty. They find that nature is designed according to beauty at the most basic level. Like artists, scientists use their keen intuition and wisdom to explore the beauty of nature and human life. Science and art are closely linked.

Modern science and technology has changed the way of production, human existence and aesthetic consciousness, and made people rediscover the beauty contained in technology. Technological beauty: between natural beauty and artistic beauty, it mainly refers to the beauty of mechanical industry technology, including the beauty of manual technology.

There is an internal connection and consistency between technological beauty and functional beauty. Functional beauty constitutes the characteristics of technological beauty and is also the core factor of the conscious structure of technological beauty. The content of products is the function and usefulness of things. The function must be expressed in the form of human perception through specific and distinctive images. The unity of function and form constitutes the unique content of industrial products, and the beauty of technology is the beauty of the unity of function and form. Technology is a process and means of creation, and its beauty can only be expressed in the object. In the process of processing and manufacturing, the utilization of materials is not only for the realization of practical value, but also shows the beauty of materials. The labor of technological processing is to awaken the natural beauty in the dormant state of the material itself and lead it from the potential form to the dominant form.

4.3 Interactive Art Design

Interactive art design is mainly reflected in providing a simulated communication platform for designers and users through the construction of virtualization platform, mapping all data information into images through data links, and users and designers can exist together in the platform. When viewing, if the user finds that the design of a certain place in the simulation environment fails to meet the expected requirements, the designer can mark the coordinates of this position in the virtual space, then integrate all problems, and then change the information parameters in the system platform. When the parameter information is modified, the virtual environment will be changed synchronously, which can facilitate the real-time communication between designers and users, and make the environmental art design show a higher quality sensory effect [9]. In addition, environmental art design through virtual reality technology can transform the traditional two-dimensional plane into three-dimensional and four-dimensional dynamic graphics, and enhance the readability of the whole effect. At the same time, the same proportion of exterior scaling can highlight the details of environmental design and improve the efficiency of environmental art design.

4.4 Design of Auxiliary Scenery

Virtual reality technology shows the value of the whole environmental art through the construction of virtual environmental scenes. The presentation of its dynamic characteristics provides a way for the integration of multi scene resources. For example, the unitary environmental design is difficult to show the value of ontology in the whole environment. Therefore, it is necessary to make the environmental space and the whole pattern present a state of natural interaction through the introduction of auxiliary resources [10]. Through the integration of virtual data such as natural landscape and traffic roads, diversified environmental elements can be injected into the whole layout to ensure that the virtual scene can be deeply integrated with the real scene, so as to improve richer visual resources for users. In addition, the character image and scene layout can be integrated into the spatial landscape, such as cultural elements and regional elements, so as to maximize the value of environmental art through exquisite image design. Figure 6 below shows the auxiliary landscape design.

Fig. 6. Auxiliary landscape design

5   Conclusion

This paper studies the application of virtual reality technology in environmental art design "VR", as a presentation method of digital media, is used more and more frequently in exhibitions. It has become possible to watch exhibitions at home, which not only makes art accessible, but also makes art more readable and observable in digital media, bringing different visual enjoyment to viewers. "VR" The integrated application of modern science and technology such as electronic information technology and many practical projects gives people a new experience, and the realistic virtual reality scene brings people more extreme multiple senses The practical application of virtual reality technology in the field of environmental art design makes up for the shortcomings of traditional environmental art design, effectively avoids potential problems in practical operation, and improves the economic benefits of entity project construction. Therefore, the application of this technology is worth popularizing in relevant industrial projects.

References

1. Yin, L.: The organic combination of calligraphy art and environmental design opens up a new path for the development of contemporary calligraphy. IOP Conf. Ser. Earth Environ. Sci. **632**, 052043 (2021)
2. Wang, W.: The application of soundscape in environmental art. In: The 6th International Conference on Arts, Design and Contemporary Education (ICADCE 2020) (2021)
3. Ylirisku, H.: Reorienting Environmental Art Education (2021)
4. Mitincu, C.G., Ioja, I.C., Hossu, C.A., et al.: Licensing sustainability related aspects in strategic environmental assessment.evidence from romania's urban areas. Land Use Policy **108**, 105572 (2021)
5. Alsaggar, M., Al-Atoum, M., منذر سامح العتوم.: The artistic social and environmental dimensions of 3D street pavement art (1)end (2021)
6. Jiang, H.: Application of virtual reality technology in chinese traditional decorative elements in interior design. J. Phys: Conf. Ser. **1744**(3), 032083 (2021)
7. Anthony, D., Louis, R.G., Shekhtman, Y., et al.: Patient-specific virtual reality technology for complex neurosurgical cases: illustrative cases (2021)
8. The combination of virtual reality technology and architectural design—taking the design of museum as an example. Creative Educ. Stud. **09**(3), 596–602 (2021)
9. Li, L.: Embedded Design of 3D image intelligent display system based on virtual reality technology. Wirel. Communi. Mobile Comput. (2021)
10. Chang, C., Wang, J., Duan, F., et al.: Research on skill training of relay protection device based on virtual reality technology. J. Phys: Conf. Ser. **2005**(1), 012044 (2021)

Exploration and Practice of Experimental Teaching Mode of Online and Offline Virtual Reality Combined with Hybrid Computer Network Course

Zhangsheng Zhong(✉)

Nanchang Institute of Technology, Jiangxi 330044, China
z13576003643@126.com

Abstract. Guided by highlighting practical ability and aiming at cultivating computer science and technology professionals, this paper makes some beneficial exploration on the experimental teaching mode of microcomputer system course, and puts forward reform measures in experimental content, experimental teaching method and experimental examination method, This paper expounds how to guide students to make full use of rich online teaching resources for independent learning and communication, realize the hybrid teaching mode of combining online and offline and complementing in class and after class, and the process of reform, exploration and practice. Practice has proved that the reform not only improves students' interest in this course, but also improves students' practical ability and the ability to comprehensively use their knowledge to solve practical problems.

Keywords: Computer network course · Online and offline · Combination of deficiency and reality · Reform in education

1 Introduction

With the rapid development of modern technology and network technology, network teaching based on computer technology, network platform, intelligent equipment and multimedia technology has been able to use the intelligent terminal to visit the Internet at home whenever and wherever possible, and study online on COVID-19.

Experimental teaching plays a very important role in the teaching of computer network courses. If the experimental teaching is carried out well, it can not only consolidate the teaching contents of relevant courses, but also cultivate students' professional skills, so that students can start immediately after taking part in work and learn something useful. The development of network experimental teaching needs a special network laboratory, and the most discussed network laboratory in higher vocational colleges is the lack of funds and experimental equipment. If experimental teaching is to achieve good results, the hardware conditions are only one aspect, and the establishment of experiments, experimental process, comprehensive experiments and evaluation system are also indispensable [1].

© ICST Institute for Computer Sciences, Social Informatics and Telecommunications Engineering 2023
Published by Springer Nature Switzerland AG 2023. All Rights Reserved
M. A. Jan and F. Khan (Eds.): BigIoT-EDU 2022, LNICST 466, pp. 602–611, 2023.
https://doi.org/10.1007/978-3-031-23947-2_63

At the same time, more and more people realize the importance of online network teaching mode, and apply this new teaching mode to traditional teaching. Online network teaching has a great impact on the traditional teaching mode, which not only changes the way students obtain knowledge and information, but also changes their learning ideas and learning methods. It promotes the reform and innovation of teaching, makes teaching no longer limited by space and time, improves the effectiveness of teaching, promotes the improvement of students' autonomous learning ability and in-depth learning ability, and helps students obtain more high-quality teaching resources.

The integration of information and intelligence into education is the trend of education development in the future. How to give play to the respective advantages of traditional offline teaching and online teaching? It is not simple accumulation and mixing, but organic integration. Giving play to the effect of $1 + 1 > 2$ is the core pursuit of online and offline integrated teaching in the future. So, what are the main differences between online teaching and offline teaching? What are the basic models of online and offline integrated teaching?

Professor hekekang of Beijing Normal University was the first to formally advocate the mixed teaching model in China. He believes that the hybrid teaching mode combines the advantages of traditional teaching methods with the advantages of network teaching, which not only gives play to the leading role of teachers in guiding, enlightening and monitoring the teaching process, but also fully reflects the initiative, enthusiasm and creativity of students as the main body of the learning process. The blended teaching here is called blended learning.

In recent years, with the rise of MOOC, the mixed teaching model has a new connotation. Flipped classroom is regarded as a powerful means to enhance the learning effect of MOOC. It combines online learning with offline discussion, that is, students first learn the video materials pre recorded or designated by the teacher on the Internet to obtain preliminary knowledge, and then discuss and study with the teacher on the problems they do not understand or have doubts in the classroom, in order to maximize the learning effect of students. The basic idea is to turn over the traditional learning process, let learners complete independent learning of knowledge points and concepts in extracurricular time, and turn the classroom into a place for interaction between teachers and students, mainly used to answer doubts, report and discuss, so as to achieve better teaching results.

In short, blended teaching is the combination and supplement of online learning and traditional classroom teaching. It can not only play the leading role of teachers, but also reflect the subjectivity of students, so as to achieve better teaching results.

2 Overview of Relevant Technologies

2.1 Current Situation of Computer Network Teaching

Computer network is an organism that runs on various hardware and software with independent functions and communicates efficiently and reliably through mature protocol rules. From the aspects of hardware, software and communication, it is a complex system. It needs experimental operation to increase perceptual knowledge, stimulate students' learning initiative, and cultivate students' analysis of the network The improvement of design and application skills can further deepen the cognition of network theoretical knowledge.

The experiment of computer network course is not only the deepening and supplement of theoretical teaching, but also the cultivation of students' ability to comprehensively use knowledge and solve problems. Our university is an ethnic college. In the past few years, the computer specialty was relatively weak, the corresponding investment in the computer network laboratory was less, and the work of the laboratory was relatively weak. Due to the lack of experimental environment, the teaching of computer network courses in recent years was more theory than practice. Due to the lack of support of experimental teaching, students can not deeply understand the network equipment and the overall composition of the network, let alone combine with practice. The understanding of network still stays at the level of abstraction and emptiness. Moreover, the computer network experiment is different from the experiments of other computer courses. It can be operated only by installing the corresponding software on the PC. The computer network experiment needs more experimental equipment and higher technical support, as well as the mutual coordination in the experimental process, organization and management, and the operability and feasibility of the experimental project, Therefore, the experiment is more difficult.

To study online and offline integrated teaching, we must first analyze the essential differences between offline teaching and online teaching. In fact, the offline teaching and online teaching scenarios that emerge in everyone's mind may not be exactly the same, because each type has various implementation forms. For example, offline teaching has the form of teachers teaching students to listen, teachers and students talking together, doing experiments, completing project tasks, full of challenges and innovations, and teachers working with students for sports; Online teaching has an independent learning mode of answering questions, statistics and feedback online, an adaptive learning mode of diagnosing and pushing personalized learning resources based on students' various learning data, a form of unified video recording and broadcasting for students, a form of synchronous live teaching for teachers and students, and a form of watching video recording and broadcasting combined with offline interaction.

What are the unique advantages of online teaching? Just take the online video class without students' participation as an example. Even such a simple and preliminary online teaching method has some unique advantages that offline teaching is difficult to have.

Accuracy. Each link, expression, speaking speed, question, exercise and activity are carefully designed and polished. The video is short and concise to ensure scientific and logical.

Controllability. Through photographing technology and cutting processing technology, it can be corrected repeatedly; There is no need for teachers' on-the-spot response to on-the-spot teaching; Ensure the integrity and appropriateness of the language, words, pictures and requirements of each class.

Hierarchy. Through overall design and repeated modification, ensure the vertical connection of different class hours.

All media learning. It integrates explanation, music, animation, video, character simulation and other forms to meet students' various cognitive styles.

Not of imposing stature but strong and capable. A micro video can be linked by a "problem chain", and each problem lasts for 3–10 min; A recording and broadcasting class shall be controlled for about 20 min. It can be learned and used repeatedly. It can be copied and spread; Students can play many times and learn repeatedly by means of on-demand and review; Teachers can use it as a whole or choose to cut part of the content for repeated use.

2.2 Advantages of Online and Offline Hybrid Teaching

Online and offline hybrid teaching is a teaching mode that organically combines online network teaching with offline classroom teaching based on computer, network technology and intelligent terminal equipment. Online teaching mainly refers to the teaching activities implemented by teachers and students through the online network platform, and offline teaching mainly refers to the traditional classroom teaching activities carried out face-to-face by teachers and students. The advantages of online and offline hybrid teaching are shown in Fig. 1 below.

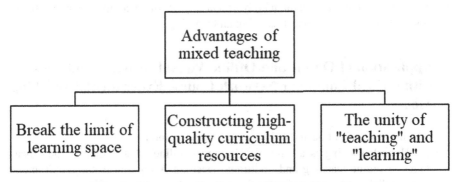

Fig. 1. Advantages of online and offline hybrid teaching

(1) Break the limit of learning space
  Hybrid teaching combines the advantages of offline traditional classroom teaching with the advantages of online Internet learning, and effectively integrates classroom teaching with information technology. The biggest advantage of hybrid teaching is that it realizes the unlimited extension of teaching through the online network platform, solves the time and space constraints of traditional offline teaching in the past, and students can learn and practice through a large number of fragmented time 4P learning resources. For difficult and important problems, they can watch teaching videos repeatedly, which fully mobilize the loose initiative of learning prince, It ensures the effectiveness of students' learning and improves the teaching quality of the course.
(2) Constructing high-quality curriculum resources
  Online and offline hybrid teaching optimizes the school's curriculum teaching resources. Some online curriculum teaching platforms have teaching resources

to watch Lei Qiu's classic. Teachers in higher vocational colleges can introduce teaching resources into the classroom according to the curriculum, and quickly build projects [2]. You f are now a famous online teacher to participate in the whole teaching process. This has built an online and external process, broken the barriers, and can share the second-class high-quality curriculum resources in the sports show and education circles of other schools. At the same time, hand Lei JH's taste has entered the teaching resources, saved the cost of school curriculum resource construction, and promoted the change and improvement of offline teaching mode.

(3) Realize the unity of "teaching" and "learning"

In online and offline hybrid teaching, teachers upload the teaching content of this class to the online teaching platform before class, so that students can clarify the learning objectives, learning tasks and learning requirements of each class. During the course, i.e. the offline teaching stage, teachers will explain selectively and emphatically according to the students' learning situation on the network teaching platform. After class is the online consolidation stage. After the course, teachers release homework on the online teaching platform for students to consolidate knowledge and deepen their understanding and application of knowledge. In mixed teaching, students are the main body of learning, learning completely and actively, and truly realize the unity of teaching and learning.

3 Application of Online and Offline Virtual Reality Combined with Hybrid Computer Network Course Experimental Teaching Mode

(1) The meaning of online and offline mixed teaching mode

Hybrid teaching is a kind of "Online + offline" that combines the advantages of online teaching and traditional teaching According to the requirements of the syllabus of computer network course, the basic process of implementing the hybrid teaching mode scheme is to use modern information-based digital teaching resources and rely on various network learning platforms to change the traditional indoctrination teaching mode and build an online and offline hybrid teaching mode, which fully reflects "teachers as the leading and students as the main body" in teaching Through the organic combination of the two teaching organization forms, the learners are guided from shallow people to deep learning. The ultimate purpose of this hybrid teaching is not to use the online platform, build digital teaching resources, or carry out fancy teaching activities, but to make effective use of online resources, offline activities and corresponding process evaluation Improve the learning depth of most students.

(2) Teaching resources and platforms

Unlike traditional teaching, online and offline hybrid teaching uses relatively single teaching resources, but uses a variety of teaching resources and platforms, such as MOOC resources, computer network experiment assisted teaching platform PTA, blog Park, mobile intelligent teaching tool classroom, etc. as shown in Fig. 2 below.

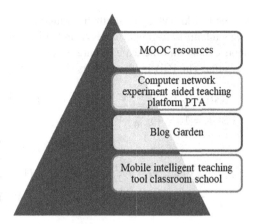

Fig. 2. Teaching resources and platforms

Using the abundant MOOC resources on the Internet can save teachers' classroom teaching time and carry out more valuable classroom discussion. Because it can be played repeatedly, it can meet the personalized learning needs of students; By using the online auxiliary experimental teaching platform PTA, the running results of students' submitted programs can be evaluated automatically, which greatly saves teachers' inspection time of students' programs, and the learning problem of basic grammar of computer network can be solved through the platform; During the teaching process, the blog Garden can be used to show the sorted homework instructions suitable for in-depth learning to the students through the blog. In addition to homework exercises, students can also exchange, share and ask questions [3]. For each question raised by students, the students can express their views, and the teachers can answer them in time. All views are displayed on it, At a glance, this can not only provide spare students with more in-depth knowledge learning, but also provide important references for teachers; The use of mobile intelligent teaching tools in the classroom enables teachers to release interactive test questions at any time for students to discuss, and seamlessly integrate students' listening and interaction. In addition, teachers can quickly release homework, correct homework and check the repetition rate of homework on the platform. At the same time, mobile intelligent teaching tools also provide bullet screen, rush answer, roll call, statistical results and analysis, courseware sharing Online discussion and other services can save more than 40% of teaching time.

(3) Organization form of online and offline hybrid teaching mode of computer network course

The course teaching adopts the online and offline mixed teaching mode, which is mainly divided into three parts: before class, during class and after class. Before class, the teacher assigns pre class tasks in advance through class assignment according to the content of the course syllabus, and issues preview courseware. The students independently learn the corresponding teaching videos on the MOOC network of China University with questions according to the requirements. During the class, the teacher according to the students' learning situation Discuss and communicate, further internalize the key knowledge, and then arrange the corresponding experimental contents for students to complete, analyze and guide the experiment in class. After class, students can submit the experimental works to PTA for operation and get the feedback results. The PTA math model is shown in formulas (1) and (2).

$$\begin{aligned} \text{MSE} &= \frac{1}{H*W} \sum_{i=1}^{H} \sum_{i=1}^{W} \left(X[i,j] - Y[i,j] \right)^2 \\ \text{PSNR} &= 10 * \log_{10}^{(2^n-1)^2/\text{MSE}} \end{aligned} \tag{1}$$

$$\begin{aligned} (2)_3^{(2)} &= f\left(w_{31}^{(1)} x_1 + w_{32}^{(1)} x_2 + w_{33}^{(1)} x_3 + (1)_3^{(1)} \right) \\ (2)_2^{(2)} &= f\left(w_{21}^{(1)} x_1 + w_{22}^{(1)} x_2 + w_{23}^{(1)} x_3 + (1)_2^{(1)} \right), \\ (2)_1^{(2)} &= f\left(w_{11}^{(1)} x_1 + w_{12}^{(1)} x_2 + w_{13}^{(1)} x_3 + (1)_1^{(1)} \right). \end{aligned} \tag{2}$$

4 Evaluation of Students' Experimental Teaching Effect

Online and offline hybrid teaching should be implemented in different levels according to different disciplines and specialties. For courses with strong practicality and operability, online simulation training software operation mode should be adopted to strengthen students' practical operation skill training and help students master practical skills; for courses with weak practical operability, online teaching resources, such as case analysis, micro courses and animation, should be used to strengthen The vivid perception and three-dimensional nature of knowledge itself can guide students' understanding of knowledge and promote the completion of predetermined teaching objectives before class [4].

In the network experiment, the evaluation of experimental teaching effect is an indispensable part of the whole experimental teaching design and an important means to test whether the teaching objectives are achieved. The evaluation of network experiment effect is mainly the evaluation of single experiment and comprehensive experiment. As mentioned above, the individual experiment carried out by students is evaluated according to the degree of completion and failure of single experiment Evaluate whether the problem has been solved. The assessment results of this part account for 35% of the overall results. The main reason is that the comprehensive experiment accounts for the majority of the overall results. Through the implementation of the comprehensive test, in addition to the routine configuration for students, a certain number of different forms of faults should also be set in the comprehensive experiment. Let students master relevant experimental knowledge and skills and test through the analysis of fault phenomena Try again and finally eliminate the fault (Fig. 3).

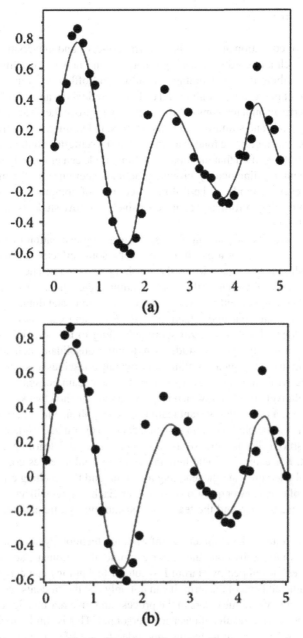

Fig. 3. Teaching effect comparison

5 Conclusion

In the upsurge of education and teaching reform, colleges and universities should make full use of the rich and colorful teaching resources and network teaching platform on the network, combine the shortcomings of online and offline teaching, integrate their advantages, adopt the reform of online and offline mixed mode, and integrate classroom, network and experimental teaching. This can greatly improve the disadvantages of traditional teaching mode and stimulate students' interest in learning, cultivating their ability of autonomous learning. In the final examination of the semester, students achieved good results, which fully verified that the mixed teaching mode can effectively improve teaching efficiency and teaching quality, provide practical experience for the implementation of the mixed teaching mode in the follow-up courses of computer majors, effectively promote the curriculum reform and comprehensively improve students' learning interest and learning effect.

Due to the diversity of teaching forms, the teaching evaluation of mixed teaching mode has always been a hot topic. In recent years, some effective evaluation methods have been explored. For example, in the teaching of some science and engineering courses, at the end of the course, the teacher requires the students to prepare the logic diagram of the course content according to their own understanding. The students can give full play to their own understanding and views, and can discuss and complete it with the students. The teacher will score according to the situation. In the process of sorting out knowledge points, students not only consolidate their knowledge, but also cultivate their own logical thinking and overall consciousness. In the process of communicating with students, they also cultivate their team consciousness. Teachers' evaluation is relatively more fair, which is an evaluation method that kills more with one stone. In addition, a teaching assistant team can be established to supervise and answer questions on the online platform, and assist teachers to encourage students to participate in offline classroom discussions, so as to enhance learners' learning experience and learning effect. For example, some humanities and social sciences courses are jointly completed by the lecturer and the teaching assistant, and the teaching content is carried out in the form of interview or question and answer. Each chapter will have corresponding exercises and discussions, and the teaching assistant will participate in the discussion and answer.

With the continuous development of information technology, there are some evaluation systems supported by computers. For example, the automatic scoring system for programming test developed by Harbin Institute of technology can carry out on-board tests at the middle and end of the term. It can not only test the students' program running results, but also analyze some errors in the process and give reasonable scores, which is very close to the scoring results of teachers' personnel. This is similar to the way coursera and others use simple online testing, and udacity and EDX use the combination of online testing and training and examination center. Through the collection and analysis of students' learning process data, they can timely feed back evaluation opinions on students' learning situation, so as to truly test students' learning effect.

References

1. Wang, S.: Current Situation of College Teachers' Educational Technology Ability Under the Background of Jmdoc. Problems and countermeasures, Inner Mongolia Normal University, Hohhot (2016)
2. Qiu, W., Zhao, G., Lei, W., et al.: Empirical study on college students' cognition and satisfaction with Mu class. China Univ. Teach. **2017**(8), 87–91 (2017)
3. Wang, S., Gao, T., Huang, Z.: Reform and practice of mixed teaching mode of programming course. Univ. Educ. **5**(5), 29–30 (2017)
4. Liu, X., Xiao, J.: Research on the construction of hybrid teaching mode of distribution channel management course under the "Internet+" Qingjing. Shandong Text. Econ. **2018**(12), 57–58 (2018)

Application of Web Data Mining Algorithms in Information Management Education

Li Liu$^{(\boxtimes)}$

Gansu Finance and Trade Vocational College, Lanzhou 730207, Gansu, China
469086945@qq.com

Abstract. How to quickly retrieve the required information from the vast data information needs web data mining technology. Its algorithm and its application in information management are worthy of research. Nowadays, web data mining plays a very important role in the field of information management such as scientific and technological literature retrieval. Based on the concept and characteristics of data mining technology, this paper briefly describes the various application fields and important significance of data mining technology in information management, and focuses on the innovative multi field applications of Web Data Mining in optimizing data resources and providing customers with personalized intelligent automation services.

Keywords: Web data mining · Information management · Application

1 Introduction

In the information age, data has become a valuable resource. In the face of explosive information growth, scientific research and innovation, university libraries, enterprise management, e-commerce and other fields are inseparable from information management. How to find valuable data from the huge data flow has become a problem that must be considered in information management. Web data mining technology can quickly and accurately collect target data and provide technical support for data selection, analysis and utilization. In order to provide personalized needs of teaching, scientific research and enterprises with high efficiency and high precision, and quickly retrieve massive information, its algorithm and its application in information management is a subject worthy of research. In recent years, information technology has penetrated into various industries, and web data mining technology has also been widely used in different fields. Mastering the operation methods and application skills of this technology is of positive help to improve the level of information management and tap the potential value of data [1].

Information management is not only the carrier management of information, but also an important part of information management. It is the requirement of information management to deeply analyze the original information content, provide the internal relations and rules of massive data as a whole, digest and identify messages, ensure

M. A. Jan and F. Khan (Eds.): BigIoT-EDU 2022, LNICST 466, pp. 612–617, 2023.
https://doi.org/10.1007/978-3-031-23947-2_64

message security, effectively use cutting-edge computer technologies such as data mining technology, and improve the overall information management level.

2   Web Data Mining Algorithm

2.1   Basic Concepts and Characteristics of Data Mining Technology

Data mining technology is a subject that integrates the research contents of statistics, computer technology database, absorbs the professional knowledge of artificial knowledge and machine learning, and carries out knowledge acquisition and data mining. It can quickly, accurately, conveniently and quickly obtain valuable information. At present, data mining technology is still the focus of information management research. Representative data mining systems include enterprise miner, intelligent miner and so on. Data mining is carried out through modeling, induction, clustering, deviation and other technologies. The technical difficulty is to carry out intelligent data mining with real-time comprehensive database. In recent years, with the development of database technology and the continuous development of various technologies based on heterogeneous data sources, the research of data mining technology of mobile computing is becoming more and more in-depth. It is worth mentioning that the representative algorithm of association rules is apriori, which finds the association relationship of items in the database by identifying frequent item sets, that is, rules with strong reliability. On the basis of this algorithm, in order to continuously improve the technical efficiency, incremental update technology is used to mine data in parallel [2]. On the basis of the above algorithms, emphasizing image rules, that is, external information such as customer interest, quickly learning similar behavior pattern index technology, and emphasizing structured and directed construction through online multi-dimensional index are the research hotspots of data mining technology. With the continuous mass of complex data, the research combines the optimized intelligent algorithm with the current data mining technology, so as to greatly improve the efficiency and quality of data processing.

Information management data is complex and massive, has a variety of information types, users have high freedom of retrieval, and users have diverse personalized needs. Web data mining technology came into being. The specific technologies include file content description, artificial link structure and access pattern usage mining. Web data mining technology uses evolutionary algorithm, rough set and other information processing methods, uses retrieval tools to retrieve and form information text sets, selects appropriate typical features, analyzes, prunes and summarizes heterogeneous information, and simplifies subsets. The approximation ability of the retrieval function reflects the retrieval quality of the technology. Content based text mining methods, such as webwatcher, musag, Letizia, etc. Form customer image information and interest model through keyword positioning, or expand keywords with near meaning dictionary, or based on browsing behavior without keywords, provide evaluation and links to customers and obtain similar information, update search methods, and feed back customer applications. At present, the application effect of the technology is good, and realizing more flexible and accurate information management is the direction of the technology.

2.2 Web Database Technology

Web database not only provides basic data storage and classification functions, but also supports interactive information query. From the perspective of data users, the use of Web database can more accurately obtain the desired data information and further tap the value of data utilization. From the perspective of composition structure, web database can be divided into four modules: server supporting data storage, middleware supporting data call, web server supporting instruction editing and issuing, and browser for data display. When using web database technology, the user opens the browser and edits instructions (such as searching keywords) on the man-machine operation interface. The system performs rapid matching from the database and displays all the matching data in turn according to the correlation.

3 Data Mining Method Based on Web Database

With the maturity of Web data mining technology and its practical application in all walks of life, it has formed a relatively perfect technical system, including neural network method, decision tree method, genetic algorithm, rough set method, association rule method and so on. The following are several main data mining methods.

3.1 Rough Set Method

In Web data mining, if the accuracy of retrieval results is not strict, and you want to complete the retrieval task and obtain the target data in the shortest possible time, you can use rough set method. In addition to data mining, it also has important application value in analyzing data correlation. Web data mining technology based on rough set has the advantages of simple algorithm and high retrieval efficiency. It usually does not need to establish a special retrieval model, which simplifies the operation process and reduces the technical difficulty. However, there are also obvious defects. For example, the mined data may have obvious discreteness. In the later stage of data analysis, it needs to be processed first to ensure data continuity, so as to reflect the value of data utilization [3].

3.2 Fuzzy Set Method

Fuzzy set algorithm is a method of fuzzy identification, judgment and decision-making of practical problems by using fuzzy set theory. Some data systems are relatively complex and fuzzy. Many fuzzy set theories have a fuzzy attribute, which may lead to result errors. Therefore, in the practice of data mining technology, uncertainty transformation should be carried out on the basis of fuzzy theory and probability statistics. The advantage of Web Data Mining Application Based on fuzzy set is that it can flexibly adjust the fuzziness according to user needs and data characteristics, obtain the desired data, and enhance the availability of the data itself. The algorithm also has defects, such as the need to provide more parameters, the need to establish a specific mathematical model, the difficulty of coding and so on.

3.3   Neural Network Method

In data mining and utilization, the available value of a single data is not high, which requires the use of data mining technology to collect the data, classify and aggregate the specific data according to the actual needs, find the correlation between the data horizontally or vertically on the basis of resource integration, and mine the potential value of the data. The application advantage of Web Data Mining Based on neural network algorithm is that it has nonlinear learning ability. With the help of nonlinear prediction model, it can identify and screen the data more intelligently to ensure the accuracy of the obtained data. It has strong anti-interference ability and plays a certain role in preventing the loss of truth of data information.

4   Specific Application of Data Mining in Information Management

Taking data mining in science and technology information platform as an example. Data can be divided into structured data, semi-structured data and unstructured data. Today is unstructured The increasing demand for personalized, random and massive data retrieval promotes the research and development of scientific and technological information retrieval platform and corresponding software. This topic is a hot topic at present. The mode reform of shared information acquisition and retrieval management of Web data mining technology emphasizes the intellectualization of science and technology information platform system, enhances user management through the addition of analysis functions, provides personalized solutions, uses data to store customer preferences, analyzes customer database, studies the field of knowledge mining, and provides multi-objective information management: improving system performance, design Understand user needs, etc. [4]. The main development trend is to analyze the retrieval volume, frequency, times, spatial-temporal distribution and path pattern discovery algorithm through statistical methods, and further build the scientific and technological literature information platform with the support of mobile communication.

The specific platform is shown in Fig. 1. On the one hand, the client integrates the contact between users, user history and analysis of user graphics, which is handed over to the data center for processing.

On the other hand, each sub node feeds back information under the command of the master node. The specific process includes: data mining, task structured analysis, mining algorithm, intelligent model, scheduling computing resources, binding mining tasks, and finally visually displaying the data mining results. Analyzing the web page content, structure and user information, and finally providing efficient information management services, is an effective supplement to the existing data processing technology. As shown in Fig. 2. In the field of science and technology information management, broadening the application of Web data mining technology, such as web data mining technology and university library integration, can optimize the resource construction. With limited funds, we can give full play to the carrier advantages and expand document storage. On the one hand, we can optimize the electronic information retrieval storage, on the other hand, we can also improve the application efficiency of university library. Make statistics on literature citation rate, browsing rate, download rate, etc., analyze the characteristics of literature itself, such as time and space distribution, citation and download curve,

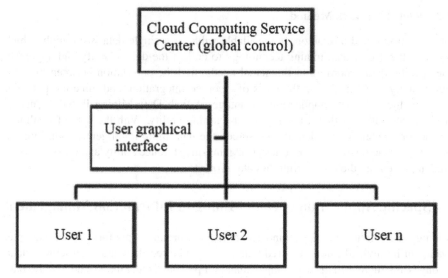

Fig. 1. Scientific and technological literature information platform

correlation proportion between documents, users' borrowing preferences, and finally optimize the layout of information management.

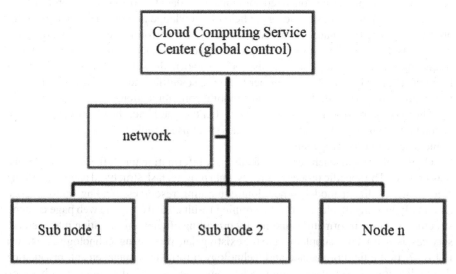

Fig. 2. Internal structure of web page

Collect and sort out user interest patterns. Use appropriate mining algorithm to check and fill gaps, adjust direction and optimize resource allocation. It can also judge the utilization rate of scientific and technological information resources, and expand intelligent information services based on people-oriented needs. Collect users' reading and browsing sets, mine association rules for the sets, match browsing patterns, form similar user groups, and pre connect those whose access frequency is higher than the threshold to improve speed and efficiency. Using web data mining technology, analyze user access data and predict the transmission user interface.

5 Conclusion

On the basis of statistics, it integrates artificial intelligence, machine learning and visualization In many fields such as parallel computing, integrate a variety of technologies to improve the efficiency and quality of data mining, deeply study the application of Web Data Mining in information management, such as the combination with library, and finally apply it to practice to produce innovative products. It provides an overall view for many fields such as scientific and technological literature management. On the basis of traditional query reports and the east wind of data warehouse technology, data mining technology is imperative. Data mining is to extract data, then analyze data, transform model data, and finally extract the key data to assist decision-making. Not only get the traditional event results, but also mine the essence of the event and the relationship between information, and finally support the decision-making behavior through confidence prediction and evaluation. Web data mining algorithm and application research foundation. Web data mining specifically studies the content structure of web pages, studies the internal relationship between users and page interaction based on user information, analyzes web data in many fields including user interface and commerce, applies the above mining technology to optimize customer retrieval experience, improve information platform design, and improve information management services in many fields such as e-commerce, It embodies the advantages of data mining technology. In the field of information management, integrating intelligence and data mining technology, analyzing user characteristics and literature knowledge is an important part of knowledge information management, which shows strong vitality.

References

1. Wu, L.: Effective integration of network information security and web data mining technology Cyberspace. Security 7(06), 62–64 (2016)
2. Li, J.: Analysis of web data mining. Fujian Comput. (11), 72–73 (2011)
3. Zhang, Q.: Application of web data mining technology to capture personalized service of network archives information resources. Arch. Constr. (07), 1s–17 (2008)
4. Li, P.: Research on the integration of network security and web data mining technology. Inf. Secur. Technol. (08), 63–65 (2016)

Application Progress of Particle Swarm Optimization in Modern Literature

Dong Zhang[1]([⊠]) and Beibei Li[2]

[1] Wuhan University, Wuhan 430072, Hubei, China
372508199@qq.com
[2] Wuhan Technical College of Communications, Wuhan 430065, Hubei, China

Abstract. Optimization problem has always been one of the important problems in modern literature, and particle swarm optimization algorithm, as a new intelligent algorithm, has good optimization ability. This paper introduces the process and steps of particle swarm optimization algorithm, as well as various improved particle swarm optimization algorithms, and analyzes the application status of particle swarm optimization algorithm in modern literature, such as the optimal allocation of literary resources. The results show that the application of particle swarm optimization algorithm in modern literature is limited; The existing application research pays attention to the maximization of economic benefits and ignores the social and ecological benefits; The research shows the phenomenon of fragmentation and does not form a complete discipline theory system; The improved particle swarm optimization algorithm has better optimization ability. It is pointed out that the combination of particle swarm optimization algorithm and other optimization algorithms and technologies will open up a new direction and road for the development of the algorithm in modern literature and obtain better optimization results for the solution of scientific problems in modern literature.

Keywords: Particle swarm optimization · Contemporary literature

1 Introduction

In recent years, there have been many research achievements in the field of the relationship between the occurrence of modern literature and media, such as Lei Qili's printing modernity and the occurrence of modern Chinese literature, Luan Meijian's pre industrial civilization and Chinese literature, and Jiang Xiaoli's modern Chinese mass media and modern Chinese literature. However, these works basically discuss the development of journals, Only a few directly take the publishing house as the starting point and the publishing technology, printing and distribution as the perspective to cut into the research on the transformation of modern literature, such as Pan Jianguo's papers "Shanghai Publishing House in the late Qing Dynasty and novels in the late Qing Dynasty", "lead stone printing and the modern communication of popular novels in the Ming and Qing Dynasties - Shanghai (1874–1911) as the investigation center", which has important academic

M. A. Jan and F. Khan (Eds.): BigIoT-EDU 2022, LNICST 466, pp. 618–628, 2023.
https://doi.org/10.1007/978-3-031-23947-2_65

value. At present, the research is basically centered on publishing institutions, while there is less comprehensive research on the relationship between publishing and modern literature, and this research spans the two disciplines of publishing and literature. The research on this has strong theoretical significance and great research space for grasping the modern transformation of Chinese literature [1].

This is a fundamental problem, which is related to the foundation of the existence of the whole modern literature. Literary works have different values for different objects. For example, Lu Xun's mother doesn't like Lu Xun's novels. She is keen on Zhang Henshui's popular novels. For citizen readers, Lu Xun's novels have no attractive value; However, in the history of literature, Lu Xun's novels are indeed a thick ink and heavy color that can not be ignored, and even have a far-reaching impact. They are internalized into modern Chinese literature. Talking about Xu Zhimo and Lao She to Shaanxi farmers is better than talking about Zhao Shuli; Similarly, people who have never been to Gaomi, Shandong and heard of Qin opera can hardly l resonate with some descriptions in Mo Yan's and Jia Pingwa's works.

Nowadays, the proportion of pure literature and modern literary works in people's life is decreasing, and the value and necessity of modern literary works are also challenged. Should modern literary works be popular or elite and stick to their positions? This is a topic that has been discussed and controversial in the literary circle. We often say that "art comes from life and is higher than life". Modern literary works must come from life and form on the basis of reality, but literature is not a plane mirror, but a convex lens or concave lens, or even a magnifying glass. Its material comes from life, combines the creator's experience, emotion and thinking, and finally forms an organic work. Once it is formed and published, it can trigger the thinking and emotional experience of different readers and explain different meanings.

Therefore, I think the most important value of modern literary works is to present the tools of thinking, including the thinking of writers and readers, and even the thinking records of a generation of people in an era. It makes us not float on the surface like foam or duckweed, but submerge to the bottom of life to think and explore and make survival a weighed and meaningful thing.

The so-called modern literature is actually to study the literary development process under the conditions of historical changes in Chinese society. Modern literature has widely accepted the influence of foreign literature and combined with the process of modern Chinese historical development. It describes modern ideas in a modern language. Its description methods, themes, description means and structure are new creations, It has the characteristics of modernization. Especially in the network era, especially in the new media era, the emergence of particle swarm optimization algorithm has not only added a strong stroke to the development and history of modern literature, but also become a real literature with modern significance. Therefore, particle swarm optimization algorithm actually plays an important role in modern literature.

2 Related Work

2.1 Particle Swarm Optimization

Particle swarm optimization (PSO) was proposed by Dr. Eberhart and Dr. Kennedy in 1995. It originates from the research on the predation behavior of birds. The basic core of particle swarm optimization algorithm is to use the information sharing of individuals in the group, so that the movement of the whole group produces an evolution process from disorder to order in the problem-solving space, so as to obtain the optimal solution of the problem.

Of course, this is a more formal statement. For us digital analog Xiaobai, we certainly hope to have a more intuitive and visual explanation.

We might as well assume that we are a bird in a flock of birds. Now we have to follow the leader to look for food in the forest. Each of us knows our distance from the food, but we don't know where the food is.

Therefore, we fly aimlessly in the forest. Every once in a while, everyone will share their distance from food in the wechat group. Then bird a found that the distance between himself and the food was 5 km, while bird Z in the group was the closest to the food, only 50 m away. Bird a made a quick decision and said in the group, "I'm going there to have a look!" Then, bird B and bird C fly in the direction of bird Z and look for food around bird Z [2].

In this way, everyone was flying in their own direction, but now they have to move closer to the position of bird Z, so we need to modify their flight speed and direction. However, when all the birds were ready to adjust their flight path, bird h suddenly thought: Although bird Z is only 50 m away from the food, he once passed point P, which is only 40 m away from the food, so he didn't know whether he should fly to point P or bird Z. Bird h sent his entanglement to the wechat group, and then everyone unanimously decided to balance the two and add the vectors of the two positions, so we discussed the speed update formula:

$$x_k(t) \in R^n, y_k(t) \in R^r, u_k(t) \in R^m \tag{1}$$

First, we need to determine which forest the birds are looking for food, that is, the feasible region we call in the optimization problem. Here, we take the feasible region as:

$$t \in [0, T] \tag{2}$$

Because the birds are randomly distributed in the forest during the foraging process, we randomly scatter 50 particles into the feasible region at the initial time, and then calculate the objective function value. All particles move towards the point with the smallest objective function value. We can simply draw a basic flow of the algorithm, as shown in Fig. 1 below.

Firstly, particle swarm optimization algorithm initializes particle swarm randomly in a given solution space, and the number of variables of the problem to be optimized determines the dimension of the solution space. Each particle has an initial position and initial velocity, and then iterative optimization. In each iteration, each particle updates

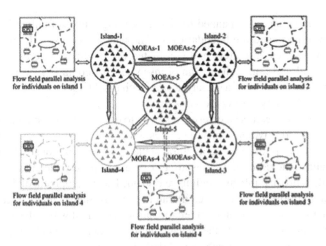

Fig. 1. Basic flow of algorithm

its position and velocity in the solution space by tracking two extreme values, one is the optimal particle (individual extreme value) found by a single particle in the iteration, and the other is the optimal solution particle (global extreme value) of all particles in the iteration process.

(1) Optimization algorithm based on swarm intelligence theory, efficient parallel algorithm.
(2) Particle swarm optimization algorithm randomly initializes the population, uses fitness to evaluate the quality of individuals, and carries out a series of random searches. However, particle swarm optimization algorithm determines the search based on its own speed, and there is no need for cross mutation and other operations, which avoids complex operations.
(3) Each particle still maintains the individual extreme value at the end of the algorithm, so in addition to obtaining the optimal solution of the problem, it can also obtain several suboptimal solutions and give more schemes.
(4) The unique memory of particle swarm optimization makes it possible to dynamically track the current search situation and adjust the search direction.

2.2 The Occurrence Context of Modern Chinese Literature

The word "communication" is involved in the field of culture, which was first seen in Taylor's primitive culture, which defines "communication" as the meaning used to reflect the migration, borrowing, implication and distribution of culture. After that, the word communication was gradually used by sociologists. The so-called "cultural communication" refers to the process or result of the transmission of cultural elements from one society, one region or one group to another society, another region or another group [3]. The transmission, diffusion, exchange and integration of culture among different subjects is a special way of culture. The obvious effect of cultural communication is to add value to culture. The extensive involvement of mass media in cultural communication has not only fundamentally changed the nature of single flow of cultural communication, but also transcended the boundaries of time and space, broke the monopoly of a few aristocratic forces on culture and eliminated the public's sense of mystery about culture, In his cultural imperialism, Tang Linsen has this cognition: "if people can still maintain the overall feeling of a society, the main channel to detect the existence of their relationship with society is only the mass media."

In modern literature, it is an external research to explore its occurrence and development from the perspective of publishing. In essence, this is the embodiment of China's transformation from traditional agricultural society to modern industrial society in the field of literature, including the innovation of external literary means such as printing industry, modern urban publishing culture and so on; The development of literary writer's identity from traditional old-fashioned literati to professional writing: the gradual establishment and improvement of modern remuneration system, of which the most important is the literary content itself: from the elegant interest of literati in landscape and countryside to paying attention to the aesthetics of daily life, the expression of literary emotion is becoming more and more popular and civilian [4].

2.3 An Overview of Modern Literature

In the era of digital economy, algorithm is an important production tool. *** Under the background of the new era, they feel the pulse of Mr. Mao Dun's spiritual inheritance. In addition to Mao Dun's letters and diaries, there are also neat and exquisite works of novels, poems, memoirs, literary comments, creative manuscripts, notebooks, groceries, ancient poetry notes, translation and other works. The handwriting reflects the gentle demeanor and clear character, which is important in literature and art [5].

Mao Dun is the most typical representative of modern literature and the weak in literati calligraphy. He was diligent in writing all his life and always maintained the habit of writing with a brush. Some representative manuscripts were excerpted and made into banners in the handwriting exhibition, trying to present the basic appearance of handwriting. The exhibits include more than 20 letters not listed in "Mao Dun's complete works", "Mao Dun's complete edition · supplement" or Mao Dun's epistles, including 11 letters from Mao Dun to Xiao Sanshu and more than 10 others from Chen Baichen, Sha Boli, pushik, Ke Ling and others; Other precious manuscripts and photos provided by Tongxiang archives. These extremely valuable manuscripts are of great significance to promote the study of Mao Dun's life, thought and works, as well as the study of modern literature in the early days of the founding of the party.

3 Particle Swarm Optimization

3.1 Basic Principle of Particle Swarm Optimization

Particle swarm optimization algorithm is inspired by the bird swarm model. In essence, it is a large-scale parallel random search algorithm. In particle swarm optimization, the potential solution to the problem is called "particle", which is equivalent to the "bird" in the bird swarm model. In order to judge the quality of particles, a function needs to be introduced into particle swarm optimization algorithm to represent the fitness value of particles [6]. All particles need to track the surrounding area of the current optimal particle. Therefore, each particle has a velocity to represent its flight direction and distance. Each particle in particle swarm optimization algorithm determines its flight direction by combining its current position, its experienced optimal position and the historical optimal position in the search space.

Particle swarm optimization algorithm initializes the optimization problem as a group of random particles, and then iteratively produces the optimal solution. In each iteration, the particle updates its position and velocity by tracking two optimal solutions. One extreme value is the optimal solution that the particle itself can find so far, that is, the individual historical optimal solution; The other extreme value is the optimal solution that the whole group can find so far, that is, the global historical optimal solution. It can also not apply to the whole group, but only take a part of the group as the particle's neighbor, then the optimal solution that can be found in the particle's neighbor is the local historical optimal solution.

3.2 Modern Literature Particle Swarm Optimization Process

Reform novel: reform literature is a work with the theme of social, political and economic reform. Because of the long-standing disadvantages and unbearable backwardness, people urgently demand reform while reflecting. Therefore, reform literature is the inevitable product of reform and opening up in the new period. It is a literary phenomenon with "Scar Literature" and "reflective literature". Jiang Zilong's factory director Qiao's taking office, Yan Zhao's Elegy, Gao Xiaosheng's "Chen Huansheng" series novels, Lu Yao's "ordinary world" and Jia Pingwa's "jiwowa family" [7].

Root seeking literature: around 1983, some writers turned their attention to national culture, tried to take care of the national cultural tradition and the deep cultural accumulation of national psychology with modern consciousness, and sought the root of national culture from the relationship between literature and culture. Main representative writers: Mo Yan and Han Shaogong's father, daughter, Wang Anyi's little Baozhuang, Acheng's chess king and tree king.

"Vanguard novels": since 1985, a number of vanguard novels have appeared in the literary world. Some of these novels have the characteristics of modernist novels and some have the characteristics of postmodernism [8]. The common feature is to advocate returning to literature itself, pay attention to language experiment, pay attention to the sense of form of works, and emphasize that "how to write" is more important than "what to write". Avant garde novels have a certain impact on later novel creation. Representative writers include Ma Yuan, Su Tong, Yu Hua, Hong Feng, Ge Fei, sun Ganlu, etc.

The difference between root seeking literature and pioneer novel

(1) Similarities: they are influenced and inspired by various new cultural and aesthetic trends, and are separated from the limitations and constraints of the traditional old-fashioned Realism (creation) principles.

(2) The differences are as follows: the writers of root seeking literature still adhere to the ideal of enlightenment and act on the cultural enlightenment and reconstruction of contemporary China through the exploration and combing of national culture;

The avant-garde novel writers have abandoned the value ideal of enlightenment. Their creative goal is to explore the infinite possibility of human nature and art in a broader space. They have basically led literature from cultural text to aesthetic text.

The main steps of particle swarm optimization algorithm are as follows:

(1) Initialize particle swarm. Set the inertia weight W, learning factors C1 and C2, the maximum number of iterations tmaxo, and randomly set the initial position Xi and velocity VI of N particles within the specified range. The individual historical optimal solution Pi of the ith particle is its current position, and the global historical optimal solution PG is set as the position of the particle with the highest current fitness [9].
(2) Set the fitness function and calculate the fitness value f (I) of each particle.
(3) The fitness value f (I) of the particle and the individual historical optimal solution p; For comparison, if f (I) is better than PI, set pi to the value of F ().
(4) Compare the fitness value f (I) of the particle with the global historical optimal solution pg. if f () is better than PG, PG is set as the value of F (I).
(5) Update the position Xi and velocity VI of each particle.
(6) Judge whether the end condition is satisfied (reaching the maximum number of iterations or minimum error). If so, end the optimization and output the optimal result; If not, increase the number of iterations by 1 and go to (2) for the next iteration.

According to the above steps, the flow chart of particle swarm optimization algorithm is shown in Fig. 2.

(1) Particle swarm optimization has a limited range of applications in modern litera- ture, mainly focusing on the above categories. Modern literature is a broad concept. Whether it is the discipline itself or guiding agricultural practice, the existing appli- cation research is not enough [10]. We should continue to explore the breadth and depth of the application of particle swarm optimization algorithm in modern litera- ture, focus on the development hotspots of the times, and promote the in-depth and three-dimensional development of modern literature.
(2) At present, most applied research aims at maximizing economic benefits and ignores social and ecological benefits. There is nothing wrong with the pursuit of economic benefits in agricultural development, but the economy and social ecology are one. If we overemphasize one over the other, it will inevitably be unbalanced. As a new intelligent algorithm, particle swarm optimization has the ability to balance and coordinate the relationship between the three when solving the optimization problems in modern literature.
(3) The existing applied research shows the phenomenon of fragmentation and does not form a complete discipline theory system. The existing applications are optimization models established for specific objectives. Whether from the particle swarm opti- mization algorithm itself or its application in modern literature, the basic theoretical system is very lack, and the basic theoretical research needs to be strengthened in the future [11].

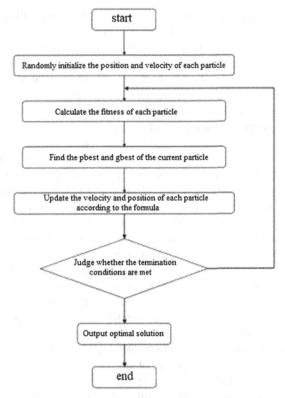

Fig. 2. Particle swarm optimization process

(4) As far as particle swarm optimization algorithm is concerned, although the improved model algorithm has better optimization effect than itself, the optimization effect of various improved algorithms is still uncertain, and there are many kinds of algorithms, lacking a general and effective improved algorithm for optimization problems. For particle swarm optimization algorithm in the future, in addition to strengthening the basic theoretical research, we need to study how to select and design parameters to reduce its dependence on specific problems, which will greatly promote the development and application of particle swarm optimization algorithm. Moreover, it is also necessary to supplement and expand the combination of particle swarm optimization algorithm and other algorithms or technologies, and apply it to parallel computing in order to achieve better optimization results.

4 Application of Particle Swarm Optimization Algorithm in Modern Literature

Particle swarm optimization algorithm is widely used in scientific problems and engineering fields. Compared with particle swarm optimization algorithm, its application in modern literature is very limited, mainly focusing on the optimal allocation of modern literary resources and the prediction of literary works [12].

The optimal allocation of particle swarm optimization algorithm in modern literature resources is a typical optimization problem in agricultural literature. Through consulting the literature, the application status of particle swarm optimization algorithm in modern literature resources is sorted out by induction and summary method, in order to provide reference for the optimal allocation of other modern literature resources with similar development conditions., Based on particle swarm optimization algorithm, an optimal allocation model of modern literature resources is established. The model is mainly divided into two levels: one is the optimal allocation of irrigation water in the whole growth period of a single crop; The second is the optimal allocation of irrigation water among various crops. Based on the model, Zhang Qian and Liu Bo compared the optimal allocation effects of modern literature resources with different precipitation frequencies or different water shortage periods. The results show that the optimal allocation results under time constraints are more conducive to the development of modern literature.

From the perspective of method model, the optimal allocation model of modern literary resources has the characteristics of many variables and complex structure. The solution of the model involves multi-objective and multi-dimensional optimization problems Question. As a new intelligent algorithm, particle swarm optimization has the advantages of simple algorithm flow, easy programming and good optimization effect. It is widely used in the optimal allocation of modern literary resources [13]. The application of particle swarm optimization algorithm in the optimal allocation of modern literature resources is mostly based on the improved algorithm or the hybrid algorithm combined with other algorithms, including the linear decreasing inertia weight operation based on the basic particle swarm optimization algorithm. The immune particle swarm optimization algorithm adds the crowding distance to the standard particle swarm optimization algorithm to evaluate the particles, and then performs the cross mutation operation on the particles, Dp-ps0 algorithm is the combination algorithm of dynamic programming and particle swarm optimization algorithm, particle swarm artificial bee colony algorithm is the particle swarm artificial bee colony hybrid algorithm, and differential particle swarm optimization algorithm (pso-dv). These algorithms have better optimization effect on the original basis, and improve the convergence speed and accuracy of the algorithm. As shown in Fig. 3 below, the optimization effect of particle algorithm in modern literature improves the convergence speed and accuracy of the algorithm.

The key of this methodology lies in Husserl's pursuit of affirmation. Firstly, we should deny the "natural attitude", that is, we believe that the object exists independently in the external world, and our knowledge of it is reliable.

When we apply it to literature, we should separate "text" and "work" as two concepts. The former is completed by the writer, and the latter is completed by the reader. This does not exclude the prescriptiveness of the writer, literary creation and the text itself, but it also requires to absorb the prescriptiveness of the recipient. In other words, on the one hand, it protects the originator, on the other hand, it establishes the status of readers as creators, which is undoubtedly a more comprehensive and thoughtful understanding of the essence of literary works [14].

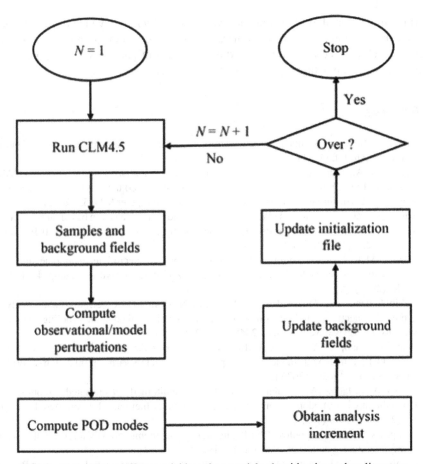

Fig. 3. Optimization effect model based on particle algorithm in modern literature

So how can we say that phenomenology is not very practical in literary criticism? The first belongs to unclear concept. Since it is methodology, it can only be said that phenomenology has had a great impact on literary criticism, including Geneva School, Russian formalism and hermeneutics. Its essence is to ignore the real historical background and production conditions of literary works, pay attention to a complete "within consciousness" understanding of the text, and seek the author's consciousness shown in the works.

5 Conclusion

This research mainly discusses the application progress of particle swarm optimization algorithm in modern literature, and puts forward some improvement methods for the shortcomings of particle swarm optimization algorithm. The research shows that the improved particle swarm optimization algorithm has good optimization ability and stronger convergence effect in modern literature. As a new intelligent algorithm, particle swarm optimization algorithm combines with modern literature, which opens up a new road for the development of modern literature. With the continuation of modern literature research and the improvement and development of particle swarm optimization algorithm, the combination of the two will play a greater role.

References

1. Zhou, X.: Research of image classification method based on particle swarm optimization. Microcomput. Inf. (2021)
2. Riyanto, E.A., Juninisviant, Y.T., Nasution, D.F., et al.: Analisis Kinerja Algoritma CART dan Naive Bayes Berbasis Particle Swarm Optimization (PSO) untuk Klasifikasi Kelayakan Kredit Koperasi. Jurnal Teknologi Informasi dan Ilmu Komputer 8(1), 55 (2021)
3. Song, X.F., Zhang, Y., Gong, D.W., et al.: A fast hybrid feature selection based on correlation-guided clustering and particle swarm optimization for high-dimensional data. IEEE Trans. Cybern. 52, 9573–9586 (2021)
4. Zdemir, M.T.: Optimal parameter estimation of polymer electrolyte membrane fuel cells model with chaos embedded particle swarm optimization. Int. J. Hydrog. Energy 46, 16465–16480 (2021)
5. Habibollahzade, A., Mehrabadi, Z.K., Markides, CN.: Comparative thermoeconomic analyses and multi-objective particle swarm optimization of geothermal combined cooling and power systems. Energy Convers. Manag. 234(C), 113921 (2021)
6. Wang, J., Zhao, X., Yu, Q., et al.: Inverse modeling of thermal decomposition of flame-retardant PET fiber with model-free coupled with particle swarm optimization algorithm. ACS Omega 6, 13626–13636 (2021)
7. Kumar, A.N., Jadhav, V., Jawalekar, R., et al.: Light emitting diode mediated photobiomodulation therapy in orthodontics - a review of contemporary literature. J. Evol. Med. Dent. Sci. 10(32), 2672–2679 (2021)
8. Filippakis, N., Stamatopoulos, T.V.: Public debt and economic growth: a review of contemporary literature. South-East. Eur. J. Econ. 19, 33–50 (2021)
9. Monisova, I.: The Program of the Academic Discipline "Contemporary Literature in Russian Language in a Foreign Cultural Space" (2021)
10. Kostretzis, L., Konstantinou, P., Pinto, I., Shahin, M., Ditsios, K., Papadopoulos, P.: Stemless reverse total shoulder arthroplasty: a systematic review of contemporary literature. Musculoskelet. Surg. 105(3), 209–224 (2021). https://doi.org/10.1007/s12306-021-00710-1
11. Pokuri, V.: Social Perspectives in Contemporary Literature latest edited (1) (2021)
12. Kurmis, A.P.: Eradicating fungal periprosthetic TKA "Super-infection": review of the contemporary literature and consideration of antibiotic-impregnated dissolving calcium sulfate beads as a novel PJI treatment adjunct. Arthroplast. Today 8, 163–170 (2021)
13. Chen, X., Miroslav, K.: Rural versus urban fiction in contemporary Chinese literature - quantitative approach case study. Digit. Scholarsh. Humanit. 37, 681–692 (2021)
14. Rong, L.Q., Rahouma, M., Lopes, A.J., et al.: Authorship patterns in contemporary anaesthesia literature: a cross-sectional study. BJA Br. J. Anaesth. 126, e152–e154 (2021)

Exploration of Personalized Foreign Language Teaching Model Based on the Integration of Multimedia Means and Traditional Methods

Fei Gao[✉]

Wenhua College, Wuhan 430074, Hubei, China
Wzx198909@126.com

Abstract. The application of multimedia technology in the 21st century has brought challenges and opportunities to foreign language teaching. It is imperative to break the traditional teaching mode of one-way communication in a single way and create an English teaching mode in a multimedia environment. This paper explores the personalized foreign language teaching mode based on the integration of multimedia means and traditional methods, mainly based on constructivism theory, humanism theory and interactionism theory, combined with the characteristics of foreign language teaching, discusses the classroom teaching mode from the perspective of multimedia, in order to find the best fit between it and traditional teaching methods, And the optimization and integration of traditional teaching methods and multimedia in middle school physics teaching, in order to make them play their respective maximum functions and realize the optimization of classroom teaching effect.

Keywords: Traditional teaching methods · Multimedia teaching · Foreign language teaching · Classroom teaching

1 Introduction

With the rapid development of information technology, CAI has its unique advantages. It provides a lively and colorful teaching environment for the classroom with its integration, rich information, intuitiveness, diversification and dynamics. It has the characteristics of breaking through time and space and expanding capacity. With the wonderful cooperation of sound, light, electricity, painting and motion, it strengthens the intuition of teaching materials, and can present some abstract and static elements in teaching in an image and dynamic way, which helps students to be directly stimulated by vision, and the improvement of teaching effect is very obvious.

Many teaching methods in traditional teaching have been tested by years, and their value and rationality are beyond doubt. Teachers can write, speak and demonstrate at the same time, have direct contact with students, and have vivid emotional communication. Teachers' infectious body language and charming dynamic teaching can make students enjoy learning.

© ICST Institute for Computer Sciences, Social Informatics and Telecommunications Engineering 2023
Published by Springer Nature Switzerland AG 2023. All Rights Reserved
M. A. Jan and F. Khan (Eds.): BigIoT-EDU 2022, LNICST 466, pp. 629–634, 2023.
https://doi.org/10.1007/978-3-031-23947-2_66

Under the new development situation, is teaching blindly pursuing multimedia teaching means, or going against the historical trend, grasping the traditional teaching means and not accepting the new multimedia information technology? The author believes that only by optimizing and integrating the traditional teaching and multimedia teaching, can the teaching effect be the best.

College English teaching is facing unprecedented fierce challenges. In recent years, the number of students in Colleges and universities across the country has been increasing [1]. Although the number of foreign language teachers has also increased steadily, the proportion of students after enrollment expansion is seriously unbalanced. College English teaching industry is still a labor-intensive industry. The majority of foreign language teachers have undertaken a lot of foreign language teaching work, but the teaching quality is not satisfactory. They are tired in the front line of foreign language teaching, have no time to study and improve their business, and are more attracted to the advanced teaching ideas and methods at home and abroad. College English Teaching in China still adopts the classroom teaching mode dominated by teachers. The class size is large, usually in the same class, that is, 50–70 people in each class attend classes at the same time; Teachers need to complete the teaching activities of intensive reading, extensive reading, listening and other teaching contents within the limited time of 4 class hours per week, so they have no time to take into account the students' oral and writing training. Although many schools have established language laboratories in recent years, purchased tape recorders, video recorders, projectors and computers, and made great efforts to reform foreign language teaching equipment, the main teaching means is still "teaching materials + blackboard", which fails to create a natural learning environment for cultivating students' foreign language communication ability. In this case, the main basis for weighing students' English level can only be CET-4 and CET-6 scores and the results at the end of each term, which is difficult to take into account the cultivation of students' practical ability to use foreign languages. Therefore, College English teaching must have corresponding countermeasures, make all-round adjustment and reform, and change one-way information transmission into two-way information exchange.

2   Discussion on Multimedia Assisted Foreign Language Teaching Mode

(1)   The necessity of multimedia teaching

According to the teaching theory of constructivism, learning is social, situational and autonomous. Learners are not the recipients of external stimuli, but the active constructors of knowledge meaning; Teachers are not indoctrinators of knowledge, but promoters and helpers of meaning construction. Teaching media is not only a means to assist teaching, but also a cognitive tool for learners. The application of Multimedia Assisted College English teaching has practiced this new teaching concept.

From the perspective of information dissemination, teaching is a two-way or multi-directional dynamic process in which disseminators transmit teaching information through communication media. Media is not only the source of teaching information, but also the carrier of teaching information.

(2) Multimedia teaching mode

In the past, the reform of teaching content, teaching means and teaching methods was emphasized, and the key problem - the reform of teaching mode was ignored.

What is the teaching mode? Teaching mode refers to the way of interaction between teachers and students or between students in order to achieve learning objectives. It refers to the steady structural form of the process of teaching activities under the guidance of certain educational thought, educational theory and learning theory, that is, according to what kind of teaching thought and theory to organize the process of teaching activities [2]. It is the concentrated embodiment of educational thought, teaching theory and learning theory.

Multi - media is a new information processing system which combines the ability of audio - visual information dissemination with the function of computer interactive control. Information symbol system includes audio, video, image, text and animation. The forms of information presentation are diversified, which use words or images to simulate the actual situation to express the abstract text content. Teachers can use multimedia equipment to create an open teaching environment, provide students with dynamic knowledge, and closely combine the vividness of the external form of teaching content with the abstraction of the internal structure. From the definition of the connotation of the teaching mode by many scholars, we can see that the multimedia teaching mode is a theoretical teaching procedure based on the teaching theory, based on the optimized combination of teaching elements, mediated by multimedia technology, using different teaching strategies to present the teaching content in order to achieve the established teaching purpose. The teaching model is defined as "an example of teaching behavior that correctly reflects the objective law of teaching and effectively guides teaching practice". The multimedia teaching mode pays attention to the open teaching content, vivid teaching form and advocates cooperation and mutual assistance. Obviously, it helps to cultivate students' language ability and arouse their interest in learning.

The key to the application of multimedia means is that it fully reflects and mobilizes students' learning enthusiasm, so as to further improve students' comprehensive ability of listening, speaking, reading, writing and translation. Through the simultaneous action of language, image and sound on students' multiple senses, they can use both left and right brains to produce an immersive feeling. Under the guidance of teachers, students carry out a large number of simulated communication. Their ability to think directly in English is often exercised, so they can more effectively improve their ability to communicate in English.

3 The Strategy of Integrating the Traditional English Teaching Mode with the Multimedia Assisted Foreign Language Teaching Mode

It can not be ignored that English is a language and requires a lot of practical practice, but the practical practice is based on certain basic skills [3]. Therefore, the importance of traditional English teaching on basic English skills can not be discarded. On this basis, multimedia technology needs to be added to expand the field of vision and supplement knowledge in English classroom. Therefore, The combination of traditional teaching mode and multimedia technology needs to be paid attention to and implemented. In order to effectively combine the two, we need to do the following:

1. Put the two teaching modes on the same position, correctly understand the advantages and disadvantages of the two teaching modes, and don't pay too much attention to either of them. The traditional English teaching mode attaches importance to the training of students' basic English skills and lays a foundation for students' further development in English. The Multimedia Assisted English teaching mode uses rich teaching means and organically combines pictures, audio, video and words, which makes the classroom atmosphere active and students' learning enthusiasm gradually improved.
2. Integrate the multimedia assisted teaching mode with the traditional English teaching mode. When teachers use multimedia to expand their knowledge and background, they should explain the knowledge points in detail, introduce students' thinking to the attention of English knowledge, instead of expanding information in a rich and colorful way. In other words, they will use multimedia expanded data to screen, remove the dross and extract the essence. In this way, students can watch while listening and learn while remembering in different classroom atmosphere. The effect of memory is better and the learning efficiency is also very high.

4   Advantages of Multimedia Technology in Foreign Language Teaching

The advantages of using multimedia technology in foreign language teaching are shown in Fig. 1.

Information efficiency. Due to the powerful function of computer processor, when multimedia teaching a language project for explanation or demonstration, the amount of information that multimedia software can express in a few seconds and the accuracy and vividness of information transmission are absolutely unmatched by traditional teaching methods.

Adapt to the needs of multi-point interaction. Traditional teaching is often limited to teachers. In addition, when teachers and other students carry out point-to-point information transmission, scholars believe that the concept of "class hour" is in the era of rapid development of information technology. Based on this concept, language teachers should make 50 min produce 2500 min. Under the traditional mode, this is impossible. Students are equipped with a tutor, instead of requiring all students to complete a week's learning content at the same time. Similarly, if a student encounters problems in learning, he can consolidate and improve his knowledge by clicking the mouse many times.

Teach in fun. The unique learning environment of sound, picture, text and movement provided by multimedia can make the learning process very relaxed and pleasant. It will make students have a strong interest in foreign language learning and change the single teaching form completely dictated by teachers in traditional foreign language teaching [4].

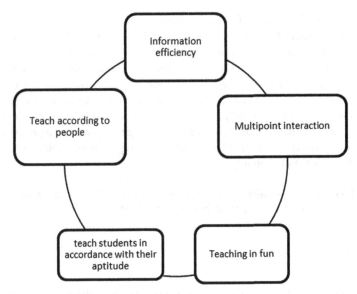

Fig. 1. Advantages of multimedia technology in foreign language teaching

Since the teaching organization in the multi-dimensional foreign language teaching model language environment is not limited by time and space - it can be carried out in the form of classroom teaching and Extracurricular Autonomous Learning, whether students can consciously and effectively carry out autonomous learning is related to our teaching goal - whether to promote the acquisition and sustainable development of students' language ability can be realized smoothly. Based on this understanding, we have established a teaching strategy that takes cultivating students' autonomous learning ability as a breakthrough. At the same time, we have changed the traditional classroom teaching idea focusing on imparting knowledge, and stressed that in teaching practice, teachers use multimedia to create a real and vivid language environment around students' learning needs, Urge students to actively participate in various language communication activities aimed at cultivating their listening and speaking ability, while the traditional classroom explanation is mainly used to cultivate students' reading, writing and translation ability and solve some problems encountered by students in language knowledge.

Under the guidance of this idea, since 2001, we have carried out the theoretical discussion and teaching reform experiment of multi-dimensional foreign language teaching model and strategy innovation research and practice of the integration of multimedia means and traditional methods under the network environment for more than two years in five classes of four departments of grade 01 of our university.

5 Conclusion

This paper explores the personalized foreign language teaching model based on the integration of multimedia means and traditional methods. The introduction of multimedia means into foreign language teaching poses a challenge to teachers' own quality and knowledge reserve. Multimedia foreign language teaching is inseparable from compound teachers with one specialty and many abilities. In the multimedia learning environment, students can learn selectively according to their interests, hobbies and their foreign language level. At any time, they may ask teachers some questions that teachers do not know. These questions not only involve foreign language knowledge or language understanding, but also involve the knowledge or information of many other disciplines. As a foreign language teacher, we must pay attention to the understanding of the development of other disciplines and accumulate relevant knowledge to adapt to the pressure brought by professional growth, modern educational technology and the rapid development of science, technology and economy.

Acknowledgements. Exploration and Practice on Personalized Employment Education Pattern Based on "4P Career Planning", Program No. 2020XGJPF2007.

References

1. Shi, S.: Computer Aided Education. Beijing Normal University Press, Beijing (1993)
2. Zhou, D., Li, Y., et al.: Modern Educational Technology. Suzhou University Press, Suzhou (1998)
3. Wang, Y.: Culture oriented foreign language teaching model and cross-cultural communication. Heilongjiang High. Educ. Res. (04) (2006)
4. Yang, J.: Combination of learning and thinking, unification of knowledge and practice, optimization of multimedia assisted foreign language teaching. Crazy Engl. (Teacher's Edition) (03) (2011)

Fast Conversion of Material Parameters of Asphalt Mixture by Laplace Transform

Nan Zhang$^{(\boxtimes)}$, Pei Sun, and Ting-ting Ling

College of Urban Construction and Transportation, Hefei University, Hefei 230601, China
zn5598080@163.com

Abstract. The rapid conversion of material parameters of asphalt mixture by Laplace transform is an analytical method to determine the density, viscosity and molecular weight distribution (MWD) in the mixture. The method is based on solving differential equations using Laplace transform, which describe these properties according to their physical quantities. The process includes solving the following set of synchronous linear algebraic equations: a matrix containing all material properties (density, viscosity and MWD), a vector containing all materials present in the mixture, and a matrix containing material concentration (mass per volume).In the service process, the pavement structure is affected by various factors such as vehicles, environment and so on. Whether it is the alternation of vehicle load or temperature, it is a constantly changing dynamic process. Asphalt mixture used in asphalt pavement is a typical viscoelastic material. Its mechanical properties are very sensitive to the changes of temperature and frequency. The mechanical responses under dynamic load and static load are very different. In order to realize the rapid conversion of asphalt mixture material parameters, Laplace transform is used to realize the rapid conversion of asphalt mixture material parameters in this paper.

Keywords: Laplace transform · Asphalt · Mixture material

1 Introduction

Asphalt mixture is a kind of composite material, which is mainly composed of asphalt, coarse aggregate, fine aggregate and mineral powder, and some are added with polymers and lignin fibers; These materials with different quality and quantity are mixed to form different structures and have different mechanical properties.

The structural composition of asphalt mixture formed according to the grading principle can be divided into three categories:

(1) Suspension dense structure: this kind of asphalt mixture filled by secondary aggregate into the gap of the previous aggregate (slightly larger than the particle size of secondary aggregate) has a great density, but because the aggregates at all levels are separated by secondary aggregate and asphalt mortar, they cannot be directly

M. A. Jan and F. Khan (Eds.): BigIoT-EDU 2022, LNICST 466, pp. 635–646, 2023.
https://doi.org/10.1007/978-3-031-23947-2_67

interlocked with each other to form a skeleton, so this structure has greater cohesion, but the internal friction angle is small, and the high-temperature stability is poor, such as AC type asphalt mixture.

(2) Skeleton void structure: this structure has a large proportion of coarse aggregate and little or no fine aggregate. Coarse aggregate can be interlocked with each other to form a skeleton; However, too little fine aggregate is easy to form voids between coarse aggregates. The internal friction angle of this structure is large, but the cohesion is low, such as asphalt macadam mixture (AM).

(3) Skeleton dense structure: a large amount of coarse aggregate forms a spatial skeleton, and a considerable amount of fine aggregate fills the gap between bone and gravel frames to form a continuous gradation. This structure not only has a large internal friction angle, but also has high cohesion, such as asphalt mastic macadam mixture (SMA for short)

The asphalt mixtures of the three structures also have significant differences in stability due to their different densities, voids and mineral aggregate voids.Asphalt mixture, as the main pavement material in China, in practical application, its rutting, cracking and other diseases are always difficult to be cured, and the actual service life is far lower than the design level. The reason is largely due to the lack of in-depth understanding of the complexity of asphalt mixture materials. In terms of material composition, asphalt mixture is a multiphase composite material composed of aggregate, asphalt and voids, in which granular aggregate accounts for about 85% of the total volume and more than 95% of the total mass of asphalt mixture. Therefore, it can be considered that asphalt mixture is a granular material dominated by discrete particle system, Granular materials have complex mechanical response characteristics significantly different from continuous media, such as nonlinearity, discontinuity and self-organized criticality, which have always been the research hotspot and difficulty in engineering and scientific circles at home and abroad [1]. Asphalt is a kind of viscoelastic materials with complex rheological properties, which is similar to fluid at high temperature and solid at low temperature, The complex interface interaction and mechanical coupling between the two eventually lead to the overall performance of asphalt mixture with very complex mechanical properties and significant temperature load time sensitivity. For example, plastic deformation is easy to occur at high temperature, brittle fracture is easy to occur at low temperature, and viscoelastic response is mainly shown at room temperature, These mechanical properties are closely related to their road performance and disease mechanism.

2   Related Work

2.1   Research on Asphalt Mixture

For a long time, the research on asphalt mixture often ignores or simplifies these micro structural characteristics. For example, in the design of pavement structure, the layered elastic system theory based on continuum mechanics is used to calculate the mechanical response of pavement, although it is an ideal engineering model with limited means of calculation and analysis, However, the object of continuum mechanics model is uniform, continuous and infinitely separable materials, which is essentially different from asphalt mixture with obvious granularity, structure and discontinuity on the micro scale, which will inevitably lead to some errors between the calculated mechanical response parameters and the real mechanical response parameters of pavement. On the other hand, the design of asphalt pavement materials pays more attention to the overall performance of the materials, and adopts the research means of macro test to phenomenally describe and summarize the material properties. However, the test results are easily interfered by many factors, and the relevant conclusions can only be effective within the confirmed range, and the complex situations in the process of material source, manufacturing, construction and operation cannot be considered, This research method also has great limitations in establishing the relationship between the internal structure, composition and macro mechanical properties of asphalt mixture and revealing the local damage mechanism caused by material heterogeneity.

In recent years, researchers have gradually realized that the mechanical properties and response of asphalt mixture materials are not only an inseparable quantity of macro scale, but reflected in different scale horizons from nano (atom) to micro, then to meso and even macro [2]. The traditional macro research scale has gradually changed to a more fine, micro and even nano research scale. According to the characteristic size, characteristic time and research focus, the division of four research scales of asphalt mixture materials and structures is shown in Fig. 1.

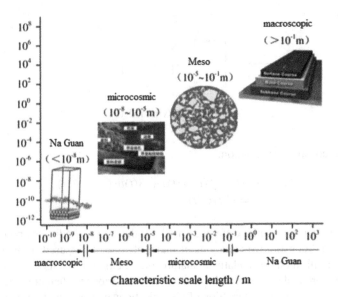

Fig. 1. Multi scale structure of asphalt mixture

Physical property requirements of raw materials:

Modified asphalt: modified asphalt is made of high molecular polymer, natural asphalt and other modified materials, which can be used for all levels of pavement. General sampling 5 kg.

Coarse aggregate: coarse aggregate for asphalt layer includes crushed stone, crushed gravel, steel slag, slag, etc., but gravel and slag shall not be used for Expressway and first-class highway. Coarse aggregate should be clean, dry and rough. The grading requirements of coarse aggregate in asphalt mixture are relatively high, and the specification shall be as detailed as possible.

Fine aggregate: fine aggregate includes natural sand, machine-made sand and stone chips. It should be clean, dry, free of weathering and impurities, and have appropriate particle grading [3].

Filler: the filler mineral powder must be the mineral powder obtained by grinding hydrophobic stones such as limestone or strong basic rocks in magmatic rocks, and the soil impurities in the original stones should be removed. The mineral powder shall be dry and clean, and can flow freely from the mineral powder silo.

2.2   Research on Laplace Transform Method

Next, a viscoelastic specimen with length L is taken as the research object, X is the Lagrange coordinate of the viscoelastic specimen, time is t, and the left end of the specimen is subjected to impact load. A simple Kelvin Voigt model is used to describe the mechanical properties of viscoelastic materials, as shown in Fig. 2.

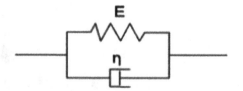

Fig. 2. Kelvin model

Material constitutive equation:

$$\begin{cases} E(t)\dot{x}_k(t) = f(t, x_k(t)) + B(t)u_k(t) + d_k(t) \\ y_k(t) = C(t)x_k(t) \end{cases} \tag{1}$$

(1) Characteristic line finite difference method: the initial conditions, boundary conditions and constitutive equations of materials need to be used in the calculation process; This method is relatively mature, the calculation results are accurate, close to the theoretical solution, and can accurately describe the characteristics of propagation, reflection and interaction of viscoelastic waves. It can effectively deal with the propagation of strong intermittent waves in viscoelastic media, which is convenient and efficient; However, when the specimen size is too large, the calculation process is more, time-consuming and high cost, which can not achieve the expected effect on the analysis of large-size concrete and other specimens.

(2) Propagation coefficient method: the calculation process requires the constitutive equation of the material without initial and boundary conditions; When using this method to calculate the viscoelastic wave propagation of slender rod (i.e. ignoring

the transverse inertia effect), it is very fast, the process is simple, and the error is about 3%; However, for the large rod (the wavelength is not significantly larger than the rod diameter), the transverse inertia effect needs to be considered, the calculation formula is lengthy, the process is complex and the solution is difficult [4]. This function is divided into three segments, but we can "spell" them segment by segment with multi segment unit ladder function, as shown in Fig. 3 below:

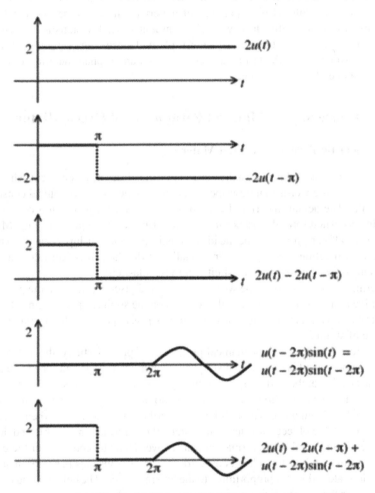

Fig. 3. Multistage unit ladder function

In contrast, penetration test, as an empirical test method, because the needle tip may encounter different components in modified asphalt such as asphalt, polymer fiber, rubber powder particles in the test process, the test results are obviously different when the same sample is tested, so penetration test is usually considered to be difficult to effectively evaluate the performance of modified asphalt. Although MSCR multi stress creep recovery test carried out with DSR dynamic shear rheometer is considered to be effective in evaluating the performance of modified asphalt, a complete evaluation in accordance with the requirements of the specification requires a short-term aging treatment of asphalt by rotating film oven (about 75–85 min) and a short-term aging treatment by pressure aging instrument (about 20 h) before the test [5]. The efficiency and complexity of operation are also more complex than abqt. Judging from the difficulty of popularizing the test method, abqt is a better choice.

In order to verify the effectiveness and repeatability of abqt test method and equipment for the test results of different asphalt materials, the developer has conducted a large number of comparative tests with different materials. The statistical results show that the coefficient of variation ° is between 1–6% and the average variation level is 3%. It can be considered that the test results are achieved and asphalt materials of different materials can be effectively evaluated.

3 Fast Conversion of Material Parameters of Green Mixture

3.1 Viscoelastic Theory of Asphalt Materials

"Elasticity" and "micondu unisexuality" are words that describe mechanical behavior. To be precise, they are words that describe the characteristics of a mechanical constitutive relationship. The actual material always shows a certain form within a certain range of conditions. Therefore, the proper use of the terms "elastic material" and "Mi visco elastic material" can only describe the ideal constitutive relationship, rather than the real material classification. So the word "material" is redundant. It is equivalent to asking "what is the difference between elasticity and viscoelasticity".

In terms of the comparison between elasticity and viscoelasticity, in the pure elastic constitutive relationship, the stress only depends on the strain, not on the time derivative of the strain. In viscoelastic constitutive relation, stress depends on both strain and time derivative of strain [6].

The effect is that for the mechanical properties of pure elasticity, the instantaneous stress does not depend on the strain history. No matter what shape and speed you deform to the current shape, the current stress only depends on the current shape. Knowing the shape at any moment can know the stress at that moment. Meter elasticity is the opposite.

Classical mechanics uses Hooke's law to describe elastic behavior: when an external force is applied, the object deforms immediately, the deformation is stable and does not increase with time, and the deformation can recover instantaneously after the external force is eliminated. Newton's law is used to describe the viscous behavior, that is, the deformation rate is directly proportional to the external force. The deformation increases with time, and the deformation cannot be recovered after the external force is eliminated. These are two completely opposite material properties. In practical application, after physical and chemical changes, the mechanical properties of engineering materials can change to the opposite, so as to meet the elastic requirements under certain conditions and the viscosity requirements under another condition [7]. For example, the commonly used building material cement concrete, the newly mixed cement concrete has good fluidity and can flow freely in the pump pipe and formwork; However, after solidification, its strength and stiffness are very large, and it can bear the load of kiloton/cm^2 without large deformation.

Solid with crystal structure such as iron and steel materials will melt into liquid at high temperature. The melting point is fixed, and this phase transition is sudden. There is no definite critical point of phase transition temperature for materials with amorphous structure, which is also called amorphous structure or glassy. Amorphous structural materials can realize the transformation between viscous flow state and elastic state without chemical change or melting process. But this change process is a slow process accompanied by temperature and time. Asphalt material is amorphous structural material.

3.2 Viscoelastic Theory of Asphalt Mixture

Asphalt mixture is a mixture of asphalt mortar and aggregate particles. Its mechanical properties are very complex, and its macro performance is typical viscoelasticity. This can be clearly seen from the stress-strain relationship of asphalt mixture: under low temperature, low-level load and short-time action, it shows obvious elastic performance, that is, the main strain increases or decreases with the increase or decrease of stress; At the same time, with a certain viscosity, the of this part of strain will lag behind the stress [8]. Asphalt mixture shows viscoelastic properties, which is very important because it is affected by the viscoelasticity of asphalt materials. The research shows that the contribution rate of asphalt performance to pavement rutting resistance is 29%, the contribution rate to fatigue resistance is 52%, and the contribution rate to low temperature crack resistance is 87%. It can be seen that asphalt has a significant impact on the performance of asphalt mixture. However, there are obvious differences between asphalt mixture and asphalt. The strength of asphalt mixture comes from the adhesion of asphalt film to aggregate and the intercalation between aggregates. Although the viscoelasticity of asphalt mixture will be affected by the properties of asphalt materials, the factors affecting the mechanical properties of asphalt mixture also include gradation, mineral aggregate type and void ratio, especially void ratio.

Due to the uniformity and continuity of asphalt materials, it is easy to study and explain by using modern mechanical theories such as thermodynamics, damage mechanics and fracture mechanics. However, the macro composition of asphalt mixture is very complex, and its mechanical properties are affected by many factors, not only by the properties of the material itself, but also by the relationship and interaction between the components. The physical and chemical interaction between asphalt and mineral aggregate surface makes it very difficult to analyze even from micro or sub micro [9]. Therefore, up to now, we still can not accurately predict the viscoelastic performance of asphalt mixture by using the asphalt performance as binder. In most of the current research and engineering applications, we still start from the macro performance of asphalt mixture, take the test as the main means, and use the method of mathematical statistics to study the mechanical properties of asphalt mixture.

4   Laplace Transform is Applied to Realize the Rapid Conversion of Asphalt Mixture Material Parameters

4.1   Laplace Method and Random Number

When simulating problems, Laplace method needs to generate random variables with specific probability distribution, and the sampling value of this random variable is called random number. It can be said that the generation method of random number is the core of Laplace method. Early researchers generated random numbers through a large number of sampling experiments and compiled them into a random sampling number table, but the length of the random number sequence composed of the number table is limited, which can not meet the solution of complex problems. At present, this method is gradually replaced by physical methods and mathematical methods. Physical methods generate random numbers through physical phenomena such as coin throwing, runner, noise using electronic components, nuclear fission and so on. These random numbers are true random numbers (completely random), but their main disadvantage is that they have high technical requirements and cannot be repeated [10]. In contrast, the mathematical method generates random numbers (pseudo-random numbers with certain periodicity) by computer according to specific mathematical recurrence formulas (algorithms). This method has the advantages of simplicity, convenience and repeatability. If the pseudo-random numbers can pass the randomness test, it can be considered that their related properties are similar to true random numbers, so as to meet most practical application needs.

Since asphalt mixture can be regarded as coarse aggregate randomly distributed in mortar matrix, that is, it can be regarded as a random process, Laplace can be used to establish asphalt mixture random aggregate structure. The most basic random variable is a random variable with uniform distribution in the [0,1] interval. The probability density function f(x) of the random variable x is as follows.

$$(E(t) - M_2 C)\Delta \dot{x}_{k+1}(t) = f(t, x_d(t)) - f(t, x_{k+1}(t)) + B\Delta u_k(t)$$
$$- \left(\Gamma_{p1} C + M_1 C + M_2 C\right)\dot{x}_d(t) + \Gamma_{p1} C \dot{x}_{k-1}(t) \quad (2)$$

4.2   Reconstruction of Three-Dimensional Random Asphalt Mixture Meso Model

Although there have been studies on the three-dimensional analysis of CT scanned images of asphalt mixture by using Laplace transform and mimics, at present, the three-dimensional discrete element model of asphalt mixture generated by image processing can only be realized by superimposing multiple two-dimensional CT scanned image models. The processing process of single CT scanned image is basically the same as that of captured image. The ultimate goal is to complete image component segmentation and extract coarse aggregate information. However, because the two-dimensional image has no "thickness" in theory, and the three-dimensional discrete element model has a certain "thickness", the single-layer image model can only be expanded repeatedly in the third dimension [11]. The biggest defect of the model generated by this method is that the identification of aggregate individuals is very limited, and the errors generated by image segmentation of multiple two-dimensional models will continue to transfer and accumulate, resulting in large errors in the overall three-dimensional model. The following Fig. 4 shows the maximum deformation test results of asphalt rapid fusion homogeneous materials.

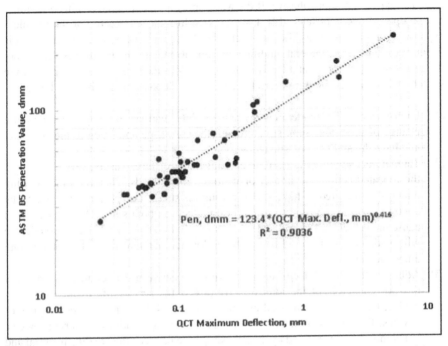

Fig. 4. Maximum deformation test results of asphalt rapid fusion homogeneous materials

Therefore, considering the randomness of asphalt mixture, this paper uses the method of Laplace transform and randomly generating three-dimensional model to carry out the mechanical simulation of asphalt mixture. Due to the limitation of the modeling method of the discrete element software, the process of randomly generating the three-dimensional model of asphalt mixture is different from that of the two-dimensional model, that is, instead of directly putting irregular aggregate particles in the two-dimensional model, the three-dimensional model of irregular aggregate is generated, and then the aggregate particle model is randomly selected from the aggregate model library, Then it replaces the basic ball stacking model of mixture.

4.3 Asphalt Filled Case Analysis

Product features: very high elastic resilience: able to adapt to repeated temperature Q and load displacement. Low temperature flexibility and high temperature stability are very good: it will not become brittle at −40 °C and will not flow at 80 °C. Therefore, it can be applied to all climatic regions in China. Good high temperature adhesion Q:

it can be firmly bonded with the existing pavement during construction, and it is not sticky at all at room temperature, and it will not be taken away after cooling. Convenient and flexible construction: a skilled construction team (8–10 people) can work 30 linear meters of expansion joints every day, and can work half way without blocking traffic. Open the traffic quickly: the traffic can be opened two hours after the installation of the seamless expansion joint adhesive. If the water spray accelerates the cooling, the traffic can be opened one hour later [12]. Long service life: the service life of the seamless expansion joint adhesive installed in strict accordance with the process requirements is about twice that of the general modified asphalt pavement. The comfort is very good: the seamless expansion joint adhesive can fully absorb the vibration and impact of the vehicle 9, and the vehicle is comfortable and stable. Good economic benefit: low cost.

(1) High elasticity. The binder must adapt to the deformation caused by the temperature change of the bridge span structure and the shrinkage and creep of the concrete, and have the ability of elastic recovery.

(2) Temperature stability. As a part of the bridge device, the expansion device must bear the repeated action and impact of various vehicle loads. Therefore, the bonding material is required to have strong rutting resistance at high temperature and be continuous with the rigidity of the bridge deck on both sides. Otherwise, it will cause the vehicle or the bridge deck to crack, and then the whole expansion device will be damaged. It should be flexible at low temperature without hardening and embrittlement.

(3) Adhesive force. The size of the adhesive force between the bonding material and the two end faces of the joint directly affects the service life of the expansion device, because the embedded expansion device is different from other types of devices. The combination with both ends is not through various anchoring devices, but completely determined by the adhesive force between the bonding material and the end face. When the bridge deck is cold or subjected to the impact and vibration of vehicles, the bonding material will produce considerable tensile stress, and only the adhesive force is large enough, And when it is greater than the cohesion of the material itself, the interface failure will not occur [13].

(4) Water resistance. The viscosity of the bonding material itself is very high. When filling, it is mixed with a single particle size stone, and the oil stone ratio is generally about 1:2–1:4. The stone cannot form a skeleton structure, and the void ratio is almost zero. In addition, the bonding material is a composite asphalt material, which is impervious and absorbent, and can prevent the infiltration of water from top to bottom. Therefore, as long as there are no holes or broken ends during construction, the waterproof of the bonding material can be guaranteed. In fact, water resistance and adhesion are inseparable. The problem often occurs on both sides. Because the adhesion force is not enough to resist stress, the interface is broken, and it is difficult to discharge water into the beam, which infiltrates into the beam and forms water damage [14].

(5) durability. The bonding material shall have anti-aging and anti-corrosion properties.

5 Conclusion

Laplace transform is applied to realize the rapid conversion of material parameters of asphalt mixture. For example, its strength is mainly composed of friction and intercalation between aggregate particles and adhesion between asphalt and aggregate, plastic deformation is mainly formed by aggregate particle flow, cracks are mainly developed from micro damage between aggregate particles, and water damage disease is mainly caused by asphalt peeling off on the surface of aggregate particles, It can be considered that the mechanical properties of asphalt mixture are closely related to the micro parameters such as the morphology, characteristics, gradation and particle interface of granular materials. Therefore, the complexity of asphalt mixture materials is not only reflected in the diversity of constituent materials, but also in its granularity on the micro scale. It can be said that the research on asphalt mixture materials is not purely to solve an engineering application problem, but a rather in-depth and universal basic theoretical problem for a granular material with complex micro structure.

Acknowledgements. Natural Science Research Project of Higher Education in Anhui Province (Key Project) (KJ2021A1004); Scientific Research and Development Foundation of Hefei University (Major Project) (19ZR02ZDA); Talent Research Foundation of Hefei University (20RC29) (18-19RC05); Scientific Research and Development Foundation of Hefei University (Key Project) (19ZR01ZDB) (20ZR06ZDB).

References

1. Ullah, R., Hafeez, I., Zaidi, S., et al.: Study the effect of substitution filler on performance of Asphalt mixture. Civil Eng. J. **6**(9), 1704–1714 (2020)
2. Zhang, F., Kaloush, K., Underwood, S., et al.: Preparation and performances of SBS compound modified asphalt mixture by acidification and vulcanization. Constr. Build. Mater. **296**(2), 123693 (2021)
3. Shishkin, E.A., Ivanchenko, S.N., Shemyakin, S.A.: Behavior of asphalt concrete mixture during relaxation. IOP Conf. Ser. Mater. Sci. Eng. **1103**(1), 012026 (2021)
4. Almaali, Y.A., Al-Busaltan, S., Kadhim, M.A.: The effect of sustainable materials on fatigue cracking of thing overlay asphalt mixture. J. Phys. Conf. Ser. **1895**(1), 012020 (2021)
5. Yu, B., Peng, W., Liu, J., et al.: Research on the performance of temperature responsive asphalt mixture with thermochromic material. Road Mater. Pavement Des. **24**, 1–12 (2020)
6. Veranita, T.B.: The effect of using PVC as a mixed additive material asphalt concrete wearing course. IOP Conf. Ser. Earth Environ. Sci. **832**(1), 012030 (9pp) (2021)
7. Analysis on the influence of steel wool fiber on the performance of dense Asphalt mixture. Mater. Sci. **11**(4), 444–452 (2021)
8. Milad, A.A., Ali, A., Yusoff, N.: A review of the utilisation of recycled waste material as an alternative modifier in Asphalt mixtures. Civil Eng. J. **6**(Special Issue), 42–60 (2020)
9. Alaye, Q., Ling, X.Z., Dong, Z., et al.: Evaluation of mixture performance recycled Asphalt pavement materials as base layer with or without rejuvenator into the Asphalt. **2020**(3), 19 (2020)
10. Shen, Y.: Research on the integration of structural design and material parameters of long-life Asphalt pavement. **6**(3), 7 (2022)

11. Jin, H.B., Zhou, X.Y., Ju, Z.C., et al.: Study on dynamic modulus dependence model for Asphalt mixture based on temperature and strain parameters. J. Highway Transp. Res. Develop. (Eng. Edn.) **14**(3), 70–77 (2020)
12. Lv, S., Wang, S., Xia, C., et al.: A new method of mix design for cold patching Asphalt mixture. Front. Mater. 7 (2020)
13. Structural optimization design of full thickness Asphalt pavement based on high modulus asphalt mixture. Mater. Sci. **11**(2), 105–110 (2021)
14. Rizal, M., Darwis, M., Ridwan, I.: Study characteristics of Asphalt concrete Lapis Aus (HRS-WC) by using sand pumice for material substitute. IOP Conf. Ser. Mater. Sci. Eng. **1125**(1), 012009 (2021)

Higher Education Evaluation System Based on Computer Network

Guangjuan Gu(✉)

Anhui Xinhua University Urban Construction College, Hefei 230088, Anhui, China
umbraler2021@126.com

Abstract. With the development and continuous improvement of computer network and its related technologies, especially today when the initial realization of educational informatization is realized, people are trying to use computer network as the operation platform to explore higher education evaluation technology, so as to ensure the fairness and fairness of evaluation results, so as to improve its efficiency and benefit and promote the development of our education. However, there are still some problems in the common higher education evaluation system. The main problem is that the evaluation materials are generally sent out of the evaluated unit by mail or carried by hand, the expert evaluation takes a long time, and the evaluation results are basically published in the form of written notice. Therefore, the evaluation workload is large and time-consuming, resulting in low evaluation efficiency. In addition, the evaluation work is difficult to be regular, the evaluation process is lack of modeling, and the determination of evaluation index weight is lack of scientificity, which seriously affects the reform of higher education evaluation. The purpose of this research is to change this situation and realize the high efficiency, networking and intelligence of higher education evaluation. Firstly, this paper introduces the origin and development of higher education evaluation, analyzes the characteristics of higher education evaluation, and puts forward a comprehensive evaluation method based on the combination of fuzzy evaluation and analytic hierarchy process; Then it discusses the working mode and architecture of the online evaluation system, and develops a higher education evaluation system based on computer network by applying relevant theories and technologies, such as database theory, dynamic web page technology ASP and web database access technology based on ASP.

Keywords: Higher education · Computer network · Evaluation system

1 Introduction

Higher education evaluation is an evaluation method for the school running level, teaching quality and management level of colleges and universities. It is an important guarantee to improve teaching quality and increase school running efficiency. Especially under the new education system, colleges and universities have become the main body of running

M. A. Jan and F. Khan (Eds.): BigIoT-EDU 2022, LNICST 466, pp. 647–659, 2023.
https://doi.org/10.1007/978-3-031-23947-2_68

schools for the society according to law, and education evaluation has become an important means for the government to conduct macro guidance and management of higher education [1]. Especially in recent years, inspired by the popularization of higher education, the rapid expansion of the scale of higher education may cause obvious quality problems. Research shows that there is a contradiction between the increase of quantity and the sliding wave of quality in the process of moving towards popularization all over the world. In particular, in order to meet the requirements of popularization, a number of higher education institutions have been upgraded and newly established. Their basic quality standards need to be improved and maintained. It is urgent to establish a strong quality assurance system.

However, due to the late start of higher education evaluation in China, so far only a few colleges and universities have established a quality assurance system, so the evaluation work is difficult to be regular. Most colleges and universities only carry out teaching evaluation, curriculum evaluation and so on. In the actual evaluation, it is often notified by the superior to evaluate a school. After receiving the notice, a school responds to the evaluation passively by reviewing the work and sorting out the materials [2]. In addition, most of the evaluation work adopts manual operation. For example, the evaluation materials are provided once by mail or carried by a specially assigned person, which not only brings a great burden to the evaluated object, It is also difficult to ensure the consistency and accuracy of the data and information provided; The expert review takes a long time, and the release of the evaluation results is basically in the form of written notice (such as documents or notes). Due to the large workload, sometimes the evaluation organizers will try to simplify the release of the evaluation results, which consumes a lot of manpower, financial resources and time. Moreover, the statistical work is cumbersome and error prone, and its workload is large and time-consuming, It is far from meeting the needs of the development of higher education evaluation. What is more serious is the lag of information, which often leads to management and decision-making mistakes. At present, some evaluation organizers use stand-alone evaluation or internal network evaluation, that is, on the basis of manual evaluation, computer statistics, analysis and conclusion [3]. Compared with manual evaluation, stand-alone evaluation does have its progress, and the workload is significantly reduced, but it still fails to share information, forming an information island and does not play its due role.

The rapid development and continuous improvement of computer network and its related technologies provide technical possibilities to fill these functional gaps. The network provides a "face-to-face" and "what you see is what I see" collaborative working environment for evaluators scattered in time and space, supports the collaborative work of multiple evaluators, evaluators and evaluation institutions that are separated in time, dispersed in space and interdependent in work, closely connects evaluators with evaluators and evaluators, and realizes The interaction between the evaluator and the evaluated makes the evaluation of higher education proceed without time and space constraints[4]. Network technologies such as WWW, e-mail, FTP, BBS, Telnet, chat and other functions, as well as network database and data mining provide strong technical support for Internet-based education evaluation.

The so-called higher education evaluation based on computer network is the higher education evaluation with computer network as the operation platform. Using such a platform to realize higher education evaluation can not only make up for the shortcomings of traditional forms, but also the network and its related technologies make the means, methods and forms of higher education evaluation more flexible and diverse. The rapid information transmission function, efficient information retrieval function and resource sharing ability of the network greatly improve the efficiency and efficiency of higher education evaluation. It is mainly reflected in the following aspects:

(1) Autonomy of assessment activities: due to the use of the Internet for assessment, the assessed can transmit the information related to the assessment to the assessor at any time through the network, and can view the progress and results of the assessment on the Internet; The evaluator no longer has to collect the information of the evaluated person at a specific place at the specified time [5]. The evaluator can retrieve the relevant data of the evaluated person from various information networks and information centers, and then evaluate the evaluated person. It has basically changed the passive response situation of the evaluated units, and realized the concept change from "want me to evaluate" to "I want to evaluate".

(2) Evaluate site virtualization
Network technology has changed the form of evaluation and virtualized the evaluation place. The Internet assessment "virtual" provides a multi-functional assessment place. In this "virtual assessment place", there is a "face-to-face" communication between assessors and assessors, assessors and assessees, which is different and similar to the traditional assessment [6]. The evaluator can evaluate on the multimedia terminal on the Internet without leaving home. Assessment work no longer means going to a specific place.

(3) Efficient evaluation
Therefore, the workload of traditional information processing, such as the application of CD-ROM and digital information processing, has been greatly reduced. This can not only greatly save manpower, material resources and time, but also improve the evaluation efficiency.

(4) Diversified evaluation contents
With the help of network technology, evaluation resources tend to be diversified. The evaluation resources provided by the network will greatly exceed people's imagination in terms of quantity and type. In addition, the evaluation special website, evaluation expert's personal web page and evaluation special news group will also be filled with the network. These professional online resources provide unprecedented choices for evaluators [7]. At the same time, in the aspects of evaluation scheme design, evaluation method selection, evaluation technical support Provide scientific guidance in the analysis and utilization of evaluation results, and effectively promote the scientific and professional process of higher education evaluation.

In addition, the establishment of such an evaluation system can not only improve the credibility of the evaluation conclusion and make the higher education administrative department and the state reasonably allocate and optimize the combination of human, material and financial resources; it can also reduce the intensity of the work management of the participating schools and enhance the enthusiasm and initiative of participating in the evaluation and self-evaluation; at the same time, it can also vigorously promote the construction of the key projects of the "211 Project".

2 Related Work

2.1 Concept of Grid

Grid it came into being in the mid-1990s and was borrowed from the power grid. The ultimate purpose of grid is to use the Internet to organize computers scattered in different geographical locations into a virtual supercomputer to realize the comprehensive sharing of computing resources, storage resources, data resources, information resources, software resources, network resources, communication resources, knowledge resources, expert resources and other resources Enjoy.

Grid is an important national infrastructure related to scientific research, economy, society and national defense. It has attracted extensive attention at home and abroad. Governments and enterprises also strongly support the research of grid computing. Based on the basic research of grid technology, the U.S. government invests as much as $500 million a year. The UK government announced an investment of £100 million to develop the UK national grid [8]. NTT data company of Japan, together with Intel, SG and others, carried out a six-month grid computing experiment in the middle of 2002. Even India has launched a plan to build a national grid. Although the research on Grid Technology in China started late, because it is an emerging technology, the country attaches great importance to it and has invested a lot of material and human resources. In April 2002, the Ministry of science and technology of the people's Republic of China held a seminar on grid strategy, which confirmed that the research and application of grid was listed as a special project of the "863" plan, with a special investment of up to 300 million. In September 2003, Intel and the Ministry of Education announced to promote the educational research grid plan based on Itanium 2 architecture, which will comprehensively improve the service level of China's educational information infrastructure and the scientific research level of colleges and universities [9].

2.2 Problems in Higher Education Evaluation

Higher education evaluation is mainly a comprehensive evaluation of many factors, such as school running conditions, students' quality, theoretical teaching, practical teaching, teachers' level and teaching management. It has many factors Fuzziness and dynamics. Through the evaluation, various feedback information about education can be obtained; By analyzing and studying these feedback information, we can find many problems in education, find out the causes of the problems, and take targeted measures to improve the quality of higher education. Because the theoretical research of higher education evaluation in China lags behind, the evaluation activities have been carried out for a short time and are still in the primary stage. At present, there are mainly the following problems in Higher Education Evaluation:

(1) The evaluation theory system and operation system are not perfect. Due to the short time for China to really carry out the theoretical research and practice of

higher education evaluation, most of them still learn from and transplant foreign evaluation theories and experience, and have not really established a theoretical system and operation system of higher education evaluation in line with China's national conditions.

(2) The evaluation model is relatively backward. There are three stages of higher education evaluation in China:

Manual evaluation mode stage. It mainly adopts questionnaire survey or expert scoring, fills in the form, receives it uniformly, and then gives it to special statisticians for statistics, analysis and conclusion. This model not only consumes too much manpower, financial resources and time, but also the statistical work is quite cumbersome, and the statistical results are not conducive to preservation.

Stand alone evaluation mode stage. This model is based on the manual evaluation model, using computer to make statistics, analysis and draw conclusions. Compared with the manual mode, the evaluation efficiency is improved, but the system openness is poor, the information sharing is poor, and it is easy to form an information island.

Network evaluation mode stage. Take computer network as the operation platform to realize all functions of higher education evaluation. The connection of computer hardware is realized, which has certain advantages compared with the previous two forms; However, the comprehensive connectivity of all higher education evaluation resources on the Internet has not been solved, and the problem of information island has not been really solved.

(3) Evaluate the singleness of the algorithm. The quality of the evaluation algorithm directly affects the evaluation effect. From the previous evaluation practice, there are still many defects. For example, the traditional method is to select several evaluation elements and indicators, artificially give each element or indicator a specific weight coefficient, and then calculate the weighted average according to the scores of the expert evaluation group to obtain the evaluation results. Although this judgment can be said to be a leap from qualitative to quantitative, this method is more subjective and has more information loss, so it is easy to make the evaluation accuracy and sensitivity relatively low.

2.3 Necessity of Establishing Educational Evaluation Grid

Higher education evaluation is the work of collecting and processing education evaluation data and providing information services to relevant departments. With the rapid development of modern science and technology, higher education evaluation is also facing great challenges and opportunities.

(1) In September 2003, the Ministry of Education decided to launch the "China Grid" project. Zhao qinping, Vice Minister of education, served as the leader of the project leading group, and Dr. Jinhai, doctoral supervisor of Huazhong University of science and technology, served as the leader of the project expert group. A total of 12 colleges and universities across the country were approved to participate in the scientific and technological breakthrough of the project. After the completion of the project, it can realize the comprehensive sharing of computing, storage, data, information and

expert resources of 100 key universities in China, greatly simplify and facilitate the resource allocation of the national education system, and comprehensively improve the service level of information infrastructure of higher education and the teaching and scientific research level of colleges and universities in China.

(2) Higher education evaluation is a systematic project. If we want to solve it in essence The problem of China's higher education evaluation should stand at the forefront of information technology, make full use of China's education and scientific research grid, digitize and network the evaluation data and information, and be widely used, so as to realize the management and sharing of integrated information and provide effective, convenient and cheap services for higher education evaluation, Promote the development of higher education evaluation in China.

(3) Grid technology can integrate and share massive and distributed evaluation resources, and provide a practical technical support for solving the problems faced in the application of higher education evaluation information.

(4) Establish a higher education evaluation grid and use grid technology to meet the needs of colleges and universities for high-performance, large-capacity distributed storage and distributed computing, so as to help colleges and universities effectively find available resources, access data and share data. In addition, mining the association information and homologous relationship hidden in the evaluation data is conducive to the macro management and guidance of higher education.

3   Evaluation and Analysis of Higher Education

3.1   Analysis on the Characteristics of Higher Education Evaluation

The evaluation of higher education, like the objective things in real life, has many factors, so the evaluation of its advantages and disadvantages should judge the comprehensive value from many factors. For example, in the evaluation of teaching quality, we need to judge comprehensively from factors such as teaching content, teaching method and teaching effect; When evaluating each factor, the evaluation scale such as excellent, good, medium and poor (or a, B, C and D) is a typical fuzzy concept, which has no clear extension, that is, it has fuzziness. Fuzziness is an objective attribute of things and the inevitable result of the intermediate transition process between the differences of things. It can be said that the fuzziness of phenomena in the world is absolute, while the clarity or accuracy is relative. In particular, the concepts formed in the human brain are almost fuzzy, and the resulting judgment and reasoning are also fuzzy. It is precisely because of this fuzziness and measurability that the evaluation of higher education can be evaluated quantitatively. Marxist epistemology holds that human beings can make accurate judgments with some fuzzy information [10]. The development of modern fuzzy mathematics provides a methodological basis for the scientificity of higher education evaluation. The application of the concept of fuzzy mathematics membership effectively solves the fuzziness problem in teaching evaluation.

In addition to the multi factor and fuzziness of higher education evaluation, it also has some other characteristics. It can be summarized as follows:

(1) Due to the diversity of evaluation indicators, higher education evaluation includes not only "constituent" elements such as teachers, students, courses and conditions, but also "process" elements such as school running thought and teaching objectives. Therefore, higher education evaluation is a multi factor, multi-level and multi-attribute complex system.

(2) The data used in its evaluation can only be obtained in a limited range, the information it provides is always incomplete and specific, and the boundary of the evaluation standard is fuzzy, so the evaluation of higher education is a typical and fuzzy grey system.

(3) For the function of higher education evaluation, it should have the function of identification and differentiation, that is, through the evaluation, we can know the school running level and management level of each participating unit.

(4) The evaluation shall have diagnostic function. That is, through the evaluation, we can know some unpredictable internal control factors from the measurable evaluation project data, such as the level of leadership, the level of teachers, the status of teaching infrastructure, so as to find the problems and disadvantages of the evaluated object, and effectively realize the principle of "promoting reform through evaluation, promoting construction through evaluation, combining evaluation and construction, and focusing on construction".

(5) There are a large number of colleges and Universities Participating in the evaluation, but there are not many similar colleges and universities, and each has its own advantages.

3.2 Selection of Evaluation Methods

With the deepening of educational reform, especially the accelerating pace of popularization of higher education, the status and role of educational evaluation in Colleges and universities are becoming increasingly prominent. The quality of the evaluation method directly affects the evaluation effect. From the past evaluation practice, there are still many defects. For example, the traditional method is to select several evaluation elements and indicators, artificially give each element or indicator a specific weight coefficient, and then calculate the weighted average according to the score of the evaluation group to obtain the evaluation result. Although this judgment can be said to be a leap from qualitative to quantitative, this method is more intuitive, subjective and loses more information, so its accuracy and sensitivity are relatively low. Therefore, we must make significant improvements in the evaluation methods, incorporate some basic contents of educational evaluation into computer management, reduce human factors, and change the past from relying solely on expert group evaluation to the combination of expert group evaluation and modern technology evaluation, so as to enhance the scientificity and impartiality of educational evaluation and improve the efficiency of evaluation.

At present, there are many methods that can be used in the evaluation work, among which the more typical ones are data envelopment analysis (DEA), fuzzy comprehensive evaluation method, analytic hierarchy process (AHP), grey correlation evaluation method, TOPSIS method and set pair analysis method. Although these methods make comprehensive decision from the Perspective of the whole Bureau, their respective principles and applicable environments are different, If we ignore the limitations and shortcomings of various methods and use them indiscriminately, sometimes it will inevitably appear very reluctantly and affect the final evaluation effect. Therefore, we should put forward a comprehensive evaluation method according to the characteristics of various higher education evaluation work and the advantages and disadvantages of various evaluation methods.

The comparison is as follows:

Data envelopment analysis (DEA): it is an efficiency evaluation method proposed by A. Charnes, W. W. Cooper and others. It extends the concept of single input and single output engineering efficiency to the effectiveness evaluation of multi input and multi output similar decision-making units (DMUs), which greatly enriches the production function theory and its application technology in microeconomics, At the same time, it has the advantages of avoiding subjective factors, simplifying the algorithm and reducing errors. It calculates and compares the relative efficiency between decision-making units by using mathematical programming model, and evaluates the efficiency of the evaluation object from the relative efficiency. Because of its practicability and no weight assumption, this method has been widely popularized and applied in a short time. However, DEA is only applicable to the evaluation among similar units, and it is required that the number of units should be much larger than the number of indicators. Otherwise, it is easy to see that most or even all decision-making units are relatively effective, which makes it impossible to evaluate.

Analytic hierarchy process: it is a multi criteria decision-making method proposed by Professor T.L. Saaty, an American operational research scientist, in the 1970s. Its basic idea is: 1 The complex problem is decomposed into various constituent factors, which are grouped according to the dominant relationship to form an orderly hierarchical structure; 2. At the same level, the relative importance of each factor exists objectively. The relative weight of each factor can be determined by pairwise comparison. The final result of AHP evaluation method is the priority of each decision-making scheme relative to the overall goal. Using this method to deal with the evaluation index system, the weight coefficients of indexes at all levels can be obtained. Therefore, AHP is especially suitable for a complex system composed of interrelated and restrictive factors.

Grey correlation evaluation method: grey system theory is an extension of cybernetics. It was first proposed by Chinese scholar Professor Deng Julong in 1982. It studies the relationship between information from the perspective of system, that is, how to use known information to reveal unknown information, that is, the problem of "whitening" of the system. Grey correlation evaluation is a factor analysis method, which is a quantitative comparative analysis of the development trend among factors. It analyzes the correlation degree among multiple factors in the system through the comparison of the geometric relationship of the system statistical series. It is considered that the closer the geometry of the curve represented by the time variables describing the factors, the closer the development trend of the factors, The greater the degree of correlation between them. The specific method is to normalize the original observation number of the evaluation index, form the optimal value of each index into a reference series, normalize the original observation number of each evaluation index of the unit to be evaluated into a comparison series, and rank the evaluation units according to their correlation value. This method has no special requirements for the distribution type and sample size of data, and does not need to provide a reference standard for evaluation. Moreover, the analysis results are generally consistent with the qualitative analysis, so it has wide practicability. At present, it is widely used in the fields of economy, society, industry and so on.

4 Higher Education Evaluation System Based on Computer Network

4.1 Architecture of Browser/Server (B/S) System

The computer application system running on the network is a computer model based on host/terminal mode, which is transitioning from client/server (C/s) structure to browser/server (B/s) structure. The rise of B/S architecture benefits from the more and more extensive application of Internet. Compared with C/S architecture, B/S architecture not only has all the advantages of C/S architecture, but also has the unique advantages that C/s does not have. It has become a new architecture that many manufacturers are competing to adopt. The user interfaces of B/S mode are unified on the browser. The browser is easy to use and friendly. There is no need to learn to use other software, which is convenient for users.

The B/s system adopts a three-tier architecture, as shown in Fig. 1. Under the B/S three-tier architecture, the presentation layer, business logic layer and data service layer are divided into three relatively independent units.

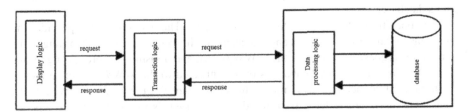

Fig. 1. B/S architecture diagram

(1) The presentation layer contains the display logic of the system, which is located at the client. Its task is from web browser to network A web server on puts forward a service request. The web server parses the client's request and then returns it to the client in the form of HTTP. The client accepts the transmitted home page file and displays it on the web browser.
(2) The function layer contains the transaction processing logic of the system, which is located on the web server side. Its task is to accept the user's request. First, it needs to execute the corresponding extended application to connect with the database, submit the data processing application to the database server through SQL, and then wait for the database server to submit the data processing results to the web server, Then it is sent back to the client by the web server.

(3) The data layer contains the data processing logic of the system, which is located on the database server side. Its task is to accept the request of the web server for database manipulation, realize the functions of database query, modification and update, and submit the operation results to the web server.

In fact, the three-tier B/S architecture separates the transaction processing logic module of the two-tier C/S structure from the task of the client, and a separate layer is responsible for the task. The client is no longer responsible for dealing with key transactions such as complex calculation and data access, but only for the display part. Therefore, the program maintenance is reduced, mainly the update of the program on the function server. Since the load is evenly distributed to the web server, the original C/S structure is transformed into a three-tier B/S structure. The three-tier B/S architecture has many advantages that the traditional C/s system does not have, and closely combines the Internet/Intranet technology. It is the general trend of technology development. It brings the application system into a new development era. This three-layer structure is independent of each other, and the change of any layer will not affect the function of other layers.

The database system based on B/S mode allows users to access the data in the remote database server through a standard interface, namely WWW browser, on any client in the network. There is no need to install any specific application on the client, and there is no direct interaction with the database in any way. All operations are completed through the browser on the client. An application program in the form of a web page is stored on the WWW server. It undertakes the function of publishing and receiving information. Specifically, it is to receive the request from the client, and then convert the user request into a database.

The operation interacts with the database server. The database server provides the functions of data storage, access and management. It operates the data according to the application request submitted by the WWW server, and transmits the processing results to the WWW server. The database is only connected to the WWW server to reduce the number of connections and improve the performance of the database server. At the same time, users are isolated from the database server. No user can directly operate the database across the WWW server. The authentication, authorization, encryption and other mechanisms are jointly provided through the database and the application in WWW to ensure the security of the database.

The teaching evaluation system we developed adopts B/S architecture, which combines the WWW server and database server into the same server. Through any host access in the campus network, we can carry out various work of evaluation and data processing.

4.2 System Structure of Evaluation System

For the evaluation system based on Browser/server, we should design different web pages and server processing programs for different users according to different functional needs. The system structure is shown in Fig. 2 below.

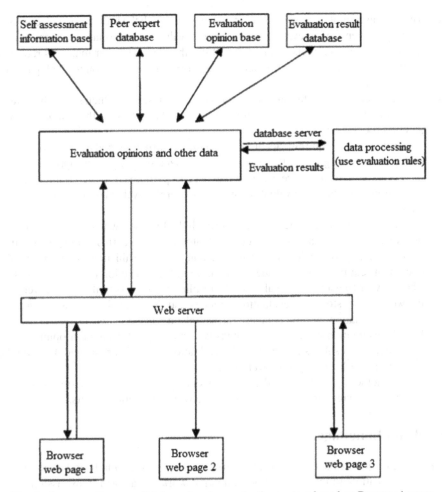

Fig. 2. Structure diagram of higher education evaluation system based on Browser / server

Web page 1; The corresponding web pages are designed according to the purpose of the evaluation, the evaluation scheme, the formulation of the evaluation index system and relevant documents.

Web page 2: design a specific web page according to the evaluation information of the evaluated unit, which includes the evaluation index system, the evaluated data and the corresponding evaluation form.

Web page 3: design specific web pages based on the evaluation results.

Its working process is roughly as follows:

① According to the purpose of the evaluation and the requirements of the evaluation scheme, the evaluation index system and relevant documents, the evaluation organizer designs the corresponding web page, and adds the relevant documents and evaluation index system to the corresponding web page;

② The appraised unit accesses a specific web page through the browser, which contains the requirements of relevant documents and evaluation information. According to the relevant requirements, count and sort out the data and other materials required for the evaluation, and then fill them in the corresponding form on the web page for submission;

③ The browser transmits the submitted form to the web server, which stores the data in the form into the self-assessment information database through the database server and preprocesses it;

④ According to the requirements of the evaluation information and evaluation scheme of the participating units, the evaluation organizer selects an appropriate amount of peer experts from the peer expert database to participate in the communication evaluation, and adds the evaluation information of the evaluated unit to the specific web page;

⑤ Peer experts visit a specific web page through the browser, which contains relevant documents, evaluation index system, evaluated data and corresponding evaluation form. Peer experts review the evaluated data, make evaluation according to the document requirements and index system, fill in the evaluation form and submit it;

⑥ The browser transmits the evaluation form filled by experts to the web server, and the web service stores the evaluation opinions and other data in the evaluation form into the evaluation opinion database through the database server;

⑦ Use the evaluation rules to comprehensively process the evaluation opinions, get the evaluation results, store them in the evaluation result database, and then add the evaluation results to a specific web page;

⑧ Users (including the appraised unit, individual experts and all sectors of society) visit the web page through the browser to view the evaluation results.

5   Beam Language

Higher education evaluation application grid is an application platform based on grid technology, national higher education evaluation work, broadband transmission, massive data organization, fuzzy evaluation technology and grid basic support environment. The processing and application of evaluation information is distributed, collaborative and intelligent. The system can use the distributed database to analyze and process the corresponding evaluation information, so as to form a powerful distributed computing ability of higher education evaluation and high-speed acquisition, transmission, storage and sharing of evaluation information. The research of higher education evaluation application grid is still in its infancy, and it still needs to be deeply studied in the aspects of architecture, grid key technology, parallel data processing and so on.

References

1. Yong, S., Wang, Y., Zhang, H.: Higher education evaluation system based on NET. In: 2021 6th International Conference on Smart Grid and Electrical Automation (ICSGEA) (2021)
2. Zhang, H.M., Ma, R.Q., Deng, M.X., et al.: Research on evaluation and improvement policy of higher education development based on TOPSIS-synthetic control method. Complexity **2021**(3), 1–11 (2021)

3. Lu, W., Jia, C., Zuo, J.: Application of fuzzy evaluation in comprehensive quality evaluation of higher education students. Int. J. Emerg. Technol. Learn. (iJET) **16**(12), 201 (2021)
4. Yildirim, K., Aslan, A.: Examination of the quality teaching in Turkish higher education based on the external evaluation reports from multiple perspectives journal of qualitative research in education. J. Qual. Res. Educ. **25**(1), 102–125 (2021)
5. Yani, F., Nurhayati, O.D., Widodo, A.P.: Heuristic evaluation and analytical network process for analyzing the role of websites in higher education. J. Phys. Conf. Ser. **1943**(1), 012112 (11pp) (2021)
6. Liu, H.: Research on practice evaluation system of higher vocational preschool education based on artificial intelligence. In: 2021 13th International Conference on Measuring Technology and Mechatronics Automation (ICMTMA) (2021)
7. Lemes, M.A., Marin, M., Lazarini, C.A., et al.: Evaluation strategies in active learning in higher education in health: integrative review. Revista Brasileira de Enfermagem **74**(2), e20201055 (2021)
8. Yousuf, M.: Evaluation of the professional competency of university faculty members as perceived by higher education students Fareeda Ibad Institute of Business Management, Pakistan. J. Educ. Educational Develop. **8**(1), 142 (2021)
9. Albakri, A., Abdulkhaleq, A.: An interactive system evaluation of blackboard system applications: a case study of higher education (2021)
10. Petra, T., Aziz, M.: Analysing student performance in higher education using fuzzy logic evaluation. Int. J. Sci. Technol. Res. **10**(1), 322–327 (2021)

Author Index

Aju, Wang   I-37, I-554

Bai, Qunfang   III-110
Bekhit, Mahmoud   III-619

Cai, Zhenzhen   III-92
Cao, Lujun   I-614
Cao, Pengcheng   II-286
Cao, Xiaojun   III-345
Chao, Huang   III-611
Chen, Bing   I-310
Chen, Bo   II-262, II-535
Chen, Guiyun   III-604
Chen, Hailin   III-491
Chen, Jianli   II-89
Chen, Liang   I-580
Chen, Mengji   III-502, III-513, III-523
Chen, Min   I-423
Chen, W. T.   I-364
Chen, Zhang   III-611
Cheng, Qingyan   I-537
Chi, GuoXing   II-254
Chong, Ning   II-39, III-557

Dangdang, Dai   III-611
Deng, Fei   III-192
Deng, Yanyan   III-138
Ding, Mingming   II-78, III-535
Dong, Jiacheng   I-243
Dong, Yanhong   II-481
Dou, Haibo   III-563
Du, Liping   II-56
Du, Qin   I-19

Fang, Guomin   II-331
Fei, Gao   II-232
Feng, Xiaosu   II-286

Gan, Suyun   II-512
Gan, Yanhong   II-488
Gao, Fei   II-629
Gao, Peng   II-254

Gong, Chao   II-344
Gong, Jian   III-377
Gong, MinYan   III-588
Gu, Guangjuan   II-647
Gu, Liang   I-485
Guan, Liang-kai   I-530
Guan, Lijuan   III-583
Guo, Jianliang   I-1
Guo, Jun   III-402
Guo, Li   II-31

Han, Ning   III-413
Han, Shengzong   III-354
Hao, Mengzhen   II-177
He, Yafang   II-314
He, Yuqi   III-121
He, Zhuang-zhuang   III-147
Hou, Jie   I-286
Hu, Minghua   I-347
Hu, Wen   I-25
Hu, Xiaowei   II-100
Hu, Zhikun   III-288
Hua, Huang   I-620
Huang, Jing   III-281
Huang, Lei   II-454
Huang, Yufei   III-480, III-513
Hui, Hu   III-446
HuiYang,   II-110
Hussain, Walayat   III-619

Jia, Wangwei   I-336
Jiang, Chao   III-281
Jiang, Lu   III-425
Jiao, Yanwei   III-223
Jie, Sun   II-389
Jing, Huang   I-161
Jinsong, Peng   III-546

Kang, Kaijie   I-273

Lai, Xiaojia   II-116, II-558
Lan, Jianjing   III-491
Lan, Zhimian   III-513
Lestari, Nur Indah   III-619

Li, Ang   I-416
Li, Beibei   II-618
Li, Chenglong   III-354
Li, Chunhui   III-186
Li, Guiping   II-325
Li, Hongting   I-149
Li, Jiahong   II-10
Li, Jinghua   II-165
Li, Liguang   III-318
Li, Liu   III-365
Li, Peng   III-354
Li, ShanShan   II-204
Li, Si   III-274
Li, Wei   II-188, II-463
Li, Xiaomei   III-36
Li, Yang   I-225
Li, Yi   I-316
Li, Zhangyan   I-586
Li, Zhe   III-395
Li, Zhen   III-7
Liang, Dong   III-611
Liang, Guozhi   II-298
Liang, Hong   II-1, II-195
Liang, Liang   III-64
Liao, Lijuan   II-569
Liao, Shude   III-480, III-513
Lin, Shaorong   II-523
Ling, Ting-ting   II-635
Liqun, Zhang   III-434
Liu, Guangjun   III-473
Liu, Haiyan   I-103
Liu, Jing   III-306
Liu, Li   II-612
Liu, LinHao   II-350
Liu, Linjiao   II-344
Liu, Sha   I-97
Liu, Yan   III-299
Liu, Yang   I-140
Liu, YuLing   II-254
Liu, Yunhua   I-179
Long, Yin   III-546
Lu, Xia   I-120
Lu, Zhengjie   III-480, III-502, III-523
Luo, Xinru   III-604

Ma, Pengfei   I-394
Merigo, Jose M.   III-619
Miao, Weiwei   II-286

Na, Xiao   III-53

Pan, Zhengzhong   I-73
Peng, Qingchen   III-604

Qi, Jinling   III-92
Qi, Na   III-192
Qian, Hongxing   I-497
Qing, Li   III-365

Rao, Changming   III-203
Ren, Chang Xia   II-126
Ren, Linzheng   III-165
Rongtao, Liao   III-611

Shan, Yanping   II-89
Shao, Haiqin   II-177
Shao, Wenyu   III-354
Sheng, Jing   II-497, III-26
Shi, Xiaoyu   II-243
Shu, Jingjun   I-467
Shufen, Sun   I-261
Song, Sentao   III-570
Su, Shanye   III-502
Su, Wanbin   III-235
Sun, Jixin   III-480, III-513
Sun, Kailing   III-252
Sun, Lei   III-336
Sun, Mingjiao   I-190
Sun, Pei   II-635
Sun, Tianyi   III-336
Sun, WeiPeng   II-254
Sun, Wenjuan   II-298

Tan, Xianglie   I-298
Teng, Jinzhi   II-546
Teng, Meng   I-603
Tian, Xi   I-563

Wang, Bo   III-480, III-523
Wang, Chun Liang   II-223
Wang, ChunLiang   I-446, II-156
Wang, Dan   I-574
Wang, Dongyang   III-513
Wang, Gao   III-604
Wang, Jianxiang   I-385
Wang, Kan   II-361
Wang, Kefei   III-425
Wang, Liao   II-591

Wang, Lin   I-172
Wang, Ping   III-386
Wang, Qianyu   I-326
Wang, Weijuan   II-309
Wang, Xiaodan   III-281
Wang, Yan   II-454
Wang, Yangqu   III-211
Wang, Yanping   III-491
Wang, Yayun   III-583
Wang, Yiping   II-188, II-463
Wang, Yong   I-53
Wei, Feiyan   III-491
Wei, Jiying   III-402
Wei, Lianjuan   I-376
Wei, Linbo   III-165
Wei, Wei   III-153
Wei, Zheng   III-491
Wu, Chunyuan   II-400
Wu, Meizhi   III-455, III-464
Wu, Xueqin   II-146

Xia, Yu   III-570
Xiao, Luo   III-446
Xiao, Yang   II-488
Xiao-hua, Chi   I-62
Xie, Xiaoli   II-100
Xing, Li   II-481
Xing, Youhua   III-281
Xiong, Hong Zhang   II-275
Xiong, Xiang-chuan   III-147
Xu, Haidan   I-433
Xu, Ziwei   III-76

Yan, Lingying   I-206
Yan, Liu   III-14
Yan, Shi   III-577
Yang, Hui   I-236
Yang, Jun   I-190
Yang, Xiao   III-47
Yang, Xiaokun   II-275
Yao, Ping   II-45
Yao, Tong   III-455, III-464
Yaoqing, Wang   I-518
Yin, Pengcheng   III-274
Ying, Wang   III-365
Yu, Bei   I-10
Yu, Changqing   II-89
Yu, Guohao   I-46
Yu, Leihan   II-488
Yu, Xiaojun   I-19

Yu, Yunshi   III-523
Yue, Guo   III-611

Zhai, Te   II-368
Zhang, Chen Kun   I-85
Zhang, Chengliang   I-236, II-110
Zhang, Chuanwei   I-114, II-135, II-424
Zhang, Dong   II-618
Zhang, Dongdong   III-324
Zhang, DongHong   I-439
Zhang, Donghong   II-21
Zhang, Huiying   III-491
Zhang, Jian   I-131, I-197
Zhang, Jianbin   I-353
Zhang, Jianxin   II-243
Zhang, Jie   I-400
Zhang, Jihong   II-379
Zhang, Jinfeng   III-324
Zhang, Jingbin   I-406, III-177
Zhang, Juanjuan   II-292
Zhang, Li   II-454
Zhang, Lingli   II-580
Zhang, Nan   II-635
Zhang, Peng   III-491
Zhang, Ru   I-249
Zhang, Rui   I-456
Zhang, Sisi   II-443
Zhang, Ting   I-53
Zhang, XingRong   II-412
Zhang, Xue-qin   III-147
Zhang, Ya-jun   III-147
Zhang, Yan   II-211, II-503, III-104, III-570
Zhang, Ying   III-596
Zhang, Yiqiong   I-46
Zhang, Yuanhao   I-243
Zhang, Zhang   III-246
Zhao, Bing   III-132
Zhao, Chengli   I-543
Zhao, Lei   I-596
Zhao, Li   III-1
Zhao, Mei   III-354
Zhao, Rui   III-147
Zhao, Ting   III-82
Zhao, Wenguo   II-286
Zhao, Xiaozhen   II-262, II-535
Zhao, Yanmei   II-431
Zhen, Liu   III-47
Zheng, Fengting   III-570
Zheng, Hui   II-67
Zhong, Hua   I-216

Zhong, Lijuan   I-506
Zhong, Zhangsheng   II-472, II-602

Zhou, Chen   I-478
Zhu, Hang   III-264

Printed in the United States
by Baker & Taylor Publisher Services